International Guide to
Qualifications
in Education
Fourth Edition

The British Council

International Guide to
Qualifications
in Education
Fourth Edition

The National Academic
Recognition Information
Centre (NARIC) for the
United Kingdom

Mansell Publishing Limited, *A Cassell Imprint*
Wellington House, 125 Strand, London WC2R 0BB, England
215 Park Avenue South, New York, New York 10003, USA
First published 1984
Second Edition 1987
Third Edition 1991
Fourth Edition 1996

© The British Council, 1984, 1987, 1991, 1996

British Library Cataloguing in Publication Data
National Academic Recognition Information Centre for the United Kingdom
  International Guide to Qualifications in
  Education.—4Rev.ed
  I. Title
  371.26

  ISBN 0–7201–2217–1

Library of Congress Cataloging-in-Publication Data
International guide to qualifications in education / the British
  Council, NARIC, the National Academic Recognition Information Centre
  for the United Kingdom.—4th ed.
     p. cm.
   ISBN 0–7201–2217–1
   1. Students, Foreign—Great Britain. 2. School credits—
Standards—Evaluation. 3. Universities and colleges—Great
Britain—Entrance requirements. 4. Comparative education.
5. Education—Standards. I. National Academic Recognition
Information Centre (Great Britain)
LB2376.6.G7158   1995
378.1'05—dc20   95–18218
                                                          CIP

Printed and bound in Great Britain by The Bath Press

Contents

Contents

Contents

Contents

Introduction

Since the publication of the last edition of the *International Guide to Qualifications in Education* in 1991, our parent organization, the British Council, has undergone substantial transformation. The National Academic Recognition Information Centre for the United Kingdom (NARIC) now forms part of the Education Promotion Group within the British Council's Professional Services. NARIC has reinstated an enquiry service to individual members of the public, on a fee-paying basis, since September 1992. NARIC's address is given at the end of this introduction.

The *International Guide* is NARIC's main publication. The present edition covers some 165 countries from which students come to Britain in search of further study, training or employment. Each country entry usually consists of the following sections:

- a brief introduction;
- **Evaluation in Britain**, which, taking the British system as the norm, outlines the recognition generally accorded to key qualifications by British institutions;
- **Marking Systems**, which describes the marking systems used at secondary and tertiary levels;
- a survey of the structure of education, level by level: **School Education, Further Education, Higher Education and Teacher Education**.

The country chapters are preceded by a note on the British Council and its work and by a guide to reading certificates and transcripts. They are followed by ten appendices on examinations, examining boards and regional universities. As in the last edition, the country chapter for the United Kingdom comes immediately before the other country chapters. This emphasizes the function of this chapter as the reference for comparison for all the others.

The following points should be noted:

a. Reference to GCSE means GCSE grades A, B and C.
b. The phrase 'may satisfy the general entrance requirements of British higher education institutions' means that a student with the overseas qualification concerned, may satisfy the minimum criteria of eligibility and be considered for admission. It does not guarantee the student a place or give him or her the right to enter a higher education course. In addition to satisfying the general entrance requirements, which are common to all faculties, the student must satisfy the

course requirements imposed by individual faculties or schools. These may be very demanding.

c. General entrance requirements may be framed in terms of passes at **GCSE** and **GCE Advanced** (England, Wales and Northern Ireland) or at **Scottish Highers**. The Scottish education system and its qualifications are described in the UK chapter. Vocational qualifications, including the new **General National Vocational Qualification (GNVQ)/General Scottish Vocational Qualification (GSVQ)** are also accepted by universities and colleges for appropriate courses.

d. No reference is made in country evaluation sections to the standard of attainment which admissions officers should look for in English language. Institutions should, however, exercise caution in the case of students from countries in which English is not the medium of instruction and should satisfy themselves that students have reached an acceptable level. Some of the internationally known examinations in English as a foreign language are listed in the UK chapter and minimum acceptable attainment levels are recommended.

e. The phrase 'may be given advanced standing by British higher education institutions' means that a student with the overseas qualification concerned may be admitted to a course at a level above the normal starting-point in recognition of a previous complete qualification obtained elsewhere. Exemption can take different forms at different institutions, viz:

   (i) a student is allowed to complete a course in a shorter time than usual but is not exempted from any examinations;

  (ii) as in (i) but exemption from some examinations is also granted;

 (iii) a student is allowed to go straight into the second year of a three-year degree course or the third year of a four-year course;

 (iv) a student is allowed to go straight into the final year of a degree course.

f. Comparison to British Master's degrees excludes Master's degrees from the older Scottish universities and from Oxford and Cambridge Universities.

g. Where no evaluations are given for postgraduate qualifications, the information is not available.

h. The evaluations given are for qualifications obtained in recent years except where stated otherwise.

i. In cases where the members of NARIC's Advisory Committee were not unanimous in their views, only the majority view has been printed.

j. The juxtaposition of the **Evaluation** section and the **Marking Systems** section in each chapter is deliberate. Users should appreciate the interdependence of these two sections.

All the information contained in the present edition has been thoroughly overhauled, updated and checked. It has not been possible, however, to obtain information about recent educational developments in the following countries: Angola, Bahamas, Barbados, Congo, Cuba, El Salvador, Guyana, Liberia, Madagascar, Mongolia,

Nicaragua, Rwanda, Solomon Islands, Somalia, Uruguay, Vanuatu, Vietnam and Zaire.

From its beginnings in 1975, in response to a Council of Europe requirement that all member states should provide national information centres on academic recognition and mobility, the UK NARIC has been maintained by the British Council and assisted in its work by the Council's overseas network and close working relationship with the higher education sector in Britain. Since the early 1980s, the UK NARIC has also been a member of the network of national NARIC centres throughout the EC. The work of the network is co-ordinated by the Directorate General XXII – Education, Training and Youth in the Commission of the European Communities in Brussels. A small part of the funds available for ERASMUS under the SOCRATES programme is set aside to promote academic recognition through the work of the NARIC centres.

As Head of the UK NARIC, I would like to thank the members of the NARIC Advisory Committee for the invaluable advice and guidance they have provided during the preparation of this edition of the *International Guide*. The Advisory Committee includes the following: The Blair Consultancy Limited (Mr A D Mackintosh, formerly of the Scottish Universities Council on Entrance); British Universities International Liaison Association (Professor J Hughes); City and Guilds (Mr J Martin of Pitman Examinations Institute, a division of C&G); Department for Education (Ms Sue Garner); Higher Education Quality Council (Mr D Bottomley); National Council for Vocational Qualifications (Mr P S Gerbrandy); Northern Examinations and Assessment Board (Dr E Rushton); School Curriculum and Assessment Authority (Mr C Woodhead); Standing Conference of Principals (Mr G R Mann); Universities and Colleges Admissions Service (Mr M W Scott); and University of London Entrance Requirements Department (Mr N Mohammed).

I would also like to thank numerous other contributors: Mr P R Custerson (Midland Examining Group); Mr J A Day (Southern Examining Group); Ms M Garvey and Mr J Stops (Voluntary Service Overseas); Mr G Gregory (Northern Examinations and Assessment Board); Ms P Grundy and colleagues (Department for Education); Mr D Kelso (Scottish Office Education Department); Mr W R Lambert (Welsh Joint Education Committee); Ms M McGill and Ms M McKerracher (Scottish Vocational Education Council); Mr H Smith (CfBT Education Services Cambodia); Mr C Taylor (University of London Examinations and Assessment Council); not forgetting staff in 35 university and college admissions offices, in other NARICs and ENICs (the joint Council of Europe/UNESCO network of information centres); in embassies and in the British Council (Ms G Bate, Ms J Caveney, Mr P Fell and Mr S Marshall at headquarters, and countless individuals in overseas offices).

I would finally like to thank the staff of the UK NARIC, past and present, who have liaised with the British Council overseas network and the Advisory Committee to prepare and produce this book (Catherine Breen, Fernando McGarrell, Linda Neilson, Hazel Palmer, Michael Snoxall, Kevin Van-Cauter); the British Council Central Typing Service and Design, Production and Publishing Department.

It should be remembered that the UK NARIC is an advisory body offering guidance on the recognition **likely to be accorded** a particular qualification by British institutions, based on collective past experience. It has no power to make authoritative statements or to give assurances which would challenge the right of individual institutions to make their own judgements.

Patricia Hubbell
(Head of UK NARIC)

Enquiry Service

If you are unable to find the information you require in the *International Guide to Qualifications in Education*, please contact:

UK National Academic Recognition Information Centre
The British Council
Medlock Street
Manchester
M15 4AA

The British Council

The British Council is Britain's principal agent for cultural relations overseas. Its purpose, in accordance with its Charter, is to promote a wider knowledge of the United Kingdom and the English language and encourage cultural, scientific, technological and other educational co-operation between the UK and other countries. It is an independent, non-political, organization managed by a Director-General working to a Board, which includes representatives from the Foreign and Commonwealth Office, the Overseas Development Administration, Parliament, industry and commerce, and the arts, scientific and academic worlds. With 229 offices in 108 countries, it provides a network of contacts between government departments, universities and professional and business organizations in Britain and around the world.

The Council's total turnover for 1994/5 is estimated at £437 million. It has five main activities:

- helping people to study, train or make professional contacts in Britain; and enabling British specialists to teach, advise or establish joint projects abroad;
- teaching English and promoting its use;
- providing library and information services;
- promoting British education, science and technology;
- making British arts and literature more widely known.

The Council's staff includes specialists in agriculture, the arts, education, English language teaching, librarianship, literature, medicine, physical sciences and technology. Through the Council's Advisory Committees, staff are able to draw on the professional expertise of leading practitioners in these fields.

The British government's Overseas Development Administration engages the Council as adviser and executive agent for much of its aid to developing countries in the fields of education and training. The Council provides consultants and trainers for overseas projects in these fields, and access to further and higher education in Britain for over 12,000 trainees from developing countries under the British aid programme. Several thousand further scholarships are arranged on behalf of the Foreign Office, overseas governments, UN agencies and as part of projects financed by international lending agencies such as the World Bank.

Britain's education system has a strong reputation overseas, and information on its teaching methods, materials and organization is readily available from British Council offices. By arranging specialist courses, study visits and training in Britain, the Council also enables overseas teachers and educational administrators to see at first hand recent developments in their specialist field.

Guide to reading transcripts of educational certificates

Reading transcripts of educational certificates obtained in other countries for the purpose of making comparisons with qualifications with which we are familiar is fraught with difficulties because education systems are not identical and consequently no two qualifications are alike. However, possible pitfalls in comparing educational credentials can be avoided and arbitrary decisions minimized if we adopt a flexible approach to assessment, basing our judgement on accurate knowledge of the education system and the country in which the qualification was awarded.

We should attempt to make a qualitative rather than a quantitative assessment. Age, for example, cannot always be a guide to the level to which a person will have studied, particularly in Third World countries where educational facilities may not be developed or widespread. The total number of years of schooling provides one clue, but a decision cannot be made merely by counting years. What the student studied, how the studies were conducted, the length of the course, the facilities available, the assessment and marking scheme used, the pass/failure rate, the admission requirements to the course, the recognition of the qualification in the country in which it was awarded – these are all factors which need to be considered.

Translations, whether made by official translators or the holders of the qualifications themselves, should be treated with care: the word 'diploma' is used to cover a wide range of qualifications, from the primary school leaving certificate to a Master's degree, and can give the wrong impression of the qualification actually obtained. Translations should be accompanied by the original documents. It is also important to verify the qualifications presented. If the original document is not available, a statement should be sought direct from the awarding institution.

As it is essential to have sufficient information when checking the student's academic level, certificates and full transcripts should be requested giving the following details:

- full name of institution issuing documents and town/city where the institution is situated;
- name of qualification in the language of the country where obtained;
- subjects studied, examinations taken and marks obtained;
- length of period of study and mode of study to obtain qualifications (with dates);
- details of any previous educational qualifications.

It is essential to have a wide knowledge of the British education system when comparing British and other qualifications. In addition to the United Kingdom chapter in this work, *British qualifications: A Complete Guide to Educational, Technical, Professional and Academic Qualifications in Britain* 25th edition (London: Kogan Page, 1994) may be useful.

The United Kingdom, with the exception of Scotland, is perhaps the only country in the world that has early specialization. Hence, a difficulty arises when comparing a school-leaving certificate from overseas with GCE Advanced level. Normally, students in other countries may take anything from four to ten subjects in their final certificate. The student's overall standard in this certificate is often considered comparable to that of a student who had taken GCE A levels, that is to say, under the British system the student would have been capable of obtaining at least two A level passes plus three GCSEs in different subjects. Individual subjects may only be compared to GCSEs, however, since it is unlikely that any one subject could have been studied in the same depth as only two or three subjects taken at A level.

The subject of English in an overseas school-leaving certificate is not usually considered of GCSE standard, unless the medium of instruction was English. Neither is a degree in the subject of English likely to be of the same standard as a British degree in that subject (even if degrees from that country are normally compared to degrees from Britain) unless English was the medium of instruction and the examination was in English.

Because of early specialization, British university entrance requirements are correspondingly high and the Bachelor degree may be taken in three years instead of four (or more) as in most other countries.

The British Bachelor degree may cover a small range of subjects which are studied in depth (Honours) or be more wide-ranging (Ordinary or General).

Introductory outline of education in the United Kingdom

Introduction

Overall responsibility for all aspects and all levels of education in England, and additionally for university education in Scotland, Wales and Northern Ireland, lies with the Secretary of State for Education. The Secretaries of State for Scotland, Wales and Northern Ireland are responsible for all non-university education in their countries and are consulted about the universities there.

Because of this division of responsibility, the education systems in the four countries in the United Kingdom, while sharing many common features, do still retain distinct characteristics of their own. Differences will be highlighted where appropriate and should be taken into account when considering comparability of qualifications.

Education is compulsory for all from the age of five to sixteen years. Pre-school education is available before this, and further and higher education afterwards. Most young people attend a state-maintained institution from primary through to higher education, while others choose to attend an institution in the independent sector for which they pay fees.

The wind of change brought by the 1988 Education Reform Act has significantly affected policy and practice at all levels of the education system. Changes in the structure and funding of education introduced under this Act have been further developed by the Further and Higher Education Act 1992. Details of the considerable changes to qualifications and training resulting from these two Acts will be given in the appropriate sections below.

The **VOCATIONAL EDUCATION** section describes the **National Vocational Qualifications** (NVQs) developed to reform/replace outdated vocational qualifications with standards-based relevant vocational qualifications meeting the needs of industry, and the **General National Vocational Qualifications** (GNVQs) developed to (a) provide an alternative route of access to further and higher education and (b) offer broad-based vocational education as a preparation for the world of work. These two systems, together with the 'traditional' **GCSE** and **GCE A level** route, form a national framework for post-sixteen education, within which it is increasingly possible to combine different kinds of qualification in a single course of study.

Within the context of this publication this chapter, describing the qualifications and examinations available in the UK education system, will serve as the basis of comparison with those of other countries.

ACRONYMS

AEB	Associated Examining Board
APU	Assessment of Performance Unit
ARELS	Association of Recognized English Language Schools

BAC	British Accreditation Council for Independent Further and Higher Education
BASCELT	British Association of State Colleges in English Language Teaching
BTEC	Business and Technician Education Council
CACC	Council for the Accreditation of Correspondence Colleges
CATE	Council for the Accreditation of Teacher Education
C&G	City and Guilds
CI	Central Institution (Scottish)
CIFE	Conference for Independent Further Education
CNAA	Council for National Academic Awards
CRCH	Central Register and Clearing House
CSYS	Certificate of Sixth Year Studies (Scotland)
CTC	City Technology College
CVCP	Committee of Vice-Chancellors and Principals of the Universities of the United Kingdom
DENI	Department of Education for Northern Ireland
DFE	Department for Education (for England and Wales)
EA	Education Authority
EEA	European Economic Area
EFL	English as a foreign language
ERA	Education Reform Act
ESOL	English for speakers of other languages
FE	Further Education
FEFC	Further Education Funding Council
GCE	General Certificate of Education
GCSE	General Certificate of Secondary Education
GNVQ	General National Vocational Qualification
GSVQ	General Scottish Vocational Qualification
GTC	General Teaching Council (Scotland)
GTTR	Graduate Teacher Training Registry
HE	Higher Education
HEFC	Higher Education Funding Council
HEQC	Higher Education Quality Council
HMI	Her Majesty's Inspectorate
HNC	Higher National Certificate
HND	Higher National Diploma
IB	International Baccalaureate
IGCSE	International General Certificate of Secondary Education
INSET	In-service education of teachers
ISIS	Independent Schools Information Service
ITT	Initial teacher training
LCCI	London Chamber of Commerce and Industry
LEA	Local Education Authority
NC	National Certificate
NC	National curriculum
NCVQ	National Council for Vocational Qualifications
ND	National Diploma
NICCEA	Northern Ireland Council for the Curriculum, Examinations and Assessment

NVQ	National Vocational Qualification
OFSTED	Office for Standards in Education
OU	Open University
PG	Postgraduate
PGCE	Postgraduate Certificate of Education
QTS	Qualified teacher status
RSA	Royal Society of Arts
SCAA	Schools Curriculum and Assessment Authority
SCCC	Scottish Consultative Council on the Curriculum
SCET	Scottish Council for Educational Technology
SCOTVEC	Scottish Vocational Education Council
SEB	Scottish Examination Board
SOED	Scottish Office Education Department
SVQ	Scottish Vocational Qualification
TASC	Teaching as a career
TVEI	Technical and Vocational Education Initiative
UCAS	Universities and Colleges Admissions Service
UCLES	University of Cambridge Local Examinations Syndicate
UG	Undergraduate

MARKING SYSTEMS

Awards of achievement exist at all levels of the education system, each with their own distinctive methods of assessment. The major examinations/awards are as follows:

General Certificate of Secondary Education
General Certificate of Education (GCE) **Advanced/Advanced Supplementary**
Scottish Certificate of Education (SCE)
    Standard Grade
    Higher Grade
Certificate of Sixth Year Studies (CSYS)
International Baccalaureate (IB) **Diploma**

General National Vocational Qualifications (GNVQ)
General Scottish Vocational Qualifications (GSVQ)
National Vocational Qualifications (NVQ) / **Scottish Vocational Qualifications** (SVQ)

Business Technician Education Council (BTEC)
City and Guilds of London Institute (C&G)
Pitman Examinations Institute (PEI)
Scottish Vocational Education Council (SCOTVEC)

Degrees

ENGLAND, WALES AND NORTHERN IRELAND

GCSE
The **General Certificate of Secondary Education (GCSE)** was introduced in

September 1986 with the first examinations in Summer 1988. It replaced the former **GCE O level** and **CSE** examinations and is normally taken by pupils around the age of 16. The great majority of maintained schools in England and Wales, together with independent schools, prepare candidates for the **GCSE**.

The **GCSE** is the principal means of assessing the National Curriculum at Key Stage 4, the two years leading up to **GCSE** examinations. The National Curriculum came into effect for the core subjects English, mathematics and science from September 1992 for first examinations in Summer 1994. The structure of the examination has been adapted, where appropriate, to accord with National Curriculum requirements.

For **GCSE**, the examinations boards in England and Wales are arranged into five Examining Groups; four in England and one in Wales. There is a similar board in Northern Ireland. These are confederations of the (university-based) **GCE** Boards and the (Local Education Authority consortia-based) **CSE** Boards. Each group awards **GCSE** certificates but the single system is designed to uphold uniform standards in the value of grades and of what is studied in each subject. From 1993, for first examinations in 1995, the City and Guilds and the Royal Society of Arts Examination Board will be offering GCSE in technology and related subjects.

Main features of the GCSE

Each Examining Group designs its own syllabuses but they are required to conform to criteria laid down by the School Curriculum and Assessment Authority (SCAA), which set out the rules and principles for all courses and all examinations in all subjects. The award of a grade is intended to indicate that a candidate has met the level of knowledge or skill laid down by the criteria.

A further feature of **GCSE** assessment methods is course work. Credit is given for assignments set and marked by the teacher, with external moderation, and the marks awarded form a contribution towards the final grade achieved. The proportion of credit obtained from course work is subject to limits laid down by SCAA.

Grading of the GCSE

The **GCSE** is graded on a lettered scale of A to G. The starred A grade was first awarded in 1994; it is pitched higher than grade A and is intended to recognize outstanding achievement.

Examination papers: arrangements for GCSE courses starting in 1996

In most subjects there will be a foundation tier covering grades G to C and a higher tier covering grades D to A starred. Entry decisions will be made towards the end of the **GCSE** course, and the two-grade overlap between tiers will enable teachers to enter each pupil for examination papers which are both accessible and challenging. No grades will be awarded above or below the range of the tier. For mathematics there will be a three-tier structure: covering grades G to D; E to B; and C to A starred.

IGCSE

Some **GCSE** examining boards still set **GCE O level** examinations for overseas countries (see Appendix 2). In addition, the University of Cambridge Local Examinations Syndicate (UCLES) has produced an international **GCSE** (IGCSE). The **IGCSE** is a two-year curriculum programme with a choice of core and extended-level examination papers. It has a seven-point grade scale A-G. Grade A indicates the highest level of achievement and grade G minimum satisfactory performance.

4

The core and extended curriculum was introduced to cater for differing abilities, with the extended curriculum intended for those going on to higher education or professional training. Candidates taking the core curriculum will receive grades D-G. Grades A-C are only available at the extended curriculum level.

IGCSE syllabuses are grouped into subject groups; each syllabus has curriculum aims and objectives. Examinations can be taken in the individual subjects or as the **International Certificate of Education** (ICE). In most **IGCSE** syllabuses, course work is optional although encouraged. School-based assessments require the approval of UCLES.

GCE Advanced and Advanced Supplementary

This examination is taken by academically able pupils at eighteen years of age. About 20 per cent of pupils take this examination. Advanced and Advanced Supplementary examinations are set by the seven GCE Examining Boards. In Northern Ireland they are set by NICCEA.

Traditionally, students followed courses in two or three related subjects, for example the sciences or the humanities. However, with the introduction of less conventional higher education courses, less traditional combinations of GCE Advanced subjects are now more common. There are five official pass grades, A-E, although a candidate not achieving the required standard may obtain an 'N' grade (i.e. a fail grade), rather than a compensatory **O level** pass.

GCE Advanced examinations have been described as the 'gold standard' of the education system as a qualification of a high standard, which is widely recognized internationally and provides entry to higher education.

Advanced Supplementaries were introduced in 1987 and examinations first taken in 1989 with the purpose of broadening **GCE Advanced** studies beyond the traditional clusters of science or arts subjects, thus providing an opportunity to include contrasting studies.

An **Advanced Supplementary** requires half the work of a **GCE Advanced** subject but it is set to the same standard and usually takes two years to complete. The syllabuses take account of the shorter teaching and study time available so that while the quantity of work is less, the quality is the same as required for the equivalent **GCE Advanced** grade. Like **GCE Advanced**, it is graded A to E, with grade standards related to the corresponding **GCE Advanced** grade. Two **Advanced Supplementaries** are seen as equivalent to one **GCE Advanced** and are accepted in lieu of one **GCE Advanced** for university entrance. Some universities allow students to enter some courses with only **Advanced Supplementaries** passes and no **GCE Advanced** passes.

SCOTLAND

The counterpart in Scotland of the **GCSE** and **GCE Advanced** examinations is the **Scottish Certificate of Education** (SCE) awarded by the Scottish Examination Board (SEB). The **SCE** examinations are offered at two levels: **Standard Grade** (for 16+) and **Higher Grade** (for 17+). In addition, a **Certificate of Sixth Year Studies** (CSYS) can be taken after **Higher Grade**.

Standard Grade

Introduced in 1984, to replace **Ordinary Grade**, **Standard Grade** examinations were first taken in 1986. The examination is similar to the **GCSE** and has three levels of study: Foundation, General and Credit. The **Standard Grade** awards are based on a seven-point scale, grade 1 being the highest and grade 7 the lowest. Grade 7 indicates that a course has been completed but no certificate awarded. Continuous assessment as well as examination (as in the **GCSE**) are integral to the assessment.

Higher Grade (also known as Highers)

The **Higher Grade** examination is taken after a one-year course covering a broad range of subjects, at seventeen years of age, after **Standard Grade**. Students usually take four to five subjects. The **Higher Grade** examination is often referred to as 'Highers'. In general terms, three **Highers** are regarded as equivalent to two **GCE Advanced** subjects. There are three levels of pass at **Higher Grade**: A – 70 per cent and above; B – 60 per cent to 69 per cent; C – 50 per cent to 59 per cent.

Certificate of Sixth Year Studies (CSYS)

This examination may be taken by a pupil who is in his or her sixth year of secondary school (18+) and who already has a **Higher Grade** pass in the subject(s) being studied for **CSYS**. The examination emphasizes the need for individual study and most subjects require a dissertation project and report. In the **CSYS** there are no pass or fail grades, just five grades from A (highest) to E (lowest). Candidates normally take up to three **CSYS** subjects.

IB Diploma

Some schools have adopted the **IB** as a post-sixteen programme of study, as this is now increasingly recognized for admission to universities in the UK. The **IB Diploma** is set by the Examining Board of the International Baccalaureate Organization (IBO). It is an international examination originally developed to suit the needs of children between the ages of sixteen and eighteen living overseas and attending international schools. The **IB Diploma** is only offered in schools, sixth form colleges, etc., that have been assessed and approved by the IBO. For further details, see Appendix 6.

General National Vocational Qualifications (GNVQs)

GNVQs are awarded at three levels: Foundation, Intermediate, and Advanced. Merit and distinction grades are awarded to students who demonstrate a level of performance above the basic requirement. Only students who achieve all the required units for the award of a **GNVQ**, and thus qualify for a pass, can be considered for the grades of merit and distinction. Grades are based on an assessment of the quality of the overall body of work presented by students in their portfolios of evidence. Units are not separately graded.

The grades for **Advanced GNVQs** are designed to align with those for **GCE A Levels** – distinction corresponds to the A level grades A/B, merit to grade C, and pass to grades D/E.

General Scottish Vocational Qualifications (GSVQs)

GSVQs are awarded at three levels – 1, 2 and 3. Level 1 requires successful completion of 12 national certificate module credits, levels 2 and 3 of 18 such credits each. Two grades are awarded: pass and merit.

National Vocational Qualifications (NVQs) and Scottish Vocational Qualifications (SVQs)

NVQs/SVQs are awarded at five levels, from level 1 (lowest level) to level 5 (highest level). Candidates are assessed in workplace conditions and are also often tested by practical, oral or written examinations. **NVQs/SVQs** are not graded.

Business and Technician Education Council (BTEC)

There are three levels of BTEC qualifications other than **G/NVQs**:

First Certificate/Diploma (FC/FD)
National Certificate/Diploma (NC/ND)
Higher National Certificate/Diploma (HNC/HND)

Each course is made up of a number of modules. These modules are marked with the following grades: pass, merit and distinction. For an overall pass, all units specified by the course should be passed with at least a pass grade. There are no further grades overall.

City and Guilds (C&G)

City and Guilds qualifications are awarded at several levels from pre-vocational level upwards. There are three main occupational levels: level 1, level 2 and level 3.

Certificates are awarded for successful performance demonstrated through a variety of assessment procedures. Some qualifications are awarded on the basis of grades: credit, distinction or simply pass. Increasingly, however, certificates awarded are issued on the basis of acquisition of skills or knowledge for particular competences and may be accompanied by a Record of Achievements indicating specific competences demonstrated.

Pitman Examinations Institute (PEI)

The single subject examinations offered by Pitman Examinations Institute are in most cases available at three levels as follows:

Level 1 (Elementary)
Level 2 (Intermediate)
Level 3 (Advanced)

Two grades of examination success can be achieved, pass or first class pass. In **NVQ** assessments where a level of competence is required only a pass grade is awarded. Group certificates are awarded only when a pre-determined combination of pass grades in single subject examinations or competences have been attained.

Scottish Vocational Education Council (SCOTVEC)

The SCOTVEC qualification system comprises a large number of units of learning (known as modules) which can be built up into group awards. Group awards may be built up to meet national criteria or can be devised to meet the very specific needs of a particular employer. SCOTVEC currently offers three types of units: **National Certificate Modules, Higher National Units and Workplace Assessed Units.**

Workplace Assessed Units are mainly associated with **SVQs**. **National Certificate Modules** may be built into two group awards: **GSVQs** and **National Certificate clusters**. **Clusters** have been introduced to help pupils to make coherent choices from the wide range of National Certificate modules on offer; each **cluster** is a group of three module credits. **Higher National Units** are the building blocks for two group awards: the **Higher National Certificate (HNC)** and the **Higher National Diploma (HND)**. SCOTVEC also offers **Professional Development Awards**; these are postgraduate and post-experience level qualifications designed to help people to further their careers or to make a career change.

Higher National Units are awarded with grades pass or merit, but students either pass or fail **National Certificate Modules** and group awards.

SCOTVEC issues two kinds of certificates: group award certificates and the **Record of Education and Training (RET)**. The **RET** is a cumulative certificate which provides pupils with a lifelong record of success in Scotland's vocational education and training system. The **RET** is updated automatically each time a candidate is credited with success in any SCOTVEC module, unit or course at all levels. It lists every successful module or unit achieved by the candidate. Once the candidate has achieved all the units needed for a group award, this too is automatically recorded on the **RET**. The **RET** also carries the endorsement of any professional bodies that recognize particular qualifications, and indicates where these qualifications count towards membership of professional associations.

Degrees

Honours degrees are usually classified in the following divisions according to performance:

Class I
Class II (Division 1)
Class II (Division 2)
Class III

Ordinary/pass degrees are not classified.

SCHOOL EDUCATION

In the UK schools are either maintained (through public funds) or independent (and fee-paying). Within both sectors schools divide into two tiers: primary and secondary. In England and Wales the division is occasionally into first, middle and upper schools; Scotland only operates a two-tier system.

Maintained schools – which this section is mainly concerned with – are administered by Local Education Authorities (LEAs) in England and Wales and by Education and Library Boards in Northern Ireland. Education Authorities (EAs) are responsible for maintained schools in Scotland. Since 1988, individual schools have been able to apply for grant-maintained status outside of local authority control; these 'self-governing state schools' – formerly 'grant-maintained schools' – receive funding directly from central government.

The Education Reform Act 1988 has resulted in a compulsory national curriculum for maintained schools at primary and secondary levels in **England and Wales**. The national curriculum comprises ten foundation subjects of which English, mathematics and science are core subjects. The other subjects are: technology (including IT), history, geography, music, art, physical education and, for pupils aged eleven to sixteen, a modern foreign language. Programmes of study and attainment targets are set within each subject at four key stages, corresponding to age levels seven, eleven, fourteen and sixteen. Pupils' progress is monitored through assessment tests at each key stage. The **GCSE** will be the principal assessment instrument at Key Stage 4 (the national curriculum is being implemented gradually, and will not take effect at KS4 until 1996).

The Education Reform Act requires that the core and foundation subjects be taught for a reasonable time but gives no statutory definition of what constitutes 'reasonable time'. The review of the manageability of the NC and its testing system conducted by

Sir Ron Dearing in 1993/4 in response to widespread recognition that the curriculum was overloaded has now led to a revised, streamlined curriculum. The new curriculum frees some 20% of teaching time for 5 to 14-year-olds and up to 40 per cent for 14 to 16-year-olds, for use at schools' discretion.

Reforms in **Northern Ireland** are being introduced along the same lines (from September 1990). The foundation subjects broadly correspond to the curriculum in England and Wales.

The Education Reform Act (England and Wales) has no equivalent in **Scotland**. However, consultation and discussion have resulted in agreement on the curricula for primary and secondary schools. A major development programme for the five to fourteen age range comprises a curricular review, guidance on assessment of pupils' progress and attainment across the curriculum – including the creation of a system of national (i.e. Scottish) tests at Primary 4 (age eight) and Primary 7 (age eleven) in aspects of language and mathematics – and advice on procedures for reporting to parents. There are eight modes of study (see **Secondary: Scotland** section), taking up about 70 per cent of pupils' time and therefore forming the core of the curriculum. The rest of the time is available for additional subjects.

Pre-primary: England, Wales, Northern Ireland and Scotland

Schooling is not compulsory for children aged two to four in the UK. However, most LEAs and EAs provide facilities for pre-school/nursery education. These are: nursery schools, nursery and reception classes within primary schools. Children may also attend day nurseries provided by local authority Social Services (in Scotland, Social Work) Departments. The level of nursery provision is lower in Northern Ireland compared with other parts of the UK, although the percentage of three and four-year-olds enrolled in pre-primary schooling is higher than in other parts of the UK.

Many children attend pre-school groups that are organized independently by parents and voluntary organizations, e.g. private playgroups and child-minders. Independent schools also provide schooling for this age-group through preparatory schools (see section **Independent schools**). There are also fee-paying alternatives to maintained nurseries. The latter include schools offering a specific educational philosophy, e.g. the Montessori method.

Primary: England, Wales and Northern Ireland

Children attend primary school from the ages of five to eleven in England, Wales and Northern Ireland. Compulsory education begins at the start of the term after a child's fifth birthday in England and Wales, and at the age of four in Northern Ireland, when children go to infants' schools or departments. There are three types of primary school: infant (five to seven years); junior (seven to eleven years); combined junior and infant schools (five to eleven years). Because some LEAs operate a middle school system, the age at which children transfer to secondary school varies: this can be at eleven, twelve, thirteen or even fourteen years of age. Primary schools are usually co-educational.

In England and Wales all schools must deliver the National Curriculum, which provides a minimum entitlement to a broad and balanced curriculum for all pupils. Within that framework, schools themselves decide how to plan and deliver their curriculum. Assessment tests in English and mathematics are taken at the ages of seven and eleven. In Northern Ireland, pupils' progress is formally assessed at the ages of eight and eleven (since 1990). Schools have freedom as to the methodology and type of textbooks used to implement the national curriculum.

Primary: Scotland

Children attend primary school from the ages of five to twelve in Scotland. The types of primary school are as for England, Wales and Northern Ireland. As in England and Wales, the majority of schools are co-educational.

In Scotland, the government does not operate a national curriculum in primary schools, but there is broad consensus as to curriculum content encouraged by central advice from the Scottish Office Education Department (SOED) and the main curriculum advice and development agency, the Scottish Consultative Council on the Curriculum (SCCC). Teachers are expected to assess pupils' progress in every area of the curriculum and there is national (Scottish) testing of all eight and eleven-year-olds in English and mathematics.

Secondary: England and Wales

Secondary education covers schooling from the age of eleven to the minimum school leaving age of sixteen. Pupils follow a common curriculum leading to the **GCSE**. Pupils may stay on at school for a further three years.

There are some 5,000 secondary schools in the state sector. These schools are organized in a variety of ways: secondary schools for the age range eleven to eighteen; middle schools with pupils moving on to senior secondary level at the ages of twelve, thirteen or fourteen; schools catering only for the age range eleven to sixteen; sixth form colleges which provide sixth form studies for sixteen to nineteen-year-olds.

There are four types of secondary school:

Comprehensive: caters for children of all abilities, providing a wide range of subjects in the curriculum. Around 90 per cent of secondary pupils in the maintained sector attend comprehensives. The remainder attend grammars, secondary moderns or CTCs (see below).

Grammar: provides mainly academic courses for the top 20 per cent of pupils aged eleven to nineteen. These pupils are selected on the basis of ability. There are a decreasing number of such schools.

Secondary modern: offers a general education with a practical bias for pupils aged eleven to sixteen. There are a decreasing number of such schools.

CTC (City Technology College): this is a relatively small type of college (introduced in 1989) for the age range eleven to sixteen providing a broad secondary education with a strong technological and business slant. CTCs have been set up by private sponsors with government grants and are financially independent of LEAs. There were fourteen CTCs in operation in 1992.

Although a certain proportion of comprehensives have sixth forms, a large percentage do not. Post-sixteen pupils wishing to pursue sixth form studies may need to enrol at a school with a sixth form or at a sixth form college. Sixth form colleges only provide courses for pupils aged sixteen to nineteen, operate under school regulations, and offer sixth form studies. They do not admit part-time students or students over nineteen. The average college enrolment is around 500 pupils. Pupils wishing to pursue sixth form studies may also go outside the school sector and enrol at a tertiary college or college of further education (see section **FURTHER EDUCATION**).

The new National Curriculum is being phased into secondary schools over a two-year period, with the new Orders being introduced at Key Stage 3 in September 1995 and at

Key Stage 4 in September 1996. Further to the Dearing review, flexibility within the curriculum for 14 to 16-year-olds is to be increased to allow schools to offer a wider range of academic and vocational options: history, geography, art and music are now optional, and from September 1996 only short courses will be required in modern foreign languages and technology. These developments mean that from September 1996 the compulsory curriculum at Key Stage 4 will only account for roughly 60 per cent of pupils' time.

GCSE is taken by the majority of pupils of school-leaving age. It is intended that **GCSE** will be used for assessment purposes in the national curriculum for the sixteen-year-old age group. **GCE Advanced** is taken after two years of study in the sixth form, sixth form and tertiary colleges or colleges of further education. **IB** courses may also be offered. Students can also study vocational courses in preference to **GCE Advanced** or **IB**.

Secondary: Northern Ireland

Secondary schooling follows the same basic pattern as for England and Wales. However, education is organized largely along selective lines, based on testing. There are four main types of secondary school:

Controlled: provided by the Education and Library Boards and managed through them by Boards of Governors. There are 85 controlled secondary schools providing **GCSE** courses and 18 controlled grammar schools providing **GCSE** and **GCE Advanced** courses.

Catholic maintained secondary: managed by Boards of Governors in conjunction with the Council for Catholic Maintained Schools. Eighty-two of these schools provide **GCSE** courses. A few of the larger schools provide **GCE Advanced** courses.

Voluntary grammar: there are 52 schools managed by Boards of Governors catering for academically inclined pupils, providing GCSE and GCE Advanced courses.

Integrated schools: the policy of successive governments has been to introduce integrated education where there is a local demand for it. There are two types of integrated schools: grant-maintained integrated and controlled integrated.

A common curriculum made up of religious education and six broad areas of study – English, mathematics, science and technology, environment and society, creative and expressive studies, and language studies – is being introduced on a phased basis from September 1990. The curriculum also contains six compulsory cross-curricular themes.

The **GCSE** examination is taken by fifteen to sixteen-year-old pupils at the end of their fifth year of secondary education. Under the present system, no pupil is required to take **GCSE** before leaving school at age sixteen. **GCE Advanced** examinations are normally taken after two years' study in the sixth form between the ages of seventeen and nineteen.

Secondary: Scotland

In Scotland, secondary schooling starts at twelve years of age, and four years of schooling are compulsory between the ages of twelve and sixteen. Pupils may continue for one to two years' additional study.

Secondary education is non-selective and all EA-maintained secondary schools are 'comprehensive'. The majority of maintained schools (sometimes referred to as 'public schools') have fifth and sixth years and, with few exceptions, are co-educational. If a school does not have a fifth and sixth year, pupils may transfer at the end of their fourth year to a six-year comprehensive.

Over 96 per cent of the secondary age population attend EA schools; the remainder are educated in independent (private) schools, about half of which are single sex. A small number of EA schools, serving the remoter areas of the Highlands and Islands, provide hostel accommodation for pupils during term time.

There is no statutory requirement in Scotland to follow a national curriculum. Since 1977, however, a consensus has gradually emerged as to what constitutes a sound secondary education, and detailed guidance has recently been issued by the SCCC on the structure of the secondary school curriculum. Subjects are grouped into eight modes of study and activity – language and communication; mathematical studies and applications; scientific studies and applications; social and environmental studies; technological activities; creative and aesthetic activities; physical education; religious and moral education – with pupils expected to follow at least one subject in each mode. It is possible to study more than one science, technological subject, or foreign language.

At sixteen years of age, pupils take the **Standard Grade** and can go on to take **Highers** and the **Certificate of Sixth Year Study** (optional). In recent years, and particularly as a result of the government's Technical and Vocational Education Initiative (TVEI) in schools (see below), new modular courses leading to the award of a **National Certificate** by the Scottish Vocational Education Council (SCOTVEC) have been widely introduced alongside **Standard Grade, Higher Grade** and **CSYS** courses. They offer complementary qualifications of a more specifically vocational nature for seventeen and eighteen-year-olds especially.

The majority of post-sixteen pupils stay voluntarily at school. Others go straight into employment, apply for the youth training schemes, or pursue further education studies with a vocational orientation.

A reform of upper secondary education is due to be implemented in Scotland in 1997/8. Existing SEB and SCOTVEC provision will be brought into a unified framework at five levels: Advanced Higher, Higher, Credit, General and Foundation. **Highers** will remain, but will incorporate current SCOTVEC as well as SEB provision. This may mean some new **Highers** or the modification of existing ones to include vocational options. The recommended study time for **Highers** will be extended from 120 to 160 hours (though the amount of course content will remain roughly as now). The courses will be modular. **Advanced Highers** will build on **Highers** and incorporate current **CSYS** courses as appropriate to form coherent two-year courses with a recommended study time of 320 hours. Students proceeding to **Advanced Higher** level will be encouraged to bypass the **Higher** examination.

Technical and Vocational Education Initiative (TVEI): England, Wales and Scotland

TVEI is a major curriculum initiative funded by the Employment Department. It is not an examination or a qualification. Its aim is to ensure that the education of fourteen to eighteen-year-olds 'provides young people with the learning opportunities which will equip them for the demands of working life in a rapidly changing society'.

The pilot phase was launched in 1983 and the 'TVEI Extension' in 1987 (£900m funding) extended TVEI-enhanced provision in participating LEAs to all pupils aged fourteen to eighteen in maintained institutions, including special schools. A number of grant-maintained schools are also taking part. The peak years for TVEI participation were 1993 and 1994 – over 4,000 institutions and 1.2m students.

The curriculum enhancement of TVEI is through increased learning opportunities in the following areas: science, modern foreign languages, technology and information technology. Other initiatives include flexible teaching, work experience, Records of Achievement, careers education and guidance and individual Action Plans.

TVEI funding has ended for those LEAs participating first in this scheme; for the majority the funding will end in 1997. The government's White Paper *Competitiveness: Helping Business to Win* (May 1994) contains the commitment to 'increase the resources for spreading best practice identified through TVEI, so that the key results of the initiative are fully embedded in the work of every school'.

Special education: England, Wales, Northern Ireland and Scotland

Special education provision in the UK covers children with emotional, behavioural and learning difficulties and has been greatly influenced by the *Warnock Report* of 1978. This recommended that children should no longer be segregated in schools according to their handicap. Instead, children who have special educational needs should receive help while studying in an ordinary school with children without handicaps wherever possible. A child may still be recommended to attend a special school. Special school provision covers the full school age range from nursery to 16+. There are around 1,500 day and boarding special schools in the UK. Most of them are smaller than mainstream schools, with, on average, 125 pupils to a school. There is a lower pupil/teacher ratio.

Other special education provision includes special education units in mainstream schools, classes in hospital, and in the home. In England, Wales and Scotland an LEA or EA is also required to provide educational provision for gifted children, again dependent on resources available to the LEA/EA.

Independent schools

These are schools outside the maintained sector which are supported by fees paid by parents and gifts of money, usually from past pupils. Some schools are charitable institutions. Approximately 1,400 of the 2,300 registered independent schools have charitable status. This confers a number of advantages in respect of income tax, capital gains tax, corporation tax and VAT. It is understood that in general schools' charitable outgoings in the form of bursaries and scholarships outweigh the financial benefits of charitable status. Commonly now referred to as independent schools, these institutions are sometimes known as public schools, private schools, preparatory and non-maintained schools. In Scotland independent schools are known as private schools.

There are approximately 2,500 independent schools educating some 600,000 pupils. All independent schools have to register with the Education Department (DFE/SOED/DENI) or, in the case of independent nursery schools, the local authority Social Services Departments. Schools are inspected by HMI, although HMI does not operate an accreditation scheme for this sector. Independent schools which belong to leading independent school associations can apply for membership of the Independent Schools Joint Council (ISJC) which operates an accrediting scheme.

Schooling for children aged three to five is through nursery playgroups. Primary schools (known as preparatory schools) provide education for boys between the ages of seven and thirteen and for girls between the ages of seven and eleven, twelve or thirteen. Some preparatory schools have pre-preparatory departments or nursery units catering for the under-five age-group. Such schools do not have to register with the Local Authority Social Services Departments. There is a common entrance examination for secondary schools. Secondary schools provide education between the ages of twelve or thirteen and eighteen or nineteen.

Pupils are accepted on ability. Most schools are small and can provide individual attention. The pupil/teacher ratio is lower than in the mainstream maintained sector and a higher proportion of pupils are boarders. Pupils follow a curriculum leading to **GCSE/Standard Grade** and sixth form studies. Independent schools are not required to follow the national curriculum, but a new independent school wishing to register with the DFE is expected to develop its school curriculum on similar lines.

In England, Wales and Scotland, the government gives income-related financial help to gifted children under its Assisted Places Scheme. The Scheme does not operate in the 19 independent schools in Northern Ireland.

VOCATIONAL EDUCATION

The National Council for Vocational Qualifications (NCVQ) has been reforming and rationalizing vocational qualifications in England, Wales and Northern Ireland since its creation in 1986. NCVQ has developed two new and complementary types of vocational qualification: **National Vocational Qualifications** (NVQs) and **General National Vocational Qualifications** (GNVQs). The government intends that **NVQs** and **GNVQs** will gradually replace all other vocational qualifications, as the main national provision for vocational education and training. Similar developments are taking place in Scotland, under the aegis of the Scottish Vocational Education Council (SCOTVEC).

National Vocational Qualifications (NVQs)

NVQs were introduced from 1988, and more than 750 are now available. They relate to competence to perform a specified range of work-related tasks. **NVQs** are available at five levels within a comprehensive national framework which covers all levels of occupational performance and all areas of employment, and makes explicit the opportunities for progression and transfer between both qualifications and areas of competence:

- Level 1 – Competence in the performance of a range of varied work activities, most of which may be routine and predictable.
- Level 2 – Competence in a significant range of varied work activities, performed in a variety of contexts. Some of the activities are complex or non-routine, and there is some individual responsibility and autonomy. Collaboration with others, perhaps through membership of a work group or team, may often be a requirement.
- Level 3 – Competence in a broad range of varied work activities performed in a wide variety of contexts, most of which are complex and non-routine. There is considerable responsibility and autonomy, and control or guidance of others is often required.
- Level 4 – Competence in a broad range of complex technical or professional work activities performed in a wide variety of contexts and with a substantial degree of personal responsibility and autonomy. Responsibility for the work of others and the allocation of resources is often present.
- Level 5 – Competence which involves the application of a significant range of fundamental principles and complex techniques across a wide and often unpredictable variety of contexts. Very substantial personal autonomy and often significant responsibility for the work of others and for the allocation of resources feature strongly, as do personal accountabilities for analysis and diagnosis, design, planning, execution and evaluation.

'Lead bodies' – made up of employers and employee representatives – set the standards forming the basis of **NVQs** in their particular sector. Whilst **NVQs** are associated with a particular occupation, parts of them – known as 'units' – may have an application in more than one sector: the standards for each **NVQ** are set out in the form of a statement of competence which is made up of units. Awarding bodies then work with the lead bodies to develop candidate assessment and quality control arrangements so that the proposed standards can be delivered as a qualification. NCVQ does not itself award qualifications. Its role is to accredit the qualifications offered by the awarding bodies within the national framework.

Being work-based, **NVQs** are designed to provide open access to assessment and facilitate lifelong learning for people in employment. **NVQ** units can be acquired gradually, and are assessed largely on the basis of a practical demonstration of competence in the workplace. Whilst training courses are available, candidates who feel they already have the necessary competences may be assessed against the national standards to identify competence and further training needs. Assessments are carried out at a centre approved by the awarding body; a centre can be an educational establishment or an industrial or commercial organization.

The Scottish equivalent to **NVQs** are **Scottish Vocational Qualifications** (SVQs)

General National Vocational Qualifications (GNVQs)

The first **GNVQs** were introduced in September 1993, after a pilot year. The GNVQ framework is still being developed. **GNVQs** are currently available at three levels – Foundation, Intermediate, and Advanced – in some subject areas. The framework will cover fifteen vocational areas: art and design; health and social care; manufacturing; business; leisure and tourism; construction and the built environment; science; distribution; information technology; media, communication and production; hospitality and catering; agriculture and land-based sectors; engineering; management; the performing arts. Foundation, Intermediate and Advanced **GNVQs** will be available in all fifteen areas by the end of 1997. It is intended that work will then start on a fourth, higher, **GNVQ** level.

As part of the development of vocational options and in response to the increased flexibility at Key Stage 4, SCAA/NCVQ have also developed a new vocational qualification specifically for 14 to 16-year-olds, to be piloted in 118 schools from September 1995. The **Part One GNVQ** will be available at two levels – Foundation and Intermediate – and initially in the vocational areas of Business, Manufacturing and Health and Social Care. The pilot scheme is likely to expand in 1996 to include more schools and possibly a larger range of subject areas. A full evaluation of the **Part One GNVQ** will be carried out before any decisions are made about general availability.

NCVQ has approved three awarding bodies to award **GNVQs**: the Business and Technician Education Council (BTEC), City and Guilds (C&G), and the RSA Examinations Board. Courses for **GNVQs** are provided in schools and colleges of further education approved by these awarding bodies.

All **GNVQs** are specified in the form of learning outcomes and consist of a number of vocational and core skills units, for which credit may be awarded separately. The core skills units (in communication, application of number and information technology) are mandatory and common to all **GNVQs** at the same level, irrespective of vocational area and awarding body. The vocational units are either mandatory or optional: the mandatory units are the same for all **GNVQs** with the same title and level; the optional units are designed by BTEC, C&G and the RSA Examinations Board, and vary between awarding bodies. Units in personal skills and problem solving are available as additional units to all **GNVQs**.

GNVQs provide a foundation for both higher academic study and further vocational training. They are aligned with **NVQs** in related occupational areas and with the national curriculum and **GCE A/AS levels**. The primary alignment is between **A/AS levels, Advanced GNVQs** and **level 3 NVQs**.

Advanced GNVQs are designed to be of a comparable standard to **GCE A/AS level** qualifications and are sometimes referred to as *vocational A levels*. They are offered to post-sixteen students in a two-year course. **Advanced GNVQs** are awarded on the achievement of twelve vocational units (eight of which are mandatory) plus three core skills units at level 3. Each vocational unit is comparable in its demands and coverage to one-sixth of an **A level** or one-third of an **AS level**. It is possible to combine an **Advanced GNVQ** with **NVQ** units or with one **A level** or one or more **AS levels**.

Intermediate GNVQs are intended to be of comparable standard and coverage to five **GCSEs** at grade C or above. They require the completion of six vocational units (four of which are mandatory) plus three core skills units at level 2. They are usually offered to post-sixteen students in a one-year course.

Foundation GNVQs require the completion of six vocational units (three of which are compulsory) plus three core skills units at level 1. A **Foundation GNVQ** is roughly comparable to four **GCSEs** at grades D to G.

Part One GNVQs are intended to take up roughly 20 per cent of curriculum time at Key Stage 4 and be broadly equivalent to two GCSE grades A^*–C at Intermediate level and grades D–G at Foundation level. They require the completion of three mandatory vocational units plus three core skills units at level one for Foundation or level two for Intermediate.

GNVQs are assessed on the basis of projects and assignments carried out as part of the course, plus externally set written tests for each mandatory unit. The tests are set by the awarding bodies to a common standard ensured through a single test specification and jointly agreed model test for each mandatory unit.

The Scottish equivalent to **GNVQs** are the **General Scottish Vocational Qualifications** (GSVQs).

FURTHER EDUCATION

The further education system in the UK provides opportunities for post-sixteen students to participate in a wide variety of vocational and academic courses up to and including **GCE A level** and **Advanced GNVQ**. Courses may be full-time or part-time and lead to vocational or academic qualifications facilitating entry to occupations or to higher education.

The majority of courses provided in this sector are vocational. Close contact is maintained with local employers to ensure that courses are relevant and up to date. Some courses are sandwich courses which include work experience lasting for up to a year.

Institutions

Further education courses are available in both state-maintained and independent colleges.

There are over 500 state-maintained further education colleges. Some specialize in particular subjects such as agriculture, building or art, others provide courses in a wide variety of subjects.

The Further Education Funding Council (FEFC) has set up its own inspectorate to help fulfil its duty under the 1992 FHE Act to secure quality assessment in colleges in the FE sector. The inspectorate has issued a framework for inspection, setting out a four-year cycle for individual college inspections leading to published reports. The inspections cover provision; governance and management; students' recruitment, guidance and support; quality assurance; and resources.

There are twenty-six Institutes of Further Education in Northern Ireland offering the same range of courses, and forty-six Colleges and Centres of Further Education in Scotland.

Independent colleges offer a wide range of courses ranging from **GCSE** to those which lead to professional and technical qualifications.

The British Accreditation Council for Independent Further and Higher Education (BAC) defines, monitors and improves standards for independent colleges and accredits those which meet its requirements. Accreditation by BAC is not compulsory, but it is a way of safeguarding standards.

BAC also accredits institutions through the Conference for Independent Further Education (CIFE). CIFE operates an inspection scheme for colleges which offer **GCSEs** and **GCE Advanced** examinations.

Qualifications: England, Wales and Northern Ireland

It is the government's aim that **GNVQs** and **NVQs** (see **VOCATIONAL EDUCATION** section above) will become the mainstream national provision for vocational education and training. **GNVQs** and **NVQs** are gradually replacing all other vocational qualifications, but a wide variety of other courses and qualifications remain available to date (March 1995) in the further education sector. Given the plethora of examining bodies in the sector, the list below is far from exhaustive: mention is only made of awarding bodies offering qualifications that have been used as a basis for comparisons in past editions of the *International Guide to Qualifications in Education*.

GCSE and **GCE Advanced** examining boards: see **MARKING SYSTEMS** section at the beginning of this chapter.

The Business and Technician Education Council (BTEC) is responsible for validating a wide variety of work-related courses. Qualifications can be taken in a range of subjects including business and finance, design, hotel and catering and so on. Both part-time and full-time courses are offered, and some courses are sandwich courses, containing an element of work experience. There are three levels of qualifications:

First Certificate/Diploma (FC/FD) – initial vocational qualification for school leavers.

National Certificate/Diploma (NC/ND) – qualifications for technicians or junior administrators.

Higher National Certificate/Diploma (HNC/HND) – qualification for higher-technician, managerial and supervisory levels. HNC/HNDs can also be taken in many higher education institutions.

Courses take one to three years depending on level and mode of study.

GNVQs are gradually replacing other BTEC awards. **Intermediate GNVQs** correspond to BTEC **First, Advanced GNVQs** to BTEC **National. GNVQ level 4** (yet to be developed) will correspond to BTEC **Higher National**.

City and Guilds (C&G) is Britain's leading technical testing and awarding body, providing assessments, certification and other services in Britain and over 80 countries internationally. It awards nationally recognized certificates in over 500 subjects, many of which are **NVQs**. Its progressive structure of awards spans seven levels; levels 1-5 correspond to levels 1-5 in the National Qualification Framework as defined by NCVQ:

C&G level	Qualifications
7	**Fellowship** (FCGI)
6	**Member** (MCGI)
5	**Graduate** (GCGI) / **NVQ level 5**
4	**Licenciate** (LCGI) / **NVQ level 4**
3	**Certificate Part III / NVQ level 3**
2	**Certificate Part II / NVQ level 2**
1	**Certificate Part I / NVQ level 1**

Courses leading to City and Guilds assessments and certification are, in many cases, part-time day-release courses where candidates are granted time off work by their employers in order to attend the course. Full-time and evening courses are also available in many subjects. There is no fixed time span for a course leading to City and Guilds certification. Subjects offered include: agriculture, engineering, caring and personnel services, including hairdressing and hotel and catering.

The Pitman Examinations Institute, now a division of City and Guilds, offers a wide range of vocational qualifications and English language qualifications by examination or, for **NVQs**, by competence assessment in office skills, information technology, business studies, business English, ESOL and training. Qualifications are available at three or more levels as single subject certificates or group certificates.

Qualifications: Scotland

The Scottish Vocational Education Council (SCOTVEC) is the national body in Scotland responsible for developing, awarding and accrediting vocational qualifications. It provides a wide range of modules at two main levels:

SCOTVEC National
SCOTVEC Higher National

Group awards are available at both levels. There are two categories: **national awards** which are developed on a national basis and **tailored awards** which can be customized to suit the needs of individual candidates. **Scottish Vocational Qualifications** (SVQs) and **General Scottish Vocational Qualifications** (GSVQs) are awarded by SCOTVEC, or by other awarding bodies and accredited by SCOTVEC. These are analogous to **NVQs** and **GNVQs**, and SCOTVEC works closely with the NVCQ to ensure that developments in England are mirrored in Scotland.

This brief outline can only give an indication of the vast range of courses offered in Colleges of Further Education. For further information the addresses of the examining bodies mentioned can be found at the end of the chapter. The *Directory of Further Education* should also be consulted. Information on the **GCSE** groups and **GCE Advanced** examining boards is given in Appendix 1.

HIGHER EDUCATION

The term higher education is defined as study above **GCE Advanced level** (that is, the **GCE A level**, the Scottish equivalent, or **Advanced GNVQ/NVQ level 3**).

Among the main effects of the Further and Higher Education Act 1992 have been:
- The elimination of the binary system of higher education by which the older universities and the polytechnics were treated separately.
- The abolition of the Council for National Academic Awards (CNAA), leaving most institutions to award their own degrees.
- The creation of Higher Education Funding Councils.

Higher education in the United Kingdom is now provided in two types of institution:

Universities

In the United Kingdom, universities are independent, self-governing bodies, empowered by a Royal Charter or an Act of Parliament to create their own courses and award degrees. Their high standards are maintained by their extensive use of external examiners to ensure that degrees are of the same standard from one institution to another.

Approximately 50 'older' universities offer courses ranging from first degree level upwards and are centres of research. Included in this group are the Open University, two universities in Northern Ireland, eight in Scotland and the independent University of Buckingham.

All thirty-seven polytechnics in England and Wales have now been renamed as universities, as have a few colleges/institutions of higher education and Scottish central institutions (see below). These institutions offer courses in a wide range of subjects from BTEC **HND** level to research. They also provide training for many professions, commerce and industry. Degrees in polytechnics were formerly awarded by the CNAA (which had a Royal Charter). The 'new' universities are particularly responsive to the needs of non-traditional students and employers through modular courses, part-time and sandwich modes of attendance, flexible admissions policies and the provision of access courses, and subscription to credit transfer schemes.

Colleges and Institutions of Higher Education (CIHEs)

A wide range of vocational and academic courses are provided in approximately 70 colleges and institutes of higher education in the UK. These colleges have developed from varied origins, many remaining specialist colleges, including those which concentrate on teacher training, art or agriculture. CIHEs have made arrangements for their degrees, previously awarded by the CNAA, to be awarded by another institution, usually a neighbouring university. Others work with the Open University.

Qualifications

Undergraduate courses

Three main types of qualifications are available at undergraduate level:

BTEC/SCOTVEC Higher National Certificate/Diploma (HNC/HND)

Courses leading to the BTEC/SCOTVEC **HNC/HND** are for higher technician, managerial and supervisory levels. **HNC** courses last one year full-time, two years part-time; **HND** courses are usually two years full-time, but a few, including sandwich courses, last three years. Many institutions give students the opportunity to transfer at appropriate stages to degree courses.

Diploma of Higher Education (DipHE)

A two-year course leads to the **DipHE**. It is often possible to transfer on to an appropriate degree course on completion of a **DipHE**, although the qualification is valid in its own right.

First degree

There are a number of different types of degrees:

Honours degree – one subject is studied in depth;
Joint/Combined/Double Honours degree – two or more subjects are studied in combination, to the same level;
General Honours degrees – a less specialized course where more subjects are taken to a lower level;
Ordinary/Pass degree – a slightly less demanding course where several subjects may be studied.

The basic degree in England, Wales and Northern Ireland is a **Bachelor degree** with Honours obtained after three years' study, although some professional courses may last five years (including architecture, dentistry, veterinary medicine) and courses in medicine last six years. Accelerated Honours degree programmes have exactly the same curricula as the conventional degrees on which they are based, but teaching and learning take place over a period of twenty-four months; this is achieved by teaching during the normal long summer vacation and reducing other holiday periods. The Scottish degree system differs from that of most of the rest of the UK in that the Honours degree requires four years of study.

Titles of degrees

First degrees are generally called **Bachelor degrees** and are known by a number of titles. The list below is not exhaustive:

Bachelor of Arts (BA)
Bachelor of Science (BSc)
Bachelor of Education (BEd)
Bachelor of Engineering (BEng)
Bachelor of Law (LLB)

There are some **postgraduate Bachelor degrees**, however: the **Bachelor of Philosophy**, the **Bachelor of Divinity** and the **Bachelor of Architecture**. Just as all **Bachelor degrees** are not necessarily at first-degree level, not all first degrees are entitled **Bachelor**. The following are first degrees too:

Graduate Diploma in Music (Grad Dip Mus)
Master of Arts (MA) from the Universities of Aberdeen, Edinburgh, Dundee, Glasgow and St Andrews (the older Scottish universities)
Master of Engineering (MEng)
At some universities, including Oxford and Cambridge, the **BA** is awarded for both arts and science courses. The **BSc** does not exist at Cambridge and is a higher degree at Oxford.

Postgraduate courses

At this level, students can study for postgraduate certificates, diplomas and higher degrees.

Postgraduate certificates and diplomas offer vocational training or a professional qualification. Courses usually last for one or two years of full-time study and can lead to qualifications or may be integrated into **Master's degree** programmes.

A **Master's degree** can be obtained by pure research or by a course of instruction which will include a short research project and an examination. **Master's degree** programmes lead to a variety of awards including:

Master of Arts (MA)
Master of Science (MSc)
Master of Business Administration (MBA)
Master of Philosophy (MPhil)

Oxford and Cambridge graduates, after a specified number of years, can obtain an **MA** without further study, on the payment of a fee.

Doctorates are normally awarded after at least three years of supervised research. The most common award is **Doctor of Philosophy (PhD/DPhil).**

The following table indicates some of the postgraduate awards available:

	Postgraduate certificates and diplomas	Masters	Doctorates
Taught	**Diploma in Librarianship (DipLib)** **Postgraduate Certificate in Education (PGCE)** **Diploma in Management Studies (DMS)**	**Master of Arts (MA)** **Master of Business Administration (MBA)** **Master of Education (MEd)** **Master of Science (MSc)**	
Research		**Master of Philosophy (MPhil)** **Bachelor of Philosophy (BPhil)**	**Doctor of Philosophy (PhD, DPhil)**

Entrance requirements

Minimum entrance requirements are given in the table entitled **British Qualifications** at the end of this chapter. Satisfying the minimum entrance requirements does not guarantee a place or give a student the right to enter a higher education course, however, since the student must also satisfy the course requirements imposed by individual faculties or schools. Course requirements may be very demanding.

Access and bridging courses

The purpose of an access and bridging course is to bridge the gap between a student's qualifications and the entrance qualifications of a course. Bridging courses are available for entry to both undergraduate degree and postgraduate courses, and many are specially designed for overseas students.

The entry requirements for bridging courses leading to undergraduate courses are **GCSE/O level** or a standard between **GCSE/O level** and **GCE Advanced**. For entry to a bridging course which leads to postgraduate admission, applicants should normally hold a first degree or a comparable qualification from overseas. In both cases, proficiency in English is required.

Courses usually last for one year and involve a study of subjects relevant to the intended degree course, often including English tuition. They are held at higher education institutions or at colleges of further education which have links with nearby universities or colleges of higher education.

Modularity and credit transfer schemes

The use of credit accumulation and transfer in the UK has been pioneered by the former polytechnics through the **Credit Accumulation and Transfer Scheme** (CATS) established by the CNAA in 1985. The CAT scheme, which operates in England, Wales and Northern Ireland, is now administered by the Open University. It is based upon the standard achievement required for the three-year full-time Honours degree. Each of these years is considered a separate stage, indicated by a level: level 1 for the first year, level 2 for the second, level 3 for the third. There is also a postgraduate level: level M. Each course unit has a number of credit points assigned to it on the basis of 120 points for each full-time year of study:

The award of a	requires
DipHE	120 credits at level 1 and 120 credits at level 2
Unclassified/Ordinary Bachelor degree	360 credits including at least 60 at level 3 and no more than 120 at level 1
Bachelor degree with Honours	360 credits including at least 120 at level 3 and no more than 120 at level 1
Postgraduate Diploma	70 credits at level M
Master's degree	120 credits at level M

The equivalent scheme in Scotland (SCOTCAT) comprises four undergraduate levels (SD1-SD4) and is recognized by all the Scottish higher education institutions.

The concept of credit accumulation and transfer has also gained ground because of European exchange programme such as ERASMUS. The CAT scheme can be made compatible with the **European Credit Transfer Scheme** (ECTS) by dividing CATS credits by two to get ECTS credits.

TEACHER EDUCATION

England and Wales

In England and Wales new teachers need to have a professional training in education as well as a high standard of competence in the subject that they will teach.

The Department for Education (DFE) has set out criteria which all courses of initial teacher training must meet. The previous system by which the Secretary of State for Education has *approved courses* which comply with the criteria will be replaced with effect from August 1995 when the new Teacher Training Agency (TTA) will assume responsibility for *accrediting course providers*. Courses themselves will still have to comply with the Department's criteria, although OFSTED inspection findings will inform TTA decisions on both accreditation and funding. Students will therefore secure qualified teacher status (QTS) by successfully completing a course at an accredited institution.

Bachelor of Education (BEd): usually a four-year honours course providing the opportunity to study both a subject appropriate to the school curriculum and professional teaching skills. **BEd** courses are offered by colleges/institutes of higher education, colleges of education, and universities. Specially shortened (two-year) **BEd** are available in some subjects; these courses are designed for mature entrants who already have appropriate technical or professional qualifications (such as **Higher National** awards) and experience. The government is also encouraging the development of new three-year primary **BEd** courses in up to six subjects which will ensure a supply of teachers with a broad-based knowledge of the primary curriculum.

Postgraduate Certificate of Education (PGCE): a one-year course following a first degree and focusing on professional teaching skills and the application of subject specialisms to teaching and assessment. **PGCE** courses are usually offered by universities. There are a small number of two-year part-time **PGCE** courses available. Two-year full-time **PGCEs** are also available for those wishing to teach a subject which is not the main subject of their first degree.

Most primary-level initial teacher training is provided through the **BEd**, whereas training for secondary teachers tends to be via the **PGCE**. However, a **PGCE/BEd** is equally valid in both sectors. Pre-primary teachers may require a **BEd/PGCE** or a specialist award from the Council for Awards in Children's Care and Education.

Newly qualified teachers are no longer required to serve a probationary period on taking up their first appointment into a state-maintained school.

Teachers may also enter the teaching profession through the **licensed teacher** or **overseas trained teacher routes**. The **Licensed teacher scheme** is aimed at mature people with a certain level of higher education. The **Overseas trained teacher scheme** is for graduate trained teachers with experience from overseas countries outside the European Economic Area (EEA). These are in-service routes that enable unqualified teachers to teach under licence or authorization (overseas trained teachers) in schools where QTS is the normal requirement. Both routes enable teachers to acquire QTS upon successful completion of a period of teaching service linked to an individually tailored training programme. The schemes are employer-led and it will be for them to decide whether they wish to make use of the arrangements. Once a licence or authorization has been granted, the employer is under duty to arrange training for the teacher. Normally the licence or authorization will be for two years (extended pro rata for part-time posts). However, not all candidates will need to serve for the full period before they can be recommended for QTS. The arrangements are open to people who have different levels of training and experience and the regulations allow QTS to be awarded earlier in certain circumstances, provided the employer is satisfied that the teacher has attained the necessary competences.

School teachers from Scotland or Northern Ireland may be entitled to QTS if they have successfully completed a course of initial teacher training, or are recognized as teachers in those countries. Teachers who are nationals of participating EEA member states may be entitled to QTS if they meet the requirements of Directive 89/48/EEC on the mutual recognition of qualifications.

Everybody entering the teaching profession must have achieved a standard equivalent to **GCSE** grade C in both English language and mathematics. In addition, all entrants to primary initial teacher training courses after 1 September 1998 who were born on or after 1 September 1979 should have attained the standard equivalent to **GCSE** grade C or above in a science subject or subjects.

Teachers of blind, deaf and children of partial hearing in special schools must have additional specialist teaching qualifications. Teachers of children handicapped in other ways, whether in a special or other school, do not require other specialist qualifications. Some further and higher education institutions offer courses for special-educational-needs teachers.

Teachers update and extend their professional skills and knowledge through in-service training (INSET). Teachers' conditions of service include five non-teaching days which should be used mainly for training. INSET needs are identified and met within a framework of specific grants, regular teacher appraisal, school inspections and school staff development plans. Training is provided by a variety of organizations including their LEA, higher education institutions, private firms and independent consultancies.

Northern Ireland

As in England and Wales, the two teacher training qualification routes are through the **BEd** and the **PGCE**. In Northern Ireland, training is provided by the education departments in the two universities and two colleges of education. Prospective teachers may also do their training through further and higher education institutions in England and Wales. These qualifications must be acceptable to the Department of Education in Northern Ireland. All teachers in pre-primary, primary and secondary grant-aided schools must hold one of the above teacher training qualifications. However, graduates who obtained their degrees before January 1974, may teach in secondary schools without having taken a course of professional training.

Teachers in special schools must hold a standard teacher training qualification. Additional specialist qualifications are required to teach blind, deaf or children with partial hearing in both ordinary and special schools.

Scotland

All teachers employed by EAs need to be registered with The General Teaching Council (GTC) for Scotland. Eligibility for registration requires entrants to have a teaching qualification awarded at a Scottish college of education or equivalent qualification approved by the GTC. Recognized teacher training in Scotland is carried out by two colleges of education – Northern and St Andrews – and four universities.

Primary school teachers must have taken a four-year degree course or the one-year postgraduate course designed specifically for primary teachers.

Secondary teachers must have a first degree, or a comparable qualification, in the subject they wish to teach, followed by a one-year postgraduate course. Secondary teachers of physical education, music and technical education can acquire qualified status through the **BEd**. Teachers of music and technological education may train through a degree followed by a postgraduate course.

It is not strictly necessary for teachers in independent schools to hold a teaching qualification, but it is preferred in the majority of cases.

As regards the teaching of special education, colleges of education in Scotland offer diploma courses for those wishing to teach children and young people with learning difficulties or handicaps of one kind or another.

DISTANCE EDUCATION

Education and training is also provided through distance education, which combines the use of self-study materials with various kinds of teaching techniques and types of media. Distance education is sometimes known as 'open' or 'flexible' learning.

In the UK the Open University (OU) provides part-time degree and vocational courses for all, regardless of age, status and academic qualifications. Courses are taught through TV and radio broadcasts, correspondence texts and summer schools, together with a network of study centres. The **BA** is a general degree, comparable in standard to other UK degrees and is awarded on a system of credits for each course completed. Although normally only available to UK residents, OU courses are studied throughout Eastern Europe and parts of Russia.

Some mainstream higher education institutions offer postgraduate degrees through distance learning such as The University of London External Programme. Other such postgraduate courses are listed in the British Council publication *Overseas Student Access Survey*.

Further and higher education institutions also offer open learning packages of their own. These are listed in the *Open Learning Directory*.

The Open College (OC) established in 1987, offers vocational and professional training, many of its courses leading to nationally recognized qualifications. A number of other private independent colleges provide flexible learning including correspondence courses. These include **GCSE, GCE Advanced**, business and secretarial studies, etc. The Council for the Accreditation of Correspondence Colleges (CACC) is the accrediting body for independent colleges offering correspondence courses.

PROFESSIONAL QUALIFICATIONS

Professional bodies are responsible for setting and maintaining standards in the professions they represent. There are approximately 400 professional bodies covering a wide range of professions.

Entrance into a profession is often based on the holding of appropriate qualifications. Most professional bodies conduct their own examinations. However, other qualifications are often accepted and may give exemption from some of the professional body's examinations.

Courses for professional examinations are taken in colleges of further and higher education and some universities. Students can study full-time, part-time or, in some cases, through distance learning.

Professional qualifications exist at all levels and some have been accredited by the NCVQ and placed in levels 1-4. The NCVQ is considering how qualifications at higher levels can be related to an extended **NVQ** framework.

ENGLISH LANGUAGE

English language examinations (see chart on next page)

Both public and private-sector institutions offer courses leading to examinations in English as a foreign language. Accreditation of schools and validation of English language courses is carried out by the Accreditation Unit of the British Council. There are two schemes: the English Language Schools Recognition Scheme for the private sector and the Courses Validation Scheme for the public sector. There are also two professional bodies: ARELS (Association of Recognized English Language Schools) covers the private sector and BASCELT (the British Association of State Colleges in English Language Teaching) the public sector. Both bodies produce a brochure annually giving details of member institutions and the courses offered.

The British Council, jointly with the University of Cambridge Local Examinations Syndicate (UCLES) and the IDP Education Australia, manages a test of academic English called the **International English Language Testing System** (IELTS). It has superseded ELTS (the English Language Testing Service). The test provides a systematic means of assessing the English of non-native speakers who intend to study or train in the medium of English. It is offered normally once a month (more often during peak times) and measures the candidate's general language skills and the skills needed for study and training. There are test centres in around 100 countries, including twenty-two centres in the UK. The specimen materials booklet, complete with cassettes, provides detailed information on test format, content and procedures, and costs about £7.00. It can be obtained from local test centres and from: UCLES, Publications Department, 1 Hills Road, Cambridge CB1 2EU.

Higher education entrance requirements

This is *only* an indication of the standards required. Applicants should check with the institution.

AEB Test in English for educational purposes (TEEP)	Grade 3
ARELS oral examinations (Higher certificate) – acceptable if applicant has this **and** a credit in the Oxford examinations in EFL (Higher certificate)	Pass
British Council/UCLES/IDP International English Language Testing System (IELTS)	5.5–7.0

ENGLISH LANGUAGE EXAMINATIONS

LEVEL	GENERAL ENGLISH						ACADEMIC ENGLISH		
	ARELS	UNIVERSITY OF LONDON	OXFORD	PITMAN	TRINITY COLLEGE	UCLES	AEB	BRITISH COUNCIL/ UCLES/IDP	JMB
	Oral examinations	GCE O level Syllabus B	Oxford examinations in EFL	English for speakers of other languages	Spoken English	UCLES	Test in English for educational purposes	International English language testing system	University entrance test in ESOL
9								9	
8	Diploma PASS		Higher Certificate		12	Diploma of English Studies		8	
7	Higher Certificate DISTINCTION		DISTINCTION	ADVANCED	11	PASS Certificate of Proficiency	4	7	
6	CREDIT		CREDIT			C Certificate of Advanced English (Pass = 6.5 IELTS)	3	6	
	PASS	C	PASS	HIGHER INTERMEDIATE	10				PASS
5	Preliminary Certificate		Preliminary Certificate		9	First Certificate	2	5	
	VERY GOOD PASS		DISTINCTION	INTERMEDIATE	8	C			

Levels of examinations (this is part of the English Speaking Union's 1 to 9 scale of language proficiency)

9 Full command of the language

8 Uses full range of language with proficiency approaching that in the learner's own tongue

7 Uses language fully, effectively and confidently in most situations

6 Uses language with confidence in all but the most demanding situations

5 Uses language independently and effectively in all familiar situations

JMB University entrance test in ESOL	Pass
University of London O-level English language Syllabus B	Grade C
Oxford examinations in EFL (Higher certificate) – acceptable if applicant has this **and** a pass in the ARELS oral examinations (Higher certificate)	Credit
Pitman Examinations Institute ESOL examinations (Higher Intermediate and Advanced certificates)	Pass
UCLES Certificate of Proficiency in English	Pass

USEFUL PUBLICATIONS

General

1. *Education Year Book*. Longman (annual)
2. *Education Fact File*. Hodder and Stoughton, 1989

School education

1. *Education Authorities Directory*. School Government Publishing (annual)
2. *Choosing Your Independent School*. ISIS (annual)

Vocational and further education

1. *Directory of Further Education*. Hobsons publications (annual)
2. *Guide to National Vocational Qualifications*. Department of Employment/NCVQ, 1991
3. *The New Qualification Framework*. Department for Education, 1994
4. *Vocational Qualifications in England, Wales and Northern Ireland*. NCVQ, 1994
5. *Yearbook of Adult Continuing Education*. NIACE (annual)

Higher education

1. *Access to UK Higher Education*. HMSO for the British Council (annual)
2. *Degree Course Guides*. Hobsons Publications (in 2 vols: alternate years)
3. *Graduate Studies*. Hobsons Publications (annual)
4. *University and College Entrance: The Official Guide*. UCAS (annual)
5. *Recognised Degree Courses in the United Kingdom*. Department for Education, 1993

Teacher education

1. *NATFHE Handbook of Initial Teacher Training*. NATFHE/Linneys (annual)
2. *University Courses in Education Open to Students from Overseas*. UCET (annual)

Distance education

1. *Open Learning Directory*. Training Enterprise Education Directorate (TEED) (annual)

Professional qualifications

1. *British Qualifications*. Kogan Page (annual)
2. *Occupations*. Careers and Occupational Information Centre (annual)
3. *Directory of British Associations*. CBD Research Ltd, 10th ed 1990

English language

1. *ESU Framework: Performance Scales for English Language Examinations*. Longman, 1989
2. *Longman Guide to English Language Examinations*. Longman, 1989
3. *English Language Entrance Requirements in British Higher Education*. British Council, 1994.

USEFUL ADDRESSES

School education

Central Bureau for Educational Visits and Exchanges
Seymour Mews House
Seymour Mews
London W1H 9PE
Telephone 0171-486 5101

Midland Examining Group (MEG)
Syndicate Buildings
1 Hills Road
Cambridge CB1 2EU
Telephone 01223-553311

National Council for Educational Technology (NCET)
Milburn Hill Road
Science Park
Coventry CV4 7JJ
Telephone 01203-416994

Northern Examinations and Assessment Board
Devas Street
Manchester M15 6EX
Telephone 0161-953 1180

Northern Ireland Council for the Curriculum, Examinations and
Assessment (NICCEA)
Beechill House
42 Beechill Road
Belfast BT8 4RS
Telephone 01232-704666

School Curriculum and Assessment Authority (SCAA)
Newcombe House
45 Notting Hill Gate
London W11 3JB
Telephone 0171-229 1234

Scottish Vocational Education Council (SCOTVEC)
Schools Unit
Hanover House
24 Douglas Street
GLASGOW G2 7NQ
Telephone 0141-248 7900

Southern Examining Group (SEG)
Stag Hill House
Guildford
Surrey GU2 5XJ
Telephone 01483-506506

University of London Examinations and Assessment Council (ULEAC)
Stewart House
32 Russell Square
London WC1B 5DN
Telephone 0171-331 4000

Welsh Joint Education Committee (WJEC)
245 Western Avenue
Cardiff CF5 2YX
Telephone 01222-561231

Further education

British Accreditation Council for Independent Further and Higher Education (BAC)
Suite 401
27 Marylebone Road
London NW1 5JS
Telephone 0171-4874643

Business and Technician Education Council (BTEC)
Central House
Upper Woburn Place
London WC1H 0HH
Telephone 0171-413 8405/6

City and Guilds (C&G)
76 Portland Place
London W1N 4AA
Telephone 0171-278 2468

Conference for Independent Further Education (CIFE)
Secretary: Myles Glover
Buckhall Farm
Bull Lane
Betherden
Nr Ashford
Kent TN26 3HB
Telephone 01233-820797

The Further Education Funding Council
Sheriffs Orchard
Greyfriars Road
Coventry CV1 3PJ
Telephone 01203-530300

National Council for Vocational Qualifications (NCVQ)
222 Euston Road
London NW1 2BZ
Telephone 0171-387 9898

Pitman Examinations Institute
Catteshall Manor
Godalming
Surrey GU7 1UU
Telephone 01483-415311

Scottish Vocational Education Council (SCOTVEC)
Hanover House
24 Douglas Street
Glasgow G2 7NQ
Telephone 0141-248 7900

Higher education

Committee of Vice-Chancellors and Principals of the Universities of the United
Kingdom (CVCP)
29 Tavistock Square
London WC1H 9EZ
Telephone 0171-387 9231

Universities and Colleges Admissions Service
Fulton House
Jessop Avenue
Cheltenham
Gloucestershire GL50 3SH
Telephone 01242-222444

Teacher education

Council for the Accreditation of Teacher Education (CATE)
c/o Department for Education
Elizabeth House
York Road
London SE1 7PH
Telephone 0171-934 0946

General Teaching Council (GTC) for Scotland
5 Royal Terrace
Edinburgh EH7 5AF
Telephone 0131-556 0072

Teaching as a Career (TASC)
35 Great Smith Street
London SW1P 3BJ
Telephone 0171-227 2867

Distance education

The Open University
PO Box 200
Milton Keynes MK7 6YZ
Telephone 01908-653 231

Council for the Accreditation of Correspondence Colleges (CACC)
27 Marylebone Road
London NW1 5JS
Telephone 0171-935 5391

English language

ARELS Examinations Trust (AET)
Ewert Place
Summertown
Oxford OX2 7BZ
Telephone 01865-514272

English Speaking Union of the Commonwealth
Dartmouth House
37 Charles Street
Berkeley Square
London W1X 8AB
Telephone 0171-493 3328

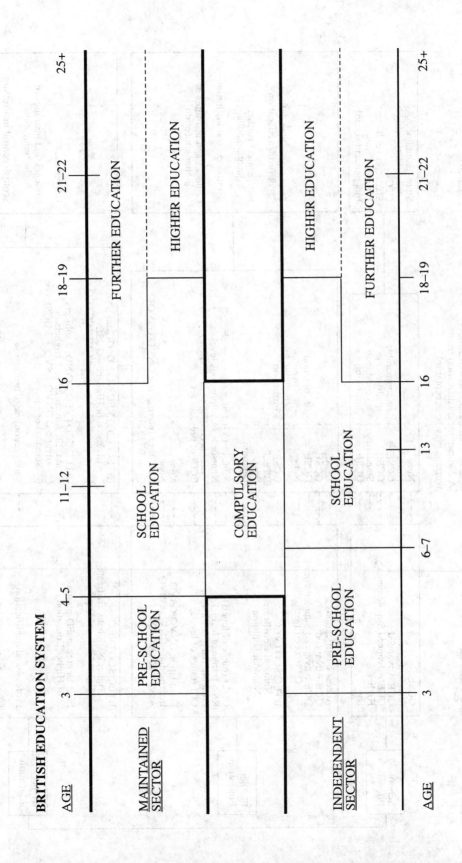

BRITISH EDUCATION SYSTEM

BRITISH QUALIFICATIONS

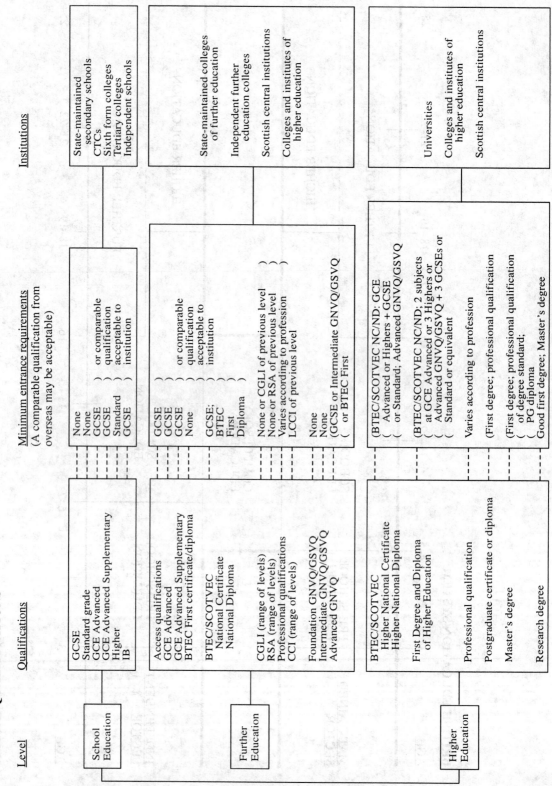

Level	Qualifications	Minimum entrance requirements (A comparable qualification from overseas may be acceptable)	Institutions
School Education	GCSE	None	State-maintained secondary schools
	Standard grade	None	CTCs
	GCE Advanced	GCSE } or comparable qualification acceptable to institution	Sixth form colleges
	GCE Advanced Supplementary	GCSE }	Tertiary colleges
	Higher	Standard }	Independent schools
	IB	GCSE }	
Further Education	Access qualifications	GCSE } or comparable qualification acceptable to institution	State-maintained colleges of further education
	GCE Advanced	GCSE }	
	GCE Advanced Supplementary	GCSE }	Independent further education colleges
	BTEC First certificate/diploma	None }	
	BTEC/SCOTVEC National Certificate National Diploma	GCSE; BTEC First Diploma }	Scottish central institutions
			Colleges and institutes of higher education
	CGLI (range of levels)	None or CGLI of previous level }	
	RSA (range of levels)	None or RSA of previous level }	
	Professional qualifications	Varies according to profession }	
	CCI (range of levels)	LCCI of previous level }	
	Foundation GNVQ/GSVQ	None	
	Intermediate GNVQ/GSVQ	None	
	Advanced GNVQ	(GCSE or Intermediate GNVQ/GSVQ (or BTEC First	
Higher Education	BTEC/SCOTVEC Higher National Certificate Higher National Diploma	(BTEC/SCOTVEC NC/ND: GCE (Advanced or Highers + GCSE (or Standard; Advanced GNVQ/GSVQ	Universities
	First Degree and Diploma of Higher Education	(BTEC/SCOTVEC NC/ND; 2 subjects (at GCE Advanced or 3 Highers or (Advanced GNVQ/GSVQ + 3 GCSEs or (Standard or equivalent	Colleges and institutes of higher education
	Professional qualification	Varies according to profession	Scottish central institutions
	Postgraduate certificate or diploma	(First degree; professional qualification	
	Master's degree	(First degree; professional qualification (of degree standard; (PG diploma	
	Research degree	Good first degree; Master's degree	

Afghanistan

Following the Soviet invasion, the traditional Islamic education system was reorganized to conform more closely with the Soviet model. Russian became the first foreign language in Afghan schools. Political indoctrination became part of the school curriculum. <u>Kabul University</u> was systematically robbed of any independence and remodelled on the Soviet pattern. The quality of teaching declined and Soviet lecturers played an increasingly active and important role following the imprisonment of other lecturers/professors. University entrance standards were reduced to allow those who had completed their military service to enter university. Notice was given of forthcoming entrance examinations, but only for girls and young men who had completed at least three years' military service. In parts of the country under the control of the mujahideen local resistance leaders tried to provide adequate schooling along traditional Afghan lines, based largely on the Koran.

1979-1992

During this period, education was free and lodging was provided for students from other areas. A small educational grant was also given. This resulted in a large number of students enrolling for higher education. Higher education was spread from Kabul to other major cities such as Mazar, Herat and Kandahar, and new technical colleges and colleges of higher education were established. The study of social sciences and the use of the Russian language in educational establishments became more widespread. At the universities, departments of Russian languages were added.

The medium of instruction is one of the two national languages (*Dari* or *Poshtu*), depending on which is spoken by the majority. At university, English is used as the medium of instruction in all faculties.

Under the Education Policy of January 1975, the period of compulsory primary education was eight years. However, it was not possible to enforce this owing to insufficient facilities. Education is now compulsory for six years covering the primary sector (ages seven to twelve).

The academic year runs from March to December (colder regions), from August to May (warmer regions) and from April to December (higher school).

EVALUATION IN BRITAIN

School

Baccalauria – generally considered comparable to GCSE standard (grades A, B and C) on a subject-for-subject basis, with the exception of English Language.

Higher

Bachelor degree/Licence – generally considered to be below British Bachelor degree standard.

MARKING SYSTEMS

School

Until 1976

Marking was on a scale of 0–10 (maximum); the minimum pass-mark was 3.5 and the minimum average was 50 per cent of the sum of the highest marks for all subjects.

School and Higher

Since 1976

Marking is on a percentage scale: 40 per cent is the minimum pass-mark for individual subjects; the minimum average is 55 per cent of the sum of the highest marks for all subjects:

Alaa	100 – 86 per cent
Aali	85 – 66 per cent
Khoob	65 – 50 per cent

SCHOOL EDUCATION

Pre-primary

This is available in cities; *Shirkhargah* (crèche) looking after one to three-year-olds and *Koodakestan* (nursery) taking over from age three to six.

Primary (*Maktabeh Ebtedaee*)

This covers six years from age seven, divided into two three-year cycles. In rural areas the period is shorter. The lower cycle covers mother tongue (*Dari* or *Poshtu*), mathematics, religious instruction, arts, crafts and physical education. The upper cycle covers the same subjects plus a second language, social studies and science.

Secondary

There is an entrance examination for admission to this level. It covers six years, divided into two three-year cycles: grades 7 to 9, studied at *Maktabeh Motevaseteh* (middle school), and grades 10 to 12 at high school/*Doreyeh Aali*. In the first cycle, the curriculum covers Dari, Poshtu, mathematics, the Koran, theology, history, chemistry, physics, biology, Arabic, a foreign language (often English), economics, geography, and manual work. On completion of this cycle, pupils take an examination to decide on admission to the second cycle. This cycle offers the same curriculum, with the addition of geology, religion, philosophy, psychology and sociology. Girls study needlework in grades 7 to 9 and home economics in grades 10 to 12. Specialization is offered in scientific and mathematical fields, as well as in humanities. On completion of this cycle, pupils take the examinations for the **Baccalauria**.

Vocational Secondary

In the lower secondary cycle at the middle schools, boys may specialize in commerce, theology, applied arts, mechanics, military training or mechanics, and girls in teacher training or commerce. In the upper secondary cycle, boys may specialize in teacher training, Islamic law, aeronautics, technology, land surveying, agriculture, dentistry and nursing, and girls in nursing, home economics and teacher training. Courses lead to a **Baccalauria** level qualification

Three-year courses covering grades 8 to 10 (including an orientation year) are available to train plumbers, mechanics, etc.

The Afghan Institute of Technology, established in 1951, trains supervisors and assistant engineers on courses covering grades 10 to 12. The best students may then go on to the Faculty of Engineering at Kabul University.

HIGHER EDUCATION

Kabul University was founded in 1932 and has nine faculties: medicine; science; agriculture; engineering; law and political science; literature; economics; theology; pharmacology. The University of Nangarhar was founded in 1963. Other universities have been established in Mazar, Herat and Kandahar. Admission to first-degree courses is based on the **Baccalauria** and success in an entrance examination (*Concours*). Courses leading to the award of a **Bachelor degree/Licence** last four years, with five years in engineering and veterinary medicine, and seven years in medicine (including one year pre-medical and one year internship). A further two years' study (three to four years in medicine) leads to the award of a **Master's degree**.

The University of Nangarhar offers **Bachelor degree** courses in medicine, agriculture and engineering. The Universities of Balkh and Herat also offer the seven year medical degree, along with a four year **Bachelor of Education** and four year **Bachelor degrees** in Social Sciences and Agriculture.

Postgraduate studies are offered to those with very high Bachelor grades who pass an entrance examination. **Master's degrees** have been in existence since 1982 at the University of Kabul, Kabul Polytechnic and the Institute of Social Sciences. They are of two years' duration and are offered in the following subjects: architecture; education; engineering; humanities; law; natural sciences; psychology and social sciences.

Programmes leading to a **doctorate** in architecture, arts, engineering, natural and social sciences are available after three years of study.

Kabul Polytechnic was opened in 1968. Entrance requirements are the same as for the universities. Until 1982 a **Bachelor of Science** was awarded after a five year course. Since this date, this has been replaced by a **Master of Science**, also lasting five years but with an increased volume of work. The extent of this is shown by the fact that holders of the old **Bachelor degree** have to complete an additional two year course before they can obtain the **Master's degree**. Postgraduate courses are offered in the fields of construction, electrical and mechanical engineering, geology and mineralogy.

Technical, art, commercial and medical schools also exist. These include the Institute of Banking; Institute of Finance; Institute of Industrial Management; Institute of Telecommunications; Kabul Technical College and Balkh Technical College in Maazareh-Sharif.

TEACHER EDUCATION

There are three teacher training institutions in Kabul and eleven elsewhere.

Primary

A two-year course is required (at a teacher training college) on completion of upper secondary school.

Secondary

Lower/middle school: a two-year course is offered after grade 12 at a higher teacher training college (first established in 1964).

High school/*Lycée*: a four-year degree course is available, selected graduates of the higher teacher training colleges being admitted to the last two years.

Albania

After periods of Soviet and then Chinese-orientated Communism from 1946 until 1978, and a period of virtual isolation in the 1980s, the legacy of Enver Hoxha was rejected by student-led demonstrations in December 1990. A Communist government was elected in the first free elections in March 1991, mainly by votes from the conservative countryside but, at the election of March 1992, the will of the cities prevailed and the first non-Communist government was elected since 1944.

Elementary education is compulsory from age six to fourteen.

The academic year is divided into two semesters, September to December and January to May or June.

Albanian is the medium of instruction.

EVALUATION IN BRITAIN

School

Certificate of Maturity/Secondary School Leaving Certificate – may be considered comparable to GCSE standard (grades A, B and C) on a subject-for-subject basis, with the exception of English language.

Higher

Diplomë universitare – generally considered comparable to a standard between GCE Advanced and British Bachelor degree. May be considered for advanced standing by British higher education institutions.

MARKING SYSTEMS

The same grading scale is used at all levels of education.

10	*dhjetë*	excellent
9	*nëntë*	very good
8	*tetë*	good
7	*seshtatë*	average
6	*gjashtë*	satisfactory
5	*pesë*	pass

SCHOOL EDUCATION

Pre-school education

Infants and children under three can attend *çerdhe fëmijësh* (nursery) while their parents work.

Kopsht fëmijësh (kindergarten) is state funded and is available for children aged three to six. Although not compulsory, the Ministry of Education aim to have 85 per cent of five-year-olds enrolled by 1995.

Elementary education

Schooling is divided into three cycles, each of four years. Basic schooling is provided in eight-year schools, the first four years (*cikël i ulët* – lower cycle) concentrating on Albanian language and mathematics and the second four years (*cikël i lartë* – upper cycle) on science. Geography and history are taught from the fifth and fourth years respectively. The final examination is set by the Ministry of Education and Culture.

Until 1991, pupils engaged in practical work of social value as an integral part of their elementary education.

General secondary

Secondary education (middle school) lasts four years and provides an extension of basic education; since 1991 it has stressed academic subjects; before this it included practical training, was broad based and vocationally oriented. The school-leaving examination, the **Maturity Examination**, gives access to higher education.

About half of middle school students attend general secondary schools.

Technical/professional secondary

This is more vocational than general secondary education, though general studies are included. Courses last four or five years.

Teknikume (Technical schools) specialize in, for example, mechanics, engineering, agriculture or building. Courses last four years. The leaving certificate (**Certificate of Maturity**) gives access to appropriate areas of study in higher education.

Shkollat Pedagogjike (Pedagogical schools) – see below under **TEACHER EDUCATION**.

There are also secondary level schools providing four or five-year courses covering such areas as music, art, physical education and administration.

FURTHER EDUCATION

Shkollat e Ulta Profesionale (Lower vocational schools) existed until the reforms of the early 1970s, and have recently been re-established. They provide training for skilled workers in various branches of industry, commerce and agriculture. Entry is on the basis of completion of compulsory education at age fifteen.

Graduates receive the title *punëtor i kualifikuar* (qualified worker). This is a vocational qualification issued for employment purposes and does not represent completion of secondary education.

HIGHER EDUCATION

Admission to higher education was controlled by the Ministry of Education until 1991, according to a central plan. A **Certificate of Maturity** was required for all programmes. However, the needs of the economy and the individuals' political stature were important considerations.

Access is now solely by means of the **Certificate of Maturity** from a general secondary school/middle school or from a technical or vocational secondary school. Institutions have been granted a degree of autonomy with regards to admissions criteria and the number of places they offer.

University

As of 1991, there are seven universities.

The first degree is the **diplomë** in most subjects and a **titull** (professional title) in agriculture, business, economics, pharmacy, engineering, fine arts, law, liberal arts, technology, dentistry and medicine, natural and social sciences and teacher training. Degree courses last four years, except in engineering, technology and dentistry (five years) and medicine (six years).

The **Kandidat i Shkencave** (Candidate of Sciences) is the first postgraduate qualification. This three year qualification is based entirely on a research, examination and a thesis; no formal teaching is involved.

The scientific degree of **Doktor mi Shkencave** (Doctor of Sciences) is the highest academic degree in Albania, and is based on a significant period of research.

Institutes of higher education

These include the Academy of Fine Arts and various Institutes of Education (one of Physical Education). Courses lead to **Professional titles** of degree status and last four to five years.

Qualifications from any of the three military institutions (the Higher Military Academies in Tirana and Vlora, the Higher Unified Military School Tirana) are recognized as equivalent to the corresponding civilian credentials.

The V.I. Lenin Party School, which offered non-academic programmes for communist party functionaries, was closed in 1991. Diplomas and certificates from this institution are not recognized in Albania as academic credentials.

Post-diplomë continuing education

Courses are offered to train graduates who have at least two years' work experience in their field. They are vocational programmes. Successful candidates are issued with a *dëshmi* (certificate).

TEACHER EDUCATION

Basic and secondary

Admission to teacher training courses is on the basis of the **Certificate of Maturity/ Secondary School Leaving Certificate**. Courses last three years (formerly two years) for teachers in the lower four years of basic school leading to the **Diplomë per Mësues te Ciklit te Ulet te Shkolles Tetëvjeçare** (Diploma for teachers of the lower cycle of the eight year school).

For teachers in the upper four years of eight year schools (grades 5 to 8) and secondary schools, a four year course leads to a diplomë with the title **Mësues ne Shkolle te Mesme** (teacher in middle school).

Physical education teachers for all levels must complete a four year programme leading to the **Diplomë per Mësues i Edukimit Fizik per Tere Nivelet e Shkollave** (Diploma of teacher of physical education for all levels of school).

Teachers for secondary schools may also receive training as part of the four-year **diplomë** course at university.

The leaving certificate from the secondary teacher schools gives access to university studies (except technological and medical studies).

University

After obtaining a **diplomë** or **Professional title**, a university graduate may follow a course lasting three years (five years part-time) and take a competitive examination to teach at university level.

Algeria

Education is state controlled and is compulsory from age six to fifteen.

The medium of instruction is Arabic whenever possible at all levels from *Ecole Fondamentale* to university. The Constitution states that Arabic is the official language and the government has decreed that Arabic should be the language of instruction in all Algerian educational institutions. English is now taught on an equal footing with French as the first foreign language from the fourth year of *Ecole Fondamentale* to pupils aged nine.

The academic year is from September to July.

EVALUATION IN BRITAIN

School

Baccalauréat de l'Enseignement Secondaire – generally considered to be above GCSE standard. When an overall mark of *bien* or above has been achieved, may be considered by some institutions as satisfying their general entrance requirements. Other institutions may require GCE A levels in addition or may require candidates to complete an access/bridging course.

Higher

Licence – generally considered comparable to British Bachelor (Ordinary) degree standard; exceptionally, students with very high average marks could be considered for admission to postgraduate study.

Diplôme d'Etat d'Ingénieur/d'Architecture – generally considered comparable to British Bachelor (Honours) degree standard.

Magister – generally considered comparable to British Bachelor (Honours) degree standard and possibly approaching British taught Master's degree standard.

Teaching

Licence – generally considered comparable to British Bachelor (Ordinary) degree standard.

MARKING SYSTEMS

School

Marking in the **Baccalauréat** examinations is on a scale of 0–20 (maximum):

16–20	*très bien*	very good
14–15	*bien*	good
12–13	*assez bien*	fairly good
10–11	*passable*	pass
0–9	*insuffisant*	fail

Less than 10 per cent of students get a *mention bien* or *très bien*.

Higher

A uniform standard of grading is now being introduced using a 0–20 scale with 10 as the pass-mark.

15–20	*très bien*	very good
13–14	*bien*	good
12	*assez bien*	fair
11	*passable*	pass
10	*sans mention*	borderline

Students at university may pass a course *avec mention* or *sans mention* the four levels of *mention* being: *très bien, bien, assez bien* and *passable*. It is possible to pass an examination *sans mention*, which represents a mark of 10.

SCHOOL EDUCATION

School education is divided into two cycles, basic (*fondamentale*) and secondary (*secondaire*).

Basic

The *Ecole Fondamentale* takes children from the age of six for a nine-year course. During this period the pupils are given a standard common-core education in which the same subjects are taught throughout the country. Only in the last two years of the *Ecole Fondamentale* are pupils subjected to formal tests orienting them either for work or further education. At the end of the nine-year course it is expected that the students will be awarded a **Brevet d'Etudes Fondamentales** (BEF), at which stage some will leave school to work or for vocational training while the more able will transfer to secondary education (*Lycées*).

Secondary

This is provided in *Lycées* where students can choose from three options: humanities, mathematics and science. The *Lycée* cycle lasts three years, at the end of which the students take the **Baccalauréat de l'Enseignement Secondaire** in the appropriate subjects.

Students may alternatively attend a *Lycée Technique/Commercial* where they may be awarded a **Baccalauréat Technique/Commercial** after a three-year course largely devoted to practical work.

Technical and vocational

Vocational training is provided by the *Centres de Formation Professionnelle* in fields such as mechanics, car-body repair, hairdressing and secretarial work. After leaving the *Ecole Fondamentale* successful students of *Centres de Formation Professionnelle* may be awarded the **Certificat d'Aptitude Professionnelle** – also known as the **Certificat** de Technicien (ordinary level) – after three years, and the **Brevet de Maîtrise** after four years.

Students who do not gain entry into the *Centres de Formation Professionnelle* serve apprenticeships in workshops under the supervision of the APC (Communal Authority).

FURTHER EDUCATION

Technological institutes

These are usually national institutes under the auspices of one of the main ministries, e.g. light or heavy industries, agriculture, etc. These institutes offer a variety of courses aimed at the secondary, higher and graduate levels and students are trained in specific skills. Recruitment is at **Baccalauréat** level, and leads to a **Diplôme d'Ingénieur** after a five-year programme. The **Diplôme d'Ingénieur** is generally equated with a **Licence** in science or technology from a university. At the lower level, students who have reached **Baccalauréat** level but not passed the examination may follow a two-and-a-half-year course leading to the **Diplôme de Technicien Supérieur.** This **Diplôme** is not equivalent to the **Baccalauréat** and is not recognized as a qualification for university entrance. However, a **Technicien Supérieur** with five years' experience may continue to study for the **Diplôme d'Ingénieur.**

HIGHER EDUCATION

The **Baccalauréat de l'Enseignement Secondaire** is the basic entrance requirement for university or an equivalent institution. It admits to all faculties. Not all university departments, however, require the same average mark. For example, English and French sections of the *Instituts de Langues Vivantes* (ILVEs) require 12/20, while medical faculties require an average score of 15–18. There is a further selection hurdle after the end of the first year of medical studies (common core). The requirements vary from year to year and department to department, depending on availability of places or facilities.

The first degree is a **Licence**. The **Licence-ès-Lettres**, previously a three-year course has been extended to four years. The **Licence-ès-Sciences** is a four-year course. The **Licence** takes five years in engineering. There is no difference between a **Licence d'Enseignement d'Anglais** and a **Licence d'Anglais** except that the holder of the **Licence d'Enseignement d'Anglais** will have signed an agreement with the *Ecole Normale Supérieure* to enter the teaching profession.

The **Doctorat de Troisième Cycle** and the **Doctorat d'Etat** were both postgraduate degrees. The **Doctorat de Troisième Cycle** has been replaced by the **Magister** degree, which takes a minimum of two years after the **Licence**; it consists of a taught course lasting eighteen months and a thesis which takes an additional six months to one year. Four years are required after the **Magister** to obtain the **Doctorat d'Etat.**

Certain agricultural and engineering institutes, as well as the Ecole Polytechnique, award the **Diplôme d'Etat**. In 1990, the Université du Soir was established, which is similar to the Open University. People of any age who do not have the **Baccalauréat**, or who have just failed it, or want to resume their studies after several years of professional life, can apply to enrol as students. The diplomas obtained are of equal standing to those obtained by normal university students. Courses are taught from 1800–1900 hrs, three evenings per week.

TEACHER EDUCATION

Basic

Students holding the **Baccalauréat** may follow a two-year course at an *Institut de Technologie de l'Education* (ITE). Students who have failed the **Baccalauréat** have to pass a competitive examination to enter the ITE.

After a one-year course and an end-of-year examination, the student is awarded the provisional title of **Instituteur-Stagiaire** and is entitled to teach pupils from six to ten years old.

After the full two-year course students obtain Part I of the **Certificat d'Aptitude de Professeur de l'Enseignement Fondamental** (CAPEF) and gain the title **Professeur-Stagiaire** which entitles them to teach pupils aged eleven to sixteen years old.

After Part I students complete a probationary year. Once they have completed this successfully they are awarded the CAPEF Part II and become **Instituteurs** or **Professeurs de l'Enseignement Fondamental** (PEF).

Secondary

No specialized training is provided for most secondary and university teachers. Although there are some degree courses designed for prospective teachers (e.g. **Licence d'Enseignement d'Anglais** above), most teachers have a degree and acquire teaching experience on the job. In their second year of teaching they are inspected and may be awarded the **Certificat d'Aptitude de Professeur de l'Enseignement Secondaire** (CAPES).

In general, prospective teachers of English, after the **Baccalauréat**, go to university where they study for the **Licence d'Anglais**. After four years, during which they have no methodological training, they have to choose either:

–   to follow a course of study in their fifth year as a preparation for a **Magister**, leading to a postgraduate **Diplôme**, or

–   to follow a methodologically oriented course specifically for teachers at an *Ecole Normale Supérieure*.

Primary teachers may after five years' experience become **Professeur de Lycée** at the secondary level. They may then enrol at *Ecole Normale Supérieure* and attend university to study for a **licence** for four years, keeping the PEF salary. If successful, they can then move into the secondary education sector.

Angola

The following chapter regarding the education system in Angola is based on information obtained from the 3rd edition of this Guide, published in 1991, as NARIC has been unable to obtain more recent information.

There are three levels of education: *Ensino de Base* (primary), *Ensino Medio* (secondary) and *Ensino Superior* (higher). When the education system was reorganized in 1976, the existing Portuguese system was modified, the ninth and tenth years no longer being general education but work/vocational specific. The education system has now become centralized under the Ministry of Education.

Education is compulsory from ages seven to eleven.

The medium of instruction is Portuguese.

The academic year runs from September to July.

EVALUATION IN BRITAIN

School

Secondary School Leaving Certificate – generally comparable to GCSE standard (grades A, B and C) on a subject-for-subject basis, with the exception of English language.

Higher

Bacharel – generally considered comparable to a standard between GCE Advanced and British Bachelor degree; may be given advanced standing by British higher education institutions.

Licenciado – generally considered comparable to British Bachelor degree standard.

Teaching

ISCED – generally considered comparable to a standard between GCE Advanced and British Bachelor degree.

MARKING SYSTEMS

Ensino de Base (primary) examinations are marked out of 20. Students must have at least 10 in every subject to go on to *Ensino Medio*.

Ensino Medio (secondary) has, as yet, no standardized examinations; examinations are set by individual teachers.

SCHOOL EDUCATION

Primary

Ensino de Base is divided into three levels. At the end of each level pupils must pass the national examinations to be able to continue.

First level compulsory education starts at age six or seven (often a lot later) and lasts four years.

Second level lasts two years and is the minimum qualification for state employment.

Third level lasts two years and leads to a national examination which students must pass to go on to *Ensino Medio*.

Secondary

Ensino Medio is a four-year vocational course, culminating in the **Secondary School Leaving Certificate**. Students who complete this may, after working for the state for two to five years, go on to university.

There are also two- to three-year pre-university courses. These were originally an interim measure so that technicians and teachers could be trained quickly but have become part of the regular system.

HIGHER EDUCATION

There is one university, the Universidade de Agostinho Neto. It has five faculties in Luanda, two in Huambo and Instituto Superior de Ciencias de Educacao (ISCED) in Lubango. The Luanda Faculties are Medicine, Engineering, Science, Economics and Law. Huambo produces agronomists and students can also study the first two years of Medicine and Economics.

The entrance requirement is the **Secondary School Leaving Certificate** and an entrance examination.

The first qualification to be obtained is the **Bacharel** on completion of four years' study, with a further two years leading to the **Licenciado**. A **Doctorate** may be obtained after a further two to three years' research.

TEACHER EDUCATION

Teachers are trained either at Instituto Medio Normal (IMN) formerly the Instituto Normal de Educacao (INE) or at Instituto Superior de Ciencias e Educacao (ISCED), Lubango.

IMN

These institutes train teachers for *Ensino de Base*, and are part of *Ensino Medio*. They offer four-year courses. The first intake was in 1981 so the first students graduated in July 1985. Students in the eleventh and twelfth years specialize and their special subjects are the only subjects that they are allowed to teach at the third level of *Ensino de Base*. Most of the teacher trainers are *Co-operantes*. The INEs also give two-year courses for teachers who have been teaching at *Ensino de Base* without any formal training.

There is a distance-learning programme to upgrade unqualified teachers. The first phase of the programme was aimed at raising the teacher's own level of education to *Ensino de Base* (third level) by 1990. The second phase is professional training including theories of education and methodology.

ISCED

This institute is part of the university. It trains teacher trainers for INE, and teachers for *Ensino Medio*. In theory, anyone who graduates from this institute is a qualified teacher trainer. These graduates sometimes teach in ISCED itself. The courses are five years, the last year (*Estagio*, equivalent to a probationary year) being spent in classroom practice and writing a dissertation.

ISCED has also set up a distance-learning programme. The students on this course receive duplicated notes of the material given in lectures and sit examinations at the university. There is no provision for seminars or tutorials, nor is there any set work.

Argentina

As from the enactment of Law 24.195 of April 1993, there will be a new academic structure within certain areas of the Argentine education system (mainly pre-school, primary and secondary levels). The gradual implementation of the different areas is to be completed by December 1999.

Education comes under the control of the national government.

Education is compulsory for children aged five to fourteen and comprises Pre-elementary and Basic General Education – *(Educaciòn General Bàsica* – EGB).

Most students at all levels are part time. In schools, pupils normally attend either from 0800 to 1200 hours or from 1300 to 1700 hours.

The majority of students attend state schools. Private institutions are attended by one fifth of the students.

The medium of instruction is Spanish. English and French are taught at all levels.

There are public (i.e. state) and private institutions at all levels.

The school year runs from March to December. The university academic year varies, but in most institutions runs from April to December.

EVALUATION IN BRITAIN

School

The former **Bachillerato** – generally considered comparable to GCSE standard (grades A, B and C) on a subject-for-subject basis, with the exception of English language.

The **Bachillerato Especializado** – considered to be slightly above GCSE standard.

Higher

Licenciado/Professional title – generally considered comparable to British Bachelor degree standard if awarded after four or more years of study. When a mimimum pass mark of 7.5 is achieved, this may be considered for admission to a taught Master's degree course.

MARKING SYSTEM

The same marking system is used throughout the education system. Secondary school marks are generally given in numerals. University and other institutions of higher education use either number or concept marks. A scale of 1–10 is used:

10	*sobresaliente*	excellent
8–9	*distinguido*	very good
6–7	*bueno*	good
4–5	*aprobado*	pass
2–3	*insuficiente*	insufficient
1	*reprobado*	fail

When (at university level) more than one classification is quoted against a subject, this implies that this subjects had to be repeated. The minimum pass-mark is usually 40 per cent.

SCHOOL EDUCATION

Before 1993, education was divided into seven years' primary and five years' secondary.

Primary (*Ciclo Primario*)

This lasted seven years (ages six to thirteen) and was compulsory. Pupils were promoted from one grade to the next on the basis of continuous assessment and end-of-year evaluation.

Secondary (*Ciclo Secundario*)

Secondary education in state institutions was not compulsory. The course normally lasted five years (divided into the three-year *Ciclo Basico* and the two-year *Ciclo Superior*) but may have lasted six or seven years. The length of the course depended on the programme followed by the student. Students could opt for courses of general academic, commercial, technical, vocational, art, or social welfare education; those who obtained an average assessment mark of 7 (out of 10) or more during the year and passed their grade examinations (end-of-year examinations) were promoted from one grade to the next.

The **Bachillerato** was the final school-leaving certificate. Some schools provided a course lasting one year longer leading to the **Bachillerato Especializado**. The extra year enabled pupils to study certain subjects more intensively but not at a more advanced level.

Academic

Academic secondary courses of five years were offered in the national *Colegios* or *Liceos*. These institutions prepared students for university entrance.

Commercial

State commercial schools (*Escuelas Comerciales*) offered six-year courses. The basic cycle was similar to that provided at the academic schools, but in the second cycle approximately forty per cent of the curriculum was devoted to commercial subjects. Graduates were awarded the title of **Perito Mercantil** (literally, Expert in Commerce). Successful graduates were eligible to enter the economics faculties of the universities.

Technical

Responsibility for technical and vocational training came under CONET (*Consejo Nacional de Educacion Tecnica*) and was provided in *Escuelas Industriales*. Students followed a six-year course and specialized in particular fields. Successful graduates were eligible for higher education. Students could obtain a **Technical Auxiliary's Certificate** after completing the first cycle and a year's specialization. CONET worked closely with industrial organizations in the design and teaching of its courses.

Vocational

Courses in vocational education *(Educaciòn Profesional)* could last from one to eight years, although most lasted four years. Vocational education was aimed largely at girls. Courses covered home economics, the clothing trade, clerical work and some technical subjects. Graduates were not eligible for higher studies.

Agricultural secondary schools offered a seven-year course. Students could also follow a three- to four-year paramedical course to qualify as medical auxiliaries. There were four-year secondary courses for social workers and 'artistic' courses which could last up to ten years.

Since 1993

The new system involves ten years of compulsory education – one year of pre-primary and nine years of Basic General Education (*Educaciòn General Bàsica*). This is followed by a non-compulsory three-year Polymodal education.

Initial education

Compulsory pre-elementary education (age five).

Basic General Education (*Educaciòn General Bàsica* – EGB)

This lasts nine years and is divided into three, three-year cycles and is compulsory (ages six to fourteen).

Polymodal Education (*Polimodal*)

Polymodal education is not compulsory. The course lasts three years. Students can opt for one of the following orientations in their studies: social science, humanities or technical, but these are not binding (ages fifteen to seventeen, plus one year for specialization).

The **Bachillerato** is the final school-leaving certificate, the word Bachillerato being followed by '*con orientaciòn . . .*' which indicates the special branch chosen.

Some schools provide a course lasting one year longer leading to the **Bachillerato Especializado**.

Vocational

Former agricultural 'secondary' schools offer a seven-year course.

Students can also follow a three- to four-year paramedical course to qualify as medical auxiliaries.

There are artistic courses which can last up to ten years.

HIGHER EDUCATION

Higher education is provided at over seventy public and private universities and other higher institutions. Entry to first degree courses is based on attendance and successful evaluation of the CBC *(Ciclo Bàsico Comùn* – pre-university entry course). Private universities hold their own pre-entry examinations.

Courses normally last between four and six years; they lead to the **Licenciado** or a professional title (e.g. *Ingeniero*). In some subjects, such as architecture, law and medicine, courses take at least six years. Most students attend on a part-time basis.

The award of a **Doctorate** would normally take at least two years after a **Licenciado**.

There are many short and long postgraduate courses run by universities, research institutes and state bodies. These do not lead to formal qualifications, but the certificates are cited in curricula vitae.

Outside the universities, professional courses are available in areas such as nursing, librarianship, higher technician training and administration.

TEACHER EDUCATION

Primary

Before 1970, primary school teachers were trained at upper secondary school level. They followed a two-year course after completing the *Ciclo Basico* leading to the title of **Maestro/Maestra**. The training required now is a two-year post-secondary course at a higher teacher training institute, followed by one semester of practical experience. Successful graduates must be prepared to undertake in-service training and refresher courses.

Secondary

Training consists of a four- to five-year post-secondary course leading to the title of **Profesorado** (considered the equivalent of a university degree in Argentina). University graduates follow a one-year course in departments attached to universities leading to a teaching certificate. Students spend about six hours a week on teaching practice throughout the course.

ADULT EDUCATION

Adult literacy and evening secondary courses are available. Some of the new universities offer two-year **Bachillerato** courses for those over twenty years of age.

Australia

The Commonwealth of Australia consists of a federation of six states and two territories. In descending order of population these are: New South Wales, Victoria, Queensland, Western Australia, South Australia, Tasmania, the Australian Capital Territory, and the Northern Territory.

Each State and Territory has its own primary and secondary education systems, and although the school systems are similar throughout Australia there are also distinct differences. In 1989 the State, Territory and Commonwealth Ministers of Education agreed on ten national goals for schooling in Australia. Arising from this agreement a National Schools Strategy was developed through the Australian Education Council, (now replaced by the Ministerial Council for Employment, Education, Training and Youth Affairs). The Strategy comprises a series of related initiatives including the encouragement of national collaboration in curriculum development and of a more consistent approach to assessment and certification. An individual section on school education in each of the States and Territories may be found following the general information.

Post-secondary education has two main sectors: the higher education sector and the much larger Vocational Education Training (VET) sector. The Vocational Education Training sector (consisting mainly of the publicly funded TAFE Colleges), is undergoing extensive change, with the establishment of the Australian National Training Authority and the development of a national VET system, with close interaction between industry and VET providers. The higher education sector has also undergone major restructuring over the last five years with the abolition of the binary system dividing universities and colleges of advanced education/institutes of technology. A Unified National System (UNS) has been created comprising thirty-nine universities.

There are a number of private colleges and training organizations providing courses in secretarial and office work, computing, accountancy and other business-related studies as well as specialist vocational courses.

There is also a large adult community education sector which provides non-award courses in pre-employment skills, personal development, cultural and recreation studies and remedial programmes.

Federal, State and Territory governments have agreed to the introduction of a National Qualifications Framework. The new framework, which will be implemented from 1 January 1995, will encompass all sectors, (schools, vocational education and training and higher education), and will provide a comprehensive, nationally consistent, yet flexible framework for all qualifications in post-compulsory education and training.

GENERAL

Evaluation in Britain

School Qualifications

It is generally considered that students with good results in **Year 12** certificates, who are qualified to enter Australian higher education, would satisfy the general entrance requirements of most British higher education institutions (see under separate States).

TAFE Diploma – generally considered comparable to BTEC Higher National Diploma/ N/SVQ level 4.

TAFE Associate Diploma – generally considered comparable to BTEC National Diploma / N/SVQ level 3 / Advanced GNVQ/GSVQ standard.

Bachelor degree (Ordinary) – generally considered comparable to British Bachelor (Ordinary) degree standard.

Bachelor degree (Honours) – generally considered comparable to British Bachelor (Honours) degree standard.

It is important to note that Ordinary or Pass degrees are common in Australia, and many faculties do not offer Honours degrees. Where Honours degrees exist they are of at least four years duration.

SCHOOL EDUCATION

The school year runs from late January/early February to early December. Most states operate on a four-term system (three in Tasmania), while Queensland and the Northern Territory have two semesters.

School attendance is compulsory for ages six to fifteen (sixteen in Tasmania). In practice the majority of students begin school earlier than the law requires, often in pre-schools run by the same organizations that administer the mainstream schools. Primary schooling lasts six to seven years and the curriculum is similar across the nation. Progression to secondary school is automatic and no certificate is awarded.

Secondary schooling begins at Year 7 or 8, with the option for students to leave school after Year 10 or to continue to Year 12. (In 1993 87.4 per cent of students remained at school until Year 11 and 76.6 per cent remained until Year 12). Most secondary schools are co-educational comprehensive or multi-purpose high schools, offering a wide range of subjects. New South Wales has some selective high schools catering for gifted students. Some States have separate high schools and colleges specializing in Technical, Agricultural, Commercial and other fields. In Tasmania and the Australian Capital Territory senior colleges provide the last two years of secondary schooling.

Private education exists in parallel with the state system at all levels. Most of these non-government schools are run by religious bodies; about three quarters are Catholic schools. Private schools charge fees, but normally receive financial assistance from the government according to need. Approximately 28 per cent of students attend private schools.

Major examinations or other formal assessments occur after three or four years of high school, marking the end of compulsory education (Year 10), and most states issue some form of School Certificate at this stage. Another two years is available for those who wish to complete Year 12 and to proceed to professional and para-professional award courses in TAFE colleges and to degree courses in universities. Increasingly it is expected that all students will continue to the end of Year 12.

School leaving certificates and tertiary entrance scores are based on courses taken in Years 11 and 12. Five of the eight State/Territory Year 12 certificates (ACT, NSW, NT, SA and VIC) require successful completion of a set programme of study in Year 11 and/or Year 12; the other State certificates are issued as records of subjects studied and do not indicate completion of a whole programme. As well as the Year 12 Certificate Australian institutions also use a 'tertiary entrance score/rank/statement/overall position/advice' calculated from performance in Years 11 and/or 12.

DISTANCE EDUCATION/OPEN LEARNING

At school level correspondence education is widely available for students who cannot attend school daily because of distance or because of illness or physical disability. There are also *Schools of the Air* which use two-way radio networks to provide 'classroom' experience to students living in isolated regions. Increasingly, electronic links are being used through computers, satellites, television and videos.

The Vocational Education and Training sector has concentrated on making delivery more flexible. This has meant, in part, the use of a variety of techniques, such as optic fibre, television and audio-video conferencing, to provide delivery to those who cannot attend institutions. Flexible delivery also encompasses offering training where the client can access it easily (home, work, community centre) at times to suit him or her and in a modular format.

At the higher education level external courses have been available for over 80 years. In May 1989 the Commonwealth Government established eight national Distance Education Centres (DECs) with the object of rationalizing external study provision. While the DECs were the main providers of external studies, all other universities continued to develop special expertise in course development, design and delivery and to enrol external students. In 1994, 30 universities provided distance education courses, with external students representing approximately 11.5 per cent of student enrolments.

In January 1993 the government funded the Open Learning Initiative. The initiative has two key elements: the establishment of the Open Learning Agency of Australia (OLAA), and the development of an open learning electronic support service which will allow open learning students to use computers to communicate with tutors and other students and to access electronic library services and other information resources. The Open Learning Agency of Australia acts as the broker for higher education courses and study units. The Open Learning Consortium (currently comprising nine universities) offers both units and degrees using a variety of media including television, radio, audio and video tapes, personal computers and conventional print material. There are currently over 200 undergraduate and 19 postgraduate units available in the fields of arts and social sciences, business studies, languages, science and technology and applied science. Future plans include the provision of some Certificate and Associate Diploma courses from the Vocational Education and Training sector.

The Professional and Graduate Education (PAGE) Consortium offers postgraduate and professional education courses currently via the medium of broadcast television within Australia. Other means, including satellite, cable, radio and CAL may be utilized in the future. The Consortium comprises thirteen universities from Australia and New

Zealand and currently offers courses in engineering, management, health, education, multicultural studies, journalism and TQM with the range of offerings continually increasing. In 1995 students will be able to enrol in 24 courses and 73 subjects leading to the completion of courses at the Graduate Certificate, Graduate Diploma and Master's levels.

VOCATIONAL EDUCATION AND TRAINING

The Vocational Education and Training (VET) sector, (consisting mainly of the publicly-funded TAFE colleges), is concerned primarily with vocational and technical education, awarding certificates in various grades below the level of degrees, but also offering sub-degree associate diplomas and diplomas. Courses operate at a number of levels: professional and para-professional, technician, trade, operative, prevocational, adult and further education.

TAFE awards are normally issued without grading or classification. Individual subjects may receive a letter grade or descriptive grade (distinction, credit, pass) depending on the State or Territory, the college and the course structure.

A number of the TAFE courses are articulated with university courses so that a student who has completed an associate diploma or diploma may move into a university degree course with some level of credit.

Professional and Para-professional Awards

Diploma courses provide education and training for professional vocations. The courses generally run for three years full-time following completion of Year 12 secondary school.

Associate Diploma courses offer students the opportunity to acquire skills which will enable them to work in support of professionals, or as para-professionals in their own right. The courses generally run for two years full-time (four years part-time) following completion of Year 12 secondary school.

Technician Awards

Advanced Certificate courses provide students with planning, supervisory, management and communication skills beyond those normally required in a trade occupation. The courses are generally one-and-a-half or two years full-time (three or four years part-time), following completion of Year 10 secondary school.

Trade Level Awards

Certificate

There are various types of certificate courses in TAFE. The most common are trade courses which provide training for specific trades, vocations or crafts. They are part-time courses run concurrently with indentures or non-indentured employment. On completion students may enter trade courses with advanced standing.

Other certificate courses offer training for technicians and other middle-level occupations. While most of these courses have no entry requirements, some require the completion of Year 10 secondary school.

Prior to the introduction of the national award system the major awards at the trade and technician level were the **TAFE Certificate** (known as the **TAFE Diploma** in Western Australia) and the **TAFE Higher Certificate**.

Statements of Attainment are awarded for short vocational courses which are not nationally accredited, but which are accredited on a State-wide basis. Courses which refine skills by following on from the nationally accredited, individual TAFE courses are known as training programmes under the national guidelines.

General Education Courses

TAFE colleges offer a number of general education courses, ranging from basic literacy and numeracy courses to the **Higher School Certificate**. Colleges also offer courses for special purposes and specific programmes for women, Aborigines, people from non-English speaking backgrounds, people with disabilities, the unemployed and those living in remote areas.

TEACHER EDUCATION

Teacher education courses are similar throughout Australia, but not all courses are available in each State.

Primary teacher education generally involves a minimum of three years of full-time study, including a year of professional education with supervised practice teaching (**Diploma of Teaching, Bachelor of Teaching, BEd (Primary)**).

Most States prefer secondary teachers to be four-year trained. The four-year programme consists of either a four-year **BEd** or a three-year **Bachelor degree** followed by a one-year **Diploma of Education**. Three-year trained teachers with sufficient teaching experience can upgrade their qualification by completing a one-year course leading to a **BEd**.

By the late 1990s Victoria, Queensland and the Australian Capital Territory will require four years of teaching preparation for both primary and secondary teachers.

Postgraduate courses include one-year **Graduate Diplomas**, two-year **Master's** programmes, and three-year **Doctor of Philosophy** programmes. In some states the postgraduate **BEd, BEd Studies** or **BSpecEd** is a specialized professional qualification requiring between one and two years of study beyond a four-year **BEd** or a **BA/BSc/DipEd**.

Teachers must be registered with the appropriate State Board of Teacher Registration.

Courses are available in some states for people wishing to specialize in adult education.

TAFE college teachers who do not hold an appropriate teacher education qualification can complete an in-service programme of professional studies.

HIGHER EDUCATION

Australia's first two universities, the University of Sydney and the University of Melbourne, were established in the 1850s. By the First World War, Australia had one university in each of the six states, and in the 1930s, university colleges were established in Canberra and Armidale. Each of the six universities was closely involved with the life of its own state, training teachers for the state secondary schools and for the professions. Collectively, the universities followed British traditions. Course structure followed British (especially Scottish) models, many of the academic staff were recruited from universities in the UK; and until the 1950s when Australian universities began offering PhD programmes academic staff had to do their postgraduate training overseas, usually in Britain or the USA.

In the 1960s a binary system of higher education was created with the establishment of 26 colleges of advanced education (CAEs). With the aim of providing a new tier of post-secondary institutions intermediate to universities and TAFE colleges, most of the CAEs were former teachers' colleges or TAFE colleges offering courses with special focus on applied teaching and preparation for employment. The CAE sector also included Institutes of Technology and a number of specialized colleges for professional education.

The economic downturn at the end of 1979 led the government to begin a programme of mergers and rationalizations reducing the number of CAEs from eighty (1970s) to forty-six (end of 1987).

In 1990 the binary system was abolished in line with the recommendations outlined in the Government's White Paper *Higher Education: A Policy Statement*, July 1988. The Institutes of Technology and CAEs either became universities or were merged with existing universities and a unified national system (UNS) of thirty-nine universities was established.

Additional sources of funding were needed for the substantial growth envisaged for the higher education sector. The Higher Education Contribution Scheme (HECS) was introduced in 1989 to collect a financial contribution from students, amounting to about 20 per cent of their tuition fees.

Australia now has thirty-nine publicly funded universities and four institutions which are not part of the unified national system, the Australian Maritime College, Bachelor College, Marcus Oldham College of Farm Management and Avondale College. There are also two privately funded universities, Bond University and the University of Notre Dame Australia.

Academic Year

Higher education institutions normally operate over either three terms or two semesters beginning in late February and ending in November.

Courses of Study

Most university courses are full-time, but Australia has a strong tradition of both part-time study and external study.

Arts and science faculties generally adhere to the tradition of a three-year **Pass degree** and a four-year **Honours degree**, the fourth year of study being open only to approved students who will already have specialized or performed particularly well in the early years of the course. In engineering and technical faculties **Honours degrees** are generally awarded on the basis of merit in a single common course, though the Honours student may have undertaken a specified additional period of study within the same period. Where a three-year scientific or technological degree exists, it is not the general practice to award it with Honours.

Pass degrees in architecture and dentistry generally takes five years, and medicine six years, all with a possible additional year for Honours.

From 1997 degrees in medicine from the universities of <u>Flinders</u>, <u>Queensland</u> and <u>Sydney</u> will only be available as postgraduate courses.

It is important to note that Ordinary or Pass degrees are common in Australia, and many faculties do not offer Honours degrees. Where Honours degrees exist they are of at least four years duration.

Postgraduate studies and research can be undertaken at all Australian universities.

Bachelor degree requiring a minimum of three years of full-time study. Normally awarded unclassified.

Bachelor degree (with **Honours**) requiring a minimum of four years of full-time study. Honours degrees are classified as: First Class, Second Class (Upper and Lower Division) and Third Class. Second Class Honours in some faculties are classified A and B, in others One and Two.

Combined Bachelor degree (with or without **Honours**) requiring a minimum of five years of full-time study (six years for Honours). Classification as above.

Graduate Certificate requiring half a year of full-time study following completion of a Bachelor degree or Diploma. Normally awarded unclassified.

Graduate Diploma requiring one year of full-time study following completion of a Bachelor degree or Diploma. Normally awarded unclassified.

Master degree by Coursework normally requiring two years of full-time study following a three-year Bachelor degree, or one calendar year following an Honours Bachelor degree. Generally awarded unclassified but some institutions award Master degrees with Honours (unclassified).

Master degree by Research normally requiring one calendar year of full-time study following an Honours or Master's qualifying year. Classification as above.

Doctor of Philosophy, by research and thesis, requiring a minimum of three years of full-time study following an Honours Bachelor degree or Master degree. Some faculties require candidates to complete some preliminary coursework.

Professional Doctorate available in a limited number of universities for professional practice programmes, eg in education, psychology, law.

Higher Doctorate (D Litt, DSc, LLD, MD) usually awarded on the basis of published work. Higher Doctorates in medicine, dentistry and law may be awarded on the basis of a thesis.

AUSTRALIAN SCALING TEST (AST)

The **Australian Scaling Test** (formerly called the Australian Scholastic Aptitude Test) is a three-hour objective test taken by students in the Australian Capital Territory and Western Australia in their final year at school. (In Western Australia the AST is referred to as a 'Scaling Test'). The format is 100 multiple-choice items on different areas in roughly the following proportions: mathematics 20; science 30; humanities 30; social sciences 20.

A total score of scholastic aptitude is calculated, as well as verbal and quantitative sub-scores. The AST total score is used to scale teacher-assessed scores in the calculation of the Tertiary Entrance Score in the Australian Capital Territory. It is also used with the Tertiary Entrance Examinations results in Western Australia to calculate the admission requirement for courses at the universities.

The AST Writing test, a two-and-a-half-hour argumentative writing task, is also undertaken by students in the Australian Capital Territory.

As the scores themselves are not directly comparable to subjects in the final certification, the AST results provide an inter-school guide on a state-wide basis. However, South Australia, Victoria, Tasmania, the Northern Territory and New South Wales do not use AST for scaling their examination scores.

The administration and test development of all forms is conducted by the Australian Council for Educational Research (ACER).

SPECIAL TERTIARY ADMISSIONS TEST

The **Special Tertiary Admissions Test** (STAT) is a series of related tests used by tertiary institutions in Australia as part of their admissions procedures for special categories of applicants. STAT provides an opportunity for those candidates who have not completed a recent or standard Year 12 certificate to demonstrate their ability to cope with tertiary studies. The purpose of STAT is to measure candidates' ability to think critically about issues and understand the material given, rather than assess knowledge of the curriculum, or any specific academic subject.

There are six forms of STAT named Series A, B, C, D, E and F. The tests in Series A, B, C, D and F are 2-hour tests, each containing 70 multiple-choice questions and differing in their proportions of Verbal (V) and Quantitative (Q) questions. STAT E is a one-hour test of written English.

AUSTRALIAN CAPITAL TERRITORY

EVALUATION IN BRITAIN

Tertiary Entrance Statement – generally considered to satisfy the general entrance requirements of universities if passes in five acceptable T courses with grades of at least three Bs and two Cs (BBBCC) have been scored.

MARKING SYSTEM

ACT Year 12 Certificate unit grades are reported on a five-point scale A–E.

The **Tertiary Entrance Statement** includes, for each T course, a scaled course score, obtained by scaling the school-derived scores in each course according to the students' performances in their own T courses and their performance in the AST. The student's individual AST score is not shown. Unscaled course scores are not reported.

For the Tertiary Entrance Statement an aggregate score is calculated for each student by taking the three best-scaled course scores in T-classified major courses plus 0.6 of the next best major or minor T-classified course score. Most aggregates lie between 400 and 750. From a rank ordering of all students on their aggregates, each student's relative ranking is expressed as a percentile ranking, covering all Year 12 T-students in the ACT. This percentile ranking is the student's **Tertiary Entrance Rank**.

SCHOOL EDUCATION

Secondary education is conducted in two kinds of institution: high schools for the first four years, and secondary colleges for the final two years. A one-year intensive programme for the Year 12 Certificate is also available through the TAFE system, (Canberra Institute of Technology).

The secondary education programme comprises four years leading to the **ACT Year 10 Certificate**, with a further (optional) two years leading to the **ACT Year 12 Certificate**.

ACT Year 10 Certificate

Until 1988 Year 10 students received an **ACT Year 10 Certificate** and a High School Record which reported on their achievements, based on teacher assessment. Since 1989, the **ACT Year 10 Certificate** itself incorporates the results of students who complete Year 10, while the High School Record is issued, only on request, before the end of Year 10.

ACT Year 12 Certificate

This is awarded in two parts, the **Year 12 Certificate** for those who complete Year 12 and the **Tertiary Entrance Statement** for students who also qualify for matriculation.

Students study **courses** made up of **units**. Points signifying approximately 11 hours of class time are used to give value to a unit, e.g. a one year full unit is generally worth 12 points.

Students may choose courses from four groups – A, T, R and E. Accredited Courses (A) are those judged to be educationally sound and appropriate for students studying in Years 11 and 12. Accredited Courses which are considered sufficiently academically demanding to be a good preparation for tertiary studies are classified as T by the Australian National University.

A or T courses with a distinct employment orientation are also classified as E courses. Students successfully completing an E course programme of study are issued with an **Employment Course Certificate** in addition to their Year 12 Certificate.
Registered Courses (R), which provide a variety of recreational and less academic activities are approved by college boards and registered with the Accrediting Agency.

The **Tertiary Entrance Statement** is awarded to students who meet the requirements for the award of Tertiary Entrance Rank (TER). To receive a TER the Year 11/12 study programme must include at least three major (two-year) T courses and one minor (one-year) T course. In addition, students must also sit the Australian Scaling Test (AST), and complete at least 120 points.

Secondary College Records are awarded on request to students who complete at least one unit in Years 11 and 12.

NEW SOUTH WALES

EVALUATION IN BRITAIN

Year 10 Certificate – generally considered comparable to GCSE (grades A–C) on a subject-for-subject basis.

Higher School Certificate – generally considered to satisfy the general entrance requirements of British higher education institutions if passes in at least two acceptable three-unit subjects plus two acceptable two-unit subjects have been scored. Consideration should also be given to the percentile band required.

Tertiary Entrance Rank – generally considered to satisfy the general entrance requirements of British higher education institutions if at least 70/100 is gained.

SCHOOL EDUCATION

Secondary education is conducted in high schools, some of which are selective. A one-year intensive programme for the **HSC** is also available through TAFE.

Secondary education comprises four years leading to the **School Certificate** examination, with a further (optional) two years leading to the **Higher School Certificate**.

School Certificate (Year 10) courses used to be offered at three levels, advanced (top 25 per cent of students), ordinary (middle 50 per cent) and modified level (lowest 25 per cent). A minimum of six subjects had to be studied, including English, mathematics, science and one of either history, geography or social studies. The minimum number of passes for the award was four at either level. The idea of course level was abandoned in 1976.

In 1975 the examination was phased out and the certificate is now awarded mainly on the basis of internal school assessment. Standards are maintained by externally prepared moderating tests.

Since 1977 all students have taken common examinations in English and mathematics and the results for all schools compared with other schools in the state. A **Science Reference Test** was introduced in 1990. Each school is allocated a certain number of each grade depending on their overall standard. The school then assigns the grades to the students according to their ranking, based on test results and teacher assessment. Schools allocate Grade A–E in all other courses, based on the Board's General Performance Descriptors which are printed on the back of the Record of Achievement.

Given that most students are now going on to complete the **HSC**, the value of the information provided on the **School Certificate** has been brought into question. The Board of Studies is currently examining options for assessing and reporting student achievement. The proposals include options for reporting on key competencies and industry specific competencies, taking into account developments at the national level in relation to core competencies.

Higher School Certificate (Year 12)

There are two types of courses, **Board-developed courses** and **Other Endorsed**

Studies (Board-endorsed courses). **Courses** generally consist of two **units** per year but many courses can be studied at 3 unit level. A unit of study comprises 60 hours indicative time in each of the Preliminary and HSC courses.

To be eligible for the **Higher School Certificate** a student must study subjects with course values totalling at least eleven units, including at least two units of English in each of Years 11 and 12.

A **one-unit** course usually requires two hours of school study per week in Year 11 and/or Year 12. A **two-unit** course usually requires four hours of school study per week in Years 11 and 12. A **three-unit** course usually incorporates all of a two-unit course and usually requires six hours of school study per week in each of Years 11 and 12. A **four-unit** course incorporates all of the three-unit course and usually requires eight hours of study per week in each of Years 11 and 12. Four-unit courses are available in only two subjects – mathematics and science.

To qualify for the **Higher School Certificate** students must study a pattern of Preliminary and HSC courses. Both the Preliminary and HSC patterns must include:

> at least 11 units of which 6 units must be from Board-developed courses;
>
> at least two units of Board-developed course in English;
>
> at least one unit from Key Learning Area Group 1 (science/mathematics/technological and applied studies);
>
> at least one unit from Key Learning Area Group 2 (languages other than English/human society and its environment/creative arts/personal development, health and physical education);
>
> three courses of two units value or greater (either Board-developed or Board-endorsed courses).

New Pathways to the HSC

With the HSC becoming essential as a prerequisite for employment and/or further study, those who are unable to complete the traditional full-time, school-based HSC are at a disadvantage. The Board of Studies has designed pathways to the HSC and beyond which will open up new opportunities for students and provide equitable access for all. The new pathways, which apply to Year 11 students from 1994, include: part-time HSC study and work; HSC study which includes courses for which credit transfer can be gained towards future education or training; HSC study together with study at TAFE or university.

MARKING SYSTEMS

Year 10 Certificate/School Certificate

		Grades
1962–74:	Advanced level	pass/fail;
	Ordinary level	credit and pass
1975:	Advanced & Ordinary levels	1–5
	Modified level	1 or 2
1976:	subjects	1–10

Reference Tests – 1977 Reference tests were introduced in English and mathematics.

English test results were divided into three levels:

Advanced	A–C (50 per cent, 40 per cent, 10 per cent)
Intermediate	A–D (30 per cent, 30 per cent, 30 per cent, 10 per cent)
General	A–B (60 per cent, 40 per cent)

1990	Reference test for science was introduced. Results were distributed as for English:

A–E (10 per cent, 20 per cent, 40 per cent, 20 per cent, 10 per cent).

Each of the mathematics levels used the same distribution A–E.

The **School Certificate** is a testament document, showing the student's name and school, and indicating that requirements for the award have been met.

The **School Certificate Record of Achievement** which is issued with the School Certificate, provides details of all courses studied in Stage 5 (Years 9–10) whether satisfactorily completed or not.

The **School Certificate Result Notice** provides details of courses studied and grades awarded in Stage 5. Result notices are a cumulative record of School Certificate studies and are issued to students who have not yet met all requirements for the award of the School Certificate.

Higher School Certificate

1967–85:	1	pass at first level
	2	pass at second level
	2F	pass at second level (full course)
	2S	pass at second level (short course)
	3	pass at third level
	P	pass in general studies
	F	fail
	X	absent

1975–85:

Awards were based on a student's performance in the examination and the estimate of that performance submitted by the school. The examination marks were scaled and the schools' estimate adjusted. Together, these formed a student's scaled mark in each course. The scaled mark was then used to determine a student's percentile band (i.e. performance in relation to other students) and aggregate mark, which was obtained by adding the candidate's ten best unit scores. Each unit was worth fifty marks, so the maximum possible aggregate mark was 500. The aggregate mark formed the basis for both tertiary selection and entry to many areas of employment.

1986–89:

Awards were based on a student's performance in the examination and a school assessment. The examination marks were scaled using a common average of 60 per cent for all two-unit courses and the assessment marks adjusted for state-wide comparability. The examination mark and the assessment mark for each course were reported separately. The marks in each course were not aggregated by the Board of Secondary Education. However, a separate scaling system operated by the University of

Sydney, scaled the average of the examination mark and the assessment mark so as to be comparable across different subjects. The University then produced aggregate scores out of 500 called Tertiary Entrance Scores (TES), which were used by most tertiary institutions to select their students.

Also recorded were Percentile Bands (deciles), based on the average of the examination and assessment marks on the certificate. Commencing in 1988, students who satisfied requirements for the Higher School Certificate were also awarded a Record of Achievement upon successful completion of Years 11 and 12.

1990–1994:

The **Tertiary Entrance Rank** (not score)

TER was reported on a scale of 0–100 with intervals of 0.05. The TER was based on a scaled aggregate calculated by using a student's best 10 units accepted for tertiary admission purposes. Students who did not attempt at least 10 of these units were ineligible for a TER.

1995–

With effect from 1995 a candidate's TER will be based on the scaled aggregate of the marks in the best ten units in recognized HSC courses, including at least one unit of English, at least one unit from each Key Learning Area Group, and at most two units of Category B subjects. The TER may include units accumulated by a candidate over a total time span of five years (conditions apply).

NORTHERN TERRITORY

EVALUATION IN BRITAIN

Junior Secondary Studies Certificate (Year 10) – issued by the Northern Territory Board of Studies – generally considered comparable to GCSE standard (grades A, B and C) on a subject-for-subject basis.

South Australian Certificate of Education – Northern Territory (Year 12) – issued by the Senior Secondary Assessment Board of South Australia (SSABSA) – generally considered to satisfy the general entrance requirements of British higher education institutions – if a minimum score of 70 out of 100 on the SSABSA assessment scale has been obtained (in the five publicly examined subjects) / passes in five acceptable publicly examined subjects taken at one sitting, provided that not less than grade B has been achieved in three of those subjects and not less than grade C in the other two.

MARKING SYSTEMS

Junior Secondary Studies Certificate grades are based on school assessments, except in English and mathematics where the school assessment (70 per cent) is combined with an external examination score (30 per cent) to produce the final grade. The school assessed component of English and mathematics, and grades in social education and science are externally moderated.

South Australian Certificate of Education (Northern Territory) grades are based on externally moderated school results in school assessed subjects and on a combination of school and external examination results in publicly examined subjects. (For further details refer to South Australia.)

The **Higher Education Entrance Score** is out of a maximum of 70 based on scaled scores in the best three **South Australian Certificate of Education (Northern Territory)** Stage 2 subjects (out of 20 for each subject) and bonus points for subject achievement scores in the fourth and fifth subjects (to a maximum of five points each). An aggregate of 46.5 from five subjects is required for tertiary entrance.

The Higher Education entrance Score for the Northern Territory University is out of 100. This is the sum of five subjects using the better of the SAS or scaled score for each subject.

SCHOOL EDUCATION

Schools may be broadly divided into two groups: those in predominantly Aboriginal communities and those in predominantly European communities.

Most schools in Aboriginal communities provide primary education only, although many also have courses for students of secondary age. The primary students follow the same common curriculum as those in urban schools and, while there are common assessment programmes in English and mathematics at Year 5 and 7 levels, there is no uniform external assessment. If an Aboriginal community school has no secondary programme, or if the students wish to pursue a full secondary education, they may attend an urban residential college, board at a residential college while attending a high school or enrol with the Northern Territory Secondary Correspondence School. In eighteen of the larger Aboriginal communities, community education centres provide pre-school and primary education along with certificate courses for secondary aged Aboriginal students who do not have the formal entrance requirements for secondary education.

Secondary education in urban areas is conducted in comprehensive high schools. In Darwin and Alice Springs there are also secondary colleges catering exclusively for students in Years 11 and 12. Common system-wide assessment programmes operate in English and mathematics in Years 5 and 7 and results are published annually. At the end of Year 10, students receive a **Junior Secondary Studies Certificate**.

At senior secondary level, assessments in Year 11 are school based, with moderation in most subjects including English and mathematics. Most Year 12 students follow courses of the Senior Secondary Assessment Board of South Australia. These courses fall into two groups: school-assessed subjects, in which gradings are awarded on externally moderated school assessments and publicly examined subjects, in which gradings are awarded on the basis of 50 per cent external examination used as a moderating instrument.

All students who follow courses at senior secondary level receive a **Northern Territory Senior Secondary Studies Certificate**. Students who complete SSABSA courses receive, in addition, a **South Australian Certificate of Education – Northern Territory**.

QUEENSLAND

EVALUATION IN BRITAIN

Junior Certificate (Year 10) – generally considered comparable to GCSE standard (grades A, B and C) on a subject-for-subject basis.

Senior Certificate/Interim Statement of Results – generally considered to satisfy the general entrance requirements of British higher education institutions with passes in five acceptable subjects providing that at least the level 'high achievement' has been obtained in three of them and at least 'sound achievement' in the other two.

Overall Position – generally considered to satisfy the general entrance requirements of British higher education institutions if an overall position of between 1 and 6 has been gained.

MARKING SYSTEMS

Junior Certificate (Year 10)

Five levels of achievement: very high to very limited.

Senior Certificate (Year 12)

Five levels of achievement: very high to very limited.

Overall positions are reported as one of 25 bands from 1 (the highest) to 25 (the lowest). The number of students eligible for an overall position in a particular year is used as the population on which overall position calculations are based.

SCHOOL EDUCATION

Secondary education is conducted in high schools for a total of five years. Alternatively, there are a small number of Senior Colleges where the last two of these five years can be completed.

Secondary education comprises three years leading to the **Junior Certificate** with a further (optional) two years leading to the **Senior Certificate**.

Student Education Profile (SEP)

At the completion of Year 12 students receive a Student Education Profile (SEP) which consists of 4 components reported on 2 documents:

Senior Certificate	1	Subject results
	2	Queensland Core Skills (QCS) Test Results
Tertiary Entrance Statement	3	Overall Position (OP)
	4	Field Position (FP)

Subject Results

Levels of Achievement in each Board and Board-registered subject are reported:

VHA = very high achievement
HA = high achievement
SA = sound achievement
LA = limited achievement
VLA = very limited achievement

Queensland Core Skills (QCS) Test

Individual results are reported on a 5-point scale from A (highest) to E.

The test consists of four papers using three modes of response: extended writing, multiple choice, and short response.

Overall Position (OP)

The OP indicates a student's rank order position using the results of the best 100 weighted semester units (WSUs) in Board subjects studied during Years 11 and 12. The OP uses equal weightings for all subjects and involves scaling using QCS Test results.

The OP is reported as one of 25 bands from 1 (highest) to 25 for eligible students:

Band 1 = 2 per cent
Band 2–6 = 15 per cent
Band 7–21 = 70 per cent
Band 22–34 = 11 per cent
Band 25 = 2 per cent

Field Positions (FPs)

The FPs indicate a student's rank order position based on overall achievements in Board subjects in up to five fields, reported in bands 1 (highest) to 10 for each field position. FPs require completion of at least 60 weighted semester units (WSUs) of relevant Board subjects. FPs use unequal weightings for each subject and involve scaling using QCS Test results.

FP A extended written expression 1–10
FP B short written communication 1–10
FP C basic numeracy 1–10
FP D solving complex problems 1–10
FP E practical performance 1–10

Tertiary Entrance (TE) Score (until 1991)

Students who had completed a minimum of twenty semester units of Board of Senior Secondary School subjects, including three subjects taken for the complete course of four semesters, were also issued with a single index of overall achievement known as the **Tertiary Entrance (TE) Score**. The TE score was derived from a special subject assessment for each BSSSS subject, made at the end of Year 12. These were scaled against results from the **Australian Scholastic Aptitude Test** and an aggregate obtained from the student's best five adjusted scores. Tertiary Entrance Scores ranged from 990 downwards in intervals of five, until all those eligible had been given a score. The Tertiary Entrance Score was abolished in 1991.

SOUTH AUSTRALIA

EVALUATION IN BRITAIN

Year 12 Certificate of Achievement – generally considered to satisfy the general entrance requirements of British higher education institutions if a minimum of three Bs and two Cs (BBBCC) in five acceptable publicly examined subjects taken at one sitting has been scored.

South Australia Certificate of Education Record of Achievement (from 1993) – generally considered to satisfy the general entrance requirements of British higher education institutions if a minimum if three Bs and two Cs (BBBCC) in five acceptable publicly examined 2 unit subjects taken at one sitting has been scored.

Higher Education Entrance Score – generally considered to satisfy the general entrance requirements of British higher education institutions if a minimum score of 55 is achieved.

MARKING SYSTEMS

Intermediate Certificate (Year 10) (up to 1968) graded 1 (highest) – 6.

Leaving Certificate (Year 11) (up to 1975) graded 1 (highest) – 6.

Leaving Honours Certificate (Year 12) (up to 1965) graded A–F.

Secondary School Certificate (Year 11 and 12) (1969–85) graded A–E and U = unsatisfactory.

School Leaver Statement (1977–88) based on continuous school assessment. Subject performance based on a three-point scale: H – successfully completed with high quality, S – successfully completed, N – not successfully completed.

Matriculation Certificate (Year 12) (1966–1983)

1966–77   grades A–G (A–D being pass grades)
1978–79   scale 1–100; aggregate of 225 from five subjects needed for matriculation
1980–83   scale 1–100; aggregate of 295 from five subjects needed for matriculation

Year 12 Certificate of Achievement (1984–1992)

From 1984–86 the score was the same as the 1980–83 Matriculation Certificate.

1987–92   Subject achievement score 1–20 and grades A–E; higher education entrance score scale 1–20. Aggregate of 59 from five subjects needed for matriculation.

South Australian Certificate of Education (from 1993).

Record of achievement subject achievement scores 1–20 and grades A–E.

A	20	Outstanding Achievement
A	17–19	Very High Achievement
B	14–16	High Achievement
C	11–13	Competent Achievement
D	8–10	Marginal Achievement
E	4–7	Low Achievement
F	0–3	Requirement not met

The Higher Education Entrance Score is out of a maximum of 70 (to nearest 0.5) based on scaled scores in the best three subjects (out of 20 for each subject) and bonus points for subject achievement scores in the fourth and fifth subjects (to a maximum of five points each). Scale 1–20.

SCHOOL EDUCATION

Secondary education comprises five years leading to the **South Australian Certificate of Education.**

Until 1968, students could take the **Intermediate certificate examination** at Year 10 after three years of secondary education. Those students continuing for a fourth year could obtain the **Leaving Certificate** which served as a matriculation until 1965. Many students intending to go on to university stayed on at school for an additional year to take the **Leaving Honours Certificate**. In 1966, the **Matriculation Examination** was introduced as a Year 12 examination (i.e. after five years of secondary education), replacing the **Leaving Honours Certificate**.

The Secondary School Certificate (SSC) was introduced in 1969 to replace the internal Years 11 and 12 certificates offered by schools. From 1976 only Year 12 SSC subjects were school assessed and externally moderated. Students selecting subjects from both SSC and matriculation groups received two certificates at the end of Year 12. Students in government schools were entitled to receive a **School Leaver Statement**, irrespective of other external certificates. From 1989, the **Student Achievement Record** replaced the School Leaver Statement.

Matriculation Certificate

Students wishing to matriculate needed to present five subjects in a prescribed pattern, accepted by the universities as suitable for tertiary entrance. From 1988, students were able to aggregate a matriculating score over two years by presenting five subjects in the first year and then any number in the second year, provided the best five subjects met the university subject grouping (matriculation) requirements.

Year 12 Certificate of Achievement (1984–1992)

Contained Subject Achievement Scores, which reported achievement in relation to the objectives of the syllabus, and Higher Education Entrance Scores, which were used for tertiary selection purposes, and which were derived by adjusting the Subject Achievement Scores.

South Australian Certificate of Education (SACE) (from 1993)

Students study **subjects** which are either 2 **units** (full year) or 1 **unit** (half-year) subjects. Three groups of subjects are studied: **Accredited** subjects based on the Extended Subject Framework at Stage 1 level, Accredited **Publicly Examined Subjects** (PES) at Stage 2 level and Accredited **School Assessed Subjects** (SAS) at stage 2 level.

The SACE is awarded to students who have reached at least a level of 'recorded achievement' in 22 approved units of study and a level of 'successful achievement' in at least 16 of the 22 units. Students receive a **SACE Certificate** and a **Record of Achievement** which details results in individual subjects. The scores are scaled into **Higher Education Entrance Scores** for university entrance purposes.

TASMANIA

EVALUATION IN BRITAIN

Higher School Certificate – generally considered to satisfy the general entrance requirements of British higher education institutions if a minimum of five level-III subjects and an aggregate mark of 640 out of a possible 1,000 has been obtained.

Tasmanian Certificate of Education (from 1993) – generally considered to satisfy the general entrance requirements of British higher education institutions if a minimum of five tertiary subjects awarded with at least High Achievement have been achieved.

Tertiary Entrance Score – generally considered to satisfy the general entrance requirements of British higher education institutions if a minimum of 56 has been obtained.

MARKING SYSTEMS

Tasmanian Certificate of Education (from 1993) within each award a 20-point score is calculated on the basis of the ratings received, within the following ranges:

OA (outstanding achievement)	17–20
HA (high achievement)	9–20
SA (satisfactory achievement)	1–8

The Tertiary Entrance Score is the sum of 20 point scores for the best five approved subjects. A percentile ranking of students within the age-cohort by percentile groups is calculated on the basis of Tertiary Entrance Scores.

SCHOOL EDUCATION

Secondary education takes place in high schools for the first four years, and secondary colleges for the final (optional) two years.

Since 1990 a new single certificate, the **Tasmanian Certificate of Education** has been introduced to record achievements for Years 9–12. This certificate replaces the former **School Certificate** (Year 10) and **Higher School Certificate** (Year 12).

From 1969 the **School Certificate** was taken at the end of the fourth year (replacing the old Schools Board Examination). A **School Certificate** (preliminary award) was available to students who left school at the end of the third year.

In 1969 the **Higher School Certificate** (Year 12) replaced the old **Matriculation Examination**. Most subjects in the **Higher School certificate** were offered at two levels. In most subjects a level-IF syllabus was provided for those wishing to undertake a preliminary study of a subject before attempting the level-III syllabus. It was not necessary to attempt level-IF before attempting level-III, nor did results obtained at level-IF count towards the level-III award. 200+ level-IF units of study each of forty hours were also available. To obtain an award in one of the sixteen level-IF subjects available in units, three units had to be chosen from the list of units available for that subject.

Progressively, from 1990, a new single certificate, the **Tasmanian Certificate of Education** (TCE) has been introduced which brings together achievements over the final years of secondary education from Year 9 onwards. Assessment for the TCE shifts the emphasis from a comparison of students' achievements one with another, to one of measuring students' work against clearly defined criteria laid down in subject syllabus statements.

Three groups of subjects are available: Group A (25 hours in Years 9/10, 50 hours in Years 11/12), Group B (100 hours in Years 9–12) and Group C (150 hours in Years 11 and 12). (There is no required course of study for the TCE). The TCE awards are classified as OA (outstanding achievements), HA (high achievement), SA (satisfactory achievement) and CC (course completed). To supplement formal certification, students are encouraged to compile individual records of achievement, to provide a more rounded student profile.

For tertiary entrance students will be required to obtain satisfactory achievement (SA) on a total of four approved Group C subjects. At least three of these subjects must be designed for Year 12 and completed in Year 12. A **Tertiary Entrance Score** is the sum of 20 point scores for the best five approved subjects. A percentile ranking of students within the age-cohort by percentile groups will be calculated on the basis of Tertiary Entrance Scores.

VICTORIA

EVALUATION IN BRITAIN

Victorian Certificate of Education – generally considered to satisfy the general entrance requirements of British higher education institutions if passes in five acceptable Unit 3 and Unit 4 subjects with at least a B in three of them and at least a C in the remaining two (BBBCC) have been obtained.

From 1994: **Victoria Certificate of Education Study Score** – an overall score of 40 out of 50 is generally considered to satisfy the general entrance requirements of British higher education institutions.

Tertiary Entrance Score (until 1993) – generally considered to satisfy the general entrance requirements of British higher education institutions if a score of at least 309 has been obtained.

From 1994 the **Tertiary Entrance Rank** is an overall percentile ranking of the applicant. May be considered to satisfy the general entrance requirements of British higher education institutions if a rank of at least 70 has been obtained.

MARKING SYSTEMS

Victorian Certificate of Education 1992–1994. Units recorded as either S/N
S = Satisfactorily completed, N = Not satisfactorily completed.

1992–93 CAT grades for units 3 and 4 scored:
A+ = 10, A = 9, B+ = 8, B = 7, C+ = 6, C = 5, D+ = 4, D = 3, E+ = 2, E = 1, UG
(ungraded), NA (not assessed) = 0.

From 1994, the VCE Study Score will be calculated from CAT scores for each subject.
The score has a maximum of 50 and a mean of 30.

Certificates prior to 1992

Year 10:

Intermediate Certificate until 1967 graded pass/fail.

Intermediate Technical Examination Certificate until 1986 graded pass/fail.

Year 11:

School Leaving Certificate until 1972 graded pass/fail.

Technical Leaving Certificate until 1986 graded pass/fail.

Matriculation Certificate (Year 12) until 1969 graded Honours 1, Honours 2 and pass.

Year 12:

Higher School Certificate 1970–86 graded A–F (A–D = satisfactorily completed) or
S/N (S = satisfactorily completed, N – not satisfactorily completed).

Victorian Certificate of Education 1987–91 graded A–F or S/N (as above) comprising
VCE (HSC), VCE (TOP), VCE (T12) and VCE Approved Composite Courses.

Matriculation certificate until 1969 graded Honours 1, Honours 2 and pass.

Technical Year 12 certificate until 1986 graded pass/fail.

SCHOOL EDUCATION

Secondary education is available in high schools, secondary colleges, post-primary
schools, and colleges of TAFE. Some VCE studies are offered by the Distance
Education Centre (formerly Secondary Correspondence School).

Secondary education comprises four years leading to year 10 (form 4), with a further
(optional) two years leading to the **Victorian Certificate of Education** (form 6/Year 12).

Until 1967, students could obtain the **Intermediate Certificate** on completion of Year
10, and until 1972, the **School Leaving Certificate** was obtained on completion of
Year 11. Certificates are no longer awarded at the end of Year 11; however, a school
may provide a student with a statement that he or she has satisfactorily completed
eleven years of education.

Formerly, students were able to stay on for a further year to study for the

Matriculation Certificate. From 1970 until 1991, the Year 12 programme was called the **Higher School Certificate** (HSC).

In 1981 a combination of school-based and external assessment was established. Normal requirements for the successful completion of HSC were grade D or better in at least twelve (equivalent to four subjects). English was compulsory. VISE also accredited a number of approved study centres.

Technical schools (which ceased to operate in 1986) provided a general secondary education to Year 12. The Technical Accreditation Programme covered the assessment and accreditation of courses for certification at:

Year 10 (form 4) – **Intermediate Technical Examination Certificate**

Year 11 (form 5) – **Technical Leaving Certificate**

Year 12 (form 6) – **Technical Year 12 Certificate**

There were two types of course in the **Technical Leaving Certificate,** Code A and Code B

The **Technical Year 12 Certificate** was awarded to students undertaking a school-devised course which met the requirements in the Technical Year 12 Study Structure Handbook.

Some of the technical schools also offered Victorian Certificate of Education subjects and courses and some the TAFE Tertiary Orientation Programme.

From 1987–91 a one-year **Victorian Certificate of Education** was awarded to those candidates who would previously have qualified for **Higher School Certificate**, or the certificates of either of the two other Year 12 programmes currently offered, the Tertiary Orientation Programme (TOP) and the Technical Year 12 Programme (T12).

Victorian Certificate of Education (VCE) (from 1992)

The VCE comprises: statement of results and summary statement of grades obtained on Common Assessment Tasks for Units 3 and 4. The VCE is awarded on the basis of satisfactory completion of the required number and pattern of units, and not on the basis of CAT grades.

The award of the VCE is contingent upon students completing satisfactorily a total of **16 units** including at least three units of the common study English (from Units 1, 2, 3 and 4); and three sequences of Units 3 and 4 in studies other than English. From 1995 students must complete at least two units from arts/humanities and two units from maths/science/technology. Units 1 and 2 are normally attempted in Year 11, and Units 3 and 4 in Year 12, but students may attempt Units 3 and 4 level studies in Year 11 and vice versa. Most studies are made up of four units, although some can include up to 21 units (e.g. history). Each unit lasts for half a year, and represents approximately 100 hours of work.

A student's level of performance is based on the results of three or four Common Assessment Tasks (CATs) in each of the Year 12 studies. At least one of the CATs in each study is an external examination, the other CATs are school assessed. From 1995 all studies will have 3 CATs.

Assessment procedures for VCE school-assessed CATs have been reviewed for 1994 and the **General Achievement Test** (GAT) is being introduced. The GAT is designed to measure the level of general achievement students have gained across three areas: (i) written communication; (ii) mathematics, science, technology; and (iii) humanities, arts, social sciences. The GAT will be used to ensure that all schools are grading their students consistently across the state. Where a school's results for its students in a school assessed CAT do not match the range of results for the same group of students in the GAT, the students work is externally reviewed. GAT results are confidential to the student and do not contribute to the award of certificates or tertiary selection.

In 1994 articulation arrangements were introduced between VCE and TAFE. VCE students can also undertake university subjects in an approved programme.

Tertiary Selection Process

Until 1994

Tertiary Entrance Score (TES)

Based on grades received from Common Assessment Tasks, a scaled study score was calculated for each study completed satisfactorily (maximum score 40). The Tertiary Entrance Score was obtained by adding the best four studies together with increments for two additional studies and bonus points for some specified studies.

In 1994 a single, state-wide **Tertiary Entrance Rank** system was introduced to replace the tertiary entrance score. The TER is a percentile rank giving the comparative placement of the student in the population of tertiary applicants who have applied for a tertiary course and replaces the former system whereby students received individual scaled study scores and a different entrance score for each course for which they applied. The TER is determined by an algorithm to produce an overall percentile ranking of the applicant. The algorithm takes into account the student's global score in English (or English as a second language), the student's best three other global scores and 10 per cent of the student's next two best global scores. In all, up to six global scores may be used.

From 1995 students applying for tertiary selection on the basis of the VCE will be selected from two categories, an upper band for those clearly above the cut-off tertiary entrance rank (TER) and those in a middle-band in the vicinity of the cut-off. It is expected that most courses will select up to 80 per cent of their school leaver intake from the first category. Students in the upper-band category will in general be selected on the basis of satisfactory completion of course prerequisites and their tertiary entrance rank.

WESTERN AUSTRALIA

EVALUATION IN BRITAIN

Certificate of Secondary Education – generally considered to satisfy the general entrance requirements of British higher education institutions if passes in five acceptable Year 12 subjects with a mark of at least 70 per cent in three of them and at least 60 per cent in the other two have been obtained.

Since 1986 – generally considered to satisfy the general entrance requirements of British higher education institutions if passes in five acceptable subjects with at least a B in three of them and at least a C in the remaining two (BBBCC) have been obtained.

Tertiary Entrance Score – generally considered to satisfy the general entrance requirements of British higher education institutions if a score of at least 337 out of a possible 510 has been obtained.

MARKING SYSTEMS

Leaving Examination (until 1974) – graded Distinction and Pass. Subjects offered at matriculation level graded pass or fail.

Leaving Certificate (1975) – graded A–F

Certificate of Secondary Education (CSE) (formerly the **Leaving Certificate**)

1976–85   graded on a ten-point scale at 10 per cent intervals (grade 1 represents the top 10 per cent in the course)

since 1986   assessment is school based, standards referenced and graded on a five-point scale, A–F (there is no E):

A   approximately top 20% of students
B   the next 20% of students
C   the next 30% of students
D   the next 20% of students
F   the remaining 10% of students

Tertiary Entrance Score (TES)

Entrance to tertiary institutions is based on the Tertiary Entrance Score (TES) which is a weighted average of scores in a student's best four or five TES subjects, including one subject from each of List 1 (humanities/social sciences subjects) and List 2 (quantitative/science subjects). Ten per cent of the student's Australian Scaling Test score is also included. The maximum TES is 510.

New TEE grading system

The Decile Place refers to a student's position relative to other students in that subject.

1 indicates the student is in the top 10% of students in that subject.
2 indicates a place in the second 10%; etc.

For each subject, a Raw Examination mark and a Scaled mark are given, each as a percentage.

All students applying for entrance to tertiary institutions must also have satisfied the requirements for Secondary Graduation.

SCHOOL EDUCATION

Secondary education comprises three years to Year 10, with a further (optional) two years leading to the **Certificate of Secondary Education**.

From 1967 pupils were awarded the **Achievement Certificate** at the end of Year 10. A student who left before Year 10 was given a certificate showing achievements for every full year of secondary schooling worked. Before 1967, the **Junior Certificate**, based on an external examination, was awarded at the end of Year 10.

From 1986 until 1993 students leaving school following the first phase (i.e. Year 10) obtained the **Certificate of Lower Secondary Studies** (CLSS). Students chose virtually any pattern of units during Years 8, 9 and 10, although in government schools they were required to study at least 160 hours of English and mathematics a year. The CLSS was last issued to Year 10 students in 1993.

Until 1974, there was a **Leaving Certificate** examination at the end of the second phase (i.e. Year 12) which was used both for the school-leaving certificate and also for matriculation purposes. The 1975 **School Leaving Certificate** took account of both school assessment and examination results. In 1977, the title of the certificate was changed from **Leaving Certificate** to **Certificate of Secondary Education**, and was issued on the basis of 50 per cent school assessment and for some subjects 50 per cent of the Tertiary Admissions Examination. This examination formed the basis of selection for entry into tertiary education institutions.

To obtain the Certificate of **Secondary Graduation** a student must earn 60 Year 11 and Year 12 credit points (18 from Year 12 courses) and have obtained a grade D or better in Year 12 English, English Literature, Senior English or English for ESL Students. If a student has met the requirements for Secondary Graduation, this will be recorded on the CSE. Otherwise, the number of credit points earned is shown on the CSE.

The **Certificate of Secondary Education** will be phased out in 1996 and replaced by the **Western Australian Certificate of Education** in 1997.

Tertiary Entrance Score Subjects (TESS) Students seeking entrance to higher education take the **Tertiary Entrance Examination** (TEE) in Year 12. The maximum TEE score is 510. The TEE score is calculated by taking 50 per cent of the scaled examination mark and 50 per cent of school assessed Year 12 work. Examinations are taken in four to six subjects. The score is produced from the average of the best four of five TEE examinations in one year, multiplied by five plus 10 per cent of the AST.

Austria

The School Organization Act of 1962 is the legal basis of the current system. The Federal Ministry of Education and the Arts is the central authority, but there are provincial and district education authorities in each of the nine provinces.

Universities and colleges of higher education are regulated by federal law and administered by the Federal Ministry of Science and Research.

Education is compulsory from ages six to fifteen (grade 9). In schools the academic year is from September until June/July, while in higher education it is from October until June, with one break in February. German is the medium of instruction.

EVALUATION IN BRITAIN

School

Reifeprüfung/Matura (from *Allgemeinbildende höhere Schulen*) – may be considered to satisfy the general entrance requirements of British higher education institutions.

Reifeprüfung/Matura (from *Berufsbildende höhere Schulen*) – generally considered comparable to BTEC National Diploma / N/SVQ level 3 / Advanced GNVQ/GSVQ standard. It gives access to technological courses in Austrian higher education.

Higher

Diplomstudium/Magister – generally considered comparable to British Bachelor (Honours) degree standard, although the course lasts longer than in the UK.

Kurzstudium – constitutes the Federally recognized **Cantonal Maturity Certificate (Eidgenossisch anerkanntes kantonales Maturitatszeugnis/Certificat de matutite cantonal reconnu par la Confederation/Attestato di maturita cantonale riconosciuto dalla Confederazione**) professionally-oriented first degree; considered comparable to BTEC Higher National Diploma / N/SVQ Level 4.

Aufbaustudium – constitutes a postgraduate professional degree; considered comparable to N/SVQ Level 5.

Doktoratsstudium – considered comparable to British PhD.

MARKING SYSTEMS

School and Higher

Marking is usually on a scale of 1–5, with 4 as the minimum pass-mark. The marks may also be classified as:

1	*sehr gut*	very good
2	*gut*	good
3	*befriedigend*	satisfactory
4	*genügend*	pass
5	*nicht genügend*	failure

SCHOOL EDUCATION

Primary (*Volksschule*, *Grundschule* or *Sonderschule*) (grades 1–4)

Primary education lasts four years from age six and is provided in *Volksschule* (also *Grundschule*/primary school) or for mentally or physically handicapped children at *Sonderschule* (special school). From the third grade onwards a foreign language (English or French) is taught (not graded).

Lower Secondary (*Unterstufe*) (grades 5–8)

There are 3 options for secondary study after grade 4;

Continued *Volksschule*, this is rare now.

General secondary school, *Hauptschule* from where pupils can go onto Academic secondary schools until grade 12.

Academic secondary schools, *Allgemeinbildende höhere Schulen* are divided into different types according to subject specialization and are terminated by the **Reifeprüfung** (matriculation exam). They have, as common core subjects, German, one modern foreign language, history and social science, geography, mathematics, biology, physics, music, art, handicrafts, physical education and religious instruction.

Grades 5 and 6 of all types of *Allgemeinbildende höhere Schulen* have a common curriculum. In grades 7 and 8 a first differentiation into three types is introduced as follows:

Gymnasium (general type), emphasizing one modern foreign language and Latin.

Realgymnasium (science-based type), emphasizing mathematics, Latin or a second foreign language, descriptive geometry or more biology and environmental studies, chemistry and physics.

Wirtschaftskundliches Realgymnasium (home economics type), emphasizing chemistry, textile or technical handicrafts.

Upper secondary (*Oberstufe*) (upper level)

Grade 9 is the last year of compulsory education. Students who do not wish to continue full-time education after *Hauptschule* attend the *Polytechnischer Lehrgang* (pre-vocational school) for the ninth year of compulsory education. In the *Polytechnischer*

Lehrgang German, mathematics and English are taught as compulsory subjects in three ability groups. This type of course is designed primarily to prepare young people for their working life.

At the upper level there are four different types of *Allgemeinbildende höhere Schulen*:

Gymnasium – in addition to Latin, Greek or a second foreign language is studied.

Realgymnasium – more mathematics, Latin or a second foreign language is studied, alongside descriptive geometry or more biology and environmental studies, chemistry and physics.

Wirtschaftskundliches Realgymnasium – Latin or a second foreign language is studied alongside home economics, nutrition, more geography and economics, biology and environmental studies, psychology and philosophy.

Oberstufen-Realgymnasium – In addition to the eight year types of Academic secondary schools there is a separate upper-level type (in some cases with a transition stage); admission after grade 8. Latin or a second foreign language is studied, alongside instrumental music or fine arts and handicraft, or descriptive geometry or more biology and environmental science, chemistry, physics (and mathematics).

In grades 10–12 of all four types students are partly able to decide themselves which subjects they would like to study in more depth according to their personal interests. These elective compulsory subjects (*Wahlpflichtgegenstände*) have to be studied for 8 hours/week at *Gymnasium* and *Oberstufen-Realgymnasium*, 10 hours/week at *Realgymnasium* and 12 hours/week at *Wirtschaftskundliches Realgymnasium*.

Two types of elective compulsory subjects are on offer:
  – those constituting additional subjects
  – those offering in-depth, additional instruction in a compulsory subject

Special types of secondary

Academic

The *Aufbaugymnasium* (language-orientated) and *Aufbaurealgymnasium* (science-orientated) offer extension courses for students (mainly adults) who have completed *Hauptschule* and wish to have an academic secondary education. There is no age limit. Some courses begin with a transitional year and progress to a four-year course.

The *Gymnasium, Realgymnasium und Wirtschaftskundliches Realgymnasium für Berufstätige* offer part-time evening classes for students over 17 in employment who have completed 8 years of compulsory schooling. It lasts 9 semesters.

The *Realgymnasium mit Ausbildung in Metallurgie* (grades 9 to 13) particularly emphasizes mathematics and offers training in metallurgy.

The school leaving exam taken on completion of the *Allgemeinbildende höhere Schule* is the **Reifeprüfung** (or **Matura**), which gives access to higher education. Students can choose from among three different possibilities:

1　In the first semester of the 12th grade students write a kind of scholarly paper (**Fachbereichsarbeit**) in one subject which, however, has to take in aspects touching on other subjects. In addition, they have to take 3 written and 3 oral exams; one of the oral exams is based on the paper. In most cases, only academically highly gifted students decide for this option.

2   Students take 3 written and 4 oral exams.

3   Students take 4 written and 3 oral exams.

Whichever option is chosen, every student taking **Matura** has to pass a total of 7 exams, with German, maths and one foreign language being compulsory subjects in the written **Matura** and a modern foreign language being compulsory for the oral **Matura**.

The oral exams include both survey questions (*Kernfragen*) as well as questions considering the student's special interests (*Spezialfragen*). In addition, one of the oral exams includes a so-called "emphasis test" (**Schwerpunktprüfung**) which is taken in a compulsory subject and an elective compulsory subject.

Technical and vocational

Berufsbildende Pflichtschulen (compulsory vocational schools), provide compulsory part-time education on day- or block-release for apprentices in trade, industry, commerce, craft, agriculture and forestry. They start after the *Polytechnischer Lehrgang*. According to the type of training and the duration of apprenticeship, the courses last between two and four years and finish with the **Lehrabschlußprüfung** (termination of apprenticeship examination).

Berufsbildende mittlere Schulen (medium-level secondary technical and vocational schools), provide the basic professional training for employment in commerce, technology, arts and crafts, tourism and catering, social work and agriculture. Most courses are full-time and last between one and four years but do not give access to higher education. Admission is granted after the completion of eight years of compulsory schooling and in most colleges the passing of an entrance examination.

The schools belonging to this category are:

Handelsschule
Medium-level secondary commercial college offering three-year full-time training.

Büro- und Verwaltungsschule
Intermediate school for office and administrative work/two years.

Büroschule
Intermediate school for office work/one year.

Schule für Datenverarbeitungskaufleute
School providing training in data processing/one to three years.

Hauswirtschaftsschule
Medium-level secondary home economics college providing domestic science and basic commercial training in a two-year course.

Haushaltungsschule
Medium-level secondary domestic science college offering one-year courses.

Fachscule für wirtschaftliche Berufe
Medium-level secondary college for domestic-science occupations/three years.

Technische, gewerbliche und kunstgewerbliche Fachschulen
Medium-level industrial, trade and crafts college/mostly four years.

Fachschule für Mode-und Bekleidungstechnik
Medium-level secondary college for the garment and clothes trades offering specialized training for work in the textile industry/four years.

Fachschule für Sozialberufe
Medium-level secondary college for social workers providing training for social occupations offering training courses of between one and three years' duration for youth leaders, family assistance workers, senior citizens assistance workers, marriage and family counsellors.

Hotelfachschule, Gastgewerbefachschule, Tourismusfachscule
Medium-level secondary college for hotel management, catering occupations and tourism offering three-year training courses for hotel management and catering.

Landwirtschaftliche Fachschule
Vocational agricultural school with the length of training from two winter semesters up to four years depending on the type of school and the preliminary education of the student. Areas of training are agriculture, gardening, wine and food.

Förstliche Bundesfachschule
Medium-level secondary forestry college offering courses in forestry/one year.

There are also schools comparable in level to *Berufsbildende mittlere Schulen*, which come under the auspices of the Ministry of Health. These are *Allgemeine Krankenpflegeschulen* (nursing schools), *Schulen für den medizinisch-technischen Fachdienst* (schools for medical laboratory assistants) and *Bundeshebammenlehranstalten* (midwifery schools).

Berufsbildende höhere Schulen (higher-level secondary technical and vocational schools), courses last five years and provide advanced general and technical/vocational education for occupations at middle-management or technician level. For admission, successful completion of eight years of compulsory education plus the passing of a standardized aptitude test is required. Some schools provide evening classes for adults in employment. This course leads to the **Reifeprüfung** (or **Matura**), which gives access to higher education. For some studies additional examinations may be required. Graduates from *Höhere technische Lehranstalten* (higher-level secondary industrial colleges), *Höhere landwirtschaftliche Lehranstalten* (higher-level secondary agriculture colleges) (with the exception of *Höhere Lehranstalt für Lund-und Hauswirtschaft*-higher level secondary agriculture and domestic-science college), as well as from *Höhere Lehranstalt für Forstwirtschaft* (higher-level secondary forestry college), who have worked in their fields for a stipulated period of time, are entitled to use the job title of '**Ingenieur**'.

The following schools belong to this category:

Höhere technische und gewerbliche Lehranstalt
Upper-level technical and trade school teaching technical knowledge and skills for technical, trade and engineering occupations.

Höhere Lehranstalt für Fremdenverkehrsberufe
Upper-level school offering training for prospective senior personnel in tourism and catering.

Handelsakademie
Upper-level commercial school providing training for all branches of business. These are four-year evening courses for people over seventeen already in employment.

Höhere Lehranstalt für wirtschaftliche Berufe
Domestic science and catering school which prepares students for jobs at executive
level in domestic science, tourism and catering, social work and economy.

Höhere land-und forstwirtschaftliche Lehranstalt
Courses in agriculture and forestry lasting five years.

Höhere Lehranstalt für Mode-und Bekleidungstechnik
Upper-level school for the garment and clothing trades offering training or qualified
specialists in the clothing and garment industry.

FURTHER EDUCATION

Technical and vocational colleges that may be attended after passing a **Reifeprüfung**
(matriculation exam):

Akademie für Sozialarbeit
Training in the field of social work for three years leading to a diploma. For entry an
aptitude test must be passed.

Speziallehrgänge
Vocational courses lasting between one and two years at *Berufsbildende höhere Schulen*
giving additional training in particular branches of technology, economics, tourism and
catering to holders of the **Reifezeugnis** as well as to school leavers of *Berufsbildende
mittlere Schulen* and *Berufsschulen*. As opposed to *Kollegs*, these schools do not lead to
Matura.

Kollegs
Courses lasting four semesters for holders of a **Reifezeugnis** from an
Allgemeinbildende höhere Schule. They provide additional training in tourism and
catering, commerce and technology and are run by *Berufsbildende höhere Schulen*.

Schulen für gehobene medizinisch-technische Dienste
Courses for medical laboratory technicians and related occupations lasting two to three
years.

Some intermediate and higher vocational schools also provide evening classes for
employed persons. Training for handicapped students is available at several
intermediate vocational schools.

HIGHER EDUCATION

Higher education is provided by eighteen institutions of university status, including five
general universities, seven specialized universities and six fine arts colleges.

Access to university is free and open to holders of a **Reifezeugnis** though students may
have to take additional examinations for certain types of study. Non-secondary school
leavers without a **Reifezeugnis** may enter higher education by taking the
Studienberechtigungsprüfung.

Studienberechtigungsprüfung (University Study Qualification Exam)
Since 1986 universities have offered preparatory courses leading to the
Studienberechtigungsprüfung which entitles the candidate to study only the subject(s)

the examination(s) was (were) taken in. For the preparatory course the candidate must be at least twenty-two years of age. However, candidates who have successfully completed four years of training after their compulsory education may be admitted to the exam from the age of twenty.

Courses and degrees

The Austrian universities offer three different types of studies:

Ordentliche Studien (normal degree courses)

Hochschulkurse and Hochschullehrgänge (special university courses)
Studium als ausserordentlicher Hörer and Studium als Gasthörer (non-degree courses)
Ordentliche Studien

A *Diplomstudium* lasts in theory eight to ten semesters (four to five years) (the average time taken in the academic year 1991/92 was 13.1 semesters) and is organized into two parts (*Studienabschnitte*). The first is basic study of the subject and ends with the **Erste Diplomprüfung**. The second part involves specialization and ends with the writing of a thesis (*Diplomarbeit*) and the **Zweite Diplomprüfung**. After passing this examination the student is conferred the first academic degree called **Magister** or **Diplom** (the latter in subjects such as engineering).

After the *Diplomstudium* students may continue studying for two to four semesters to obtain a doctor's degree. A dissertation (doctorate thesis) must be written and a **Rigorosum** (final oral examination) passed. The title **Doktor** is then conferred, which is the highest academic qualification. Final examinations for master's and doctor's degrees (**Diplomprüfung, Rigorosum**) are comprehensive examinations. They are composed of several tests covering different disciplines. Comprehensive examinations are either administered by an examination board or by individual examiners. The assessment of examination performances and the quality of these are rated by marks, ranging from 1 (very good) to 5 (failure). The final certificate (**Diplomzeugnis**) will give three marks only; *Mit Auszeichnung* (with distinction), *Bestanden* (pass), *Nicht bestanden* (fail).

Alongside the full-length degree courses, some universities offer *Kurzstudien* (short courses) lasting five to six semesters which lead to a professional title, such as:

Datentechnik (computation methods);
title: **Akademisch geprüfter Rechentechniker**

Versicherungsmathematik (actuarial mathematics);
title: **Akademisch geprüfter Versicherungsmathematiker**

Kurzstudium fur Übersetzer (translating);
title: **Akademisch geprüfter Übersetzer**

While the individual courses and lectures of the *Ordentliche Studien* are strictly regulated, students have more freedom of choice with the so-called *Studium irregulare*. These special courses incorporate elements of the *Ordentliche Studien* combined by the student to form a tailor-made course. On certain conditions a *Studium irregulare* becomes a *Studienversuch* (study experiment) and must be approved by the academic authorities.

Hochschulkurse and *Hochschullehrgänge*

These are open to university students, university graduates and even students who do not hold a **Reifezeugnis**. These courses offer practical or academic training and last up to six semesters. Courses cover a great variety of subjects including music, pedagogics, medicine, trade, advertising, tourism, law, and journalism. Some of the *Hochschulkurse* and *Hochschullehrgänge* can be considered postgraduate courses.

Apart from the universities, there are several non-university institutions which offer courses at postgraduate level, such as the Diplomatische Akademie (Diplomatic Academy) in Vienna, the Institut für Höhere Studien und wissenschaftliche Forschung (Institute for Advanced Studies and Scientific Research) and the Wiener medizinische Akademie für ärztliche Fortbildung (Vienna Academy of Medicine for Postgraduate Training).

Studium als ausserordentlicher Hörer and Studium als Gasthörer

All students who are a minimum of seventeen years old and wish to attend university lectures or *Hochschulkurse* and *Hochschullehrgänge* without having a **Reifezeugnis** may do so as *ausserordentliche Hörer*. University graduates from other countries who wish to have their foreign degrees validated in Austria may have to enrol for certain courses as *ausserordentliche Hörer*.

All university graduates who want to attend lectures, *Hochschulkurse* or *Hochschullehrgänge* for a certain period without beginning a second course of studies may do so as *Gasthörer*.

Ausserordentliche Hörer and *Gasthörer* are free to take examinations with *Hochschulkurse* and *Hochschullehrgänge*. They are, however, not allowed to take examinations with ordinary university lectures.

Fachhochschulen (Post-Secondary Special-Subject Colleges)

Fachhochschulen will be established in Austria from the academic year 1994/95 onwards as an alternative to currently existing university studies. They will offer a scientifically-based and practically-orientated professional training in the fields or technology, economy, social affairs and society (media, law, training of teachers and educators). Studies are to last three, at the most four years. Anybody having finished *Gymnasium* (Academic Secondary School), a technical and vocational school, or an apprenticeship will be permitted to study at the new colleges. Apprentices have to acquire the so-called '**Fachhochschulreife**' (the maturity for attending a *Fachhochschule*) by passing a separate special-subject course which lasts either two or four semesters. Graduates from higher-level secondary and vocational schools may save study time and immediately enter a higher stage. Graduates from *Fachhochschulen*, who want to continue their studies at a university, will receive credits for their studies at *Fachhochschule*.

TEACHER EDUCATION

Teachers undergo different kinds of training, according to the level of teaching they intend to take up. Generally teacher training can be divided into university level and non-university level.

Non-university training

Training for compulsory school teachers is provided at teacher training colleges. There are also colleges which train specialist teachers for various kinds of vocational schools. For admission the **Reifezeugnis** is required.

Pädagogische Akademien
These provide training for teachers at *Volksschule, Hauptschule, Sonderschule, Polytechnischer Lehrgang*. Students must pass an aptitude test. All courses last three years, and on completion students take the **Lehramtsprüfung** (teachers' examination). Teaching practice is given in practice schools attached to the *Akademien*.

Berufspädagogische Akademien (vocational teacher colleges) and *Land- und forstwirtschaftliche Akademien* (agricultural teacher training colleges)
These train teachers of domestic science, commercial subjects, agriculture and forestry at *Berufsbildende mittlere Schulen* and *Berufsbildende höhere Schulen*, teachers of shorthand and typing and teachers at *Berufsschulen*. Admission requirements may either be a **Reifezeugnis** or a master craftsman's certificate plus professional experience. Courses last between one and three years.

Pädagogischer Institute (institutes for further teacher training)
Originally designed for the further training of teachers at *Volksschulen, Hauptschulen, Sonderschulen* and *Polytechnische Lehrgänge*, they now also provide further training for teachers at *Allgemeinbildende höhere Schulen* and *Berufsbildende Schulen*.

University training

All teachers at *Allgemeinbildende höhere Schulen* and teachers of general theoretical-technical subjects at *Berufsbildende höhere Schulen* must be university graduates. Students have to qualify in two subjects, combined in accordance with the relevant regulations.

On completion of a minimum of nine semesters (four and a half years) of studies, the student takes the second **Diplomprüfung** in her/his major subject and is then conferred the academic degree of **Magister**. Practical training (*Schulpraktikum*) is part of the second *Studienabschnitt* and comprises a general didactic (four weeks *Einführungsphase*) and a practical phase (two weeks *Übungsphase* per subject at a school). Teachers in their first year complete a so-called *Unterrichtspraktikum* (introductory year) before they are fully qualified.

Kindergarten

Kindergarten teachers are trained at *Bildungsanstalten für Kindergartenpädagogik*. Admission depends on the completion of eight years of compulsory schooling and the passing of an aptitude test. Courses last five years and lead to the **Reifeprüfung**.

Other

Bildungsanstalten für Erzieher train teachers at boarding schools and children's day centres. Admission requirements and the duration of training are as for kindergarten teachers. There is a special two-year course (*Kolleg für Erzieher*) for those who hold a **Reifezeugnis**.

Religionspädagogische Akademien provide two-year courses for Catholic religious instructors and require the **Reifezeugnis** for admission.

The *Evangelische Frauenschule für kirchlichen und sozialen Dienst* provides similar training for Protestant religious instructors.

Bundesanstalten für Leibeserziehung train *Sportlehrer* (sports teachers) and *Schilehrer* (skiing instructors).

ADULT EDUCATION

Adults are offered the opportunity to attend courses at various general and vocational schools. In addition, special adult education institutions called *Volkshochschulen*, as well as *Berufsförderungsinstitute* (institutes for the advancement of vocational training), offer preparatory courses for **Reifeprüfung** (matriculation exam), for the university study qualification exam and for the leaving certificate of *Hauptschule* (general secondary school).

Distance Education (*Fernstudien*)

This has been provided since 1979 by the Interuniversitäres Forschungsinstitut für Fernstudien located at the University of Klagenfurt. Since 1992, the new distance education centre called Zentrum fur Fernstudien der Universität Linz, has moved to Linz working together with two other centres in Bregenz and Vienna. They are managing courses offered by the Fernuniversität Hagen in Germany, which offers normal degree courses in economics, law, social sciences, pedagogics, mathematics, electronic engineering, computer sciences and humanities.

In Vienna they are planning to establish a Eurostudy-centre in order to enable students to participate in programmes being offered by foreign-language distance education centres. In 1992 a branch of the Open University was opened in Vienna.

Studies for senior citizens (*Seniorenstudium*)

Austrian universities welcome senior citizens as students. Courses, degrees and conditions of admission are the same as for younger students.

Republic of Azerbaijan

Following the break-up of the former Union of Soviet Socialist Republics, the Azerbaijan Republic has begun to establish its own education system, in common with the other Asian republics. The recent introduction of a new education law will enable the republic to begin the transition to a multi-stage structure of education, including the formation of new policies in further education. This will include the introduction of international standards to higher education.

For information on the situation before 1991, please see the **Russian Federation** chapter.

EVALUATION IN BRITAIN

Until approximately 1990 under the Soviet system:

School

Svidetel'stvo/o Srednem Obrazovanii (Certificate of Secondary Education)

at grade 10 – generally considered to be below GCSE standard.
at grade 11 – generally considered comparable to GCSE standard (grades A, B and C) on a subject-for-subject basis, with the exception of English language.

Higher

Diplom ob Okanchanii Vyssheg(v)o Uchebnog(v)o Zavedeniya (Diploma Specialist) – generally considered comparable to a standard between GCE Advanced and British Bachelor degree; may be considered for advanced standing by British higher education institutions. Candidates from prestigious institutions may be considered for admission to taught Master's degree courses. Enquirers should contact the National Academic Recognition Information centre for further information.

From approximately 1990 under the new system:

Bachelor degree, Magister, Doctor – NARIC is unable to provide an evaluation for these new qualifications, as standards are still being developed.

MARKING SYSTEM

School and Higher

Marking is on a 1–5 scale

5   excellent
4   good
3   satisfactory
2   unsatisfactory
1   totally unsatisfactory

SCHOOL EDUCATION

Please refer to the chapter on the **Russian Federation**.

UK NARIC has no information on the current school education system in the Azerbaijan Republic.

HIGHER EDUCATION

Since 1990:

Training of specialists in the higher education institutions of the Azerbaijan Republic is carried out to conform with the 'List of basic directions and specialities of higher education', adopted by the resolution of the Cabinet of Ministers, dated 19 September 1993. Since the proclamation of the sovereignty of the republic the policy has been to begin to train specialists necessary for the future development of the economy.

Institutions of higher education include universities, institutes, academies, higher colleges and conservatoires.

There are two recognized universities:

> Azerbaijan Technical University, Baku
>
> Baku State University (includes a branch in Shaki)

Other higher education institutes are:

> Azerbaijan Agricultural Institute, Kirovabad
>
> Azerbaijan N. Narimanov Medical Institute, Baku
>
> Azerbaijan State Pedagogical Institute of Languages, Baku (with branches in Shamaki and Agjabadi)
>
> Azerbaijan State Petroleum Academy, Baku
>
> Azerbaijan State University of Art, Baku (with a branch in Guba)
>
> Azerbaijan U. Gadzhibekov State Conservatoire, Baku
>
> Baku Civil Engineering Institute
>
> Gyanzha Technological Institute
>
> Ganja State Pedagogical Institute (with a branch in Gazakh)

There are a further four higher education institutions which are under the subordination of other ministries and committees.

Azerbaijan State Medical University – Ministry of Health

Azerbaijan State Academy of Agriculture – Ministry of Agriculture

Azerbaijan Co-operative Institute – *Azerittifag*

Azerbaijan State Institute of Physical Training – Azerbaijan Physical Training and Sports Committee

Bachelor degree courses are provided at 'one-stage' institutes of higher education. Those who pass the required examinations will continue their studies on to the next stage. Each year will consist of two semesters, the first of seventeen weeks duration, the second eighteen. The degree is awarded after either passing the state examinations or successfully completing 'diploma projects'.

Programmes and curricula for different specialities have been developed with the participation of teaching staff of higher education institutions and submitted for the approval of government and scientific boards.

Magister degree courses will be provided at 'two-stage' institutes of higher education.

Doctor degree courses will be provided at 'three-stage' institutes of higher education.

The degrees of **Bachelor, Magister** and **Doctor** are currently being developed along the lines of those awarded in other European countries. The higher education institutions are forming links with prominent world universities, members of the Association of Euro-Asian Universities and institutions in the Russian Federation. The Republic plans to accede to the convention on the recognition of overseas (mainly European), academic qualifications.

TEACHER EDUCATION

Since approximately 1990

Teachers for all levels of education are trained at the Azerbaijan Pedagogical University and the Ganja State Pedagogical Institute.

Bahamas

The following chapter regarding the education system in the Bahamas is based on information obtained from the 3rd edition of this Guide, published in 1991, as NARIC has been unable to obtain more recent information.

Education in the Bahamas is under the jurisdiction of the Ministry of Education, which has responsibility for all educational institutions in the Commonwealth of the Bahamas. There are 230 schools throughout the islands, of which 190 are maintained by Government and 40 are independent.

Education is compulsory from age five to fifteen.

Free education is available in Ministry schools, while the independent schools, which provide education at primary and secondary levels, are fee paying.

The medium of instruction is English.

The academic school year consists of three terms commencing in September. The College of the Bahamas has a two-semester academic year also commencing in September.

EVALUATION IN BRITAIN

School

Bahamas Junior Certificate – generally considered to be below GCSE standard.

General Certificate of Education O and **A levels** – generally equated to GCSE and GCE A level examinations taken in Britain.

Further

Associate degree (from the College of the Bahamas) – may be considered to satisfy the general entrance requirements of British higher education institutions.

Higher

Bachelor degree (from the University of the West Indies) – generally considered comparable to British Bachelor degree standard.

SCHOOL EDUCATION

Primary

This covers six years from age five to eleven.

Secondary

This normally covers five years and is divided into a three-year junior high school course and a two-year senior high school course. At the end of junior high school or in the first year of senior high school, pupils take the **Bahamas Junior Certificate**, which is an academic examination with individual subjects. At the end of senior high school pupils take University of London **GCE O level** examinations.

One school offers a further two-year course in science subjects leading to University of London **GCE A level** examinations.

(For further information on GCE examinations see Appendix 2.)

FURTHER EDUCATION

The College of the Bahamas, established in 1974 as a community college, provides a two- or three-year programme leading to an **Associate degree** in any of six academic divisions: natural science, social science, education, humanities, business and administrative studies, and technology. Several college programmes are offered in conjunction with the University of the West Indies. Two-year courses leading to GCE A level examinations are also available.

The Bahamas Hotel Training College offers a range of subjects up to middle-management level. The College has an 'articulation' agreement with Florida International University, an accredited institution in the USA. Courses offered are only to diploma level.

Several private schools of continuing education offer daytime and evening secretarial and academic courses, and the government-operated Princess Margaret Hospital offers a nursing course through the School of Nursing.

The Industrial Training Centre provides basic trade skills.

HIGHER EDUCATION

The Bahamas is affiliated to the University of the West Indies which is a regional institution with campuses in Jamaica, Trinidad and Barbados. The University maintains an administrative office and a full-time representative in Nassau, through whom Bahamian students may seek admission to any campus.

There are two levels of admission to first degree courses. Students with the **Caribbean Examinations Council Secondary Education Certificate** (CSEC) or **GCSE** equivalents take a preliminary year's study. Direct entry to degree courses is based on **GCE A level** or equivalents.

Bachelor degree courses normally take three years.

Higher degrees and certificate and diploma courses are available.

Based in Nassau, the <u>University of the West Indies Centre for Hotel and Tourism Management</u> (a department within the Faculty of Social Sciences) offers the final two years of the **BSc Hotel Management** and the **BSc Tourism Management** to both full- and part-time students. Additionally, in collaboration with the <u>College of the Bahamas</u>, it offers the Part II **BSc Management Studies** to part-time students. The Centre also offers postgraduate diplomas in both hotel and tourism management.

(For further information see Appendix 10.)

TEACHER EDUCATION

The <u>University of the West Indies</u> **BEd** course is offered in Nassau in collaboration with the Education Division of the <u>College of the Bahamas</u>, which provides one- and two-year courses of basic training for non-graduates, and in-service training.

The <u>College of the Bahamas</u> also trains technical teachers.

Bahrain

School education is centrally administered by the Ministry of Education with central control of the curriculum.

There are many private schools in which much of the teaching is in English.

State schooling is based on a 6–3–3 pattern, beginning at the age of six. Basic education to the age of fifteen is compulsory and this may be extended.

The medium of instruction in schools is Arabic; English is introduced in the fourth year of primary education as the main foreign language and is compulsory to the end of secondary education. Many, but not all, of the further and higher education courses are taught in English.

The academic year runs from October to June and is split into two semesters.

EVALUATION IN BRITAIN

School

Tawjahiya (Secondary School Leaving Certificate) – generally considered comparable to GCSE standard (grades A, B and C) on a subject-for-subject basis, with the exception of English language, when a minimum overall mark of 60 per cent has been obtained. Students with very good results may be considered for admission to access/bridging courses.

Further

Diploma (two year) and **Associate degree** – generally considered comparable to BTEC National Diploma standard / N/SVQ level 3 / Advanced GNVQ/GSVQ; may be considered to satisfy the general entrance requirements of British higher education institutions.

Higher

Bachelor degree – generally considered comparable to a standard between GCE Advanced and British Bachelor degree; may be given advanced standing by British higher education institutions. Exceptionally, students with very high grades may be considered for admission to postgraduate study.

MARKING SYSTEMS

School

Tawjahiya (Secondary School Leaving Certificate):

In general secondary and commercial secondary schools: marking varies per subject; maximum and minimum grades per subject are shown on the certificate.

In technical secondary schools: credit system.

There are plans to introduce the credit system to all schools.

Higher

Grade-point average:

4	excellent	A
3	good	B, B+
2	satisfactory	C, C+
1	minimum pass	D, D+
0	fail	F

SCHOOL EDUCATION

Pre-primary

There are a few private kindergartens.

Primary

This covers six years from age six.

The curriculum covers Arabic, English (introduced in the fourth year), mathematics, geography, history, drawing, music, physical education and religion. On conclusion of this cycle pupils proceed to intermediate education.

Intermediate

This covers three years. The syllabus – a mixture of practical and academic subjects – includes English, Arabic and mathematics (geometry, algebra, arithmetic) throughout. Pupils take the examinations for the **Intermediate School Certificate** and, dependent upon the results of this, may proceed to some form of secondary education.

Secondary

This covers three years. Pupils may attend general, technical or commercial schools but there is no provision to switch during the course from one to another.

General secondary

All pupils take religious instruction, Arabic, English, physical education and vocational education. In addition, they may specialize in either literary studies or science. Those in the literary stream also take history, geography, society and philosophy. Those specializing in science take arithmetic, physics, chemistry and natural history. Some science subjects are taught in English. In addition, the following small specialized sections have been introduced in general secondary schools: agriculture, health sciences, hotel and catering, printing and textiles. Those specializations all culminate in the examinations for the **Tawjahiya (Secondary School Leaving Certificate).**

Technical secondary

The three-year course leading to the **Tawjahiya (Technical School Leaving Certificate)** covers the compulsory subjects (as in the general schools) and workshop practice, technology, mathematics, chemistry, physics and engineering drawing. Pupils may also take courses leading to the qualifications of the City and Guilds of London Institute.

Commercial secondary

The three-year course leading to the **Tawjahiya (Commercial School Leaving Certificate)** covers the compulsory subjects (as in the general schools) and bookkeeping and accountancy, pure and financial mathematics, economics, practical secretarial work in English and Arabic, and English and Arabic typing.

FURTHER EDUCATION

Bahrain University (see below) offers a variety of courses taught in English. An average of 60 per cent in the **Tawjahiya** is required for entry to the programmes. Most students take an orientation year covering English and other subjects before entering a two-year full-time diploma course. Diplomas are available in accounting, business, computing, various engineering disciplines, and secretarial studies. A proportion of those successful in the diploma are allowed to study for a further two years to complete a degree course. Progression depends on the credits and GPA achieved.

The College of Health Sciences, established by the Ministry of Health in 1976, trains nurses and other allied health technicians. The entrance requirement is a pass in the **Tawjahiya** science stream. The technician level **Associate degrees** in public health, pharmacy, radiography, medical laboratory sciences, nursing, etc. take five semesters to complete. Students with the **AD in Nursing** can either study for a further one year to obtain a **Diploma in Midwifery, Psychiatric Nursing** or **Community Health**; or a further two years to obtain the **Bachelor of Nursing**. Courses are taught in English.

The Hotel and Catering Training Centre offers **Tawjahiya** holders a two-year **Diploma in Hotel Operations**. Courses leading to the qualifications of the City and Guilds of London Institute are also offered by the Centre.

The Ministry of Labour and Social Affairs runs sandwich programmes at the Vocational and Training Centre for technical secondary school leavers who have 60 per cent plus in the **Tawjahiya**. The five craft programmes follow the City and Guilds syllabus.

HIGHER EDUCATION

In May 1986, a legislative decree announced the establishment of Bahrain University, as a result of a merger of the existing University College of Arts, Science and Education and the Gulf Polytechnic.

The entrance requirement to undergraduate courses is a pass of at least 60 per cent in the **Tawjahiya**. Most students take the two-semester orientation programme which prepares students in study skills, English, mathematics and individual subjects before starting their degree course.

Bachelor degree courses are offered in Arabic, biology, chemistry, education, English, mathematics, physics, accounting, business and management, computing, engineering and office management. The normal length of course is four years. Students obtain an **Associate degree** on successful completion of the first two years.

The University also offers an **MEd in Science Education**, a **Postgraduate Diploma in Education**, **Master of Science in Civil Engineering**, **Master in Electrical Engineering**, **Master of Science in Mathematics** and a three-year part-time **MBA**.

There is an active continuing education programme of part-time courses.

The Arabian Gulf University, a regional university, was established in 1980 by the Gulf Co-operation Council countries and Iraq. The first department to accept students (in 1982) was the College of Medical Science which offers a two-year pre-medical course followed by a two-year pre-clinical stage leading to the award of a **BSc in Medical Studies**. Then follows a three-year clinical stage leading to the award of the **MD** certificate. The average **Tawjahiya** entrance for the College of Medical Science is over 95 per cent. It is expected that the University will develop almost exclusively postgraduate studies and research for the next ten years. Priority is given to three subject areas: desert sciences, bio-engineering and special education.

TEACHER EDUCATION

The Faculty of Education at Bahrain University offers qualifications in education including **BEd, MEd in Science Education** and a **Postgraduate Diploma in Education**. The College also undertakes in-service re-training of subject teachers at the intermediate and lower secondary levels. Graduates may be appointed to primary and intermediate schools, as well as to secondary schools.

Many teachers hold degrees obtained abroad.

Bangladesh

Bangladesh (former East Pakistan) seceded from Pakistan in 1971.

Until 1993 there was no compulsory education, but, since 1973, the government has increasingly been putting emphasis on the universalization of primary education. Recently it has been made compulsory for all children of 6 to 10 years old by an Act of *Jatiyo Sangshad* (Parliament).

The nation inherited a traditional system of education known as the *Madrasah* system mostly for Muslims. Similar facilities are also available through Pali and Sanskrit colleges for Buddhists and Hindus respectively, which are commonly known as the *Tol* and *Sanskrit* systems.

'Bangla' is the medium of instructions at all levels of education but English is compulsory up to higher secondary level and on Bachelor of Arts courses. English is widely used at the higher education level.

The academic year varies according to the level of education: for primary and secondary levels it begins in January and ends in December. In educational institutions for study beyond class 10, courses begin in July and end in June. Most university courses are out of phase with the official academic year; some, for example, begin in October/November rather that in July. Internal political disturbances have delayed courses, with examination dates being deferred several times. Degrees have been referred to by the notional date of completion rather than by the year in which they were finally awarded. The situation is however improving; some departments are now conducting their examinations on time.

EVALUATION IN BRITAIN

School

Secondary School Certificate (SSC) – generally considered to be below GCSE standard (grades A, B and C).

Higher Secondary Certificate (HSC)/**Intermediate Certificate** – generally considered comparable to GCSE standard (grades A, B and C) on a subject-for-subject basis, with the exception of English language.

Polytechnic diplomas – generally considered to be slightly above GCSE standard (grades A, B and C).

Higher

Bachelor of Arts, Science and Commerce (Pass) – generally considered to approach GCE Advanced.

Bachelor of Arts, Science and Commerce (Honours) – generally considered to satisfy the general entrance requirements of British higher education institutions.

Bachelor of Science (Engineering) – generally considered comparable to British Bachelor (Ordinary) degree standard. Exceptionally, students with very high grades may be considered for admission to postgraduate study.

Master of Arts, Science and Commerce – generally considered comparable to British Bachelor (Ordinary) degree standard. Exceptionally, students with very high grades may be considered for admission to postgraduate study.

Master of Engineering and Master of Science (Engineering) – generally considered comparable to British Bachelor (Honours) degree standard.

MARKING SYSTEMS

School

Secondary School Certificate and **Higher Secondary Certificate/ Intermediate Certificate** are group examinations graded as follows:

60–100 per cent	1st division pass
45–59	2nd division pass
33–44	3rd division pass
0–32	fail

The minimum pass-mark is 33. Students securing a 75 per cent aggregate mark are awarded 'Star'. 'Letter' is awarded to a candidate securing a minimum of 80 per cent in each subject.

Further

Polytechnic Diplomas are group examinations graded as follows:

60–100 per cent	1st division
45–59	2nd division

A student obtaining 80 per cent and above is awarded 'Distinction'.

Higher

Grades for degrees at university are usually decided by examination. The grading system used is as follows:

60–100 per cent	1st class/division
45–59	2nd class/division
33–44	3rd class/division

Pass degrees are classified by division and Honours degrees by class.

Honours candidates whose achievement is insufficient for Honours may be awarded a Pass degree.

Engineering

Students obtaining an aggregate of 75 per cent and above are awarded an Honours degree.

60 per cent and above	1st class
50 per cent and above	upper 2nd class
40 per cent and above	2nd class

Agriculture

A course system or semester system is followed.

60 per cent and above	1st class
45 per cent and above	2nd class

Medical

For obtaining an **MBBS degree** the minimum qualifying mark in each of papers is 50 per cent. Honours is awarded in a particular subject where 80 per cent has been obtained.

SCHOOL EDUCATION

Pre-primary

Government recognition for pre-primary education is absent even though many primary schools offer such facilities. Kindergarten, tutorial and pre-cadet schools are located in urban areas which have pre-primary classes; for example standard one, two and three, preceding formal primary classes.

Primary

Primary education is free and comprises a five year course. This begins at the age of six and generally children between six and ten years are enrolled in primary education. The primary school curriculum for classes one and two consists of Bangla, arithmetic and environmental science, from class three onward the students have to take physical education, arts & crafts, music and religion.

English is taught as a second language from class three. A countrywide scholarship examination known as the **Primary Scholarship Examination** is held every year.

Secondary

Secondary education may be divided into three cycles: Junior Secondary (3 years), Secondary (2 years) and Higher Secondary (2 years) (i.e. 3, 2, 2). The majority of students attend only the first two cycles. The last cycle is for those continuing their education.

Junior Secondary

Each institute conducts its own entrance examination for this cycle. Annual examinations are held at the end of the calendar year. A countrywide scholarship examination known as the **Junior Scholarship** examination is also held every year. The curricular structure is uniform and consists of Bangla, English, mathematics, general science, social and religious studies. This cycle comprises three grades: 6, 7 and

8. Most junior secondary classes are simply the lower end of high schools, which normally extend to class 10. Pupils proceed to the secondary cycle by passing the school's internal examination, although some pupils leave school at this time.

Secondary

Grades 9 and 10 are considered the secondary stage. Diversification of courses and curricula are introduced at class 9, where students are separated into two streams of courses: science and humanities. On completion of class 10, students take the **Secondary School Certificate** (SSC) examination, which is the first public examination. The examination is conducted every year by one of the four Boards of Intermediate and Secondary Education (BISE) located at the headquarters of the four administrative divisions. All secondary schools require affiliation to the Board within the region for academic and examination purposes.

Higher Secondary

At the higher secondary stage the academic programme for general education is of two years duration (class 11 & 12). Students who pass SSC examination may apply for this higher secondary/intermediate course. These courses are mainly offered by intermediate colleges, although some high schools extend as far as class 12, and some degree colleges also offer higher secondary education. On completion of class 12 students take a second public examination known as **Higher Secondary Certificate** (HSC) examination. All the higher secondary institutions are under the control of BISE, which grant affiliation to these institutions, without which students cannot be admitted for HSC examinations.

A limited number of Caden Colleges offer a curriculum for classes 7 to 12 similar to that taken for the SSC and HSC examinations, but with many subjects taught in the English medium.

Madrasah schools traditionally concentrate on Islamic instruction, preparing students for religious duties. In recent years the final examinations at these schools is considered to compare to the **Secondary School Certificate** (SSC). Students who achieve satisfactory results can apply for admission to class 11 in a general college.

After eight years of schooling (five years of primary and three years of junior secondary) courses in technical and vocational education are offered in vocational and trade schools which are terminal. Entry into the three-year polytechnic diploma course is available at the polytechnic institutes after SSC.

Second level *Madrasah* education is imparted at *Dakhil* and *Alim Madrasahs*. Similarly Sanskrit and Pali education is imparted at the '*Tol*' after ten years of schooling (i.e. SSC).

FURTHER EDUCATION

Technical and Vocational

Technical education in Bangladesh is organized in three phases: certificate, diploma and degree. The certificate courses prepare skilled workers in different vocations spread over 1–2 years after eight years of schooling (class 8) and diploma courses run at Polytechnic Institutes prepare Diploma Engineers. The **Diploma** course is of three years duration and courses are offered in various branches of engineering and technology. The admission requirement is a minimum of SSC. Three-year diplomas are also offered by monotechnics which specialize in leather and textile technologies. The Islamic Centre for Technical and Vocational Training and Research (ICTVTR) offers technical training courses to students from other Islamic countries.

The Ministry of Agriculture operates eleven Agricultural Training Institutes (ATIs) where a three year diploma course in agriculture is offered after SSC.

Professional Education

There are many professional institutes which offer professional certificates, diplomas and degrees: the Bangladesh Institute of Engineers; Marine Academy; Institute of Cost and Management Accounts; Institute of Chartered Accounts; Institute of Bankers; Institute of Personnel Management; Bangladesh Management Development Centre; Library Association of Bangladesh and similar associations offer professional certificates, diplomas and fellowships etc., after HSC or graduation followed by professional training and internships. The objectives of all these courses are to develop manpower at different levels on a work-oriented and need-related basis with special reference to industry.

HIGHER EDUCATION

Entry to first degree courses (**Pass/Honours Bachelor's degree**) is based on the **Higher Secondary Certificate** (HSC).

In arts, science and commerce, **Pass degrees** are obtained after two years study and **Honours degrees** after three years. Holders of **Pass degrees** may proceed to a two-year **Master's degree** if their marks are good in the first degree, whilst holders of an **Honours degree** may complete a **Master's degree** in one year.

Most students taking Pass degree courses study at colleges (affiliated to National University of Bangladesh) whilst those taking Honours degree courses study at one of the universities. A few colleges offer Pass and Honours degree courses and postgraduate courses.

MPhil (2 years after Master's degree) and **PhD** (minimum 3 years after **Master's degree**) courses in selected subjects are also offered in universities.

Law degree courses are offered in Dhaka, Rajshahi and Chittagong Universities and in thirty-two Law colleges approved by the universities. The duration of the **LLB honours** course is of four years after HSC and the **LLM** is a one or two-year full-time course after a first degree in any subject.

Engineering and Technology

Engineering education at degree level began in Bangladesh with the establishment of Ahsanullah Engineering College, Dhaka, and with the establishment of Bangladesh University of Engineering and Technology (BUET), also in Dhaka, the scope of Higher Education in Engineering and Technology has expanded. These are the only institutions awarding degrees in mechanical, civil, electrical, chemical and metallurgical engineering. Recently four government engineering colleges have been restructured as autonomous degree awarding Institutes of Technology under a council of BIT (Bangladesh Institute of Technology) where four year **Bachelor of Science** courses are offered. In future Post-graduate degree and diploma courses will also be conducted in the BIT.

BUET also offers a five year **Bachelor of Architecture** after HSC followed by a one year **Master of Architecture**.

PhD degrees are also awarded by the BUET after two to three years following completion of an **MSc**. It has very strict entry requirements including a special examination.

Agricultural Education

Diversified courses in agriculture are offered at the Agricultural University and three other Government Agricultural Colleges. The HSC is the minimum entry requirement for admission in the university and the colleges. In the university **Bachelor of Science (Honours)** courses are offered in agriculture, animal husbandry, fisheries, veterinary science, agricultural engineering, agricultural economics followed by one year **Master's degree** course and **PhD** courses of two to three years' duration. Recently, the Government has established a post-gratudate institute for agricultural education called the Institute of Post-graduate Studies in Agriculture (IPSA). There is a *Forest Research Institute* where Honours and Master's courses in Forestry are offered. There is also an Institute under the Chittagong University which offer courses in Marine Science of equivalent level.

Health Education

Five year MBBS (**Bachelor of Medicine** and **Bachelor of Surgery**) courses are offered at the eight Government Medical Colleges in Bangladesh and also at three Private Medical Colleges. Academically they function under the affiliating Universities of Dhaka, Rajshahi and Chittagong. The administrative functions are under the control of the Ministry of Health and Family Welfare. The Bangladesh Medical Council gives Registration Certificates to candidates who have passed the MBBS course and completed one year internship training.

Also available is a four-year BDC (**Bachelor of Dental Surgery**) course after HSC and a Nursing College offers a four year BNSc (**Bachelor of Nursing Science**) course after HSC. Also forty-two Schools of Nursing offer four-year **senior certificate** courses.

Ten other specialized medical institutes (e.g. The Institute of Postgraduate Medicine & Research; National Institute of Ophthalmology; Institute of Public Health and Nutrition) offer different postgraduate courses: Diploma/Master of Science/ MPhil/FCPS/MCPS/MPHE/MS in their area of specialization.

Homeopathic System of Medicine

Formal homeopathic medical education has developed recently. There are thirty-eight Homeopathic Medical Colleges in Bangladesh, among which thirty-two are registered with the Homeopathic Board and the remaining six are awaiting registration. Courses offered in these institutions are:

Diploma: four-year course in Homeopathic Medicine after SSC which is awarded on successful completion of the course and known as DHMS (**Diploma in Homeo Medicine and Surgery**)

Degree: BHMS (**Bachelor of Homeo Medicine and Surgery**) is awarded by the Faculty of Medicine of Dhaka University.

Unani and Ayurvedic System of Medicine

The traditional Unani and Ayurvedic System of medicine are very popular in

Bangladesh. The former system is based on the medical system developed at 'Unan' in Greece. There are as many as thirteen Unani and Ayurvedic institutions in the country.

TEACHER EDUCATION

In Bangladesh there are five types of teacher training:

Primary

Primary school teachers are trained at the Primary Training Institutes (PTI). After one year of training in the PTI a **Certificate of Education** (C-in-ED) is awarded to successful candidates.

Technical and Vocational

A two year vocational training course for teachers in vocational institutes is offered by the Vocational Teachers Training Institute (VTTI).

Physical Education

Two physical education colleges offer a one-year **Junior Diploma in Physical Education Certificate** (post-HSC) and a one-year **Bachelor of Physical Education** (BPEd) after a first degree.

Technical Teachers Training

A one year **Diploma-in-Technical Education** and a two-year **BEd (Technology)** course if offered by the Technical Teachers Training College (TTTC) (validated by the University of Dhaka) for employed teachers of the Polytechnic institutes.

Teacher Training for Secondary School and Madrasah Teachers

There are ten Teachers Training Colleges in the country. They train university graduates by means of a one year BEd course, which is validated by a university. This allows teachers to teach in both schools and *Madrasahs*.

MADRASAH EDUCATION

The present system of *Madrasah* education in Bangladesh was first introduced with the establishment of Calcutta *Madrasah* in 1780. The *Madrasah* was established aiming at extending Islamic education for the Muslims and also producing civil servants especially for handling judicial affairs in Muslim law in the court. The present system of *Madrasah* education is a parallel system with the general education system which offers Islamic instructions to Muslims. The *Madrasah* has the following stages:

Stages	Equivalent level	Duration
Ibtedayee	Primary	5 years
Dakhil	Secondary	5 years
Alim	Higher Secondary	2 years
Fazil	Degree	2 years
Kamil	Master's Degree	2 years

Adult/Non-formal education

The Government of Bangladesh has recently given emphasis to adult and non-formal education with the objective of eradicating illiteracy from society. The Mass Education Programme has therefore been put under the direct supervision of the **Ministry of Education**. The main objectives of the project is to impart functional literacy to the illiterate population in the 11–45 age range.

Barbados

The following chapter regarding the education system in Barbados is based on information obtained from the 3rd edition of this Guide, published in 1991, as NARIC has been unable to obtain more recent information.

The education system is based on the British system.

There is no period of compulsory education.

The medium of instruction is English.

The academic year runs from September to June.

EVALUATION IN BRITAIN

School

Caribbean Examinations Council Secondary Education Certificate – grades 1 and 2 at general proficiency – generally considered comparable to GCSE standard (grades A, B or C) on a subject-for-subject basis.

GCE O and **A levels** – generally equated to GCSE and GCE Advanced examinations taken in Britain.

Higher

Bachelor degree (from the University of the West Indies) – generally considered comparable to British Bachelor degree standard.

MARKING SYSTEM

School

Caribbean Examinations Council Secondary Education Certificate: two schemes are available in the subject examinations; the general proficiency scheme and the basic proficiency scheme.

There is no pass/fail-mark.

Five grades are awarded, defined as follows:

1   comprehensive working knowledge of the syllabus
2   working knowledge of most aspects of the syllabus

3   working knowledge of some aspects of the syllabus
4   limited knowledge of a few aspects of the syllabus
5   insufficient evidence on which to base a judgement.

GCE O and **A level** – see Appendix 2.

Higher

Bachelor (Honours) degrees are awarded with the following classifications:

first class
second class upper division
second class lower division

If the performance has been insufficient for Honours, the degree is awarded as a Pass.

SCHOOL EDUCATION

Primary

This covers six years usually from age five. Towards the end of the sixth year all pupils, at both state and private schools, take the **Secondary Schools Entrance Examination**, which decides admission to secondary education.

Secondary

This covers a possible seven years, the last two being the sixth form.

Students are placed in schools according to the score they obtained in the **Secondary Schools Entrance Examination** and their choice of school.

On completion of five years' secondary education, pupils take the examinations for the **Caribbean Examinations Council Secondary Education Certificate** (CSEC). (For further information see Appendix 5.)

A number of composite schools offer both primary and secondary education with courses culminating in the **Barbados Secondary School Certificate Part I** (there is no Part 2) taken after four or five years of secondary education, which is at a lower level than the CSEC.

On completion of the two-year sixth-form course, pupils take the examinations for the **GCE A levels** of the University of Cambridge Local Examinations Syndicate (UCLES). For further information on **GCE** examinations see Appendix 2.

TECHNICAL SECONDARY/FURTHER EDUCATION

The Samuel Jackman Prescod Polytechnic was established in 1970 following the reorganization and expansion of courses provided by the Barbados Technical Institute which was absorbed into the Polytechnic. The Polytechnic offers a wide range of trade and craft courses leading to local certification and qualifications from the City and Guilds of London Institute and the Royal Society of Arts (RSA).

The Barbados Community College, established in January 1969, is an institution designed to improve the facilities available to the community for training in a wide range of skills at the technical, para-professional, middle-management and pre-university levels.

The College offers courses in the Divisions of Liberal Arts, Fine Arts, Health Sciences, Sciences, Commerce, Hospitality Studies, Technology, General and Continuing Education, The Language Centre, the Departments of Computer Studies and Physical Education. The courses of study are of two years' duration and lead to the **Associate Degree** in Arts or Applied Arts, Sciences or Applied Sciences.

Nursing education includes a three-year programme in basic nursing education leading to the **Registered Nursing Certificate** and shorter specialized courses.

In addition, the College offers a wide range of evening and summer courses as part of its service to the community.

HIGHER EDUCATION

Barbados is affiliated to the University of the West Indies which is a regional institution with campuses in Jamaica, Barbados and Trinidad.

There are two levels of admission to first degree courses. Students with the **Caribbean Examinations Council Secondary Education Certificate** (CSEC) or **GCSE**-level equivalents take a preliminary year's study. Direct entry to degree courses is based on **GCE A level**.

Bachelor degree courses normally take three years.

Higher degrees and certificate and diploma courses are also available. (For further information see Appendix 10.)

TEACHER EDUCATION

Erdiston Teachers College provides a two-year teacher education programme for non-graduate teachers of primary and secondary schools. Graduate secondary teachers are trained at the University of the West Indies.

Republic of Belarus

The Belorussian Soviet Socialist Republic was proclaimed in January 1919. In August 1991, following an unsuccessful coup, the Supreme Soviet adopted a declaration of independence, and the republic was renamed the 'Republic of Belarus' in September. It became a member of the Commonwealth of Independent States in December 1991. The development of education until 1990 reflected central Soviet policy. Since this time, the whole education system has been in the process of continuous reform. However, it remains based on the former Soviet system. In many cases, proposals for reform have been put forward but hampered by poor implementation.

For information on the former Soviet system (before 1990) see the **Russian Federation** chapter.

In theory, Belorussian is the official language, but there is a significant Russian minority. In reality, the 80 per cent Belorussian population often resists education in Belorussian, as this language is not widely spoken. To overcome this, Belorussian has been introduced as the language of instruction in 65 per cent of primary schools, while 30 per cent are Russian/Belorussian and only about five per cent use the Russian language. National minority schools exist where the language of instruction is Lithuanian or Polish, among others. Often Belorussian is introduced officially in Russian-medium schools for some subjects, but there is resistance from teachers and pupils.

The school year runs from September to the end of May for primary schools, September to mid-June for secondary schools, and September to the end of June for tertiary institutions.

The first two stages of secondary education are compulsory, and last until the age of 15.

EVALUATION IN BRITAIN

School

Svidetel'stvo/o Srednem Obrazovanii (Certificate of Secondary Education)

at grade 10 – generally considered to be below GCSE standard.
at grade 11 – generally considered comparable to GCSE standard (grades A, B and C) on a subject-for-subject basis, with the exception of English language.

Higher

Diplom ob Okanchanii Vyssheg(v)o Uchebnog(v)o Zavedeniya (Diploma Specialist) – generally considered comparable to a standard between GCE Advanced and British Bachelor degree; may be considered for advanced standing by British higher education institutions. Candidates with high marks from prestigious institutions may be considered for admission to postgraduate study. Enquirers should contact the National Academic Recognition Information Centre for further information.

MARKING SYSTEM

School and Higher

Marking is on a 1–5 scale

5   excellent
4   good
3   satisfactory
2   unsatisfactory
1   totally unsatisfactory

SCHOOL EDUCATION

Pre-school provision

Almost half of all children receive education at pre-school establishments. There are nurseries for children up to three years, and kindergartens for children up to the age of six. Pre-school establishments are under the supervision of either the National Ministry or Branch Ministries and Departments.

General school education

Primary education starts at age six or seven, and lasts four years.

The second stage is known as basic secondary and also lasts four years.

The third stage completes the pupils' general secondary education on the basis of specialization, and lasts two years. This cycle culminates in the **Svidetel'stvo/ o Srednem Obrazovanii** (Certificate of Secondary Education)

A wide network of gymnasiums and Lyceums (forty-four and fourteen respectively in 1993) provides education for the academically strongest students. These schools have close contacts with higher education institutions, and tend to select the best pupils. Olympiads play an important role in this process; they are run in various subjects and are organized at district and Republic level.

The first two stages (primary and basic secondary) are compulsory. Pupils who complete the second stage can continue their education at the third stage or at vocational school.

In 1992/93, new curricula and teaching methods were worked out for all subjects at school level. A major feature of these reforms is that up to 30 per cent of a student's time can now be devoted to his or her own choice of subjects. Another feature is the increased importance of Belorussian history and culture.

In 1994, the Ministry of Education approved procedures for the accreditation for all forms of educational institution, whether private or public.

Vocational training

There are courses of two or three years' duration for those who have finished grade 9 (second stage), run in 420 different specialities. The courses are a mixture of academic and vocational secondary education. Successful completion of such a course is also regarded as an alternative way of completing secondary education.

Secondary specialized education

Training of specialists is conducted at technical schools, pedagogical schools and colleges.

This is open both to those who have completed the second stage (grade 9) or third stage (grade 11). For the former, courses last three to four years, for the latter, two to three years. These courses lead to the **Diplom o Srednem Spetsialnom Obrazovanii** (Diploma of Specialized Secondary Education).

The need to improve the quality of secondary special education has led to the establishment of two levels of training: one at the secondary level and one with elements which are of higher education level. Graduates from the latter are able to gain higher education qualifications in a shortened period.

Graduates of these colleges may be employed to supervise basic industrial work or assist higher qualified specialists in industry.

HIGHER EDUCATION

Higher education is provided in universities, academies and institutes. In 1994 there were thirty-eight higher education establishments in the Republic, including twelve universities, three academies, eight technical, four pedagogical, four medical, two agricultural and two special institutes, and two institutes of cinema and arts. In recent years some institutes have been granted university status.

Recent reform has led to the Ministry of Education widening the rights of the institutes, turning from central planning to a degree of autonomy. A system of licensing and inspection for private institutes has also been implemented, to ensure national standards of education are maintained.

New models for technical and pedagogical education are being worked out and they should be implemented by 1997. There are also plans to restructure and rationalize institutes' specialities (for example there is currently overprovision in engineering disciplines and underprovision in the humanities). New specialities are also to be introduced, connected to the needs of the new market economy, stimulation of international relations and the needs of national culture. The is also a gradual change towards the establishment of **Bachelor** and **Master's degree** programmes. The **Bachelor degree** will last four or five years, with an additional one or two years leading to a **Master's degree.**

One important aim is to stimulate use of Belorussian in higher education.

First degree

Admission is on the basis of success in a competitive entrance examination and possession of the **Svidetel'stvo/o Srednem Obrazovanii** (Certificate of Secondary Education) or the equivalent from a vocational training or secondary specialist institution. Those who pass and win a contest for admission, are entitled to free education at a public institution. Those who pass but fail the contest may proceed to higher education, but must pay a fee.

The first degree (**Diplom ob Okanchanii Vyssheg(v)o Uchebnog (v)o Zavedeniya**: Diploma Specialist) is generally awarded at the end of a five-year course.

Higher degrees

Full-time postgraduate studies (*Aspirantura*) leading to the qualification of **Kandidat nauk** (candidate of sciences) normally last three years. The **Doktoratura** (doctorate) is more concerned with original research.

TEACHER EDUCATION

Pre-school

Five higher and ten secondary special education establishments train teachers for the pre-schools of the Republic.

General secondary

Approximately 80 per cent of secondary school teachers have received training at higher education level.

Vocational secondary

Staff are trained in industrial-pedagogical schools and higher teacher training establishments.

Postgraduate vocational training

There exists a wide range of establishments which offer upgrading and retraining of specialists. Higher education establishments have special retraining departments, and some commercial organizations offer in-service training for those employed in industry. The latter training lasts between one and six months.

Belgium

Education reflects the old state-religion rivalry and the linguistic differences within the country, stemming from the existence of two main cultural communities, the Dutch-speaking area in the north and the French-speaking area in the south. There is also a small German-speaking area in the east. Brussels, the capital, is geographically in Flanders but largely French-speaking and mainly surrounded by Dutch-speaking communes.

The linguistic differences within the country were legally acknowledged by the Act of 30 July 1963 which established that French should be the medium of instruction in Wallonia, Dutch in Flanders and German in the *Cantons de L'Est*. Brussels is bilingual. Since 1966 there have also been two Ministries of Public Education, one for the French-speaking area, which also covers the German-speaking region and one for the Dutch-speaking area. Since the constitutional reform of 1989 education is no longer organized or subsidized by the state but by each of the three linguistic communities. The state retains control of compulsory schooling and sets the minimum requirements governing the award of diplomas so that certificates obtained at the same level but in different schools have equal validity.

It is possible to open schools which have absolutely no ties with official authorities. However, schools which wish to grant authorized diplomas and receive subsidies must comply with legal and statutory conditions. In practice the organizing powers are: the communities, the provinces, the municipalities (communes) or amalgamations of municipalities, any public or private bodies or persons. Schools opened by the communities, the provinces, the municipalities or any other public body are called *Ecoles Officielles* and all other schools are called *Ecoles Libres*.

Within the prevailing legal or statutory provisions (e.g. duration of studies, minimum number of hours per week, possible obligation to teach certain subjects etc.) every organizing power has the right to determine its own programme, its teaching methods and its organization.

The sector of Roman Catholic Schools (*Enseignement Libre Catholique/Vrij Katholiek Onderwijs*) caters for over 50 per cent of the country's school and non-university higher education population.

Compulsory education was from age six to fourteen. It was first extended to sixteen, then further extended by the Law of 29 June 1983 to eighteen. Pupils must undertake full-time education between ages six and fifteen. This period is extended to sixteen if the pupil has not completed the first two years of secondary education and by a period of part-time education for pupils aged fifteen/sixteen to eighteen.

The academic year runs from September to June in primary and secondary schools and from October to June/July in institutes of higher education and universities.

EVALUATION IN BRITAIN

School

Certificat d'Enseignement Secondaire Inférieur (previously **Diplôme d'Humanités Inférieures**) **Getuigschrift van Lager Secundair Onderwijs**	) generally considered to) be below GCSE) standard)))

Certificat de Fin d'Etudes du Premier Degré du Secondaire or **Certificat de Fin d'Etudes du Deuxième Degré du Secondaire** – generally considered to be below GCSE standard.

Certificat Complémentaire – generally considered to approach GCSE standard. It is not issued in the reformed system.

Since 1993/94 for French speaking community, 1992/93 for the Flemish community:

Getuigschrift van Hoger Secundair Onderwijs/ Certificat d'Enseignement Secondaire Supérieur (from academic stream)	) generally considered to) satisfy the general entrance) requirements of British) higher education institutions

Until 1992/3 (French community) 1991/92 (Flemish community):

Certificat d'Enseignement Secondaire Supérieur (previously **Certificat d'Etudes Moyennes Supérieures**) (previously **Certificat (Diplôme) d'Humanités**) **Getuigschrift van Hoger Secundair Onderwijs** (previously **Getuigschrift van Hoger Middelbaar Onderwijs**) (previously **Humanioragetuigschrift**)	)) generally considered) comparable to a standard) between GCSE and GCE ⌐) Advanced)))))

Until 1992/3 (French community) 1991/92 (Flemish community) (cont.):

Diplôme d'accès à l'enseignment supérieur (previously **Diplôme d'Aptitude à Accéder à l'Enseignement Supérieur**)/
Bekwaamheidsdiploma dat Toegang verleent tot het Hoger Onderwijs
(previously **Maturité/Bekwaamheidsdiploma**) – generally considered to satisfy the general entrance requirements of British higher education institutions.

Higher

Graduat/Graduaat – constitutes a non-university, professionally oriented, 'short-course' degree; generally considered comparable to a standard above that of BTEC Higher National Diploma / N/SVQ level 4.

Candidat/Kandidaat – generally considered comparable to a standard between GCE Advanced and British Bachelor degree; may be given advanced standing by British higher education institutions.

Licencié/Licenciaat/Ingénieur Industriel/Industrieel Ingenieur – generally considered comparable to British Bachelor (Honours) degree standard, although the course lasts longer than the UK.

MARKING SYSTEMS

School

Until 1971:   percentage scale.

Since 1971:   various but most often on a scale of 1 to 10 (maximum); details given on certificates.

Higher

In university-level education the grades at the end of each academic year are as follows:

met voldoening *avec satisfaction*	approximately 60 per cent
met onderscheiding *avec distinction*	approximately 70 per cent
met grote onderscheiding *avec grande distinction*	approximately 80 per cent
met grontste onderscheiding *avec la plus grande distinction*	approximately 90 per cent

The decision to award these grades is taken internally at each university by a Board of Professors. Degrees are graded according to performance in any one year group and do not necessarily reflect the same performance between one year and the next.

SCHOOL EDUCATION

Pre-primary

Widespread facilities are available for children between two-and-a-half and six.

Primary

This covers six years from age six and is divided into three two-year cycles. After completion of the third cycle pupils obtain:

Certificat de Fin d'Etudes Primaires/Certificat d'Etudes de Base Getuigschrift van Lager Onderwijs/Getuigschrift van Basisonderwijs.

Secondary

The reformed system, introduced in 1971, has now been adopted by most schools. The previous system used two three-year cycles, the lower of which was divided into classical and modern branches and the upper into classical, mathematics and physics, natural sciences, human sciences and economics branches.

The six years are now divided into three two-year cycles:

Observation	taken by all students irrespective of their later specialization in general, technical, artistic or vocational fields;
Orientation	guidance;
Détermination	specialization.

Secondary education is organized following two main channels: the 'transition' channel and the 'qualification' channel, in which there are four distinct types of education: general, technical, artistic and vocational.

The 'transition' channel prepares for higher education without eliminating the possibility of entering the world of employment. The 'qualification' channel prepares for work immediately after secondary education without excluding the possibility of continuing studies in further or higher education institutions.

General education is always of the transition type. Technical and artistic education can be either of the transition or of the qualification type, the choice being made from the third year. Vocational education is always qualifying and starts from the second year.

In principle, and within reason, pupils may change from one specialism to another until the fourth year. The last cycle (specialization) must be done in one section.

There are some restrictions in the vocational sector. Until 1985, students in this section could not change, now they can if favourably advised by an Admission Board. A pupil who has already completed two years in a vocational section must start again in the second year of whichever new section is chosen. Students who have completed the full six-year cycle in a vocational section may only change to a technical section by beginning again from the fifth year.

Each year pupils obtain an end-of-year report (*Attestation d'orientation/Orienteringsattest*), based on continuous assessment and on examinations organized either at the end of each term or only in December and in June, for streaming according to abilities. On completion of the third cycle pupils can obtain:

Certificat d'Enseignement Secondaire Supérieur
Getuigschrift van Hoger Secundair Onderwijs

which states which section was followed, i.e. general, technical or artistic. From 1987, students who have completed the third cycle (six years in total) in a vocational section may follow a more general seventh year and gain a similar certificate which gives access to short courses of higher education only. In the French speaking community, there are two types of **Certificat d'Enseignement Secondaire Supérieur**. The first represents an academic education, the second is from *enseignement professionnel* and does not give access to higher education.

Since 1985–6

Examinations for the **Diplôme de Maturité/Bekwaamheidsdiploma** (instituted in 1965) which gave access to university or non-university higher education are no longer organized, except for students who, for whatever reason, did not pursue a normal course of study.

With the extension of compulsory education to the age of eighteen new forms of education had to be created. Fifteen-year olds may now choose to follow full-time secondary education (described above) or part-time education in one of the forms described below.

An apprenticeship with the self-employed, the craft industries, small and medium-sized businesses, organized by the Ministry of Small Firms and Trades (*Ministère des Classes Moyennes/Ministerie van Middenstand*) which comes under the authority of the linguistic community concerned. This normally lasts three years and includes 360 hours a year academic tuition complemented by 28 hours a week of practical work for an employer in the first year, and 256 hours tuition and 32 hours work in the second and third years.

An industrial apprenticeship organized by the Joint Committee in each industrial sector and the National Labour Council within the Ministry of Employment and Labour. These already exist in the diamond industry, inland water transport and the clothing industry. This kind of contract can be signed for six months to two years and is renewable.

Reduced timetable of schooling (fifteen hours a week during forty weeks a year) at one of the ninety (forty-five French-speaking and forty-five Dutch-speaking) centres called *Centres d'Enseignement à Horaire Réduit/Centra voon Deeltijds Onderwijs* attached to secondary education establishments. This is organized by the two Ministries of Education. At the end of their training students receive an attestation showing the dates of their training and their skills.

Work experience training organized by associations recognized by the Ministry for the linguistic community concerned (with minimum 360 hours a year for fifteen-to-sixteen year-olds and minimum 240 hours a year for those aged sixteen to eighteen).

Training organized in evening and weekend classes (*Enseignement de Promotion Sociale/Onderwijs voor Sociale Promotie*).

The types of training described above do not lead to any certificates equivalent to the ones issued by the Ministries of Education but only to attestation giving legal access to some specific trades.

Outside the school system training is given by vocational and pre-vocational guidance and training centres (*Centres d'Orientation et d'Initiation Professionnelle/Centrum voor Orientatie en Beroepsvorming*) for unemployed people under twenty-five whose lack of basic training excludes them from the conventional vocational training system. Courses lasting six weeks are organized to determine the appropriate level of training for each individual.

HIGHER EDUCATION

Since 1993/4 (French community), 1992/3 (Flemish community). The normal entrance qualification for a higher education course are the:

Certificat d'Enseignement Secondaire Supérieur/Getuigschrift van Hoger Secundair Onderwijs
Before these dates, the above qualifications were supplemented by the **Diplôme d'accès à l'enseignment supérieur** (previously **Diplôme d'Aptitude à Accéder à l'Enseignement Supérieur)/**
Bekwaamheidsdiploma dat Toegang verleent tot het Hoger Onderwijs

(previously **Maturité/Bekwaamheidsdiploma**). These were issued by a board of teachers following one year of evaluation of a pupil's work using criteria defined by a Royal decree. Certificates had to be ratified by the *Commission d'Homologation/Homologatie Commissie* to be valid.

There is no system of *numerus clausus* (restrictions on numbers) except in applied sciences where prospective students have to take a rigorous entrance examination in mathematics.

University education is organized in three cycles.

The first cycle of university study leads to the intermediate qualification of **Candidat/Kandidaat** after two to three years of generalized study.

The second stage is a further two to three years of specialist study, including the preparation of a thesis, and leads to the qualification of **Licencié/Licenciaat**. In certain subjects – engineering, medicine and medical sciences – the final qualification is the professional qualification (e.g. engineer) and the course may be a little longer.

The **Candidat/Kandidaat** in natural and medical sciences is obtained after three years, and the qualification of **Doctor of Medicine or Surgery** after a further four years, including several periods of probation in a clinic and one year as resident in a hospital. With this qualification, doctors enter the medical register in Belgium and may set up in general practice.

The **Candidat/Kandidaat** in veterinary medicine is obtained after two years' study and the qualification of **Doctor** after a further three years.

In law, the **Candidat/Kandidaat** is obtained in two years, and the **Licencié/ Licenciaat** in three years.

The third cycle of university study may take two forms:

post-academic or advanced academic training courses linked up to the basic academic courses. There are additional courses, leading to the qualification of **Diplôme de Maîtrise/Gediplomeerde van de Aanvullende Studies**, and specialized courses, leading to the qualification of **Licence Spéciale/Gediplomeerde van de Specialisatie Studies**.

advanced academic education leading to a **Doctorate (Doctorat/Doctoraat)**. The **Doctorate** may not be obtained until at least one year after the award of the **Licence** and consists of the presentation of an original thesis, defended in public. There is no upper limit as to duration.

There are two categories of degree: state/legal degrees and academic degrees. State degrees are a prerequisite for practising certain professions or holding certain posts in professions, e.g. law (the Bar), teaching (to become a principal). Courses for which the entrance requirements and syllabuses are fixed by law lead to a state degree. For courses which lead to academic degrees the admission requirements and syllabuses are determined by the university (if private) or by the government (if a state university).

The difference between 'legal' degrees and the so-called 'scientific' or 'university' degrees has been abolished in the Flemish Community in June 1991: only academic degrees remain. As at 8 April 1994, this distinction remains in the French speaking community. However, the government has proposed a decree putting an end to this dual degree structure. This decree has not yet been adopted.

The diplomas of all the universities, whether public or private and irrespective of their denomination, have the same value.

Non-university education

Non-university higher education is offered by colleges of technology, economics, agriculture, para-medical studies, social studies, art, and teacher training.

There were three types of non-university education, leading to the qualifications of : **Ingénieur Commercial, Ingénieur Technicien,** or **Graduat**. These have now been replaced by a two-tier system of short and long courses. The admission requirements for long courses are the same as for universities. For short courses, the higher secondary school leaving certificate is sufficient.

Short courses of at least three years at non-university level lead to a **Graduat/Graduaat** (certificates issued on completion of this course do not state **Graduat/Graduaat**). Long courses of at least four years at university level lead (according to discipline) to the following qualifications:

Ingénieur Industriel/Industrieel Ingenieur
Licencié-traducteur/interprète/Licentiaat-vertaler/tolk
Licencié en Sciences Commerciales/Licentiaat
Licencié en Sciences Administratives/Licentiaat
Bestuurswetenschappen
Ingénieur Commercial/Handelsingenieur
Architecte/Architect

TEACHER EDUCATION

Until 1967

Primary

Students who had completed the first cycle of secondary education undertook a four-year course at a primary teacher training college. The syllabus included all the modern and classical courses normally taken in the second cycle of secondary education and pedagogical training. On completion of the course students obtained a **Certificat d'Humanités** and the title of primary teacher.

1967–74

Pre-primary/nursery

On completion of the first cycle of secondary education pupils undertook a four-year course at a nursery teacher training college. Students could also enter directly into the second year of this course on completion of the first year of the second cycle of secondary education or the first year of a primary teacher training course. The syllabus was the same as that of the second cycle of secondary education for the first two years. On completion of the course, students obtained a **Diplôme de Fin d'Etudes** allowing university admission, but not a **Certificat d'Humanités.**

Primary

The length of the primary teacher training course was increased by one year and divided into two cycles:

First cycle lasting three years, based on the old four-year course, and leading to the **Certificat d'Humanités.**

Second cycle lasting two years, including practical training, and leading to the **Diplôme d'Instituteur Primaire/Diploma van Lager Onderwijzer**.

Since 1974

All types of teacher training (not just for secondary level as before) are now part of the higher education system and courses last two years.

Since 1985

Prospective teachers of pre-primary, primary and lower secondary level attend a three-year course at a teacher training college.

Pre-primary

On completion of the course the teachers obtain the:

**Diplôme d'Institutrice (eur) de maternelle
Diploma van Kleuterleidster.**

Primary

On completion of the course teachers obtain the:

**Diplôme d'Institutrice (eur) Primaire
Diploma van Lager Onderwijzer (van Lagere Onderwijzeres).**

Lower secondary

On completion of the course teachers obtain the qualification of:

Régent with a **Diplôme d'Agrégé de l'Enseignement
Secondaire Inférieur
Diploma van Geagregeerde voor het Lager Secundair Onderwijs.**

Upper secondary

At this level teachers must be university graduates, with an additional teaching qualification. Students may take the examinations for the teaching qualification:

**Agrégation de l'Enseignement Secondaire Supérieur
Agregaat van het Hoger Middelbaar Onderwijs**

at the same time as their degree examinations, or later.

Higher

The qualification of:

**Agrégé de l'Enseignement Supérieur
Geagregeerde voor het Hoger Onderwijs**

cannot be granted until at least two years after the **Doctorate** has been obtained. The candidate must present an original dissertation, plus three theses, defend it in public and give a lecture.

A reform of initial teacher training for basic (nursery and primary) and lower secondary education has been proposed in the French community. The proposed reform aims at strengthening the link between theory and practice and would involve more periods of teaching practice. Training institutes would also be granted greater autonomy, allowing for more co-operation with the universities.

The reform envisages organizing teacher training in half-year modules rather than in academic years. There is also talk of merging the existing *Instituts d'Enseignement Supérieur Pédagogiques* (IESPs) in order to end up with one institution per network (community education, official and private grant-aided education) in each province. Initial teacher training should also include in future analysis of the key aspects of social change.

The College of Europe, although heavily subsidized by the Belgian government and the City of Brugge, is separate from the Belgian education system, being a small postgraduate college with an international student body. It was founded in 1949 for study into European unity and tuition is in French and English. The postgraduate students specialize in economics, law, political science or European society and civilization. The course lasts one year (October to May) and leads to the **Certificat de Hautes Etudes Européennes/Certificate of Advanced European Studies**. On submission of an approved thesis graduates are awarded the **Diplôme d'Etudes Approfondies/Master of European Studies**.

Belize

Before 1960 most of the educational facilities were provided by missionary organizations, mostly from the United States. There are still many schools run by religious organizations and voluntary agencies but with government assistance.

Education is compulsory from age six to fourteen.

The medium of instruction is English.

EVALUATION IN BRITAIN

School

Caribbean Examinations Council Secondary Education Certificate – grades 1 and 2 at general proficiency generally considered comparable to GCSE (grades A, B and C).

GCE O levels – grades 1–6 generally equated to GCSE standard (grades A, B and C) on a subject-for-subject basis.

GCE Advanced – of the same standard as GCE Advanced taken in Britain.

Higher

Bachelor degrees (from the University of the West Indies) – generally considered comparable to British Bachelor degree standard.

MARKING SYSTEMS

School

Caribbean Examinations Council Secondary Education Certificate: two schemes are available in the subject examinations; the general proficiency scheme and the basic proficiency scheme.

There is no pass/fail-mark.

Five grades are awarded, defined as follows:

1   comprehensive working knowledge of the syllabus

2   working knowledge of most aspects of the syllabus

3   working knowledge of some aspects of the syllabus

4   limited knowledge of a few aspects of the syllabus

5   insufficient evidence on which to base a judgement

GCE O level and Advanced – see Appendix 2.

Higher

Bachelor (Honours) degrees are awarded with the following classifications:

first class
second class upper division
second class lower division

If the performance has been insufficient for Honours, the degree is awarded as a Pass.

SCHOOL EDUCATION

Primary

This covers six years, usually from age six but pupils may enter at five. On completion of this cycle, pupils take the **Common Entrance Examination**, which determines entrance to secondary school.

Secondary

This normally covers seven years divided into two cycles, the lower lasting five years and the upper two. On conclusion of the lower cycle, pupils may take the examinations for the **GCE O levels** of the British Boards (Associated Examining Board, London, Oxford, and Cambridge Overseas), or (since 1979) the **Caribbean Examinations Council Secondary Education Certificate**. (For further information see Appendix 4.)

After a further two years, pupils may take **GCE Advanced** examinations of the British Boards.

Some schools offer an accelerated form of the lower cycle, lasting four years instead of five.

Pupils who do not wish to go beyond the period of compulsory school take a post-primary course lasting three years.

Technical and vocational secondary

Various courses are available, mostly leading to qualifications of the City and Guilds of London Institute, the London Chamber of Commerce, and the Royal Society of Arts.

HIGHER EDUCATION

There is an extra-mural unit of the University of the West Indies in Belize. This is not part of the University College Belize.

There are two levels of admission to first degree courses. Students with the **Caribbean Examinations Council Secondary Education Certificate** (CSEC) or GCSE-level equivalents take a preliminary year's study. Direct entry to degree courses is based on **GCE Advanced**.

Bachelor degree courses normally take three years.

Higher degrees and certificate and diploma courses are also available. (For further information see Appendix 10.)

St John's Training College which recently merged with the Government Training College offers courses based on the American pattern, with a two-year post-**GCE O level** course leading to an **Associate of Arts degree**.

University College of Belize offers its own **Bachelor degree** courses in secondary education and business studies, on the authority of the Government of Belize.

TEACHER EDUCATION

Prospective teachers take three-year post-**GCE O level** courses (two years study plus one year practical work) at two training colleges (the Government Training College and St John's Training College).

Benin

The Republic of Benin (known as Dahomey before 1975) became an independent republic within the French Community in 1958; full independence was proclaimed in 1960.

Education is free and compulsory between the ages of six and twelve but in practice in some parts of the country parents prefer their children to work.

The present education system is the fruit of the 1975 Education Act, which specifies in great detail the characteristics of each level of the system, from pre-primary to university level. The basic structures have remained practically unchanged since then.

In October 1990 *les Etats Généraux de l'Education* fixed new priorities: basic training, training for self-employment, training for girls and searching for excellence.

The official medium of instruction is French, but the government intends to implement a de-Westernization policy involving a gradual shift to national languages.

The academic year runs from October to July.

The school curricula are modelled on those of France, but they are gradually being adapted to local needs and traditions.

EVALUATION IN BRITAIN

School

Brevet d'Etudes du Premier Cycle (BEPC) and **Brevet de Technicien** – generally considered to be below GCSE standard.

Baccalauréat/Baccalauréat de Technicien – generally considered comparable to GCSE standard (grades A, B and C) on a subject-for-subject basis, with the exception of English language; these are the only pre-university courses which satisfy matriculation requirements in Benin.

Higher

Diplôme Universitaire d'Etudes Littéraires (DUEL), **Diplôme Universitaire d'Etudes Scientifiques** (DUES), **Diplôme Universitaire d'Etudes Juridiques Générales** (DUEJG), **Diplôme Universitaire d'Etudes Economiques Générales** (DUEEG) – may be considered to satisfy the general entrance requirements of British higher education institutions.

Licence – generally considered comparable to a standard between GCE Advanced and British Bachelor degree; may be given advanced standing in British higher education institutions.

Maîtrise – generally considered comparable to British Bachelor (Ordinary) degree standard but where very high marks have been achieved candidates could be considered for admission to postgraduate study.

Teaching

CAPEM/CAPES – generally considered comparable to British Bachelor (Ordinary) degree standard.

MARKING SYSTEMS

School and Higher

Grades determined for course work and examinations in individual subjects are as follows:

A 14–20
B 12–13
C 10–11
D 9
E 0–8

There are no similar number or letter grades for the **Baccalauréat**. The quality of the examination results is specified in *mentions*, these being as follows:

passable average
assez bien quite good
bien good
très bien very good

A student may have grades below 9 in one or more subjects and still receive the **Baccalauréat** as long as the overall grade average is 10 or higher.

SCHOOL EDUCATION

Primary

Primary education lasts six years and leads to the **Certificat d'Etudes Primaires** (CEP). With this qualification, pupils are eligible to proceed to the first cycle of the secondary school, or, after a competitive examination, to certain institutions like the National School for Auxiliary Nurses in Parakou.

Secondary

Secondary education lasts seven years, divided into two cycles, *Niveau 1* (level one) which lasts four years, *Niveau II* (level two), which lasts three. At the end of the first four-year cycle, students are awarded the **Brevet d'Etudes du Premier Cycle**. The second three-year cycle consists of the *classe de seconde, classe de premiére* and *classe terminale*. At the end of this cycle successful students obtain the **Baccalauréat**. (Students may choose between five combinations of subjects, three of which relate to the arts and two to the sciences.)

Technical secondary

Collèges Polytechniques (technical secondary schools) offer six-year secondary courses leading to the **Baccalauréat de Technicien**; the **Certificat d'Aptitude Professionnelle** (CAP) is taken after three years' study and the **Baccalauréat de Technicien** after a further three years' study.

A comparatively large number of private *Collèges Polytechniques* have sprung up in the last few years, following the lifting of the government ban on private schools.

HIGHER EDUCATION

This is provided in the Université Nationale du Bénin (formerly the Université du Dahomey) founded in 1970.

The university has five faculties: letters, arts and humanities; science and technology; law, economics and politics. There are eleven schools attached to the university which offer professionally-oriented degree courses. They are:

–	University Technical College (Collège Polytechnique Universitaire, CPU)

–	National Institute for the Teaching of Physical and Sports Education (Institut National d'Enseignement d'Education Physique et Sportive, INEEPS)

–	National Institute of Economics (Institut National d'Economie, INE)

–	National School of Administration (Ecole Nationale d'Administration, ENA)

–	Faculty of Agronomical Science (Faculté des Sciences Agronomiques, FSA)

–	Faculty of Health Sciences (Faculté des Sciences de la Santé, FSS)

–	Higher Teacher Training College (Ecole Normale Supérieure, ENS)

–	National School of Social Work (Ecole Nationale des Assistants Sociaux, ENAS)

–	Centre for Foreign Languages (Centre Béninois de Langues Etrangères, CEBELAE)

–	Institute of Mathematics and Physical Sciences (Institut de Mathématiques et de Sciences Physiques, IMSP)

–	Regional Institute of Public Health (Institut Régional de Santé Publique, IRSP)

Entrance to the three 'academic' faculties is based on the **Baccalauréat**; entrance to the faculties of agronomy and health sciences and the above schools is by competitive examination.

The first phase of studies lasting two years leads to the **Diplôme Universitaire d'Etudes Littéraires** (DUEL), the **Diplôme Universitaire d'Etudes Scientifiques** (DUES), the **Diplôme Universitaire d'Etudes Juridiques Générales** (DUEJG), or the **Diplôme Universitaire d'Etudes Economiques Générales** (DUEEG).
The DUEL involves specialized work in one of the following areas: philosophy, modern literature, foreign languages, linguistics or history and/or geography. In the first

year of the DUES there are two main options: pure science (mathematics, chemistry, first year's preparation for teaching); and biological science and geology (chemistry, biology, physics). In the second year increased specialization leads to the DUES in mathematics and physics, physics and chemistry, or chemistry, biology and geology.

Students who have the DUES or DUEL may continue their studies for a further one year to obtain the **Licence** or two years to obtain the **Maîtrise**.

For the **Maîtrise** in the humanities or science, candidates must obtain two **Certificats d'Etudes Supérieures**.

In law and economics, the **Maîtrise** requires two years after the DUEJG/DUEEG.

The **Diplôme d'Ingénieur Agronome** is awarded after six years' successful study of agronomy.

The qualification **Ingénieur de Conception** represents four or five years study post-**Baccalauréat**.

The **Doctorat de 3ème Cycle** represents two or more years' study beyond the **Maîtrise** and involves the writing of a thesis.

The **Doctorat en Médecine** is obtained after seven years of university study.

At the <u>Collège Polytechnique Universitaire</u> students follow a three-year course which leads to the **Diplôme d'Etudes Techniques Supérieures**.

TEACHER EDUCATION

Primary

Primary school teachers and first-cycle secondary teachers are trained at the *Ecole Normales Integrées* of which there are three in Lokossa, Parakou and Natitingou. The entrance requirement is the **Brevet d'Etudes du Premier Cycle** (BEPC) and success in a competitive entrance examination. Successful students are awarded the **Certificat Elementaire d'Aptitude Professionnelle/ Certificat d'Aptitude Pédagogique** (CEAP/CAP) after completing a three-year course.

Secondary

Secondary school teachers are trained at the <u>Ecole Normale Supérieure</u> in Porto Novo.

Students at the <u>Ecole Normale Supérieure</u> (ENS) spend the first two years at university completing the DUEL or DUES. On return to the ENS, depending on the grades obtained in the DUEL/DUES, they train as either first-cycle or second-cycle secondary teachers. Those who train as first-cycle teachers follow a three-year course, gain the **Brevet d'Aptitude au Professorat de l'Enseignement Moyen** (BAPEM) and are known as *Professeurs Adjoints*.

Those who train to be second-cycle teachers also follow a three-year course and obtain a **Certificat d'Aptitude au Professorat de l'Enseignment Secondaire** (CAPES) and are known as *Professeurs Certifiés*.

Bermuda

Bermuda is an internally self-governing colony of Britain.

Education is compulsory for children between the ages of five and sixteen, and free for all secondary school children up to the age of nineteen.

The school year runs from September to July.

EVALUATION IN BRITAIN

School

Bermuda Secondary School Certificate – generally considered comparable to GCSE standard.

Further

Diploma of Arts and Science – may be considered to satisfy the general entrance requirements of British higher education institutions.

MARKING SYSTEM

School

Bermuda Secondary School Certificate:

A	4.0	outstanding
B	3.0	very good
C	2.0	good
D	1.0	satisfactory
E	0.0	unsatisfactory

The grade-point average is the sum of grade points over five years, divided by the number of subjects taken.

SCHOOL EDUCATION

Pre-primary

There are places available for approximately 60 per cent of four-year-olds in the government's twelve pre-schools.

Primary

This lasts for seven years from age five.

Secondary

There are three government, four government-aided and four private secondary schools. All government and government-aided schools follow the same curriculum which lasts for five years and leads to the **Bermuda Secondary School Certificate**.

This programme was introduced in 1974 and the first holders gained the qualification in 1979. Previously, students took the Cambridge and London **GCE O level** examinations. The **Bermuda Secondary School Certificate** is based on continuous assessment and includes multiple-choice tests, essay questions, projects, oral examinations and practical work. Compulsory courses are English, mathematics, Bermudian history, Bermudian geography, civics, science and physical education.

FURTHER EDUCATION

Bermuda College is the only institution offering post-secondary education. It has faculties of arts and science, hotel and business administration, and applied science offering two-year courses leading to the award of a **Diploma of Arts and Science**.

Some students then continue their education in North America entering the third year of four-year institutions.

Some students follow a two-year terminal programme at the College in craft and technological courses which are closely linked to the Bermuda economy.

In addition to approximately 500 full-time students the College has approximately 3,000 part-time students in all faculties including the Faculty of Adult and Continuing Education.

The University of Maryland and Webster University provide courses in the evenings which may lead to undergraduate or graduate degrees. Queen's University of Canada runs summer courses in conjunction with Bermuda College.

TEACHER EDUCATION

There are no teacher training courses. A maximum of eight scholarships are provided annually to enable Bermudians to train abroad for the teaching profession. Other government funding schemes are available to students pursuing higher education including training for the teaching profession.

Bhutan

Bhutan's modern education system is relatively young. The first schools were established in the late 1950s.

The system of education has been based largely on the British pattern via India. Currently, many changes are being planned to improve the system.

Responsibility at the primary level is shared, administration being the responsibility of the *Dzonkhags* (districts) while the curriculum and examinations are national responsibilities. The *Dzonkhag* also has responsibility for teacher placement within the district. All responsibilities for secondary education are at the national level.

Education is free for all but has not been made compulsory yet.

English is the medium of instruction but a pass in Dzongkha (the national language) is compulsory to be promoted to the next higher class.

The school year is from March to December.

EVALUATION IN BRITAIN

School

Indian Certificate of Secondary Education – generally considered to be below GCSE standard.

Indian School Certificate if awarded at Class XI – may be considered to approach GCSE standard; if awarded at Class XII – generally considered comparable to GCSE (grades A, B and C) on a subject-for-subject basis, with the exception of English language. Exceptionally, students with excellent results in the Class XII certificate examinations of the Central Board of Secondary Education (CBSE) and the India Council for School Examinations (ICSE) may be considered for admission to undergraduate courses in the humanities and social sciences.

Higher

Bachelor of Arts	)	(awarded by Delhi University) – generally
Bachelor of Science	)	considered comparable to British
Bachelor of Commerce	)	Bachelor (Ordinary) degree standard. Exceptionally
		students with very high grades may be considered
		for admission to postgraduate study.

MARKING SYSTEMS

School

School examinations are marked on a percentage basis. Subjects in papers may have different minimum and maximum pass-marks.

Higher

60–100 per cent	First Division/Class
50–59	Second Division/Class
40–49	Third Division/Class

SCHOOL EDUCATION

A 1 + 6 + 2 + 2 + 2 pattern of education is followed. It consists of seven years of primary education, four years of secondary education plus two years of higher secondary education.

Primary

Primary education covers a seven-year period. Students enter at age six plus into a pre-primary year. After six further years (Class I to VI) students take the **Primary School Certificate Examination** (PCSE) conducted by the Bhutan Board of Examinations. This examination, which was almost entirely based on external examinations, except in two language papers where there was an oral assessment conducted internally (that contributed towards 10% of the candidate's final marks), will be based on 50% internal assessment from 1994. This is a move towards achieving a more comprehensive and rounded assessment of students.

In an effort to better the education system the New Approach to Primary Education which is child centred was introduced and piloted in some selected schools in 1986. This system now covers the whole country and is being followed from the pre-primary class to Class III. The syllabus for primary education covers English, Dzongkha, mathematics, science, and social studies. Besides these academic subjects, the students are also expected to study and practise agriculture and *Driglam Namzha* (Bhutanese etiquette).

Secondary

Secondary education has two stages, Classes VII and VIII followed by Classes IX and X.

The Junior High Schools house primary classes as well as Class VII and VIII. The High Schools have Classes VII and VIII and Classes IX and X. The Class VII and VIII curriculum covers English, mathematics, Dzongkha, biology, chemistry, physics, geography and history. In southern-belt schools Nepali is also taught. There is a national selective examination at the end of Class VIII (The **Lower Secondary School Examination**) which includes an internal assessment of 20%.

The curriculum for Class IX and X is similar to Class VII and VIII except that it includes two additional subjects i.e. English literature and economics/computer science. The school-leaving certificate is the **Indian Certificate of Secondary Education** (ICSE) taken at the end of Class X. To continue to Class XI English and Dzonghka must be passed.

The two years of higher secondary classes are attached to the college with the exception of one high school which also has Classes XI and XII. At the end of Class XII students take the **Indian School Certificate** examination.

The Education Division intends to have its own examinations for all levels of education. In this respect a joint examination at the Class X level will start from 1996, which should move towards an independent examination by the Bhutan Board of Examinations at the Class X as well as XII levels within the decade.

Technical secondary

There are two technical institutes in Bhutan, the Royal Technical Institute (RTI) at Kharbandi, and the Royal Bhutan Polytechnic (RBP). The RTI is basically a secondary/higher secondary institution which requires a LSSCE certificate for entry. After five years of study, students can obtain a **Certificate** in one of the following subjects: motor mechanics; general mechanics; electrical; building construction. Entry into the RBP is dependent on an ICSE certificate. After three years in this institute, successful candidates are awarded a **Diploma** in civil/electrical/mechanical engineering.

FURTHER EDUCATION

There is a Buddhist Theological School at Tarpoling.

The Simtakha Rigney School offers vernacular subjects up to Class XII.

The Royal Institute of Management runs training courses in accountancy, stenography, management and computer programming.

Various government departments have training schools: Health School, Agricultural Training Institute, Veterinary Training Institute, Forestry Institute. These award certificates and diplomas.

The Zangley Muenselling School for the Blind runs courses up to Class X.

HIGHER EDUCATION

Higher education is offered at Sherubtse College (an affiliated college of Delhi University), Deothang Polytechnic and the National Institute of Education. (NIE has close links with the Institute of Education, University of London.)

Sherubtse College at present offers a **Bachelor of Science (General) degree** course and **Bachelor of Arts (Pass) degree** courses in arts and commerce. The degrees are awarded by Delhi University.

The National Institute of Education offers **Bachelor of Education degree** courses at the pass level in arts and science.

The Royal Polytechnic at Deothang offers three-year **diploma** courses in civil engineering and electrical engineering to candidates who have passed Class X. The Polytechnic also runs two-year **certificate** courses, one in surveying and another in draughtmanship. Girls can apply for the draughtmanship course. Entry to these two courses is preferably at Class X but at present Class VIII is accepted.

In traditional institutions there are academic courses in Dzongkha with qualifications at **BA** and **MA** level. Both are regarded as being of high standard.

TEACHER EDUCATION

Primary

There is a two-year course for primary teachers offered at the two teacher training institutes, the <u>National Institute of Education</u> (NIE) at Samchi or at the <u>Teachers' Training College</u> (TTC) at Paro. This certificate-level course is assessed by course work (50 per cent) and examination (50 per cent). A **Primary Teacher's Certificate** (PTC) is awarded by the Bhutan Board of Examinations.

A **Bachelor of Education (Primary)** course started in 1994. The TTC also runs a Zhungkha teacher's course for Dzongkha teachers.

Secondary

The <u>National Institute of Education</u> offers a three-year **Bachelor of Education** course. Entry is Class XII Certificate (normally **Indian School Certificate**). A **Postgraduate Certificate in Education** is also offered by this institute for candidates with a first degree. These courses are assessed internally with moderation done by the London Institute of Education.

Training for Dzongkha language teachers is given at the <u>Simtokha Rigney School</u>.

Bolivia

The Education Code of 1955 laid down the structure of the education system. Responsibility for education in urban and rural areas was separated under the Ministry of Education and the Ministry of Rural Affairs, respectively, until 1970 when they were combined. The reforms of 1968 were an attempt to standardize education in urban and rural areas.

Under the Constitution of 1961, education was made compulsory for children aged seven to fourteen. Primary education is now also compulsory.

The medium of instruction is Spanish.

The academic year runs from March to December divided into two semesters.

EVALUATION IN BRITAIN

School

Bachillerato – generally considered comparable to GCSE standard (grades A, B and C) on a subject-for-subject basis, with the exception of English language.

Higher

Licenciado/Professional title – generally considered comparable to British Bachelor degree standard if awarded after four or more years of study.

MARKING SYSTEMS

Until 1968

School and Higher

Marking was on the scale 1–7 (maximum), with 3.6 as the minimum pass-mark.

7	*excelente*
6	*muy bueno*
5	*bueno*
4	*regular*
3	*deficiente*
2	*malo*
1	*pesimo*

1969–72

School and Higher

Marking was on the scale 1–5 (maximum), with 2.6 as the minimum pass mark.

Since 1972

School

Marking is on the scale 1–7 (maximum), with 3.6 as the minimum pass mark.

Technical schools and Higher

Marking is on a percentage scale.

SCHOOL EDUCATION

Pre-primary

Some facilities exist for two-year courses for children up to age seven. Day care centres for working mothers are available; nurseries are privately run.

Primary

Until 1968

This covered six years for children from age seven.

Since 1969

This covers eight years for children from age seven, divided into a basic cycle of five years and an intermediate cycle of three years. The curriculum of both cycles includes mathematics, language, natural science and social studies; physical education, religion and moral education for children in urban schools; health education, agriculture and home economics for children in rural schools.

Secondary

Until 1968

This covered six years, divided into a lower cycle of four years and an upper cycle of two years. Pupils could specialize in social science or physical sciences during the upper cycle.

Since 1969

This now covers four years taken in general academic or technical/vocational schools. The academic course consists of one four-year cycle.

On completion of this cycle pupils take the examinations for the **Bachillerato en Humanidades**.

Technical secondary

The first year of the four-year course is common for all pupils and covers the same curriculum as that offered on the general academic course. Pupils may then specialize in industrial, commercial, artistic or agricultural subjects. On successful completion of the course, pupils obtain the qualification of **Tecnico Medio/Perito** (skilled worker). They may also obtain the **Bachillerato en Humanidades** even if they have studied purely science subjects (a **Bachillerato en Ciencias** used to be awarded).

Adults (students over the age of eighteen) may attend accelerated courses to complete the primary and secondary course in six years and obtain the **Bachillerato de Adultos** from the <u>Centro de Estadios</u>.

FURTHER EDUCATION

The qualification of **Tecnico Superior** may be obtained on completion of a course lasting four years (eight semesters) from the <u>Escuela Tecnico Superior</u>.

HIGHER EDUCATION

The entry requirement for a first degree course is the **Bachillerato** plus a pass in the university entrance examination. The course normally lasts four to five years although students may take longer; medicine requires six years plus professional experience. The qualificatioin obtained is the **Licenciado** or **Professional title**. The credit system is used for marking.

The **Maestria** may be obtained two to three years after the **Licenciado**.

Doctorado may be awarded after a period of original research in law and philosophy.

Universities also offer courses of two to four years leading to the **Tecnico Superior** in nursing, physiotherapy, laboratory technician skills, and engineering.

TEACHER EDUCATION

Primary (basic and intermediate)

A three-year course for holders of the **Bachillerato** at *Escuelas Normales Superiores*.

Secondary

A four-year course, plus two years of professional experience, for holders of the **Bachillerato** at *Escuelas Normales Superiores*.

Botswana

Botswana gained independence from Britain in 1966. For some years before and after this its education system was closely connected with those of Lesotho and Swaziland. (collectively known as the BOLESWA countries).

A review of the education system in 1977 led to a great educational expansion with the aim of providing all children with nine years of basic education. More recently the 1993 National Commission on Education recommended a consolidation of the education system. Ten years of basic education will be provided, seven in primary and three in junior secondary.

The medium of instruction in the early years of primary school is Setswana, with a change to English in late primary school and secondary school. The 1994 National Policy on Education recommends that Setswana should eventually only be the medium of instruction in the first year of primary school.

The academic year runs from January to December for schools and colleges, and from August to May for the University. This will shortly be changed so that all educational institutions start the academic year in February/March and end in November/December.

EVALUATION IN BRITAIN

School

Junior Certificate – generally considered to be below GCSE standard.

Cambridge Overseas School Certificate – grades 1–6 are generally equated to GCSE standard (grades A, B and C) on a subject-for-subject basis.

Higher

Successful completion of **Part 1** (i.e. the first two years) of a **Bachelor degree** – considered to satisfy the general entrance requirements of British higher education institutions.

Successful completion of **Part 2** (i.e. a further two years) – generally considered to bring a student to a standard between GCE Advanced and a British Bachelor degree.

MARKING SYSTEMS

School

Cambridge Overseas School Certificate is graded 1 (maximum) to 9 (fail) as follows:

139

1	excellent
2	good
3–6	credit
7–8	pass
9	fail

Higher

Until 1967

A	pass with distinction
B	pass
C	fail

Since 1967

Results for **Part 1** and **Part 2** examination subjects are classified:

A	outstanding	80–100 per cent
B	very good	70–79
C	good	60–69
D	pass	50–59
E	fail but may take a supplementary	
	examination	40–49
F	fail	below 40

The overall results for the examinations are classified:

1st class	A average
2nd class 1st division	B average
2nd class 2nd division	C average
pass	D average
fail	E or F average

SCHOOL EDUCATION

Primary

All state primary education is free. There are private English-medium schools which are fee paying.

Children normally begin school between the ages of six and eight, with seven stipulated as the recommended age by the Ministry of Education. The course used to last eight years, divided into six-year and two-year cycles. It now lasts seven years (standards 1 to 7). This is due to be periodically reviewed; when performance has been adequately improved, a six-year primary course will be implemented. On completion of this phase of education pupils obtain the **Primary Leaving Certificate** (PLC) from the Ministry of Education.

Secondary

This covers five years, divided into two cycles: intermediate (two years, forms I to II) usually completed at a Community Junior Secondary School, and senior secondary (three years, forms III to V). In 1996, this will change to a three-year intermediate cycle and a two-year senior one. Pupils take the locally examined **Junior Certificate** examination on completion of the two-year course. On completion of form V pupils may take the examinations for the **Cambridge Overseas School Certificate**. This is due to be gradually replaced with a localized Cambridge GCSE examination by 1998. Only one private secondary school, Maru-a-Pula, offers **A levels**.

Technical secondary

Expansion of this sector is perceived as of vital importance. A Botswana Technical Authority will be established to co-ordinate the country's skill training and develop a national skills awards scheme. At present there are a variety of technical courses at different levels. The hope is that these will be standardized by the Botswana Technical Authority.

The former Botswana Training Centre, now the Botswana Institute of Administration and Commerce, offers a wide range of post-primary technical and craft courses. It also offers secretarial courses, usually with the **Junior Certificate** as the entrance requirement, and operates a range of in-service courses for higher executive officers, statisticians, prison wardens, etc.

The Home Craft Centre offers a two-year post-primary course in home economics and management, leading to a **Home Craft Certificate**; and a one-year course for qualified teachers to specialize in home craft subjects, leading to a **Home Craft Teachers' Certificate**.

St Joseph College runs commercial courses for pupils who have completed form II.

A number of institutions offer courses leading to the awards, at different levels, of the City and Guilds of London Institute.

FURTHER EDUCATION

Botswana Polytechnic offers Certificate, Diploma and Degree courses in the area of engineering. There are plans for it to be incorporated into the University of Botswana as the Faculty of Engineering.

HIGHER EDUCATION

The University of Basutoland (now Lesotho), Bechuanaland (now Botswana) and Swaziland was founded in 1964 at Roma in Lesotho, to provide facilities for higher education for all three countries. With the independence of Botswana and Lesotho in 1966, it became the University of Botswana, Lesotho and Swaziland. In 1973 a new campus was opened at Gaborone in Botswana with facilities for **Part 1** courses (see below) and in 1974 instruction was also offered for **Part 2** courses in humanities. When Lesotho withdrew from the arrangement in 1975, Botswana and Swaziland continued their co-operation and the University became the University of Botswana and Swaziland with campuses at Gaborone and Kwaluseni (Swaziland). In July 1982, the two constituent colleges of the University of Botswana and Swaziland became independent universities: the University of Botswana and the University of Swaziland.

The University of Botswana offers certificate, diploma, bachelor and master's degrees. **Bachelor degree** courses last four years (four-and-a-half years in law) divided into two

two-year cycles, **Part 1** and **Part 2** (for the LLB there is an additional **Part 3 examination**). The normal entrance requirement is the **Cambridge Overseas School Certificate** in 1st or 2nd division, with a credit in English language. Entry to a **Master's** programme normally requires a **Bachelor degree** (second class, second division) or equivalent.

There are no facilities for studying engineering, architecture, medicine, pharmacy, dentistry or veterinary medicine.

TEACHER EDUCATION

The 1994 Revised Policy on Education recommends that all prospective teachers undergo a three-year teacher training course. Entrance requirements will be the **Cambridge Overseas Leaving Certificate** for all courses.

Primary

Two courses used to exist to train primary school teachers: the **Primary Lower** and **Primary Higher Certificates**. Since 1973 these courses have been condensed into a two-year course to be taken at a teacher training college and leading to a **Primary Teachers' Certificate**. This is offered at Tlokweng College of Education and Lobatse, Serowe and Francistown Teacher Training Colleges.

The entrance requirement for the **Lower** and **Higher Certificates** used to be the **Primary Leaving Certificate**; students must now hold the **Junior Certificate** although some will also hold the **Cambridge Overseas School Certificate**. The teacher training colleges are now affiliated to the university.

Secondary

A two-year **Diploma in Secondary Education** course for students holding the **Cambridge Overseas School Certificate** is offered by Molepolole and Tonota Colleges of Education. Students may also take a one-year **Postgraduate diploma in Education**, a four-year **Bachelor of Education** degree, or a two-year **Diploma in Education** from the University of Botswana. All teacher training colleges are affiliated to the University.

Brazil

The general aims and objectives of national education are expressed in specific statutory laws. The National Education Bases and Guidelines Law (Law No. 4.024/61, later amended by other statutory laws, No 5.540/68, .692/71 and 7.044/82) is the overall tool which regulates the educational system.

However, by constitutional stipulation, this legislation only applies to the educational system as long as it does not conflict with the Constitution. That ambiguity is a consequence of the absence of a new Bases and Guidelines Law and characterizes the transition phase.

Educational Programmes:

The Ministry of Education does not itself set up nation-wide educational programmes, but defines by law or by other legal instrument the guiding principles for the organization of such programmes.

For first-grade education, the federal Educational Council determines which subject shall be compulsory for the national common core, defining their objectives and scope.

The Federal Council in each state lists the disciplines which can be included in the optional part of school curricula, for the area under its jurisdiction.

For higher-education programmes, the Federal Educational Council determines the minimum curriculum for each course, but not the programmes.

Thus, in Brazil, due to the laws in force, educational curricula and programmes are not established by law; on the contrary, they are developed by the different educational systems or even by individual schools.

The official medium of instruction is Portuguese.

EVALUATION IN BRITAIN

School

Certificado de Conclusao de 2 Grau (known before 1971 as the **Certificado de Curso Colegial**); **concurso vestibular** – generally considered comparable to GCSE standard, with the exception of English language.

Higher

Bacharel/Licenciado/Professional title – may be considered comparable to British Bachelor degree standard if awarded after four or more years of study; applicants with high marks may be considered for admission to taught Master's degree courses.

Mestrado – generally considered comparable to British taught Master's degree standard.

Qualifications obtained from prestigious institutions may be considered to be of a higher standard than those obtained elsewhere. For further information enquirers should contact the National Academic Recognition Information Centre.

MARKING SYSTEMS

School

The assessment of student achievement is defined in the school's by-laws and includes learning evaluation – expressed in grades or codes of assessment – and attendance, the minimum requirement being attendance at 75 per cent of classes.

Marking is usually on a scale of 1–10 (maximum), or on a 5 point scale: SS (9–10), MS (7–8), MM (5–6), MI (3–4), II (1–2), SR (0), with 5 as the minimum pass-mark.

Higher

There is a great variety of grading scales (e.g. alphabetical, numerical and percentage), even within the same institution. The system used most commonly is the same as at school level.

SCHOOL EDUCATION

In 1971 reform promoted extensive changes in the structure and designation of primary and secondary education which since then have been called *1 Grau* and *2 Grau* respectively.

The new Constitution (1988) uses new designations to refer to these two levels: *Ensino Fundamental* (when referring to *1 Grau*) and *Ensino Médio* (when referring to 2 Grau). These new designations may be followed by new changes in structure but the new law that will regulate them has not yet been approved.

Some institutions are adopting the designations used in the Construction (*Ensino Fundamental and Médio*) as equivalent to *1* and *2 Graus* but as the new law has not been approved, and the structure of the courses may change, this procedure could cause problems.

Until 1971

Primary (Ensino Primario):

This covered grades 1 to 4, and was compulsory. On completion, children sat the entrance examination for secondary education.

Secondary (Ensino Secundario):

This lasted seven years, divided into the *Primario Ciclo/Curso Ginasial*, covering grades 5 to 8, and the *Segundo Ciclo/Curso Colegial*, covering grades 9 to 11.

It was sometimes possible to stay on for a twelfth year. On completion of the *Curso*

Colegial pupils obtained the **Certificado do Curso Colegial**. During this cycle pupils could specialize in one of three branches:

academic (classical and scientific)

technical (industrial, commercial, agricultural and artistic studies, home economics and nursing)

teaching ('normal' schools provided instruction for prospective elementary teachers).

All pupils who completed this course were eligible to sit the university entrance examination (**Concurso Vestibular/Concurso de Habilitacao**).

Since 1971

Primary *(1 grau)*

This covers grades 1 to 8 (*1a to 8a séries*) and is compulsory for children aged seven to fourteen. The selection examination previously required to proceed from grade 4 to grade 5 has been abolished.

At the end of this phase of education pupils are awarded a **Certificado de Conclusao de 1 Grau** or a **Certificado de Conclusao de Ensino Fundamental** (if the institution has adopted the new designation).

The minimum age to enter elementary school is seven, though it is possible to accept younger children.

The regular school year in Brazil, independent of the calendar year, covers a minimum of 800 hours of effective work, excluding tests and exams. It usually runs from February to December.

The educational system supervises schools for children under seven years of age to make sure they will receive proper education in pre-schools.

Secondary *(2 Grau)*

The requirement for entering secondary schools is to have finished primary schools or supplemental equivalent schooling.

This covers three studying years (*1a to 3a série of 2 Grau*) with the possibility of staying on for a further year. When the number of students is higher than the places available there is a local selection examination for entry to the schools.

Compulsory subjects are: Portuguese language; Brazilian literature; a modern foreign language (normally French or English); history; geography; mathematics; physics; chemistry; biology; art; moral, civil and health education; and physical education.

Second-grade school, takes up 2,200 hours of effective school work, distributed in at least three annual grades.

Until 1982 each school had to provide a form of professional education (*Habilitaçao*), including a period of practical training for technical students, but since then it has become optional.

At the end of this phase of education, pupils are awarded a **Certificado de Conclusao de 2 Grau** (if the institution has adopted the new designation) or a **Diploma de**

Técnico de Nível Médio and may then take the university entrance examination, the **Concurso Vestibular**.

Technical secondary

During the phase of secondary education, pupils may take a course of three or four years, in a variety of technical and vocational fields, leading to the qualifications of **Certificado de Auxiliar Técnico de Nível Médio** (assistant technician) or **Certificado de Técnico de Nível Médio** (technician) respectively. Holders of these qualifications may take the university entrance examination.

Technical Post-Secondary

Further to the **Bacharelado** and **Licenciatura** there is a third option at tertiary level, which is '**Curso Superior de Tecnologia**', which leads to the qualification of **Técnico de Nível Superior**. The courses usually take three years. They were created because of the demand for specialized work and aim basically at the development of practical skills.

HIGHER EDUCATION (3 GRAU)

Access to higher education is on the basis of **secondary school certificate** and the university entrance examination, **Concurso Vestibular**. A high failure rate in this examination, due to the high number of students taking the exam and the limited number of places available, has led to the establishment of one-year courses, *curso pre-vestibular*, which prepare students specifically to take the examination. The schools offering these courses are also called *Cursinhos* and are privately owned and operated.

There is a *numerus clausus* (restricted entry) for each faculty, with medicine, law, computer studies, business & administration and communication being the most prestigious and hence most popular faculties in any institution.

Courses normally vary from three to five years. After the reforms of 1972 all universities introduced a basic cycle of at least one year in either the humanities or science. On completion of a full academic course, students may obtain the **Bacharel**, **Licenciado** or a **Professional title** (e.g. **Engenheiro** – Engineer). In departments where both the **Bacharelado** and **Licenciatura** are offered, the **Bacharelado** is normally taken by those not considering a teaching career. The **Licenciatura** is offered only in fields where a student might wish to undertake secondary or tertiary-level teaching. However, it is possible and quite usual for a student to work for and complete the two degrees simultaneously; the student's academic standard would not be raised by obtaining both qualifications.

Acceptance on postgraduate courses varies from institution to institution and may be based on entrance examination, previous academic record, etc. The first level of study usually takes two years beyond the undergraduate degree and leads to the qualification of **Mestre (Mestrado)**. The qualification of **Doutor (Doutorado)** requires an additional minimum of two years study beyond the **Mestrado**. Under the reforms of 1971 each tertiary-level institution had to adopt the semester credit system, whereby each subject carries a fixed number of credits and is completed in one semester.

The first qualification to be obtained in medicine is the **Doutor em Medicina** after a six-year course, which includes a two-year basic cycle, a three-year course in clinical sciences and one year of practical experience.

New priorities of the Ministry of Education are:

–   increase the number of **Licenciatura** courses in physics, chemistry and mathematics aiming to qualify teachers to teach at secondary level considering the lack of teachers in these areas;

–   increase evening courses and places at federal universities due to the high demand for these;

–   increase the number of courses offered outside the main campuses of federal universities in the North, Centre and Northeast of Brazil. These new campuses are called *campi do interior*.

TEACHER EDUCATION

Until 1971

During the second cycle of secondary education (*Curso Colegial*) pupils could take the teaching specialization.

Until 1971

Teacher Training and Qualification of Educational Specialists

Teacher training encompasses different modes which are implemented partially at second-grade schools and partially at the higher-education level:

–   second-grade school training, through 3-year courses for teachers to work with the first four grades of elementary schools – **Diploma de Professor de Ensino de 1 Grau (1a á 4a séries)**;

–   second-grade school training, through 3 to 4 year courses plus an additional year of studies, to qualify teachers to work in fifth and sixth grades of elementary school, for pre-school education and special education, among other specializations;

–   higher education training, in undergraduate and specialized courses, for first – and second-grade schools, pre-schools, and special education, among others – **Licenciatura**;

–   higher education training, at the graduate level (*lato sensu* – updating specialization, permanent education programs), aiming at qualifying teachers for undergraduate programmes;

–   graduate training, *stricto sensu* (master's degree and doctorate), dedicated to training researchers and professors in the different fields of knowledge covered by undergraduate and graduate programmes.

Besides the courses included in the initial training, there are programmes – usually held during school vacation periods – geared toward the updating and recycling of practising teachers and specialists. Also, teachers who have not obtained the required minimum qualification are also offered the opportunity for professional training in their area of activity.

Higher

The first level is *Auxiliar de Ensino*, for which teachers must hold a **Bacharel/Licenciado/Professional title**. Teachers must remain in this post for at least two years.

The position of *Professor Assistente* requires the degree of **Mestre**, and that of *Professor Adjunto* normally the degree of **Doutor**, although promotion to a higher rank is possible as a result of long service. The rank of professor was known as *Catedrático*, but is now *Professor Titular*.

ADULT EDUCATION

Facilities are available for people who left school before completing their primary or secondary education to return to school to further or complete their education (*Ensino Supletivo*). There are no age limits for entering *Supletivo* courses but students must be eighteen to receive the **1 Grau Diploma** and twenty-one to receive the **2 Grau Certificate**. The diploma or certificate awarded is of equal value to that obtained by students under the normal system. Students may then go on to take the university entrance examinations.

Brunei

Education has only been widely available since 1954. However, it is now available to all children in the state, although it is not yet compulsory and is free only to Brunei citizens attending government institutions. Permanent residents attending government schools are charged a nominal amount. Charges in private schools vary greatly.

There are two media of instruction in government schools, English and Malay. All schools are bilingual and great emphasis is being placed on proficiency in both languages.

For the first three years of primary education the medium of instruction is Malay for all subjects except English language. From year 4 onwards, English is the medium of instruction for some subjects (including science, mathematics and technology) and Malay for others (including history, physical education and Islamic knowledge).

Private schools catering for Brunei citizens follow the same curriculum as government schools. The Chinese language may be taught in these schools as a separate subject. Schools catering solely for children of expatriates are exempt from the official government language policy.

The school year runs from January to December and the university year from August to May, divided into two semesters.

EVALUATION IN BRITAIN

School

Brunei/Cambridge GCE O level – grades 1–6 generally equated to GCSE standard (grades A, B or C).

Brunei/Cambridge GCE A level – generally equated to GCE Advanced standard.

Matriculation – may be considered to satisfy the general entrance requirements of British higher education institutions.

Higher

Higher Bachelor (Honours) degree – generally considered comparable to British Bachelor (Honours) degree standard.

MARKING SYSTEMS

School

Brunei/Cambridge GCE O level) see Appendix 2.
Brunei/Cambridge GCE A level)

Matriculation – see Appendix 2.

Higher

Degrees are classified as follows:

First Class Honours
Second Class Honours (Upper Division)
Second Class Honours (Lower Division)
Third Class Honours
Pass

SCHOOL EDUCATION

Primary

Primary education begins at age six. However, many children start their education at age five, doing one year at the pre-school level.

All pupils sit standardized tests after three years in primary school and take the **Primary Certificate of Education** after a further three years at the nominal age of eleven. Pupils must pass this examination to be allowed to proceed to the next stage of education. Those who are unsuccessful remain at primary school until they pass or leave.

Secondary

After three years of bilingual (English/Malay) study at secondary school, students take the **Brunei Junior Certificate of Education** examination, its format now known as 'assessment examination', the papers being in English or Malay as appropriate. Subjects covered include Malay, English, mathematics, integrated science, history, geography and Islamic studies. For some, this is the school-leaving certificate. For academic pupils, a further two years of bilingual education is required before they take the **Brunei/Cambridge GCE O level examination**. Most also enter privately for University of London GCE examinations. Technical courses lead to City and Guilds of London Institute, RSA or BTEC examinations.

Those who continue their education in the sixth form take the **Brunei/Cambridge GCE A level examination** after a further two years of study.

Matriculation Scheme

The Matriculation Scheme was designed in 1986, in order to speed up the period of transition from a monolingual to the bilingual system of education promulgated in 1985.

For Malay-stream students at the upper secondary and pre-university levels, it aims to facilitate their access to all kinds of tertiary education either at home or abroad.

Qualified students who have completed the **Brunei/Cambridge GCE O level examination** undergo a seven-term Matriculation programme, including two terms of intensive English language. Beginning with the third term, students take three Matriculation subjects which are of the same standard as **GCE A levels** and continue with the study of English language.

The Matriculation course in English language has been established with the intention of accelerating Brunei's bilingual education policy by helping post-**GCE O level** Malay-medium students to gain linguistic equality with their English-medium counterparts in as short a period as possible.

Matriculation students are given a total period of two-and-a-half years before they sit the **Brunei Matriculation Examination** which is held in June. This examination is conducted by Universiti Brunei Darussalam in collaboration with the University of Cambridge Local Examinations Syndicate (UCLES).

The syllabus of the **Brunei Matriculation Examination Certificate** strictly follows the **Singapore/Cambridge GCE A level** (Malay medium) with the inclusion of topics which are directly relevant to Brunei.

The subjects offered at present are as follows:

Matriculation English, economics, geography, Malay language and literature, history, Syariah and Usuluddin.

FURTHER EDUCATION

A number of institutions offer both full and part-time technical and vocational training. These include:

The Institut Teknologi Brunei (ITB), established in 1986, presently is mainly geared to producing **BTEC Higher National Diploma** graduates. The courses are designed, organized and implemented by ITB but are validated by the Business and Technician Education Council (United Kingdom).

Currently, ITB offers two-and-a-half-year, full-time **BTEC Higher National Diploma** programmes in business and finance, computer studies and electrical and electronic engineering as well as a three-and-a-half year part-time **Higher National Certificate** programme in electrical and electronic engineering. ITB also plays a role in retraining and upgrading the skills of personnel in both the private and public sectors. Proposals to develop other courses have been made to meet the needs of the country.

A College of Nursing has been developed with assistance from the Department of Nursing Studies at the University of Wales in Cardiff. This has the same status as an Institute of Nursing in the UK. It provides general nursing training.

At the Sultan Saiful Rijal Technical College in Bandar Seri Begawan and the Jefri Bolkiah College of Engineering in Kuala Belait, courses leading to City and Guilds of London Institute craft-level awards are offered to lower secondary school-leavers. **BTEC National Certificate and National Diploma** technician courses are offered to those with **Brunei/Cambridge GCE O level** qualifications. Both colleges provide courses to upgrade and re-train those in employment.

Sinaut Agricultural Training Centre offers its own technician's award, the **Brunei National Diploma in Agriculture**.

HIGHER EDUCATION

The University Brunei Darussalam (UBD) opened in October 1985, with assistance from University of Wales College of Cardiff and the University of Leeds. There are five faculties: arts and social sciences, education, management and administrative studies, Islamic studies and science. The first degrees were awarded in 1989.

The normal entry requirement is a minimum of two **Brunei/Cambridge GCE A level** passes.

Nine Honours degree programmes are offered, each normally spread over a minimum period of four years and leading to the award of the following **Bachelor degrees**. Where two or more subjects are indicated, one is studied as a major subject and another as a minor.

Malay medium

Bachelor of Arts Education – education with either (i) two subjects from Malay language and linguistics, Malay literature, history, Islamic studies (minor only) or (ii) Islamic studies.

Bachelor of Arts Primary Education

English medium

Bachelor of Arts Education – education with either (i) economics and geography or (ii) English.

Bachelor of Science Education – education with two subjects chosen from biology, chemistry, mathematics and physics.

Bachelor of Arts Primary Education

Bachelor of Arts

(i)   management studies
(ii)   public policy and administration
(iii)   geography and economics

Bachelor of Science – mathematics and computer science.

Bachelor of Engineering – jointly with the University of Glasgow.

Bachelor of Commerce – jointly with the University of Birmingham.

Other courses offered are: **Certificate in Education, Postgraduate Certificate in Education** and **Certificate in Educational Management** and **Master of Public Policy**.

The academic programmes are run on a unit system under which a student has to accumulate a minimum number of credit units for graduation. The minimum number of credit units required is 124 for the **BA** and **BA Primary Education** and 128 for the **BA/BSc Education**.

TEACHER EDUCATION

Training is provided by the Faculty of Education at the University.

A **BA in Primary Education** entitles the holder to teach at primary level.

A **BA in Education** entitles the holder to teach at secondary level.

Bulgaria

Following demonstrations in November 1989, the National Assembly approved constitutional reform and abolished the Communist Party's sole right to govern. There has been legislation to devolve autonomy to higher education institutions. At the time of writing (August 1995), the Bulgarian education system is still undergoing comprehensive reform.

Education is free and compulsory for children aged six to sixteen (grades 1–8). The medium of instruction is Bulgarian, but there are some foreign-language medium secondary schools (English, French, German, Russian, Spanish, Italian).

The school year runs from September to June and consists of two terms.

EVALUATION

School

Diploma za Zavarsheno Sredno Obrazovanie (Diploma of Completed Secondary Education) – may be considered to satisfy the general entrance requirements of British higher education institutions.

Higher

Diploma za Zavarsheno Visshe Obrazovanie (Diploma of Completed Higher Education) – generally considered comparable to British Bachelor (Ordinary) degree standard.

Diploma za Kandidat na Naukite – generally considered comparable to British PhD degree standard.

Diploma za Doktor na Naukite – postdoctoral degree without British counterpart.

MARKING SYSTEM

The grading system (2–6 with a minimum pass-mark of 3) is the same for all levels:

2	*slab*	poor
3	*sreden*	sufficient
4	*dobur*	good
5	*mnogo dobur*	very good
6	*otlichen*	excellent

Bulgaria

SCHOOL EDUCATION

Pre-school

This caters for children aged three to six. It is conducted in specialized, half-day, full-day and weekly kindergartens (*Detski Gradini*). These often operate with nurseries for children aged one to three, though the nurseries are under the jurisdiction of the Ministry of Public Health and Social Welfare. About 90 per cent of all children receive pre-school education.

Primary and secondary education

Primary education is from Grade 1 to 4, while pre-secondary school is from Grade 5 to 8. Education is compulsory up to Grade 8. The curriculum for Grade 1 to 4 includes the following eight compulsory subjects: Bulgarian language, mathematics, basic Bulgarian history and geography, natural science, fine art, music, handicrafts and physical training.

There are 12 compulsory subjects for Grades 5 to 8: Bulgarian language and literature, mathematics, geography, physics, chemistry, biology, fine art, music, handicrafts, physical training and one foreign language. A second foreign language is included after the 7th Grade.

Secondary education can be of three, four or five years' duration. The compulsory subjects now include European literature and history, philosophy and computer programming and technology.

The course of study in secondary schools ends in a compulsory matriculation examination in Bulgarian language, mathematics and two other subjects of the student's choice. Successful completion leads to a **Diploma za Zavarsheno Sredno Obrazovanie** (Diploma of Completed Secondary Education). Those who do not sit for the matriculation examination receive a certificate for the completed course of study, but are not able to apply for higher education.

Almost all students complete primary education and 98 per cent undergo secondary education. The forms of training after the compulsory period of education include regular, extramural and evening courses. Extramural and evening courses are popular mainly for post-secondary and post-higher education, and cater for about 25 per cent of the students.

There are four types of secondary schools and colleges:

Unified secondary polytechnic schools of the general type.

Unified secondary polytechnic schools with provisions for teaching in foreign languages. Students are admitted on the basis of competitive examinations in the Bulgarian language and mathematics after grade 7; the leaving certificate after grade 7 is also taken into account. The first school year is a preparatory one.

Technical colleges provide four-year training courses (after grade 8) in economics, various branches of technology, agriculture, applied arts, music, sports, etc. Admission is competitive. The arts schools admit students of different age groups, depending on their own criteria.

Secondary vocational-technical schools provide three-year training courses in various technical branches, services, etc.

All secondary schools award the **Diploma za Zavarsheno Sredno Obrazovanie** (Diploma of Completed Secondary Education) required for entry to higher education.

Special

There is a network of boarding schools, entirely supported by the state, for children with physical or mental disabilities.

FURTHER EDUCATION

Technical colleges admit secondary school graduates for a two-year course. They usually train medical personnel (human and veterinary), economists and technicians.

HIGHER EDUCATION

There are 34 higher educational institutions in Bulgaria, comprising the following groups:

–   25 universities (15 of them are specialized in technology, economics, medicine, engineering and architecture)
–   5 academies of arts and sport
–   2 institutes of medicine
–   1 institute of food and beverage
–   1 institute of agriculture

29 of the higher institutions are state run and 5 are private.

There are also 47 colleges for teacher training, technology, economics, medicine, librarianship and communication as well as an Institute for Foreign Students where Bulgarian language is studied before university courses and where foreign language courses are organized for Bulgarians.

Entry to higher education institutions is on the basis of competitive examinations and the **Diploma za Zavarsheno Sredno Obrazovanie**. The examinations, vocational trends, number of first-year students and other conditions are determined each year by the Ministry of Education.

The period of training at higher education institutions varies from four-and-a-half to six years, depending on speciality. Over 50 per cent of students receive state scholarships.

Those who complete the **Diploma za Zavarsheno Visshe Obrazovanie** by submitting a final-year dissertation or a thesis (in science/technology), or by passing the necessary state examination (in humanities), can begin a postgraduate course.

A scientific degree known as **Kandidat na Naukite** is awarded to those who successfully defend a dissertation. A still higher degree is that of **Doktor na Naukite**, awarded for notable contributions to science.

Higher education institutions have special departments for postgraduate professional training which include courses in advanced areas of science and technology. These courses are usually full- or part-time but there are extramural courses. Diplomas are awarded for successful completion.

By the end of 1995, a 'New Educational Law' should be approved by the National Assembly. Four stages in higher education would be introduced: specialist (pre-university level), Bachelor, Master and PhD. After the law has been ratified by the National Assembly, structures of the higher institutions, curriculum and programmes will undergo full reform.

TEACHER EDUCATION

Universities and pedagogical institutes provide opportunities for advanced teaching qualifications. The system also includes specialization abroad, scholarships and research work.

Research workers and lecturers at higher education institutions undergo an obligatory course of pedagogical training. Centres for pedagogical studies and for professional qualifications have been set up at these institutions. Sofia University plays a leading role in this respect.

There are specialized research institutes at the Ministry of Education, such as the Research Institute in Higher Education, the Research Institute in Vocational Training and the Research Institute in General Education. Other institutes cover modern methods and educational materials.

MILITARY EDUCATION

Military service is obligatory for young men after the age of eighteen. They can take their competitive entrance examination before their military service which lasts three years in the navy and two years for all other services. The period of training at the higher military educational establishments is recognised as normal military service. These establishments are under the jurisdiction of the Ministry of Defence.

Burkina Faso

This chapter covers the period since independence was gained in 1960. The education system is based on the French pattern.

There is no compulsory education.

The medium of instruction is French.

The academic year runs from October to June.

EVALUATION IN BRITAIN

School

Baccalauréat/Diplôme de Bachelier de l'Enseignement du Second Degré – generally considered comparable to GCSE standard (Grades A, B and C) on a subject-for-subject basis, with the exception of English language.

Higher

Diplôme Universitaire d'Etudes Littéraires (DUEL), **Diplôme Universitaire d'Etudes Scientifiques** (DUES), **Diplôme d'Etudes Universitaires Générales** (DEUG) – may be considered to satisfy the general entrance requirements of British higher education institutions.

Licence – generally considered comparable to a standard between GCE Advanced and British Bachelor degree; may be given advanced standing in British higher education institutions.

Maîtrise – generally considered comparable to British Bachelor (Ordinary) degree standard but where very high marks have been achieved candidates could be considered for admission to postgraduate study.

MARKING SYSTEM

School and Higher

Marking is on a scale of 0-20, with 10 as the minimum pass-mark.

16–20	*très bien*	very good
14–15	*bien*	good
12–13	*assez bien*	quite good
10–11	*passable*	average

SCHOOL EDUCATION

Primary

This covers six years.

Secondary

This covers seven years, divided into a four-year lower cycle followed by a three-year upper cycle. The lower cycle may be taken at a **Collège d'Enseignement Général** or a **Lycée** and culminates in the **Brevet d'Etudes du Premier Cycle**. The upper cycle may be taken only at a **Lycée** and leads to the examinations for the **Baccalauréat/Diplôme de Bachelier de l'Enseignement du Second Degré**. This is available in a variety of series depending on the student's specialization:

A   *philosophie-lettres*, options A1–A5
B   *économique et social*
C   *sciences mathematiques et physiques*
D   *sciences mathematiques et naturales*
E   *mathematiques et technique*

Technical secondary

The **Certificat d'Aptitude Professionnelle** (CAP) is taken in place of the **Brevet d'Etudes du Premier Cycle** (BEPC) in *Collèges d'Enseignement Technique* (i.e. after four years).

On completion of the upper cycle in a technical specialization, pupils take the examinations for the **Baccalauréat de Technician/Diplôme de Bachelier de Technicien** available in three series:

E   mathematics and technical
F1   mechanical construction
F2   electronics
F3   electrical
G1   administration
G2   accounting/management

On completion of one year of the upper cycle in a technical specialization, pupils may take the examination for the **Brevet d'Etudes Professionnelles** (BEP) available in three subjects:

– secretarial
– accounting
– surveying

FURTHER AND HIGHER EDUCATION

There is only one university, the <u>University of Ouagadougou</u>. It was established in 1965 as the <u>Ecole Normale Supérieure</u>, became the <u>Centre d'Enseignement Supérieur</u> in 1969, and obtained its present status in 1974. Tertiary-level education is also provided in five institutes. They are:

– <u>Ecole Inter-états d'Ingénieurs de l'Equipement Rural</u> founded in 1970; jointly financed by thirteen francophone African states as a rural development and education programme.

– <u>Ecole Inter-états de Techniciens Supérieurs de l'Hydraulique et de l'Equipement Rural</u> founded in 1974 following an agreement between thirteen francophone African states.

– <u>Ecole Nationale d'Administration et de Magistrature</u>; founded in 1959 as <u>Ecole Nationale d'Administration</u>, it acquired its present title in 1984.

– <u>Institut National des Sports.</u>

– <u>Institut de la Réforme et de l'action Pédagogique</u>; founded in 1964 as the <u>Centre de Documentation et de Perfectionnement</u>, it became the <u>National Institute of Education</u> in 1976 and acquired its present title in 1983.

The entrance requirement to degree courses is the **Baccalauréat/Diplôme de Bachelier de l'Enseignement du Second Degré**.

Two years' study in the humanities leads to the **Diplôme d'Etudes Universitaires Générales** (DEUG). After a further year in the humanities, students obtain the **Licence** and after a fourth year the **Maîtrise**. A similar pattern is followed in all the university institutes (law, medicine, economics, technology, sciences, mathematics, engineering, film production).

TEACHER EDUCATION

Primary

Teachers are trained at secondary level training colleges.

Secondary

Teachers are trained in the appropriate university department or institute. English teachers are trained in the <u>Département de Langues Vivantes</u> by means of a teacher-training option in the third year.

The <u>Institut des Sciences de l'Education</u> (INSE) offers secondary teacher training courses of two years' duration to holders of the **Baccalauréat** and ex-students of the university who have completed at least one year of their course. INSE is an institute of the university and future secondary teacher training may well be centralized there, together with the training of secondary advisers and inspectors.

Burundi

Since the country's accession to independence in 1962, there have been a number of educational reforms, in particular the reforms of secondary education in 1964 and of primary education in 1970.

Free schooling was introduced when the Republic was proclaimed, in November 1966, although as yet no sector is compulsory.

French is one of the official media of instruction; the others are the indigenous languages.

EVALUATION IN BRITAIN

School

Diplôme des Humanités Complètes – generally considered comparable to GCSE standard (grades A, B and C) on a subject-for-subject basis, with the exception of English language.

Higher

Bachelor degree – generally considered comparable to British Bachelor (Ordinary) degree standard.

MARKING SYSTEMS

School and higher

90–100 per cent	*excellence*
80–89	*la plus grande distinction*
70–79	*grande distinction*
60–69	*distinction*
50–59	*satisfaction*
below 50	*fail*

SCHOOL EDUCATION

Primary

Some primary schools also offer facilities for pre-primary classes (*classes gardiennes*).

Primary education covers six years from age six and is divided into three two-year cycles. There is now officially a seventh year of primary education which is intended as preparation for secondary school. Some schools still offer only the first two cycles.

Kirundi is the medium of instruction, with French as a compulsory subject each year.

Secondary

General secondary education covers six years, divided into two cycles, the lower two years, and the upper four years. In the first year of the upper cycle, pupils choose one of two streams (modern or Latin); there are four divisions in the second and third years (modern, classical, scientific and economic). In the final year of this cycle there are five divisions; modern, classical, science A, science B and economics. Only pupils who specialize in the Latin division in the first year of this cycle may be admitted to the classical division in the second year. Only pupils who specialize in the science division in the third year may take science A or B in the final year. The second cycle leads to the **Diplôme des Humanités Complètes**.

Technical/vocational secondary

Pupils wishing to undertake a technical specialization during secondary education may attend a seven-year course leading to the qualification of **Technician**.

Craft schools offer two-, three- and four-year courses in a variety of fields beyond primary school.

The intermediate social schools provide a four-year general course in the humanities specifically for girls.

HIGHER EDUCATION

The Université du Burundi was established in 1964 as the Université Officielle de Bujumbura and acquired its present title in 1977. The University now comprises seven faculties and three institutes.

The entrance requirement for a course at the University is the **Diplôme des Humanités Complètes**, which must be validated by a commission of the Ministry of National Education and Culture. For courses in civil engineering, mathematics and physics, pupils must also pass a special entrance examination.

The first stage of study lasts two years, is generally based, and leads to the **Candidature**. A further two years leads to the **Licence**.

In medicine, four years of study beyond the **Candidature** lead to the professional title of **Docteur en Médecine**.

In civil and agronomic engineering, courses leading to the professional title of **Ingénieur** last five years. By contrast, the **Diplôme d'Ingénieur Technicien** awarded by the Institut Technique Supérieur only requires three years.

TEACHER EDUCATION

Primary

Teachers are trained on seven-year secondary-level courses. On completion of the full course, pupils obtain a secondary school certificate and the ordinary teachers' diploma.

Secondary

The higher teacher training school (Ecole Normale Supérieure) was established in 1965 and trains teachers for the lower and upper cycles. The entrance level is the secondary school certificate or successful completion of the course at the primary teacher training school.

Cambodia

The national education system broke down during the civil war following the coup in 1970 and was destroyed during the Khmer Rouge years (1975–9). It has been steadily re-established since then, from 1979–91 with support from Vietnam and the Soviet Union, and more recently with support from Western donors.

The 1993 constitution defines the right to quality education at all levels and sets a goal of nine years of compulsory free education throughout the country. The education system is currently being reorganized at all levels and is steadily moving towards meeting this goal.

The medium of instruction is Khmer. The academic year runs from September to June.

EVALUATION IN BRITAIN

Given the history of education in Cambodia since 1970 and the limited quality of the curriculum, teacher training and resources, it would not be appropriate to propose a standard equivalence with British education. Qualifications obtained before 1970 relate approximately to their French equivalents.

MARKING SYSTEM

Marking is on the scale 0–10; the minimum pass-mark is 5.

SCHOOL EDUCATION

Primary

This consists of five years from the age of six, at the end of which an examination leads to a certificate of completion of primary school. (There are also a small number of government-run kindergartens for children aged three to five.)

Secondary

There are three years of lower secondary or 'first cycle' (grades 6–8) and three years of upper secondary or 'second cycle' (grades 9–11). Examinations at the end of each cycle lead to a certificate of completion. All students follow the same curriculum in all six years. (There is no standard terminology for these certificates in English, but they are still referred to as **'diplome'** (end of grade 8) and **'bac'** (end of grade 11) by French speakers.)

TECHNICAL AND VOCATIONAL EDUCATION

A number of government-run centres offer courses in agriculture, health and industrial training, usually at post-lower secondary level, but there is no standardization of length, curriculum or certification. The principal centres for longer courses (1–3 years) are Prek Leap Agricultural College, Russey Keo Technical College, Tuk Thla Vocational Training Centre and the Central Health School (Phnom Penh).

FURTHER EDUCATION

The government's 'complementary education' system (providing school-equivalent education to adults) is now being drawn to a close. There is no other standardized adult education system, although courses are offered in many places by Non-Governmental Organizations and private enterprise.

HIGHER EDUCATION

There are seven institutions covering:

      arts, sciences, foreign languages and teacher training (University of Phnom Penh)
      technology (Institute of Technology)
      economics and law (Faculty of Economic Sciences and Law)
      business (Faculty of Business)
      medicine (Faculty of Medicine, Dentistry & Pharmacology)
      agriculture (Royal University of Agriculture, Chamcar Daung)
      fine arts (University of Fine Arts)

Most courses are now four years, leading to a degree ('**licence**'). Since 1992 there has been an additional pre-university 'preparatory year' which all higher education students must complete. There are no postgraduate courses.

TEACHER EDUCATION

Training for upper secondary teachers takes place at the University of Phnom Penh: it lasts five years (including the preparatory year) and leads to a **post-upper secondary leaving certificate**.

Training for lower secondary teachers takes place at six regional teacher training centres: a two-year **post-upper secondary leaving certificate** ('11+2') model has recently replaced the three-year **post-lower secondary leaving certificate** ('8+3') model.

Training of primary teachers takes place at 18 provincial teacher training centres: a two-year **post-upper secondary leaving certificate** ('11+2') model is in the process of replacing a two-year **post-lower secondary leaving certificate** ('8+2') model.

Cameroon

Cameroon was a German colony from 1884 to 1916. France administered the former East Cameroon from 1916 to 1959. It became independent in January 1960 as the Republic of Cameroon and was joined in October by the former British-administered territory of the Southern Cameroon, after which it was known as the United Republic of Cameroon until 1984 when 'United' was dropped.

Two different education systems operate in Cameroon, one in the former British south-west and north-west provinces and the other in the eight former French provinces. The former British provinces follow broadly the British model of education, while the former French provinces follow that of France.

Education is compulsory from age six to eleven.

The medium of instruction is English in the two anglophone provinces and French elsewhere.

The academic year runs from September to June in the east and from October to June in the west.

EVALUATION IN BRITAIN

School

Anglophone

Cameroon GCE O and **A level** examinations – generally considered comparable to British GCSE (grades A, B and C) and GCE Advanced standards.

Francophone

Probatoire – generally considered comparable to GCSE standard (grades A, B and C) on a subject-for-subject basis.

Baccalauréat – generally considered to be above GCSE standard. May be considered for admission to access/bridging courses.

Higher

Licence/BA – from the University of Yaoundé – generally considered comparable to British Bachelor (Ordinary) degree standard when awarded with high average marks.

Maîtrise – generally considered comparable to British Bachelor (Honours) degree standard.

Doctorat du Troisième Cycle – generally considered comparable to British MPhil standard.

Doctorat d'Etat – generally considered comparable to British PhD standard.

Teaching

Licence/(DIPES) – may be considered for entry to postgraduate study.

MARKING SYSTEMS

School

Anglophone

GCE O and **A level** are marked as in Britain.

Francophone

Marking for the **Baccalauréat** is on a scale of 0–20 (maximum) with 10 as the pass-mark:

16–20	*très bien*	very good
14–15	*bien*	good
12–13	*assez bien*	fair
10–11	*passable*	pass
0–9		fail

Higher

The same marking score is used as for Francophone secondary education. The degrees of **Master** and **Doctorate** may be awarded with the following classifications:

Très honorable avec felicitations du jury
Très honorable
Honorable

SCHOOL EDUCATION

Primary

Anglophone

Primary education starts at age five. After seven years of primary school, students take the **First School Leaving Certificate Examination** and the **Government Common Entrance Examination**. Students can leave school with the **First School Leaving Certificate**, but success in both is essential for entry to secondary school.

Francophone

Primary education commences at age six (a year later than in the anglophone provinces). After six years of primary education students take two national examinations to determine their entry to secondary school. These are the **Certificat** d'Etudes Primaires Elémentaires (CEPE), also called the **Concours d'Entrée en Sixième**. Only enough students are passed to fill the places available in the first year of secondary school (*sixième*).

Secondary

Anglophone

The first cycle of secondary education consists of a five-year course leading to the **Cameroon GCE O level**. The Cameroon education authorities are assisted by the London Board to:

1. moderate GCE examination questions
2. print the examination papers
3. vet the marked scripts (compare the marking in Cameroon with that in Britain)
4. print the certificates.

The Cameroon College of Arts, Science and Technology offers two-year courses leading to **GCE A level** examinations. The Higher Schools in Cameroon also offer these courses.

Francophone

General secondary education is provided by *Collèges d'Enseignement Général* (CEG), *Collèges d'Enseignement Secondaire* (CES) and *Lycées*. The first cycle covering the first four years leads to the **Brevet d'Etudes du Premier Cycle** (BEPC). At the *Lycées* the first two years lead to the **Probatoire** and the third year leads to the **Baccalauréat**.

Technical and vocational secondary

Anglophone

Secondary technical pupils take the City and Guilds craft examinations or the **Certificat d'Aptitude Professionnelle** (CAP). Second-cycle education is covered by the *Lycées Techniques* and some private Collèges d'Enseignement Technique Industrielle (CETIs) which offer a two-year course leading to the **Probatoire** and the **City and Guilds Part II** and a further year to obtain the **Baccalauréat** or the **Brevet de Technicien** (technicians diploma) or the **City and Guilds Part III**. In commercial schools students can enter for the **Royal Society of Arts** (RSA) or the **London Chamber of Commerce** (LCC) **Stage II** examinations or the CAP after the first cycle. Those who continue to the second cycle can take the **RSA** or **LCC Stage II** or **GCE A level**. For more vocationally oriented students there are *Sections Artisanales Rurales* (SAR) as well as the Manual Arts Centre (for boys only) which operate on a day-release basis. *Sections Ménagères* (homecraft centres) also offer some basic academic courses but without formal examinations.

Francophone

First-cycle education lasting four years leading to the **Certificat d'Aptitude Professionnelle** in industrial and commercial subjects is available in the *Collèges d'Enseignement Technique Industriel* (CETI). Second-cycle education is covered by the *Lycées Techniques* and some private CETIs which offer a two-year course leading to the **Probatoire** and the third year to the **Baccalauréat** or the **Brevet de Technicien** (technicians diploma). The **Brevet** provides the opportunity for specialization in surveying, manufacturing engineering, automobile engineering or metalwork. The **Baccalauréat** can be taken in the following options: mathematics and technology; general mechanics; electronics; electrotechnology; civil engineering; or industrial cooling systems.

Sections Artisanales Rurales and *Sections Ménagères* offer two-year post-primary courses in vocational subjects. No certificates or diplomas are awarded.

HIGHER EDUCATION

Access to the University of Yaoundé is based on the **Baccalauréat** or **GCE** (two **A levels** plus at least four **O levels**). The first stage of higher education leads after three years' minimum to the **Licence** or **BA** (either **Libre** or **d'Enseignement**) and to a **Maîtrise** after a further year or a professional **Maîtrise** after two further years. A third cycle of two or more years culminates in the **Doctorat du Troisième Cycle** and the highest qualification, the **Doctorat d'Etat**, is obtained after at least five years beyond the **Doctorat du Troisième Cycle**.

The Ecole Nationale Supérieure Polytechnique is part of the University. It offers three-year courses in electronic, electromechanical or civil engineering, leading to the qualification of **ingénieur de travaux** (site engineer) and five-year courses in either civil or industrial engineering, leading to the qualification of **ingénieur de conception** (design engineer).

Other constituent colleges of the university: Douala, Dschang, Ngaoundere and Buea.

The Ecole Nationale de Technologie offers two-year courses for foremen, four-year technician courses (the entrance requirement for both being the CAP) and a three-year site engineers' course for applicants holding the **Baccalauréat**.

Agricultural education is provided by various government institutions.

Medical training is provided by the Centre Universitaire des Sciences de la Santé.

Other institutions include:

Centre Régional de Formation Phytosanitaire de Yaoundé
Ecole Nationale d'Administration et de Magistrature (1962)
Ecole Nationale des Infirmiers Diplômes d'Etat
Ecole Nationale Supérieure de l'Enseignement Technique
Ecole Nationale Supérieure de Police
Ecole Supérieure des Postes et Télécommunications
Ecole Nationale Supérieure des Travaux Publics
Institut National des Assurances
Institut National de la Jeunesse, des Sports et de l'Education Populaire
Institut de Formation et de Recherches Démographiques
Institut de Statistique, de Planification et d'Economie Appliquée
Institut Pan-Africain pour le Développement
Académie Régionale des Sciences et Techniques de la Mer

Five new universities have been formally set up from January 1993 by Presidential decree. They are Yaoundé II, Dschang, Ngaoundere, Douala and Buea.

TEACHER EDUCATION

Primary

Anglophone

Students with primary school leaving certificates are eligible to enter for the **Grade II** or **Certificat d'Aptitude Pedagogique d'Instituteur Adjoint** and spend three years studying, while students who enter with three or more **O levels** spend only one year for the same certificate.

GCE A levels or at least three years of teaching experience with the **Grade II** certificates are required for the **Certificat d'Aptitude Pédagogique d'Instituteur**.

Francophone

Ecoles Normales d'Instituteurs Adjoints (ENIA) offer one-year courses after the BEPC. The *Ecoles Normales d'Instituteurs* (ENI) offer two-year courses after the **Brevet d'Etudes du Premier Cycle** and three-year courses after the **Baccalauréat**. Students who complete ENIA courses do not receive certificates but are registered as *Instituteurs Adjoints*.

Secondary

Until 1979

Students with the **Baccalauréat** or **GCE A levels** used to take the **Diplôme d'Etudes Supérieures** after a three-year course. With this qualification they were eligible to take the **Certificat d'Aptitude Pédagogique d'Enseignement Secondaire**.

Since 1979

The qualification obtained after the first three-year cycle has been renamed the **Diplôme de Professeur des Collèges d'Enseignement Général**. Entry to the second cycle is now restricted to graduates with experience.

The Ecole Normale Supérieure (ENS) is part of the University of Yaoundé, training secondary teachers on a four-year programme leading to a **Licence** from the university and concurrently a **Diplôme de Professeur d'Enseignement Secondaire** (DIPES) first cycle from the ENS. This qualifies teachers for the lower forms of secondary schools. A further two years leads to the DIPES second cycle (equivalent to the university **Maîtrise**) which qualifies teachers for the upper forms of secondary schools. There are at present proposals for certain subjects to be taught to DIPES first cycle in provincial annexes of the ENS.

Canada

Under the Constitution Act of 1982, power to make laws 'in and for each province' in education matters rests exclusively with the provinces. There is no central ministry of education in Canada, although the Department of the Secretary of State of Canada plays a role in co-ordinating federal involvement in post-secondary education.

All children must attend school from age six or seven until fifteen or sixteen. The school year runs from September to June.

French and English are the official languages of Canada. Outside the province of Quebec, English is the predominant medium of instruction. However, French-language institutions at all levels are found in other regions of the country. French-language immersion programmes at the primary and secondary school levels are also popular throughout Canada.

Owing to the differentiation of the Canadian educational system this chapter has individual sections, which follow a **GENERAL** section, on each of the following provinces and territories:

Alberta	Newfoundland	Prince Edward Island
British Columbia	North West Territories	Quebec
Manitoba	Nova Scotia	Saskatchewan
New Brunswick	Ontario	Yukon Territory

GENERAL

Pre-school education

Kindergarten programmes are available in every province and territory except Prince Edward Island which has an early childhood programme incorporated in its day care programme. A one year programme is offered at Kindergarten, to 5 year olds, prior to primary education (grade 1).

School education

Students are required to attend school until 15 or 16 years of age, depending on the province or territory in which they study. The school year runs from September to June. The structure of elementary and secondary education varies in each province and territory.

Technical secondary education

The pattern of vocational education varies from province to province. Many secondary schools provide technical and vocational courses as part of their programmes.

Trade and occupational training schools are available for those students who have passed the provincial school-leaving age and have left the regular school system. Courses at the trade level do not usually require high school graduation; the grade level required varies according to trade and province and ranges from grade 8 to 12.

FURTHER EDUCATION

There are many institutions offering instruction at this level as well as public and private specialist colleges and institutes: Colleges of Agriculture, Colleges of Applied Arts and Technology, *Colléges d'Enseignement Général et Professionnel* (CEGEPs), Conservatories of Music, Hospital-based schools, Institutes of Technology and Community Colleges (in addition to Colleges of Trades and Technology, Forest Ranger Schools, Land Survey Institutes, and so on).

Colleges of Applied Arts and Technology

These are located mainly in Ontario. They were originally conceived as terminal institutions, with few possibilities for transfer to universities. Their scope has now been widened to include a broader range of courses.

Community Colleges

Many of these colleges have been established since the late 1960s; others grew out of existing colleges. They do not award degrees, and are oriented more towards community service. Hence, the types of course vary according to the institution and its locality. However, in general, full- and part-time courses are available in a variety of subjects in career, remedial and general education. Some colleges also offer one- and two-year preparation courses for university entrance or advanced university entrance.

HIGHER EDUCATION

A secondary school certificate (or in the case of Quebec, completion of a 2-year CEGEP programme) is typically the minimum requirement for entry to a university undergraduate course. A more flexible admission policy is often extended to mature 'students' at the undergraduate level. The usual criteria are that the candidate is 21 years of age or older, has been out of school for several years, and is able to demonstrate a potential for success in university.

While 'university' is the most common designation for degree-granting institutions, there are also colleges, schools, and specialized institutes that perform this function. Identifying the number of such institutions is complicated by the fact that a university or college may be associated with another university as a federated, affiliated, or constituent institution. A federated institution is responsible for its own administration and has the power to grant degrees, but may, by agreement, hold some or all of its degree-granting powers in abeyance; affiliated institution retains its administrative independence, but not its powers to grant degrees in its own right; and a constituent university is considered part of the parent university, both as far as administration and degree-granting powers are concerned. Thus, broadly defined, Canada has approximately 90 university-level institutions. Of this total, about 70 grant degrees in all of their programmes. Of the remainder, a small number grant degrees in only one or two fields, mainly theology, while the others do not grant degrees but are associated with a university with full degree-granting powers. In effect, although the latter have programmes leading to degrees, they are not strictly speaking degree-granting institutions themselves.

Degrees offered by universities and colleges are generally recognized as consisting of three levels: the **baccalaureate** in arts or science (BA or BSc), or a profession such as engineering (BEng); **Master's** (MA or MSc, or professional such as MEng); and **Doctoral** (PhD). Some institutions also offer diploma and certificate courses. For certain professions, such as medicine and dentistry, the first degree conferred is '**Doctor**' (MD, DDS). In other fields, such as library and information science or social work, the first professional degree is a **Master's** (MLS,MSW) following completion of an undergraduate degree. Students at the bachelor's level are known as undergraduates. Degrees at this level require three of four years' full-time study depending on whether the programme is general or specialized. Quebec undergraduate French-language programmes tend to be more specialized, although there is trend toward more general education.

A **Master's** degree typically requires two years. A minimum of three years and up to four or five years of course work, study, research, and completion of a dissertation is normal for a **Doctoral** degree. Although the degree is known generically as a 'PhD', a **Doctoral** degree may also be granted in a particular field of study such as music (DMus) or law (LLD).

In professions, such as medicine and law, a period of practical internship is required before a licence to practice can be obtained. Medical specialization also requires further study, internship, and certification.

At most universities in Canada, the academic year is divided into two terms or sessions, running from September to December and from January to early May. Intersession and summer courses are also available at many institutions. The majority of students are admitted to the September term. A few institutions operate on a formal trimester system, with three terms of equal length and admission possible to any of the three terms.

ALBERTA

EVALUATION IN BRITAIN

School

General High School Diploma – generally considered to satisfy the general entrance requirements of British higher education institutions if awarded with an average of at least 65 per cent in five acceptable grade 12 courses.

Higher

Bachelor (Ordinary) degree – generally considered comparable to British Bachelor (ordinary) degree standard.

Bachelor (Honours) degree – generally considered comparable to British Bachelor (Honours) degree standard.

173

MARKING SYSTEMS

School

High School Transcript of Academic Achievement

Marks for subjects in grades 10, 11 and 12 are reported in percentages.

A   80–100 per cent
B   65–79
C   50–64
F   0–49
P   Pass

From 1983, government examinations were administered in seven grade 12 subjects. Transcripts indicate three grades for such courses: a teacher grade, a departmental mark and a final grade, which is the average of the other two grades. The final grade is used for determining entrance to post-secondary institutions.

SCHOOL EDUCATION

Education is compulsory to age sixteen.

The pre-primary year (Early Childhood Services) is not mandatory, but nearly all students are enrolled.

Primary lasts for six years, covering grades 1 to 6, and is sometimes referred to as Division 1 (grades 1 to 3) and Division 2 (grades 4 to 6).

Secondary lasts for six years, divided into junior high school – three years (grades 7–9, Division 3), and senior high school – three years (grades 10–12, Division 4).

Compulsory subjects in junior high school are language, arts, social studies, mathematics, science, physical education and health and personal life skills.

All courses in senior high school are numbered in decades: numbers 10 to 19 represent grade 10 courses, 20 to 29 grade 11 and 30 to 39 grade 12. All courses have a certain credit value, which may vary from course to course, but is usually 5. A credit represents course-specific knowledge, skills and attitudes that most students can achieve with approximately twenty-five hours of instruction. A minimum of 50 per cent or grade C is required to receive credit in courses. Normally, a student is limited to attempting only 40 credits in any one academic year. Compulsory subjects are language, arts, mathematics, science, social studies and social sciences, physical education and career and life management.

For the award of the **General High School Diploma**, students must obtain 100 credits, which must include 15 credits in language arts, 15 credits in social studies, 3 credits in physical education, 8 credits in mathematics, 8 credits in science, 3 credits in career and life management and a minimum of two other grade 12 courses other than language arts and social studies.

For the award of the **Advanced High School Diploma** students must obtain 100 credits which must include 30 credits in each of the following compulsory subjects: English, social studies, mathematics, and either biology, chemistry, or physics 30. All six of these grade 12 courses require completion of a government examination. In addition, English 33 (not used for university entrance) also has a government examination. Students who complete the four required grade 12 courses for an **Advanced High School Diploma** with a minimum mark of 65 per cent and an average of 80 per cent will be awarded the **Diploma with Excellence**.

Students wishing to proceed to university level studies, must obtain a minimum average of at least 60 per cent in five required subjects, but possibly as high as 70 per cent dependent upon student demand for various programmes. The **Advanced High School Diploma** is not required.

Since 1991, students have been able to earn a **Certificate of Achievement** in the Integrated Occupational Programme. Students must obtain 80 credits which must include 9 credits in English, 6 credits in social studies, 3 credits in mathematics, 3 credits in science, 3 credits in physical education, 3 credits in career and life management and 40 credits selected from the occupational clusters.

TEACHER EDUCATION

Prospective teachers both at the primary and secondary school level may register for the four-year **Bachelor of Education** degree course, offered by the Universities of Alberta, Calgary and Lethbridge. The entrance requirement is the **High School Graduation Diploma**.

HIGHER EDUCATION

See under **GENERAL** at beginning of chapter

BRITISH COLUMBIA

EVALUATION IN BRITAIN

School

Senior Secondary Graduation Diploma – generally considered to satisfy the general entrance requirements of British higher education institutions if awarded with at least five Bs (BBBBB) in acceptable grade 12 subjects.

Higher

Bachelor (Ordinary) degree – generally considered comparable to British Bachelor (Ordinary) degree standard.

Bachelor (Honours) degree – generally considered comparable to British Bachelor (Honours) degree standard.

MARKING SYSTEMS

School

Transcripts of Grades		**Graduation Diploma/ Statement of Standing**		
A	86–100 %	A+	90–100 %	honours
B	73–85	A	80–89	excellent
C+	67–72	B	70–79	good
C	60–66	C	56–69	average
P	50–59	D	50–55	pass
F	below 50	F	below 50	fail
I	incomplete			

SCHOOL EDUCATION

Compulsory education is from age five to sixteen. Provision for school entry in September or January exists within the School Act.

A new system is being phased in which is structured into three divisions: Primary (four years), Secondary (seven years), Graduation (two years).

The minimum secondary school graduation requirements include the successful completion of at least thirteen courses, numbered 11 or 12. Graduation requirements include English 11 or communications 11; English 12 or communications 12; social studies 11; an 11-level mathematics course; an 11-level science course; and a course in consumer education. A student must also successfully complete three provincially authorized 12-level courses in addition to English 12. Transcripts of grades are issued by the Ministry of Education. Final grades for grade 12 provincially examinable courses are based on the school percentage (60 per cent) and the final examination percentage (40 per cent). A **Senior Secondary Graduation Diploma** is issued by the Ministry of Education for each student who has successfully completed graduation requirements.

An average of at least C+ (67 to 72 per cent) is required for admission to most undergraduate courses at universities in British Columbia.

HIGHER EDUCATION

See under **GENERAL** at beginning of chapter.

TEACHER EDUCATION

Certification requirements are determined by the College of Teachers.

Most teachers undertake either a four-year **Bachelor degree** in arts or science, followed by one year of teacher training, or a five-year **Bachelor of Education** degree course. Both types of training will lead to the **Professional Certificate**.

MANITOBA

EVALUATION IN BRITAIN

School

High School Graduation Diploma – generally considered to satisfy the general entrance requirements of British higher education institutions if five credits have been awarded at the 300 level in at least four subject areas; and at least 65 per cent has been achieved in each of these subjects.

Higher

Bachelor (Ordinary) degree – generally considered comparable to British Bachelor (Ordinary) degree standard.

Bachelor (Honours) degree – generally considered comparable to British Bachelor (Honours) degree standard.

MARKING SYSTEM

School

High School Graduation Diploma/Statement of Standing

A+	90–100 per cent	honours
A	80–89	excellent
B	70–79	good
C	56–69	average
D	50–55	pass
F	below 50	fail

SCHOOL EDUCATION

Compulsory education is from age seven to sixteen.

Primary, from age five, covers grades K (kindergarten) to 3 or 4.

Middle is usually from grades 5 to 8 or 9.

Secondary lasts four years, covering grades 9 to 12. Many schools organize themselves in grade groupings of K–6, 7–9, 10–12.

Students take a general course, which is common for all, to the end of grade 9. Compulsory subjects are language arts, mathematics, science, social studies and physical education and health. Art and music are compulsory to the end of grade 6. Optional courses begin in grade 7, and by grade 10 students may specialize.

There are four high school course patterns in addition to a mature students' programme:

university entrance course;

general course – (which also leads to high school graduation, and possible admission to a community college);

vocational/industrial/business;

occupational entrance (slow learners).

Courses are identified by a three-digit number, e.g. 100, 201, 302, 103, 204, 305. The 10, 20, 30 refer to courses taken in grades 10, 11 and 12 respectively. The suffix 0 signifies a subject taken in the university entrance course, 1 the general course, 2 the commercial course, 3 the industrial course, 4 an occupational entrance course, and 5 other courses.

All courses at the senior high school level are assigned a certain credit value. A student may earn one credit by successfully completing a course of study for which a minimum of 110 hours instructing has been taken. Most courses carry a credit of 1; English 300 is a 2-credit course.

The final secondary school-leaving certificate, the **High School Graduation Diploma**, is obtainable on successful completion of grade 12, i.e. on obtaining 20 credits. These must include credits obtained for English, social studies, mathematics and science in each of grades 10 and 11, English in grade 12, physical education, and 9 or 10 credits selected from other courses. The general requirement for entry to university is five credits in 300–level subjects.

HIGHER EDUCATION

See under **GENERAL** at beginning of chapter.

TEACHER EDUCATION

To teach at both primary and secondary level students may undertake one of several types of training of which the more common are:

a four-year **Bachelor of Education** degree course

a three-year **BA** or **BSc** degree course, followed by a two-year after degree programme leading to a **Bachelor of Education** degree and a teaching certificate.

NEW BRUNSWICK

EVALUATION IN BRITAIN
School

High School Graduation Diploma – generally considered to satisfy the general entrance requirements of British higher education institutions if an average of 65 per cent in at least five acceptable subjects is obtained.

Higher

Bachelor (Ordinary) degree – generally considered comparable to British Bachelor (Ordinary) degree standard.

Bachelor (Honours) degree – generally considered comparable to British Bachelor (Honours) degree standard.

SCHOOL EDUCATION

Elementary school, which commenced in September 1991, lasts six or seven years. Secondary school lasts for six years, divided into three years junior high school and three years senior high school. In September 1989, New Brunswick initiated a major senior high school reorganization programme.

The reorganized programme requires that all students complete a broad common compulsory core of studies as well as a number of challenging elective courses. Programme designations such as College Preparatory, Industrial Occupational, and General Education have been discontinued. The common high school programme now provides a wider and more balanced array of learning experiences for all students with the effect of increased training, educational, and employment options at the end of high school. Specified courses in the compulsory core are offered at more than one level of difficulty to account for individual student interests, abilities and aptitudes.

The senior high school continues to be organized on a three-year plan with grades 10, 11 and 12.

Implementation of the senior high school reorganization took place over five years and began in the school year 1989–90. By September 1991, all schools had begun implementation of either a 21- or 24-credit system. From the date of commencement, each school had three years to fully implement the new programme.

Graduation from the senior high school

The goals of reorganization were to prepare all students to function as informed and responsible citizens in a democratic society, to function effectively in the world of work, and to realize personal fulfilment. To achieve these goals, school districts have been given a choice in instructional organization. They may offer a scheduling system that will provide a 21-credit programme with a minimum 18 credits required for graduation of which 13 must be compulsory credits. Or they may offer a 24-credit programme with a minimum 20 credits required for graduation of which 14 for anglophone students, or 15 for francophone students, must be compulsory credits. The compulsory credits will be selected from four areas (clusters) of study: (i) language and mathematics, (ii) science and technology, (iii) social sciences, and (iv) personal development.

Two systems

New Brunswick is officially bilingual and its education system is organized on the principle of duality. In essence, anglophones and francophones get the same basic education but the system allows for minor differences mainly in graduation requirements.

Anglophone system

A **High School Graduation Diploma** is awarded, therefore, upon successful completion of one of the following minimum programmes:

a) 21-credit system:

Canada

Student course load – seven credits per year beginning with the first year of implementation.

Gradution Requirements – 18 credits of which four must be at the Grade 12 level.

Subject clusters	Credits required
1. Languages and mathematics	7
2. Sciences and technology	2
3. Social sciences	2
4. Personal development	2

Compulsory courses – 13 credits
Elective courses – 8 credits

b) 24-credit system:

Student course load – 8 credits per year beginning with the first year of implementation.

Graduation requirements – 20 credits of which 4 must be at the grade 12 level.

Subject clusters	Credits required
1. Language and mathematics	7
2. Science and technology	2
3. Social sciences	2
4. Personal development	2
5. One from any cluster	1

Compulsory courses – 14 credits
Elective courses – 10 credits

Francophone system

All of the senior high schools have opted for the 24-credit system and therefore a high school graduation diploma is awarded upon successful completion of:

24-credit system

Student course load – 8 credits per year beginning with the first year of implementation.

Graduation requirements – 20 credits of which 15 are compulsory:

Subjects	Credits required
1. French	4
2. Mathematics	3
3. English	1
4. Social Sciences	2
5. Natural Sciences	2
6. Technology	1
7. Physical Education	1
8. One of: personal development; art; economical, political and judicial institutions of Canada.	1

Compulsory courses – 15 credits
Elective courses – 9 credits

HIGHER EDUCATION

See under **GENERAL** at beginning of chapter.

TEACHER EDUCATION

The formal training required to be a teacher at elementary or secondary level is a four-year course leading to a **Bachelor of Education** degree.

NEWFOUNDLAND

EVALUATION IN BRITAIN

School

High School Graduation Diploma – generally considered to satisfy the general entrance requirements of British higher education institutions if obtained with at least a mark of 65 per cent in at least five acceptable subjects at university preparatory level (grade 12).

Higher

Bachelor (Ordinary) degree – generally considered comparable to British Bachelor (Ordinary) degree standard.

Bachelor (Honours) degree – generally considered comparable to British Bachelor (Honours) degree standard.

MARKING SYSTEM

School

Pass certificate – 36 credits including 21 'core' credits **Graduation Diploma with Distinction** – satisfies minimum graduation requirements, + 550 or more marks in seven level-III courses.

Graduation Diploma with Honours – satisfies minimum graduation requirements, + 550 or more marks in seven university preparatory level-III courses, as specified by the Department of Education.

SCHOOL EDUCATION

Primary and elementary (grades K to 6) (K = kindergarten)
Junior high (grades 7 to 9)
High school (grades 10 to 12)

The grade 12 **High School Graduation Diploma** contains three designations:

Graduation Pass Certificate
Graduation with Distinction
Graduation with Honours

Minimum graduation requirements include successful completion of 21 'core' credits, with an overall attainment of 36 credits.

Graduation with Distinction requires satisfaction of minimum graduation requirements and attainment of 550 or more marks in any seven level-III (grade 12) courses.

Graduation with Honours requires satisfaction of minimum graduation requirements and attainment of 550 or more marks in seven university preparatory level-III courses (grade 12) as specified by the Department of Education.

The pass mark in all subjects is 50 per cent.

The grade 12 **High School Diploma** admits the holder to Memorial University in Newfoundland, provided all courses required for admission are successfully completed, with an overall average of not less than 60 per cent. Most other Canadian universities accept Newfoundland grade 12 **High School Diploma** for entrance to the first year of a four-year degree programme.

HIGHER EDUCATION

See under **GENERAL** at beginning of chapter.

TEACHER EDUCATION

The minimum qualification for permanent certification is four years of university training in education beyond grade 12 graduation. However, most new teachers entering the profession have university degrees.

It should be noted that preference is given to teachers with a minimum of five years' university training for teacher certification purposes.

NORTH WEST TERRITORIES

EVALUATION IN BRITAIN

School

General High School Diploma – generally considered to satisfy the general entrance requirements of British higher education institutions if awarded with an average of at least 65 per cent in five acceptable grade 12 courses.

Higher

Bachelor (Ordinary) degree – generally considered comparable to British Bachelor (Ordinary) degree standard.

Bachelor (Honours) degree – generally considered comparable to British Bachelor (Honours) degree standard.

MARKING SYSTEM

School

Student achievement in each course is normally reported in percentages or letter grades as follows:

A	80 to 100 per cent
B	65 to 79
C	60 to 64
F	0 to 49.

At the secondary level, a student who achieves a mark of 50 per cent or higher in a given course is eligible to take the next course in that sequence.

Achievement scores are determined by the school, except for those grade 12 courses which require Alberta departmental examinations. For Alberta departmental examination courses, the student's final mark is determined by averaging the mark assigned by the school with the mark attained on the departmental examination. At the secondary level, marks are reported to the Department of Education for recording and transcript purposes.

SCHOOL EDUCATION

Secondary schools in the North West Territories use selected curricula from Alberta Education, subject to approval by the North West Territories Minister of Education and according to requirements established by the Minister of Education.

Meaning of specific terms

Complementary courses:	optional courses that provide opportunities for developing students' unique talents, interests and abilities.
Core courses:	courses which all students are expected to take to graduate from secondary school.
Required component:	content within each course that covers the knowledge, skills, and attitudes that all students are expected to acquire.
Elective component:	content within each course that is designed to provide enrichment, additional assistance to those students having difficulty with the required material, or opportunities for innovation and experimentation within individual schools.
Credit:	a unit value which reflects the time allocated or assigned to secondary school courses.

Canada

Secondary school:	grades 10, 11, 12.
Credit requirements:	most courses have a value of either 3 or 5 credits, but there are courses that are offered for 2, 4, 6, 10, 15 and 20 credits.
Time allocation for credits:	at least twenty-five hours per credit must be scheduled for purposes of instruction, examinations, and other activities which directly relate to the course for which credit is to be granted. During this time, direct student-teacher interaction and supervision are to be maintained.

Pattern of school organization

School year:	usually extends from mid-August to 30 June of following year with minor variations among jurisdictions.
Days in the year:	normally a minimum of 190 days of instruction is required. Other days are used for planning, in-service education, and such other activities.
Instruction time:	1,600 minutes per week normally required in secondary schools.
School term:	secondary schools may offer courses for an entire school year, or they may divide the year into two equal semesters.
Time requirements:	regardless of whether a school is organized by semesters or on a ten-month basis, the school must meet the instructional time requirements for each course as determined by its credit value.

Curriculum organization

The curriculum is organized to provide for three years of study at the secondary level.

Requirements for graduation

Promotion to secondary school is determined by the principal of the junior high school.

General Secondary School Certificate

Core	Average figures 1990/92
English/Français	15
Social studies	15
Mathematics	8
Science	8
Career and life skills management	4
Physical education	3
Northern studies	3

Additional requirement

Two grade 12 level courses	10
Specified credits	66
Unspecified credit	34
Minimum credit requirement	100

Advanced Secondary School Certificate

Core

English/Français	15
Social studies	15
Mathematics	15
Science	11
Career and life skills management	4
Physical education	3
Northern studies	3

Complementary

Category C Courses	10
Specified credits	76
Unspecified credits	24
Minimum credit requirement	100

1. The pass mark for all courses is 50 per cent.

2. An Award of Excellence will be noted on the **Secondary School Certificate** of a student who qualifies for:

 – the **Advanced Certificate** and earns a final average of 80 per cent or higher, with not less than 65 per cent in any one of the four required departmental examination courses.

 – the **General Certificate** and earns a final average of 80 per cent or higher in any four of the grade 12 courses.

3. The selection of courses for acceptance into a university programme, is determined by the faculty of the particular university. Students should check the appropriate university calendar prior to selecting their courses.

Language of instruction

Instruction in English, aboriginal language or French is permitted, subject to the Education Act and Regulations issued by the Minister.

Except for alternative programmes, northern studies, industrial technology, career and life management (community service module) and aboriginal languages, all other secondary school curricula are derived from Alberta.

Canada

Aboriginal language credit

Students enrolled in the N.W.T. schools may be awarded credit toward graduation for demonstrated competence in one of the official North West Territories aboriginal languages.

Career and life management

Career and Life Management (CALM 20) is a required course for all secondary school students. Included in this course is a community service module with twenty-five hours of volunteer community work. The activity will be planned, scheduled and executed by the individual student with the approval of the school principal.

Alternative programmes

The Department of Education has developed two alternative programmes, Community Occupational Programme (COs) and Senior Practical Programme (SPP), targeted at students who are at least fifteen years of age and possess a combination of some of the following characteristics:

low achievement scores, poor attendance records, potential school drop-out, lack of awareness of educational procedures and/or opportunities, lack of support and guidance because of lack of parental education, poor self image, especially as it relates to school performance, lack of educational and life goals, failure to find meaningful experiences at school.

Credits

There are no credits awarded for these programmes towards the **Secondary School Graduate Certificate**.

Graduation certificates

Graduation certificates, issued by the Minister of Education for both COP and SPP, will be awarded to students who successfully complete the graduation requirements of the respective programmes.

Northern studies 15

The northern studies curriculum is designed to prepare secondary school students for citizenship in a rapidly changing society in which recognition of individual worth, pride and respect for the diverse cultural heritage and mutual accommodation of cultural, political and economic differences in Canada. Northern studies brings the immediate world of Canadian youth into the secondary school classroom, enriches and deepens the students' understanding of it, and extends this understanding from the local and territorial to the national and international levels.

All grade 10 students in a secondary school programme will be required to successfully complete Northern Studies 15 in order to earn their **Secondary School Graduation Certificate**.

Industrial technology

The industrial technology curriculum consists of courses designed for an exploration of the technologies and trades areas. The courses develop the student's self-confidence, knowledge, talents and skills and provide guidance to students to help them select more in-depth courses for occupational preparation or simply add to their technological 'know-how'.

Through the programme, students are able to work in an environment which is conducive to challenging their intellect and developing their talents in a number of technical and craft areas. Students become aware of the interrelationship and the dependency of one technology upon the others. They are given the opportunity to develop an understanding of the principles and skills required in the various occupations. Students will have many opportunities to apply academic skills learned in other subjects to their laboratory work. These courses were developed primarily for students in laboratories that are found in most smaller schools, but can be taught in larger schools as well.

NOVA SCOTIA

EVALUATION IN BRITAIN

School

High School Completion Certificate – generally considered to satisfy the general entrance requirements of British higher education institutions if awarded with at least an average of 65 per cent in at least five acceptable subjects at level 4 or 5.

Higher

Bachelor (Ordinary) degree – generally considered comparable to British Bachelor (Ordinary) degree standard.

Bachelor (Honours) degree – generally considered comparable to British Bachelor (Honours) degree standard.

MARKING SYSTEM

School

High School Diploma – a percentage scale

SCHOOL EDUCATION

School attendance is compulsory from ages six to sixteen; however, most children begin at age five.

The Nova Scotia school system comprises thirteen grades: a primary year and grades 1 to 12.

Elementary covers seven years: the primary grade and grades 1 to 6. Secondary covers a further six years, divided into three years' junior high school and three years' senior high school. Students in the senior high school age group may also enter a programme in one of the province's community colleges.

The senior high school programme (grades 10, 11 and 12) leads to the Nova Scotia **High School Completion Certificate**. A minimum of 16 credits are required for this certificate. They must include three English-language arts, one mathematics, one social studies (taken from history, geography or economics) and one science (taken from physical science, biology, chemistry or physics).

Further changes in required credits are planned for during the 1996–7 school years.

Local school boards may award their own graduation certificates which might include additional specified courses in mathematics, sciences and social studies.

A few secondary schools are French first language and students are instructed in both French and English, depending on the subject matter. In addition to the required courses already mentioned, students in French-first-language schools are required to take three courses in French-language arts.

Occasionally, some post-secondary institutions will admit students to some programmes after grade 11, but most universities require a minimum average of at least 60 per cent in the final year of studies (grade 12) in five appropriate university preparatory subjects. Some university programmes have special admission requirements regarding subjects taken at high school level.

Mathematics is provided in two university preparatory courses, both leading to university entrance. One, however, provides more specific preparation for students intending to enter mathematics and science-related fields.

At senior high school each course is referred to by its subject name followed by digits. The first digit indicates the type of course: 2 – high school leaving; 3 – open category; 4 – university preparatory; 5 – honours university preparatory. The second digit indicates the year in which the course is taught: 2 – grade 10; 3 – grade 11; 4 – grade 12. The third digit distinguishes different courses of the same subject area type and grade level: e.g. ENG 441 – English literature; ENG 442 – Canadian literature.

HIGHER EDUCATION

See under **GENERAL** at beginning of chapter.

TEACHER EDUCATION

Teacher training is provided at a number of universities. There are two basic types of programmes: 1) sequential – a one-year or two-year **Bachelor of Education** programme following completion of an undergraduate degree; 2) integrated – four-year or five-year programmes combining liberal arts and professional training.

With the exception of the <u>Nova Scotia Teachers College</u>, whose four-year **Bachelor of Education** programme prepares generalist elementary and junior high teachers, and specialist technology education teachers, the integrated programmes are most frequently used to prepare specialist teachers in physical education, art education, music education and home economics education.

ONTARIO

EVALUATION IN BRITAIN

School

Ontario Academic Courses (OACs) – generally considered to satisfy the general entrance requirements of British higher education institutions if six OACs are passed; three at grade B and three at grade C.

Higher

Bachelor (Ordinary) degree – generally considered comparable to British Bachelor (Ordinary) degree standard.

Bachelor (Honours) degree – generally considered comparable to British Bachelor (Honours) degree standard.

MARKING SYSTEM

School

Ontario Secondary School Diploma (OSSD) – from 1986

One credit is granted on successful completion of a course for which a minimum of 110 hours has been scheduled.

Achievement:

A	80–100 per cent
B	70 – 79.9
C	60 – 69.9
D	50 – 59.9
P	Pass

Equivalent standing toward the OSSD may be granted for:

maturity – on the basis of age and length of time out of school;

equivalent education – equivalent courses not normally identified as secondary education, but not post-secondary education and equivalent secondary education courses completed outside Ontario;

apprenticeship training – on the basis of successful completion of each period of appropriate apprenticeship training;

music – standing toward the **Secondary School Graduation Diploma** (SSGD), **Secondary School Honours Graduation Diploma** (SSGD), **Ontario Secondary School Diploma** OSSD and **Ontario Academic Courses** (OAC) may also be granted for appropriate work completed at a recognized conservatory, college or school of music.

Level of difficulty – no level of difficulty has been assigned for courses completed before 1979–80.

B   Basic-level courses focus on social and personal skills, as well as preparation for direct entry into employment.

G   General-level courses are appropriate preparation for employment or further non-university education.

A   Advanced-level courses are appropriate preparation for grade 13 and OAC courses, and focus on theoretical knowledge as well as fundamental knowledge and practical applications. All grade 13 courses are at the advanced level of difficulty and are preparation for university entrance.

OAC **Ontario Academic Courses** are at the advanced level of difficulty and are preparation for university entrance.

SCHOOL EDUCATION

Compulsory education is from age six to sixteen.

In 1984, implementation of a new secondary school curriculum commenced. The **Secondary School Graduation Diploma** (SSGD) hitherto awarded to grade 12 graduates, and the **Secondary School Honours Graduation Diploma** (SSHGD) awarded to grade 13 graduates, have been replaced by a single certificate called the **Ontario Secondary School Diploma** (OSSD).

Students entering secondary school programmes on or after 1 September 1984 must earn a minimum of 30 credits to receive the **Ontario Secondary School Diploma**. 16 of the 30 credits are compulsory and 14 are elective. A credit is earned by successfully completing a course that involves a minimum of 110 hours of classroom work. Short courses may be available to students and fractional credits may be given.

Credits (total 30) required for the **Ontario Secondary School Diploma:**

Compulsory – English/Français 5; French/Anglais 1; mathematics 2; science 2; Canadian history 1; Canadian geography 1; arts 1; physical and health education 1; business/technological studies 1; senior social science 1, (16 credits).

Elective (14 credits).

Students who plan to go to university are required to take six **Ontario Academic Courses** (OACs), which are the new prescriptive, provincially designed university entrance courses that are offered by the secondary schools in Ontario.

OACs may be counted as credits towards the OSSD.

HIGHER EDUCATION

See under **GENERAL** at beginning of chapter.

TEACHER EDUCATION

Since the Education Act in 1974, Ontario has had one certificate for teachers, the **Ontario Teacher's Certificate** (OTC). All new graduates from teacher education programmes and all practising teachers and others who hold existing basic teaching certificates – elementary, secondary, vocational or occupational – now hold the OTC. All new and old qualifications are included on a Teacher Qualifications Record Card issued to each teacher by the provincial Ministry of Education.

Faculties of Education or Schools of Education (teachers' colleges) in Ontario are now all affiliated with universities. The duration of the basic Ontario Teacher's Programme is one year, leading to a **BEd** and OTC. Candidates must hold a university degree and must choose 1 of 3 grade divisions: primary/junior (K-6), junior/intermediate (4 to 10), or intermediate/senior (7 to 3). Prospective teachers for the junior/intermediate programme should have at least three full courses in a subject taught in the school system, and those for the intermediate/senior division should have a major and minor in two subjects taught in the school system.

An OTC in technological studies is obtained upon completion of a one-year teacher education programme in technological studies. The requirements for entry to this programme include a combination of wage-earning experience and education related to the area of technological studies.

PRINCE EDWARD ISLAND

EVALUATION IN BRITAIN

School

High School Graduation Diploma – generally considered to satisfy the general entrance requirements of British higher education institutions if a minimum average of 65 per cent in at least five acceptable subjects at grade 12 level is obtained.

Higher

Bachelor (Ordinary) degree – generally considered comparable to British Bachelor (Ordinary) degree standard.

Bachelor (Honours) degree – generally considered comparable to British Bachelor (Honours) degree standard.

MARKING SYSTEM

School

High School Diploma – percentage scale.

SCHOOL EDUCATION

Elementary lasts for six years.

Secondary lasts a further six years divided into two three-year cycles.

To obtain the **Prince Edward Island High School Graduation Diploma** on completion of grade 12, students must gain a minimum of 18 credits over grades 10, 11 and 12, to include four courses in English and/or French, two in mathematics, and two each in science and social studies. Each credit represents 120 hours of instruction.

A minimum overall average of 60 per cent is normally required in the **High School Graduation Diploma** for admission to the University of Prince Edward Island, with at least five subjects including English and mathematics, at the grade 12 academic or college preparatory level.

The college preparatory programme prepares students for courses at colleges or universities. The programme is subdivided into regular courses and a limited number of enriched courses, the latter offered to students with considerable interest and ability in a particular subject.

The general educational and occupational programme is for students requiring a broad high school education as preparation for entering the work force and/or proceeding to further training in commercial areas, the trades, or service occupations.

HIGHER EDUCATION

See under **GENERAL** at beginning of chapter.

TEACHER EDUCATION

Four levels of certification are available.

Certificate 4 – may be granted to those who have successfully completed a four-year **Bachelor in Education** or equivalent.

Certificate 5 – may be granted to those who have successfully completed an approved four-year academic **Bachelor degree** and also completed a one-year **Bachelor in Education** or equivalent.

Certificate 5A – may be granted to those who have completed an approved year of study beyond **Certificate 5**. Prior approval of the Registrar is required to begin this year.

Certificate 6 – may be granted to those who have completed an approved academic **Master's degree** and one-year **Bachelor in Education** or a **Master in Education** (minimum of six years post-secondary study).

QUEBEC

EVALUATION IN BRITAIN

School

Diplôme d'Etudes Secondaires (DES) – generally considered comparable to GCSE standard (grades A, B and C) on a subject-for-subject basis, with the exception of English language.

Diplôme d'Etudes Collègialles (DEC) – may be considered to satisfy the general entrance requirements of British higher education institutions.

Higher

Bachelor (Ordinary) degree – generally considered comparable to British Bachelor (Ordinary) degree standard.

Bachelor (Honours) degree – generally considered comparable to British Bachelor (Honours) degree standard.

MARKING SYSTEMS

School

High School Diploma/Secondary Grade V Certificate (DES): unit credit system.

A unit represents the measure of the value of a course. A course which requires the equivalent of one period of instruction per day throughout the school year, yields 6 units. On the certificate this is indicated by the last digit of each subject code (a six-digit code).

CEGEP Diploma: (see under Quebec school education):
percentage scale, 60 being the lowest pass mark. The mark received is reported with the average of the section of the course in which the student is registered.

SCHOOL EDUCATION

Primary is usually from age six, for six years.

Secondary lasts five years, covering grades 7 to 11 or secondary forms 1 to 5.

Diplôme d'Etudes Secondaires (DES) is awarded to pupils who have accumulated a minimum of 130 credits, including the compulsory credits listed below. Twenty credits of the 130–credit total must be from Secondary 5 courses (in general education or vocational education) or those recognized as such:

–	Mother tongue	Sec. 4 and 5
–	Second language Sec. 5 (English sector)	Sec. 4 or 5 (French sector)
–	History of Canada and Quebec, or History 412	Sec. 4 Sec. 4 (English sector)
–	Catholic or Protestant religious instruction, or moral instruction	Sec. 4 or 5

The Minister awards the **Secondary School Vocational Certificate** with mention of the trade or vocational specialization to any pupil who has obtained the credits attached to the vocational education programme he or she has selected.

Each paper in the certificate examinations is given a value of unit credits, usually 2 for each.

The General and Vocational College Act of 1967 led to the establishment of the **Collèges d'Enseignement Général et Professionel** (CEGEPs). These instutitions offer two-year academic courses preparing students for entry to university, and three-year terminal technical/vocational courses, which prepare students directly for employment. Admission to both types of course is by the **Diplôme d'Etudes Secondaires** (DES).

If a student takes the two-year pre-university course, he or she is required to complete 24 credit courses to qualify for the **Diploma of Collegial Studies** (DCS)/**Diplôme d'Etudes Collégiales** (DEC):

Core courses	Total credits
4 English/French	
4 humanities	8

plus field of concentration
      12 courses from 3 or 4
      disciplines within 1 of 3
      groups (maximum 6 courses
      in the same discipline)   12

plus complementary courses
      to ensure a diversified
      programme of studies, 4
      courses ought to be selected
      outside the field of
      concentration $\frac{4}{24}$

The curriculum of this two-year course was previously offered in the first year of the university degree courses.

HIGHER EDUCATION

Since the introduction of the CEGEPs (**Collèges d'Enseignement Général et Professionel**) in the late 1960s, all universities in Quebec have offered a three-year programme leading to a **BA** or **BSc** from the level of the **Diploma of Collegial Studies (Diplôme d'Etudes Collègiales)**.

TEACHER EDUCATION

To qualify to teach at either the elementary or secondary level, it is necessary to obtain certification from the Ministry of Education. Certification can be obtained either by completing a three-year university **Bachelor of Education** programme, or one-year diploma programme, after the award of a **Bachelor degree**.

SASKATCHEWAN

EVALUATION IN BRITAIN

School

Complete Grade 12 Standing/Division IV Standing (Secondary School Diploma) – generally considered to satisfy the general entrance requirements of British higher education institutions if at least a 65 per cent grade average in five acceptable subjects is obtained.

Higher

Bachelor (Ordinary) degree – generally considered comparable to British Bachelor (Ordinary) degree standard.

Bachelor (Honours) degree – generally considered comparable to British Bachelor (Honours) degree standard.

MARKING SYSTEMS

School

Under Core Curriculum guidelines, the K-12 system uses a credit system in which 1 credit is equal to 100 hours of classroom instruction. A minimum 24 credits are required to attain secondary level standing or high school completion.

Higher

Universities – marks are based on a percentage system; a mark less than 50 per cent is considered a failing grade.

Saskatchewan Institute of Applied Science and Technology (SIAST)

The four campuses of SIAST use these marking systems:

- percentage system: a mark less than 50 per cent is considered a failing grade;

- grade-point system for some competency-based learning programmes: a 4, 3, 2 or 1 is assigned (1 indicates minimal level of performance); competency-based programmes requiring both a written and skills test. The written test requires an 80 per cent; 100 per cent is required on the skills test. Upon successful completion of the two tests, credit is awarded for each competency or module by assigning a 'complete.'

Regional Colleges – Overall, a percentage-based system is used, in which a mark less than 50 per cent is considered to be a failing grade. Some programmes require a passing grade of 75 per cent.

SCHOOL EDUCATION

Primary and Secondary

The Core Curriculum is considered to be developmental in nature and is based on a kindergarten to grade 12 (K–12) continuum, which consists of kindergarten, elementary (grades 1 to 5), middle years (grades 6 to 9) and secondary (grades 10 to 12).

Core Curriculum is divided into two major categories: the required areas of study and the Common Essential Learnings (CELs). The required areas of study consist of: language arts, mathematics, science, social studies, health education, arts education, and physical education. The CELs are skills, values and understanding which are considered important as foundations for learning in all school subjects. Common Essential Learnings in the following categories will be incorporated into all courses of study: communication, numeracy, critical and creative thinking, technological literacy, independent learning, personal and social values and skills.

To meet community and student needs at the local level, provision is made for locally determined options. Saskatchewan Education reviews and approves locally developed programmes. In recognition of special needs of individual students, the adaptive dimension of the Core Curriculum allows teachers to individualize instruction.

Saskatchewan's elementary and secondary (K–12) education is delivered by 117 public and separate (Roman Catholic) school divisions.

Attendance within the K–12 system is compulsory for children aged between seven and sixteen. It is not mandatory for children to attend kindergarten.

Within the K–12 system, the academic year typically begins in September and ends in June. Legislation provides for a maximum of 200 school days in a year, but the Minister may, in any year, determine a lesser number of school days. In recent years, the school year has been set at 196 days. A summer vacation of not less than six weeks must begin immediately following 1 July.

Qualifications – grade 12 or secondary level standing requires 24 credits. Subsequent entrance to post-secondary institutions generally requires secondary level standing. In addition, particular subjects may be required to enter specific programmes of faculties. The medium of instruction is primarily English. However, Core French and French Immersion programmes are also offered.

Publicly funded K–12 education is delivered by public and separate (Roman Catholic) school divisions. All schools must follow the provincial curricula, which includes both required courses, and electives which may be determined by local priorities and individual student interest.

All schools follow the standard academic year, beginning in late August or early September and ending in June.

Some schools at the secondary level specialize in offering a wider range of elective courses in technical and vocational education. However, all students must fulfil the standard requirements for completion of grade 12.

Under legislation, all between the ages of six and twenty-one years have the right to an appropriate education within the K–12 system.

As indicated previously, the Core Curriculum includes the following required areas of study: language arts, mathematics, science, social studies, health education, arts education and physical education. Common essential learnings in the following six categories are incorporated into all courses of study: communication, numeracy, critical and creative thinking, technological literacy, independent learning, personal and social values and skills.

Vocational education

The medium of instruction is primarily English. However, to improve language skills prior to other education and training, English as a second language is offered at all the Saskatchewan Institute of Applied Science and Technology (SIAST) campuses and Regional Colleges.

SIAST offers one- and two-year programmes leading to a certificate or diploma, respectively. Regional Colleges provide a variety of programmes; some may require a few months while others will last up to a maximum of two years.

Types of institutions/programmes

SIAST: The four campuses of SIAST offer a variety or programmes in business, health, industrial, service and technology sectors. Some of the programmes offer a co-op work/study option which combines work experience and academic training. Students alternate between terms of work experience and classroom study. Competency-based learning, which allows students to progress at their own pace while utilizing instructional assistance when required, is provided at some of the SIAST campuses. In addition, some of the campuses offer university credit courses.

Regional Colleges: The Regional Colleges offer a range of university and technical institute programmes. As well, they provide programmes in adult basic education, English as a second language, literacy training, life skills, and high school completion.

The Apprenticeship Program includes on-the-job skills development under the supervision of a certified journeyman, supplemented by technical training. The Saskatchewan Skills Extension Program offers skill-training programmes to people in rural, northern and small urban centres through a co-operative arrangement between SIAST and the Regional Colleges.

Private vocational schools are located throughout the province. The schools provide a wide variety of programmes such as office education, cosmetology, and computer training.

Qualifications vary depending on the programme. However, overall, the age requirement is seventeen years of age or older having attained grade 12. There is some flexibility in entrance requirements for adult students who have been out of school for a long period of time.

The apprenticeship programme's entrance requirements state that students must be sixteen years or older, have attained a grade 10 standing or higher, and be engaged in a designated trade.

A certificate or diploma is awarded to students by SIAST and the Regional Colleges. The Apprenticeship Program awards a **Journeyman's Certificate**.

The certificate or diploma programmes may lead to professional designations such as a registered nurse. The Apprenticeship Program may lead to the nationally recognized Red Seal certification.

Post-secondary

University of Saskatchewan – the academic year is a twelve-month period beginning on 1 July. The regular session begins in September and ends in April. There are two, three-week intersessions provided in May and June. In addition, a summer session is provided which is a six-week session in July and August.

University of Regina – currently operates on a semester system. The first semester begins in September and ends in December. The second semester begins in January and ends in April. Two intersessions are provided: a spring session which runs from May until June and a summer session which begins in July and concludes in August. In the spring of 1992, the University of Regina is converting from the semester system to a twelve-month academic cycle.

Saskatchewan Institute of Applied Science and Technology (SIAST) – the academic year varies among the campuses based on different starting times for specialized programmes. However, in general, the academic term begins in September and ends in April.

Regional Colleges – owing to the variety of programmes offered, the starting periods may vary. However, in general, the academic term begins in September and ends in April.

FURTHER EDUCATION

The medium of instruction is primarily English.

A variety of extension programmes are offered through the universities and SIAST which allow students to gain credit toward a university degree, certificate or professional designation. Non-credit programmes allow students to enhance their professional development or personal enrichment. Completion of a programme is based on a pre-determined set of course requirements, rather than number of years.

The participating institutions include the <u>Saskatchewan Institute of Applied Science and Technology</u>, <u>University of Regina</u>, <u>University of Saskatchewan</u> and Regional Colleges.

Entrance requirements vary among the extension programmes. Overall, regular admission is granted to students who have grade 12-level standing.

Each institution establishes curriculum content.

A certificate or diploma is awarded by SIAST, Regional Colleges and the universities.

HIGHER EDUCATION

The medium of instruction is primarily English. However, the <u>University of Regina</u> houses the first Canadian International Language Centre and intensive language immersion programmes.

Depending upon the faculty or college, a **Bachelor degree** involves three or four years of full-time study (or equivalent). A prerequisite to the **Master's degree** programme is a **Bachelor degree**. A **Master's degree** involves completion of a programme of advanced study while registered as a graduate student. The type of work involved varies from one faculty or college to another. A **Master's degree** is usually a prerequisite to a **Doctoral degree** programme which usually requires two to three years of full-time study while registered as a graduate student.

The <u>University of Regina</u> houses the Canadian International Language Centre, Westbridge Computer Centre and offers a School of Journalism which is currently the only programme of its kind in Western Canada.

The <u>University of Saskatchewan</u> offers one of the broadest ranges of degree programmes, including all five life sciences, of any university in Canada. In addition, the <u>University of Saskatchewan</u> houses the largest and most up-to-date agricultural research centre.

In addition, there are a number of affiliated colleges, which have received affiliation status from the senate of one of the two universities. They are expected to offer four university-accredited classes per year and must have a permanent approved faculty. They are not required to locate on the university campus. Most are theological in nature. As well, there are federated colleges which are academically integrated with one of the universities, and are governed by independent Boards of Governors. They share tuition fees with the parent university, receive annual operating grants from the Department of Education and receive funding for minor capital renovations. Students register for university programmes through a federated college and earn their degrees from the university.

The <u>University of Regina</u> and the <u>University of Saskatchewan</u>, adhere to two sets of admission requirements: general admission and specific faculty or college admission.

General university admission requires a complete grade 12 (minimum 24 credits), in which 12 of those credits are taken from combined grade 11 and 12 level subjects. Students must have a minimum 65 per cent average from the seven classes used for admission, all of which must be in different subject areas. Some programmes select the most qualified candidates. In addition, there is some flexibility in entrance requirements for adult students who have been out of school for a long period of time.

The admission requirements for specific faculty/college university programmes adhere to certain high school subject prerequisites. The specific faculty/college admissions are direct-entry programmes through a specific faculty or college; pre-professional programmes which students can take at one of the universities prior to transferring to a professional programme at a university outside the province; and non-direct-entry programmes which require the completion of a pre-professional programme prior to transferring to a professional programme at a Saskatchewan university.

The curriculum content is established by each institution.

Upon completion of specified requirements, a **Bachelor degree, Master's degree** or **Doctoral degree** will be awarded by the institution according to the programme. Undergraduate students may continue on to graduate studies to obtain a **Master's** or **Doctoral degree**.

Some programmes result in professional designations such as lawyer, medical doctor, dentist, engineer, nurse, etc. These graduates are then eligible for membership in the appropriate professional associations.

TEACHER EDUCATION

The medium of instruction is primarily English. However, the universities offer French Elementary Education and French Immersion Programmes, where some instruction is provided in French.

The required number of years to obtain a **Bachelor of Education** degree is four years.

Teacher education may be obtained on-campus at either of the two universities or off-campus through the Northern Teacher Education Program (NORTEP) or the Saskatchewan Urban Native Teacher Education Program (SUNTEP). NORTEP is designed to provide opportunities for northern residents, preferably with a background of native language, to become teachers. SUNTEP is designed to assist Metis and Non-Status Indians to become teachers.

The entrance requirements for teacher education are as previously noted in the section on higher education.

The curriculum content is established by each institution.

Upon completion, a **Bachelor of Education** degree is awarded by the institution. Provincial certification is required in order to teach in the province of Saskatchewan. A **Bachelor of Education** degree is required for teacher certification.

The **Bachelor of Education** degree gives the option to continue with graduate studies.

YUKON TERRITORY

The education system is modelled on that of British Columbia, i.e. seven years' primary, followed by five years' secondary.

Central African Republic

The Central African Republic was formerly the French colony of Ubangi Shari. In 1958 Ubangi Shari elected to remain within the French community and adopted its present title. The education system, unified in 1962, is based on the French system. All education is the responsibility of the Ministry of Education.

The medium of instruction is almost entirely French but Sango is now also used in some primary schools.

EVALUATION IN BRITAIN

School

Brevet Elementaire du Premier Cycle (BEPC) – generally considered to be below GCSE standard.

Baccalauréat – generally considered comparable to GCSE standard (grades A, B and C) on a subject-for-subject basis, with the exception of English language.

Higher

Diplôme Universitaire d'Etudes Litteraires (DUEL) – generally considered comparable to GCE Advanced standard.

Diplôme Universitaire d'Etudes Scientifiques (DUES) – generally considered comparable to GCE Advanced standard.

Licence – generally considered comparable to a standard between GCE Advanced and Bachelor degree; may be considered for advanced standing by British higher education institutions.

Licence from the Ecole Normale Supérieure – may qualify for Maîtrise – generally considered comparable to a British Bachelor (Ordinary) degree, but where very high marks have been achieved, candidates may be considered for admission to postgraduate study.

MARKING SYSTEMS

School Baccalauréat – subjects are marked on a scale of 0–20 (maximum) with 10 being the minimum pass-mark.

SCHOOL EDUCATION

Primary

This lasts six years, from age 6. At the end of the course pupils are awarded the **Elementary Primary School Leaving Certificate**. At the end of the sixth year, pupils take a competitive examination which grants access to the first year of secondary education (**Concours d'Entrée en Sixième**).

After primary education, pupils may be directed into general and technical secondary education, apprenticeship centres, the Ecole des Arts et Metiers (school of arts and crafts), the Collège d'Enseignement Technique Feminin (technical school for girls) or to agricultural education.

Secondary

This is divided into two cycles. The first is a four-year course which leads to the **Brevet Elémentaire du Premier Cycle** (BEPC). The second cycle consists of a three-year course ending in the **Baccalauréat** examination or **Diplôme de Bachelier de l'Enseignement du Second Degré**. This gives access to higher education.

Technical secondary

Courses of technical education are also available. They lead to various **Certificats d'Aptitude Professionnelle** (CAP) and the **technical Baccalauréat**.

HIGHER EDUCATION

The Université de Bangui, which opened in 1969, consists of:

- four faculties: Law and Economics;
  Letters and Humanities;
  Sciences;
  Health Sciences;

- five institutes: University Institute of Technology;
  University Institute of Business Administration;
  Institute of Rural Development;
  Institute of Mathematical Studies;
  Institute of Applied Linguistics;

- one higher teacher training college, the Ecole Normale Supérieure.

Programme Length		Diploma/certificate degree
First cycle	**Baccalauréat** + two years	**Diplôme universitaire d'Etudes Littéraires** (DUEL)
		Diplôme Universitaire d'Etudes Scientifiques (DUES)

Second cycle	DUEL/DUES + 1 year	Licence
	Baccalauréat + three years	Diplôme Supérieur de Gestion
	Licence + 1 year	Maîtrise
Medicine	Baccalauréat + six years	Doctorat en Médecine
Engineering	Baccalauréat + four years	Diplôme d'Ingénieur d'Agriculture
	Baccalauréat + three years	Diplôme d'Ingénieur

TEACHER EDUCATION

Primary

The teacher training school for primary school teachers offers a two-year course. Candidates are selected after obtaining the BEOC. The course leads to the **Certificat d'Aptitude Pedagogique.**

Secondary

Lower secondary teachers take a three-year course after obtaining the **Baccalauréat**. They are awarded the **Certificat d'Aptitude Professionnelle à L'Enseignement dans les Colleges d'Enseignement Général** (CAP/CEG).

Upper secondary teachers take a four-year course after obtaining the **Baccalauréat**. They are awarded the **Certificat d'Aptitude Professionnelle du Second Cycle dans les Lycées** (CAP second cycle).

Chad

Before the early 1960s, education was offered only by mission and Koranic schools. Since then, compulsory schooling has been from age six to twelve but lack of facilities, despite state-school provision, prevents this being fully implemented. There are standard national curricula at school level.

French is the official medium of instruction; at early primary level many children have to learn the language. Arabic is also taught at this level.

The school year runs from September to June.

EVALUATION IN BRITAIN

School

Baccalauréat – generally considered comparable to GCSE standard (grades A, B and C) on a subject-for-subject basis, with the exception of English language.

Higher

Diplôme Universitaires de Lettres Modernes (DULMO), **Diplôme Universitaire de Sciences** (DUS), **Diplôme Universitaire de Sciences Juridiques, Economiques et de Gestion** (DUSJEG) – may be considered to satisfy the general entrance requirements of British higher education institutions.

Licence – generally considered comparable with a standard between GCE Advanced and British Bachelor degree; may be given advanced standing by British higher education institutions.

Maîtrise – generally considered comparable to British Bachelor (Ordinary) degree standard but where very high marks have been achieved candidates may be considered for admission to a postgraduate course.

Teaching

CAPEL – generally considered comparable to British Bachelor (Ordinary) degree standard.

MARKING SYSTEMS

School and Higher

Each element marked out of 20.

SCHOOL EDUCATION

Primary

Primary education lasts six years with pupils beginning school between the ages of six and eight and leads to the **Certificat d'Etudes Primaires Elémentaires**. Some rural schools offer courses only lasting two to three years and these do not lead to a formal qualification. The standardized curriculum includes reading, writing, spelling, grammar, mathematics, history, geography, science and drawing.

There is a competitive entrance examination (**Concours d'Entrée en Sixième**) for admission to secondary education.

Secondary

Secondary education is divided into two cycles; the lower, lasting four years, leading to the **Brevet d'Etudes du Premier Cycle** (BEPC), and the upper lasting a further three years, leading to the examinations for the **Baccalauréat**. During this cycle pupils may specialize in the mathematics, science or literature options.

Technical secondary

Technical *Lycées* offer three-year secondary courses on completion of the BEPC leading to a **Baccalauréat Technique**.

Technical vocational schools offer courses starting from the *classe de quatrième* (i.e. third year of lower secondary), lasting five years and leading to the different certificates of vocational aptitude.

Apprenticeship centres offer three-year courses leading to an apprenticeship certificate.

FURTHER EDUCATION

Holders of the **Brevet d'Etudes du Premier Cycle** may enter:

Postal and Telecommunication School (Sarh) for a four-year course.

Ecole Nationale d'Administration et de Magistrature (ENAM). Holders of the **Baccalauréat** may apply for two- or three-year professional courses.

HIGHER EDUCATION

The University of Ndjamena, which opened in 1972, closed in 1979 and re-opened in 1984. Tertiary education is also offered by various specialist institutes and national schools:

– the Ecole Nationale d'Administration et de Magistrature (1963);
– the Ecole Nationale des Travaux Publics (1965);
– the Ecole Nationale des Postes et Télécommunications;
– the Institut National Tchadien pour les Sciences Humaines (1961).

The first stage of studies comprising two years leads to the **Diplôme Universitaire de**

Lettres Modernes (DULMO) in humanities, to the **Diplôme Universitaire de Sciences** (DUS) in science, or to the **Diplôme Universitaire de Sciences Juridiques, Economiques et de Gestion** (DUSJEG). After a further year of study students may obtain the **Licence** in humanities, law and economics. One or two years' further study leads to a Master's degree (**Maîtrise**).

The **Diplôme d'Ingénieur des Techniques d'Elevages** from the Institut Universitaire des Techniques de l'Elevage requires three years.

NON-UNIVERSITY HIGHER EDUCATION

Programme Length	Diploma/certificate
BEPC + four years	**Poste et Télécommunications Diplôme**
BEPC + three years	**Contrôleur EMVPT**
Controleur + two years	**Ingénieur**

TEACHER EDUCATION

Primary

After completion of the **Brevet d'Etudes du Premier Cycle** students may enter an *Ecole Normal d'Instituteurs* for a three-year course graduating as **Instituteurs**. Students may leave after two years as **Instituteurs-Adjoints** and can, if they wish, return later to complete the third year.

Secondary

Students who hold the **Baccalauréat** can take a competitive examination for entry to the Ecole Normale Supérieure Ndjamena to follow a two-year course leading to the **Certificat d'Aptitude Pédagogique pour Collèges d'Enseignement Général** (CAPCEG). The CAPCEG entitles the holder to teach at the lower secondary cycle.

Lycée teachers are required to hold a **Licence** but from 1989 teachers with the CAPCEG can follow a two-year course at the Ecole Normale Supérieure leading to the **Certificat d'Aptitude Pédagogiques pour l'Enseignement aux Lycées** (CAPEL). Holders of the **Licence** will be required to follow a one-year course at an *Ecole Normale Supérieure* which also leads to the CAPEL.

Chile

The new government, inaugurated in March 1994, intends to continue education reforms at all levels, but these reforms refer more to programmes and style rather than structure.

Education is free and compulsory for children aged six to fourteen (eight years) covering the primary cycle.

The medium of instruction is Spanish.

The academic year runs from March to December and is divided into three terms at school level and normally two semesters at university.

EVALUATION IN BRITAIN

School

Licencia de Educación Media – generally considered comparable to GCSE standard (grades A, B and C) on a subject-for-subject basis, with the exception of English language.

Higher

Licenciatura/Professional Degree – generally considered comparable to British Bachelor degree standard if awarded after four or more years of study.

- Licenciatura (3 – 5 years)
- Magister/Master/Maestría (Licenciatura plus 2 years)
- Doctorado (3 – 5 additional years)

In general, academic and professional degrees are awarded simultaneously, practically all professional degrees require a period of six months practice. In addition most 4/5 year courses require a thesis or degree project.

MARKING SYSTEMS

The same grading system is used for primary, secondary and higher education. The maximum mark available is 7 and the minimum pass-mark is 4.

Until 1973

7	*muy bueno*	very good
6	*bueno*	good
5	*más que suficiente*	above average
4	*suficiente*	average
3	*deficiente*	
2	*malo*	failure
1	*muy malo*	

Since 1973

6–7	*muy bueno*	very good
5–5.9	*bueno*	good
4–4.9	*suficiente*	average
1–3.9	*insuficiente*	failure

SCHOOL EDUCATION

Pre-primary education *(Pre-básica)*

This caters for children up to the age of six and is not compulsory. There is an official curriculum for the different levels of pre-primary education which in general is child centred and in keeping with modern theories.

Primary *(Educación Básica)*

This covers an eight-year compulsory period (ages six to fourteen). Each school devises its own internal examinations although the Ministry of Education still defines the general aims of education, the plans and programmes of study, and the rules of evaluation and certification. Children who successfully complete all eight grades of primary education are awarded a primary school-leaving certificate which grants access to secondary education.

Secondary *(Educación Media)*

The general secondary education course lasts four years. Students choose to specialize in one of two branches: humanistic-scientific general education or technico-professional vocational education (which is one year longer to include practical experience). The first two years are common to both types.

Humanistic-scientific

Most pupils choose to enter the humanistic-scientific branch of education which is a preparation for higher education. This offers a two-year common course of studies and two years of specialization in literary, historical and social sciences or natural sciences and mathematics.

Technico-professional

This branch of education is intended to be less academic and more vocational. It is divided into four branches: industrial, agricultural, commercial, and special services and techniques. After two common years of general studies, students specialize in one of these branches. Although these courses are intended to provide technicians for industry, agriculture and commerce, some students continue to the higher education sector.

Students of both branches who successfully complete their secondary education are awarded the **Licencia de Educación Media**.

FURTHER EDUCATION

Apart from the vocational opportunities offered within the sphere of school and university education, various non-academic courses are available for those in employment.

The Instituto Nacional de Capacitación (INACAP) provides practical courses in motor mechanics, machine repairs, building construction, mining, agriculture and cottage industries. Students attend regional centres which offer courses suited to the particular area.

The technico-professional courses require a **Licencia de Educación Media**. Courses are composed of three stages, each of which lasts approximately 400 hours, designated *Formación, Capacitación* and *Especialización*. Each stage lasts approximately four months. Shorter courses are offered. Most trainees attend on a part-time basis. There are no formal examinations. The instructors decide whether the student has been successful; 100 per cent attendance is required.

The Instituto Tecnológico of the University of Santiago and the Instituto Politécnico of the Federico Santa Maria Technical University offer a limited number of similar courses.

The Departamento Universitario Obrero Campesino (DUOC), part of the Catholic University, offers part-time courses at centres throughout the country. Most of the courses are offered at evening classes and cover technical and arts and crafts subjects, as well as health and education. Courses are offered to adults to complete primary and/or secondary education. The technico-professional courses offered require a **Licencia de Educación Media**.

Technical formation centres offer post-secondary courses of two or three years mainly in administration, commerce and technology.

HIGHER EDUCATION

Students holding the **Licencia de Educación Media** sit a national university entrance examination called the **Prueba de Aptitúd Académica** (PAA). This is a multiple-choice examination valid for all universities and professional institutes in Chile. Candidates compete nationally in the examination, which consists of two papers: language aptitude (mostly comprehension) and mathematical aptitude. Each candidate may be required to take an additional **Prueba de Conocimientos Específicos** (test of specific knowledge) in one of five or more areas (mathematics, natural sciences, social sciences, physics and chemistry) relevant to the subject the candidate wishes to pursue at university. The student's average marks obtained in secondary school are also taken into account.

Higher education is provided by the universities and professional institutes. Twelve subjects (*Carreras*) are available only at the universities: agronomy, architecture, biochemistry, civil engineering, commercial engineering, dentistry, forestry, law, medicine, pharmacology, psychology, veterinary medicine.

Undergraduate courses offered by the universities vary in length from four to seven years; they generally lead to the **Licenciatura** and/or **Professional degree**.

Courses at the professional institutes normally last from three to five years and do not necessarily lead to the **Licenciatura**. They usually concentrate in the areas of anthropology, pedagogy, philosophy, journalism, sociology, nursing, technical engineering, etc.

Postgraduate studies are concentrated in the University of Chile, the Catholic University of Chile, the University of Concepción, the University Austral, the University of Santiago, the University of La Serena and the Technical University Federico Santa María. The universities in the provinces tend to emphasize regional-relevant courses, e.g. geology and mining in the north and dairy farming and forestry in the south. Courses range from one-year diplomas to doctorates. Students holding the **Licenciatura** may be awarded a **Magister** after two years' further study. The **Doctorado** (PhD) is awarded after the submission of a thesis and usually takes between three and five years beyond **Magister**.

TEACHER EDUCATION

Primary and secondary

Pre-primary and primary teachers are required to take a 3–year degree course at a higher education institution. Secondary teachers are required to follow a five-year university or professional institute course in which they cover education and a specialized subject. Successful students receive the qualification of **Profesor** (i.e. teacher)

The **Professional degree** is required to be able to teach at any level of education. Most universities have specialization courses for teachers and the Ministry of Education has a special centre, Centro de Perfeccionamiento, Experimentación e Investigaciones Pedagógicas (CPEIP) to provide in-service courses for teachers. The Colegio de Profesores (Association of Teachers) also offers some summer courses for its members.

ADULT EDUCATION

There are adult primary and secondary schools which function as evening schools. Nearly all of these are state financed.

ADDITIONAL INFORMATION:

1988: The Instituto Profesional Chileno-Británico (former British Institute, Santiago) offers a 4-year English Teacher Training course. Teachers receive a qualification referred to as a degree, equivalent to a UK university BEd. They also run a 3-year translation course and students qualify for a degree as a translator English/Spanish.

1994:

72 universities – 50 of these private
123 professional institutes – 121 of these private
247 technical centres – none of these receive state funding.

China

The period from the founding of the People's Republic of China in 1949 to the late 1950s was one of reliance on Soviet assistance and loans; the education system was patterned on that of the Soviet Union, with Russian as the second language at school. Educational facilities were expanded and great importance was attached to examinations.

After the 1950s the Soviet pattern was rejected. In the period known as the Great Leap Forward, beginning in 1958, the concept of manual labour was introduced to the education system.

In the mid-1960s the education system lapsed into chaos and disorganization, as education was one of the priorities of the Cultural Revolution. After 1966, most schools and universities were closed to prepare for a reorientation and restructuring of the whole system (for example, the reduction of the period of schooling and the abolition of college entrance examinations). Some institutions began to reopen in 1967, but teachers often had no formal qualifications, students entered university without having taken any examinations, and there was no form of assessment during the university course. Great importance was given to manual labour and the link between production and education. Many institutions remained closed until the early 1970s.

During the early 1970s, the so-called Educational Revolution of 1971-5, a number of 'colleges' and 'universities' were established offering spare-time and short-term highly vocational courses. The curriculum was changed at all levels to make it more relevant to the needs of society. Courses were shortened, and students had to work before going on to university, normally for a minimum of two years.

The Chinese authorities now concede that the Cultural Revolution had ruinous effects on higher education. However, since 1977 there has been much progress. It is difficult to generalize about the present situation as progress is happening at different rates throughout China, but since 1978 the school curriculum has again become centrally regulated, and six years' primary education is compulsory. The 1986 Compulsory Education Act has extended compulsory schooling to nine years. Academic merit is again emphasized, rather than solely political consciousness. In 1980 the degree system was re-established and in 1987 the conferment of academic titles was restored. In recent years many postgraduate programmes have begun.

The academic year runs from September to July divided into two semesters.

EVALUATION IN BRITAIN

School

1952–8

School leaving certificate (before 1990)/**Senior High School Graduation**

Examination (since 1990)/**Chinese University Entrance Examination** – generally considered comparable to GCSE standard.

Higher

First degree – generally considered comparable to a standard between GCE Advanced and British Bachelor degree; may be given advanced standing by British higher education institutions. Candidates with good results from prestigious institutions may be considered for admission to postgraduate study.

For further information enquirers should contact the National Academic Recognition Information Centre.

MARKING SYSTEM

School

The **Chinese University Entrance Examination** is marked on a percentage scale per subject, with no minimum pass mark and a maximum mark for the examination of 500. The minimum usually required for entry to university or teacher training college in China ranges from 280 to 370, although some major universities may require as high a figure as 380. The maximum mark does not include the mark obtained for the test in the foreign language, except for students wishing to study foreign languages at higher education level. In this case the mark for the foreign language test is counted, but the mathematics result is not included.

The **Senior High School Graduation Examination** is also marked on a percentage scale per subject.

Higher

University students are evaluated frequently through examinations in all subjects both in the compulsory and optional courses. Examinations are marked on either a percentage scale with a minimum pass-mark of 60, or on a pass-or-fail basis (A, B, C, P and F).

Graduation examination consists of two parts; course examinations which are marked as above, and graduation thesis which is marked as pass or fail.

SCHOOL EDUCATION

Pre-primary

In the past, facilities for children aged three to six years were limited, but these are now being expanded. Kindergartens are divided into three grades: three to four year olds, four to five year olds and five to six year olds.

Primary

1952–67

Primary education generally lasted six years for children aged six-and-a-half to seven years; it was divided into two cycles of four and two years respectively. Some schools operated an experimental system of five years. There was an entrance examination to decide entry to secondary education.

Since 1967

Primary education generally lasts six years, although in 1989 the State Education Commission determined that this should be reduced to five (with an additional year in secondary school) and this policy has been implemented in urban areas. The curriculum includes Chinese language, mathematics, geography, nature, foreign languages, physical education, music, painting, agricultural work, and industrial work. There is no longer an entrance examination for secondary education.

Secondary

Until the mid-1970s

In the 1950s a six-year secondary system was established, with the emphasis in the curriculum on the sciences and political training. Schools were closed by the Cultural Revolution in 1966, and only gradually reopened after the spring of 1967, at first offering only two to three years of combined junior and senior middle school; this expanded in the early 1970s to four years, divided into two two-year cycles. From 1967–77 the end-of-course examination was internally set and controlled by the Revolutionary Committee in each school without any form of external moderation.

Since the mid-1970s

Secondary education covers six years, divided into two cycles of three years each in junior and senior middle schools, although (see **Primary** above) this is being extended to four years and three years. The curriculum covers: Chinese language and literature; mathematics; politics; physics and chemistry; history; geography; a second language (usually English); culture; physical training; and foundations of agriculture (including biology); plus a period of work study in a school workshop or agricultural unit, often combined with sessions at a regular factory.

In 1977, the first external examinations since before the Cultural Revolution were introduced at the end of the course to decide entrance to higher education. The **Chinese University Entrance Examination** is standardized and taken nation-wide. Compulsory subjects are Chinese, mathematics and politics. In addition, pupils take either chemistry and physics or geography and history, according to specialization. A foreign language may also be included: there is a choice of English, French, Spanish, Russian, and German. Since the introduction of the **National Senior High School Graduation Examination**, the number of core subjects has been reduced from seven to five.

The **National Senior High School Graduation Examination** was introduced in 1990, and is available in a wider range of subjects. It has now been made available in all thirty provinces in China. The examination is set by each province according to standards formulated by the State Education Commission to assess the achievement of school leavers. The result is provincial level examinations with national recognition. Success in this examination leads to a school leaving certificate issued by the provincial education commission, whereas in the past it was issued by the individual school. Before 1990, a **School leaving certificate** was issued.

Technical secondary

Upon completion of the nine year compulsory education, students are streamlined through entrance examinations for senior secondary schools to decide whether they go on to either the three year senior secondary school, or a three year programme in a technical and vocational school to learn practical skills oriented towards the job market. In 1992, the enrolment in technical and vocational schools had reached 6,828,000, almost matching the number of senior secondary school students (7,049,000), and in some areas the enrolment at the former is higher than the latter.

HIGHER EDUCATION

Until the beginning of the Cultural Revolution in 1966, students could enter university on completion of secondary school and success in an entrance examination. When institutions began to reopen in 1967, places on higher education courses were allocated by regional revolutionary committees to communes and factories, which then decided to whom they should be awarded on the basis of good socialist consciousness and activity. Normally, students would have completed secondary school, but some entered university with little previous education. In the early 1970s, students were generally expected to work for at least two years before entering university.

In 1977, a national entrance examination was again instituted, the **Chinese University Entrance Examination**, which is now taken by students on completion of secondary education. In the new **Matriculation Examination** in general a mark of 550–600 is required for university entrance. There is a national admission system with fierce competition for places at universities with high reputations.

Until the Cultural Revolution, courses lasted from three years (humanities) to six years (science). When the institutions reopened, courses were reduced to three to four years and the curriculum was oriented towards the practical application of subjects studied i.e. to labour practice, political education, and community work. Since the late 1970s, most courses have again been lengthened to four years (six years in medicine, dentistry and some polytechnic institutes). The curriculum still contains a small element of political-ideological training, military-physical training, and productive work (besides the main area of specialization): this has increased since the unrest of May/June 1989.

From 1949 to 1980, in general, only certificates and diplomas were awarded although some first degrees were conferred from 1954–9, 1961–4 and in 1965. Since 1980, **Bachelor degrees** have been awarded.

Until 1955 no postgraduate study facilities were available, and students mostly went to the Soviet Union. In 1955 the qualification of **Associate Doctor** was established, but few were awarded. After the closure of the universities in 1966, postgraduate study was re-instituted in 1978, and since 1981, students have been able to obtain a **Master's degree** after two to three years' successful study. An Academic Council has been appointed to arrange supervision of **PhD** work and to approve the granting of **PhD** degrees. Since 1982, the Chinese government has instituted a number of educational development programmes to raise academic standards and introduce a wide range of research courses in universities.

Many universities offers special classes to enable students to make up any deficiency in their secondary education; these normally last two to four years.

A number of spare-time colleges have been established by factories and trade unions. These offer four-year courses in various fields and/or short advanced courses. In China, these institutions are regarded as offering the same standard of education as the universities.

The Central Radio and Television University was established in 1979. (In the early 1960s, TV universities had been set up in Peking, Tianjin, Shanghai, Shenyang, but these were all closed during the Cultural Revolution). Subsequently, 43 provincial radio and television universities were set up, supported by 279 branch schools and 625 work stations. The CRTVU is the central hub of the existing network, setting policy goals, arranging curriculum and course development, and producing programmes and materials. Courses developed by CRTVU are accredited by the State Education Commission and recommended to the local TVUs. It offers a wide variety of degree courses in natural sciences, humanities, engineering, economics, management and agriculture.

China Education television (CETV) was established by the State Education Committee in 1986 as a national station broadcasting all of CRTVU's education programmes. About 10 per cent of its output is produced in house, the rest coming from the CRTVU and the provincial RTVUs.

China's first private university has opened in Shanghai in September 1992. It is an off-shoot of a high-tech project involving the prestigious Peking and Qinghua universities in Beijing and Shanghai Jiaotong University. Programmes on offer include applied computer science, international business and accounting. Tuition fees are about £400, nearly four times what many Chinese people earn in a year.

In 1981, the prestigious Tongji University established an affiliated high-tech enterprise. Since then many of Shanghai's universities and colleges have followed suit.

TEACHER EDUCATION

Primary

Lower: Prospective teachers at this level are recruited from those who have completed primary school. Courses last three to four years and are conducted at a junior teachers' training school.

Upper: A three year course at a senior teachers' training school is available for pupils who have completed junior middle/lower secondary education.

Secondary (middle school)

Three to four years' training at a teachers' training college/institute/university is available for pupils who have completed senior middle/upper secondary education. In 1988–9 the teacher training curriculum was revised in an attempt to make it more relevant to schools' needs, and distinct from general university courses.

Colombia

The Ministry of National Education is the major administrative authority for all levels of education. The Ministry exercises control over public and private institutions.

State education is free and compulsory for children aged six to twelve.

The medium of instruction is Spanish.

The academic year runs from February to November in most of the country but owing to climatic conditions it runs from September to June in the departments of Valle, Cauca and Narino. In both cases the year is divided into two semesters.

EVALUATION IN BRITAIN

School

Bachillerato (sometimes called **Diploma de Bachillér**) – generally considered comparable to GCSE standard (grades A, B and C) on a subject-for-subject basis, with the exception of English language.

Higher

Licenciado/Professional title – generally considered comparable to British Bachelor degree standard if awarded after four or more years of study; students with good grades (typically a GPA of 4.0 to 4.2) may be considered for admission to postgraduate study.

MARKING SYSTEMS

School

Pupils are examined at the end of each year of secondary studies. The final yearly grade is arrived at from the examination mark (40 per cent) and average marks for work done during the year (60 per cent). Failure in more than two subjects means that the year must be repeated.

The examinations are conducted internally, but in the sixth year of the **Bachillerato** course the examination papers are corrected by the pupils' own teacher and a teacher delegated by the Ministry of Education.

Until 1974, the **Bachillerato** was marked on a scale of 1–5 (maximum), with 3 as the minimum pass-mark.

Between 1975 and 1978 it was marked on a scale of 1–10 (maximum), with 6 as the minimum pass-mark.

Since 1978 it has been marked on a scale of 1–100 (maximum), with 50 as the minimum pass-mark. Some certificates are still marked on the old 1–10 (maximum) scale.

Higher

Students must pass the ICFES (The Colombian Institute for planning higher education in Colombia) entry examination which is marked on 700 points, with 250 as the minimum pass mark average. However, every university is autonomous in its marking. Most universities' marks depend on the subject taught.

The degree structure at Colombian universities is based on that of the United States. Students must follow a programme of unit courses, some compulsory and others elective. Each course has a unit value, and 3200 units are required for graduation. Student performance on each course is indicated by a grade point on the scale 0.0–5.0, where 3.0 is usually the minimum acceptable. At the end of the whole course, grade-points are averaged to show the general level of achievement. An average of 5.0 is rare.

4.60–5.00	extremely high
4.00–4.59	excellent
3.50–3.99	good
3.00–3.49	sufficient (average)
0.00–2.99	failure

SCHOOL EDUCATION

In 1975 and 1976 major educational reforms were announced which involved the restructuring of the education system according to the periods of basic education covering primary (grades 1 to 5), secondary (grades 6 to 9) and middle and intermediate education (grades 10 to 11 and 12 to 13 respectively). The system is, however, only slowly being introduced, and many institutions still operate on the lines of the traditional five-year primary and six-year secondary courses.

Within the public (i.e. state) system, education is provided by national, municipal and departmental schools. Private schools are run by the Catholic Church, other religious organizations, secular concerns and co-operative groups. All private schools must conform to the state's curricular models.

Pre-primary

Most kindergartens are located in the larger towns and are run by private organizations, but the Instituto Colombiano de Bienestar Familiar (Colombian Institute of Family Welfare), a government agency, is also beginning to provide such facilities.

Primary

This cycle covers five years (grades 1 to 5) for children aged seven to twelve.

Secondary

This covers six years (grades 6 to 11) divided into two cycles. The basic cycle (*Ciclo Básico*) covers four years (grades 6 to 9) and the advanced secondary cycle (*Ciclo Vocacionál*) two years (grades 10 and 11) when students may specialize in a number of different subject areas including general academic, commercial, agricultural, industrial, teacher training and social studies. Successful completion of the course leads to the **Bachillerato** in the specialization studied.

In the early 1970s the *Institutos Nacionales de Ensenanza Media Diversificada* (National Institutes of Diversified Middle Education) (INEM) introduced a new concept of comprehensive secondary schools offering the range of different specializations in one institution rather than at separate schools. They offer the same curriculum as other schools leading to the **Bachillerato**. Their numbers have been growing steadily.

Technical secondary

Technical secondary schools offer courses leading to the **Bachillerato Técnico**. After some years of approved industrial experience, this can be converted to the level of **Técnico Intermedio**. The INEM produce school-leavers holding the **Bachillerato Técnico** who have some technical training. The National Apprenticeship Service (SENA) provides most of the technical secondary training. Students who pursue apprenticeship schemes must have completed at least four years of formal secondary education. They are seconded from their work in industry for periods varying from eighteen months to three years. These courses are not oriented towards university entrance.

FURTHER EDUCATION

There are four levels of post-secondary education:

> Level 1: Formacion Intermadia Tecnica Profesional (FIP), leading to the **diploma/tecnico profesional intermedio**.
> Level 2: Formacion Technologica (FT), leading to **Tecnologo** after the first cycle and **tecnologo especializado** after a further two-year cycle.
> Level 3: Formacion Universitaria (FU), leading to the **licenciado/Professional title**.
> Level 4: Formacion Avanzada o de Posgrado (FA(P)), leading to **Magister/Especialista/Doctorado**.

Post-secondary education includes a number of vocational/technical courses. Courses lasting usually two years (four semesters) lead to the title of **Técnico Profesional Intermedio** (intermediate professional technician). The courses offer predominantly practical experience aimed at training people to perform specific technical operations. Courses may also be taken on a part-time basis. They are available at a variety of state and private institutions such as *Academias, Institutos* and *Colegios*.

Courses lasting usually three years (six semesters) lead to the title of **Tecnólogo** (technologist). Courses are offered in various subjects including architecture, computer science, engineering and economics and are designed to train future technical staff, but there is increased emphasis on scientific principles. Courses are available at a variety of state and private institutions including *Institutos, Politécnicos* and also at some universities. A further two-year programme leads to the title of **Tecnólogo Especializado** (technological specialist) which is the equivalent of a first degree.

HIGHER EDUCATION

Entry to first degree courses is based on the **Bachillerato** and the **State University Entrance Examination**, which has to be taken by all those wishing to enter higher education. The **ICFES** tests are taken during the last year of **Bachillerato** (these tests are also given to older people who have not been able to take the **Bachillerato** at a certain age). The **ICFES** tests are equivalent to the **Bachillerato**.

Most first degree courses leading to the **Licenciado** or **Professional title** take four to five years (a minimum of eight semesters). Some courses, such as law, medicine and veterinary studies take longer. Students frequently attend university on a part-time basis. In this case courses may take eight or more years to complete. Course work is measured in *Unidades de Labor Académica* (units of academic work). A minimum of 3,200 ULAs is required for a **Licenciado** or other first degree title.

Postgraduate studies lead to the title of **Especialista** (specialist), **Master's degree** or **Doctor**.

The entry requirement for specialist and **Master's** programmes is the **Licenciado** or equivalent and usually an entrance examination. A **Master's degree**, which usually takes a minimum of two years, is normally required for entry to a doctoral programme. Specialist programmes are usually offered in practical or applied disciplines such as medicine, dentistry, education, engineering and law and vary in length from one to four years.

TEACHER EDUCATION

Primary

Teachers (*Normalistas*) are trained in *Escuelas Normales*, which are secondary-level institutions.

Secondary

Teachers are trained either in the pedagogic universities or in the other universities, where they take courses in their specialist subjects as well as in education. There are some university-level courses in pre-school and primary education.

NON-FORMAL AND ADULT EDUCATION

The Ministry of Education sends out teams which provide courses in different parts of the country.

The Ministry of Communications provides primary and secondary education by means of specially devised radio and television programmes on Inravision. Courses are approved by the Ministry of Education and lead to qualifications at primary or secondary level which have equal recognition to those obtained in the formal system.

The National Apprenticeship Service (SENA) is another agency which contributes to non-formal education on a large scale. It provides training centres for the whole country as well as mobile training programmes.

The government has also developed the CAMINA project to help illiterate people.

Congo

The following chapter regarding the education system in Congo is based on information obtained from the 3rd edition of this Guide, published in 1991, as NARIC has been unable to obtain more recent information.

Formerly the French colony of Middle Congo, Congo has followed a basically French system of education since independence in 1960.

The medium of instruction is French.

The academic year runs from October to June.

EVALUATION IN BRITAIN

School

Baccalauréat – generally considered to be of GCSE standard, with the exception of English language. May be considered for admission to access/bridging courses.

Higher

Diplôme Universitaire d'Etudes Littéraires (DUEL), **Diplôme Universitaire d'Etudes Scientifiques** (DUES) – may be considered to satisfy the general entrance requirements of British higher education institutions.

Licence – generally considered comparable to a standard between GCE advanced and British Bachelor degree; may be given advanced standing in British higher education institutions.

Maîtrise – generally considered comparable to British Bachelor (Ordinary) degree standard, but where very high marks have been achieved candidates could be considered for admission to taught Master's degree courses.

Teaching

CAPEL/CAPES – generally considered comparable to British Bachelor (Ordinary) degree standard.

MARKING SYSTEM

School

Subjects are marked on a scale of 0–20 (maximum), with no official minimum pass-mark.

Overall grades in the **Baccalauréat** are:

très bien	very good
bien	good
assez bien	quite good
passable	average

A student may have subject grades below 9 in 1 or more subjects and still obtain the **Baccalauréat** if he or she attains an overall average grade of 9 or higher.

SCHOOL EDUCATION

Primary

This covers six years numbered F1 to F6, leading to the **Certificat d'Etudes Primaires Elementaires** (CEPE).

Secondary

This covers seven years, divided into a four-year lower cycle (*fondamental*) (F7 to F10) and a three-year upper cycle (*secondaire supérieur*) (SS1 to SS3). On completion of class F10, pupils obtain the **Brevet d'Etudes du Premier Cycle** (BEPC). During the second cycle pupils may specialize in mathematics, science or literature. On completion of this cycle pupils take the examinations for the **Baccalauréat**, available in a variety of options, depending on specialization:

A	humanities and philosophy
B	economics
C	mathematics and physical science
D	natural science
E	science and technology.

Pupils who do not take the examinations (or fail) are given a **Certificat de Fin d'Etudes Secondaires**, a record of attendance and performance in the final year at school.

Technical secondary

On completion of lower secondary education, pupils may take a 'short' technical secondary course (two to three years), leading to the qualification of **Brevet de Technicien**, or a 'long' course (three to four years) leading to the **Baccalauréat Technique**, a qualification available in two options, depending on specialization:

F	technology
G	commerce.

HIGHER EDUCATION

There is one university, founded in 1959 as the Centre d'Etudes Administratives et Techniques Supérieures; it became the University of Brazzaville in 1971 and acquired its present title of Université Marien Ngouabi in 1977.

The entrance requirement is the **Baccalauréat**.

The University is made up of the following faculties:

Faculté des Lettres et des Sciences Humaines

Departments of language, linguistics, literature, communication, philosophy, psychology, geography, history and sociology.

Faculté des Sciences

Departments of mathematics, physics, chemistry, biology and plant physiology, biology and animal physiology, cellular and molecular biology and geology.

The first stage of studies after two years leads to the **Diplôme Universitaire d'Etudes Littéraires** (DUEL) in arts and humanities and **Diplôme Universitaire d'Etudes Scientifiques** (DUES) in the sciences. A further year of study leads to the **Licence**, and a further two years (i.e. one year after the **Licence**, including the submission of a thesis) to the **Maîtrise**.

Study for **Maîtrises** and for **Doctorats** is not taking place at present.

There are also the following *Instituts* and *Ecoles* :

L'Institut Supérieur des Sciences Economiques, Juridiques, Administratives et de Gestion

Departments of law and administration (*sciences juridiques et administratives*), economics and planning, management, secretarial studies.

L'Institut Supérieur des Sciences de l'Education

Specializing in teacher training: departments of educational science, technical teacher training, secondary teacher training in humanities, secondary teacher training in science.

L'Institut Supérieur des Sciences de la Santé (INSSA)

Departments of biological morphology, physiology, medicine and nursing science, surgery and maternity, public health.
Six years' study leads to MD (**Doctorat en Médecine**)

Three years' study is required to become a trained nurse (**Licence en Sciences de la Santé pour les Infirmiers**)

L'Institut de Développement Rural (IDR)

To provide training in agricultural science, departments of rural development, agriculture and agronomy, short training courses (*formations courtes et du perfectionnement*)

L'Ecole Nationale d'Administration et de Magistrature

To provide training and in-service training for civil servants in administration and law, departments of administration and law.

Unless otherwise indicated, as for IDR or INSSA, admission to these institutes is generally after obtaining a **Licence** or completing a *cycle court*. Study at the institutes is normally for two years, leading to a DES or DESP (**Diplôme des Études Supérieures**).

TEACHER EDUCATION

Primary

Training is undertaken at secondary level.

Secondary

A two-year post-secondary course at the Institut Supérieur des Sciences de l'Education (INSSED), a teacher training college which forms part of the Université Marien-Ngouabi, leads to the qualification of **Certificat d'Aptitude au Professorat dans les Collèges d'Enseignement Général** (CAP de CEG). A further year of study leads to the title of **Professeur de Lycée** with the qualification of **Certificat d'Aptitude au Professorat d'Enseignement dans les Lycées** (CAPEL), formerly called the **Certificat d'Aptitude au Professorat de l'Enseignement Secondaire** (CAPES).

Ecole Normale Supérieur de l'Enseignement Technique (ENSET)

This institute trains technical teachers for the **Certificat d'Aptitude au Professorat de l'Enseignement Technique** (CAPET).

Institut Supérieur d'Education Physique et Sportive (ISEPS) – for the training and in-service training of sports and physical education instructors, departments of sports technology and of physical education. Four years' training leads to the **Certificat d'Aptitude au Professorat d'Education Physique et Sportive** (CAPES). Three years' training is required for the assistant teacher qualification.

Costa Rica

Education is the responsibility of the Higher Council of Education (*Consejo Superior de Educacion*). Many private institutions exist but are subject to state inspection.

State education is free and compulsory for the nine years of basic education from age six to fourteen.

The medium of instruction is Spanish.

EVALUATION IN BRITAIN

School

Bachillerato – generally considered comparable to GCSE standard (grades A, B and C) on a subject-for-subject basis, with the exception of English language.

Higher

Bachiller/Bachillerato Universitario/Licenciado – generally considered comparable to British Bachelor degree standard if awarded after four or more years of study.

MARKING SYSTEMS

School

Cycles 1–3:

100 per cent	S	*sobresaliente*	excellent
80	N	*notable*	very good
60	Suf.	*suficiente*	pass
below 60	I	*insuficiente*	fail

Cycle 4:

Marking is on the scale 1–100 with 65 as the minimum pass-mark.

Higher

The grading scale is 0–10 (maximum) with 7 as the minimum pass-mark.

The symbols used are:

A *Curso Aprobado* (course passed). It is only used when the course does not carry credit and therefore is not marked on the above numerical scale.

P   *Reprobado* (failed). This generally applies to practical courses, e.g. laboratory work where some of the requirements have not been fulfilled. P generally equates to 5.

RJ   *Retiro Justificado*. Used when a student has been authorized to withdraw from a course without penalty.

E   *Escolaridad Ganada*. Used in cases where the student has not passed a course, but has no marks below 6. The student is permitted to undertake further examinations and enrol in the following course even if the course in which an E has been obtained is a prerequisite.

SCHOOL EDUCATION

Basic education consists of three cycles of three years each. There is also a fourth three-year cycle which is not compulsory.

Pre-primary

Kindergarten courses generally last only one year. The number of pre-primary schools is increasing although they are mainly situated in urban areas.

Primary

This covers six years divided into cycle 1 and cycle 2 each lasting three years. Promotion to each successive grade is based on continuous assessment requiring marks of 60 and above. On successful completion of cycle 2 the student is awarded a certificate.

Secondary

This covers five or six years divided into cycle 3, the last three years of basic education, and cycle 4 (or the diversified cycle) of two or three years.

On entering cycle 3, pupils choose an academic course or a technical/vocational programme. At the end of this cycle a certificate is awarded.

In cycle 4, pupils choose an academic course lasting two years or a technical course lasting three years. Both courses follow a core curriculum including Spanish, social studies, mathematics, science and foreign languages, in addition to the specialized subjects. Satisfactory completion of this cycle leads to the secondary school-leaving certificate, the **Bachillerato**.

HIGHER EDUCATION

Entrance to first degree courses is based on the **Bachillerato** and an entrance examination.

There are seven state institutions of higher education: five universities, including a distance learning university, and two institutes. The five state universities are: the Universidad de Costa Rica, the Universidad Nacional, the Universidad para la Paz, the Universidad Latinoamericana de Ciencia y Technologia, and the Universidad Estatal a Distancia. The Instituto Tecnologica de Costa Rica, and the Instituto Centroamericano de Administracion de Empresas also award first degrees. There are also several private universities, notably the Universidad Autonoma de Centro América, the Universidad Internacional de las Americas and the Universidad Hispanoamericana.

The award of **Bachiller** or **Bachillerato Universitario** is normally obtained after four years' study and a **Licenciado** after five years.

A **Maestria** degree normally requires two years' study after a first degree and a **Doctorado** a further two years beyond a **Maestria**.

To complete the academic requirements of a degree course, students must obtain the prescribed number of credits. For example, the requirements are for **Bachiller** 120–144 credits, **Licenciatura** 30–36 credits beyond **Bachiller**, **Maestria** 60–72 beyond **Bachiller**, and **Doctorado** 100–120 beyond the **Bachiller**.

The Universidad Autonoma de Centro América follows its own system of academic units, e.g. to qualify for the **Bachiller**, students must complete at least 72 units. Each four-month period (three per academic year) comprises 12 units. The **Maestria** requires at least 48 more units.

The Instituto Tecnologica de Costa Rica, which has university status, offers courses for those aiming at professional and middle-level technical careers in agriculture, industry, mining, computer sciences and business administration. The **Bachiller** degree normally lasts three years, the exception being the four-year technical teachers' course, run in conjunction with the Universidad de Costa Rica, which provides the pedagogical content. On completion of the course, students receive the title *Profesor de Educacion Tecnica*. The grading scale runs from 0–100, with 70 as the minimum pass mark.

In the non-university sector, institutions are usually privately run and specialize mainly in business courses. The degrees and diplomas awarded by such institutions are not recognized in the formal education system.

TEACHER EDUCATION

Teacher training takes place solely at higher education level.

Teachers may be either:

Profesores Titulados, who possess a recognized degree or professional title in education;

Profesores Autorizados, who do not possess a title or specific degree in teaching but have qualifications in other fields;

Profesores Aspirantes, who are not qualified but are employed as teachers because of the lack of qualified personnel.

The universities, therefore, train teachers in the first category and provide up-grading courses for those in the other two categories.

Generally, the **Bachelor degree in Education** at all levels requires four years' full-time study comprising approximately 145 credits. The **Licenciado** represents a further year's study and involves completion of an extra 33 credit courses. All degrees involve periods of practical training.

ADULT EDUCATION

Special provision is made for this. At all levels (cycles 1 to 4) there are night schools, multi-purpose rural centres (*Centros Polivalentes Rurales*), literacy training projects, Saturday schools and music training available. In the private sector, opportunities exist for adult study in commercial, technical and craft subjects.

Adults may qualify for academic certificates by completing a course of study entitled *Educacion Basica por Suficienza* which is considered the equivalent of completion of cycles 1 and 2; and the **Bachillerato por Madurez** which is equivalent to the certificate awarded on completion of cycles 3 and 4 of the formal system.

Côte d'Ivoire
(Ivory Coast)

The education system is based on the French system.

The medium of instruction is French.

The academic year runs from October to June.

EVALUATION IN BRITAIN

School

Diplôme de Bachelier de l'Enseignement du Second Degré/Baccalauréat – generally considered comparable to GCSE standard (grades A, B and C) on a subject-for-subject basis, with the exception of English language.

Further

Diplôme Universitaire de Technologie – generally considered comparable to BTEC National Diploma / N/SVQ level 3 / Advanced GNVQ/GSVQ standard; may be considered to satisfy the general entrance requirements of British higher education institutions.

Higher

Diplôme Universitaire d'Etudes Littéraires (DUEL), **Diplôme Universitaire d'Etudes Scientifiques** (DUES), **Diplôme d'Etudes Economiques Générales** (DEG), **Diplôme d'Etudes Juridiques Générales** (DEJG) – may be considered to satisfy the general entrance requirements of British higher education institutions.

Licence – generally considered comparable to a standard between GCE Advanced and British Bachelor degree; may be given advanced standing in British higher education institutions.

Maîtrise – generally considered comparable to British Bachelor (Ordinary) degree standard but where very high marks have been achieved candidates may be considered for admission to postgraduate study.

Teaching

CAPES – generally considered comparable to British Bachelor (Ordinary) degree standard.

Côte d'Ivoire (Ivory Coast)

MARKING SYSTEM

School and Higher

Marking is on the scale 0–20; the minimum pass-mark is 10

16-20	*très bien*	very good
14-15	*bien*	good
12-13	*assez bien*	quite good
11	*passable*	average

SCHOOL EDUCATION

Primary

This covers six years from the age of six or seven, divided into two-year cycles:

cours préparatoire	CP1, CP2
cours élémentaire	CE1, CE2
cours moyen	CM1, CM2

On completion of the final year, pupils take an examination leading to the **Certificat d'Etudes Primaires Elémentaires** (CEPE).

Secondary

This covers seven years, with classes numbered in reverse order. It is divided into a four-year lower cycle followed by a three-year upper cycle. The first cycle may be taken at a *College d'Enseignement Général*, a *Collège Moderne* or *Lycée* and culminates in the examinations for the **Brevet d'Etudes du Premier Cycle** (BEPC).

In the upper cycle pupils may specialize in a general/academic or technical course. The former is available only at a *Lycée*, and in two options: classical or modern (i.e. specializing in mathematics, modern languages or science).

After this cycle, pupils take the examinations for the **Diplôme de Bachelier de l'Enseignement du Second Degré/Baccalauréat** in one of seven options, depending on the specialization already studied. Several options have specialized sub-options.

A	philosophy – letters
B	economics and social studies
C	mathematics and physical sciences
D	mathematics, agricultural sciences and natural sciences
E	mathematics
F	technical
G	secretarial and accounting

Technical secondary

After a two-year lower secondary course, pupils undertake a three-year course at a *Collège d'Enseignement Technique* or a *Lycée Professionnel*, leading to a **Certificat d'Aptitude Professionnelle** (CAP) and later to the **Brevet d'Etudes Professionnelles** (BEP).

After a two-year upper secondary course, pupils may obtain a **Brevet d'Etudes Commerciales/Industrielles**.

The **Baccalauréat/Bachelier Technicien/Technique** may be obtained on completion of the three-year upper-secondary technical course, usually at *Lycées Techniques*.

FURTHER EDUCATION

The *Instituts Universitaires de Technologie* offer courses for holders of the **Baccalauréat**, leading to a **Diplôme Universitaire de Technologie** after two years' study.

HIGHER EDUCATION

The only university, the <u>Université Nationale de Côte d'Ivoire</u>, (previously <u>University of Abidjan</u>), originated in the <u>Centre d'Enseignement Supérieur</u> established in 1958. It acquired university status in 1964 and adopted its present title in 1976.

Two years of study lead to:

Diplôme Universitaire d'Etudes Littéraires (DUEL)	arts
Diplôme Universitaire d'Etudes Scientifiques (DUES)	sciences
Diplôme d'Etudes Economiques Générales (DEEG)	economics
Diplôme d'Etudes Juridiques Générales (DEJG)	law

A further year of study in the humanities and science subjects leads to the **Licence**, two years for law and economics. The period can vary, depending on the length of time spent by the students in obtaining the requisite number of **Certificats d'Etudes Supérieures**.

The **Maîtrise** in arts and science subjects takes one year after the **Licence** is obtained and includes a mini-thesis.

The **Diplôme d'Etudes Approfondies** (DEA) is obtained after a one-year taught course. A minimum of one year's approved research then leads (in science, law and economics) to the **Diplôme d'Etudes Supérieures** or to the **Doctorat de Specialité de Troisième Cycle**. In medicine and technology this stage leads to the professional qualification of **Docteur** and **Ingénieur** respectively.

The qualifications of **Ingénieur-Docteur** and **Doctorat d'Etat** may be obtained after many more years of original research. The **Doctorat d'Université** is only awarded to foreign students but is similar in standard to the **Doctorat d'Etat**.

There are *Grandes Ecoles* which award their own diplomas after five years' post-**Baccalauréat** study. These are professional qualifications and are of a higher level than the **Licence**.

TEACHER EDUCATION

Primary

A three-year course for holders of the **Baccalauréat** or **Brevet Technique** leads to the **Diplôme d'Instituteur Stagiaire**.

Secondary

Lower

A one-year course for holders of the **Baccalauréat** leads to the **Certificat d'Aptitude Pédagogique pour l'Enseignement du Second Degré**. A three-year programme (two-three year course plus one year's teaching practice and classroom evaluation) leads to the **Certificat d'Aptitude Pédagogique pour les Collèges d'Enseignement Général de Premier Cycle du Second Degré** (CAP/CEG). Holders of this qualification may then go to university for a further year to obtain the **Licence**.

Upper

Teachers for this level may do a **Licence d'Enseignement** or a one-year course followed by a one-year supervised and examined teaching practice if they already hold a degree. This leads to the **Certificat d'Aptitude Pédagogique pour l'Enseignement Secondaire** (CAPES).

Former Yugoslav Republic of Croatia

The republic of Croatia became an independent state in 1991. Before then, it was one of the six republics of the former Yugoslavia. Croatia inherited the federal educational system. However, independence has brought about modifications in the school curricula, subject content and in the administration of educational institutions. The present educational system is regulated by laws enacted in 1992.

Prior to 1991, all educational systems in Croatia were state-run. This is still the case for the majority of institutions, however some new private schools have been established.

Compulsory education covers the period of basic education; that is, eight years between ages six or seven and fourteen.

The medium of instruction is Croatian.

The academic year runs from September/October to June.

EVALUATION IN BRITAIN

School

Matura (before 1980 from the *Gimnazije* – academic upper secondary school)/ **Secondary School-Leaving Diploma** (before 1980 from a technical secondary school) – may be considered to satisfy the general entrance requirements of British higher education institutions.

Secondary School-Leaving Diploma (obtained since 1980) – generally considered to satisfy the general entrance requirements of British higher education institutions.

Medunarodna matura (identical to the International Baccalaureat) obtained from some *Gimnazija* (secondary schools) in Zagreb and Varazdin – may be considered to satisfy the general entrance requirements of British higher education institutions.

Higher

Vise Obrazovanje/Level VI/1 (first-level degree obtained on completion of a two to three-year course) – generally considered comparable to a standard between GCE Advanced and British Bachelor degree; may be considered for advanced standing by British higher education institutions.

Visoko Obrazovanja/Level VII/1 (second-level degree obtained on completion of a four to six-year course) – generally considered comparable to British Bachelor (Ordinary) degree standard; students with high grades may be considered for admission to taught Master's degree programmes.

Magistar/Level VII/2 – generally considered comparable to British Master's degree standard.

Docktor/Level VIII – generally considered comparable to British PhD standard.

MARKING SYSTEM

School

Marking is on the scale 1–5 (maximum), with 2 as the minimum pass-mark.

Higher

Student's knowledge is tested and graded during the academic year, and the final grade established by an examination. An examination in the same subject can be taken a maximum of four times. A student who does not pass the examination at the fourth attempt is obliged to re-enrol in that subject in the following academic year. If the student fails the examination in the following academic year, he/she loses the right to study at that institution.

The examinations can be oral or written or a combination of the two.

Marking is on the scale 1–5 (maximum), with 2 as the minimum pass-mark.

5	excellent
4	very good
3	good
2	satisfactory
1	unsatisfactory

SCHOOL EDUCATION

Pre-primary

Limited facilities are available in crèches (*Jaslice*) for children to age three and kindergartens (*Djeci Vrtic*) for children aged from three years to seven years. Kindergartens have been established according to Montessori, Waldorf, religious and other educational principles. Apart from kindergartens and nursery school programmes, a number of alternative pre-primary programmes are being developed. These programmes, lasting two to three hours, include: music; art; dance and sport; and early foreign language education.

Primary

This period of schooling (*Osnova Skola*) covers eight years from age six or seven to age fourteen. The period is divided into two stages: classes one to four and five to eight. A school year has three terms and pupils are marked in each term, with the mark from the final term being the one that matters.

In most primary schools pupils begin studying one of the following foreign languages in the fifth grade: English, German, Italian or French. However, in some primary schools in Zagreb, Osijek and Split, an experimental scheme to teach foreign languages to first grade pupils began in 1991. This is part of a Council of Europe project.

Secondary

Secondary education comprises grammar schools (*Gimnazija*), vocational schools (*Strukovna Skola*) and art schools (*Umjetnicka Skola*).

Grammar schools (*Gimnazija*)

Grammar schools are divided into general, linguistic, classical and scientific. A typical *Gimnazija* curriculum comprises Croatian, two foreign languages, Latin and Greek (in the classical *Gimnazija*), arts, psychology, philosophy, sociology, history, geography, mathematics, physics, chemistry, biology, information technology and sport. Some *Gimnazija* specialize in science/mathematics and others in humanities/social studies and languages.

Entrance to *Gimnazija* is by a selective test.

The academic cycle covers four years at this level. The final school-leaving examination is the **Matura**. The matriculation certificate (*Maturalna Svjedodzba*) is awarded to pupils who pass the **Matura**.

Vocational schools (*Stukovna Skola*)

Vocational schools offer courses lasting three or four years, including a period of practical instruction. On completion of the course, pupils take the examinations for the **Matura** and a vocational qualification.

Admission is by competition.

The curricula of technical and related schools (medical, catering, trade, tourist or administration schools) consist of general and specific vocational subjects.

Art schools (*Umjetnicka Skola*)

Art schools offer courses lasting four years and include music, dance, visual art and design. The music and dance programmes are identical to those offered in the *Gimnazija*, although the attendance of science classes is not obligatory. The remaining curriculum consists of theoretical and practical professional training.

The final examination (*Zavrsni Ispit*) for both vocational and art schools leads to the award of a **School-Leaving Certificate** (*Svejedodzba o Zavrsnom Ispitu*), with a vocational or artistic qualification.

FURTHER EDUCATION

The Law of Higher Education, which regulates all aspects of further and higher education in Croatia, was adopted by the Croatian Parliament on 8 October 1993, and published in the official publication *Narodne Novine*, No. 96, on 25 October 1993.

Further and higher education is provided at universities, polytechnics, faculties, academies and higher schools.

Higher Schools (*Visa Skola*)

Higher Schools were part of the university system until the end of the academic year 1994/95. Courses lasted for at least four semesters and led to the award of a professionally-orientated degree or **Vise Obrazovanje**.

The new law anticipates the change in status of the Higher Schools. They will eventually become Polytechnic Schools (*Veleuciliste Skola*), and will offer professionally oriented undergraduate studies lasting from one to four years. The final award will be the **Diplom**, issued at Level VI/1.

HIGHER EDUCATION

The higher education system consists of two types of study at either university or professional level.

General entrance requirements to higher education are a **Secondary School-Leaving Certificate** obtained after twelve years of schooling and an entrance examination administered by the individual faculty. Higher education institutions are authorized to set special entry requirements for certain professional fields of study. Selection is based on a points system, which includes the number of points acquired on the high school records of a candidate, and on tests (written or oral). The entrance examination enables the institution to compare candidates from various secondary schools.

The academic year begins on 1 October and ends on 30 September the following year. It is divided into two semesters, winter and summer. The language of instruction is Croatian, with some courses at the University of Rijeka in Italian.

The four universities in Croatia are:

The University of Osijek (which incorporates the Faculty of Economics formerly attached to the University of Zagreb. This is an independent, self-governing institution.

The University of Rijeka (which also incorporates faculties formerly attached to the University of Zagreb). This is governed by an assembly (*Skupsina*) and a university council (*Savjet Sveucilista*).

The University of Split (which also incorporates faculties formerly attached to the University of Zagreb). This is an independent, self-governing institution financed by the Republic.

The University of Zagreb, which is a self-governing public institution.

University study

Undergraduate university study qualifies the student for highly specialized, artistic or scientific work. Courses last at least four years and lead to the award of **Diploma**. The **Diploma** is issued at Level VII/1.

After graduation, students can go on to study for a **Magistar** (master's degree) in either arts or science subjects. In both arts and science subjects, students must defend a master's thesis (*Strucni Rad/Umjetnicki Rad*). Students who complete a postgraduate course in art at a polytechnic attain the professional title of Master of Arts in accordance with a separate law. The final award is the **Diploma,** which is issued at Level VII/2.

The final, postgraduate qualification is the **Doktor** (Doctor of Science). Graduate scientific study is concluded with the production and defence of a scientific doctoral thesis (*Doktorski Rad*). The final award is the **Diploma**, issued at Level VIII.

Professional study

Undergraduate professional study is offered at the new Polytechnics (*Veleuciliste*). They provide professionally oriented undergraduate studies (usually in the arts), lasting from one to four years. The final award is the **Diploma**, issued at Level VI/1.

After graduation, students can go on to study for a postgraduate, specialist degree. The final award is the **Diploma**, issued at either **Magistar** standard (Level VII/2) or **Doktor** standard (Level VIII).

TEACHER EDUCATION

Pre-school, primary and secondary school teachers are educated in institutions of higher education.

Cuba

The following chapter regarding the Education System in Cuba is based on information obtained for the 3rd edition of this Guide, published in 1991, as NARIC has been unable to obtain more recent information.

Since Fidel Castro came to power in 1959, education in Cuba has undergone major changes, with the emphasis on education for the population as a whole and the development of skills necessary for the country's economy.

Primary and secondary education are compulsory.

The medium of instruction is Spanish. Learning English is compulsory in all secondary schools.

The academic year runs from September to July.

EVALUATION IN BRITAIN

School

Secondary School Completion Diploma – generally considered to be below GCSE standard.

Pre-University Course – generally considered comparable to GCSE standard (grades A, B and C) on a subject-for-subject basis, with the exception of English language.

Higher

Licenciado/Professional title – generally considered comparable to British Bachelor degree standard if awarded after four or more years of study.

MARKING SYSTEM

The following grades are used throughout:

90–100	*obresaliente*	excellent
80–89	*aprovechado*	above average
70–79	*aprobado*	pass
Below 70	*desaprobado*	fail

SCHOOL EDUCATION

Primary

This covers grades 1–6.

Secondary

After primary school, pupils have two options: basic secondary school or lower secondary technical school.

Basic secondary school

This three-year course involves academic and practical studies. Apart from academic studies, students from Havana and other large towns and cities regularly work for a period of forty-five days in agricultural production at *Escuelas al Campo* which are co-educational lower secondary boarding schools in the country.

Those who complete basic secondary school are awarded the **Secondary School Completion Diploma** and may go on to various kinds of upper secondary institution.

Students continuing their education follow a three-year pre-university course.

Technical schools

Escuelas Tecnologicas (technical schools) offer general education and training in various technical subjects. Training leads to two levels of qualification – skilled worker and middle-level technician. These correspond, respectively, to the completion of the second and third year of the basic secondary course. Successful completion of technical school grants access to the technological institutes.

HIGHER EDUCATION

Entry to tertiary education depends on success in the **national competitive examination** (held since 1983) and a perceived and proven attitude in relevant subjects – this allows automatic entry for those scoring over 92/100, with the distribution of places to lower categories determined by the places remaining.

There are four categories of tertiary education institution (*Centros de Ensconza Superior*):

Universities: The four universities, Havana, Oriente (at Santiago), Central de las Villas and Camaguey (originally the Centro Universitario), cover natural sciences, mathematics, humanities and economics.

Centros Universitarios: These university centres, at Pinas del Rio and Matanzas, are in the process of being upgraded to universities.

Institutos Superiores Politecnicos: These two institutions, at Havana and Santiago, specialize in technical sciences relevant to the economy.

Institutos Superiores: These thirty-eight tertiary institutions are more vocational in orientation. There are also forty-two affiliated institutes (*Filiales*) where workers are able to pursue sandwich courses in specialist disciplines.

First degree courses normally last five years; they lead to a **Licenciado** or a **Professional title**.

TEACHER EDUCATION

Primary

Since 1990 all primary teachers have followed a degree course. They are allowed sabbatical years to concentrate on degree studies. It is hoped that they will be able to take a sabbatical every seven years to maintain and improve their standards.

Secondary

Teachers are trained at three institutes of education (within the <u>Universities of Havana</u>, <u>Las Villas</u> and <u>Oriente</u>) which offer five-year courses to qualify students for basic secondary and upper secondary teachers' certificates. The admission requirement is the **Secondary School Completion Diploma**.

Cyprus

Under the 1960 Constitution, education is the responsibility of the Greek-Cypriot and Turkish-Cypriot communities separately, a separation which subsequent events have perpetuated. At secondary level in particular, identification with the education systems of Greece and Turkey, respectively, is strong.

In the south (Greek-Cypriot) there are many private educational institutions at all levels but there are few in the north (Turkish-Cypriot). For Greek-Cypriots primary education has been compulsory since 1962. For Turkish-Cypriots it has been compulsory since 1986. For Greek-Cypriots, secondary education, at the *Gymnasium* level (first three-year cycle) has been compulsory since 1984. Compulsory education is therefore up to age 15, and the *Lyceum* level (second three-year cycle) is not compulsory.

The academic year runs from September to June. For Greek-Cypriots the academic year is broken down into three terms with two-week breaks during Christmas and Easter. For Turkish-Cypriots the academic year is broken down into two semesters with a two-week break from 1 to 16 February.

Greek and Turkish are the media of instruction in most schools in the south and north respectively. Most private schools are English medium. There are five Turkish-Cypriot public English-medium schools. At almost all further and higher education, with the exception of the <u>University of Cyprus</u>, the medium of instruction is English.

EVALUATION IN BRITAIN

School

Apolytirion of Lykeion – generally considered comparable to GCSE (grades A, B and C) on a subject-for-subject basis (where pupils have obtained marks of over 10 in subjects which may be taken in the GCSE examinations, with the exception of English language).

Some universities accept the **Apolytirion of Lykeion** as satisfying the general entrance requirements provided that it is obtained with a minimum overall average of at least 17.

Lise Bitirme Diploma – generally considered comparable to GCSE (grades A, B and C) on a subject-for-subject basis (where pupils have obtained marks of over 50 per cent in subjects which may be taken in the GCSE examinations, with the exception of English language). A minimum overall average of 8 may be acceptable for entry to higher education.

Further

The **Diploma** awarded by the <u>Higher Technical Institute</u> after a three-year full-time course is generally considered comparable to a BTEC Higher National Diploma / N/SVQ level 4.

Turkish-Cypriots can obtain this diploma from the University of the Eastern Mediterranean.

Higher

Ptychion (from University of Cyprus) – generally considered comparable to British Bachelor degree standard.

MARKING SYSTEMS

School

Greek-Cypriot system: 1–20, minimum pass-mark 10
Turkish-Cypriot system: 1–10, minimum pass-mark 5

Examinations for the final year in the Greek-Cypriot system are set externally by the Ministry of Education. They are marked by panels of teachers who receive anonymous scripts.

The final subject mark is a combination of: 70 per cent of the internal school subject examination plus 30 per cent of the external subject examination. Greek and general maths are obligatory. Four to five other subjects are taken, most of which are given a combined mark.

Examinations in the Turkish-Cypriot system are internally assessed and there can be considerable variations in standard between schools.

SCHOOL EDUCATION

Pre-primary

Public provision has expanded considerably on the Greek-Cypriot side in recent years. There are now nursery schools and classes in ordinary schools. There are also many private nursery schools.

On the Turkish-Cypriot side, in about half of the ordinary schools, there are nursery classes. There are also five private nursery schools.

Primary

This covers six years for children from age five-and-a-half in the Greek-Cypriot system, and five years for children from age six in the Turkish-Cypriot system.

The curriculum consists of Greek or Turkish, English (in the last three years in Greek-Cypriot schools and two years in Turkish-Cypriot schools), religious instruction, mathematics, natural science, history, geography, handiwork and art, music, agriculture and domestic science, physical education and general education (including hygiene).

Secondary

Public education is comprehensive and co-educational and covers six years in both systems, divided into two three-year cycles.

Greek-Cypriot: three years' *Gymnasium*, followed by three years' *Lyceum*.

Turkish-Cypriot: three years' middle school (*Ortaokul*), followed by three years' *Lise*.

Most pupils complete all six years.

Entrance to the first cycle at the public schools is automatic.

Most Greek-Cypriot private schools have competitive entrance examinations in Greek and mathematics.

In the Turkish-Cypriot English-medium schools (Nicosia Turk Maarif Koleji, Bayraktar Turk Maarif Koleji, Famagusta Turk Maarif Koleji, Morphou Turk Maarif Koleji and Kyrenia Turk Maarif Koleji) there are also competitive entrance examinations in Turkish, mathematics, science, history, geography and English (started in 1992).

In both systems the first cycle is common for all pupils and consists of:

Greek-Cypriot ancient and modern Greek, English, French, general science, history, civics, geography, religious knowledge, music, art, design technology, home economics and physical education.

Turkish-Cypriot Turkish, English, mathematics, general science, social studies (history, civics, geography), ethics, music, art and physical education; optional subjects are religious knowledge, agriculture, home economics, craft and (in some schools) French and/or German.

In the second cycle, the Greek-Cypriot system offers a scheme of options, the five main fields of specialization being classical (humanities), science, economics, commercial/secretarial, and foreign languages. Half of the teaching periods are still, however, devoted to the compulsory core-curriculum, consisting of ancient and modern Greek, English, French, mathematics, physics, chemistry, history, civics, religion, gymnastics, and in the first year, general science, music and art. On completion of this cycle, pupils take the examinations for the **Apolytirion**, in which English is a compulsory subject. It is set by each school individually. Many students take **GCE Advanced** at the same time.

In the Turkish-Cypriot system, the curriculum in the first year of the *Lise* is very similar to that of the first cycle. Specialization begins in the second year, when pupils with good grades in science and mathematics may choose to enter the science stream while the remainder go into the arts streams. In the third year the science stream subdivides into natural sciences (with the emphasis on biology and chemistry) and mathematics (mathematics and chemistry). The compulsory core-curriculum is Turkish, English, history, civics, ethics, physical education and (second year only) psychology, mathematics, (third year only) philosophy. The English-medium school, Turk Maarif Kolejleri, in common with other *Lises*, prepares pupils for the **Lise Bitirme Diplomasi**, in which English is a compulsory subject, and for the entrance examination to universities in Turkey. In addition, the Turk Maarif Kolejleri prepares pupils for TOEFL (Teaching of English as a foreign language) and British GCSE examinations.

Before 1951, the examinations held at the end of the secondary cycle were the **Colony of Cyprus Ordinary** and **Distinction Examinations**. They were superseded by the **Cyprus Certificate Examinations** which lasted until 1959. From 1960 until 1990 all examinations were school based. Since 1991 the examinations for the final year in the Greek system called the **Common Unified Final Exams** are set externally by the Ministry of Education and are graded by independent teachers.

Parallel to the morning school classes many Greek-Cypriot public school pupils study privately for outside examinations such as Greek University Entrance, GCSE and C&G

examinations as well as IELTS and TOEFL English language tests.

Most Greek-Cypriot private schools have competitive entrance examinations in Greek and mathematics and work towards GCSE examinations as well as providing a certificate of six years attendance.

There are plans to introduce a new **Cyprus Certificate of Education** but this is unlikely in the near future (as at November 1994). It will be an examination more or less along the same lines as British GCE A levels.

Technical and vocational

Greek-Cypriot

Schools in this category aim to provide local industry with technicians and craftsmen and to prepare pupils for continuing their education in higher education institutions in Greece and Cyprus. These schools accept pupils at the second stage of secondary education, beginning in the fourth year. Each school has two departments, technical and vocational. The technical department lays emphasis on theory and practice in science and technical knowledge and skills while the vocational department provides training for craftsmen and various service trades.

Turkish-Cypriot

About one-third of pupils at upper secondary level attend these schools. All but one cater for upper secondary level only and offer three-year courses either in commercial or technical subjects; there are also two vocational schools for girls.

In the technical schools, pupils choose a combination of subjects from the following: plumbing, sanitary engineering and metal work, electronics, electrical engineering, welding, technical drawing, woodwork and carpentry, fitting, automobile engineering, and building (one school).

Developments in the Greek-Cypriot Education System

There is increasing pressure to create a curriculum that reflects the changing social and technical need of future generations and to meet the many challenges facing education. Current or proposed changes are:

the introduction of the concept of a nine year cycle (six years primary and three *Gymnasium* years) into schools aiming at coherence and progression in the education system;

the proposed major reform of merging the *Lyceums* with the technical schools and creating new *Lyceums* in which students will have access to a wide range of subjects with opportunities to combine academic and vocational courses;

as from September 1994 the Ministry of Education has introduced, on an experimental basis in three *Lyceums*, an new system known as the Comprehensive *Lyceum*. The first year of these institutions will be a common core year. In the second year students will be taught twenty hours a week in common core subjects and fifteen hours in three subjects chosen from a wide range. In the third year they will be taught ten hours of core subjects and twenty from their chosen subjects.

FURTHER EDUCATION

Greek-Cypriot

A large number of students who continue their education do so abroad. In Cyprus the Higher Technical Institute offers three-year English-medium courses, training technician engineers (civil, electrical and mechanical) for industry and the merchant marine service and teachers for the technical schools. Other public-sector institutions offering full-time courses of between one and three years are the Hotel and Catering Institute, the Forestry College and the Schools of Nursing and Midwifery and the Mediterranean Institute of Management. There is a rapidly growing number of students, including foreign entrants, at institutions in the private sector, most of which concentrate on secretarial or business studies and work towards internal diplomas and British professional qualifications.

Turkish-Cypriot

Most students continue their education abroad. In Cyprus, as they no longer have access to the Higher Technical Institute (which was bi-communal before 1974) a Higher Technological Institute was established in Famagusta in 1979 to offer English-medium technical engineering courses at a similar level (now the University of the Eastern Mediterranean see **HIGHER EDUCATION**). There are also small agricultural, hotel and catering, and nursing and midwifery schools.

HIGHER EDUCATION

There is compulsory military service and entry to higher education is often deferred.

Greek-Cypriot

The University of Cyprus which opened in September 1992 contains three schools (Humanities and Social Sciences, Pure and Applied Sciences and Economics and Management).

Study is organized in semesters, and subjects taught are computed in credits. Degrees last at least eight semesters. The University will offer graduate programmes and will award **Master's** and **PhD degrees.** The medium of instruction is Greek and (nominally) Turkish.

There is a tradition of private education which has resulted in recent links with American and British universities to provide training towards a degree. Private institutions offer courses such as business administration, electrical, mechanical and civil engineering, computing, accounting and banking. In most cases their examinations are associated with overseas examining bodies and institutions. They also award their own degrees and diplomas. The new law 1/87 requires registration of so-called Private Schools of Tertiary Education (PSTEs). Under this law, awards made by educational institutions abroad in collaboration with a PSTE are not recognized by the Ministry of Education.

Private institutions are, however, allowed at all levels. They are required to register with the Ministry of Education (according to the relevant law). They are inspected by the competent department of the Ministry of Education to ensure that they comply with the terms under which they have been registered. The end qualification is recognized by the Ministry of Education only if the programme of study is accredited (the accreditation process, under law 1/87, has only recently started). The medium of instruction is generally English.

Turkish-Cypriot

The Higher Technological Institute, Famagusta, was upgraded in 1986 and renamed the University of Eastern Mediterranean. Its courses are accredited by the Higher Education Council of the Republic of Turkey.

The University of the Eastern Mediterranean offers a preparatory year which has since September 1988 been devoted entirely to courses in English language to enable prospective students to move into undergraduate courses, all of which are conducted in English. This preparatory year does not lead to any formal qualification, neither would it be given official credit towards the Turkish university entrance examination.

There are two other universities, the University of Lefke founded in 1990 and the Near East University founded in 1988. Both universities are English medium. Like the University of the Eastern Mediterranean they have a preparatory English year.

TEACHER EDUCATION

Primary and pre-primary

All teachers in the public sector must have attended a three-year course after the end of upper secondary education at the Pedagogical Academy (PA) in the south and the Turkish Teacher Training College in the north.

Since the opening of the University of Cyprus the PA courses have been discontinued and a four-year degree course is offered by the University.

Secondary

Greek-Cypriot

All general secondary teachers must be graduates but few have any initial teacher training. The Pedagogical Institute of the Ministry of Education and Culture runs in-service training courses which are compulsory for probationers but voluntary for others.

Turkish-Cypriot

All teachers must be graduates of a university or a teacher training college, usually in Turkey. New entrants from universities must now also have a teaching qualification and most Turkish universities offer a pedagogical course which can be taken concurrently with the specialist subjects. There is little formal in-service training.

Czech Republic

In 1992 the Czech and Slovak Federation was dissolved and each republic became independent. In both republics, which used to form the Czech and Slovak Federative Republic, the same radical higher education reform (known as Act 172) was passed in 1991. In higher education most of the decisions affecting institutions are now devolved to the institutions from the central ministries; these include the authority to establish curricula, to regulate student numbers, to impose specific admission requirements and to create new faculties.

Education is compulsory between the ages of six and fifteen.

The medium of instruction is Czech. In some areas, tuition up to secondary level may be available in Hungarian, Polish or Ukrainian.

The academic year is from September to August, although the normal school year ends on 30 June. Students in higher education are entitled to only four weeks' summer vacation, as examinations also take place in July and August. Higher education institutions have two, fifteen-week terms, followed by examination periods.

EVALUATION IN BRITAIN

School

Maturitni Zkouška/Maturita – may be considered to satisfy the general entrance requirements of British higher education institutions.

Higher

Bakalàř – generally considered comparable to British Bachelor (Ordinary) degree standard.

Magistr (formerly **Absolvent Vysoké Skoly**)/**Professional title** – generally considered comparable to British Bachelor (Honours) degree standard.

PhDr – may be compared to a British PhD degree but requires evaluation on a case-by-case basis.

Kandidát Ved – generally considered comparable to British PhD degree standard.

Doktor – generally considered comparable to British DLitt/DSc degree standard.

MARKING SYSTEMS

School

1	*výborný*	excellent
2	*chvalitebný*	very good
3	*dobrý*	good
4	*dostatečný*	pass
5	*nedostatečný*	fail

Higher

výborně	excellent
velmi dobře	good
dobře	pass
nevyhověl	fail

SCHOOL EDUCATION

Pre-primary

Facilities are available in crèches (*Jesle*) for children aged one to three and in nurseries (*Materšká Skola*) for children aged four to six.

Basic

The system consists of a nine-year primary and lower secondary course of so-called basic education (*Základní Všeobecná*) to coincide with the period of compulsory education, followed by a four-year upper secondary course. Basic education is divided into lower and upper cycles and the compulsory subjects are mother tongue (Czech or in some areas, Hungarian, Polish, Ukrainian or German), history, geography, mathematics, civics, general science, physical education, art, music and work training. Some specialization is possible from grade 5 and progress to each grade is made by continuous assessment.

Secondary

Upper secondary education (*Střední Všeobecná*) can be taken in a general secondary school (*Gymnasium*), a secondary vocational school, or a secondary technical school. All courses last four years and culminate in the matriculation examination, **Vysvědčení o Maturitní Zkouška** or **Maturita**. In general, secondary school students specialize in either science, humanities or mathematics, but spend most of their time on the general core subjects of Czech language and literature, one modern language, mathematics, history, geography, physics, chemistry, biology, physical education and, since 1987, information science and computer technology. There are a number of foreign-language-medium secondary schools (English, German, Spanish, French) and English is likely to be taught more and more widely, at the expense of Russian and, possibly, German. The **Maturita** examinations are normally taken in only four subjects: Czech, one modern language, mathematics (for science specialists) or history (for humanities specialists) and one subject of the pupil's choice. The **Maturita** following the vocational secondary course of vocational training and general education, involves Czech, one modern language, technical subjects and the preparation of a project.

Apprentice schools (*Ucňovská Skola*)/training centres (*Odborné Učiliště*) run by major industrial concerns, offer courses of two to four years for pupils who have eight years' basic education. The courses contain an element of general education and train pupils to become skilled workers; they may then apply to technical universities on passing the **Maturitni Zkouška**.

Secondary schools for workers (*Střední Skola pro Pracující*) offer courses of evening study for pupils who left school after eight years' basic education. These last five years and lead to the examinations for the **Maturitni Zkouška (Maturita)**.

FURTHER EDUCATION

External studies may be carried out at secondary schools, possibly leading to the **Maturita** for those who have not previously completed the full secondary education course or for those who wish to qualify or retrain in a discipline different from that originally followed. External studies are also possible at universities or their equivalent; a degree course followed thus usually takes one year longer than when completed by full-time study.

Specialist institutions such as language schools, people's schools of art or shorthand institutes cater for people wishing to acquire new skills. At a language school, for example, students may eventually take the **Státní Zkouška** (State Examination) which brings them to the same level as a university graduate.

Factories and other work organizations provide courses related to their own interests, while local 'houses of culture' (*Dům Kultůry*) offer classes in mainly non-academic pastimes and activities.

HIGHER EDUCATION

Until 1990, the level of enrolment was planned and set by the Ministry of Education, Youth and Sport. In 1990 state planning was abolished. Now the higher education institutions specify the number of enrolments independently. They decide whether they will set entrance examinations or not.

In 1994, there were twenty-three higher education institutions in the Czech Republic, including new universities which were founded in regional centres (eight multi-disciplinary universities, four technical universities, one veterinary university, one economic university, two universities of chemical technology, two universities of agriculture and forestry, one higher school of education, four academies of arts). Three universities have a traditional structure – they are made up of faculties of humanities, social sciences, natural science and medicine. Newly founded universities are composed of faculties of education, natural sciences, technology, agriculture, etc. The two technical universities have a traditional structure; they contain the faculties of mechanical engineering, electrotechnics, architecture and civil engineering.

Admission to higher education institutions

In general, an applicant for study at a higher education institution is expected to have a school-leaving certificate from a Czech secondary school (called **Maturita**) or final certificate of secondary education received abroad which is recognized by the Ministry of Education of the Czech Republic or which is from a state that has signed the agreement with the Czech Republic (or with the former Czech and Slovak Federal Republic). Individual higher education institutions or faculties have different entrance requirements based on the results obtained at secondary school and an entrance examination. The most common form of entrance examination is a written test on general knowledge in humanities, science and languages. The second part of the examination is oral. It is focused on students' interests and their preliminary knowledge in the field of study they have chosen. Academies of performing arts and music, academies of fine arts and applied arts and faculties of architecture also examine the level of respective artistic talent.

Structure of study

The new Higher Education Act from 1990 has established a short form of study (bachelor study – *bakalarske studium*) which is usually three years (exceptionally four years) in length. The length of study after which the academic degrees of magister (**magistr**) or engineer (**inzenyr**) is granted is usually five years (maximum six years). Each higher education institution can set fields of study, curricula and the length of study independently.

Academic degrees

Until 1990, the majority of fields of study were completed by a state final examination. It consisted of the defence of a diploma thesis or diploma project and an oral examination. Graduates of universities were not awarded any title. Only in medicine and veterinary first-degree studies were graduates awarded the degree **Doktor mediciny** (MUDr) and **Doktor veterinarni mediciny** (MVDr). The degree **Inzenyr** (Ing) was given to graduates of technical universities, technical institutes, agricultural universities and economic universities. These titles were always used before one's name. The graduates of universities who had completed their first-degree studies with a state final examination were allowed to take the state rigorosum examination (**statni rigorozni zkouska**). This examination was aimed at assessing the graduates' expertise in their specialization. On passing the examination, the graduates were awarded the following degrees according to the field of study.

> Doctor of Law – **Doktor prav** (JUDr)
> Doctor of Philosophy – **Doktor filozofie** (PHDr)
> Doctor of Natural Sciences – **Doktor prirodnich ved** (RMDr)
> Doctor of Pedagogy – **Doktor pedagogiky** (PaedDr)
> Doctor of Pharmacy – **Doktor farmacie** (PharmDr)
> Doctor of Socio-political Sciences – **Doktor sociane politickych ved** (RSDr)

The new Higher Education Act has established vertically structured, three-level study. The undergraduate study is completed with a state examination. If it is required by the statute of a faculty, the defence of a thesis is a part of the state examination. Since 1990, a higher education institution can offer a short course of study (three to four years) after completion of which certificates are issued, or graduates are awarded the degree of 'Bachelor', **Bakalář** (Bc). Graduates of long studies (five to six years) are granted the following academic degrees:

> **Magistr** (Mgr) at institutions offering programmes of an artistic or theological character
> **Inzenyr** (Ing) at institutions of technical, economic and agricultural character
>
> **Doktor mediciny** (MUDr) at faculties of medicine
> **Doktor veterinarni mediciny** (MVDr) at faculties of veterinary medicine

Postgraduate study

At the postgraduate level, the *Aspirantura* involving the preparation of a thesis and a minimum of three years' full-time or five years' part-time study used to lead to the **Candidatus Scientiarum/Kandidát ved** (CSC). A further indeterminate period of research could lead to the **Doctor of Science/Doktor ved** (DrSc). Beginning in 1990, higher education institutions established postgraduate study of a new kind. This study (doctoral study) prepares graduates for research work. Postgraduates are awarded the academic-scientific degree of **Doktor** (Dr). Previous forms of research training were cancelled. After many years of research, those university teachers and researchers who have achieved excellent results in their performance and have published distinguished research works, can submit their doctoral dissertations for their defence. After a successful defence, they are awarded the highest scientific degree **Doktor ved** (DRSc).

TEACHER EDUCATION

Kindergarten

Teachers follow a four-year course after eight years' basic education or a two-year course for holders of the **Maturitni Zkouška (Maturita)**. There is also a five-year part-time course at university.

Primary (lower cycle)

Teachers follow a four-year course for holders of the **Maturita** at a pedagogical faculty.

Primary (upper cycle) and secondary

Students of any faculty studying subjects taught at either of these levels normally have to include a pedagogical element as part of their first degree. In this case, they have to study two main subjects, e.g. English and Russian, whereas if they choose to follow the purely academic, non-pedagogical option, only one subject need be studied.

Alternatively, a student may be based at a university pedagogical faculty in which case the pedagogical content will be relatively greater and the academic content relatively smaller than if the student studied in the relevant subject faculty. Pedagogical qualifications may also be obtained by study at a university's pedagogical faculty or an equivalent institution's pedagogical department after the completion of first-degree studies containing no such element.

Denmark

The Ministry of Education is the body with overall responsibility for education at all levels. The Ministry is divided into departments, which are in charge of different levels of teaching. At primary and secondary level, the departments determine the framework for the curricula together with special subject advisers. The teachers decide the exact content of the curriculum with their pupils.

The *Folkeskole* Act of 1993, which came into force on 1st August 1994, is the basis of present primary and lower secondary education, organized as nine years' comprehensive, compulsory education, combined with an optional pre-school class and an optional tenth year.

Compulsory education was from age seven to fourteen until 1972, when it was increased to fifteen. It was increased again in 1973 to sixteen.

The medium of instruction is Danish, but English is compulsory from the fourth to the ninth/tenth form in the *Folkeskole* and is provided or required by schools offering upper secondary education for another two to three years.

The academic year runs from August/September to December and from January/February to June.

The higher education system is currently undergoing reform and change. In particular, the Government has been looking at ways of shortening courses and encouraging people to complete their degrees more quickly. In 1988 three year BA and BSc degrees were introduced and in 1993 postgraduate studies for the PhD (Licentiat before 1988) were reformed into a fairly structured three-year programme.

EVALUATION IN BRITAIN

School

Folkeskolens Udvidede Afgangsprove (10th form advanced leaving examination) – generally considered comparable to GCSE standard.

Bevis for Studentereksamen	may be considered to satisfy
Bevis for Højere Forberedelseseksamen	the general entrance
Bevis for Højere Handelseksamen	requirements of British
Bevis for Højere Teknisk Eksamen	higher education institutions.

Higher

Basisuddannelse: **Grunduddannelse/Bifagsexamen/Examen Artium** – may qualify for advanced standing from British higher education institutions.

Diplomingeniør (formerly **Teknikumingeniør**) – generally considered comparable to a British Bachelor (Ordinary) degree or N/SVQ level 4.

Bachelor of Arts (BA)/Bachelor of Science (BSc) – may be considered comparable to British Bachelor (Ordinary) degree standard.

(HA is full time, HD is its part-time equivalent)

Candidatus Philosophiae (CandPhil) – generally considered comparable to British Bachelor (Honours) degree standard, although the course lasts longer than in the UK.

Kandidateksamen/Candidatus Magisterii (CandMag)/Candidatus Medicinae (CandMed)/Candidatus Juris (CandJur), (i.e. **Candidatus** + field of study); **Magisterkonferens (Magister Artium/Magister Scientiarum)** – generally considered comparable to British Master's degree standard.

PhD (formerly Licentiat)
Doctoral (+ field of study e.g. **DrJur**/law, **DrTheol**/theology) – may be considered comparable to British PhD standard or N/SVQ level 5.

MARKING SYSTEMS

School

Since 1963

Marking is on a scale 00, 03, 05, 6, 7, 8, 9, 10, 11, 13 (maximum), and marks are divided into three main groups; excellent, average and hesitant. There is no particular mark required to pass the leaving examinations of the *Folkeskole*.

13	Given for exceptional, independent performance (very rare)
11	Given for independent and excellent performance
10	Given for excellent, but not particularly independent performance
9	Given for good performance, a little above average
8	Given for average performance
7	Given for mediocre performance, slightly below average
6	Given for somewhat hesitant but more or less satisfactory performance
05	Given for hesitant and not satisfactory performance
03	Given for very hesitant, inadequate and unsatisfactory performance
00	Given for completely unacceptable performance.

To pass the upper secondary examinations students must obtain a minimum average of 6.0 in the marks for both the year's work and for the examinations.

Higher

Until 1971

Each faculty within a university or department within other institutions of higher education had its own marking scale, e.g. 0–16, 0–15, 0–10, etc. There is usually some explanation on the transcript of marks.

Since 1971

Marking is on a scale of 00–13 (maximum); an average of 6 or, in some cases, at least 6 in each subject is required to pass. Marks given at institutions of higher education represent the student's achievement in terms of standards set by the institution in question.

13	
11	very good
10	

9	
8	good
7	

6	

05	
03	weak/unsatisfactory
00	

SCHOOL EDUCATION

Pre-primary/kindergarten (*Bornehave*)

Facilities are available for children aged two-and-a-half to seven years. All municipalities are required to offer a one-year pre-school class.

1958–76

Primary

This was a seven-year course at a *Hovedskole*. At the end of class 5 pupils could be divided into two sections/lines:

line a – mainly for pupils proceeding to classes 8, 9 and 10 of general, vocationally-oriented education;

line b – to prepare pupils for the *Realafdeling* (three-year lower-secondary course).

Secondary

Lower

There were two courses – the *Realafdeling* and the General.

Realafdeling

The seven-year course at a *Hovedskole* plus this three-year course was sometimes referred to as the *Folkeskole*. The curriculum covered most subjects including foreign languages. There was no streaming or specialization, but an emphasis on the sciences was possible in the third year. On completion of the three-year course pupils sat for the **Realeksamen**.

General

Pupils took all general subjects and vocational/educational guidance activities. At the end of class 9/10 all pupils were entitled to leave and receive a certificate testifying to their performance in the subjects taken. Most pupils, however, sat for optional state-run examinations at the end of class 9 or 10 – **Statskontrollerede Prøver efter 9. eller 10. Klasse**. The usual school grading system was used, but no specific pass-marks were required. Eligibility for entry to the *Gymnasium* was based on a statement from the school.

Upper

It was possible to enter the three-year upper secondary course at a *Gymnasium* on completion of the second year of the *Realafdeling* (lower secondary), but some pupils took the **Realeksamen** before starting *Gymnasium*.

Pupils could choose between two specializations/lines:

languages (*Sproglig Linie*) – covering from the second year social studies (offered from 1967–8), modern languages and classical languages;

mathematics (*Matematisk Linie*) – covering from the second year social studies, mathematics and physics and natural science.

On completion of the three-year course pupils took the examinations for the **Studentereksamen (Upper Secondary School Leaving Certificate)**. These consisted of four written examinations and six oral tests. The **School Leaving Certificate** showed the marks obtained in the examinations and in the final year's work. If a pupil was not examined in a subject, the year's course mark was also noted on the certificate under the main heading 'examination marks' and subsection 'transferred'.

Since 1976 (including 1988 and 1993 reforms)

Primary and secondary

The Danish education system does not differentiate between primary and lower secondary education.

Lower

According to the education act (*Folkeskolelov*) of 1975, in force from 1976, amended in 1993 (amendments in force from 1994), there is a nine-year basic comprehensive school (*Folkeskole*) and a voluntary year (class 10). On completion of class 9 all pupils are entitled to leave after sitting the **Afgangsprove** (leaving examination). On completion of class 10 pupils can sit the **Folkeskolens Udvidede Afgangsprove** (advanced leaving examination). There is no pass-mark.

There is a common curriculum for all pupils in classes 1–7. The basic syllabus covers Danish, arithmetic/mathematics, physical education, Christian studies, creative art and music. The following subjects are mandatory for certain classes, depending on the class: history, geography, biology, needlework, English, woodwork, home economics, physics, chemistry, German.

In classes 8 and 9 the compulsory subjects are Danish, arithmetic/mathematics, physical education, Christian studies, social studies, physics/chemistry, geography (class 8), biology (class 8) and English, with German being optional. Electives are creative art, music, history, needlework, drama, film, motor knowledge, vocational studies, electronics, child care, woodwork, home economics, typing, photography and informatics.

In class 10 the basic syllabus covers Danish, physical education, contemporary studies and English. In addition, schools must offer German, arithmetic/mathematics, Christian studies, religious studies, physics/chemistry and French; they may also offer the electives available in classes 8 and 9, as well as history.

At the end of the 9th class pupils take the **Afgangsprøve** (Leaving Examination) which may be taken in 11 subjects. At the end of the 10th class, they may resit the 9th class examination or take the **Udvidede Afgangsprøve** (Advanced Leaving Examination) in 5 subjects. There is no pass-mark in either examination.

Under the Folkskole Act of 1993 a new subject, nature & technology was introduced to the curriculum in the 1st – 6th class. Nature & technology is a combination of geography, biology, physics and chemistry and forms the basis for continued study in these subjects in the 7th – 10th class. French has been introduced as a third foreign language, and possible second alternative to German.

Upper

There are four different upper secondary courses that all meet the general entrance requirements for higher education in Denmark.

Upper secondary school leaving examination (**Studentereksamen**)

The structure and curriculum of the *Gymnasium* were changed by the Reform Act which came into effect for pupils starting in August 1988. Teaching is still provided on two lines – language and science. A core curriculum is common to both lines. In addition there are a number of compulsory subjects in years one and two, and four 'blocks' for option choices at higher or intermediate level (three in year 3 and one in year 2). To gain the **Studentereksamen** pupils must sit written examinations in Danish and in all higher level subjects at the end of the 3rd year, and compulsory English (language line) or mathematics (science line) at the end of the second year. There are also 5 or 6 oral examinations to make up a total of 10 examinations during the three years of study.

Pupils who have completed classes 9 or 10 of the *Folkeskole* can be admitted to a *Gymnasium* on the basis of a statement, issued by their previous school, that they are 'qualified' or 'perhaps qualified' for studies at this level ('perhaps qualified' pupils are tested at the school they apply to and entry is decided on the basis of the test). They must have achieved an appropriate average mark in the leaving examination of the *Folkeskole* (class 9). The *Gymnasium* is designed for academically able pupils aiming at higher education.

The examination taken on completion of the course is the **Studentereksamen**, which consists of oral and written tests arranged by the Ministry of Education.

A new reform came into force in August 1988 which enables pupils to combine subjects more freely and places more emphasis on languages in the mathematics branches and on mathematics in the languages branch. Pupils also have to write an extended essay during the third year.

Higher preparatory examination (HF)

Two year courses leading to the **Højere Forberedelseseksamen** (higher preparatory examination) were introduced in 1967 especially for those who have done practical work for some years but want further education.

The formal requirement for admission to courses is ten years' school attendance, with the **Folkeskolens Udvidede Afgangsprove** in Danish and in two of the following subjects: mathematics; English and German. Alternative qualifications corresponding to ten years of school attendance may also be accepted.

The HF course is a two-year course with a nucleus of common-core subjects and a number of elective subjects which can be freely combined. To complete the examination, the student must pass in all subjects from the common-core nucleus, as well as in some of the elective subjects. The common-core subjects are: Danish; religious education; history; biology; geography; mathematics; science; English; German; social studies; music; art and physical education/sport. The first two must be taken for both years, the others for one. The optional subjects are biology, mathematics, German, social studies, music, art, physical education, French/Russian, Italian/Spanish, physics, chemistry, psychology, informatics, design, philosophy, drama, economics, film and TV, classical studies and technical studies.

The HF examination may also be taken subject by subject after day or evening courses, designed mainly for adults.

Higher commercial examination (HH) or (HXX)

Formal entrance requirements for the ordinary three-year course leading to the **Højere Handelseksamen** (higher commercial examination) are nine to ten years' *Folkeskole*. The course takes place at commercial schools (*Handelsskole*) and it qualifies students both for higher education and for work, or for further education in business administration and management. Students with the **Studentereksamen** or the **Hojere Forberedelseseksamen** are admitted to a special one-year course.

The main subjects covered are communication, organization, data processing, accountancy, business economics, foreign languages, commercial law, Danish language, general economics and typing. Students on the two-year course will also study mathematics, Danish contemporary history and economic geography.

Examinations are both oral and written.

Technical secondary

Higher technical examination (HTX)

The **Højere Teknisk Eksamen** is a three-year course at a technical school (*Tekniskskole*). The entrance requirement is nine or ten years of *Folkeskole*.

The main subjects studied are: Danish language; science (chemistry, biology, mathematics and physics); foreign languages (English, German and French); social studies; technical subjects (practical skills, technology and technics) and optional subjects.

The first year is the same for all students. In the second and third years students can choose between several options, all technical. The examination enables students to enter higher education and to pursue jobs/further education in firms, companies and public institutions which provide a practical/theoretical education and training. Examinations are both oral and written.

Vocational

Apprenticeship training (*Laerlingeuddannelse*)

Under the Apprenticeship Act of 1956 anyone below the age of eighteen who is recruited for skilled work must become an indentured and registered apprentice. The minimum age to begin such training is now sixteen, and the apprentice must have completed the compulsory period of education. The training period is separately fixed for each sector and ranges from two to four years, including theoretical training at a technical school. In industry and crafts either a test is held with the award of a **Svendeprøve** (journeyman's certificate), or a certificate of training is awarded after internal and external assessment. Commercial apprenticeships for employment in shops and offices last two to four years from the end of class 9. The theoretical instruction is given at *Handelsskoler* and *Tekniske Skoler*. The courses culminate in the **Handelsmedhjaelperaeksamen** (shop and office assistants examination). A one-year full-time course from the end of the ninth or tenth year at a *Handelsskole* leads to the **Handelseksamen**.

Basic vocational education (EFG)

This has existed as an alternative to apprenticeship training since 1972; Reform acts were passed in 1977 and 1989.

The first part (basic year) is common to all students in a particular sector and takes place in a school. The subjects taught comprise both general and vocational subjects. The student subsequently specializes and at the same time applies for a practical job in that field. The second part, which may take up to three years, alternates between attendance at the technical school and practical work. A certificate is awarded after completion of the course of training. It is equivalent to the certificate issued on completion of apprenticeship training.

Voluntary youth and adult education

These two types of institution do not award formal qualifications:

Youth schools (*Ungdomsskoler*) provide courses for unskilled workers who have completed compulsory schooling and are aged under eighteen.

Folkehojskøler (Folk high schools/adult education colleges) offer full-time residential courses of all-round general education. There are no formal entrance requirements, but students should normally have completed *Folkeskole* and be eighteen years old. There is no fixed syllabus or length of course, but courses may include Danish (literature and language); social and foreign affairs; foreign languages; psychology; musical appreciation; mathematics and science as well as more creative and practical subjects. There are no leaving examinations.

In 1991 reform of vocational education came into effect and provides for a unified training system, combining basic vocational training (EFG), combined with apprenticeship and technician courses, centred on broadly-based qualifications with individual specializations. Access to initial vocational training is based on completion of *Folkeskole*; there are three different tracks:

> apprenticeship/basic vocational training (EFG)
> higher commercial courses (HHX) – (see above)
> higher technical courses (HTX) – (see above)

Apprenticeship and EFG courses can be taken in 8 main fields covering about 200 occupations; both types of training lead to a certificate of skilled worker.

Apprenticeship training lasts between three (industrial sector) and four (commerce and administration) years. Apprentices attend school either in block releases of two weeks, or two days a week for four hours.

EFG – *Erhvervsfaglige Grunduddannelser* starts with a basic year, at the end of which a basic-year certificate is awarded and leads to basic vocational training Part 2, lasting between two and three years in either a commercial school or a technical school.

In order to progress to EFG Part 2 the basic year certificate and a training contract with a firm are necessary. School attendance is as for apprentices.

Commercial school – following on from the EFG basic year. A two year course leads to the HHX **(Højere handelseksamen)** (Higher commercial examination). Students who have passed the upper secondary school leaving examination may take the HHX in one year. The HHX gives access to higher education.

Technical school – following on from the EFG basic year. A two year course leads to the HTX **(Højere teknisk eksamen)** (Higher technical examination). There is a common first year after which students opt for one of four lines of study: building technology; electrical engineering; mechanical engineering or process engineering. The HTX gives access to further technical studies.

HIGHER EDUCATION

The normal entrance qualifications for most faculties are the **Studentereksamen, Højere Forberedelseseksamen** (HF) or **Hojere Handelseksamen** (HH/HHX) or **Højere Teknisk Eksamen** (HTX). A system of *numerus clausus* (restricted entry) has operated since 1977.

There are five multifaculty universities and nine universities specializing in the fields of engineering, veterinary science, pharmacy, art, architecture and business studies. In addition to these universities there are over one hundred specialized colleges of higher education which offer two to four year courses in teacher training, social work, physiotherapy, nursing and engineering.

Most degree courses are self-contained and students choose their field of specialization when commencing their studies. Degree courses offered by the universities of Aalborg and Roshilde begin with a one year basic study programme (*Basisuddannelse*), characterized by a broad inter-disciplinary and problem-oriented approach within either the humanities, social sciences or natural sciences. The courses form part of the **Bachelor degree** at both these institutions.

Until 1988

Undergraduate courses were normally of three to six years' length. The most usual was the **Candidatus degree** which was five to six-and-a-half years long. The title is usually shortened to **Cand** followed by the abbreviated Latin term for the discipline, e.g.: theology (**CandTheol**), law (**CandJur**), economics (**CandPolit**), actuarial science (**CandAct**), humanities – two subjects (**CandMag**), humanities – one subject (**CandPhil**), psychology (**CandPsych**), science (**CandScient**), medicine (**CandMed**), business administration, dentistry (**CandOdont**), pharmacy (**CandPharm**), veterinary science (**CandMedVet**), architecture (**Arkitekt**), engineering – three-and-a-half years (**Akademiingeniør** until 1993, now **Diplomingeniør**) and engineering – five years (**CandPolyt**).

With effect from September 1988, students who had completed three years of studies for a **Candidatus degree** within the humanities, the theological or the social science areas, and had passed the stipulated examinations, had the right to use the title BA. Students who had completed three years of studies for a **Candidatus degree** within the natural sciences and health education areas, and had passed the stipulated examinations, had the right to use the title BSc.

Since 1993, Denmark has adopted a more Anglo-American structure of higher education. A university course now consists of a three-year **Bachelor degree** course, followed by a two-year course leading to the **Candidatus degree**. Programmes for the **Candidatus degree** include half-a-year's work on a thesis. A few disciplines (e.g. engineering, medicine, veterinary medicine and pharmacy) do not award **Bachelor degrees**, but only **Candidatus degrees** after five-to-six-and-a-half years of study.

The HA degree is awarded after three years of study in business administration. The **Adaemiingenior** and **Teknikum ingenior** have been amalgamated, and after three-and-a-half years of study lead to the qualification of **Diplom ingenior (BScEng)**.

Before 1985, faculties of arts offered different types and levels of degrees. The degrees were divided into major subjects (*hovedfag*) and minor subjects (*bifag*). The following degrees were conferred:

CandPhil (Candidatus Philosophiae), the degree awarded for a *hovedfag* (major subject); **CandMag (Candidatus Magisterii)**, awarded for *hovedfag* plus *bifag* (major plus minor); **MagArt (Magisterkonferens)**, an advanced graduate degree in a single subject or a group of related subjects. It normally took six years.

Grunduddannelse/Bifagseksamen/ExamArt is a two year intermediate degree in one subject which formed part of the **Candidatus degree** in humanities until 1995.

Postgraduate degrees

The **PhD** (formerly **Licentiat**) is the first advanced postgraduate degree, which is normally of three years duration. Those with a **Candidatus** (or **Magister**) **degree** are eligible for admission as **PhD** students provided that the faculty concerned has approved their project. **PhDs** are offered in many fields, e.g. theology, medicine, law, economics, sociology, arts, psychology, engineering and science.

Doctoral degrees

Whereas the **PhD** is ideally obtained at the onset of a research career, the classic **doctor degree** is traditionally obtained by the mature researcher after many years of research work.

Doctoral degrees are awarded solely on the basis of a thesis submitted by the candidate. The requirements are such that several years' intensive and independent research is necessary to produce a thesis of a sufficiently high standard to be accepted for the doctorate, and only those of exceptional merit can expect to receive this degree.

Doctoral degrees are conferred in many fields, e.g. theology (**DrTheol**), social sciences (**DrJur**/law, **DrPolit**/economics, **DrScient**/sociology), medicine (**DrMed**), humanities (**DrPhil**), science (**DrScient**), psychology (**DrPsych**). The usual entry qualification for a doctoral candidate is a **Candidate, Magister** or **Licentiat degree**.

Folkeuniversitet (Danish open university) offers academic courses. There are no formal entrance requirements, but students must be at least eighteen years old. There are no leaving examinations.

PROFESSIONAL EDUCATION

There are a large number of institutions of professional education offering degree courses of three to four years' duration depending on the subject area.

Entrance requirements are the same as for universities. Other qualifications may also be accepted. A system of *numerus clauses* (restricted entry) is in operation.

The courses taken qualify the student for a career in a particular field. All courses culminate with examinations.

Librarianship: four-year course, where the first two years are common to all students. Practical training takes place in the third term. Students specialize in certain areas from the fifth term.

Kindergarten and leisure-time pedagogy: three and a half year course, consisting of both theoretical and practical training. Students specialize in different areas connected with children and adolescents.

Occupational therapy: three-year course, where the students study seven different subjects and have a twenty-two-week period of practical training.

Physiotherapy: three-year course. The teaching is divided into modules and consists of both theory and practical training. The last year-and-a-half is divided into equal parts of teaching and practical work.

Home economics: three-and-half-year teacher training course. Three main subject areas are structured around five modules. Students have to write a thesis. The course also includes four to six weeks of practical training.

Midwifery: three-year course consisting of forty-six weeks of theoretical training (divided into modules of twenty, thirteen, and thirteen weeks at the beginning of each year) and ninety-six weeks of practical training at a hospital.

Journalism: four-year course divided into three modules: eighteen months' theoretical training, eighteen months of practical training and twelve months of theoretical training.

Social pedagogy: three-year course consisting of twenty months of theoretical training and ten months of practical training. Students have to write an extended essay in their third year.

Social worker: three-year course with main courses in theory and method in social work as well as a large number of other subjects. The course also includes a five-month period of practical training.

Technical engineering: the Teknika and the Engineering Academy of Denmark offer three-and-a-half-year courses leading to the qualification of **Diplomingeiør** (formerly **Teknikumingeniør**). There are different admission routes to the course depending on previous qualifications and practical experience. Students must normally have an upper-secondary school-leaving examination and practical training or a specified combination of theoretical and practical training. The course consists of forty-eight modules, each of approximately 120 hours including preparation. The common core course consists of eight of these modules and the specialization of forty modules. At least eighteen modules must concentrate on engineering subjects.

Students must choose one of six engineering specializations: civil and constructional engineering, electrotechnology, mechanical engineering, production engineering, naval construction and chemical engineering. Besides the purely technical subjects students study Danish, foreign languages, management, law and accounting.

TEACHER EDUCATION

Teacher training below upper-secondary level is undertaken at colleges of education. Courses last four years and consist of a common core of all the subjects taught in the *Folkeskole*, two advanced subjects together with general didactics, theory of education and psychology. Students have sixteen weeks of teaching practice and have to write a pedagogical thesis.

Gymnasium and HF (upper secondary)

Teachers at this level are university graduates holding the **Candidatus Philosophiae, Candidatus Magisterii** or **Candidatus Scientiarum** who have passed the **Paedagogicum**, a postgraduate course lasting half a year conducted by the Ministry of Education's department for upper secondary education. It includes teaching practice at an upper secondary school and a concurrent theoretical course comprising general education, didactics, educational psychology and school hygiene.

Dominican Republic

Education is compulsory from age seven to fourteen.

The medium of instruction is Spanish.

The academic year runs from August to June. Many schools, both primary and secondary, operate up to three teaching sessions or shifts a day, with pupils attending one of the sessions.

EVALUATION IN BRITAIN

School

Bachillerato – generally considered comparable to GCSE standard (grades A, B and C) on a subject-for-subject basis, with the exception of English language.

Higher

Licenciado/Professional title – generally considered comparable to a standard between GCE Advanced and British Bachelor degree; may be given advanced standing by British higher education institutions. Exceptionally, students with very high grades may be considered for admission to postgraduate study.

MARKING SYSTEMS

School

Primary (years 1 to 6)

85–100 per cent	A	
70–84	B	
55–69	C	Pass-mark 55
40–54	D	
0–40	F	

For the **Bachillerato**, marking is on a percentage scale applied to the average of the monthly grades at the end of the academic year.

80–100 per cent	course passed with no final examination required
60–79	referred to a final examination
0–59	fail

Higher

Systems vary from institution to institution. A percentage scale similar to the following may be used:

90–100 per cent	A	
80–89	B	
70–79	C	Pass-mark 70
60–69	D	
0–59	E	

or a scale:

A	4
B	3
C	2
D	1
F	0

SCHOOL EDUCATION

Schools are classified into three categories according to funding sources: official schools receive only public funds, semi-official receive part public and part private funding, and private schools receive no funds from the government. The government approves the curriculum for all schools no matter how they are classified. The **Secretaría de Estado de Educación, Bellas Artes y Cultos – SEEBAC** (Secretariate of Education, Fine Arts and Culture) controls all pre-school, primary and secondary public education and sets the curriculum for private pre-school, primary and secondary education. Programmes in the private sector which follow SEEBAC-approved curricula are deemed equivalent to those in the public sector.

Pre-primary

Very few facilities are available. However, most private schools offer a four-year pre-primary programme.

Primary

This extends over six years (grades 1 to 6) and on completion pupils receive a **Certificado de Suficiencia en los Estudios Primarios** (certificate of primary school sufficiency).

Secondary

Two systems exist concurrently in the secondary education sector; the *Plan Traditional* (traditional system) and the *Plan de Reforma* (reform system). Implementation of the reform began in 1970 but has not expanded as planned. The traditional system is still the most prevalent. Both systems cover six years.

The traditional system (2 + 4)

The six-year period is divided into a two-year cycle of intermediate education (grades 7 and 8) followed by a four-year cycle of secondary education (grades 9 to 12). On completion of the first cycle, pupils receive a **Certificado de Suficiencia en los Estudios Intermedios**. In the second cycle students may follow one of three programmes: general academic (the majority of students), vocational/technical or teacher training. In the general academic programme at the beginning of the fourth year (grade 12) students may specialize further. At the end of the course, students take the **Bachillerato** in their specialization: *Filosofía y Letras* (philosophy and letters), *Ciencias Físicas y Naturales* (physical and natural sciences) or *Ciencias Físicas y Matemáticas* (physical science and mathematics).

The reform system (4 + 2)

The six-year period is divided into the *Ciclo Básico* (basic cycle) of four years and the *Ciclo Superior* (higher cycle) of two years. The basic cycle in the reform system differs from the traditional in its emphasis on science for all students. In the last two years (grades 11 and 12) students have a wider variety of specializations to choose from than those in the traditional system. Courses lead to the award of **Bachillerato en Ciencias y Letras**.

Technical and vocational secondary

A number of technical and vocational schools offer courses in agriculture, commerce, technology, home economics and other trades. Students choose this option for the second cycle of secondary education. In the traditional system, courses lead to the award of **Bachillerato** commercial or **Bachillerato en Ciencias Agricolas**. Courses in the reform system lead to the **Bachillerato Técnico Profesional**. The title of **Perito** (expert) is awarded in both the traditional and reform system on completion of technical/vocational studies. The title may be obtained at the end of grade 12 or in some cases, such as from the Instituto Politécnico de Loyala, at the end of grade 13 after obtaining a **Bachillerato Técnico** at the end of the previous year.

HIGHER EDUCATION

The only requirement for first degree courses is normally the **Bachillerato**. Courses usually last four years (although, by studying all the way through the year students may complete their degree in less than four years) and lead to the **Licenciado**. Courses in certain subjects such as engineering and architecture take five to six years and lead to a professional title, and medicine, law and veterinary medicine take approximately six years, leading to the title of **Doctor**.

A few universities offer courses leading to the award of **Maestría (Master's degree)**.

Many universities offer intermediate programmes which are shorter than normal first degrees and which are designed to prepare students for specific careers, especially in the vocational/technical area. Courses usually last two to three years. The most common title awarded is **Técnico** (technician).

In 1983 the **Consejo Nacional de Educación Nacional – CONES** (National Council on Higher Education) was established to oversee the administration and operation of private higher education institutions.

TEACHER EDUCATION

Primary

Training is at secondary school level as one of the options in the secondary education sector. Schools offer a two-year programme following completion of grade 10 and accept students from both the traditional and reform systems. Courses lead to the title of **Maestro Normal**.

Secondary

Two types of training are available: a two to three-year programme resulting in an intermediate degree of **Técnico, Profesor** or a **Certificado de Estudios Superiores**, preparing teachers for grades 1 to 10, and a four-year **Licenciado** in education for grades 1 to 12.

Since 1966, a two-year course at university has led to the qualification of **Profesorado**, or a four-year course to a **Licenciado en Educacion**, with a major in mathematics, social studies, biology, physics, language (English, Spanish or French), chemistry or philosophy.

Ecuador

The Government, through the Ministry of Education, exercises central control of all aspects of primary and secondary education. The National Council for Higher Education coordinates the activities of higher education institutions. There are public (i.e. state), municipal (only at primary and secondary), and private institutions at all levels.

The first nine years of education, up to the end of the basic cycle (first cycle of secondary education), are compulsory.

The medium of instruction is Spanish in most cases. Quichua is the first language of instruction for the first year of primary education in parts of Amazonia and the Sierra region.

The academic year runs from October to July in the Sierra region; and from April to January in the coast region.

EVALUATION IN BRITAIN

School

Bachillerato – generally considered comparable to GCSE standard (grades A, B and C) on a subject-for-subject basis, with the exception of English language.

Higher

Licenciado/Professional title – generally considered comparable to British Bachelor degree standard if awarded after four or more years of study.

MARKING SYSTEMS

School

At secondary level there are monthly tests and term tests – averaged every term out of 20. A minimum 40 out of 60 over the year has to be obtained for promotion to the next year.

In order to be promoted each year, pupils who obtain 40 points in each subject in the three terms will not need to take supplementary exams.

The only mark to appear on transcript is the average of the total grades obtained in three terms.

Higher

There is no standard system of grading common to all institutions of higher education, and it may even vary within the constituent faculties of an institution. The most common systems used are the percentage scale and a scale of 0–10, with 6 or 7 being the pass-mark.

SCHOOL EDUCATION

Primary

This begins at age six for six years, divided into three two-year cycles.

There is a proposal to begin at age four and to restructure the system into the years of compulsory education divided into three cycles, ending at age fifteen.

Secondary

This takes six years divided into two three-year cycles. The first or basic cycle is common for all pupils. In the second or diversified cycle, pupils may specialize in:

academic studies, leading to the examinations for the **Bachillerato en Humanidades** or **Ciencias** (school-leaving certificate in humanities or sciences);

or

technical studies, leading to the examinations for the **Bachillerato Técnico** (school-leaving certificate in technical subjects).

The exception is vocational studies which leads to a qualification after one to two years.

HIGHER EDUCATION

In theory, all students holding a **Bachillerato** with a particular specialization may proceed to university, although in practice only those with an academic specialization may do so. Some of the private institutions also require prospective students to sit an entrance examination.

Students may take courses over four years leading to the award of the **Licenciado**, or five to six years leading to the award of a professional qualification (e.g. electrical engineer, economist, architect, veterinary surgeon, etc.; the latter three confer the title of **Doctor**), with seven years for medicine.

Very few institutions offer postgraduate courses although some are available in technical fields, leading to the qualification of **Masterado**.

Short courses of between two and four years lead to an advanced vocational qualification, e.g. librarian, nurse, etc.

The <u>American Junior College, Quito</u> is fully recognized by the Ministry of Education; it awards associate degrees, for which it issues both English and Spanish diplomas. The degree in Spanish is called **Técnico Superior**.

The Escuela Politécnica Nacional and the Escuela Politécnica del Literal are degree-awarding institutions.

TEACHER EDUCATION

Primary

Teachers are trained in two-year post-**Bachillerato** courses, or undergo four to five years' training in education at university.

Secondary

Teachers are trained in four-year courses at university leading to a **Licenciado de Educaciôn Media**.

Egypt

There are two parallel systems of education in Egypt: a modern secular system which comprises both public and private schools and the *Al-Azhar* Islamic education system which follows the same curricula and syllabuses and uses the same textbooks but adds a number of theological subjects and a great deal of religious instruction.

The Ministry of Education (MOE) is the body responsible for education at all levels. It determines curricula and teaching methods for all schools, of all types, all over the country. The system is, therefore, centralized.

The primary and secondary curricula were modernised in 1987. The curricula placed the emphasis on creative abilities rather than rote learning, which helped prevent cheating on examinations (which had been widespread). Greater emphasis was also placed on languages (particularly English) and computer science. A new primary curriculum was introduced in September 1994.

Education is compulsory from the age of five to fifteen. The first year of which is a new compulsory kindergarten year which was introduced in September 1994.

Public education is free at all levels.

The medium of instruction is Arabic, apart from in 'Experimental Language schools' which are government fee-paying schools where the medium of instruction is mostly a foreign language.

The academic year runs from September to May, with the main exams taking place in July.

EVALUATION IN BRITAIN

School

Thanaweya A'ama (General Secondary School Certificate) – generally considered comparable to GCSE standard (with the exception of English language), provided a minimum overall mark of 70 per cent is obtained. Candidates with good results may be considered suitable for access/bridging courses.

Higher

Bachelor degree – generally considered comparable to a standard between GCE Advanced and British Bachelor degree; may be given advanced standing by British higher education institutions. Candidates from prestigious institutions may be considered for admission to postgraduate study. For further information enquirers should contact the National Academic Recognition Information Centre.

Bachelor degree awarded by the American University in Cairo – is generally considered comparable to a middle-ranking institution in the United States. Those candidates with good grade-point average (3.0 or better), having completed four-year programmes may be considered for admission to postgraduate study. See United States of America chapter for further information.

MARKING SYSTEMS

School

Individual subjects in the **General Secondary School Certificate** examination have different maximum and minimum pass-marks. All subjects require a minimum of 40 per cent of the maximum pass-mark apart from Arabic and religion which require a minimum pass-mark of 50 per cent.

An average grade of 70 per cent is required to satisfy Egyptian matriculation requirements, although some faculties may demand higher average grades. The Faculties of Science, Engineering and Medicine, for example, may demand average grades of 90 per cent.

Higher

Marking systems vary from faculty to faculty.

Arts	90–100 per cent	excellent
	80–89	very good
	65–79	good
	50–64	pass
Medicine	) 85–100 per cent	excellent
Dentistry	) 75–84	very good
Veterinary Medicine	) 65–74	good
Pharmacy	) 60–64	pass
Other science	85–100 per cent	excellent
faculties	75–84	very good
	65–74	good
	50–64	pass –

A first-class Honours degree is awarded if a student obtains grades of 'excellent' in the last year's work and minimum grades of 'very good' in each of the preceding years.

A second-class Honours degree is awarded if a student obtains grades of 'very good' in the final year's work and minimum grades of 'very good' in each of the previous years.

No Honours recognition is awarded if a failure has been indicated at any time during course work.

The American University in Cairo uses the American marking system.

SCHOOL EDUCATION

Pre-primary

Since September 1994 a new compulsory one-year kindergarten, to be taught at primary school for children aged five, was introduced as part of the primary system. Non compulsory/private kindergarten is still offered from the age of four at kindergarten schools.

Primary

Basic education covers a five-year period (grades 1 to 5) from age five/six. Pupils take examinations each year in order to be promoted to the next grade. At the end of the fifth grade, pupils take the **Primary School Certificate** examination, which ensures promotion to the preparatory level.

Preparatory

This lasts three years (ages eleven/twelve to fourteen/fifteen) and has now been made compulsory, giving an eight-year system of 'basic education'. This is divided into general and vocational streams, although it has been decided to delay specialization until the beginning of secondary education. Pupils are promoted to the next grade automatically and at the end of the course take the **General Certificate Test** examination. According to the results obtained in the examination, students enter the secondary general schools, secondary technical schools or vocational training schools.

Secondary

This lasts three years (ages fifteen to eighteen). Pupils enter either general or technical schools.

General secondary

These schools offer an academic course which prepares pupils for university. During the first and second years, pupils follow a common curriculum. In the third year, pupils choose between sciences and literature.

At the end of the course, pupils take the **General Secondary School Certificate Examination (Thanaweya A'ama)** in thirteen subjects within the chosen branch. Marks of at least 50 per cent in each subject are needed to obtain a Certificate. This Certificate also gives access to university.

Since September 1994, pupils are able to sit for the **Thanaweya A'ama** over two years instead of one, which will undoubtedly lead to an increase in those eligible for university entrance.

Technical secondary

The Ministry of Education aims to attract 70 per cent of pupils finishing the preparatory course into technical education.

Technical secondary schools prepare students for work in skilled trades in industry, agriculture and commerce. Applicants must have the **General Certificate Test** and not exceed eighteen years of age. These schools offer three-year and five-year technical courses. Students who are successful in the national examination are awarded the **Technical Secondary School Certificate**, which makes them eligible for higher education. In practice, few technical secondary graduates are accepted, and this form of secondary education has therefore proved unpopular with parents and students, so is now receiving less emphasis. The programme of the technical secondary schools covers four subject areas: general education, industrial education, agricultural education and commercial education. Students follow the general education course and choose one of the other subjects as their specialization.

Industrial

During the first year, students cover a general course involving metal lathe work and blacksmith work, carpentry and joinery, masonry, weaving and spinning. In the second and third years, students may specialize in general mechanic training, automechanics, electricity, masonry, weaving and spinning. Students may take the final State secondary examinations at the end of the industrial course. This gives access to **Bachelor degree** courses at the Institutes of Higher Learning in Industrial Technology.

Agricultural

A three-year programme serves as a general introduction to agriculture, providing knowledge of modern agricultural methods and some field experience. At the end of the course students can take the final state examination. This gives access to the Institutes of Higher Learning in Agriculture which offer **Bachelor degree** courses. There are also five-year programmes, e.g. a canning course in Mostorod, Cairo.

Commercial

Students take a general three-year course. Those who gain high marks in the final examination may enter the Higher Institutes of Commerce and pursue a **Bachelor degree** course. There are also five-year courses in banking, catering and tourism.

Vocational

Many more students are involved in vocational training courses offered by private industry, religious foundations and the Ministry of Industry. The Ministry of Industry has training centres and supervises the training of apprentices in 101 trades. Students who hold the **General Test Certificate**, and are not over eighteen years of age, can follow a five-year course at the end of which they receive the **Vocational Diploma**.

International GCSE

There is a protocol between the Ministry of Education, the University of Cambridge Local Examinations Syndicate (UCLES) and the British Council to ensure that the exam is properly taught and administered. Twenty three schools have been given permission by the Ministry of Education to teach the IGCSE following inspections and recommendation by UCLES. Students undertake a course of study lasting two years for the IGCSE and one year for the Advanced Supplementary (AS) level. The Supreme Council of Universities has accorded acceptance by Egyptian universities for pupils with eight IGCSE subjects or six IGCSE subjects plus one AS level subject. All IGCSE grades must be between A–C, and A–E at AS level. In addition, pupils must pass exams in the following subjects of the Egyptian curriculum: Arabic, religion, civics and social sciences.

HIGHER EDUCATION

Entry to university in Egypt is extremely competitive and is based upon a student's score in the **General Secondary** or the **Technical Secondary Certificate**. Students would normally need an average of 70 per cent or above.

A **Bachelor degree** normally takes four years (five years for engineering and pharmacology and seven years for medicine). After three years' further study, students may obtain a **Master's degree** (one-year full-time study and two years set aside for the dissertation); four (occasionally three) further years' study leads to a **Doctorate**.

Cairo University is the largest and best-known public university in Egypt. It has 10,000 students and admits anyone who scores 65 per cent or more in the school-leaving examinations. Classes of 300 students are common. Facilities, including libraries, are poor. It is a multi-faculty institution.

The American University of Cairo is a private institution founded in 1919 with presently around 3,000 students. Instruction is in English. It provides a liberal arts education, although some engineering degrees are offered. More students are now seeking admission to this university because of a deterioration of standards at Egyptian institutions of higher education. In spite of relatively high fees, admission is now very competitive. It selects students with 85 per cent or more in the school **Certificate of General Secondary Education**.

Higher education institutes

Some two-year industrial and commercial institutes and two-year and four-year private institutes exist at the post-secondary level, although many higher education institutes were integrated into the university system after 1975. These institutes were established after the 1952 revolution had called for higher education to be made available to all the population.

TEACHER EDUCATION

Primary

All new primary teachers must now have a qualification from a university Faculty of Education. Teachers are being retrained at Faculties of Education through evening courses (four-year programmes) and are then awarded a **Bachelor of Education** degree. There is also a distance learning programme to upgrade, through the medium of Arabic, all primary school teachers who did not have a degree. The distance learning course is organized by Ain Shams University (Faculty of Education) and leads to a **BEd in Primary Education**.

The *Al-Azhar* teacher institutes also provide three-year scientific and literary courses with religious orientation for students who will teach in primary schools supervised by *Al-Azhar*.

Secondary

University faculties of education provide four-year secondary school teacher training courses for holders of the **General Certificate of Secondary Education**. Both preparatory and general secondary teachers follow the same course which leads to the **Bachelor degree**.

Graduates who hold a four-year university degree in an academic field can also teach at the secondary level after undergoing one year of postgraduate training at the Faculty of Education when they are awarded the **General Diploma**. In certain 'shortage' subjects graduates may begin teaching without a teaching qualification.

Students who have completed the technical secondary school course, may pursue a two-year course at a technical teacher training institution which enables them to teach in three-year technical secondary school. Alternatively, they may enrol for the five-year **Bachelor of Science** degree course at the Faculty of Technology and Education in Matareya and go on to teach at vocational/technician secondary school.

Some higher institutes train general secondary school graduates as teachers of art, domestic science, music and physical education. These are four-year courses. Additional courses are being established to overcome the shortage of teachers in these areas.

There are facilities for in-service teacher training in some university faculties of education and in six regional teacher training centres run by the Ministry of Education.

El Salvador

The following chapter regarding the education system in El Salvador is based on information obtained from the 3rd edition of this Guide, published in 1991, as NARIC has been unable to obtain more recent information.

Education is controlled by the Ministry of Education and is free.

In the 1960s and 1970s, reforms and full-scale expansion plans were initiated to improve facilities which were almost non-existent in rural areas. Teacher training programmes were also expanded to provide the teaching force for the new schools.

Basic or primary education is compulsory for all children where facilities are available.

The medium of instruction is Spanish.

The school year runs from February to October. At the National University of El Salvador the year runs from January to October; at the Universidad Centro Americana José Siméon Canas from March to December. Both institutions operate on two semesters, each of five months.

EVALUATION IN BRITAIN

School

Bachillerato (academic) – generally considered comparable to GCSE standard (grades A, B and C) on a subject-for-subject basis, with the exception of English language.

Higher

Licenciado/Professional title – generally considered comparable to British Bachelor degree standard if awarded after four or more years of study.

MARKING SYSTEMS

School

Subjects are graded on a scale of 1–10 (maximum) as follows:

10	*sobresaliente*	excellent
9	*muy bueno*	extremely good
8	*bastante bueno*	very good
6–7	*bueno*	good
5	*regular*	pass
1–4	*malo*	fail

Higher

The grading scale is the same as that used for school qualifications, except at the <u>Universidad Centro Americana José Siméon Canas</u> where 6 is the minimum pass-mark.

SCHOOL EDUCATION

Pre-primary (*Parvulario*)

Kindergarten lasts three years, for children aged four to six where facilities exist. The state-run institutions, *Escuelas de Parvulos*, prepare children for primary studies.

Primary (*Basico*)

This lasts nine years and is compulsory for pupils aged seven to fifteen. It is composed of three cycles, each of three years. Level 1 takes in cycles 1 and 2 (grades 1 to 6) and level 2 the third cycle (grades 7 to 9).

In the state-run primary schools, *Escuelas de Educación Básica*, the curriculum covers studies in the humanities, which includes Spanish and social sciences, and science, which includes mathematics, and physical education. In the third cycle pupils begin the study of a foreign language.

Pupils who pass in all subjects and fulfil the requirements of each cycle receive a certificate. Transcripts showing grades achieved are issued at the end of each year throughout primary and secondary education.

Secondary (*Medio*)

The secondary cycle for students of sixteen to eighteen years of age, lasts three years covering grades 10 to 12, culminating in the **Bachillerato** which gives access to higher education provided that the appropriate entrance examination has been passed. State secondary institutions are called *Institutos*.

The secondary curriculum entails the study of certain core subjects in the fields of language, social studies, foreign languages, mathematics, natural sciences, art and sport. In addition to these basic subjects, which must be studied by all, pupils can choose to specialize in certain areas. The **Bachillerato** is then awarded in the corresponding specialization. The following specializations, and options within each are possible:

Academic	natural sciences
	mathematics and physics
	humanities
Agriculture	
Arts	sculpture
	painting
	music
Commerce and administration	bookkeeping
	secretarial skills
Hotel management, catering and tourism	

Seamanship and fishing	naval engineering	)
	fishing	) not offered
	seamanship	) since 1976
Health	nursing	
	environmental health	
Vocational	beauty	
	art and decoration	
	fashion and design	
Industrial	engineering	
	automobile engineering	
	electrical engineering	
	electronic engineering	
Pedagogical	nursery education	
	special education	

HIGHER EDUCATION

Access to higher education is on the basis of success in the **Bachillerato** and an appropriate entrance examination.

University education is based on the American pattern in that the first two or three years of the course are general, preparing students for specialization in the later stages of the degree. Graduation occurs when a certain number of credits have been accumulated. Credits are earned on completion of a series of courses which are to a certain extent complete in themselves. A student who has completed the academic requirements of the course, i.e. has obtained sufficient credits, is known as an **Egresado**. Students must then present a thesis and they graduate when it has been approved.

There are two main institutions of higher education, the National University of El Salvador and the Universidad Centro Americana José Siméon Canas. In the non-university sector, there are nine specialized institutions.

The National University of El Salvador, founded in 1841, is a state institution which offers degree courses leading to the professional titles of **Ingeniero** and **Arquitecto** in the fields of engineering and architecture, and to the qualification of **Licenciado** in most other fields. The length of the course varies according to subject and may last from five to seven years, although five years' full-time study is normal. Graduation is followed by a period of professional work in the service of the state. The title of **Doctor** is awarded in medicine, chemistry and pharmacy after seven years' full-time study. The **Doctorado** is awarded after a further two years' study following the **Licenciado** or **Professional title**.

The Universidad Centro Americana José Siméon Canas is a private university. Teaching began in 1966. Studies lead to the **Licenciado**, awarded after five years in economics and humanities, after six years in administrative studies, and after five years for the title of **Ingeniero**.

Higher education courses outside the universities may be followed at specialized institutions such as the School of Social Work, the Higher Teacher Training Institute, the School of Physical Education and the Central American Technical Institute.

Institutions in other fields, e.g. nursing, agriculture, art, tourism, are generally known as Higher or National Schools. Courses may be of two or three years.

TEACHER EDUCATION

Teacher training courses may vary from nine months to three years. At the end of the course students receive a certificate.

Primary

Primary teachers are trained at 'normal schools' (*Escuelas Normales*), an alternative to grades 10 to 12 of the secondary cycle. The certificate received after three years also gives access to certain areas of higher education, e.g. the Faculty of Humanities at the National University of El Salvador, the School of Social Work or other similar institutions.

Secondary and higher

Training courses for secondary teachers and teachers in higher education are run at the universities or at the Higher Teacher Training Institute.

ADULT EDUCATION

The Adult Literacy Programme attracts many young people who have either never had the opportunity of attending schools or who finished school prematurely because existing facilities were insufficient.

Adult Study Centres (*Centros Escolares de Adultos*) give students the opportunity to improve on existing education by offering an accelerated first cycle of three years (normally six years) and a second cycle of three years which is identical to the third cycle of primary education. Those completing each cycle will receive the same certificates as students who complete their education by the normal route. These centres also offer vocational training programmes.

Eritrea

In 1991 the socialist Mengistu regime was overthrown by a combination of insurgent groups. Peace talks in London between the government and the insurgents in May 1991 were ended when the Ethiopian People's Revolutionary Democratic Front (EPRDF) occupied Addis Ababa with US approval.

The Eritrean People's Liberation Front (EPLF) announced that it would form a provisional government for Eritrea pending a UN-supervised referendum on self-determination in 1993.

Eritrea declared independence in 1993.

Education is free from primary to college level.

Since liberation, the government of Eritrea is making an all-out effort to rehabilitate war-ravaged education. Changes and reforms have been introduced in the structure of education, curriculum, management, etc.

The educational policy of 1991 declared a seven-year compulsory education covering ages seven to thirteen. It also stipulates that education at primary level be provided to all nationalities in their own languages and English is to be the medium of instruction beginning from middle school level through to higher education.

The medium of instruction is therefore Amharic in primary schools and English in all post-secondary institutions.

The academic year runs from September to June.

EVALUATION IN BRITAIN

School

Eritrean Secondary Education Certificate Examination (ESECE) – generally considered comparable to GCSE standard (grades A, B and C) on a subject-for-subject basis when a minimum overall mark of 50 per cent has been obtained, with the exception of English language.

Ethiopian School Leaving Certificate – generally considered comparable to GCSE standard (grades A, B and C) on a subject-for-subject basis when a minimum overall mark of 50 per cent has been obtained, with the exception of English language.

Higher

Bachelor degree – generally considered comparable to a standard between GCE Advanced and British Bachelor degree. May be given advanced standing in British higher education institutions.

MARKING SYSTEM

School

At primary level 55 per cent and above is the pass-mark.

At middle and secondary school 50 per cent and above is the pass-mark.

Higher

Letter grades, A, B, C, D, or F are used to indicate the academic achievement of a student in a course.

The value of each grade is as follows:

Grade	Description	Point
A	Excellent	4
B	Very good	3
C	Good	2
D	Unsatisfactory	1
F	Failure	0

SCHOOL EDUCATION

Primary

Primary schooling takes five years, starting at age seven. Pupils take examinations every year in order to be promoted to the next higher grade.

Middle level

This level lasts two years (ages twelve and thirteen) covering grades 6 and 7.

Secondary

This level lasts four years and comprises grades 8 to 11 (ages fourteen to seventeen). At the end of the course pupils sit for the **Eritrean Secondary Education Certificate Examination** (ESECE).

Technical secondary/Further

There are two technical schools, the Asmara Technical School and Wina Technical School.

These schools offer technical education leading to a certificate qualification. They prepare skilled workers for industry, agriculture and other development areas. Applicants for these schools must first complete grade 10 at secondary schools and sit an entrance examination. The schools offer three-year technical courses in electricity, radioelectronics, metalwork, woodwork, drafting, automechanics, surveying, machine shop, and building construction. This sector of education also culminates in the **Eritrean Secondary Education Certificate Examination** (ESECE).

HIGHER EDUCATION

Higher education is provided by the <u>University of Asmara</u>. The University was founded in 1958 and granted full university status in 1968.

Entrance to the University requires five subject passes in the **Eritrean Secondary Education Certificate Examination** (ESECE).

The ESECE is administered by a joint committee from the <u>University of Asmara</u> and the Ministry of Education. The examination is open to all who have successfully completed secondary education and technical school education.

The University consists of four colleges: the College of Science; the College of Agriculture and Aquatic Science; the College of Arts and Language Studies; and the College of Business and Economics.

The <u>University of Asmara</u> runs degree and diploma level programmes for regular students by day and for adult extension students in the evening. Courses for **Bachelor degrees** are generally obtained after four years of regular study for day students and seven years for extension students.

TEACHER EDUCATION

Primary

The <u>Asmara Teacher Training Institute</u> offers a training programme for primary school teachers. It admits secondary school graduates for a one-year course. At the end of this course trainees are awarded a primary school certificate.

In-service courses are also offered during the long vacation, July and August, to upgrade unqualified primary school teachers and school directors.

Secondary

Teachers for secondary school level are taught by the <u>University of Asmara</u> at the College of Science and the College of Arts and Language Studies.

Estonia

Until the end of the 1980s the educational system was under the control of the Union of Soviet Socialist Republics. Please see the **Russian Federation** chapter.

During the last 50 years there were very limited possibilities for developing independent educational policy in Estonia. Despite the pressure to adopt the over-politicized Soviet educational structure and curricula, the Estonian educational system maintained instruction in the Estonian language.

Political renaissance started at the end of the 1980s. Depoliticized, child-centered humanistic education regained its value.

The Estonian Education Act, passed in 1992, enshrines the development of national minorities and the Estonian language and culture as the main goals of education, along with general humanistic values.

Since then, two essential innovations have been introduced. Firstly, the nine-year compulsory basic school has replaced compulsory secondary education. Secondly, four-year college level institutions were introduced into tertiary education, along with universities. Private educational institutions have begun to function as an alternative to the existing public schools.

The language of instruction is either Estonian or Russian in all types of schools, the latter accounting for about 35 per cent of all schools. In universities the majority of courses are conducted in Estonian, but there are academic groups in which the language of instruction is Russian, English or German. Many of the Russian-speaking students continue their studies in the higher education institutions of the former Soviet Union.

EVALUATION IN BRITAIN

School

Secondary School Certificate

at grade 12 – generally considered comparable to GCSE standard (grades A, B and C) on a subject-for-subject basis, with the exception of English language.

Higher

Diploma – generally considered comparable to British Bachelor degree standard.

Magister – generally considered comparable to British Master's degree standard.

Doctor – generally considered comparable to British PhD standard.

MARKING SYSTEMS

School and Higher

Knowledge is numerically measured on a five-point scale.

Marking under the old Soviet system was as follows:

5	very good
3	sufficient
2	fail

Under the new system:

5	excellent
4	good
3	satisfactory
2	fail

SCHOOL EDUCATION

Pre-primary

Pre-primary education is available at kindergartens, day-care centres, playgroups and kindergarten-primary schools, and lasts until the age of seven.

Primary

This is compulsory from ages seven to eleven (grades 1–4). The language of instruction is either Estonian or Russian.

Secondary education

This is divided into two parts:

Basic education (grades 5–9)

This is compulsory for all children in Estonia. Students are obliged to stay at school either until they obtain the basic education or until the age of seventeen. The **Basic Schools' Certificate,** obtained at grade 9, provides a student with the right to continue his/her education at the next level.

There are two main options after basic school:

Upper secondary school/Gymnasiums from 1993 (grades 10–12)

In the 1992/93 academic year, there were 691 comprehensive schools, 229 of which provided secondary education. The **Secondary School Certificate** gives a student the right to continue his/her education either in university or in other higher educational institutions.

The Law on Basic Schools and Gymnasiums, passed in September 1993, now establishes gymnasiums as the main structural units of upper secondary education, replacing secondary schools. Some three-year gymnasiums for post-compulsory level students (grades 10–12) have already been established. According to this law, by the year 2000 the instruction in the state and municipal gymnasiums will be conducted in

Estonian. Basic schools will continue instruction in either the Estonian or Russian language. Graduates of the Russian-language basic schools are supposed to have gained sufficient knowledge of Estonian to continue their studies in gymnasiums.

However, the Law on Cultural Autonomy for National Minorities, also passed in the autumn of 1993, provides the possibility for national minorities to establish private gymnasiums with an instructional language other than Estonian.

Vocational school

Until the beginning of the 1990s, vocational education in Estonia followed Soviet policy. There were artificial boundaries between tertiary and vocational educational systems. As a rule, compulsory secondary education was accompanied by vocational training which lacked flexibility.

In 1992/93 about 30 per cent of graduates from basic school continued their studies in vocational schools. Some vocational schools provide secondary education in addition to vocational education. Today, there are different curricula depending on the educational level of the student. In 1992/93 there were 81 different vocational training institutions with 30,700 students. These schools offered more than 100 areas of study. The responsibility for non-tertiary level vocational education institutions is delegated to the local municipalities.

FURTHER EDUCATION

Vocational, technical and business education

There are now seven vocational institutions in Estonia at the tertiary level:

The Faculty of Teaching, Tartu, which provides training for teachers in the basic secondary school system as well as training for music teachers

The College for Cultural Professions, Viljandi

Narva College, which provides training for Russian-speaking teachers in the basic secondary school system

The Estonian Police Academy

The Estonian Marine Centre

Virumaa College, which provides a one-year basic technical course (two-years for students without the **Secondary School Certificate**)

Tallinn Engineering College

New programmes to meet the needs of a national market economy have been introduced (business management, navigation, aviation, tourism, police and military, etc.).

HIGHER EDUCATION

Restructuring of higher education and research in Estonia began in 1988. The government regulates the establishment of universities and other higher education institutions. There are currently six universities in Estonia: <u>Tartu University</u> founded in 1632, <u>Tallinn Technical University</u> founded in 1918, <u>Tallinn Art University</u> founded in 1938, <u>Tallinn Music Academy</u> founded in 1919, the <u>Estonian Agricultural University</u>, founded in 1951 and <u>Tallinn Pedagogical University</u> founded in 1952.

In addition, there are several private institutions, for example the <u>Estonian Institute of Humanities</u> and the <u>Estonian Business School</u>.

Admission to the first level of university studies is based on the **Certificate of Secondary Education** and one to three entrance examinations, tests or interviews, which are competitive. The entrance examinations are held in July.

Undergraduate study lasts four to six years and leads to the award of the **Diploma.**

The degree programme is divided into lower, middle and higher stages (cycles). Lectures are held in two semesters, usually from September to December and from February to June. The duration and extent of the study courses are usually expressed in credit units, literally 'study weeks'. One 'study week' refers to an input of approximately forty hours of work on the part of the student. Lecture hours, exercises and other forms of instruction as well as independent work are all included in this calculation.

The usual minimum requirement for graduation is 160 study weeks, but more study weeks are required of the students of medicine, mathematics and specialized education faculties. The students are expected to accomplish the 160 study weeks within four academic years. It is also possible to extend some study courses by two semesters or forty study weeks to include teacher training courses.

In order to acquire a **Diploma** from a university, students have to choose a major subject and pass the requirements in all three stages (lower, middle and higher). Students can also choose a minor subject and complete this at the lower, middle or even higher stage.

Diplomas are awarded after completion of studies and upon presentation of a diploma thesis, or passing the graduation examinations, or both. The requirements for graduation are set by the faculty.

The requirements for admission to a postgraduate course are completion of the first level of university studies (the **Diploma**) and the recognition of the student's qualifications and study purpose. The **Magister** (Master's degree) programme is four semesters. The student is expected to deepen his/her knowledge of the major subject, complete an individual programme and pass the Master's examination(s).

To acquire a **Master's degree** the student has to compile a Master's thesis. The thesis is a scientific paper proving the candidate's ability to solve problems in his/her field of research.

The **Master's degree** is generally a prerequisite for admission to doctoral studies. The **Doctoral** degree **(PhD)** programme generally takes four academic years. The requirements include writing a doctoral dissertation and defending it in a public debate. The doctoral dissertation is a scientific research paper with original, outstanding results which have been published in authoritative journals.

TEACHER EDUCATION

The education level of a teacher depends on the institution in which he/she is employed. In pre-schools, most teachers have two to three years of tertiary education. Approximately one half of primary and over 80 per cent of secondary school teachers have a university education. The teaching profession has not been popular among young people and salaries are traditionally low.

Educational personnel are trained at three universities and five educational colleges:

Tallinn Pedagogical University which trains pre-school, primary and subject teachers for basic and secondary school level. In-service training programmes for teachers and school administrators exist.

Tartu University offers a qualification as a subject teacher for basic and secondary school levels. Prospective teachers study for one additional year after their academic studies are completed in the main subject. The university also has a Department of Special Education.

Tallinn Music Academy trains teachers of music.

Adult and non-formal education

Since the early 1990s public and private educational institutions have been engaged in adult and non-formal education, especially in previously neglected areas, such as humanities, Estonian for the Russian-speaking population, foreign languages, family therapy, business legislation and administration, computer applications and religion. Professional organizations and some state agencies are elaborating professional certification standards (medicine, engineering, jurisprudence, teaching and public administration). A wide range of cultural activities has been organized for personal enrichment.

Ethiopia

After the 1974 revolution and the establishment of Ethiopia as a socialist state, the military government attempted to introduce wide educational reform with the accent on non-formal and vocational education, adult education and the extension of education to all.

In 1991 the socialist Mengistu regime was overthrown by a combination of insurgent groups. Peace talks in London between the Government and the insurgents in May 1991 were ended when the Ethiopian People's Revolutionary Democratic Front (EPRDF) occupied Addis Ababa with US approval.

The Eritrean People's Liberation Front (EPLF) announced that it would form a provisional government for Eritrea pending a UN-supervised referendum on self-determination in 1993.

Education is free from primary to college level.

The medium of instruction is Amharic in primary schools and English in all post-secondary institutions.

The academic year runs from September to July.

EVALUATION IN BRITAIN

School

Ethiopian School Leaving Certificate – generally considered comparable to GCSE standard (grades A, B and C) on a subject-for-subject basis when a mark of C or above has been achieved, with the exception of English language.

Higher

Bachelor degree – generally considered comparable to a standard between GCE Advanced and British Bachelor degree. May be given advanced standing in British higher education institutions.

MARKING SYSTEMS

School

Marks are out of 100, with 50 as the pass-mark.

A	90–100	excellent
B	80–89	very good
C	60–79	satisfactory
D	50–59	average
E	Below 50	failure

Higher

Marks are sometimes out of 100 (in which case the lowest pass-mark is 60) and sometimes according to the following system:

A = 4	excellent
B = 3	very good
C = 2	good
D = 1	satisfactory
	failure

SCHOOL EDUCATION

Pre-primary

Pre-school units are a new feature of the system catering for children aged four to six. The responsibility for the establishment and financing of these units falls to the *Kebele* (local neighbourhood association).

Primary

Primary schooling lasts six years from grade 1 to 6. At the end of grade 6 pupils take the **Primary School Certificate**, set by the Ministry of Education.

Secondary

The government intends to change the secondary school system from a two-year lower and a four-year higher to a four-year lower and a two-year higher format.

Junior secondary

Schooling covers grades 7 and 8 (ages twelve to fourteen). Schools offer a practical education. All instruction is theoretically in English from grade 7. There is a national examination at grade 8.

Senior secondary

This covers four years from grades 9 to 12. The Ministry of Education plans eventually to postpone higher secondary education until pupils have undertaken a period of practical experience. At present, grades 11 to 12 offer general academic courses. At the end of this course pupils take the **Ethiopian School Leaving Certificate** examination.

When the junior secondary is absorbed into the new structure of general polytechnic education (grades 1 to 8) which is still at the pilot stage, the senior grades of the secondary system will be divided into two cycles of higher polytechnic education (grades 9 to 10) and extended polytechnic education (11 to 12). The syllabus, curriculum and textbook design are still at the pilot stage.

FURTHER EDUCATION

Technical and vocational
This is provided by secondary school level courses and specialist institutions. The entrance requirements for these schools varies from completion of grades 8 to 12 and the duration of courses ranges from two to four years. The schools include the Polytechnic Institute in Bahir Dar, the Commercial School in Addis Ababa, the Veterinary School in Debre Zeit, the Wondo Guenet Forestry Resources Institute, the Technical School at Addis Ababa, the Technical School in Asmara, the Institute of Telecommunications and the Institute of Civil Aviation.

In addition, there is a plan to create twenty-six extended technical schools for grades 11 and 12 located in all the regions.

In-service training is provided by several government agencies.

Agricultural

The Agricultural Institutes at Ambo and Jimma and the Junior Agricultural Colleges at Debre Zeit and Aswassa offer a two-year diploma in general agriculture.

Military

The Ethiopian Military Academy in Harar aims to offer courses which are broadly comparable to the first and second years of Ethiopian degree courses.

HIGHER EDUCATION

Higher education is provided by various post-secondary institutions which include three universities: Addis Ababa University, the University of Asmara and Alemaya University of Agriculture. The entry qualification for all higher education institutions is the possession of the **Ethiopian School Leaving Certificate**. The course leading to the **Bachelor degree** lasts four years.

Addis Ababa University was founded in 1961 and has ten campuses. It was closed in 1974 and reopened in 1976. It offers degrees and a two-year diploma programme.

The University of Asmara received its charter from the government in 1968. It no longer has any private status and like Addis Ababa University, is now administered by the Higher Education Commission.

Alemaya University of Agriculture was established in 1951 by the United States of America and operated as a charter unit of Addis Ababa University. In 1985 it gained university status and became the third university.

Junior colleges offer diploma-level courses.

TEACHER EDUCATION

In the past, teacher education involved pre-service training: for primary, one year after grade11; for lower secondary, two years after grade 12; and for senior secondary, four years after grade 12. Emphasis is now on in-service training.

Primary

Primary school teachers take one-year training courses after grade 12 at eleven regional teacher training institutes co-ordinated by the Ministry of Education. The Ministry hopes to initiate four-year pedagogy courses in lower secondary schools.

Secondary

Lower

Lower secondary school teachers receive instruction at the College of Teacher Education in Kotebe. The college offers a two-year course. It trains teachers in productive technology, agriculture, commerce, home economics, Amharic, English language, history, geography, mathematics, science and physical education.

Science teachers are trained at the Bahr Dar College for Science Teachers.

Bahr Dar Teachers' College offers a four-year degree course for secondary school teachers, leading to the degree of **Bachelor of Education (BEd)**.

The Ministry is also planning to open two-year pedagogy courses in selected higher secondary schools which will provide training for lower secondary school teachers.

Higher

Higher secondary teachers are trained at the Faculty of Education of Addis Ababa University.

Technical

The College of Pedagogical Sciences at Addis Ababa University offers a two-year diploma programme for prospective technical education teachers. The Polytechnic Institute of Bahr Dar offers three-year programmes for technical teachers.

ADULT AND NON-FORMAL EDUCATION

The Adult Education Department offers adult literacy courses. The Community Skill Training Centres offer basic education and literacy courses for adults which last between two and three months. The Ministry of Education is extending correspondence-course education; the Department of Education Mass Media Services (DEMMS) has an audio-visual centre which was transformed into a supportive mass media centre ten years ago. The service now covers between eighty-five and ninety per cent of the country.

Fiji

The education system has been closely related to that of New Zealand with students taking examinations administered by the New Zealand Examinations Board, but increasingly modified to Fijian needs. The last New Zealand examinations were taken in 1988 and replaced by the **Fiji School Leaving Certificate** in 1989.

There is no compulsory period of education, but most children complete at least eight years of primary education between the ages of six and thirteen.

The medium of instruction is English, although in the early years of primary education vernacular languages are often used.

EVALUATION IN BRITAIN

School

New Zealand University Entrance Certificate (until 1988) – generally considered comparable to GCSE standard (grades A, B and C) on a subject-for-subject basis.

Fiji School Leaving Certificate – generally considered comparable to GCSE standard (grades A, B and C) on a subject-for-subject basis.

Form 7 Examination – generally considered comparable to GCSE standard.

Higher

Bachelor degrees (from the <u>University of the South Pacific</u>) – generally considered comparable to British Bachelor degree standard.

MARKING SYSTEMS

School

New Zealand University Entrance Certificate – see chapter on New Zealand.

Fiji School Leaving Certificate – for a pass to be awarded at least four subjects must be taken and all the following achieved:

(i)   all marks must be in the range of 50 per cent

(ii)   not less than 200 in the aggregate for the four subjects.

A Certificate of Attainment is awarded to those who pass.

A Certificate of Completion is awarded to all students.

Form 7 Examination – percentage scale, minimum pass is 50 per cent; the pass-marks are then transferred into grades:

A   80–100 per cent
B   65–79
C   50–64

Higher

Degrees of the <u>University of the South Pacific</u> are not classified.

SCHOOL EDUCATION

Primary

The normal time for a student to complete a primary level would be eight years, from the age of six. Pupils are required to sit:

(i)   The **Fiji Intermediate Schools Examination.**
(ii)   The **Fiji Secondary Schools Examination** (i.e. in the eighth year).

Most schools in Fiji do not offer both these exams.

Secondary

A student normally covers a five-year programme at secondary level. It is not always necessary for them to have studied at a junior secondary school first.

Until 1986, at senior secondary level, pupils took examinations set and marked by the New Zealand Examinations Board. At the end of form V, pupils sat the **New Zealand School Certificate**, which had been increasingly modified by the Board to include topics relevant to Fiji and the Pacific. At the end of form VI pupils took the **New Zealand University Entrance Certificate**.

In 1987, Fiji introduced its own three-year **Fiji School Leaving Certificate** which is awarded after a student has completed and successfully passed the form VII examination. The first Fiji certificates were awarded in 1989. This meant the last **New Zealand School Certificate** was held in 1986 and the **New Zealand University Entrance Certificate** in 1988.

Technical secondary

Some facilities are available, including courses in trade and office skills leading to examinations of the Royal Society of Arts. Technical and vocational aspects have become more prominent in the curriculum of the **Fiji School Leaving Certificate**, including vocationally biased multicraft and homecraft courses promoted and encouraged by the Ministry of Education.

FURTHER EDUCATION

The <u>Fiji Polytech</u> formerly known, before privatization, as the <u>Fiji Institute of Technology</u>, which was formed by an amalgamation of the <u>Derrick Technical Institute</u>

and <u>Western Division Technical Centre</u>, offers short trade and apprenticeship courses in addition to courses leading to diplomas in engineering, hotel catering and business studies. The Institute also offers courses leading to several City and Guilds examinations.

HIGHER EDUCATION

Courses are available at the <u>University of the South Pacific</u> which has campuses in Fiji and Western Samoa. Admission to degree courses is based on the **Form 7 Examination,** or an equivalent qualification. The normal length of **Bachelor degree** courses is three years except for medicine which takes four years for a first degree.

Postgraduate certificates and diplomas, **Master's degrees** and **PhD** programmes are offered in a number of areas. For further information on the <u>University of the South Pacific</u> see Appendix 9.

TEACHER EDUCATION

Primary

A two-year basic teacher training course is available at the <u>Teacher Training College</u>. Previously the entry level was a pass in the **New Zealand School Certificate** (form V) but now trainees must have successfully completed form VII of secondary education.

Secondary

Normally a four-year course at the <u>University of the South Pacific</u> after the foundation programme. A three-year **Bachelor degree** course is followed by a one-year **Postgraduate Certificate in Education.**

Finland

Finnish children start school at the age of seven, in special cases at the age of six. Comprehensive school lasts for nine years. Compulsory school attendance is linked to the completion of the comprehensive school. Compulsory education also applies to handicapped children. All comprehensive school leavers have the same eligibility for further studies either in upper secondary school or in vocational institutions.

The national languages of education are Finnish and Swedish. Official bilingualism has guaranteed the Swedish-speaking minority (six per cent of the population) equal opportunities of education at all levels. Both language groups have their own schools and vocational institutions. One of the experimental polytechnics and two of the universities are Swedish, a few of the other universities also offer degree courses in Swedish.

Tuition in schools, vocational institutions, polytechnics and universities is free of charge. The academic year runs from August to May in schools and from September to May at university level.

EVALUATION IN BRITAIN

School

Ylioppilastutkinoto/Studentexamen – may be considered to satisfy the general entrance requirements of British higher education institutions.

Higher

Old System (in existence until 1996)

Kandidaatti/Kandidat (Ekonomi, Diplomi-insinööri, Arkkitehti, Lisensiaatti, Proviisori) – generally considered comparable to British Bachelor (Honours) degree standard, although the course lasts longer than in the UK.

Licentiate (Lisensiaatti/Licenciat) – generally considered comparable to British Master's degree standard.

Doctorate (Tohtori/Doctor) – generally considered comparable to British PhD standard.

New System (implemented from 1993–96)

Kandidaatti/Kandidat (120 credits/3 years) – generally considered comparable to a British bachelor (ordinary) degree.

Maisteri/magister (160 credits, 2 additional years) – generally considered comparable to a British bachelor (honours) degree.

Doctorate (Tohtori/Doctor) generally considered comparable to British PhD standard.

MARKING SYSTEMS

School

Marking is on a scale from 4–10 (maximum), with 5 as minimum pass-mark.

Matriculation examination:

0   *improbatur* (fail)
2   *approbatur*
3   *lubenter approbatur*
4   *cum laude approbatur*
5   *magna cum laude approbatur*
6   *laudatur*
(1 not used)

Vocational institutions and Polytechnics

Marking is on a scale from 1–5 (minimum-maximum)

Higher

For examinations, the most common systems are:

–   1–3, or satisfactory, good, excellent;
–   1–5 (minimum-maximum)
–   pass/fail

For theses, the most common systems are:

–   *approbatur, lubenter approbatur, non sine laude approbatur, cum laude approbatur, magna cum laude approbatur, eximia cum laude approbatur, laudatur* (minimum-maximum);
–   1–5

In the experimental polytechnics and in university education a credit unit (*opintoviikko/studievecka*) system is used to measure the extent of the courses.

SCHOOL EDUCATION

Pre-primary/kindergarten education (*lastentarha/barnträdgard*)

The Children's Day Care Act, which came into force in 1973, obligated municipalities to provide day-care to satisfy prevailing demand. The day-care is administered by the Ministry of Social Affairs and Health. The objective of day-care is to support parents in bringing up their children and, together with them, promote the children's balanced personal development and their learning ability. The municipal day-care is a social service, and children are selected for it on the basis of both social and educational criteria.

In addition to the pre-school education provided in day-care, in sparsely populated areas education is given at pre-school classes attached to comprehensive schools.

Systematic two-year pre-primary education is provided for severely handicapped children, for whom the eleven years of compulsory education begins at the age of six, i.e. one year earlier than for other children.

In 1992, one-third of the children aged 3–6 participated in pre-school programmes, but some sixty per cent of children did so at six years of age. Approximately seven per cent of the children receiving pre-school education attend private schools or day-care centres.

In addition, some private and religious organizations arrange part-time activities for young children under the school age. These programmes are not included in the above figures.

Comprehensive school (*Peruskoulu/grundskola*)

Children in Finland begin school in the year when they turn seven. Basic (compulsory) schooling is provided by a nine-year comprehensive school, which is divided into a lower (primary) and an upper (lower secondary) stage. The comprehensive school system was introduced in 1968 in the Law of Principles of Public Education and it was implemented gradually throughout the country during the 1970s.

Education at comprehensive school is given according to a national core curriculum, which is defined in the Comprehensive School Act, Decree and Curricula Guidelines given by the National Board of Education. The municipalities compile the actual curriculum, and the schools draw up an annual work plan. In addition to the compulsory curriculum, there are optional and elective subjects. The curriculum reform of 1994 gives schools considerably more freedom in building up their curriculum.

Post-compulsory education

The Secondary Education Development Act from the year 1978 started the development of education in upper secondary schools and vocational institutions on the basis of common overall objectives. One principle is to offer the entire age group completing comprehensive school or upper secondary school (i.e. general education) the option of continuing their studies at a vocational institution or university, before entering the work-force.

After leaving comprehensive school, a young person may apply to an upper secondary school or a vocational institution. There is a national joint selection procedure for these two types of education. Over half of the comprehensive school leavers continue directly in upper secondary school, and about 32 per cent in vocational education (figures from the year 1992). Students may also choose to take a voluntary extra tenth grade to improve their chances in further education.

In 1994, there is an experimental system of secondary education going on in sixteen upper secondary schools and vocational institutions. The experiment aims to provide a wider range of opportunities than previously for completing both vocational diplomas and the upper secondary school syllabus. In addition, a combination diploma of the two is offered.

A new reform of vocational education will be implemented from 1995 onwards. Its aim is to simplify the education system and eliminate multiple education. The present system of vocational education including both secondary and higher education will be developed into a linear system, and a separate non-university sector of higher education will be introduced. The experiment in polytechnics which was launched in 1991 started the development of the non-university sector. For these reforms, see under Vocational and professional education.

Finland

Upper secondary school (*lukio/gymnasiet*)

Upper secondary schools offer a three-year general education curriculum, at the end of which the pupil takes the national matriculation examination, which is the general eligibility criterion for university admission.

The core curriculum is defined in the Upper Secondary School Act and Decree. The curriculum is being designed in the same way as that of comprehensive school (see above). There are compulsory, optional and applied subjects and courses in the curriculum. Upper secondary schools can be specialized, e.g. in languages, sports, music or other arts. The reform of the upper secondary school curriculum in 1994 increased the range of options in the curriculum, and individual schools will begin to cultivate a more distinct image.

Since 1982, instruction in upper secondary schools has been given in the form of courses. Another experiment, this time consisting of gradeless upper secondary schools, i.e. schools with no special year-classes, started in the autumn of 1987. As a result of the success of this pilot, opportunity to complete upper secondary school under this system will be provided to all students in 1995/96. The maximum study time is four years.

On completion of the three years' upper secondary schooling pupils obtain the **Upper Secondary School Leaving Certificate (lukion paastotodistus/gymnasiets dimissionsbetyg)**.

The national matriculation examination (**ylioppilastutkinto/studentexamen**) consists of four compulsory written tests: in the mother tongue (i.e. in Finnish or Swedish, from the spring of 1994 also in Sami language), the second national language, a foreign language, and either mathematics or *realia* (general paper). In *realia* students choose questions in one of the following areas: religion and ethics; psychology and philosophy; history and civics; physics; chemistry; biology and geography. In addition, it is possible to take two optional tests either in mathematics, *realia* or foreign languages. The foreign language exam includes a test in listening comprehension. After a fail in a test the student has two chances to improve the grade, he/she can also try to improve the other grades (not failed).

A student who has passed the matriculation examination and has got the school leaving certificate obtains the Matriculation Certificate (**ylioppilastutkintotodistus/ studentexamensbetyg**).

Vocational and professional education

The system of vocational education is now under development. An earlier reform was carried out 1982–1988 under the principles of the Secondary Education Development Act (1978). The reform of curricula was launched at the same time. The new Vocational Institutions Act was passed in 1987. The law governs 13 types of institutions. The institutions are in the fields of national defence and law and order. Some training in communication and transportation, as well as education given in liberal education institutions has its own legislation.

The present vocational education system offers both secondary and higher education programmes. Education is provided by vocational institutions, schools and colleges. This education leads to three levels of qualifications: school level certificates, college/institute level diplomas and higher vocational/institute level diplomas. In addition, higher education levels programmes are provided by the experimental polytechnics.

In the reform of the 1980s a system of basic programmes was introduced instead of the previous system of nearly 700 separate, narrowly defined study programmes. This basic programme structure is intended only for comprehensive school-leavers. A basic programme is composed of a one-year foundation course common to all students, which is further divided into school, college and higher level specialization lines. The foundation course includes general subjects e.g. languages, civics, mathematics and natural sciences, information technology, and so forth. There are at present 26 basic programmes, offering more than 200 study lines. In addition, vocational education is given in nearly 50 separate programmes and in 20 programmes in folk high schools, sports colleges, music institutes and kindergarten teacher colleges.

The school level programmes take two to three years, the college level programmes three to five years and the higher vocational level programmes five to six years to complete. Vocational programmes usually include a period of practice; in college and at higher level its duration is usually one year.

Matriculated students study for the same qualifications as comprehensive school leavers, but they have a separate curricula. The vocational contents of the two kind of curricula are the same, but matriculated students do not have to take general studies. This shortens their study time by between six months and one-and-a-half years.

This complex system of basic programmes and specialization lines and additional programmes outside vocational institutions, with separate lines for comprehensive school and upper secondary school leavers will be reformed, from 1995 onwards. The foundation course will be abolished, and education will be arranged linearly; students first complete a course corresponding to the present school level programme, and then go on to the college level and to polytechnics. As a rule, matriculated students will apply to college or to polytechnics. The duration of studies will not change.

The types of institutions which the Vocational Institutions Act covers are the following:

multidisciplinary vocational institutions (mostly school level education, training skilled workers for industry and the service industries); hotel and catering institutions; commercial institutions; institutions of home and institutional economics; art and media culture colleges; arts and crafts institutions; agricultural institutions (agriculture, dairying, horticulture, fishing and fish farming); nautical colleges; forestry and food processing; social work institutions; health care institutions; technical colleges (both technicians and engineers); special vocational institutions (training disabled persons and invalids).

There are at present nearly 500 vocational institutions. Their number is however diminishing. The tendency is towards larger institutions offering courses from different fields of study; gradually, the system of narrowly specified institutions will be abandoned.

Higher Education

As stated above, higher education is given in vocational colleges as well as in the experimental polytechnics.

Higher education in vocational colleges

There are at present 280 colleges which give at least college-level vocational education. These are longer college and higher level programmes, i.e. those taking at least three years to complete for matriculated students, which include, for example, programmes for prospective engineers, programmes in health care, social service and other social fields, cultural studies (including music and other arts, crafts and design, art education, media studies etc.), hotel and catering services, and kindergarten teacher education.

This sector is now being reorganized (see above) and a network of polytechnics is being established.

Experimental polytechnics

Under the experimental programme in vocational higher education, one or more vocational colleges form a temporary polytechnic which offers programmes leading to non-university higher degrees. There are 22 polytechnics taking part in this experiment, one of them is Swedish medium. The polytechnics comprise 85 vocational colleges, which give college and higher level education. The experiment was launched in 1991, and the first permanent polytechnics will be established in 1996.

The polytechnic degree programmes offer students a larger scope of options, allowing them to choose their subjects from different fields of study. The courses take three to four years to complete. The system of credits is applied. Students must prepare a short thesis. Compared with university education, polytechnic programmes are more specifically related to certain professions.

Students apply for entry to polytechnics after secondary studies. They must have a secondary vocational qualification supplemented by certain upper secondary school syllabi, or a secondary vocational qualification in the field a student is applying for, or a matriculation certificate (or upper secondary education), or a combination diploma from one of the experimental secondary institutions. Selection is made in the national joint system and it is based on the student's school achievement, work experience and sometimes also an aptitude test. Polytechnics may arrange entrance examinations.

The polytechnic graduates can use two kinds of titles. Since the polytechnic programmes have been developed from the higher vocational programmes, students are in the most cases able to use the old titles (of institute/college level or higher level) with an acronym AMK/YHS after the title, e.g. *insinööri* (AMK) *ingenjör* (YHS) etc. On the other hand, new names have also been introduced. These are called *ammattikorkeakoulutkinto/ yrkeshögskoleexamen* with a definition of the field of study in front.

Polytechnic Degrees

A list of polytechnic degrees follows. The 'general' name of the degree is given first. In addition, there are special titles, which are also in use. The list includes the degrees existing in 1994, new degrees may be added over the next few years. (The specific field of study is in brackets.)

Forestry and Agriculture

Maa-ja metsatalouden ammattikorkeakoulututkino/Yrkeshögskoleexamen i jord-och skogsbruk
   Agrologi (AMK)/*Agrolog* (YHS) (agriculture)
   Metsatalousinsinööri (AMK)/*Skogsbruksingenjör* (YHS) (forestry)
   Hortonomi (AMK)/*Hortonom* (YHS) (horticulture)

Technology and Seafaring

Tekniikan ammattikorkeakoulutukinto/Yrkeshögskoleexamen i teknik (technology)
   Insinööri (AMK)/*Ingenjör* (YHS) (technology, i.e. programme for engineers)
   Rakennusarkkitehti (AMK)/*Byggnadsarkitekt* (YHS) (building architecture)
Merenkulun ammattikorkeakoulutkinto/Yrkeshögskoleexamen i sjofart (seafaring)
   Merikapteeni (AMK)/*Sjökapten* (YHS) (seafaring)
Vaatetusalan ammattikorkeakoulututkinto/Yrkeshögskoleexamen i bekladnadsbranscen (clothing industry)

Finland

Tourism, Hotel and Restaurant Business

Matkailu-ja ravitsemusalan ammattikorkeakoulututkinto/Yrkeshögskoleexamen i turism och kosthållning

Commercial and Administrative Services

Liiketalouden ammattikorkeakoulutitkinto/Yrkeshögskoleexamen i företageskonomi

Social and Health Care

Terveysalan ammattikorkeakoulututkinto/YrKeshögskoleexamen i hälsovård (health care) *Sosiaalialan ammattikorkeakoulututkinto/Yrkeshögskoleexamen inom det sociala området* (social care)
Sociaali- ja terveysalan ammattikorkeakoulututkinto/Yrkeshögskoleexamen i social- och hälsovård (social and health care)

Culture

Käsi- ja taideteollisuuden ammattikorkeakouututkinto/Yrkeshögskoleexamen i hantverk och konstindustri (crafts and design)
 Artenomi (AMK)/*Artenom* (YHS)
Konservointialan ammattikorkeakouututkinto/Yrkeshögskoleexamen i konservering
 Konservaattori (AMK)/*Konservator* (YHS)
Kuvataiteen ammattikorkeakoulututkinto/Yrkeshögskoleexamen i bildkonst (visual arts)
 Kuvataiteilija (AMK)/*Bildonstnär* (YHS)

University Education

There are at present twenty-one university institutions. The general entrance requirement for university degree programmes is the matriculation examination. The other possibility, the vocational path is used only by 2–3 per cent of first year students. In the course of the reform of vocational education in 1980s, the option of entering university was introduced to students who had taken a college or higher level vocational diploma. This option was first possible only to the same field of study in which the applicant's diploma was taken, but since 1991 the option has been general.

A system of numerus clauses, i.e. restricted entry, is used in all fields of study. Since there are usually many more qualified applicants than there are study places, selection procedures must be used. The universities select their own students and define their selection criteria. Applicants can be ranked e.g. according to the grades in the matriculation examination (and school-leaving certificate) and/or entrance examination.

The earlier reform of university degrees was implemented between 1977 and 1984. In this 'old' degree system (which will be phased out during the period 1993–96 i.e. it is still in use in some fields until 1996) there are only a few lower academic degrees. The degree programmes usually lead to a higher academic degree, **kandidaatti/kandidat** (or equivalent). A system of credits is in use. One credit (*opintoviikko/studievecka*) implies an output of approximately forty hours of work towards set objectives. The extent of the 'old' *kandidaatti*, i.e. the higher academic degree, is most usually 160 (minimum) or 180 credits.

A new degree reform was started in 1993 and will be carried out in all fields of study by the year 1996. This reform is based on evaluations of education made field by field. In this new system the first degree is a lower academic degree, which is most usually called **kandidaatti/kandidat** (N.B. Do not confuse with the old kandidaatti, the higher academic degree!). The extent of the degree is 120 credits, and it takes three years to complete. The second cycle degree is a higher academic degree, **maisteri/magister**, which takes a total of five years to complete, or two after **kandidaatti**. The total extent of the degree is 160 credits (120 + 40). In autumn 1993, this new system was introduced into the fine arts and natural sciences (the names of the degrees are different in fine arts and pharmacy), from autumn 1994 it has also been in use also in the humanities, social sciences, sport and industrial arts.

In both degree systems, there is a doctorate (**tohtori/doctor**) in all fields of study. Before taking the doctor's degree, students can study for a **lisensiaatti/licentiat** degree in all fields other than in medicine, dentistry or veterinary medicine (where **lisensiaatti** is higher academic degree). It is an optional postgraduate degree. In the new degree system, there have been plans in some fields of study either to abolish the **lisensiaatti** degree or to develop it into a professional postgraduate degree.

Students who started their studies before the reform began are usually allowed to change to the new system.

University Degrees

The 'old' degrees:

A)   Lower academic degrees:

–   duration of studies: 3 years, 100–120 credits, a short thesis required
–   awarded by a few universities in certain disciplines:

varanotaari, diploma in law;
ortodoksisen kirkkokunnan kanttori, orthodox cantor;
oopperalaulaja, opera singer's degree;
in social sciences, the following eight degrees:
hallintovirkamiestutkinto, diploma in public administration;
verorirkamiestutkinto, diploma in taxation;
kunnallisturkinto, diploma in municipal administration;
yleinen vakuutustutkinto, diploma in public insurance;
nuorisotyön tutkinto, diploma in youth work;
toimittajatutkinto, diploma in journalism
sosiaalihuoltajatutkinton, diploma in welfare work;
socionom, diploma in social services (Swedish)

B)   Higher academic degrees:

–   duration of studies: 5–6 years (160–250 credits), a thesis required

(a)   **kandidaatin tutkinto:**
teologian kandidaatti, theology;
filosofian kandidaatti, the humanities, natural sciences;
oikeustieteen kandidaatti, law;
valtiotieteen kandidaatti; yhteiskuntatieteiden kandidadaati;
hallintotieteiden kandidaati, all three in social sciences;
psykologian kandidaatti, psychology;
kasvatustieteiden kandidaatti, education
maatalous- ja metsätieteiden kandidaati, agriculture and forestry;
elintarviketieteiden kandidaatti, food sciences;
liikuntatieteiden kandidaatti, sport sciences;
terveydenhuollon kandidaatti, health care;
musiikin kandidaatti, music;
taiteen kandidaatti, industrial arts;

teatteritaiteen kandidaatti, theatre, drama;
tanssitaiteen kandidaati, dance

(b)   Higher academic degrees with different names, degrees are equivalent
to **kandidaatti** above:

ekonomi, economics and business administration;
diploma-insinööri, engineering;
arkkitehti, architecture;
maisema-arkkitehti, landscape architecture;
proviisori, pharmacy;

(c)   Three **lisensiaatti** degrees, equivalent to **kandidaatti** etc. above. (N.B.
the **Lisensiaatti** degrees in other fields of study are pre-doctoral postgraduate
degrees, see below):

lääketieteen lisensiaatti, medicine;
hammaslääketieteen lisensiaatti, dentistry;
eläinlääketieteen lisensiaatti, veterinary medicine

C)   Lisensiatti/licentiat

–   a pre-doctoral postgraduate degree in all the other fields than medicine,
         dentistry and veterinary medicine, a substantial thesis required.
–   not compulsory
–   duration of studies: 2–3 years of full-time studies

D)   Tohtori/doctor, a doctorate

–   a doctorate, the doctoral thesis (dissertation) must be defended in a
         public debate
–   at least 4 years of full-time studies

The new degrees:

The following list includes the degrees which will be in use by 1 August 1994 (with
one exception); the reform will be completed by 1996 in the other fields of study.

A)   The lower degrees

–   duration of studies: 3 years; 120 credits, a short thesis required

(a)   **kandidaatin tutkinto:**
luonnontieteiden kandidaatti, natural sciences, 1 August 1993;
humanististen tieteiden kandidaatti, the humanities, 1 August 1994;
**valtiotieteiden kandidaatti, yhteiskuntatieteiden kandidaatti and
hallintotieteiden kandidaatti**, all three in social sciences, 1 August 1994;
liikuntatieteiden kandidaatti, sport sciences, 1 August 1994;
taiteen kandidaatti, industrial arts, 1 August 1994 – (N.B. Do not confuse with
the 'old' **kandidaatti**, which is a higher academic degree, see above!)

(b)   **kuvataiteen tutkinto**, fine arts, 1 August 1993

(c)   **farmaseutin tutkinto**, pharmacy, 1 August 1994

(d)   **lastentarhanopettajan tutkinto**, kindergarten teacher, 1 August 1995

B)   The higher academic degrees, from autumn 1993 onwards

–   duration of studies: 5 years, or 2 years after the new **kandidaatti**; a total of 160 credits, or 120+40

(a)   **maisterin tutkinto**, 1 August 1994:
filosofian maisteri, the humanities, natural sciences;
valtiotieteiden maisteri, yhteiskuntatieteiden maisteri, hallintotieteiden maisteri, all three in social sciences;
liikuntatieteiden maisteri, sport sciences
taiteen maisteri, industrial arts

(b)   **kuvataideakatemian loppututkinto**, fine arts, 1 August 1993

(c)   **proviisorin tutkinto**, 1 August 1994

C)   Lisensiaatti/licentiat

–   a pre-doctoral postgraduate degree, not in all fields of study, may also be a professional postgraduate degree, otherwise as in the old system

D)   Tohtori/doctor

–   a doctorate, as in the old system

TEACHER EDUCATION

Pre-primary education

This consists of a three-year course at kindergarten teacher colleges. The entrance requirements are the matriculation examination. The education will be transferred to universities in 1995, a three-year programme will then lead to a lower academic degree.

Comprehensive school and upper secondary school

University education is required in the form of a Master's degree, i.e. the higher academic degree. For teachers in the lower stage of comprehensive school this must be in education. Master's degree in the relevant field of study are required of subject teachers.

France
(including Monaco and overseas departments and territories)

The historical tendency towards centralization in French education has been reversed gradually since November 1968 (*Loi d'Orientation d'Education*) and, particularly, since the election of the Socialist government in 1981. Although curricula and teaching methods are laid down by the Ministry of Education, institutions are allowed more and more autonomy in their application.

Apart from decentralization, the objective of successive education ministers since 1988 has been to reassert the value of the teaching profession, to develop vocational and technical training, to increase the number of those studying to **Baccalauréat** level and to fight against underachievement. Following the general election in March 1993, a new ministry of education was introduced. A reform of secondary education is due, at the time we are writing, to be introduced.

Education is compulsory from age 6 (when children start in primary school) to age 16. Except in the case of those who have to repeat a year, this means that compulsory education covers primary school, lower secondary school, and one year of upper secondary school.

The school year runs from September to June.

EVALUATION IN BRITAIN

School

Certificat d'Aptitude Professionnelle (CAP) – generally considered comparable to City and Guilds of London Institute (C&G) Craft Certificate Part II.

Brevet d'Etudes Professionnelles (BEP) – generally considered comparable to C&G Craft Certificate Part II/III.

Brevet Professionel (BP)/**Brevet de Maîtrise** – generally considered comparable to C&G Craft Certificate Part III.

Brevet de Technicien (BT) – generally considered comparable to BTEC National Diploma / N/SVQ level 3 / Advanced GNVQ/GSVQ standard.

Brevet d'Etudes du Premier Cycle (before 1981)/**Brevet des Collèges** – generally considered to be below GCSE standard.

Baccalauréat de l'Enseignement du Second Degré (former **Baccalauréat Parts I and II**), and **Diplôme de Bachelier de l'Enseignement du Second Degré** – may be considered to satisfy the general entrance requirements of British higher education institutions.

Baccalauréat Technologique – generally considered comparable to BTEC National Diploma / N/SVQ level 3 / Advanced GNVQ/GSVQ standard; may be considered to satisfy the general entrance requirements of British higher education institutions.

Further

Brevet de Technicien Supérieur – considered to approach the standard of BTEC Higher National Diploma / N/SVQ Level 4.

Diplôme Universitaire de Technologie – generally considered comparable to BTEC Higher National Diploma / N/SVQ Level 4.

Higher

Licence – generally considered comparable to British Bachelor (Ordinary) degree standard; students with high grades could be considered for admission to postgraduate study.

Diplôme d'Ingénieur – generally considered comparable to British Master's degree standard.

Maîtrise – generally considered comparable to British Bachelor (Honours) degree standard.

Magistère (introduced in 1985) – generally considered comparable to British Master's degree standard.

Doctorat de Troisième Cycle (last awarded in the academic year 1984–5) – generally considered comparable to British MPhil degree standard.

Docteur de l'Université – generally considered comparable to British PhD degree standard.

MARKING SYSTEMS

School

Baccalauréat: individual subjects are marked on a scale of 0–20 (maximum), 10 being the minimum pass mark.

16–20	*très bien*	outstanding (seldom awarded!)
14–15	*bien*	very good
12–13	*assez bien*	good
10–11	*passable*	pass

Higher

The **Licence** is classified: *passable*, *assez bien*, *bien* and *très bien*.

If no classification (*mention*) is given, the **Licence** is awarded with the grade *passable*.

No classification or marking is given for qualifications from the *Grandes Ecoles*.

ABBREVIATIONS

Qualifications

Bac	–	**Baccalauréat**
BC	–	**Brevet de Collège**
BEP	–	**Brevet d'Etudes Professionnelles**
BEPC	–	**Brevet d'Etudes du Premier Cycle**
BP	–	**Brevet Professionnel**
BT	–	**Brevet de Technicien**
BTn	–	**Baccalauréat Technologique/de Technicien**
BTS	–	**Brevet de Technicien Supérieur**
BTSA	–	**Brevet de Technicien Supérieur en Agriculture**
CAP	–	**Certificat d'Aptitude Pédagogique**
CAP	–	**Certificat d'Aptitude Professionnelle**
CAPEGC	–	**Certificat d'Aptitude au Professorat de l'Enseignement Général de Collège**
CAPES	–	**Certificat d'Aptitude au Professorat de l'Enseignement du Second Degré**
CAPET	–	**Certificat d'Aptitude au Professorat de l'Enseignement Technique**
CEAA	–	**Certificat d'Etudes Approfondies en Architecture**
CEP	–	**Certificat d'Education Professionnelle**
DEA	–	**Diplôme d'Etudes Approfondies**
DES	–	**Diplôme d'Etudes Specialisées**
DESS	–	**Diplôme d'Etudes Supérieures Specialisées**
DEUG	–	**Diplôme d'Etudes Universitaires Générales**
DEUP	–	**Diplôme d'Etudes Universitaires Professionnelles**
DEUST	–	**Diplôme d'Etudes Universitaires Scientifiques et Techniques**
DNAP	–	**Diplôme National d'Arts Plastiques**
DNAT	–	**Diplôme National des Arts et Techniques**
DNSEP	–	**Diplôme National Supérieur d'Arts Plastiques**
DPLG	–	**Diplôme par le Gouvernement**
DU	–	**Diplôme d'Université**
DUT	–	**Diplôme Universitaire de Technologie**
MIAGE	–	**Maîtrise de Méthodes Informatiques Appliquées à la Gestion**
MSG	–	**Maîtrise de Sciences de Gestion**
MST	–	**Maîtrise des Sciences et Techniques**

Institutions

CET	–	*Collège d'Enseignement Technique*
CFA	–	*Centre de Formation d'Apprentis*
LEGT	–	*Lycée d'Enseignement Général et Technologique*
LEP	–	*Lycée d'Enseignement Professionnel*
IUFM	–	*Institut Universitaire de Formation des Maîtres*
IUP	–	*Institut Universitaire Professionnalisé*
IUT	–	*Institut Universitaire de Technologie*
UER	–	*Unité d'Enseignement et de Recherche*

SCHOOL EDUCATION

Pre-primary

Facilities are available in *Ecoles Maternelles* for children aged two to six.

Primary

This covers five years from age six, divided into three cycles:

Préparatoire (preparatory)   one year
Elémentaire (elementary)   two years
Moyen (intermediate)   two years

The curriculum covers reading, writing, French, arithmetic, moral guidance, history, geography, observation exercises, drawing, singing, handiwork and games.

The teaching of a modern language in the last two years of primary school, has been gradually introduced since 1993.

Pupils proceed automatically to secondary education, without an entrance examination, unless they come from a private school or have an unsatisfactory report from the primary school.

Secondary

This is divided into two stages covering seven years: lower and upper.

Lower secondary

The lower cycle (*enseignement secondaire du premier cycle*) covers four years, and classes are numbered in reverse order, i.e. the first year of secondary education is the sixth class, the second year is the fifth class, etc.

Since 1959, the first two years have been known as the Observation Cycle. The core subjects are: French, mathematics, history, geography, one foreign language, physical education, and, since 1975, experimental sciences, artistic activities (including music and drawing) and manual and technical education. There has been no streaming since 1975.

The second cycle of two years is known as the Orientation Cycle. Pupils may continue their general education with the same core subjects plus one obligatory subject from the following: an additional foreign language, the reinforced study of the foreign language, Latin, Greek, or one of three technical subjects. Pupils not wishing to do this may begin a course with a vocational bias.

At the beginning of 1992 some one hundred European Sections were set up. In these sections, after two years of intensive learning of a modern language, pupils begin to learn another subject – e.g. history, geography or biology – through that language. A further 72 European Sections are scheduled to open at the beginning of the academic year in 1993.

From 1959, pupils attended *Collèges d'Enseignement Généraux* for lower-secondary education; these were renamed *Collèges Uniques* in 1977–8. In the mid-1960s, schools called *Collèges d'Enseignement Secondaires* were established, which covered all the various types of lower secondary course, i.e. classical (Latin, with optional Greek), modern I (including two modern languages), modern II (including one modern language) and transition classes. These were reclassified as *'Collèges Uniques'* in 1977–8 and are now all referred to simply as *Collèges*.

Until 1976 pupils could take an examination in six subjects on completion of the full four-year course of lower secondary education, to be awarded the **Brevet d'Etudes du Premier Cycle** (BEPC); now called **Brevet des Collèges**.

Pupils sit for this national examination whether they attend classes in a *Collège* or a *Lycée Professionnel*. There are three types of **Brevet** corresponding to the three types of schooling available: **Collège**, **Technologique** or **Professionnel**. The **Brevet** is awarded on the basis of marks obtained both in a written examination in French, mathematics, history and geography and in all the subjects marked throughout the last two years of the *Collège*.

Upper secondary

After the *Collège*, pupils may go either to a *Lycée Professionnel* (LP) or to a *Lycée d'Enseignement Général et Technologique* (LEGT). The LP offers short and long courses in general, technical and vocational subjects. LEGTs only offer long courses which can be either technical, vocational or general.

Short courses

The **Certificat d'Aptitude Professionnelle** (CAP) is the first craft qualification awarded by the LPs. This course takes three years for pupils who have completed the first two years of the *Collège* or who come from the *Classes Préprofessionnelles de Niveau* (CPPN) or from the *Classes Préparatoires à l'Apprentissage* (CPA), two years for pupils who have completed *Collège* education and one year for pupils who already hold another CAP.

The **Brevet d'Etudes Professionnelles** (BEP) qualifies students for a function which can be common to several craft activities. Its relevance is wider than that of the CAP but less specific. It is awarded after a two-year course to pupils who have completed the *Collège*, holders of a CAP or to pupils who have been reorientated from the *Lycée*.

Long courses

The **Baccalauréat Professionnel** (BacPro) is a vocational qualification created in 1985. It aims at offering a higher vocational qualification than the BEP, preparing students for employment and yet leaving them the possibility of entering higher education. It is awarded after a two-year course to holders of the relevant CAP or BEP. Industrial attachment is included in the training for between sixteen and twenty-two weeks. There are now up to thirteen subjects available.

The **Brevet de Technicien** (BT) is a technical qualification in a specific area, aimed at training technicians who may either start working after qualifying or further their studies (BTS, BTSA, or sometimes DUT). It is a three-year course starting after the first year of upper school (*classe de seconde*).

After the first year in the *Lycée*, pupils may choose between different sections and subsections which will lead them to either the **Baccalauréat de l'Enseignement du Second Degré** or to the **Baccalauréat Technologique** (BTn).

Before 1966 the examinations for the **Baccalauréat** were taken in two parts. At the end of the second year of the three-year cycle, the Part I examinations were taken in the three compulsory subjects (French, history and geography) plus three other subjects. On completion of the final year, pupils took the examinations for Part II, which was more specialized and concentrated on mathematics, science and philosophy.

Prior to the 1989 reform of the baccalaureate, there were eight **Baccalauréats du Second Degré**: three with the emphasis on literary subjects (A1, A2, A3), one with the emphasis on economics (B) and four in sciences (C, D, D1, E). Section S divided into C (mathematics and physics) and D (mathematics and natural sciences) in the last year; the other sections remained the same throughout.

The **Baccalauréat de Technicien**, created in 1968, became, in 1985, the **Baccalauréat Technologique** (BTn) The aim of the BTn is to produce technicians who have followed both a general and a technical education, and are familiar with modern technology (electronics, computing and robotics). Pupils are examined after a three-year course in a *Lycée*. Holders of a CAP or a BEP may also prepare for a BTn. Prior to the 1989 reform of the baccalaureate, there were seventeen BTns. Series F subdivided into:

F1	mechanical construction
F2	electronics
F3	electrotechnology
F4	civil engineering
F5	physics
F6	chemistry
F7	biological sciences – biochemistry module
F7[1]	biological sciences – biology module
F8	medical and social sciences
F9	building engineering
F10	microtechnics
F11	music technology
F12	art and design

Series G subdivided into:

G1	public administration
G2	business management
G3	commerce

Series H computer science/information science.

The 1989 reform provides for a reorganization and simplification of the general and technical streams and a new balance between them. There will now be only three groups in the general stream – scientific (S), literary (L), and economic and social (ES) – and four in the technical stream: service industry, general industry, laboratory, and medico-social. The first examinations of this new **Baccalauréat** were held in July 1994.

There are now two sets of examinations for the **Baccalauréat**. The first group is compulsory and subdivided into two sets of examinations:

The first set includes written and oral examinations. At the end of this set, pupils who have obtained a mean mark of 10 out of 20 pass. There are four grades: *passable* (mean: 10), *assez bien* (mean: 12), *bien* (mean: 14), *très bien* (mean: 16). Pupils whose mean mark is between 8 and 10 have to sit for the second set of examinations. A compulsory examination in physical education and sports is included in the first set of examinations.

The second group of examinations is optional and students may choose up to two subjects. Subjects which are assessed as compulsory subjects cannot be chosen as options. Only the points above 10 obtained in these optional examinations will contribute to the mean mark.

The **Certificat d'Etudes Secondaires** (CFES) is awarded to pupils who obtain a mean mark between 8 and 10 out of 20 in the examinations of the **Baccalauréat**.

Students who pass the examination are given the certificate of **Diplôme de Bachelier de l'Enseignement du Second Degré**.

The existing **Baccalauréats** were replaced in 1994 with five new ones: literature; economics and social studies; management and communication; science; science and technology. Each has a compulsory core taking up to 80 per cent of the timetable with a choice of two options specific to the series.

A **Baccalauréat à Option Internationale** was introduced in 1983 in order to offer a French alternative to the **International Baccalaureate** (Swiss). Unlike the **International Baccalaureate** it is a fully bilingual examination, requiring candidates to write and speak in two languages. The examination includes, together with other subjects of the **Baccalauréat**, papers in literature, history and geography taken in the foreign language concerned.

FURTHER EDUCATION

Before 1966, holders of the **Baccalauréat** or **Brevet de Technicien** could undertake a two-year specialized and practically oriented course at a *Lycée Technique* leading to a **Brevet de Technicien Supérieur** (BTS).

In 1966 a number of university institutes of technology (*Instituts Universitaires de Technologie* – IUTs) were established; these offer two-year courses leading to the **Diplôme Universitaire de Technologie** (DUT). These courses and the DUT are intended to replace the courses leading to the BTS, but are less specialized. The BTS aims at being more vocational than the DUT.

HIGHER EDUCATION

There are several types of institutions of higher education: universities and university institutes on the one hand, and on the other, a number of institutions outside the university sector, which may be either public or private, some of them being part of the prestigious *Conférence des Grandes Ecoles*.

French universities award three different types of qualification:

a)   national qualifications in law, economics and management, arts, social sciences, physics, natural sciences, technology, medicine, dentistry and pharmacy;

b)   qualifications from schools or institutes which are part of a university (e.g. *Institut d'Etudes Politiques, Ecole Nationale Supérieure d'Ingénieurs*, etc.);

c)   university qualifications.

National qualifications appear on a list produced by the Ministry of Education. The syllabus of the courses contains both an element agreed at national level and one set by universities and recognized by the Ministry (DUT, DEUG, DEUST, etc. – see below). University qualifications are organized by individual institutions usually with the help of the representatives of industry and commerce in the area. This is why their content is pre-vocational as well as theoretical. Their title is not the same as that of national qualifications (e.g. DU – created in 1976, **Magistère** – created in 1985 – see below).

Entry is officially on the basis of success in the **Baccalauréat,** whatever the subject or grades. However, perhaps owing to a growing number of **Baccalauréat** holders and to limited space, some Parisian universities have proceeded to unofficial selection procedures since the mid-1980s. Competition is also stiff for places in the successful technical universities (IUTs). Many students with a **Technical Baccalauréat** take a university place to study literature as a last resort. Moreover, many students who end up in non-selective universities have little real aptitude for their chosen courses.

A compulsory application scheme for undergraduate courses was started in March 1992.

University education is divided into three cycles:

First cycle

Until 1966

All students undertook a common first year (*l'année de propédeutique*). Successful performance in the end-of-year examinations led to the **Certificat d'Etudes Littéraires/Scientifiques Générales** (CELG/CESG), but this was abolished, mainly because of a high failure rate. Until the 1966 reforms, students often took longer than the usual three or four years to obtain a **Licence.**

1966 reforms

The qualifications **Diplôme Universitaire d'Etudes Littéraires** (DUEL) and **Diplôme Universitaire d'Etudes Scientifiques** (DUES) were introduced and awarded on completion of the first cycle (usually two years) of the **Licence** course in the humanities and sciences respectively.

Since 1966

The first cycle of university study in the sciences and humanities has been limited to three years and only one re-examination permitted.

Since 1973–4

The first cycle became more specialized and led to the **Diplôme d'Etudes Universitaires Générales** (DEUG), normally after two years' study. Since the education reform of 1985, it has been possible to prepare as well for the **Diplôme d'Etudes Universitaires de Sciences et Techniques** (DEUST) (a two-year scientific training for employment or more advanced courses including short periods of industrial attachment) and the **Diplôme d'Université** (DU) which must have a technical element and involves one to three years' training according to regional requirements.

Second cycle

1973–4:

On completing one year of study after the DEUG, students could obtain a **Licence** in arts and science subjects (three years in total) or after a further two years' study in law and economic subjects (four years in total).

Since 1976

The **Licence** in law and economics may be obtained one year after the DEUG (three years in total).

A **Maîtrise** was created in law and economics.

To obtain a **Licence** (or any other higher education qualification) students must obtain a certain number of **Certificats d'Etudes Supérieures** (CES) (called **Certificat de Licence** until the mid-1960s).

Until 1978 there were two types of **Licence** (differing in course content), the **Licence Libre** and the **Licence d'Enseignement**. A student who prepared a **Licence Libre** had a freer choice of subjects than a student preparing a **Licence d'Enseignement**, who was, and is, bound by a number of regulations, compulsory subjects, etc. (a second foreign language is necessary for the **Licence d'Enseignement d'Anglais** for example).

In management and technology, students may, after obtaining the DEUG, study for a **Maîtrise** directly, which is awarded after a two-year course: MST, MIAGE, MSG.

In arts and science subjects, one further year of study after the **Licence** now leads to the **Maîtrise**. There is no official time limit to obtain the qualifications of the second cycle (**Licence** and **Maîtrise**). The **Magistère**, which was first introduced in 1985, is awarded after a three-year course. The entrance requirements are the DUT or the DEUG. Admission is selective and the qualification is intended to be high-level and vocational.

A **Diplôme d'Ingénieur** may be obtained three years after the DEUG (or one year after the MST diploma has been obtained).

Third cycle

Until July 1984

The qualifications obtained in the third cycle were the **Doctorat de Spécialité de Troisième Cycle** and the **Doctorat d'Etat**.

To obtain the former, students took a one-year course after the **Maîtrise** leading to the **Diplôme d'Etudes Approfondies** (DEA); followed by between one and two years' research and submission of a thesis.

The **Diplôme d'Etudes Supérieures Spécialisées** (DESS) was obtained after one year of specialized training directly related to a profession. The entrance requirement was a **Maîtrise**.

The **Doctorat d'Etat** was the highest qualification in arts and sciences but could also be obtained in pharmacy, law, economic science and medicine. There was no maximum time limit for research for the thesis but the minimum was two years after the **Maîtrise**. In literary subjects the thesis usually took at least five years to prepare. In law, students had to hold the **Licence** and the **Diplôme d'Etudes Supérieures** (DES) before being admitted to research for this qualification. The DES was obtained after one year of research in law and economics if the student was successful in written and oral examinations and the presentation of a thesis.

Since 1984

The Law on Higher Education (5 July 1984) created a new **Doctorat** which replaces the **Doctorat de Troisième Cycle** and the **Doctorat d'Etat**.

The new **Doctorat** is preceded (as were former **Doctorats**) by one year's study for the DEA and followed by two to four years' research to doctoral title. The standard of the new **Doctorat** is higher than the former **Doctorat de Troisième Cycle**. The new doctoral title is: **Docteur de l'Université X** and the diploma will include the title of the thesis and names and of titles of jury members. This **Doctorat** is delivered by universities on their own responsibility and by certain other higher education institutions.

The **Habilitation à Diriger des Recherches** is of a higher level than the previous **Doctorat d'Etat**. An applicant must already hold the **Doctorat** and demonstrate an ability to plan and direct research work. An assessment is made of the candidate's entire scientific work and there is no time limit.

Medicine, dentistry, pharmacy

The first two years of the course in medicine (PCEM) cover general scientific subjects. The first year is also followed by students in dentistry. The competitive examination at the end of the first year may only be taken twice; but, even if a student passes, promotion to the second year is not automatic, as it depends on the number of hospital training places available.

The **Diplôme d'Etat de Docteur en Médecine** is obtained after a further six years of specialized study. The **Diplôme d'Etat de Docteur en Chirurgie Dentaire** is obtained after four years following the basic first year, and the **Diplôme d'Etat de Docteur en Pharmacie** is awarded after a six-year course. Students enter the second year of training after a competitive examination.

Specialist medical training is not postgraduate but is available after the sixth year of medical education. Students have to sit for a highly competitive examination to enter a four or five-year course of specialist training culminating in the **Diplôme d'Etudes Spécialisées** (DES). After the sixth year, medical students may also undertake research and prepare for a DEA and then a **Doctorat**.

In dentistry, the **Diplôme d'Etat** is a prerequisite to specialization. In dentistry, students obtain the **Certificats d'Etudes Spécialisées** (CES) A and B (two years) or the **Certificat d'Etudes Cliniques Spéciales Mention Orthodontive** (CESMO). In pharmacy, they prepare **Diplômes d'Etudes Spécialisées** (DES) after a competitive examination, the **Internat**, which takes place at the end of the fifth year. Specialization lasts three years. Both dental students and pharmacists may undertake research and prepare for a DEA and a **Doctorat**. A DES is also available in pharmacy (one year).

University institutes

Some universities also include institutes which may be of four kinds:

Institut Universitaire de Technologie (IUT). Within universities, IUTs offer two-year courses with a general and vocational content. The qualification awarded is the **Diplôme Universitaire de Technologie** (DUT). Entrance requirements are the **Baccalauréat** and acceptable school reports. Candidates may be asked to come for interview. Some IUTs have also been organizing one-year post-DUT courses with a significant vocational content.

Institut d'Etudes Politiques (IEP). There are six of these in the provinces and one in Paris, which organize three-year courses in political sciences. Entrance requirements are the **Baccalauréat**, a written entrance examination and an interview. Promotion to the second year entails passing an examination which eliminates many students. Students who hold a **licence** are admitted directly into the second year of IEP.

Institut Universitaire de Formation des Maîtres (IUFM). Since 1990 a number of these have been created. They run courses of pre- and in-service training for teachers.

Institut Universitaire Professionnalisé (IUP). Created in 1992, the IUPs, in conjunction with industry, train executives in the field of engineering, business and management, general administration, information and communication. Admission is selective, after one year of higher education. The course lasts 3 years, includes at least six months in work placements, with an initiation to research. The study of two foreign languages is compulsory. After the first year a **Diplôme d'Etudes Universitaires Professionnelles (DEUP)** is awarded, then a **Licence** after the second year and a **Maîtrise** after the third year. The title *Ingénieur-maître* is awarded at the end of training.

Non-University Institutes of Higher Education

Training in business, engineering, agriculture, architecture and fine art/design was not traditionally offered by universities. With the creation of architecture, fine art, engineering and management courses in universities over the past decade, French universities started to go against this trend. However, non-university institutions, either state or private, still offer the main training opportunities in these subjects.

The difficulty in the recognition of the qualifications awarded by these establishments lies in the status of the establishments: are they state, private, are they recognized by an official body – the Ministry of Education or another 'technical' Ministry – do they belong to the local chamber of commerce, are they part of the *Conférence des Grandes Ecoles*? If they are private and not recognized, are their qualifications validated (*homologué*) by the Ministry of Labour? In this case, the Ministry will assess the level of competence represented by the qualification according to a set scale, the same that can be found in other EU countries, including Britain (NVQs), but in the opposite order.

In some subjects which are considered as 'applied' or vocational and not 'academic', prestigious qualifications or prestigious institutions are neither recognized nor validated by the Ministry of Education, for instance fine or applied arts: it is the case of the **Diplôme** of the prestigious Ecole Nationale Supérieure des Beaux-Arts in Paris, which is however a state institution under the control of the Ministry of Culture.

1) Architecture: training is offered by a number of schools under the control of the Ministry of Equipment, Transport and Tourism (previously Ministry of Culture). Access is selective: holders of the **Baccalauréat** with a good school record will go through an interview. Applicants with another art/design qualification are also considered. Training was reorganized in 1984 in two parts (the Malraux reform in 1971 had organized training in three parts, each of them lasting two years): a two year foundation course leading to the **Diplôme d'Etudes Fondamentales en Architecture (DEFA)**. A further three-year course leads to the final award, the **Diplôme d'Architecte DPLG (Diplômé par le gouvernement)** which is the qualifying examination to be a registered architect in France. The **Diplôme** of a private school, the Ecole Spéciale d'Architecture is also recognised for registration. Some schools offer postgraduate courses leading to the **Certificat d'Etudes Approfondies en Architecture** (CEAA), sometimes in conjunction with universities. Some universities offer postgraduate courses in town and country planning to architects.

2) Training in business/management, engineering, agriculture and advanced teacher training provided by non-university institutes is generally highly competitive. Students can join these institutes either after the **Baccalauréat** or after a preparatory course (*Classes Préparatoires*) which can cover either one (business and management) or two years (agriculture, engineering and advanced teacher training). The entrance examinations are particularly competitive, especially in the case of the *Grandes Ecoles* which will only accept students after one or two years of higher education. The entrance examinations test applicants' ability in relevant subjects but also general knowledge in humanities and languages.

– In schools of agriculture and engineering training will last 5 years if entrance is immediately after the **Baccalauréat**, 4 years if entrance is after one year of higher education, 3 years if entrance is after 2 years of *classes préparatoires*.

– In business and management schools, training will last either 4 years if entrance is immediately after the **Baccalauréat**, and 3 years if it is after one-year *classe préparatoire*.

– In advanced teacher training (*Ecoles Normales Supérieures*) training usually lasts 3 years.

The final qualification awarded is that of the institute itself. In the case of engineering schools, the **Diplôme d'ingénieur** must be validated by the *Commission des Titres*, which is an offshoot of the Ministry of Education, even if the engineering school is under the control of another Ministry, Telecommunications, for instance.

3) Access to fine art/design courses in state schools (either local or national) is through success in the **Baccalauréat**, a competitive entrance examination including a written test, a practical and an interview. There are three awards available: the **Diplôme National des Arts et Techniques** (DNAT) after a three-year course, the **Diplôme National d'Arts Plastiques** (DNAP) after a three-year course leading to the preparation of the **Diplôme National Supérieur d'Expression Plastique** (DNSEP), awarded after another two years. A great number of private schools prevail in these fields without any official control. A certain number of them award qualifications recognized by professional associations, like the *Office Public de Qualification des Architectes d'Intérieur* which recognizes the awards in interior decoration from the Académie Julian, Ecole Supérieure des Arts et Techniques, Ecole Camondo.

The most prestigious of these non-university institutions of higher education have associated in the *Conférence des Grandes Ecoles* which sets standards for new entrants and controls those of current members. Access to these institutes is always by competitive examination prepared over one or two years and training usually lasts three years. In the mid-1980s these institutions have created postgraduate qualifications such as the **Diplôme de Specialisation** or the **Mastere Specialisé**. Some also offer research facilities which can lead to a DEA or a **Doctorat** awarded in partnership with a university. Few have been authorized (*habilité*) by the Ministry of Education to award a **Doctorat** (i.e. Ecole Centrale de Paris).

TEACHER EDUCATION

Pre-primary and primary

Until 1972

Students holding the **Baccalauréat** were trained on a two-year course at an *Ecole Normale* leading to the **Certificat d'Aptitude Pédagogique** (CAP), which included one month of teaching practice each term for the two years. There was also provision for students to undertake a four-year course if they had completed only five years of general secondary education.

1972–8

Students were recruited to the two-year course by competitive examination after the **Baccalauréat**. At the end of the course, students were awarded a **Certificat de Fin d'Etudes Normales** (CFEN), which also qualified them for the **Certificat d'Aptitude Pédagogique** (CAP), necessary for teaching.

1979–82

The course lasted three years from the level of **Baccalauréat** and led to the **Diplôme d'Enseignement Supérieur** as well as the CAP.

Since 1983

Students are recruited to the two-year training course after either a DEUG, BTS or DUT and a competitive examination.

From 1991

All teacher training now takes place in the *Instituts Universitaires de Formation des Maîtres* (IUFMs). The entrance requirement to the two-year course is the **Licence**. Candidates must specify whether they intend to teach in primary or secondary schools: all students have a common core consisting of about 10 per cent of the course, but apart from this core the courses are very different. The courses are not purely academic but include regular periods of practice. At the end of the first year, students sit an examination leading to the **Certificat d'Aptitude au Professorat des Ecoles** (CAPE). Most of the second year is spent in in-service training with a minimum of 500 hours. Upon completion of the course primary school teachers are awarded the title *Professeur d'Ecoles*.

Secondary

Before 1991

In *Collèges, Professeurs d'Enseignement Général de Collège* (PEGCs), usually primary teachers who passed a competitive internal examination, the **Certificat d'Aptitude au Professorat d'Enseignement Général de Collège** (CAPEGC), usually teach two (sometimes three) subjects at the lower levels; at the higher levels, most teachers hold the **Certificat d'Aptitude à l'Enseignement du Second Degré** (CAPES) and usually teach only one subject. The latter title is obtained after a competitive civil service examination, success in which is dependent on the number of posts available each year, of which the first part is prepared in the universities. In order to sit the competitive examination, candidates must hold a **Licence** in a relevant subject or an equivalent qualification. The second part (a one-year teacher-training course) is prepared in the *Centres Pédagogiques Régionaux* (CPR) and comprises practical teaching work under supervision. Some teachers may hold the **Agrégation** (see below). In the *Collèges et Lycées Professionnels*, most teachers are holders of the **Certificat d'Aptitude au Professorat d'Enseignement Technique** (CAPET), the technical education equivalent of the CAPES. Three new qualifications have been created for teachers in *Lycées d'Enseignement Professionnel* and technological sections in *Lycées*:

– **Professeur de Lycée Professionnel -1er grade** (PLP1) – Candidates who have already completed two years of higher education (DEUG, DUT, BTS) or who have three years' professional experience sit a competitive examination for selection.

– **Professeur de Lycée Professionnel -2e grade** (PLP2). Candidates holding a **Licence** or a similar qualification, or who have worked for at least five years as a *cadre* (executive), sit a competitive examination for selection.

In the *Lycées*, most teachers are holders of the CAPES, and a few hold the **Agrégation**. Like the CAPES, the **Agrégation** is a competitive civil service examination, of a very high academic standard, prepared in the universities and the *Ecoles Normales Supérieures*; success also depends on the number of posts available each year. In order to sit the competitive examination candidates must hold a **Maîtrise** in a relevant subject or the CAPES. The teacher-training element is, however, much shorter, consisting of a six-week period. Very few candidates succeed in obtaining the **Agrégation** at their first attempt, and many prepare for it whilst already in teaching posts.

Since 1991

Secondary school teacher training no longer takes place in universities but – like primary school teacher training – in the *Instituts Universitaires de Formation des Maîtres*. Students take the teaching examination which was formerly prepared and held in universities at the end of their first year in the IUFM. Most of the second year is taken up by in-service training with a minimum of 300 hours' practice.

Higher

Teachers at this level receive no formal professional training, but there are minimum qualifications laid down for each grade, according to discipline.

MONACO

The educational system in Monaco is exactly the same as in France. The same syllabuses are used all through primary and secondary education. These are the qualifications which are currently prepared in Monaco: **Certificat d'Aptitude Pédagogique/Professionelle** (CAP), **Brevet des Collèges** (BC), **Brevet d'Etudes Professionelles** (BEP), **Baccalauréat Professionel, Baccalauréat Technologique/de Technicien** (BTn), **Baccalauréats A, B, G, D, F, Baccalauréat à Option Internationale** and **Brevet de Technicien Supérieur** (BTS). There is no provision for higher education in Monaco.

DEPARTEMENTS D'OUTREMER (DOM)/TERRITOIRES D'OUTREMER (TOM)

Education is supervised by the French Ministry of Education, as for metropolitan France, and the same certificates are taken.

Universities were created in Guadeloupe, Martinique and Guyana (Université Antilles-Guyane – 1982); in La Réunion (Université de la Réunion); in New Caledonia and Tahiti (Université du Pacifique – 1987).

Gabon

Formerly a French colony in French Equatorial Africa, Gabon has continued to follow a basically French pattern of education since independence in 1960.

The medium of instruction is French.

The academic year runs from October to June.

EVALUATION IN BRITAIN

School

Brevet d'Etudes du Premier Cycle (BEPC) – generally considered to be below GCSE standard.

Baccalauréat – generally considered comparable to GCSE standard (grades A, B and C) on a subject-for-subject basis, with the exception of English language.

Higher

Diplôme Universitaire d'Etudes Littéraires (DUEL), **Diplôme Universitaire d'Etudes Scientifiques** (UES), **Diplôme Universitaire d'Etudes Juridiques** (DUEJ), **Diplôme Universitaire d'Etudes Economiques** (DUEE), **Diplôme d'Etudes Universitaires Générales** (DEUG) – may be considered to satisfy the general entrance requirements of British higher education institutions.

Licence – generally considered comparable to a standard between GCE Advanced and British Bachelor degree; may be given advanced standing by British higher education institutions.

MARKING SYSTEMS

School

Marking is on a scale of 0–20 (maximum) per subject, with no official minimum pass-mark (though in practice 9 is the minimum pass-mark).

Overall grade at **Baccalauréat** is classified

très bien	very good
bien	good
assez bien	fair
passable	pass

A student may have grades below 9 in one or more subjects and still receive the **Baccalauréat** if the overall grade average is 9 or higher.

Higher

The **Licence** is classified as:

très bien	very good
bien	good
assez bien	fair
passable	pass

SCHOOL EDUCATION

Primary

This covers six years. The classes are known as: *maternelle* (ages three to five); class CP (*cours préparatoire*), for which the child must be six years old; classes CE1 and CE2 (*cours élémentaire*); and classes CM1 and CM2 (*septième*). At the end of this period pupils obtain the **Certificat d'Etudes Primaires Elementaires** (CEPE).

Secondary

This covers seven years, divided into a lower (*premier*) cycle lasting four years and an upper (*deuxième*) cycle lasting three years. Classes are numbered in reverse order: *classe de sixième* to *classe de troisième* in the lower cycle. On conclusion of the lower cycle, pupils obtain the **Brevet d'Etudes du Premier Cycle** (BEPC). During the upper cycle, pupils may specialize in mathematics, science or literature. On completion of the cycle, pupils take the examinations for the **Baccalauréat**, which may be obtained in one of the following options:

A	humanities and philosophy
B	economics
C	mathematics and physical sciences
D	natural science
E	science and technology

Pupils who do not qualify for the **Baccalauréat** are awarded the **Certificat de Fin d'Etudes Secondaires**, a record of attendance and performance in the final year.

Technical secondary

On completion of the lower cycle pupils may opt to take a 'short' course (two to three years) or 'long' course (three to four years) of technical secondary education. The former leads to the **Brevet de Technicien** and the latter to the **Baccalauréat Technique** which may be obtained in one of two options:

F	technology
G	commerce

Some apprenticeships and short vocational courses are available.

FURTHER EDUCATION

The **Baccalauréat** and five years at engineering college (Ecole Nationale Supérieure d'Enseignement Technique) leads to the **Diplôme d'Ingénieur**.

The **Baccalauréat** and two or three years at engineering college leads to the **Diplôme de Spécialiste Qualifié**.

HIGHER EDUCATION

There is one university, the National University of Gabon, founded in 1970, and now called the Université Omar Bongo.

Other institutions of higher education are:

Centre Universitaire des Sciences de la Santé (CUSS)
Ecole Nationale de l'Administration (ENA) (for diplomats as well)
Ecole Nationale de la Magistrature
Ecole Nationale des Postes
Ecole des Techniciens des Travaux Publics
Ecole Nationale des Eaux et Forêts
Institut Africain d'Informatique.

The entrance requirement for degree studies is the **Baccalauréat**.

The first cycle of studies lasts two years and leads to:

Diplôme Universitaire d'Etudes Litteraires (DUEL) in the arts and humanities

Diplôme Universitaire d'Etudes Scientifiques (DUES) in science subjects

Diplôme Universitaire d'Etudes Juridiques (DUEJ) in law

Diplôme Universitaire d'Etudes Economiques (DUEE) in economics.

Most of these qualifications now come under the overall title of **Diplôme d'Etudes Universitaires Générales** (DEUG).

A further one year of study in the arts and sciences and a further two years in economics and law lead to the **Licence.** Students may then proceed for a further year which includes the preparation of a thesis and leads to the **Maîtrise.**

Students who wish to study law but do not hold the **Baccalauréat** may undertake a two-year course leading to the **Capacité en Droit.**

The **Diplôme d'Ingénieur** requires five years of study beyond the **Baccalauréat**.

The **Doctorat en Médecine** requires six years of study beyond the **Baccalauréat**.

TEACHER EDUCATION

Primary

The BEPC and four years at a teacher training college leads to the **Certificat d'Aptitude Pédagogique**.

Secondary

Lower

A three-year post-secondary course at an advanced teacher training college leads to the **Diplôme de Professeur de Premier Cycle de l'Enseignement Secondaire.**

Upper

Teachers are normally graduates.

Technical

The **Baccalauréat** and five years at a teacher training college lead to the **Certificat d'Aptitude Pédagogique à l'Enseignement Technique.**

Gambia

The basis of the education system is the Education Act of 1963.

There is no compulsory education.

The medium of instruction is English.

EVALUATION IN BRITAIN

School

Secondary Technical School Leaving Certificate/Middle School Leaving Certificate – generally considered to be below GCSE standard.

West African Examinations Council School Certificate/GCE O level – grades 1–6 generally equated to GCSE standard (grades A, B and C) on a subject-for-subject basis.

West African Examinations Council A level – grades A–E are equated to GCE Advanced.

MARKING SYSTEM

School

West African Examinations Council School Certificate is graded 1 (maximum) – 9.

1	excellent
2	very good
3	good
4–6	credit
7–8	pass
9	fail

West African Examinations Council A level is graded A (maximum), B, C, D, E, O or S (subsidiary pass), F (fail).

SCHOOL EDUCATION

Primary

Until 1992

This covered six years from age seven. Under the Education Act of 1963, pupils took the **Common Entrance Examination** administered by the West African Examinations

Council. The results determined whether pupils went on to secondary technical schools or secondary high schools.

From 1992

On completion of this period, pupils now take the **Primary School Leaving Certificate** administered by the West African Examinations Council.

Secondary

Until 1992

Secondary technical schools offered four-year courses leading to the **Secondary Technical School Leaving Certificate** at the completion of Form 4, set locally and administered by the West African Examinations Council.

The secondary high schools offered a five-year course leading to the examinations for the **West African Examinations Council School Certificate**, followed by a further two years in the sixth form leading to the examinations for the **West African Examinations Council A level**.

From 1992

Middle schools offer three-year courses leading to the **Middle School Leaving Certificate** at the completion of Form 3, set locally and administered by the West African Examinations Council.

High schools offer a three-year course leading to the examinations for the **West African Examinations Council School Certificate**, followed by a further two years in the sixth form leading to the examinations for the **West African Examinations Council A level**.

The O and A level examinations are now referred to as **West African Examinations Council Secondary Schools Certificate.**

FURTHER EDUCATION

Technical and vocational

The Gambia Technical Training Institute offers a range of courses leading to the examinations of the City and Guilds of London Institute and the Royal Society of Arts.

Gambia College has four constituent schools:

– The School of Agriculture runs courses for extension workers and a certificate course for agricultural assistants; examinations are set and examined locally.

– The School of Education awards **Gambia Teachers' Certificates** which are local qualifications.

– The School of Nursing and Midwifery conducts courses leading to the award of **State Registered Nurse, State Enrolled Nurse, State Certified Midwife** and **Community Health Nursing Certificate**.

– The School of Public Health offers courses leading to the examinations of the **West African Health Examination Board Diploma** (Royal Society of Health) and a locally set and examined diploma.

The <u>Gambia Hotel School</u> conducts courses leading to locally set and examined awards in various areas of hotel work.

The <u>Management Development Institute</u>, newly established, runs short courses and seminars mainly for middle and upper-level officers in government service.

The <u>National Vocational Training Centre</u> conducts courses of one or two-years' duration in such areas as masonry, carpentry and welding, mainly at a basic level and locally examined.

HIGHER EDUCATION

There are no institutions of higher education. Students at this level go to a broad range of countries, including the United Kingdom, United States of America, Canada, Australia, New Zealand, Sweden, France, Soviet Union, Federal Republic of Germany and West and East African countries.

TEACHER EDUCATION

<u>Gambia College School of Education</u> offers a two-year course for primary teachers leading to the award of the **Gambia Primary Teachers' Certificate** and a two-year course for secondary teachers leading to the award of the **Gambia Higher Teachers' Certificate**. Students enter with the **West African Examinations Council School Certificate**.

A three-year in-service course leading to the award of the **Gambia Basic Teachers' Certificate** is now offered to unqualified teachers. The minimum entry requirements for this course are the **Gambia High School Leaving Certificate** or the **Middle School Leaving Certificate** and some teaching experience as an unqualified teacher.

Germany

Under the Basic Law (*Grundgesetz*) of the Federal Republic of Germany the legislative and administrative responsibility for education rested with the eleven *Länder* (states). These were West Berlin, Baden-Württemberg, Bavaria (*Bayern*), Bremen, Hamburg, Hesse, Lower Saxony (*Niedersachsen*), North Rhine-Westphalia (*Nordrhein Westfalen*), Rhineland Palatinate (*Rheinland-Pfalz*), Saarland and Schleswig-Holstein. Only a limited number and range of duties were attributed to the federal government; their legislative responsibilities covered the enactment of a framework of provisions for the general principles in the higher education sector, for the advancement of scientific research, and for vocational training provided outside the formal school system and vocational guidance. The federal government also assisted with the award of grants and with the construction costs of educational institutions.

On 3 October 1990 five new *Länder* (and the eastern part of Berlin), which formed the German Democratic Republic (GDR) between 1949 and 1990, acceded to the Federal Republic. These are Brandenburg, Mecklenburg-Vorpommern, Saxony-Anhalt (*Sachsen-Anhalt*), Saxony (*Sachsen*) and Thuringia (*Thüringen*). Since 1990, these *Länder* have been assimilating their education systems to those in the other eleven and to the Federal framework for vocational and higher education. A description of the education system in the former GDR and an evaluation of its qualifications are given as an appendix to this chapter.

The basic structures of the *Länder* education systems (e.g. length of compulsory education, beginning and end of the school year, designation of the various educational institutions and their organizational form, essential elements of curricula) were standardized by agreements between the *Länder* for the standardization of the school system between 1954 and 1964. There is broad uniformity between the systems of the *Länder*, the instruction offered, and the qualifications gained, but sometimes nomenclature and periods of study vary.

Education is compulsory from age six. It lasted eight years until 1964, when it was increased to nine years (ten years in Berlin, Brandenburg, Bremen, North Rhine-Westphalia) full-time, plus a further three years part-time (i.e. regardless of whether a person has taken up full-time employment, he or she must attend a *Berufsschule*, a part-time vocational school, or continue full-time at a *Berufsfachschule*).

The medium of instruction is German.

The academic year varies but is generally from September/October to June/July.

EVALUATION IN BRITAIN

School

Hauptschulabschluss (HSAS) – generally considered to be below GCSE standard.

Realschulabschluss/Mittlere Reife/Realschulreife – generally considered comparable to GCSE standards, (grades A, B and C), on a subject-for-subject basis, with the exception of English language.

Abitur/Zeugnis der Allgemeinen Hochschulreife/Zeugnis der Reife/Reifezeugnis – may be considered to satisfy the general entrance requirements of British higher education institutions.

Vocational

Gesellenbrief/Facharbeiterbrief – generally considered comparable to City and Guilds of London Institute (C&G) Certificate Part III.

Fachschulreife – see **Realschulabschluss** above.

Fachhochschulreife – generally considered to be above GCSE standard. May be considered for admission to access/bridging courses.

Fachgebundenes Abitur/Zeugnis der Fachgebundenen Hochschul-reife – generally considered comparable to BTEC National Diploma/ N/SVQ level 3 / Advanced GNVQ/GSVQ standard. May be considered to satisfy the general entrance requirements of British higher education institutions.

Higher

Vordiplom/Zwischenprüfung – generally considered comparable to a standard between GCE Advanced and British Bachelor degree. May be given advanced standing by British higher education institutions. These are intermediate exams taken at university.

Also **Grundstudium** – a basic three-year university course.

Berufsakademien diploma – generally considered to a standard above BTEC Higher National Diploma / N/SVQ level 4 standard.

Fachhochschuldiplom/Diplom (FH) – comparable to a British Bachelor degree. May be considered for postgraduate study where an overall mark of *Gut* has been achieved.

Diplom/Erstes Staatsexamen/Magister Artium – generally considered comparable to British Bachelor (Honours) degree standard, although the course lasts longer than in the UK.

Staatsprüfung/Lizentiat
Lizentiat/Aufbaustudium – generally considered comparable to British Master's degree standard.

Doktor – generally considered comparable to British PhD standard.

GLOSSARY

Abgang/Abschluss/Abgangszeugnis – Leaving certificate, provided when a pupil leaves school without taking an examination. It, therefore, represents merely a certificate of attendance

Abitur – Upper secondary school-leaving certificate, giving access to all types of higher education in all disciplines

Abschlusszeugnis – Leaving certificate, usually issued on the basis of examination performance

Allgemeine Hochschulreife – see **Abitur** above

Aufbau- – Extension, continuation

Berufs- – Vocational

Berufsaufbauschule – Part-time continuation (i.e. more advanced) vocational school

Berufsfachschule – Full-time specialized vocational school

Handelschule – as above but for commercial studies

Berufsschule – Part-time vocational school

Betriebswirt – Business economist

Ergänzungsprüfung – Supplementary examination

Fach- – Specialized

Facharbeiterbrief – Skilled worker's certificate

Fachgebunden – Restricted to certain subjects

Fachgebundene Hochschulreife – giving access to higher level education courses only in a limited range of subjects

Fachhochschule – University level higher education college offering practically oriented courses in specific subjects

Fachhochschulreife – Leaving certificate from an advanced full-time technical school, giving access to courses at a **Fachhochschule**

Fachoberschule – Advanced full-time technical school

Fachschule – Advanced technical school

Fachschulreife – Leaving certificate giving access to courses at a **Fachschule**; comparable in standard to the **Mittlere Reife**

Gesamtschule – Comprehensive school

Gesellenbrief – Apprenticeship certificate, journeyman's certificate. See Facharbeiterbrief

graduiert – Graduated

Grundkurse – Basic courses

Grundschule – Primary school

Gymnasium – Grammar school

(Haupt)diplom – Final degree at all types of university and Fachhochschulen

Hauptschule – Non-academic secondary school, similar to secondary modern school

Hauptschulabschluss – **Hauptschul**-leaving certificate

Hochschule – Higher education institution

Höhere Berufsfachschule – Full-time specialized higher vocational school

Leistungskurse – Achievement/main/intensive courses

Mittlere Reife – Intermediate school-leaving certificate

Prüfung – Examination

Realschule – Secondary school, more academic than the **Hauptschule**, less academic than the **Gymnasium**

Realschulabschlusszeugnis – **Realschul**-leaving certificate

Realschulreife – see **Mittlere Reife** and **Realschulabschlusszeugnis** above

Reife – Maturity, matriculation leaving certificate, giving access to the next level of education

Staatlich geprüfter Techniker – Technician who has passed a state examination

Staatsexamen – State examination

Vordiplom – University intermediate examination in science, economic and social science, and technological subjects

Wissenschaftszweig – Branch of learning

Zeugnis – Certificate

Zwischenprüfung – University intermediate examination in the humanities

MARKING SYSTEMS

School

1	*sehr gut*	very good
2	*gut*	good
3	*befriedigend*	very satisfactory
4	*ausreichend*	just adequate/pass
5	*mangelhaft*	fail
6	*ungenügend*	fail

Abitur examinations since 1976

15, 14, 13	very good
12, 11, 10	good
9, 8, 7	very satisfactory
6, 5, 4	just adequate/pass
3, 2, 1, 0	fail

The marks obtained for term-time work are converted to the marking scale now used for the **Abitur** as follows:

15	1+	9	3+	3	5+
14	1	8	3	2	5
13	1–	7	3–	1	5–
12	2+	6	4+	0	6
11	2	5	4		
10	2–	4	4–		

Each grade (except grade six) covers three points.

Achievement/main/intensive courses carry triple weighting, giving a possible maximum per subject of 45. For admission to the examinations for the **Abitur** a minimum of 200 points (100 in achievement courses, 100 in basic courses) is required. On the leaving certificate (**Zeugnis der Allgemeinen Hochschulreife**), entitling the holder to general admission to higher education, are given the marks accumulated in the last four semesters of the course and those of the **Abitur** examination. To pass the **Abitur** a minimum of 300 out of 900 points is required with at least 100 in each of the categories (achievement courses, basic courses, examination). The grand total (P) is then converted into an average (N) on the 1–6 scale according to a standard formula:

$$N = 5\ 2/3 - P/180$$
(if P is over 840, N = 1)

Higher

1	*sehr gut*	very good
2	*gut*	good
3	*befriedigend*	very satisfactory
4	*ausreichend*	just adequate/pass
5	*mangelhaft*	fail

SCHOOL EDUCATION

Pre-primary

Facilities are available for children aged three to six at *Kindergarten*.

Primary

This generally covers four years for children from age six at a *Grundschule*, but in Berlin and Brandenburg it is six years. The curriculum generally covers German, religious instruction, local studies, history, geography, science, arithmetic, music, art, craftwork and physical education. Normally, no examinations are taken at the end of the cycle, and some pupils may stay at this type of school until completion of compulsory schooling.

Secondary

This may cover nine or ten years. The school attended depends on parental choice and the recommendation of the primary school teachers. In many *Länder* the first two years are referred to as the orientation phase (*Orientierungsstufe*) and the type of schooling is not decided until completion of this phase.

There are four main types of secondary school covering the period of compulsory schooling: *Hauptschule, Realschule, Gymnasium and Gesamtschule.* In some *Länder, Mittelschule, Regelschule* and *Sekundaschule* offer alternative types of schooling.

Hauptschule

This covers grades five to nine in most *Länder* and grades five to ten in North Rhine-Westphalia, seven to nine in *Länder* having an independent orientation stage, and seven to ten in Berlin and Bremen. Where there is a possibility of a tenth year pupils may take the examinations for a certificate equivalent to the **Realschulabschlusszeugnis** (see below).

The course includes instruction in one foreign language (usually English), and the curriculum covers German, a foreign language, mathematics, physics/chemistry, biology, geography, history, social affairs, religious instruction, music, art, civics and physical education. On completion of the course, pupils take the *Hauptschul*-leaving examination (**Qualifizierter Hauptschulabschluss**) and obtain a record of their qualifications (**Qualifikationsvermerk**), which may give entry to a course of upper-secondary education at a *Gymnasium*. The certificate awarded is the **Hauptschulabschluss** (HSAS). In Bavaria, pupils do not sit examinations at this stage for the award of the certificate. The **Hauptschulabgangszeugnis** may be given to a pupil who leaves the school at any stage during the course; it is not based on examination performance.

Since 1991 Mecklenburg-Western Pomerania has been the only new *Länd* to establish *Hauptschulen*. However, the type of course described here is offered in *Mittelschule* in Saxony, at *Sekundarschule* in Saxony-Anhalt and at *Regelschule* in Thuringia. In Brandenburg the **Berufsbildungsreife** is comparable to the **Hauptschulabgangs zeugnis**, and can be obtained from a *Gesamtschulen*.

Realschule

This covers grades five to ten in most *Länder* (grades seven to ten in *Länder* with an independent orientation phase). In Bavaria, Berlin, Brandenburg and Hamburg, this phase covers only four years (grades six to ten). One foreign language (English) is compulsory. The curriculum covers the same subjects as at the *Hauptschule*, but they are taught at a more advanced level. On completion of the course, pupils take the examinations for the **Realschulabschlusszeugnis/Mittlere Reife/Realschulreife**.

Saxony, Saxony-Anhalt and Thuringia do not have *Realschule*, but comparable courses are offered at *Mittleschulen* (Saxony), *Sekundarschulen* (Saxony-Anhalt) or *Regelschulen* (Thuringia).

Gymnasium

This covers the full nine years of secondary schooling (grades five to thirteen) or seven years (grades seven to thirteen) where primary schooling lasts six years or there exists an independent orientation phase. In Mecklenburg-Western Pomerania, Saxony, Saxony-Anhalt and Thuringia it covers grades five to twelve. Pupils may however leave at the end of grade ten in all cases.

The curriculum in grades five to ten (or seven to ten) covers German, mathematics, biology, geography, music, art, physical education, at least two foreign languages, history, social studies, physics and chemistry. On completion of grade ten the **Mittlere Reife** is awarded (no examinations are taken).

Until 1976–7

Pupils wishing to continue their studies could specialize in one of three options:

mathematisch naturwissenschaftlich – mathematics/natural science;

neusprachlich – modern languages;

altsprachlich – classical languages.

Compulsory subjects common to all three options included German, civics, chemistry, physics, mathematics, physical education, music and art.

Since 1976–7 (1977–8 in Baden-Württenberg and Bayern)

Following the resolution of the Conference of Ministers of Education and Culture of the *Länder* of July 1972, the re-organized upper level of the *Gymnasium* (*Reformierte Gymnasiale Oberstufe*) was introduced. The course of instruction covers three broad subject areas: language/literature/arts; social sciences; mathematics/natural sciences/technology.

Compulsory subjects include German, foreign languages, art, music, philosophy and/or religious instruction, civics or history/geography/ social studies, economics, mathematics, physics, chemistry and biology. In addition, pupils study elective subjects, which comprise approximately one third of the course. Electives include the subjects mentioned as being compulsory plus e.g. education, psychology, sociology, statistics, geology, data processing, technology, etc. Both elective and compulsory subjects are taught at basic (*Grundkurse*) and intensive/main/achievement (*Leistungskurse*) level. The latter comprise five to six lessons per week, and basic courses only two to three lessons per week. Pupils must take two intensive courses, of which one must be a foreign language or mathematics or a natural science.

In 1988 the Standing Conference of the Ministers of Education and Culture of the *Länder* agreed on a continuation of the agreements concerning the *Reformierte Gymnasiale Oberstufe*. The new elements are:

three half-year courses must be taken in at least two subjects chosen from German, a foreign language and mathematics;

four half-year courses in history in civics/social studies (with history);

one natural science subject or two natural science subjects from grade eleven with two half-year courses in each.

On completion of grade thirteen (or twelve in the *Länder* mentioned above), pupils take the examinations for the **Abitur/Zeugnis der Allgemeinen Hochschulreife/Zeugnis der Reife/Reifezeugnis**:

In the 'traditional' form of *Gymnasium* (normally pre-1972) pupils took four written examinations: German, mathematics, a foreign language, and a subject related to the specialization (i.e. physics for the mathematics/natural science option, a further language from the original choice of languages – English and French for the modern languages option, Latin for the classical option) and oral examinations in these subjects. Pupils received the **Abitur** certificate if they obtained the classification of *Ausreichend* or above in all subjects.

In the reorganized upper level of the *Gymnasium* (post-1976–7) pupils take three written examinations and one oral. The first and second written examinations are in the subjects taken as achievement/main/intensive courses; the third written examination is taken in one of the elective subjects. The oral examination is chosen from: language, literature, arts, social studies, mathematics, science, religious studies and history, but must not be in one of the subjects already tested in a written examination. The complete set of examinations must include one modern foreign language, mathematics, natural science and German. One of the compulsory subjects may be taken at the end of grade twelve. The final grades on the **Zeugnis der Allgemeinen Hochschulreife** are based on marks obtained in the final examinations and on class performance in the basic and achievement/main/intensive courses during grades twelve and thirteen.

There are still a limited number of specialist *Gymnasien* (see under *Berufliches Gymnasium* below). On completion of the three-year course pupils take the examinations for the **Abitur** and, if successful, are awarded the **Fachgebundenes Abitur/Zeugnis der Fachgebundenen Hochschulreife**. This may be converted into the **Zeugnis der Allgemeinen Hochschulreife** by passing supplementary examinations.

Gesamtschulen

Gesamtschulen (comprehensive schools) are a relatively new type of school, but now exist as one of the standard school types in most *Länder*. They cover only grades five to nine or ten, or begin at grade seven is some *Länder*; others cover the full period of secondary schooling (grades five to thirteen). There are two types of comprehensive school:

ko-operativ – offering facilities usually available at other types of school (i.e. *Hauptschule, Realschule, Sekundarschule* and *Gymnasium*) on the same site, but with different classes;

integriert – each subject is taught at three levels, and students choose their own level according to their ability in each subject, but are not separated according to the traditional school types.

Pupils at the comprehensive schools take the same examinations as at the other types of secondary school.

From 1991/92 some *Länder* introduced new types of school in which the courses traditionally available at *Hauptschule* and *Realschule* where brought together. These schools are:

Mittelschule

Only established in Saxony, the *Mittelschule* provides a combined form of *Hauptschule* and *Realschule* education. Grades five and six form an orientation period, with specialization beginning at grade seven. The **Hauptschule leaving certificate** can be awarded at grade nine, **Realschule certificate** at grade ten.

Sekundarschule/Regelschule

The *Sekundarschule* exists in Saxony-Anhalt, where it is the standard type of school alongside the *Gymnasium*, and in Saarland where it is an alternative type of school.

Pupils may receive either a *Realschule* or *Hauptschule* type education, according to their performance in the first two years (orientation phase). In Thuringia the *Regelschule* provides a similar form of education.

Aufbauhauptschule, Aufbaurealschule and *Aufbaugymnasium* – students aged twenty-eight upwards normally transfer from industry (not school) to these institutions.

Technical and vocational secondary

All those who leave full-time schooling at age fifteen or sixteen must attend part-time school (one day per week minimum) until they are eighteen. This applies to all school-leavers between fifteen and eighteen, whether in training apprenticeships or full-time employment.

A great variety of institutions offer this type of course, and there are variations between the individual *Länder*. However, some major types may be identified:

Berufsschule (part-time vocational school/day continuation school)

These offer courses mainly for those who leave school at fifteen or sixteen and then proceed to vocational training in industry, as well as for those who are employed but receive no on-the-job training. Courses consist of practical and vocational training (about sixty per cent) and a programme of general subjects such as German, civics/social affairs, economics, English, religion and sport (about forty per cent). At the end of the course, trainees take a final examination administered by the competent local body i.e. by the Chamber of Commerce (*Industrie und Handelskammer*, see under Apprenticeships below). They receive a **leaving certificate** from the *Berufsschule*, issued without a preceding examination.

Berufsaufbauschule (part-time continuation, vocational school)

These offer courses for students who have already completed six months at a part-time vocational school (*Berufsschule*). The teaching, both of the general and of the vocational courses, is at a higher level than at the *Berufsschule*. General subjects covered are German, a foreign language, history and social affairs, geography (including economic geography), mathematics, physics and chemistry. The courses vary from one year full-time to three years' part-time. There are five areas of specialization, all of which incorporate economics and business management: general commercial/industrial; industrial/technical; home economics/nursing; social work; and agriculture. Courses lead to the **Fachschulreife**, considered in Germany to be comparable to the **Realschulreife**. With this qualification students may enter a *Fachschule* (see immediately below) or the second year of a *Fachoberschule* (see below).

Fachschule (advanced technical school)

These offer courses lasting between six months and two-and-a-half years for students who have completed an initial vocational training course. The entrance requirement is the **Mittlere** or **Fachschulreife** and completed vocational training. Personnel for middle management are trained in a variety of fields (e.g. at *Technikerschulen*).

Berufsfachschule (full-time specialized vocational school)

These train lower-level technicians, at the same time improving their general education. The various specializations sometimes lead to a complete change in an institution's name e.g. a *Handelschule* is a *Berufsfachschule* specializing in commerce. The entrance requirement is successful completion of *Hauptschule* (grade nine) or *Realschule* (grade ten). Courses vary from one to three years. At schools requiring a *Hauptschul*-leaving certificate for admission, a qualification considered comparable in Germany to the leaving certificate of a *Realschule* may be obtained on conclusion of a course lasting two years.

Höhere Berufsfachschule (full-time specialized higher vocational school)

Students completing a course at a *Berufsfachschule* may go on to this type of school, which prepares them for positions in lower and middle management as well as for entry to a course at a *Fachhochschule* (see under **HIGHER EDUCATION**). Such students have to undergo an additional year of practical training. Courses vary in length according to the specialization.

Fachoberschule (advanced full-time technical school)

This type of school was first established in 1969. It offers a course at grades eleven and twelve for students who have completed the course at a *Realschule* or an apprenticeship. Courses include an element of practical training in grade 11 as well as some general education. Compulsory subjects for all students include German, social studies, mathematics, natural sciences, a foreign language and physical education. The specializations include: engineering, economics and administration, domestic science, design, and navigation. Success in the final examination leads to the **Fachhochschulreife**, the entry qualification for *Fachhochschulen* (specialist university sector higher education colleges: see under **HIGHER EDUCATION**). Written examinations are taken in four subjects: German, mathematics, a foreign language and one subject taken from the particular subject area taught at the *Fachoberschule*. Oral examinations are also taken in all of the written examination subjects, and in one career-oriented subject.

Apprenticeships

These normally last approximately from two to three-and-a-half years for those who have completed compulsory schooling (grade nine). The apprentice must attend a part-time vocational school (*Berufsschule*). At the end of the apprenticeship an examination is taken, supervised by the committee of the professional organization (*Handwerkskammer*). If the apprenticeship has been contracted by a master craftsman, the certificate issued is the **Gesellenbrief**. If the apprenticeship has been contracted by an industrial organization, the examination is supervised by the competent local body i.e. self-governing industrial bodies (Chambers) or the committee of a Chamber of Commerce and Industry (*Industrie und Handelskammer*), and the certificate issued is the **Facharbeiterbrief**. A skilled worker who wishes to obtain a higher qualification may undertake a course lasting three to four semesters (one-and-a-half to two years) at a *Technikerschule* (see under *Fachschule*) after gaining at least two years' experience in the respective field. Among the qualifications which may be obtained is **Staatlich geprüfter Techniker**.

Berufliches Gymnasium/Fachgymnasium (vocational grammar school)

Pupils who complete a course at a *Realschule* may take a course lasting three years, specializing in a particular field (e.g. agriculture, economics, textiles, music/art, social studies) which will prepare them for entry to specific faculties at institutions of higher education. Vocational subjects are taught instead of a foreign language. The qualification obtained is the **Fachgebundenes Abitur/Zeugnis der Fachgebundenen Hochschulreife**. Since 1988, certain courses of study have also led to a general certificate of eligibility for admission to higher education (**Allgemeine Hochschulreife**).

HIGHER EDUCATION

The entrance qualification to courses of higher education is the **Abitur/Zeugnis der Allgemeinen Hochschulreife**. The qualification obtained on completion of the course at a specialist *Gymnasium*, the **Fachgebundenes Abitur/Zeugnis der Fachgebundenen Hochschulreife** gives access to courses only in certain relevant fields. However, students may sit a further set of examinations (*Ergänzungsprüfungen*), and success in these would entitle the holder to access to all faculties. Owing to limited places, a system of restricted entry (*numerus clausus*) has been introduced to decide admission to courses in medicine, veterinary medicine, dentistry, pharmacology and psychology. The system may also operate in other fields, depending on the demand for places, and this can change from year to year.

Courses are offered by universities and technical universities (*Technische Hochschulen/Technische Universitäten*, now mostly called *Technische Universitäten*), *Universitäten-Gesamthochschulen* (comprehensive universities), *Kunthochschulen* and *Musikhochschulen* (colleges of art and music) or *Fachhochschulen*.

The first qualification to be obtained is the **Diplom/Erstes Staatsexamen** (in arts subjects as well as certain professional fields, except engineering and science – see also under **TEACHER EDUCATION/Magister Artium**). The minimum period to obtain all these qualifications is four years (eight semesters). Most students take longer (on average five years/ten semesters), and apart from restrictions on courses in certain professional fields (e.g. medicine, science and technology faculties), students can decide when to take their final examinations. The principle of academic freedom is the underlying feature of this sector of higher education. Students may normally attend the university of their choice, have the right to change universities part way through their studies or for a semester, and are responsible for planning their studies (apart from courses for which there are professional requirements and in which students have little choice because of the many prescribed courses). In most fields there is an intermediate examination, the **Vordiplom** (science, economic and social science, and technology)/ **Zwischenprüfung** (humanities) after four or five semesters. Until then, studies are more generally based than in the second period when students specialize. In medical, scientific and technological faculties many institutions bar from further study students who fail these intermediate examinations.

Until the early 1960s, students of the humanities had to continue studying for the doctorate as there was no earlier qualification to be obtained. The **Magister Artium** was then introduced as a qualification which could be obtained after the same period of study as the **Diplom/Erstes Staatsexamen** in fields that did not lead to the **Diplom** for those who did not wish to teach or fulfil requirements for other professional fields.

The **Doctorate** may be obtained after a minimum of approximately two years' research after the award of the **Diplom/Magister Artium/Erstes Staatsexamen**. The process of obtaining the doctorate is known as *Promotion*, and the oral examination taken on completion of the research is the *Rigorosum*.

There is also a higher doctorate, the **Habilitation**, awarded on submission of a considerable volume of post-doctoral research, published as a thesis for the degree. The **Habilitation** is a pre-requisite for senior university teachers.

Universitäten-Gesamthochschulen (comprehensive universities) operate in Hesse and North Rhine-Westphalia, and offer the education and research traditionally carried out separately in universities and *Fachhochschulen*, by means of integrated study programmes.

Fachhochschulen

Fachhochschulen (until 1968 called *Ingenieurschulen*, i.e. engineering schools; then reclassified as institutions of higher education in the university sector and renamed). Until 1979, the qualification obtained in the field of engineering was the **Ingenieur graduiert** (Inggrad). However, following the 1976 Framework Act for Higher Education (*Hochschulrahmengesetz*), the *Fachhochschulen* were given the same legal basis as the universities. Thus, since 1979 students studying at these institutions receive a qualification (the **Fachhochschuldiplom**) with the same name as students studying at a university, e.g. **Diplom Ingenieur** (DiplIng). In certain *Länder* it is required that certificates supply the initials FH after the title of the qualification to show that it has been awarded by that type of institution. The standard of the course was not altered. All **Fachhochschulen diplom** have the initials FH after the title of the qualification.

Non-university higher education

Courses of advanced technical education are offered by *Höhere Fachschulen* and *Akademien*.

The entry requirement to courses at these institutions is the **Fachhochschulreife/Abitur/ Realschulreife** (plus two years' vocational experience). Courses normally last three to four years (inclusive of practical training, the duration of which varies, depending on the course and the *Länd* in which the person is studying) although students may take longer if they wish. The qualification obtained on completion of the course, which emphasizes the practical orientation and application of the subjects studied, is the specialization **graduiert**, e.g. **Betriebswirt** (grad), **Sozialpädagoge** (grad).

TEACHER EDUCATION

Primary (*Grundschule*)
Lower secondary (*Hauptschule*)
Comprehensive (*Gesamtschule*, grades five/seven to ten)

From the entrance requirement of the **Abitur/Zeugnis der Allgemeinen Hochschulreife/Zeugnis der Reife**, students take a course which lasts a minimum of six semesters (three years), plus one examination semester, at a *Pädagogische Hochschule* (teacher training college) in Baden-Württemburg and Thuringia; in all other Länder, all training is undertaken at universities. On completion of the course, students take the first state examination for the teaching profession at primary, secondary modern and comprehensive schools (**Erste Staatsprüfung für das Lehramt an Grundschulen/Hauptschulen/Gesamtschulen**). This is followed by a probationary period of two years, known as the *Referendarzeit*. During this period the probationary teacher has a light teaching load but has to attend seminars and write a dissertation. It culminates in a second set of examinations, the **Zweite Staatsprüfung**.

Lower secondary (*Realschule/Gymnasium*)
Upper secondary (*Gymnasium*)

From the entrance requirement of the **Abitur/Zeugnis der Allgemeinen Hochschulreife/Zeugnis der Reife**, students take a course lasting a minimum of eight semesters (four years), although in practice few prospective teachers take the examination in less than ten, at a university. On completion of this period students take the first set of examinations, the **Erstes Staatsexamen** (see under **HIGHER EDUCATION**) followed by the probationary period (*Referendarzeit*), lasting two years – see under **Primary**. At the end of this period, students take the second set of examinations, the **Zweites Staatsexamen**.

The names of the examination, **Staatsprüfung** and **Staatsexamen**, are interchangeable at lower secondary (*Realschule/Gymnasium*) and upper secondary level. It is, therefore, strongly recommended that the type of institution at which the student has studied, and the level of education for which the prospective teacher has been trained, should be checked.

APPENDIX

former **German Democratic Republic (GDR)**

From the establishment of the Republic in 1949, education was totally controlled by the state: there were no private schools. The Ministry of National Education (*Ministerium für Volksbildung*) controlled the schools and the teaching colleges. The Ministry of Higher and Specialized Education (*Ministerium für Hoch- und Fachschulwesen*) was responsible for the universities, special institutes and technical education.

Every five years a Pedagogical Congress was held to review progress and to set the targets for the next period.

The system was structured mainly in accordance with the Law on Socialist Development of 1959 and the Law on the Integrated Socialist Education System of 1965.

Until 1969, compulsory education lasted eight years (ages six to fourteen). In 1969 it was extended to ten years (ages six to sixteen).

The medium of instruction was German. The academic year ran from September to June.

EVALUATION IN BRITAIN

School

Abschlusszeugnis/Mittlere Reife – generally considered comparable to GCSE standard, (grades A, B and C) on a subject-for-subject basis, with the exception of English language.

Abitur/Reifezeugnis – may be considered to satisfy the general entrance requirements of British higher education institutions.

Higher

Vorprüfung – generally considered comparable to a standard between GCE Advanced and British Bachelor degree. May be given advanced standing by British higher education institutions.

Diplom – generally considered comparable to British Bachelor (Honours) degree standard.

Doktor eines Wissenschaftszweiges – generally considered comparable to British PhD degree standard.

MARKING SYSTEM

School and Higher

Marking was on the scale 1–5, 1 being the maximum and 4 the minimum pass-mark.

1	*sehr gut*	very good
2	*gut*	good
3	*befriedigend*	very satisfactory
4	*genügend*	just adequate/pass
5	*ungenügend/nicht bestanden*	poor/failed

SCHOOL EDUCATION

Pre-primary

Crèches (*Kinderkrippen*) – were available for children aged one to three, and there were numerous *Kindergartens* for children aged three to six.

Basic

Basic education covered ten years from ages six to sixteen and took place in general polytechnical schools (*Allgemeine Polytechnische Oberschule*). It was divided into three cycles:

First cycle (*Unterstufe*) – classes one to three. The curriculum covered German, mathematics, manual training, singing, music, drawing, painting and modelling and physical education.

Second cycle (*Mittelstufe*) – classes four to six. The curriculum covered German language and literature, mathematics, natural science, social science, Russian, singing, music, painting and modelling, physical education, manual training, and polytechnic instruction (e.g. instruction in the principles of socialist production).

Third cycle (*Oberstufe*) – classes seven to ten. The curriculum covered mathematics, natural sciences (physics, astronomy, chemistry, biology and physical geography), social science, German, Russian, physical education, civics, optional foreign language (usually English or French), and polytechnic instruction (e.g. instruction in the principles of socialist production). At this stage great importance was attached to practical instruction; often one day per week would be spent in a factory.

Pupils with a gift for languages, mathematics, dance, music or physical education were placed in special classes or in special schools.

The **Abschlusszeugnis/Mittlere Reife** was awarded at the end of the tenth grade. Most pupils left school at this point and took up vocational training.

Secondary

Secondary education took two years and was provided in an Extended General Polytechnical School (*Erweiterte Allgemeinbildende Polytechnische Oberschule*: EOS for short). Compulsory subjects were mathematics, physics, chemistry, biology, Russian, English or French, history, geography, German, art or music, civics, and polytechnical education. Upon completion pupils took the examination for the **Abitur/Reifezeugnis**.

Some pupils went on to university studies, while the remainder undertook technical or vocational training.

Vocational

At the lower level, training as a skilled worker (*Facharbeiter*) was provided in schools run by the state (*Berufsschulen*) and by industrial enterprises (*Betriebsberufsschulen*). Courses usually lasted two years and combined practical experience with theoretical education.

The next stage of training was provided in the technical colleges (*Fachschulen*). The course lasted three years and led to a professional qualification and possibly the **Abitur**. There were different kinds of *Fachschulen*: *Ingenieurschulen* for engineering, agriculture and forestry; *Medizinische Fachschulen* for medical staff; *Pädagogische Fachschulen* for junior schoolteachers; and others for librarians, journalists, economists, legal assistants, etc. A number of *Ingenieurschulen* were upgraded to the status of universities (*Ingenieurhochschulen*) in order to remedy the shortage of trained graduates in engineering and economics.

The third level of vocational training took place at the university level in *Hochschulen* of various specialities. Medical training took place in both universities and in *Medizinische Akademien*. Teacher training took place in universities and in *Pädagogische Hochschulen*.

HIGHER EDUCATION

Courses of higher education were offered by universities, technical universities and specialized institutes (*Hochschulen*).

Access was based on success in the **Abitur** and an aptitude test (**Eignungsprüfung**). A system of restricted entry (*numerus clausus*) was in operation; the number of students to be admitted was decided according to the National Economic Development Plan. Preference was also given to those who had been employed in a productive occupation or in the army or in social service for at least a year. For certain subjects (e.g. medicine, dentistry, agronomy, mining or metallurgical engineering) previous practical experience was necessary.

Studies were undertaken in stages:

Grundstudium – during which students acquired the basic knowledge of their subject. Students had to take the **Vorprüfung** on conclusion of this stage. This was not a qualification in itself, but students had to pass to proceed with their studies.

Fachstudium – this covered the specialist study and with the *Grundstudium* took four to five years (six in medicine and a few other subjects). It led to the **Diplomprüfung** and the qualification of **Diplom** + specialization (e.g. **Diplom-Ingenieur** – degree in engineering). This qualification entitled the holder to practise a profession.

Forschungsstudium (postgraduate study) – this was only open to students who had the **Diplomprüfung**. The course (*Aspirantur*) was in two stages:

– *Promotion zum Grad* (Promotion A) – leading to the qualification of **Doktor eines Wissenschaftszweiges**, after three to four years' original research (e.g. **Dring, Drmed, Droec**).

– Promotion B – leading to the qualification of **Doktor der Wissenschaften (Drsc)** after a minimum of a further four years' highly specialized research and teaching. The holder of a **Drsc** could apply for **Habilitation** (a post-doctoral qualification conferring recognition as a university teacher).

All courses included compulsory non-specialist studies i.e. physical education and a foreign language.

University staff were divided into the following categories: university teachers (*Hochschullehrer*) which included senior lecturers, readers (*Dozent*), professors, *Assistenten* and *Oberassistenten* who were usually on four year contracts while they pursued their doctoral research.

TEACHER EDUCATION

Kindergarten

Training involved a two-year course at *Oberstufe* (secondary) level (i.e. on completion of grade 10) at a pedagogical school; teachers had to then work under supervision for two years. Nursery auxiliaries who had not completed a full course of education undertook a corresponding course lasting three years.

Basic

Teachers for the *Unterstufe* (grades 1 to 3) undertook a training course lasting three years at secondary level at a teacher training institute (*Institut für Lehrerbildung*) which was comparable in standard to the *Fachschulen* (technical schools) and led to the qualification of **Lehrbefähigung** (i.e. qualified to teach). Compulsory subjects were German language and literature, new mathematics and one elective from sport, music, art or handiwork. Before the introduction of the polytechnic school the course was taken on completion of eight years' *Grundschule*.

Teachers for the *Mitteloberstufe* (grades four to ten) undertook a four-year course at a training college (*Pädagogische Hochschule*) for holders of the **Abitur/Reifezeugnis**, leading to a state diploma. The course included the preparation of a thesis and teaching practice; students studied a major and a minor subject (the former for the full four years, the latter for two years only).

Secondary

Until 1960

Teachers at grades eleven and twelve undertook a course of higher education lasting four years.

Since 1960

Teachers at grades 11 and 12 (in the EOS) undertook a five-year course at either a university or a *Pädagogische Hochschule*. On completion of the course they were awarded the **Diplom-Lehrer**.

Headteachers

Teachers were required to undertake a one-year course followed by six months' part-time study including the preparation of a thesis, leading to a qualification in educational administration.

Retraining and refesher courses

Teachers were legally required to retrain in their subject specialization and
methodology on a short course every four years.

ADULT EDUCATION

Some people continued general and vocational education in some kind of centre:
Abendoberschulen and *Betriebsoberschulen* (evening and factory schools), *Arbeiter-
und-Bauern-Fakultäten* (Workers' and Peasants' Faculties). Courses were available for
particular qualifications, including entrance examinations to courses of higher
education.

Ghana

Education in Ghana is centrally administered and mostly government financed. In the larger cities such as Accra and Kumasi, however, there are an increasing number of private primary and junior secondary schools. There are also a smaller number of private secondary institutions.

Basic education, which comprises six years of primary school and three years of junior secondary school, is compulsory and available to all children. However, dropout rates are high, especially among girls.

English is the official medium of instruction at all levels. The major local language of a particular area is however used for the first three years of primary school.

Since 1987 the educational system has been undergoing major reform. This has involved a change from a heavily academic system to one with a more practical and vocational orientation, and the introduction of nine years universal compulsory education. Pre-university education has been reduced from seventeen to twelve years as follows: basic education, which used to last from seven to ten years has now been standardized at nine years, six for primary and three for junior secondary. Secondary education used to involve five years leading to **O levels**, followed by another two years for **A levels**. This has now been reduced to three years of senior secondary school. University courses under the old system lasted from three to six years, but will now last four to six years. Generally, the educational system is evolving to one which can be described as 6–3–3–4. Some aspects of the old system are still in operation, although they will be phased out completely by the year 2000.

The pace of the reforms has been criticized. Between January 1991 and December 1993 160 new schools were built, mostly in rural areas, to cope with the increase in student numbers. This has lead to a lack of qualified teachers. The first batch of senior secondary school (SSS) graduates received very poor results; only 3.9 per cent of entrants were successful, and examiners highlighted a widespread poor command of the English language. Admission to the SSS programme was liberal because of the aims of the reform.

In 1993 parliament therefore approved a series of measures aimed at improving performance, with emphasis on the teaching of basic English grammar. In addition, because of the low number of successful senior secondary school candidates, universities suspended their entrance examinations for the year. For the majority of students, termed 'partly qualified', polytechnics have organized bridging courses to allow them to study for the upgraded **Higher Diploma**.

Academic years vary, depending on the level of education and whether the 'old' system is still in operation. For basic education, the academic year runs from September to August. For secondary, those still following the 'old' system of **O levels** and **A levels** are in session from September to July, while those pursuing courses in the senior secondary schools start their academic year in January and end in December. Tertiary institutions generally run from September/October to July.

Ghana

EVALUATION IN BRITAIN

School

Junior Secondary School Leaving Certificate (known as BECE – **Basic Education Certificate Examination**) now replaced by **Middle School Leaving Certificate** – generally considered to be below GCSE standard.

West African School Certificate GCE O Level – grades 1–6 are generally equated to GCSE standard (grades A–C). NB: The last **GCE O levels** in schools took place in May/June 1994 but private candidates will be able to continue taking the exam in October/November until either 1998 or 2000.

Post Middle School Certificate A – generally considered comparable to a standard between GCSE and GCE Advanced.
NB: Now being phased out.

Senior Secondary Certificate Examination – The first SSCE were held in December 1993, so standards are difficult to assess. However, it is hoped to be between GCSE and GCE Advanced.

Post Secondary Certificate A – generally considered comparable to a standard between GCSE and GCE Advanced.

West African Higher School Certificate/GCE A level – grades A – E are generally compared to GCE Advanced grades.

Further

Certificate of Forestry – awarded after three years of post **O level** study at School of Forestry, Sunyani. Considered to be slightly above BTEC National Diploma / N/SVQ level 3 / Advanced GNVQ/GSVQ standard.

Agricultural Diploma – awarded after two to three years post **O level** study at an agricultural college. Considered to be slightly above BTEC National Diploma / N/SVQ level 3 / Advanced GNVQ/GSVQ standard.

Certificate – awarded by the University of Ghana in professional areas. Generally considered to be roughly comparable to BTEC National Diploma / N/SVQ level 3 / Advanced GNVQ/GSVQ standard.

Diploma – awarded by either University of Ghana or University of Science and Technology, generally considered to be slightly above BTEC National Diploma / N/SVQ level 3 / Advanced GNVQ/GSVQ standard.

Ordinary National Certificate/Diploma – awarded by a Polytechnic, may be considered to approach British BTEC National Diploma / N/SVQ level 3 / Advanced GNVQ/GSVQ standard.

Higher National Certificate/Diploma – awarded by a Polytechnic, may be considered to approach British BTEC Higher National Diploma / N/SVQ level 4 standard.

Higher

Bachelor degree – generally considered comparable to British Bachelor degree standard.

Teaching

Advanced Teacher Training College Diploma – considered roughly comparable to a standard between BTEC National Diploma / N/SVQ level 3 / Advanced GNVQ/GSVQ, and Higher National Diploma / N/SVQ level 4; candidates may be eligible for a two year BEd; alternatively it would satisfy the entrance requirements of such a course.

MARKING SYSTEMS

School

Basic Education Certificate Examination
graded 1 (max.) to 9 (fail)

West African School Certificate/GCE O level
graded 1 (max.) to 9 (fail)

Senior Secondary Certificate Examination
graded A–F.

West African School Certificate/GCE A level
graded A (max.) to F (fail)

HIGHER

The four universities and the University College record their letter grades according to slightly different scales, which are usually noted on the transcript: (NB: details are not available for <u>University of Development Studies</u> and <u>University College of Education, Winneba</u>).

Univ. of Ghana, Legon	UST, Kumasi	UCC, Cape Coast
A 70 upwards	A 70 upwards	A 70 upwards
B+ 60–69	B 60–69	B+ 60–69
B 50–59	C 50–59	B 50–59
C 40–49	D 40–49	C 45–49
D 30–39	E below 40 (fail)	E below 30

Degrees are classified as:

Honours degrees:

First Class
Second Class, Upper Division
Second Class, Lower Division
Pass

General degrees

SCHOOL EDUCATION

During the last forty years there have been three main patterns of school education:

1950–63

The 'Accelerated Development Plan for Education' of the early 1950s established the system of one year of Kindergarten (age four to five) followed by six years primary education. Up to four years of middle school could then follow. The **Common Entrance Examination** was taken anytime from the end of class six to the end of middle form four to determine entry to secondary schools as places were limited. At the end of six years primary education, followed by four years of middle school, pupils could sit the **Middle School Leaving Examinations.**

Secondary school students followed predominantly academic courses for five years before sitting the **West African School Certificate/GCE O level examinations**. Those with good enough grades went on to study for a further two years in a secondary school, at the end of which they would take the **West African Higher School Certificate/GCE A level examinations.**

Primary and secondary education could therefore last between thirteen and seventeen years.

1963–1987

In 1963 the system was overhauled: six years primary school (from age six); three years junior secondary school, and three years senior secondary school became the model. At the end of this period pupils took the **GCE O level examinations** of the West African Examinations Council. Those with good enough grades went on to study for a further two years at secondary school, at the end of which they took the **West African Higher School Certificate/GCE A level examinations.**

From 1987

In 1987 there was a radical reorganization, which has led to the following changes, which are still in the process of being implemented:

Basic education now consists of six years primary school, followed automatically by three years of Junior Secondary School (JSS). At the end of JSS pupils sit the **Basic Education Certificate Examination (BECE)**. For some pupils this is a terminal examination, while others will proceed to senior secondary schools, technical institutes or other vocational institutions.

Those students admitted to senior secondary schools follow any one of the following five streams or options: technical, vocational, general, business or agricultural. At the end of three years students sit the **Senior Secondary Certificate Examination (SSCE)**. The first SSCEs were held in December 1993.

Due to the gradual implementation of the reforms, most secondary schools have been running both the 'old' and 'new' programmes since the 1990/91 academic year. The last batch of students sitting **O levels** in schools will have sat their examinations in May/June 1994. Some of these students will enter the sixth form and sit the **GCE A levels** in May/June 1996. After 1996 only the senior secondary courses will remain in schools. Private candidates will however continue to be able to take the **GCE O level** and **A level examinations** until the year 2000.

Under the reforms, some students who have completed JSS may be unable to gain admission to senior secondary schools. The following options are now available to them:

There are twenty-one technical institutes and eighteen National Vocational Training Institute Training Centres which offer two or three year courses in subjects ranging from autobody repairs to building and carpentry, as well as, for example, catering and dressmaking. Some private institutions offer similar courses, at the end of which students sit for national **craft examinations**. Until the late 1980s many such exams were administered by either the <u>City and Guilds of London Institute</u> or the <u>Royal Society of Arts</u>, but virtually all have now been localized.

FURTHER EDUCATION

Just as basic and secondary education is undergoing change, so too is the further education sector. It is envisaged that two levels of further education will be in place within the next few years:

The <u>Regional College of Applied Arts, Science and Technology</u> (RECAST) will bring together such institutions as teacher training colleges, nursing training colleges and health training institutions, as well as other professional institutions such as the agricultural colleges and the <u>School of Forestry</u>. Admission requirements for these institutions are presently from three to five **O levels**, although this will change to the SSCE. Courses generally last three years and the qualifications awarded are certificates.

The second level of further education is occupied by the six polytechnics, located in Accra, Kumasi, Cape Coast, Takoradi, Ho and Tamale. Since the 1992/93 academic year the polytechnics have offered three year HND courses in subjects such as pharmaceutical dispensing, various aspects of engineering, business studies and fashion. Admission requirements for HND courses were five **O level** passes and three **A level** passes, or **Polytechnic certificate** or **diploma**.

In addition to the tertiary level HND courses, however, most polytechnics continue to offer a range of technician level certificates and diplomas, which may only have three to five **O levels** as entry requirements.

At the time of writing entry procedures and qualifications for those with **SSCE** are not available.

The <u>University of Ghana, Legon</u> and the <u>University of Science and Technology (UST), Kumasi</u> both offer diploma courses. At the <u>University of Ghana</u> there are two year courses in accounting, librarianship and archives administration, adult education, public administration, police administration, music, African studies, theatre arts (3 years), statistics, social administration, agriculture, nursing education and medical laboratory technology. At the <u>University of Science and Technology</u> diploma courses are offered in agricultural extension and farm management, horticulture, rural art and industry, various aspects of engineering, environmental health technology, data processing, estate management and natural resources management.

In the past, entry requirements have been five **O level** passes and two **A level** passes although relevant certificate qualifications have been recognized instead of A levels.

HIGHER EDUCATION

This is offered by four universities and one university college:

The <u>University of Ghana</u> at Legon was founded 1948 and granted full university status in 1961. The <u>University of Cape Coast</u> (UCC) – founded as a university college in 1962 was designated <u>University College of Science Education</u> in 1964–66, resumed its former title in 1966, and achieved full university status in 1972.

The University of Science and Technology at Kumasi was founded as Kumasi College of Technology in 1952 and achieved university status as the Kwame Nkrumah University of Science and Technology in 1961. It was given its present title in 1966.

The University College of Education at Winneba was founded in 1992 by amalgamating several institutions, including the Advanced Teacher Training College and the Specialist Training College.

The University of Development Studies at Tamale was founded as a university in 1993.

The usual minimum entrance requirements for **Bachelor's degree** courses were five credits at **O level**, plus two or three **A levels**, for those whose secondary education was under the 'old' system. For those who have taken the SSCE, a **University Entrance Examination** is also required.

Most **Bachelor degree** courses may be taken as General or Honours; the latter are classified: First class, Second class upper division, Second class lower division, or pass.

Bachelor degree courses at the University of Ghana normally take three years, as do those in the social sciences at the University of Science and Technology and the University of Development Studies. Those in the applied sciences and at the University of Cape Coast usually take four years. At the University College of Education **BEd** degrees may be obtained after two years by those with diplomas from Advanced Teacher Training Colleges.

Master's Degrees generally require two years study (including the presentation of a thesis) after the award of a **Bachelor degree**.

TEACHER EDUCATION

Non-graduate teachers

There are at present three types of teacher training institutions:

Teacher training colleges

There are thirty-eight such colleges which train teachers for both the primary and junior secondary schools. At present admission requirements are three to five **O levels**. The courses last three years, at the end of which a **Teacher's Certificate A** is awarded. Students may choose courses with either a science or humanities bias.

Until the late 1980s however, many colleges admitted students who had either the **Middle School Leaving Certificate**, the **JSS Leaving Certificate** or who had completed two to three years of secondary school. These students followed a four-year course, at the end of which they were awarded a **Post Middle Certificate A**.

Advanced Teacher Training Colleges

These colleges accept experienced teachers who already have a teacher's certificate (usually **Certificate A**) to specialize in one subject, normally for three years, at the end of which a **Diploma** is awarded. Until the early 1990s teachers from these colleges usually taught in the lower forms of secondary schools and in teacher training colleges. Now it is expected that such teachers will teach mostly in the senior secondary schools, or possibly in some of the technical institutions.

The University College of Education still offers experienced teachers who posses

Certificate A a three year advanced Diploma course.

Graduate Teachers

The <u>University of Cape Coast</u>, primarily a teacher training institution, provides degree courses in all the main academic disciplines. Until the early 1990s arts and science courses were taken concurrently with the **Diploma in Education (DipEd)** course. On completion of the four-year course, which included teaching practice, graduates were qualified to teach in secondary schools, teacher training colleges (including the advanced ones), as well as polytechnics. At present education is being incorporated into most courses resulting in **BEd degrees.**

The <u>University of Cape Coast</u> also offered a one-year **Postgraduate Certificate of Education** for graduates of the <u>University of Ghana</u> and the <u>University of Science and Technology</u>. This is now being turned into a sandwich course.

Despite the existence of these courses, many graduates continue to go straight into teaching without qualifications in education.

Unqualified teachers

There are many unqualified teachers at all levels of the school system, including pupil-teachers and National Service Personnel. The latter is made up of those who have just finished their **A levels** or Diplomas, together with graduates, all of whom are doing compulsory national service. However, the Ministry of Education has undertaken to ensure that there are no unqualified teachers in the system by 2000.

Gibraltar

The education system is based on that of the United Kingdom.

Free education is offered to British subjects resident in Gibraltar, and school attendance is compulsory between the ages of five and fifteen. Non-British children may be admitted to government schools subject to residential qualifications and the approval of the Minister for Education. Requests for admission of such children should be made to the Department of Education. Non-resident children may be admitted to schools, at the Department's discretion, as paying students. The fees vary for the different age groups and reach a maximum of £2076 per annum for secondary students.

Education is provided up to GCSE and GCE Advanced level standards. RSA, C&G and BTEC examinations are also taken. For all higher education and professional training, students must go to Britain. Graduates and qualified teachers employed in government schools, therefore, hold British degrees and teaching certificates. Other qualifications are accepted only if recognized by the Department for Education as valid for qualified-teacher status and for salary purposes in Britain.

Primary education

With the introduction of secondary comprehensive education in September 1972, primary education was reorganized. Middle schools were created which replaced the junior schools. Transfer age for children in the First schools was raised to eight and for those in Middle schools to twelve.

The Department of Education operates all primary schools staffed by lay teachers. All are open to children of all denominations and provide religious instruction accordingly. However, the majority of Gibraltarian children are Roman Catholic and hence the basic religious and moral instruction is in accordance with this denomination. The Hebrew School is intended primarily for Jewish children and its calendar and curriculum are adapted to this end.

The Ministry of Defence runs one primary school for the children of UK services personnel to which a number of local Anglican children are admitted by special arrangement with the Gibraltar Government.

In addition, there is a private school at Loreto Convent providing education at both infant and junior stages. This school is co-educational at the infant stage and single sex at the junior school stage.

Secondary education

All secondary education is conducted in two single-sex comprehensive schools.

Specialized education

The Gibraltar Government also runs a College of Further Education. This offers a number of courses in technology and business studies, up to the **BTEC National Diploma** standard and courses leading to City and Guilds of London Institute (C&G) awards. The College is also involved in the provision of evening classes in both leisure activities and adult education. Other courses offered can include Royal Society of Arts examinations, **Bankers' Certificate** courses, Association of Accounting Technicians' courses and such other National courses as the community may reasonably require.

The Department also operates a school for handicapped children in purpose-built premises.

Parents of children who may require any of the above types of specialized education may obtain further details from the Director of Education.

Teaching

Approximately two per cent of the permanent teaching force is unqualified; the majority of these teachers are working in primary schools. Appointment of permanent unqualified teachers ceased in 1976. Over 62 per cent of school teachers are now graduates and this figure is increasing.

Greece

Education in Greece has traditionally been centralized and state controlled. According to the Greek Constitution, every citizen, regardless of origin, background and sex should have the right and access to equal educational opportunities. State education is free at all levels.

Until the late 1950s, emphasis in the school curriculum was on classics; since then the balance with science and technology has been restored.

Official education begins at the age of five-and-a-half or six. There is also provision for one or two years of pre-school education. Primary education lasts six years. Secondary education caters for the age range eleven-and-a-half or twelve to eighteen. Compulsory education ends at age fifteen.

Higher education is offered at universities and university-level institutions (generally known as AEI) and institutions of further education (known as TEI).

The law permits the establishment of privately owned nursery, primary and secondary schools. These are required to be approved by and registered with the Ministry of Education. They have to follow the national curriculum at all stages and their certificates are recognized as equivalent to those awarded by state sector schools. Their teachers must have the same training and qualifications as state teachers.

The academic year runs from September/October to June, and is divided into two semesters.

EVALUATION IN BRITAIN

School

Apolytirion of Gymnasio – generally considered to be below GCSE standard (grades A, B and C).

Apolytirion of Lykeio – generally considered comparable to GCSE standard (grades A, B and C) on a subject-for-subject basis (with the exception of English) where a pupil has obtained marks of at least 11 out of 20.

Some universities accept the **Apolytirion of Lykeio** as satisfying the general entrance requirements provided that it is obtained with an overall average of at least 17. However, results obtained in the **General entrance examination** (formerly **Panhellenic**) should also be taken into account.

Higher

Ptychion (awarded by a TEI) – constitutes a professionally-oriented first degree; generally considered comparable to a standard above that of BTEC Higher National

Diploma / N/SVQ level 4.

Ptychion (Bachelor degree) (awarded by an AEI) or **Diploma** from Faculties of engineering and agriculture – generally considered comparable to British Bachelor (Honours) degree standard although the course lasts longer than in the UK.

MARKING SYSTEMS

Primary

A numerical scale of 1–10, where 10 is the highest and 5 the pass-mark.

Secondary

Marking is on a scale of 1–20 (maximum), with 10 as the pass-mark.

The university entrance examination, now called **general entrance examination** (formerly **Panhellenic**) is taken in four subjects, each of which is marked out of 160, with a pass-mark of 80. One of these subjects is a major which must be passed and for which no compensation is possible.

Higher

Marking is on a scale of 1–10 (maximum), with 5 as the minimum pass-mark.

Grades 5 – 6.9	*Kalos* (good)
Grades 7 – 8.4	*Liankalos* (very good)
Grades 8.5 – 10	*Arista* (best/excellent)

SCHOOL EDUCATION

Primary (*Demotiko Scholio*)

This covers six years for children from age five-and-a-half. The curriculum covers: classes 1 and 2: environmental studies; modern Greek language; arithmetic; arts; and physical education. In the remaining classes, the curriculum includes: religious knowledge; Greek language; history; arithmetic; civics; arts and crafts; music; gymnastics and cultural activities. On completion of this cycle, pupils obtain the primary leaving certificate.

Secondary (*Gymnasio* and *Lykeio*)

Until 1977

Secondary education consisted of one six-year cycle in establishments called *Gymnasio*. To continue their education at secondary level, primary school leavers had to take an entrance examination consisting of tests in: Greek; mathematics; physics; geography; religious instruction and history.

Since 1977

The former six-year *Gymnasio* has been divided into two three-year cycles to form *Gymnasio* (lower cycle) and *Lykeio* (upper cycle). The six-year primary and the three-year lower secondary cycle (*Gymnasio*) now constitute the statutory nine-year compulsory education. There are both day and evening *Gymnasia*. Pupils who have completed the primary cycle proceed automatically to *Gymnasia* without examination.

Lower cycle (*Gymnasio*) leavers may continue their education at general *Lykeio*. There are three different types of *Lykeia*: general *Lykeio* (*Geniko Lykeio*), which attracts the majority of *Gymnasio* leavers; the technical/vocational *Lykeio* (*Techniko Epagelmatiko Lykeio* – TEL); classical *Lykeio* and the interdisciplinary *Lykeio* (*Polykladiko* – EPL). There are also a few ecclesiastical *Lykeia* which prepare boys for the priesthood, and one or two music *Lykeio*. There are also secondary technical/vocational schools (*Technikes Epagelmatikes Scholes* – TES).

The curriculum of the first cycle covers ancient Greek in translation; modern Greek; mathematics; history; physical education; science; French or English; religious knowledge; history; music crafts and geography. On completion of this cycle, pupils are awarded the **Apolytirion of Gymnasio**. They may be enrolled, without examination, in all types of *Lykeia* as well as at TES.

The curriculum of the general *Lykeio* consists of academic subjects similar to those offered in the *Gymnasio*, with psychology, physics, chemistry, biology and economics in addition.

In the third year, in addition to common subjects, tuition is given in one of four option streams. Each option stream is designed to prepare pupils to enter a specific group of tertiary education institutions (university and non-university level).

The curriculum of the technical/vocational *Lykeio* (TEL) consists of a selection from the subjects of general *Lykeio* and specialist subjects including engineering, economics, agriculture, etc., according to the chosen orientation.

Classical *Lykeia* promote classical studies. Comprehensive *Lykeia* provide a balance of general and technical/vocational education.

The technical/vocational schools aim to consolidate the general education of pupils and prepare them for the world of work. There are both day and evening TES, with programmes lasting two years (day) or three years (evening). On successful completion, students receive a certificate called **Ptychio TES**. They can then seek employment or be registered in the first year of *Lykeio* (2nd year of a comprehensive *Lykeio*).

On completion of the upper secondary cycle, pupils have to sit examinations for the school leaving certificate (**Apolytirion**), which reflects the pupil's performance assessed by oral and written tests held during the final year.

There are two types of post *Lykeio* education; that offered at universities and university level institutions (AEI) and that offered at Technical Educational Institutes (TEI).

The selection of candidates for post-secondary education (AEI and TEI) is based on the results of the **General Examination** (formerly called **Panhellenic examination**). To sit the **General Examinations,** which are written, candidates must have obtained a **Lykeio Apolyterion**.

In the **General Examinations** there are four subject groups, called *Desmes*. Candidates may only sit for one *Desmes* which leads to a specific group of AEI and TEI courses.

Holders of the **TEI Apolytirion** are permitted to apply for entry to TEI courses without sitting the **General Examinations,** with offers based on marks obtained in the **Apolytirion**.

General Examinations – *Desmes*

> *Desmi* 1 : composition; mathematics; physics; chemistry
> *Desmi* 2 : composition; physics; chemistry; biology
> *Desmi* 3 : composition; ancient Greek; history; Latin
> *Desmi* 4 : composition; mathematics; history; political economy.

A pass in the **Apolytirion** allows the student to enter the **general entrance examinations**, but it does not affect university selection. Before 1987, the marks obtained in the **Apolytirion** contributed 25 per cent of the total marks for university selection, the remaining 75 per cent came from the former **Panhellenic** examinations. Changes were made to this system in 1988. Admission to universities is now based solely on performance in the **general entrance examinations** which are conducted by the Ministry of Education.

All the examinations at this level must be taken at one sitting, the highest mark per subject being 160 and the pass-mark 80 i.e. 50 per cent. Each of the groups has a major subject which must be passed if the candidate is to pass the examination as a whole i.e. no compensation is allowed for this subject. The candidate is eligible to be selected for university in Greece providing that he or she has reached the grades required for the desired course and that there are places available on that course. The certificate shows the marks obtained for each of the four subjects taken. Selection is made according to the rank order until all available places are filled.

Laboratories of Liberal Studies (see additional information below) tend to absorb the *Lykeio* school leavers who are not admitted to the AEI and TEI, onto foundation programmes.

HIGHER EDUCATION

In 1973, *Anotera* (post-*Lykeio*) technical educational institutions were established under the name of KATE. In 1977 these were renamed KATEE (*Kentra Anoteras Technikis Epangelmatikis Ekpethefseos*) to include vocational/professional courses in a wide range of subjects. Candidates had to be holders of the **Lykeio Apolytirio** and to have passed entrance examinations conducted by the Ministry of Education nationwide. The length of studies was three years, including practical training. Upon graduation, students were awarded the **Ptychion of KATEE**.

Following Law 1404 of 1983, the KATEEs were restructured to upgrade the courses offered and were renamed TEI (*Technologika Ekpedeftika Idrymata*). New courses were introduced, and the average length of the courses was extended to four years. Additionally, there is a new feature in the TEIs, which is a period of compulsory practical training after the course of study. The final award is called **Ptychion of TEI**. There are twelve TEI.

Each semester comprises 15 full weeks of instruction plus two examination periods each lasting two weeks. Students are required to submit a graduation project in an area directly related to a practical aspect of production or service; this may be completed after the last semester and has to be passed by a committee. Placements also form part of the TEI course and take place after successful completion of the taught curriculum; two separate placements, one of 6 months and one of 2 months, must also be completed. Students receive payment during the placements. There are eighteen university-level institutions (AEI – *Anotera Ekpedeftika Idrymata*). Courses last a minimum of four years, with five years in engineering, agriculture, veterinary medicine and dentistry and six years in medicine. All courses at the <u>National Technical University</u> last five years.

Under the University Law of 1978, there was a limit on the number of times students could resit examinations and the number of additional years they could take to complete their degrees; this limit has now been lifted.

The first degree awarded by AEI is called **Ptychio** or, in the case of Engineering or Architecture, **Diploma**.

A new kind of state institution, the Institute of Vocational Training (IEK) has recently been established in the major cities to offer post-secondary vocational technical training courses. The law permits the establishment of privately owned IEK provided they satisfy the laid down requirements and conditions.

Postgraduate courses are available in a limited number of fields and last two years (leading to a **postgraduate diploma**). There are facilities for research leading to the award of a **doctorate**.

Study for a **Doctorate** (*Didaktoriko*) normally takes at least three years; it is technically a qualification for teaching in universities but in practice many Greeks regard it as a useful qualification for careers in other areas.

Higher education is under state control, in accordance with the Greek Constitution.

<u>The School of Tourism</u> in Rhodes has equivalent status to a TEI.

TEACHER EDUCATION

SELETE is the body (under the jurisdiction of the Ministry of Education) responsible for teacher training.

Pre-primary and primary

Until 1989

Pre-primary and primary school teachers were trained at pedagogical academies; one year for pre-primary teachers and two years for primary teachers.

Since 1984

Primary and nursery school teachers are trained in two-year courses of higher education (non-university), at primary teacher training colleges and at the <u>Universities of Thessaloniki, Patras, Ioannina, Thrace</u> and <u>Crete</u> where the courses last four years.

Primary school teachers can also be trained at Primary In-Service Training Schools (SELDE) where courses last one year. There are ten of these and teacher trainees are chosen by lot.

Secondary

Teachers are graduates from higher education institutions and, to a lesser extent, from secondary education institutions (technical/vocational training). For in-service training, they attend Secondary In-Service Training Schools (SELME) and Regional Training Centres (PEK).

Greece

Vocational Education
Outside the formal education system, the Employment and Manpower Organization (OAED) is the major provider of training for young people, through the apprenticeship system and short training courses. Legislation passed in 1989 established the National Council for Vocational Training and placed under the responsibility of the Ministry of Labour all training institutions outside the formal education system.

Apprenticeship: these now last three years. The first year is spent full-time in classes and workshops in an apprenticeship centre; the second and third years are spent more and more in industry – 50 per cent of the week in the third semester, 60 per cent in the fourth, 80 per cent in the fifth and 100 per cent in the sixth.

Apprenticeships are available to 15–18-year-olds who have completed the three year *Gymnasio*.

Short course: full-time intensive training courses lasting 6 to 9 months are provided in *KETEK* (Centres of technical and vocational training) in more than 20 occupational fields. They are available to unskilled, unemployed young people over the age of 18.

Specialized Training: this is provided in the following fields:

Nursing – at the *Middle Technical and Vocational Nursing Schools*. Open to *Gymnasio* graduates but mainly taken up by *Lykeio* graduates. The first 6 months are theoretical and the following 18 months alternate theory and practice in hospitals.

Tourism – *Schools for Tourist Professions* (STE): one-year course in hotel and restaurant, two-year course in catering, one-year course in hotel client account management.

Agriculture – *School of Agricultural Training* (KEGE): short courses of up to 40 days in production techniques, management, marketing, co-operatives, agricultural home economics, rural tourism, etc.

Private Higher Education Establishments

Article 16 of the Greek Constitution forbids the establishment of private Greek institutions of higher education.

A law of 1935 allows privately owned institutions offering post-school education to operate as 'Laboratories of Liberal Studies'. There are no plans to abolish these institutions, or to prevent them from offering educational services to the public. However, it is stressed that they are not allowed to award any paper qualifications, except certificates of attendance. Even degrees awarded by foreign institutions on the basis of an approved course of study at a Laboratory of Liberal Studies will not be recognized by DIKATSA (the Greek NARIC). This means that a student who has taken any part of a foreign degree course at a LLS will not be able to use the qualification to obtain employment in the Greek public sector. Private sector employers are of course free to accept such qualifications. It should be noted that these institutions are registered as businesses with the Ministry of Commerce, and the Ministry of Education does not set standards, or monitor the quality of courses. As businesses, they are free to establish links with other businesses, i.e. foreign educational establishments.

The only regionally accredited US post-secondary institutions in Greece are Deree College (New England Association of Schools and Colleges) and The University of La Verne (Western Association of Schools and Colleges).

Guatemala

Compulsory education extends from age seven to fourteen, but it is not possible to enforce this owing to insufficient facilities.

The medium of instruction is normally Spanish. However in recent years, in areas where the local population speak the original Indian languages, classes are given on a bilingual basis, that is, Spanish and the local language.

The academic year runs from January to October.

EVALUATION IN BRITAIN

School

Bachillerato – generally considered comparable to GCSE standard (grades A, B and C) on a subject-for-subject basis, with the exception of English language.

Higher

Licenciado/Professional title – generally considered comparable to British Bachelor degree standard if awarded after four or more years of study.

MARKING SYSTEM

School

Marking is on a scale of 1–100 with 51 per cent as the pass-mark in government schools (higher in private schools).

The **Bachillerato** is only awarded to those with an average of at least 51 per cent from government schools and 61 per cent from private schools.

Higher

The minimum pass in the state university and one of the private universities is 51 per cent; 61 per cent is the minimum pass in the other three private universities.

SCHOOL EDUCATION

Pre-primary

Some facilities are available for children aged four to six.

Primary

This covers six years, from age seven, and is divided into three two-year cycles. The curriculum covers Spanish, mathematics, geography, history, science, handicrafts, art and music, health and safety, agriculture, industrial arts and home economics.

Secondary

This covers five years, divided into a three-year *Ciclo Prevocacional* of general education, followed by a two-year *Ciclo Diversificado.* During the first cycle, common to all pupils, the curriculum includes mathematics, Spanish, sociology, natural science, drawing and painting, music, handicrafts or domestic science, electives (e.g. a foreign language – usually English or French, typing, etc.). In the second cycle, pupils may specialize. Annual examinations determine progression from grade to grade. On conclusion of the second cycle (the 11th grade) pupils take the examinations for the **Bachillerato.**

Technical secondary

A course of three years' upper secondary education leads to the **Perito Industrial, Agricola** or **Contador** (commerce).

HIGHER EDUCATION

There are five universities, of which only one is state run (San Carlos University). The entrance requirement is the **Bachillerato** (or an equivalent certificate at **Bachillerato** level) plus an entrance examination.

The **Licenciado** takes four to five years, of which the first one to two years are devoted to general studies. A further one-year course followed by a minimum of one year of research leads to the **Doctorado** in law, the humanities, education and the economic and social sciences. The medical training course leading to the **Licencia** (of medicine) lasts seven years (three years at university followed by four years' professional experience).

There is a **Maestrado** (**Master's degree**) which lasts between one and two-and-a-half years after the first degree at San Carlos University. Facilities for training to doctorate level are limited and many Guatemalans have to go abroad for training at this level.

The National School of Nursing offers a three-year course leading to the qualification of **Enfermera Graduada.**

TEACHER EDUCATION

Primary

Training takes place at teacher training colleges, lasting for three years after the first cycle of secondary education.

Teaching practice occupies fifty per cent of the third year training timetable.

Secondary

Training is post-secondary and courses are offered at all five Guatemalan universities.

Guatemala

The course lasts three years and the degree awarded is **Professor** (of education).

Special education

Only <u>San Carlos University</u> and <u>Landivar University</u> provide teacher training courses for handicapped children.

Guinea

The education system in Guinea during the colonial period was based on the French system.

Until the early 1960s, almost all education was provided by mission and Koranic schools but, during the 1960s, a series of reforms altered the nature of schooling. One major reform was the replacement of French with the various vernaculars as the principal media of instruction. In 1984, the new regime reversed this reform and French again became the medium of instruction at all levels of the education system.

The **Ministère de l'Education Nationale** (MEN) is responsible for administering education, be it public or private. Through the **Institut Pédagogique National** (IPN), the Ministry of National Education is also responsible for determining curricula, teaching methods, etc.

The school year runs from September to July.

Education is compulsory until the age of thirteen.

EVALUATION IN BRITAIN

School

Baccalauréat 2ème partie – generally considered comparable to GCSE standard (grades A, B and C) on a subject-for-subject basis, with the exception of English language.

Higher

Licence – generally considered comparable to a standard between GCE Advanced and British Bachelor degree; may be considered for advanced standing in British higher education institutions.

Diplôme d'Etudes Supérieures/Maîtrise – generally considered comparable to British Bachelor (Ordinary) degree standard, but where very high marks have been achieved candidates could be considered for admission to taught Master's degree courses.

MARKING SYSTEMS

School

The marking system is out of 10.

Higher

The marking system is out of 10.

SCHOOL EDUCATION

1961–7

Primary

This covered four years until 1964 when it was increased to five years. It was referred to as the first cycle.

Secondary

This was divided into two parts:

lower (second cycle) covering three years, which was soon increased to five years;

upper (third cycle) covering five years, which was then correspondingly decreased to three years.

Owing to the very limited facilities, few children actually proceeded to secondary education.

1968–84

Primary

This covered six years and was referred to as the first cycle. Children studied French, history, the indigenous language, geography, arithmetic, natural sciences, drawing, music, sewing, physical education and civics.

Secondary

This was divided into two cycles (the second and the third), each of three years. During the lower cycle pupils studied philosophy and ideology, national and French languages, history, geography, mathematics, sciences (biology, chemistry and physics), administrative accounting and instruction in techniques of teaching. On completion of the cycle pupils took the examinations for the **Brevet d'Etudes du Premier Cycle**, necessary to proceed to the third cycle.

During the higher cycle pupils in the academic **Lycées** continued to study the same subjects as during the lower cycle, plus statistics and business administration, although they could specialize in the literary or scientific options. On completion of the cycle pupils took the examinations for the **Baccalauréat**. In 1973–4 the cycle was lengthened to four years.

Technical secondary

Lower

Since the late 1960s there have been two types: vocational/technical and rural (the School of Rural Education/Centre d'Enseignement Rural – CER). In 1968 this was changed to the Centre d'Education Revolutionnaire. The Centre is primarily concerned with agricultural practices and land use.

Upper

During this cycle pupils could attend a technical *Lycée* for the three-year course or a vocational school which offered courses of various lengths.

Ecoles Professionnelles

These offered intensive vocational/technical training. They included the National Arts and Trades School, the National Health School and the National Telecommunications School. These three professional schools became university faculties in 1975.

Since 1984

French is the language of instruction at all educational levels.

Primary

This covers six years of schooling from the age of seven. The study of indigenous languages has been dropped. English can be studied from the third year.

Secondary

The second cycle is now four years, is taken at *Collège*, and leads to the **Brevet Elémentaire** in the tenth grade. National languages and ideology have been dropped. English has been added.

The third cycle has been reduced to three years and is studied at the *Lycée* leading to the **Baccalauréat 1ère partie** in grade 12 and the **Baccalauréat 2ème partie** in grade 13 (*Terminale*). Students specialize in one of the following options from grade 11:

Bac Sciences Expérimentales
Bac Sciences Mathématiques
Bac Sciences Sociales

Technical secondary

With the elevation of the three *Ecoles Professionnelles* to university faculties, it is intended that there be *Centres de Formation Professionnelle* in each region to train qualified workers (*Ouvriers Qualifiés*). Candidates are recruited mainly from grade 10.

HIGHER EDUCATION

Admission to all higher education institutions requires the **Baccalauréat 2ème partie** and success in a competitive entrance examination. The programme leading to the **Licence** consists of four years of study. A further year culminating in the writing of a dissertation is required to obtain the **Diplôme d'Etudes Supérieures/Maîtrise**.

In engineering, the **Diplôme d'Ingénieur** requires four to five years of study beyond the **Baccalauréat 2ème partie**.

University of Conakry comprises the following faculties:

Faculté des Sciences Sociales
Faculté de Chimie
Faculté d' Electrotechnique

Faculté de Mécanique
Faculté de Pharmacie
Faculté de Génie Civil
Faculté de Droit et Sciences Economiques
Faculté de Médecine
Faculté de Sciences de la Nature
Faculté de Biologie

The University of Kankan offers courses in two faculties: *Lettres et Sciences Humaines* and *Sciences de la Nature*.

The *Instituts des Sciences Agro-zootechniques* recruit after the **Baccalauréat 2ème partie** and an entrance examination. These are situated at Faranah, Kankan and Kindia.

Ecole Normale Supérieure at Maneah and Ecole Normale Supérieure d'Enseignement Technique at Matoto (Conakry) each recruit after the **Baccalauréat 2ème partie** and an entrance examination.

The following institutions will accept students from '*le niveau Bac.*'– that is to say students who have taken but failed the **Baccalauréat** – with an entrance test:

Ecoles Nationales de la Santé
Ecole Nationale d'Agriculture (Tolo-Mamou, Macenta and Dubreka)
Ecole Normale Secondaire (Dubreka and Pita)

These are designed to train middle-level personnel, nurses and primary school teachers.

TEACHER EDUCATION

Primary and secondary

Primary teacher training colleges offer two-year courses from grade 9, leading to the **Primary School Teachers Certificate** at the Ecole Nationale d'Instituteurs. A more advanced course from grade 10 and lasting for three years at the Ecole Nationale Secondaire leads to the qualification of **Diplôme de Professeur de l'Enseignement Secondaire**.

Higher

Teachers at the Polytechnical Institutes are usually graduates of these institutes or from abroad.

Guyana

The following chapter regarding the education system in Guyana is based on information obtained from the 3rd edition of this Guide, published in 1991, as NARIC has been unable to obtain more recent information.

This chapter covers the period from British Guiana's independence in 1966.

Under the 1876 Education Act, education was made compulsory for children aged five to fourteen years old. The 1975 Education Act made all schools co-educational – in practice this Act only affected the six schools that had still remained exclusively boys' schools or girls' schools. Shortly thereafter, the government effectively nationalized all private schools, including those run by religious groups under the 1976 Free Education Act which guaranteed the right of free education from nursery to university. The principal body in Guyana responsible for education, including curricula and teaching methods, is the Ministry of Education.

The medium of instruction is English.

The academic year runs from September to July.

EVALUATION IN BRITAIN

School

Caribbean Examinations Council Secondary Education Certificate – grades 1 and 2 at general proficiency generally considered comparable to GCSE standard (grades A, B and C).

GCE Advanced – of the same standard as GCE Advanced examinations taken in Britain.

Higher

Bachelor degree – generally considered to be below British Bachelor degree standard.

Master's degree – generally considered comparable to British Bachelor degree standard.

MARKING SYSTEMS

School

Caribbean Examinations Council Secondary Education Certificate: two schemes are available in the subject examinations; the general proficiency scheme and the basic proficiency scheme.

There is no pass/fail mark.

Five grades are awarded, defined as follows:

1   comprehensive working knowledge of the syllabus

2   working knowledge of most aspects of the syllabus

3   working knowledge of some aspects of the syllabus

4   limited knowledge of a few aspects of the syllabus

5   insufficient evidence on which to base a judgement.

GCE examinations: see Appendix 2.

Higher

Bachelor degrees:

Subjects are graded A (maximum) – F
Degrees are classified: pass with distinction
                           pass

SCHOOL EDUCATION

Primary

This covers six years from age five years and six months. On completion of grade 6, pupils take the **Secondary School Entrance Examination** (SSEE) which determines admission to secondary education.

Secondary

Entry to secondary schools depends on the grades obtained in the **Secondary School Entrance Examination**. Community high schools usually prepare students for the **Secondary Schools Proficiency Examination** (SSPE) over a period of four years. General secondary and senior secondary schools prepare students for the **Caribbean Examinations Council Secondary Education Certificate** (CSEC) over five years. Senior secondary schools provide courses for a further two years leading to **General Certificate of Education Advanced-level** examinations of British examining boards (mainly the University of London). (For further information on Caribbean Examinations Council examinations see Appendix 4.)

Technical secondary/further

The Carnegie School of Home Economics and the Fredericks School of Home Economics provide two-year day-time courses in household management and catering. Day-time pupils at the Carnegie School also sit for the **Secondary Schools Certificate Examination** (SSCE) in food, nutrition and needlecraft. Evening classes for adults in a variety of home management and craft skills are of three and six months' duration.

The Guyana Industrial Training Centre provides short courses (of one year or less in duration) in six basic trade areas: electricity; plumbing; carpentry; masonry; welding; and heavy equipment operation and maintenance.

The Government Technical Institute (GTI) offers courses in business studies (to the level of Technician), land surveying and building. These courses lead to various diplomas, **BTEC National** and **BTEC Higher National Certificates**.

The Guyana School of Agriculture, which comes under the Ministry of Agriculture, offers courses in agricultural education and training at the **Certificate** and the **Higher Diploma** level. Graduates of the **Certificate** course are notionally fitted to be farmers and extension workers. For the **Higher Diploma** course, students should possess a **Trained Teacher's Certificate** or four subjects at CSEC general proficiency. Graduates of this course are eligible for appointment as agricultural field assistants or agriculture teachers. They are also eligible for entry to the agriculture degree programme offered by the University of Guyana.

The **Guyana Technical Educational Examination** (GTEE) has replaced the City and Guilds of London Institute examinations. Under the GTEE system, examinations are prepared and marked in Guyana. Since there has been concern in business circles that students of technical institutions were not emerging with the qualifications and skills required by industry, there have been moves to revive the National Advisory Board and for there to be closer relations between these institutions and employers' associations. A regional approach to technical/vocational education has not been ruled out.

HIGHER EDUCATION

The University of Guyana was established in 1963, based to a large extent on the American system. The minimum entrance requirement to **Bachelor degree** courses is the **Caribbean Examinations Council Secondary Education Certificate** general proficiency scheme or **General Certificate of Education Ordinary level. Bachelor degree** courses generally last four years. Students who successfully complete Part I of the LLB course transfer to the University of the West Indies to complete their studies.

Master's degrees generally take a further one to two years.

TEACHER EDUCATION

The Cyril Potter College of Education is responsible for the professional training of nursery, primary and secondary teachers.

Primary

The College offers separate two-year nursery and primary programmes for teachers who have not received formal professional training and teachers who intend to make teaching a career. These courses lead to a **Trained Teacher's Certificate**.

Secondary

The College provides three-year courses leading to the **Trained Teacher's Certificate**. The University of Guyana also offers a **Bachelor in Education** (BEd) degree; a **Certificate course in Education** for practising teachers who have graduated from the Cyril Potter College of Education; and a **Diploma in Education** for practising teachers with the **BEd** qualifications.

Haiti

The education system is centralized under the Ministry of National Education, Youth and Sports. There are both state and private schools. All state and most private schools work towards nationally administered examinations. Some private schools work to either the French or American systems and the pupils take the appropriate French or American examinations. There are currently approximately 1,120 state and 2,900 private primary schools, and a total of aproximately 400 secondary schools (both state and private).

The education system is based on the French system but is currently undergoing reform. The Educational Reform was formulated in 1975 and introduced from 1980 but was not widely accepted, and most schools continued to follow the traditional system. The government Decree of 6 March 1989 formally introduced the *Ecole Fondamentale* (or Reform) as from 1989. It is expected that the first school-leaving examinations under the Reform will be held in approximately the year 2000.

As both the traditional system and the Reform are currently in use, they will both be described below; the change-over will be gradual and it is expected that there will be resistance to the Reform from the private sector.

In the traditional system, the six-year cycle of primary education is compulsory. Under the Reform, basic schooling will cover nine years.

In the traditional system, French is the official medium of instruction, despite the government Decree of 19 September 1979 which proclaimed Creole the official language for the first four years of primary school, with French taught in parallel as a foreign language. Under the Reform, both French and Creole will be used, with a gradual switch from Creole (spoken by all Haitians) to French (spoken by a minority).

The academic year runs from October to June. Some private schools working under the French or American systems have a slightly longer school year (September to June).

EVALUATION IN BRITAIN

School

Brevet Elémentaire du Premier Cycle – generally considered to be below GCSE standard.

Baccalauréat I (Rhétorique) – generally considered to be below GCSE standard.

Baccalauréat II (Philosophie) – generally considered comparable to GCSE standard (grades A, B and C) on a subject-for-subject basis, with the exception of English language.

Higher

Diplôme d'Etudes Supérieures/Professional title (or equivalent) – generally considered to satisfy the general entrance requirements of British higher education institutions.

MARKING SYSTEMS

School

Marking is on a scale of 1–10 or 1–20 or given as a percentage, with 50 per cent required to pass. Some private schools require a higher pass-mark. If a student fails to obtain the required pass-mark at the end of the school year then the whole year must be retaken.

Higher

Marking is on a percentage scale, with 60 per cent as the minimum pass-mark.

Students must obtain a general average of 65 per cent at the end of each year or retake the whole year.

SCHOOL EDUCATION

Pre-primary

This is not compulsory although facilities exist for children to attend one year of pre-primary schooling. Private kindergartens in the capital and major towns offer a three-year kindergarten cycle (for ages three to six).

Primary

Schooling normally begins at six years of age.

In the traditional system, primary school extends over six years, divided into three two-year cycles: preparatory, elementary and intermediate. On completion of the sixth year pupils take examinations for the **Certificat d'Etudes Primaires**.

Under the Reform, primary school will cover nine years, divided into three cycles (four years, two years, three years). Upon completion of the nine years, pupils will take the examinations for the **Brevet d'Enseignement Fondamental**.

Secondary

Under the traditional system, secondary schooling extends over seven years, divided into a three-year lower general cycle and a four-year specialized upper cycle. Upon completion of the lower cycle, pupils take examinations for the **Brevet Elémentaire du Premier Cycle**, and the final examinations are the **Baccalauréat**, in two parts, at the end of the third and fourth years of the upper cycle. **Baccalauréat I (Rhétorique)** is at the end of the third upper cycle year and **Baccalauréat II (Philosophie)** at the end of the fourth upper cycle year. In the upper cycle, pupils are oriented towards one of four section options, with emphasis on the following major subjects, although other subjects are taken simultaneously, but with a lower points value in the final examinations:

Section A : Latin, Greek
Section B : Latin, languages, literature
Section C : Mathematics, physical sciences
Section D : Mathematics, natural sciences.

Under the Reform, the new secondary cycle will be three years (after nine years of *Ecole Fondamentale*), and the new school-leaving examinations will be the **Baccalauréat** and the **Diplôme d'Enseignement Secondaire**. Pupils will be oriented towards one of three options (*Classique, Technique or Professionnelle*) or enter *Ecole Normale* (teacher training college) for the three years of secondary schooling.

Technical secondary

Holders of the **Brevet Elémentaire du Premier Cycle** (traditional) may take a four-year course in commercial training, accounting, and hotel management for the **Brevet d'Aptitude Professionnelle** or a two-year course for the **Brevet Supérieur**.

Under the Reform, pupils may choose the technical or professional option after nine years of *Ecole Fondamentale* for the three-year cycle of secondary (technical) education.

HIGHER EDUCATION

Most facilities for higher education are offered by the State University of Haiti (founded in 1944, although some faculties were created at later dates) or by various *Ecoles Supérieures* which are under state control: e.g. the Ecole Normale Supérieure; Institut National d'Administration, de Gestion et des Hautes Etudes Internationales. There are at present seven faculties in the University:

–   Medicine and Pharmacy;
–   Odontology;
–   Law and Economic Sciences;
–   Sciences;
–   Human and Social Sciences;
–   Ethnology;
–   Agronomy and Veterinary Medicine.

First degree courses, normally lasting three to four years, lead to the award of **Diplôme d'Etudes Supérieures, Certificat d'Etudes Supérieures** or a **Professional title**, the exceptions being the Faculty of Law where the **Licence en Droit** is obtained after four years and the Faculty of Medicine where the **Diplôme de Docteur en Medecin** is obtained after seven years.

There are no certificates or diplomas for partial completion of a degree at the University of Haiti.

The admission requirement for university courses is **Baccalauréat II**, and in addition, students wishing to enter the faculties of law, dentistry, medicine, economic sciences, agriculture and veterinary medicine, must take an entrance examination.

There are facilities for postgraduate study in ethnology and in development sciences, both leading to a **Doctorate**.

TEACHER EDUCATION

Primary

Holders of the **Brevet Elémentaire du Premier Cycle** (traditional system) or the **Brevet d'Enseignement Fondamental** (Reform) take a competitive entrance examination for entry into the teacher training college (Ecole Normale d'Instituteurs) for a three-year course, culminating in the **Diplôme de Fin d'Etudes Normales**. Alternatively, students with **Baccalauréat I** can follow a one-year teacher training course.

Secondary

Students with **Baccalauréat II** take an entrance examination for a three-year course at the Ecole Normale Supérieure. Upon successful completion of the course, students are awarded the **Diplôme d'Ecole Normale Supérieure** by the Faculty of Letters and Pedagogy of the University of Haiti.

Honduras

The education system is centralized under the Ministry of Public Education.

Compulsory education covers the six years of primary education from seven to thirteen years.

The medium of instruction in state institutions is Spanish.

The academic year runs from February to November.

EVALUATION IN BRITAIN

School

Bachillerato – generally considered comparable to GCSE standard (grades A, B and C) on a subject-for-subject basis, with the exception of English language.

Higher

Licenciado/Professional title – generally considered comparable to British Bachelor degree standard if awarded after four or more years of study.

MARKING SYSTEM

School

Marking is on a percentage scale (lowest pass 61) or a numerical scale of 1–5 maximum (lowest pass 3).

100–96	5	*sobresaliente*	excellent
95-76	4	*muy bueno*	very good
75-61	3	*bueno*	good
60–40	2	*aplazado*	referred/fail
39–1	1	*insuficiente*	fail

SCHOOL EDUCATION

In addition to the state system, there is a flourishing private sector. These schools are required to conform to standards laid down by the government. Many of them are bilingual Spanish/English and Spanish/French.

Pre-primary

Limited facilities are available, although an increased number of private centres have opened in recent years.

Primary

This covers six years from age seven.

Secondary

This covers five years divided into a *Ciclo Comun de Cultura General*/lower cycle, of three years, and an upper cycle of two years. The lower cycle covers general education; pupils may then specialize in literary or scientific streams in the upper cycle, on the completion of which they take the examinations for the **Bachillerato**.

Technical secondary

A variety of specializations is available during the upper cycle of secondary education which in these fields lasts three years, leading to, for example, **Perito Mercantil**, a qualification in business/office skills and **Maestro de Educacion Primaria** (Primary School Teacher). These qualifications entitle the holder to university admission.

HIGHER EDUCATION

This is offered by several universities and a number of specialized institutes. The usual admission requirement is the **Bachillerato** (or technical equivalent). Students at the National Autonomous University spend the first year (for medical students two years) in the Centre of General Studies. Successful completion of the specialized course leads to the **Licenciado/Professional qualification**. In addition to the common first year, courses normally last four years except for the following:

law	
economics	five years
engineering	
pharmacy	
dentistry	five years, leading to the **Doctorado**
medicine	six years, leading to the **Doctorado**

TEACHER EDUCATION

Primary

Teachers are trained during the upper secondary cycle, on courses lasting three years leading to the **Maestro de Educacion Primaria**.

Secondary

Holders of the **Bachillerato** or the **Maestro de Educacion Primaria** are trained at the Higher Teachers' Training School on courses lasting four years.

Hong Kong

Education is compulsory for nine years covering the primary and junior secondary levels.

The school academic year runs from September to July divided into three terms. In higher education the year runs from October to June with some institutions following the three-term and some the two-semester system.

Medium of instruction – see individual sections.

EVALUATION IN BRITAIN

School

Certificate of Education – generally considered comparable to GCSE standard (grades A, B and C) provided grade C or above is obtained except for English language (syllabus A) which is considered a lower level.

Higher Level Certificate – generally considered comparable to a standard between GCSE and GCE Advanced. Considered comparable in many subjects, but not all, to the Scottish Certificate of Education Higher Grade. (The Certificate was available for the last time in 1992.)

Advanced Supplementary Level Certificate – generally considered comparable to British Advanced Supplementary.

Advanced Level Certificate – grades A to E are generally equated to GCE Advanced standard.

Whilst the structure of the HKALE examination is similar to the GCE Advanced examination, there appears to be a difference in respect of mathematics and science subjects in that the level of attainment required for the award of a given grade seems higher in the HKALE. Many admission tutors would accept that the difference amounts to at least one grade – so that a grade D in a HKALE would be comparable to a grade C in an A level taken in the UK.

Use of English – grades A to C are generally considered comparable to GCSE (grades A, B and C).

Further and Higher

Technician-level certificates and diplomas (from technical institutes and polytechnics) – generally considered comparable to BTEC National Diploma / N/SVQ level 3 / Advanced GNVQ/GSVQ standard. Diploma holders could be considered for admission to the first year of a related degree course.

Diplomas (from <u>Shue Yan College</u>) – generally considered comparable to a standard between GCE Advanced and British Bachelor degree; may be given advanced standing by British higher education institutions.

Higher Certificates and Higher Diplomas (from former polytechnics) – generally considered comparable to BTEC Higher National Certificate and BTEC Higher National Diploma / N/SVQ level 4.

Honours Diplomas (from <u>Lingnan College</u>) and **Professional Diplomas** (from former polytechnics) – generally considered to be of a standard above BTEC Higher National Diploma N/SVQ level 4.

Higher Diploma holders and professional diploma holders could be considered for direct admission to the second or third year of a related degree course. A few institutions, however, have accepted these students direct to MSc courses. Higher Certificate holders could be considered for direct admission to the second year of a related degree course.

Bachelor degrees – Honours degrees generally considered comparable to British Bachelor (Honours) degree standard and Pass degrees to British Bachelor (Ordinary) degree standard.

Master's degree – generally considered comparable to British Master's degree.

Doctoral degree – generally considered comparable to British Doctorate/PhD.

MARKING SYSTEMS

School

Hong Kong Certificate of	)
Education (English) –	)
Hong Kong Certificate of	) 1968–73
Education (Chinese) –	)
Hong Kong Certificate of	) 1974 onwards
Education –	)

A (1) (highest) to H (8) lowest.
Grade E represents the basic level of achievement.

Since 1988, grades G and H have not been offered.

Since 1986, the language medium in which each subject is taken has not been shown on the certificate.

Hong Kong Higher Level Certificate – 1979–92
Hong Kong Advanced Level Certificate – 1980 onwards

1979 **Higher Level Certificate** and 1980 both **Higher Level** and **Advanced Level certificates**.

A (1) highest to H (8) lowest

1981 – each grade is divided into three sub-grades:

A(01) B(04) C(07) D(10) E(13) F(16) G(19) H(22)
A(02) B(05) C(08) D(11) E(14) F(17) G(20) H(23)
A(03) B(06) C(09) D(12) E(15) F(18) G(21) H(24)

Since 1985 grades G and H have not been offered.

Higher Level Certificate: since 1987 the language medium in which each subject is taken has not been shown on the certificate.

Advanced Level Certificate: up to 1991 subjects were examined in English only except for Chinese studies. From 1992 the examination is available in English and Chinese. The language medium in which each subject is taken is not shown on the certificate.

Higher

Degrees are classified as follows:

First class honours
Second class honours upper division
Second class honours lower division
Third class honours
Pass

Some degrees are unclassified.

SCHOOL EDUCATION

Schools may be either government, government aided or private.

Pre-primary

Kindergartens are operated by voluntary organizations and private bodies for children between the ages of three and five.

Primary

Primary education lasts for six years from Primary 1 to Primary 6 and normally takes a child from the age of six to twelve years old. It is free in all government and in nearly all aided primary schools. The majority of primary schools operate on a bi-sessional basis, with children either attending school in the morning or the afternoon. However, all-day schooling is set to be introduced for all Primary 5 and 6 pupils. In most primary schools the language of instruction is Chinese with English being taught as a second language. Competition among parents for places in the 'best' primary schools, as at other levels of education, is fierce and admission is monitored through the Primary One Admissions Scheme. In 1994, about sixty per cent of pupils were admitted to schools of their parents' choice with the rest being allocated to schools within their own district.

Secondary

At the end of their Primary 6 year, pupils are allocated places in government and aided secondary schools through a scheme called the Secondary School Places Allocation (SSPA) System. Allocation is based on parental choice and internal school examination results moderated by an **Academic Aptitude Test** which is centrally administered.

Again, there is competition for schools which have a good reputation for academic success. In 1994, about 75 per cent of the pupils were allocated to places of parental first choice.

Secondary schools offer courses at junior secondary level (Secondary 1 to Secondary 3) covering the twelve to fourteen years age group, senior secondary level (Secondary 4 and 5), the fifteen to sixteen years age group, and sixth form (Secondary 6 and 7) for the seventeen and eighteen year olds.

Secondary schools can also be classified according to the language of instruction and the curriculum followed. They are divided by language into Chinese, Anglo-Chinese (where the medium of teaching is in both English and Chinese) and English schools. The vast majority of students are taught in Anglo-Chinese schools. The curriculum followed separates schools into grammar, technical or prevocational.

Both grammar and technical schools offer a five-year course (Secondary 1–5) leading to the **Hong Kong Certificate of Education Examination** (HKCEE) in a broad range of subjects, the difference between the two being that technical schools place a greater emphasis on technical and commercial subjects. The majority of grammar and technical schools also offer two-year sixth form courses leading to the **Hong Kong Advanced Level Examination** (HKALE). A one-year course (Secondary 6) leading to the **Hong Kong Higher Level Examination** was also offered by some schools but this examination was abolished in 1992. The Hong Kong Examinations Authority has introduced an **Advanced Supplementary Level Examination** (AS) with effect from 1994. AS courses span two years and are of a similar depth to the HKALE but cover a more restricted ground. Again, there is strong competition for sixth form places in schools with good academic records and other schools not wishing to lower their standards may not accept some Secondary 5 students.

Pre-vocational schools offer an alternative form of education for those of a more practical bent. Students in these schools may enter approved apprenticeship schemes in a technical institute or continue to HKCEE after Secondary 3 and then continue their studies in one of the technical institutes.

The introduction of A level courses in practical and technical subjects from 1991 will allow some pre-vocational schools to offer sixth form courses for the first time.

Many pupils take British **GCE/GCSE** examinations in Hong Kong in addition to the examinations of the Hong Kong Examinations Authority mentioned above.

FURTHER EDUCATION

Shue Yan College is an approved post-secondary institution offering post-HKCEE diploma courses in arts, commerce and social sciences which can be completed in a minimum of four years. Instruction is in both English and Chinese.

Non-degree post-secondary courses are also offered by the Lingnan College, the Hong Kong Academy for Performing Arts, the City University of Hong Kong (formerly City Polytechnic of Hong Kong) and the Hong Kong Polytechnic University (formerly Hong Kong Polytechnic); they include post-HKCEE diplomas and certificates, Higher Diplomas and certificates and three-year post-HKALE, Higher Diplomas and professional diplomas. Further details of the former polytechnics are given in the **HIGHER EDUCATION** section.

The Hong Kong Polytechnic and the City Polytechnic of Hong Kong changed their names when they were given university status in Autumn 1994.

Technical further education is offered by eight technical institutes (TIs) all of which are operated by the Vocational Training Council. They offer diploma and certificate courses at both craft and technician level in vocationally orientated subjects such as accountancy, design, engineering and hotel and catering. The two-year diploma course at the technician level is very similar in content and style to the BTEC National Diploma course and indeed, all the engineering diploma courses taught in TIs have been validated by BTEC. City and Guilds of London Institute agreed, from October 1994, to accredit the Vocational Training Council courses leading to City and Guilds certification. There is competition for places which varies from course to course but students will generally need a minimum of four or five passes in the HKCEE to be admitted or Form 3 for lower level courses. Technician courses are taught in English while craft courses are taught in Chinese. Upon completion of their diplomas, most students enter industry or commerce where many will continue with their studies by part-time day release or, more commonly, by evening study in one of the local former polytechnics for **Higher Certificate** or **Diploma** qualifications.

There are a significant number of private colleges, approved by the Education Department, which offer limited post-secondary education, for example, the Hang Seng School of Commerce offers a two-year post-HKCEE Diploma in Business Studies, although about half its students already have A levels.

HIGHER EDUCATION

The University and Polytechnic Grants Committee (UPGC) is an advisory body which makes recommendations about the development of the tertiary (higher education) sector, the funding requirements of those institutions it covers, and the administration of government grants. The UPGC currently funds seven institutions: University of Hong Kong, Chinese University of Hong Kong, Hong Kong University of Science and Technology, Lingnan College, City University of Hong Kong (formerly City Polytechnic of Hong Kong), Hong Kong Polytechnic University (formerly Hong Kong Polytechnic) and Hong Kong Baptist University (formerly Hong Kong Baptist College).

The Hong Kong Government approved university status for the Hong Kong Polytechnic, the City Polytechnic of Hong Kong and the Hong Kong Baptist College. Their names changed in Autumn 1994.

There are additional tertiary institutions over and above those funded by UPGC. The Hong Kong Academy for Performing Arts is funded through the Government's Recreation and Culture Branch. The Open Learning Institute of Hong Kong was established by the Government and initially sub-vented, but is moving towards becoming self-financing.

Admission to first degree courses is mainly based on **Hong Kong Advanced Level** results and is competitive. The Chinese University of Hong Kong, in addition to accepting students on the basis of their **Hong Kong Advanced Level** results, used to accept students for admission at the end of their Secondary 6 year on the basis of their **Hong Kong Higher Level** examination or their **Hong Kong Certificate of Education** and their performance in their Secondary 6 year. All institutions offer a three-year **Bachelor degree**. In addition, the Chinese University, which offered four year degrees, is now offering three year degrees. A new admissions scheme, the Joint Universities and Polytechnics Admissions Scheme (JUPAS) which is like a more complicated version of a combined UCCA-PCAS system, was introduced in 1991 replacing the previous individual application procedure.

All tertiary institutions will be expanding the number and range of their degree courses. The two former polytechnics will expand and move from a forty per cent ceiling on degree work to sixty-five per cent, at the same time some of their higher diploma work will go to new technical colleges.

A brief description of the institutions is given below.

The University of Hong Kong (HKU), the oldest tertiary institution in Hong Kong, was founded in 1911. It has a student population of about 9,500 of whom 8,200 are undergraduates and 1,300 are postgraduates. It is divided into nine faculties: architecture, arts, dentistry, education, engineering, law, medicine, science and social sciences. Admission is mainly based on HKALE grades (plus Use of English at grade E or above) and places at the undergraduate level, as in the other institutions, are almost exclusively for school-leavers. The University is modelled along British lines and there are many links with British institutions. The medium of instruction is English except for Chinese studies where Chinese is used. In addition to first degrees, the University offers a range of postgraduate certificates, diplomas and higher degrees.

The Chinese University of Hong Kong (CUHK), founded in 1963, has seven faculties: arts, business administration, medicine, science, social sciences, education and engineering. The university is unique in Hong Kong in that it offers a flexible credit unit system. Students are admitted at the end of either their Secondary 6 or Secondary 7 year and normally graduate after three or four years of study. While the American system is adopted for the curriculum structure, degree classification is the same as in Britain. The University offers **Master's degrees** and research programmes. In 1993-4, there were about 8,900 students of whom 8,100 were full-time undergraduates, 800 postgraduates and the remainder part-time undergraduates. The media of instruction are Chinese and English.

The Hong Kong University of Science and Technology (HKUST) had its first intake of students in October 1991, both at undergraduate and postgraduate level. There are four academic schools: business and management; humanities and social science; engineering, and science. The academic year is divided into two semesters. The medium of instruction is English.

The City University of Hong Kong (CityU), founded in 1984, offers the following courses: **Diplomas, Higher Diplomas, Bachelor degrees, Postgraduate certificates, Postgraduate Diplomas** and **Master's degrees**. Half the full-time students are following courses at **Bachelor degree** level and above. The number of students is expected to increase from 11,000 to 12,900 in 1996.

The University has departments which are organized into four faculties: business, humanities and social sciences, law, science and engineering. Academic programmes are orientated towards professional practice and are geared towards the needs of commerce and industry in Hong Kong. The modular system is used for building up academic programmes. The medium of instruction is mainly English.

Courses at **Diploma** and **Higher Diploma** level are co-ordinated through the College of Higher Vocational Studies (in effect a fifth faculty). This has enabled a better focus on sub-degree work to be developed. The College consists of three divisions: commerce, technology, and humanities and social sciences. The total student population in the College is expected to be about 4,700 (or 36 per cent of the total student population by 1996).

Hong Kong Polytechnic University, offers a wide range of courses designed to meet the demands of commerce, industry and the needs of the community. The university has expanded rapidly since it was founded in 1972 and is organized into six faculties: applied science and textiles; business and information systems; communication; construction and land use; engineering; and health and social studies. About sixty per cent of full-time equivalent students are studying for degree courses and postgraduate courses. The remainder take Higher Diplomas and Certificate courses. Postgraduate studies are offered both by course work and by research. In 1993–94, there were 9,000 students of whom 6,800 were undergraduates, 200 postgraduates and the remaining were engaged in sub-degree level courses. The medium of instruction is mainly English.

Hong Kong Baptist University, which was founded in 1956, was accepted into the UPGC in 1983, started its first Honours degree courses in 1986 and is now an all-degree-awarding institution with 3,700 students. It previously offered a three-year post-**Advanced Level Honours Diploma**. The university has twenty departments which are divided into five faculties: arts, business, science, social sciences, and communication. It has strong links with the USA and has adopted the American system of semesters, course units, grade-point averages, President's Lists and so on, the only exception being that the undergraduate Honours programme is of three years' duration and not four.

Lingnan College (LC), became a degree-awarding institution under the auspices of the UPGC in 1991. It was formerly an approved post-secondary institution offering three-year post-**Hong Kong Advanced Level Honours Diplomas**. It is planned that by 1994–5, all courses of study will be at degree level. The College has three faculties: art, business and social sciences. The medium of instruction is mainly English.

The Open Learning Institute of Hong Kong (OLI), which opened in 1989, is similar in concept to the Open University in Britain and many of its courses are heavily influenced by OU units. Teaching is mainly by notes and textbooks although there is a regular meeting once every two weeks between tutors and students. There are three schools, arts, business, and science and technology, with currently seventy per cent of students studying in the School of Business. The minimum time for graduation for an **Ordinary degree** is three years and for an **Honours degree** four years.

The Hong Kong Academy for Performing Arts (APA), was established by Ordinance in 1984 with the object of fostering and providing training, education and research in the performing and related technical arts. The APA has four schools: Dance, Drama, Music and Technical Arts. It offers degree, diploma, higher certificate and advanced diploma awards, plus one-year foundation courses.

The Hong Kong Council on Academic Accreditation (HKCAA) was established in 1990 by government as an independent statutory body. One of its functions is to validate the degrees awarded by the non-university tertiary institutions in Hong Kong: Lingnan College, the Open Learning Institute, and the Hong Kong Academy for Performing Arts where degrees in dance, drama, music and the technical arts have been introduced.

Some private colleges operate in Hong Kong but are accredited elsewhere e.g. Taiwan.

TEACHER EDUCATION

There are two types of teacher, non-graduate and graduate.

Non-graduate teachers take either a three-year post-HKCEE or two-year post-HKALE course leading to a **Certificate** award at one of four colleges of education. Non-graduate teachers normally teach in primary schools or the junior forms of secondary schools.

Graduate teachers who do not hold approved **Bachelor of Education** degrees, for career advancement, may take a one-year postgraduate course in either the Faculty of Education of the University of Hong Kong or the Chinese University which leads, respectively, to the **Postgraduate Certificate in Education** and the **Postgraduate Diploma in Education**.

The Institute of Language in Education (ILE) provides in-service training for non-graduate teachers.

Following the Education Commission Report published in July 1992, radical reforms of the teaching profession are in progress. These include upgrading teaching as a profession and significant development in the provision of teacher education. In progress at present, is the introduction of graduate posts in the primary sector. However, one ultimate goal of the exercise is to have an all graduate teaching profession in Hong Kong. At present the four teacher training colleges; Grantham College of Education, Sir Robert Black College of Education, Hong Kong Technical Teachers' College, and Northcote College of Education, plus the Institute of Language in Education provide teacher education for Hong Kong. These are now being absorbed into the newly established Hong Kong Institute of Education. The Institute is in the process of developing new sub-degree and degree programmes for teachers.

Hungary

After more than three years' discussion and more than 13 different proposals, the Hungarian parliament passed the new Bill on Public Education (K to 12), vocational education, and higher education in June 1993. The main issues of this long discussion were the place of religious education, the necessary changes in the school-system, and the national core curriculum. Since the new Bill came into force in September 1993, some of these questions are not yet answered. But the Bill introduced some major changes in the legal framework of education as compared with the 1985 Bill.

Education in Hungary is under state control, but any individual, company, foundation, or other legal entity has the legal right to found an education institution.

The age of compulsory education runs from 6 to 16. Prior to entering comprehensive schools, children, aged 3 to 6, may take part in preparatory education in Kindergartens.

A new characteristic of the secondary education system is gradually making possible the postponement of the choice of profession until at least the age of 16.

Probably the most important feature of the restructuring of Hungarian higher education is that by 30 June 1998, all higher education institutions must be accredited according to a uniform procedure. After this date, those institutions which have not fulfilled the requirements stipulated in the Law will not be permitted to operate as universities.

The medium of instruction is Hungarian (except in certain nursery, primary and secondary schools for ethnic minorities).

The academic year runs from the beginning of September to the end of June.

EVALUATION IN BRITAIN

School

Erettsegi/Matura – generally considered to satisfy the general entrance requirements of British higher education institutions.

Higher

Egyetemi Oklevel – generally considered comparable to British Bachelor (Honours) degree standard, although the course lasts longer than in the UK.

Foiskola Oklevel – constitutes a professionally oriented first degree; generally considered comparable to a standard above that of BTEC Higher National Diploma / N/SVQ level 4.

MARKING SYSTEMS

School

5	*jeles*	excellent	90 per cent or above
4	*jo*	good	80–89 per cent
3	*kozepes*	average	70–79 per cent
2	*elegseges*	pass	60–69 per cent
1	*elegtelen*	fail	below 60 per cent

Higher

In subjects of instruction the same marking system is used as in schools. For the doctor's degree (physicians, dentists, vets and lawyers) and the university doctorate, the grades are:

4.51–5.00	*summa cum laude*
3.51–4.50	*cum laude*
2.00–3.50	*rite* (pass)

SCHOOL EDUCATION

1985–1994

Pre-primary/kindergarten

Nursery schools (*Bolcsode*) are available for children aged one to three and kindergartens (*Ovoda*) for those aged three to six.

Primary and lower secondary/elementary

This covers eight years from age six, divided into two four-year cycles, undertaken in general schools (*Altalanos Iskola*). The curriculum covers Hungarian language and literature, Russian, history, geography, arithmetic – geography, physics, chemistry, biology, technics, drawing, singing/music and physical education.

Secondary

There are four types of secondary school:

Grammar school (*Gimnazium*): pupils follow a four-year course terminating with the qualification **Erettsegi/Matura**. The curriculum covers Hungarian language and literature, history, a foreign language (formerly Russian, now usually English), a second foreign language, mathematics, physics, chemistry, biology, drawing and fine arts, physical education, occupational guidance and optional courses. The **Erettsegi** examination is taken in only four subjects: written and oral examination in Hungarian language and literature, mathematics, an oral examination in history, and a written or oral examination in one subject chosen by the pupil.

Secondary technical school (*Szakkozepiskola*): pupils follow a four-year course, terminating with the qualification **Erettsegi**. The curriculum covers general subjects (Hungarian language and literature, history, Russian, English, mathematics, physics) and vocational subjects (which account for fifty per cent of the curriculum). The **Erettsegi** examination is taken in Hungarian language and literature, history, mathematics and a vocational subject.

School for vocational skills (*Szakmunkaskepzo Iskola*): pupils follow a two to three-year course, terminating with the qualification **Szakmunkas** (skilled worker). The general subjects studied are the same as in secondary technical schools but with fewer weekly lessons and a greater emphasis on vocational training.

Vocational schools: these give skilled-worker qualifications in a particular field and prepare pupils for their chosen professions.

In 1987, bilingual (dual-language) grammar schools (*Ket Nyelvu Gimnazium*) were set up (English/Hungarian, German/Hungarian, French/Hungarian, Russian/Hungarian). Mathematics, physics, biology, history and geography are taught in the foreign language using translations of Hungarian textbooks. The curriculum is still the Hungarian one and the **Erettsegi** examination is taken at the end of the course though there is now some interest in the **International Baccalaureate**.

SCHOOL EDUCATION

Since 1994

The Education Bill introduced some flexibility in the school system by creating the six and eight year long *Gymnasiums*. It also allows students to study at home with the provision that they must pass a standard exam administered by a school. While the compulsory school-system used to run from grades K through eight, the new Bill changes it to K through ten. This will be the base of the national core curriculum (not yet introduced). Public education is completed with an examination after the tenth grade.

There are some changes in the legal status of the private and religious schools; these 'non-state' schools can make a 'Public Educational Contract' with either the local government or the Ministry of Education and Culture. They can receive public funds through this contract according to their commitment to participate in the public education.

FURTHER EDUCATION

Evening and correspondence schools are available for adults and those who did not attend a secondary school after leaving the *Altalanos Iskola.*

HIGHER EDUCATION

1985–1994

Because of the country's history and geographical location the structure of higher education follows the Central European model, i.e. it is a modified version of the German/Austrian systems. The 1985 Education Act increased considerably the independence of institutions: they are now allowed to make decisions about the curriculum, about examination procedures, about their internal structure, about state allowances for students (within the resources available) and about requirements for staff. Substantial changes are also taking place in methodology: the amount of independent work required and the number of small study groups are being increased while the number of compulsory practice sessions and the number of examinations are being reduced.

Entrance is highly selective with demand exceeding the number of places available by three or four times on average, though there are wide differences between faculties. (The authorities aim to raise the number of students entering higher education by the end of the 1990s.) Approximately eighty per cent of students entering university are from grammar schools and twenty per cent from technical schools. Admission is based on:

– results in the **Erettsegi/Matura** and performance in the third and fourth years of secondary school (marks out of a maximum of 60 points);
– an entrance examination in which two subjects are taken pertinent to the proposed degree course; both are examined orally and in writing (there is a maximum of 15 points per examination).

At least 90 points out of the combined maximum of 120 must be obtained for entry, although many faculties seem to require more. The **Erettsegi/Matura** itself is a formality, although it is a university entrance requirement. In subjects in which the demand for places is particularly great, such as medicine or veterinary medicine, 110 points or more are normally stipulated. Even obtaining the stipulated number of points is no guarantee of a place: the best students are accepted. There is a considerable waiting list for entry, many students having to wait two or three years until a place becomes available.

Courses are offered at two levels: universities (*Egyetem*) provide courses lasting four to six years, including the preparation of a thesis, usually leading to the state examination (**Allamvizsga**) and the award of the university diploma (**Egyetemi Oklevel**). This normally entitles holders to practise professionally and to undertake postgraduate courses. A degree in engineering at the <u>Technical University of Budapest</u>, for example, takes five years, the first three years devoted to the teaching of basic subjects, followed by greater specialization in the final two years. This university also offers a course based on the Anglo-Saxon model, i.e. a three or four-year BSc course followed by a two-year MSc course. Courses in medicine take six years, those in law, dentistry and veterinary medicine five years. In these subjects the qualification obtained is **Doktor**, not **Oklevel**; it is regarded as a professional qualification, not an academic degree. All students, except those reading law or medicine, have to take two subjects of equal weight. Until recently there were also compulsory subsidiary subjects (Russian, another foreign language, political ideology and physical education) but these requirements are now receding.

The second, lower level of courses are those offered by the colleges of higher education (*Foiskola*). These colleges, which constitute the predominant section of higher education, are independent of the universities (except for agriculture) and are not authorized to award university degrees. Their courses, which last three or four years, are less broadly based and more practically slanted than their university counterparts. Graduates receive a college diploma (**Foiskola Oklevel**); they are referred to as college graduate engineers, teacher, etc., thus differentiating them from university graduates in the same subjects. At certain universities the two levels are combined: a college diploma is awarded after three years and a university diploma after a further two years.

In subjects other than medicine, law, dentistry and veterinary medicine, the university degree of **Doktor** can be obtained at least one year, but usually two to three years, after the **Egyetemi Oklevel**. The **Kandidatus** is a post-university academic qualification awarded by a committee of the Academy of Sciences after not less than three years' research following the **Oklevel** (often more than ten years e.g. in medicine) and the successful submission of a thesis and passing of an oral examination which includes foreign languages. The **Tudomanyok Doktora** is the highest post-university academic qualification awarded by the Academy of Sciences. Students must already have the **Kandidatus** and at least three to four years of further original research.

HIGHER EDUCATION

Since 1994

There have been key changes to the higher education system in Hungary following the summer of 1993, when parliment passed a legal package regulating various aspects of tertiary education.

Under the new act only those institutions offering undergraduate and postgraduate training can be called universities. Institutions offering undergraduate training only will become colleges for instance. Equally an institution offering to train postgraduates only is not eligible to be a university.

Formerly there was much tighter control exerted by the Ministry of Education over the way universities spent their budgets. Now the state continues to finance the universities but the universities have more discretion over how they will spend their budgets.

An Anglo-Saxon system of degrees has been established, with the introduction of degrees such as BA, MA and PhD. Under the old system there were three types of **doctorates**. The old university **doctorate**, which was considered comparable to a British MA or MSc by thesis, will remain for a transitory period (as yet unspecified). The old **Kandidatus** degree will now be replaced by a new university awarded degree which is supposed to be more comparable to the British PhD. The **doctorate** awarded by the Academy of Sciences will remain although it is likely to be granted in the future to academics on the basis of distinguished academic performance (usually based upon publications) rather than the formal submission of another thesis.

The new MBA's fall within the category of specialized postgraduate education. It would appear from the act that as they fall within this special category they are not equivalent to a Master's degree awarded after a five year university degree course and cannot therefore qualify as a route through to a PhD programme.

TEACHER EDUCATION

Pre-primary/kindergarten

This is a two-year course on successful completion of four years at *Gimnazium* or four years at a specialized technical secondary school (*Ovonoi Szakkozepiskola*).

Primary/elementary

First cycle

This is a three-year course at a teacher training college (*Tanitokepzo Foiskola*) on completion of the four-year course at a *Gimnazium* leading to the **Erettsegi**. *Tanito* is a teacher who has not specialized in a subject and teaches children in primary education (six to ten years old).

Second cycle

This is a four-year course at a college of education (*Tanarkepzo Foiskola*), specializing in two subjects, on completion of the four-year course at a *Gimnazium* leading to the **Erettsegi**. *Tanar* is a teacher who has specialized in two subjects and teaches children in primary education (ten to fourteen years old).

Secondary (grammar and technical)

Students follow a five-year course at university. Until 1992, a pedagogic element was built into all but a few university courses, regardless of whether the particular student was intending to take up teaching.

Iceland

The present law on compulsory education from 1991 stipulates compulsory schooling between the ages of six and sixteen. The compulsory school (*grunnskoli*) is divided into ten grades. Programmes offered at the upper-secondary level are mainly four-year programmes, but may vary from one to ten semesters in length. The programmes leading to matriculation examination (**studentsprof**) are organized as four year programmes, as are most programmes in the education for the certified trades, where the course of study is concluded with a journeyman's examination (**sveinsprof**).

The present law stipulates that compulsory schools are to operate for nine months of the year (September to May), although, according to the same law, exceptions may be granted. All schools in urban areas are in operation for full nine months. The schools that have a shorter academic year (between eight and nine months) are all located in rural areas and the reason for this has mainly to do with traditions going back to the time when agriculture and fishing industries needed pupils as labour. Most schools divide the academic year into two semesters. Examinations are given at the end of each semester in December and May.

The medium of instruction is Icelandic but the study of English as a foreign language is compulsory from the 7th grade. The academic year runs from September to the end of May.

Compulsory school education is free of charge.

EVALUATION IN BRITAIN

School

Studentsprof – may be considered to satisfy the general requirements of British higher education institutions if obtained from a Gymnasium; generally compared to BTEC National Diploma / N/SVQ level 3 / Advanced GNVQ/GSVQ standard, if from a technical/vocational school.

Higher

Bachelor degree – generally considered comparable to British Bachelor (Ordinary) degree standard. Students with grades 7.25 and above may be considered for postgraduate studies.

Kandidatsprof/Candidatus Mag – generally considered to approach British Master's degree standard.

MARKING SYSTEMS

School

Marking is on a scale 0–10 (maximum), with an average of 5 needed to proceed to the next year of school.

Higher

Marking is on a scale 0–10 (maximum), with 5 as the pass-mark.

SCHOOL EDUCATION

Until 1974–6

Primary

This was a six-year course from the age seven at a *Barnaskoli*, leading to the **Barnaprof** (leaving examination). All pupils could proceed to lower secondary education, but the result of this examination determined which stream (i.e. general or vocational) a child should enter.

Lower secondary (*Unglingaskoli*)

This covered two years and was offered in two streams: *Boknamsdeild* (general) and *Verknamsdeild* (vocational). Both streams led to **Unglingaprof**. Pupils could then leave school or enter *Landsprofsdeild* for one year to prepare for the **Landsprof** which gave entrance to the Gymnasium (*Menntaskoli*) or stay at secondary school (*Gagnfraedaskoli*) for two more years leading to **Gagnfraedaprof**. Danish was the first compulsory foreign language and was begun in the seventh year, i.e. in the first year of lower secondary school.

1974–6 to 1988

A new law on the comprehensive primary school was passed in 1974 and the system was fully implemented in 1976.

Primary and lower secondary (Compulsory education)

This covered nine years of which grades one to eight were compulsory. In grades one to three, compulsory subjects were Icelandic, mathematics, social studies, religious studies, domestic science, arts and crafts, music, and physical education. From grade six, science and Danish were added, and English was added in the seventh grade.

National Co-ordinated (NC) examinations were administered at the end of grade nine in Icelandic, Danish, English and mathematics. Depending on the results of these examinations and internal school assessments, pupils could proceed to (upper) secondary education. If a pupil did not fulfil the requirements he or she could undertake a preparatory course giving no credit (0–course) at an upper secondary school.

Since 1988

Pre-primary

The present legislation concerning pre-schools was passed in 1994. Pre-school lasts until the age of six. The state and the local municipalities share responsibility for pre-primary education, but the Ministry of Education decides educational policy.

Primary and lower secondary

The state and local municipalities jointly operate compulsory schools. The state pays for instruction (general teaching, substitute teaching, special education and teaching of children in hospitals), administration, educational materials and specialists services, whereas local municipalities are in charge of establishing and running schools.

Compulsory school (*grunnskoli*) is divided into ten grades. Three types of schools are the most common; schools that have all ten grades, schools that have grades one to seven and schools that have grades eight to ten.

In 1991, a new Education Act was introduced. This extended school hours for the youngest children. It also contains provisions for increased decentralization and more influence for parents. Compulsory schooling was extended to ten years instead of nine, i.e. it became mandatory for all children to start school at the age of six. There is no selection or streaming by ability and children are automatically promoted by age from one class to the next. In smaller schools, mostly rural schools, children at a number of different stages can be taught in one class by one teacher. The Ministry of Culture and Education issues a National Curriculum Guide.

At the conclusion of ten years of compulsory education, the pupils scheduled school time will have been divided among the various subjects in approximately the following manner:

Icelandic 18 per cent; mathematics 15 per cent; arts and crafts 20 per cent; foreign languages 9 per cent; natural sciences 6 per cent; social studies 7 per cent; religious studies 3 per cent; physical education 10 per cent; optional subjects and miscellaneous extra studies 12 per cent.

Icelandic, mathematics, art and handiwork, home economics, music, social studies, natural sciences and physical education are subjects which all pupils study throughout their primary and lower secondary school years. Danish is studied from the sixth grade (eleven year old pupils) and English from the seventh. In the tenth grade (the final year of compulsory education) all students study Icelandic, mathematics, English, Danish and physical education, in addition to other subjects and electives. Assessment is not necessarily standardized between different schools and teachers.

The last week of April, at the end of the tenth and final year in compulsory education, all pupils sit the same compulsory written examination in Icelandic, mathematics, English and Danish. These examinations are composed, marked and organized by *Rannsoknastofnun uppeldis- og menntamala* (The Institute of Educational Research). The certificate states the pupils marks on both the public examinations and all other courses completed in the tenth grade at school.

Upper Secondary Education (*Framhaldsskoli*)

Programmes of study at the upper-secondary level can be divided into academically and vocationally oriented programmes.

The main types of schools at the upper-secondary level are the following:

Gymnasium (*menntaskoli*), which offer four-year academic programmes of study which conclude with matriculation examination (**studentsprof**). Those students who complete the course satisfactorily are entitled to enter universities in Iceland.

Industrial vocational schools (*idnskoli*), which offer theoretical and practical programmes in the certified and some non-certified trades.

Comprehensive upper-secondary schools (*fjolbrautaskoli*) which offer academic programmes comparable to that of the grammar schools concluding with a matriculation examination and also general theoretical courses for those students taking a two-year programme of study. These schools also offer theoretical and practical training as in the industrial vocational schools.

Specialized vocational schools (*serskoli*) which offer specialized programmes as preparation for specialized employment.

Most schools operate according to a unit-credit system with no rigid form structure, i.e. the student groups vary according to their choice of course units. The unit-credit system is now the most common form of upper-secondary education.

General academic education is primarily organized as a four-year course leading to the **studentsprof**, but a few two-year programmes are also offered. Such programmes are usually intended as preparatory studies for other courses within the school or at specialized vocational schools.

There are six academic programmes of study that lead to the matriculation examination: languages, sociology, economics, physical education, natural science and physics. There are also fine arts programmes that can lead to matriculation, for example in music, and a technical programme following training in the certified trades. In schools with a unit-credit system, 140 credits are required for matriculation. Within any given academic programmes of study, three groups of courses are offered: general subjects, specialized subjects and electives. About two thirds of the course leading to matriculation is of a general nature and is common to all programmes of study.

The following subjects are compulsory for all programmes of study leading to matriculation and the figures following them are given as a percentage of the whole course: Icelandic 12 per cent; modern languages 19 per cent; social studies 8 per cent; science 9 per cent; mathematics 9 per cent; computer science 2 per cent and physical education 6 per cent. In addition to this between 17 per cent and 33 per cent of the student's education is spent on specialized subjects. The time given to electives varies according to the programme of study in question and is somewhere between 2 per cent and 18 per cent.

In the general academic programmes of education there are no nationally co-ordinated examinations neither as far as final examinations are concerned nor otherwise. Examinations are the responsibility of each individual school.

Vocational Secondary

Vocational training takes place in upper-secondary comprehensive schools, industrial vocational schools and specialized vocational schools. Students can choose between training for the certified trades or vocational training in other areas, for example in the field of agriculture, in the travel industry, the fisheries, the food production industry, or health and commerce. Many forms of vocational training give the students legal certification for certain types of employment. This applies mainly to studies in the certified trades.

Training for the certified trades takes three to four years. It involves taking a vocational programme of study at an upper-secondary school and a study contract with a master craftsman or an industrial firm. The student has the choice of one of the following avenues:

An apprenticeship agreement with a master craftsman;

A one-year programme of basic academic and practical studies at an industrial vocational school or an upper-secondary comprehensive school (*grunndeild*), followed by an apprenticeship agreement with a master craftsman;

A one-year programme of basic academic and practical studies, followed by a one-year programme of specialized academic and practical studies at an industrial vocational school or an upper-secondary comprehensive school (*framhaldsdeild*), followed by an apprenticeship agreement with a master craftsman.

The subjects included in vocational programmes of study can be divided as follows: general academic subjects, theoretical vocational subjects and practical vocational subjects. All vocational trainees in certified vocational trades must take at least 25 credits in general academic subjects; i.e. four credits in Icelandic, eight in modern languages, two in social studies, four in mathematics, two in book-keeping and five in electives. The number of credits in specialized subjects varies in different programmes and so does the extent of practical training.

On completion of his studies, the apprentice takes the journeyman's examination (**sveinsprof**) that provides him with qualifications to pursue the trade concerned.

Other forms of vocational education within the school system are available. Entry to some of these studies is only open to those who have completed one to two years of general academic education at an upper secondary school.

FURTHER EDUCATION

There are a few specialized institutions (*serskolar*) which are not defined as higher education institutions (universities). They offer a range of different educational opportunities bridging secondary and university level. The most usual qualifying examination which gives admission to these higher education courses is the **studentsprof**. In addition, however, some other courses qualify students for admission to higher education courses in this sector.

Institutions in this sector are Myndlista- og handidaskoli Islands (The Icelandic College of Arts and Crafts), Leiklistarskoli Islands (The Drama College of Iceland), Tonlistarskolinn Reykjavik (The Reykjavik College of Music), Fosturskoli Islands (The Icelandic College for Pre-school Teachers), Roskajalfaskoli Islands (The Icelandic School for Educators of the Mentally Retarded), Irottakennaraskoli Islands (The Icelandic College of Physical Education), Samvinnuhaskolinn Bifrost, Borgarfjordur (The Co-operative College of Iceland) and Tolvuhaskoli Verzlunarskola Islands, Reykjavik (The Commercial College of Iceland, Computer Department).

The duration of the programmes is between two and four years.

HIGHER EDUCATION

The **studentsprof** usually gives admission to university courses. Admission to most institutions is restricted and applicants are admitted on the basis of their average marks in the **studentsprof** or in certain subjects of the **studentsprof** relevant to the study to be followed and/or on basis of entrance examinations, interviews etc. In some faculties at the University of Iceland admission is restricted by *numerus clausus*.

Iceland

There are two types of university higher education institutions in Iceland:

Haskolar (universities). These are Haskoli Islands, Reykjavik (The University of Iceland), which offers study programmes in the traditional university subjects, Haskolinn a Akureyri (The University College of Akureyri) and Kennarahaskoli Islands, Reykjavik (The University College of Education).

Taekniskolar og serskolar (technical and vocational colleges). These are Taekniskoli Islands, Reykjavik (The Icelandic College of Engineering and Technology) and Bndasklinn Hvanneyri, Borgarfjrur (The Agricultural College, Hvanneyri).

Degree programmes are from three to six years in duration. In most institutions the studies are divided into study credits (*einingar*), 30 credits corresponding to one academic year of full-time studies (one credit equals approximately one week (50 hours) of full-time study).

University studies do not include a general studies component. This general studies background knowledge is obtained in upper secondary schools. On successful completion, a course of study may in some cases lead directly to a professional qualification, while in other cases additional training specific to the profession is required. In order to obtain a professional qualification in such cases, additional specialized study programmes are required, sometimes combined with practical training.

Bachelor degrees (BA/BS/BEd) are the first university degrees requiring three to four-and-a-half years of study. In some disciplines this is also a professional degree and practical training is a part of the programme.

In the Faculty of Arts at the University of Iceland, a special three year programme is offered in Icelandic for Foreign Students leading to the **BPhil Isl** degree (*Baccalaureatus Philologiae Islandicae*). This degree programme is on the same level as the BA programme. The first year course is designed for students with little or no prior knowledge of Icelandic.

The **kandidatsprof** (candidatus examination/degree) is only offered at the University of Iceland and qualifies the holder for a profession. It is an academic/professional degree in the fields of theology, medicine, pharmacy, law, business administration, engineering and dentistry. The courses leading to **candidatus degrees** have a prescribed length of four to six years, the shortest (four years) being the **cand oecon** degree in business administration and the **cand scient** degree in engineering; the longest (six years) the **cand med et chir** degree in medicine and the **cand odont** degree in dentistry. The others are **cand juris** degree in law (five years), **cand theol** degree in theology (five years) and **cand pharm** degree in pharmacy (five years).

The **Meistaraprof** (Master's degree – MA/MS/MPaed) follows successful completion of a BA or BS degree. In some Master's programmes the admission prerequisite is a first class BA/BS degree. It is an academic/scientific degree, a research oriented training course with a prescribed length of two to three years after the BA/BS degree, The University of Iceland offers a degree course in education leading to the degree **Magister Paedagogiae**, the MPaed degree. This programme is only offered in Icelandic studies and follows successful completion of a first class BA degree.

The **doktorsprof** (doctorate degree) is only awarded by the University of Iceland. There are two types of **doktorsprof**. One is a special doctoral programme in Icelandic literature, Icelandic language and Icelandic history leading to an academic degree awarded by the Faculty of Arts. The duration of this programme is three to four years after the MA degree and the degree awarded is **Doctor Philosophiae, drphil.**

Admission prerequisite is a first class MA degree from the Faculty of Arts. The other type of **doktorsprof** is not a taught or preplanned programme. As a general rule this **doctorate degree** can only be awarded to those who have completed a **candidatus degree**, a **master's degree** or equivalent. It is awarded on the basis of a dissertation that is submitted to one of the University faculties.

TEACHER EDUCATION

Primary and lower secondary

Students who have completed three years of study on a degree course in teacher education at the University College of Education or the University College of Akureyri, and who have passed the prescribed examinations and completed the final thesis or research project, are awarded the BEd degree (**Bachelor of Education**) which is a professional teacher certificate.

Students who have completed three years of study in the Instrumental Teachers Training Departments and the Department of Theory and Composition at the Reykjavk College of Music receive a professional music teachers certificate for primary and lower secondary school.

Upper secondary school

Teachers in academic subjects (to teach age level sixteen to nineteen) are educated at the University of Iceland. They are also qualified as teachers at the compulsory lower secondary level (age level thirteen to fifteen). Upon completion of a BA or BS degree they receive their professional education in a one year (30 credits) programme in the Faculty of Social Science.

In-service education for upper-secondary school teachers is organized by the teachers unions in co-operation with the University of Iceland In-Service Institute. Teachers in vocational education at the upper-secondary level complete a one year course offered by the University College of Education for those holding a licence as master craftsman.

India

The National Policy on Education of 1986 emphasizes a national education strategy with a clearer role for the Union Government in setting and evaluating standards. The Policy recommended a common structure for school education consisting of five (in some states four) years of lower primary schooling followed by three years' upper primary. Depending on the number of years spent at the primary stage, secondary education consists of two or three years' schooling which marks the completion of ten years' general education. This can be followed by a further two years of higher secondary education. This 10 + 2 system has been almost universally adopted.

Education is compulsory for the first six years of primary schooling although in practice there is a high drop-out rate.

In state schools Hindi (or the regional language) is the medium of instruction at the primary level and also in most secondary schools, although here English is taught as a second language. English is the medium of instruction at most universities with an option given to students to also use their regional language. Hindi is the medium of instruction in universities in the Hindi-speaking belt which extends over five Indian states. For most postgraduate and all professional courses English tends to be the medium of instruction. In teacher education the medium of instruction varies from state to state and can be English, Hindi or the regional language. Private fee-paying schools usually use English as the medium of instruction.

The academic year normally begins in June or July and ends in March or April. It is usually divided into three terms but a few higher education institutions follow a two-semester system.

EVALUATION IN BRITAIN

School

Secondary School Certificates awarded on completion of Standard X:

Matriculation Certificate	) generally considered to be below
Secondary School Certificate	) GCSE standard
All India Secondary School Certificate	)
Indian Certificate of Secondary Education	)

India

Higher Secondary School Certificates awarded on completion of Standards XI or XII:

Indian School Certificate (ISC)
Intermediate Certificate
Higher School Certificate
Higher Secondary Certificate
All India Senior School Certificate
Pre-University course

if awarded at Standard XI may be considered to approach GCSE standard. If awarded at Standard XII may be considered comparable to GCSE standard (grades A, B and C) on a subject-for-subject basis (with the exception of English language, UNLESS English is the medium of instruction). Students with excellent results in the Standard XII examinations of the Central Board of Secondary Education (CBSE), and the Indian Council School Examinations (ICSE) may be considered for undergraduate admission in humanities and social science courses.

Higher

Bachelor of Arts/Science/Commerce

may be considered to satisfy the general entrance requirements of British higher education institutions.

Bachelor degree
(when awarded from a central university, a centre of advanced study)

generally considered comparable to British Bachelor (Ordinary) degree standard. Students with very high grades may be considered for admission to postgraduate study.

Bachelor of Science (Engineering)/ Engineering/Technology (when awarded from an institute of national importance, centre for advanced study, or an Indian Institute of Technology (IIT) or the Indian Institute of Science, in Bangalore)

generally considered comparable to British Bachelor (Honours) degree standard.

Master of Arts/Science/Commerce

generally considered comparable to British Bachelor (Ordinary) degree standard. Students with very high grades may be considered for admission to postgraduate study.

Master's degree (when awarded from a central university or centre of advanced study)

generally considered comparable to British Bachelor (Honours) degree standard.

Master of Science (Engineering)/ Engineering/Technology

generally considered comparable to British Bachelor (Honours) degree standard.

Master of Science (Engineering)/ Engineering/Technology
(when awarded from an Institute of national importance, centre for advanced study, or an Indian Institute of Technology, or the Indian Institute of Science, in Bangalore)

generally considered comparable to British Master's degree standard.

MARKING SYSTEM

School

School examinations are often graded on a percentage basis. Subjects in papers may have different minimum pass-marks.

Higher

65–100 per cent	First Division/Class
50–64	Second Division/Class
40–49	Third Division/Class

SCHOOL EDUCATION

Primary

Primary education generally covers eight years (seven in some states). Students enter the lower primary stage at age six for five years (Standards I to V). The upper primary stage is a three-year course from eleven to fourteen years (Standards VI to VIII). The syllabus covers subjects such as reading, writing and arithmetic, supplemented by environmental studies which includes history, geography, general science and civics. Hindi or the regional language is generally used although English is introduced as an optional subject in the later years and is used extensively in some private schools. Examinations are set either by schools or by the Municipal Boards and are usually held at the end of each term and school year.

Secondary

Secondary education usually covers between two and four years. After two (sometimes three) years, pupils who have completed ten years of education (Standard X) take the **Secondary School Certificate** (the title of the certificate varies between the different examining boards – see **EVALUATION** section). Secondary school examinations are public examinations controlled by State and Central Boards of Secondary Education.

Pupils completing a further two years of education (Standard XII), sometimes known as higher secondary, take the **Higher Secondary School Certificate** (for different titles see **EVALUATION**). Many schools do not offer courses beyond Standard X and students may follow the two-year higher secondary course at a college as a pre-university course.

The medium of instruction is usually Hindi or the regional language although English is taught as a second language. Top private schools use English as the medium of instruction.

Many states offer vocational courses at secondary schools concentrating on agriculture, commerce, technology, para-medical services and home economics. Each state chooses its own subjects for vocational education depending on the state's needs.

The Central Board of Secondary Education and the Indian Council for School Examinations are the only two boards with national jurisdiction, and are considered to attract the more able students. At standard XII, they have a stricter marking system and are therefore considered as post-GCSE level in Britain (see **EVALUATION** section).

FURTHER EDUCATION

Technical and vocational training is offered at industrial training institutes, polytechnics and rural institutes, most of which are controlled by state governments. Certificate and diploma courses of one to three years are available. The usual admission requirement is the Standard X certificate although some courses require Standard XII.

The Central Board of Secondary Education (CBSE) has established an Open School, which offers CBSE school-leaving qualifications. Recently, most state governments agreed to set up similar open schools.

Technical

Technical education is academically controlled by the State Boards of Technical Education and operates at three levels – certificate, diploma and degree. The certificate and diploma programmes in various trades and secretarial courses are conducted by Industrial Training Boards and polytechnics. These courses involve one to three years of study after ten years of secondary school education. The engineering technology programmes generally require three years of full-time study after completion of ten years of school education.

HIGHER EDUCATION

Higher education is offered at universities, institutes of higher learning 'deemed to be universities' and institutions declared to be of national importance.

First degree courses are generally conducted at affiliated colleges i.e. a network of private and state-sponsored institutes recognized by a specific university which takes direct responsibility for postgraduate studies. Curricula and examinations are controlled by the universities.

Students wishing to enter first degree courses must have completed either Standard XI or XII with a pass in a higher secondary or pre-university examination.

The Indian Institutes of Technology (IIT) and other centrally sponsored institutes and universities conduct the **Joint Entrance Examination** (JEE) for admissions to degree courses in engineering, pharmaceutics and architecture.

Three Types of Institution

Central Universities are those universities which are centrally funded by Act of Parliament, as opposed to State universities.

Institutes of National Importance are university level institutions, empowered to grant degrees or qualifications deemed to be equivalent to university degrees.

The University Grants Commission has provided substantial assistance to Centres of Advanced Study to encourage the pursuit of excellence. Centres are selected on the basis of their contribution to research, reputation and quality of work. The aim is to strengthen postgraduate teaching and research.

Lists of Central Universities, Institutes of National Importance and Centres of Advanced Study, as of late 1994, are included at the end of this chapter.

First degrees generally require three years' full-time study leading to **Bachelor of Arts, Science and Commerce** degrees. Entrance to an Honours course may require a higher pass-mark in the higher secondary or pre-university examinations. An Honours degree does not normally involve longer study but does indicate greater specialization. Bachelor degrees in professional subjects such as architecture, engineering, medicine, dentistry, pharmacy and technology generally take two to five years.

Some Bachelor degrees, for example in education, journalism, law and librarianship, are second degrees.

A **Master's degree in Arts, Science and Commerce** generally requires two years of study after a first degree. The **MTech** usually requires three semesters over one-and-a-half years, one of which will be occupied by a research project. An **MPhil** is usually awarded one year after a **Master's degree**. This is a pre-**PhD** course which may be either solely by research or may contain a taught component. A **PhD** takes a further two years after an **MPhil**. Entry to postgraduate courses requires at least a second class Honours degree. However, a number of institutions set their own admission tests. Admission to all postgraduate courses in engineering, technology, pharmacy, and architecture at engineering colleges is restricted to those who qualify through the **Graduate Aptitude Test in Engineering** (GATE). Master's courses in engineering and technology normally require two years' study after a first degree.

Examination System

Most examinations are conducted by the universities. The Indian Institutes of Technology, the technical universities, agricultural universities, and faculties like medicine and engineering in some universities, operate an internal assessment system. For the rest there is a public examination which is conducted in March or April and again in September or October.

Open Universities

At university level there are four open universities and about fifty-seven other universities which conduct correspondence/distance learning programmes covering 206 undergraduate and postgraduate courses. In almost all large towns and cities there are evening colleges. They mostly provide courses at undergraduate level, but in a few cases postgraduate courses are taught. At national level there is the Indira Gandhi National Open University based in Delhi with over 150 regional centres around India, which was established in 1986. There are three other state open universities: Andhra Pradesh Open University, Kota Open University and Nalanda Open University.

Co-ordinating Bodies

Association of Indian Universities (AIU)	Facilitates the recognition of degrees by other universities in India as well as abroad; speaks on behalf of the universities in national and international forums.
University Grants Commission	Grant giving and co-ordinating body; maintains constant academic standards in higher and professional education.
Central Advisory Board of Education (CABE)	Policy making body.

There are a number of other co-ordinating bodies in various subject fields such as the All-India Council for Technical Education (AICTE), the Bar Council of India, the

Dental Council of India, the Pharmacy Council of India and the Nursing Council of India. All these bodies are vested with powers to regulate standards of academic performance.

TEACHER EDUCATION

Primary

Training for teachers of lower primary classes (Standard I to V) is carried out in the Teacher Training Institutes attached to state departments of education, also known as Junior Basic Training Institutes (JBTI) or Primary Teachers Colleges in some states. Under a new system recently introduced, there will be a District Institute of Education and Training in each district for primary teachers education, which will play a similar role to that of the JBT colleges and Primary Teachers Colleges. The duration of the course is generally two years and leads to a diploma or teacher training certificate. The entrance requirement for these institutions is the school-leaving examination (Standard X).

For upper primary school teaching the minimum entrance requirement is the higher secondary school-leaving examination (Standard XII). This also leads to a diploma after a two-year course.

Secondary

Teachers at lower secondary level (Standards IX and X) are graduates who have completed a one-year **Bachelor of Education** (BEd) at a college affiliated to a university, while teachers at the higher secondary level (Standards XI and XII) are postgraduates who have completed the **BEd.** There are also four Regional Colleges of Education which offer a combined four-year integrated programme in both subject content and teaching methodology, leading to a **Bachelor degree.**

MEd and **PhD** qualifications are required to teach at colleges of education. Studies for these are undertaken at a number of universities including the <u>Centre of Advanced Studies in Education</u> (CASE) in Baroda. Teachers of technical and vocational subjects sometimes receive more specialist training.

University (Academic Staff College)

Since 1987/88, the University Grants Commission has approved a number of academic staff colleges for the purposes of organizing orientation courses for newly appointed college and university teachers.

APPENDIX

Central Universities

<u>Aligarh Muslim University</u>
<u>Bombay University</u>
<u>Banaras Hindu University</u>
<u>Delhi University</u>
<u>Hyderabad University</u>
<u>Indira Gandhi National Open University</u>
<u>Jamia Millia Islamia</u>
<u>Jawarharlal Nehru University</u>
<u>Madras University</u>
<u>North-Eastern Hill University</u>

Osmania University
Pondicherry University
Visva Bharati

Institutes of National Importance

Indian Institute of Technology, Bombay
Indian Institute of Technology, Delhi
Indian Institute of Technology, Kanpur
Indian Institute of Technology, Kharagpur
Indian Institute of Technology, Madras
Indian Institute of Sciences, Bangalore
Indian Institute of Management, Ahmedabad, Bangalore, Calcutta, Lucknow
All Indian Institute of Medical Sciences
Postgraduate Institute of Medical Education and Research
Sree Chitra Tirunal Institute for Medical Sciences and Technology
Indian Statistical Institute
Dakshina Bharat Hindi Prachar Sabha

Centres of Advanced Study

Centres of advanced study refer only to the departments which offer the subjects listed:

Anthropology	Ranchi University
Archaeology	Deccan College, Pune
Economics	Agricultural Economics, Gokhale Institute of Politics and Economics, University of Pune; Department of Economics, University of Delhi; Department of Economics, University of Bombay
Education	MS University of Baroda
Gujarati	S N D T Women's University
History	Aligarh Muslim University
Linguistics	Annamalai University; Osmania University
Philosophy	University of Madras; Jadavpur University
Psychology	University of Allahabad; Utkal University
Sanskrit	University of Poona
Sociology	University of Delhi

Science, Engineering and Technology

Astronomy	Osmania University
Biochemistry	Indian Institute of Science, Bangalore
Botany	Banaras Hindu University; University of Delhi; University of Madras; University of Calcutta
Chemical Eng.	University of Bombay
Chemistry Applied	chemistry of natural products, University of Delhi; chemistry, University of Bombay; pure chemistry, University of Calcutta; organic chemistry, inorganic and physical chemistry, Indian Institute of Science, Bangalore; thermodynamics, Punjab University
Civil Eng.	Indian Institute of Sciences, Bangalore
Electrical Eng.	control systems, University of Jadavpur; microelectronics and electronics, Banaras Hindu University; power control and signal processing, Indian Institute of Science, Bangalore
Geology	economic and structural geology, Jadavpur University; Himalayan geology, Punjab University

India

Marine Biology	Annamalai University
Mathematics	applied, University of Calcutta; pure, Universities of Bombay and Madras, pure and applied; Punjab University
Mechanical Eng.	University of Roorkee
Metallurgical Eng.	material processing, Indian Institute of Sciences Bangalore; physical and process metallurgy, Banaras Hindu University
Mining Eng.	Indian School of Mines, Dhanbad; rock mechanics, Banaras Hindu University
Molecular Biology	Banaras Hindu University
Molecular Biophysics	Indian Institute of Science, Bangalore
Physics	condensed matter physics, Indian Institute of Sciences, Bangalore; material science and solid state physics, University of Poona; nuclear physics, Punjab University; materials physics, Banaras Hindu University; Universities of Calcutta and Delhi
Production Eng.	University of Jadavpur
Zoology	Banaras Hindu University

Indonesia

Overall responsibility for education rests with the Ministry of Education and Culture, in which there are four main divisions: basic and secondary education, higher education, culture and out-of-school education and sports. Each of the twenty-seven provinces has its own department of education, which reports directly to Jakarta. There are also many private institutions at every level.

As from July 1994, the Indonesian Government has introduced a nine year education programme between the ages of six and fifteen.

The medium of instruction is Bahasa Indonesia. The local regional language is, however, used during the first three years of primary education in certain areas of the country where the major regional languages (Javanese, Sundanese, Balinese, Buginese, Makassarese and Batak) are spoken, but not in other areas.

English is one of the subjects in the new 1994 curriculum.

The academic year for primary and secondary education runs from mid-July to mid-June, divided into three terms.

EVALUATION IN BRITAIN

School

Ijazah SMA/Surat Tanda Tamat Belajar Sekolah Menengah Tingkat Atas/STTB SMA (senior secondary leaving certificate) – generally considered comparable to GCSE (grades, A, B and C) on a subject-for-subject basis, with the exception of English language. Students with very good results may be considered for access/bridging courses in the UK.

Higher

Until 1981

Sarjana Muda (often referred to as 'bachelor') – may be considered to satisfy the general entrance requirements of British higher education institutions.

Sarjana – generally considered comparable to British Bachelor (Ordinary) degree standard.

Pasca Sarjana – generally considered comparable to British Bachelor (Honours) degree standard.

Since 1981

S1 (Strata 1) **Sarjana** – generally considered comparable to British Bachelor

(Ordinary) degree standard.

S2 (Strata 2) **Magister** – generally considered comparable to British Bachelor (Honours) degree standard.

S3 (Strata 3) **Doktor** – generally considered comparable to British MPhil degree standard.

Qualifications obtained from prestigious institutions may be considered to be of a higher standard than those obtained elsewhere. For further information enquirers should contact the National Academic Recognition Information Centre.

Polytechnic Diploma D1 – D4:

D1   Generally considered to be below City and Guilds level

D2   Comparable to City and Guilds Certificate Part I

D3   Comparable to City and Guilds Certificate Part II

D4   Comparable to BTEC National Diploma / N/SVQ level 3 / Advanced GNVQ/GSVQ standard.

MARKING SYSTEMS

School

School Leaving Certificate (Primary and Secondary)

Students are tested and reports are issued each quarter. The grading scale is as follows:

Grade

10	Excellent
9	Very Good
8	Good
7	Above Average
6	Average
5	Below Average
4–1	Fail

Passing the EBTANAS SMA is a prerequisite to receiving an upper secondary certificate of completion, the **Surat Tanda Tamat Belajar Sekolah Menengah Tingkat Atas**/STTB SMA. The results are weighted according to the same formula as that used for the primary level EBTANAS. The result, NEM (*Nilai* EBTANAS *Murni*) is given twice the weight of the school's own final examination and the student's report card grade.

The formula is as follows:

$$\frac{P + Q + n\text{R}}{2 + n}$$

P   = The grade report from the 5th and 6th semesters
Q   = The end-of-year exam set by the school
R   = The EBTANAS score
n   = The weight for upper secondary school; the usual weight is 2, indicating that the EBTANAS score is given twice the importance of the other two sources. These weightings may vary by region.

Higher

A credit system is used and it is essential to see the academic transcript in addition to the degree certificate. To graduate a total of 140 to 160 credits must be obtained over a minimum of nine semesters. Degrees are not classified but a record of final year grades is routinely issued.

The following are the credit points needed to graduate from each institution:

	Credits	Semesters
Akademi (Diploma)	120	6
Politeknik (Diploma)	120	6
Sekolah Tinggi	144–160	8
Institut	144–160	8
Universitas:		
Sarjana 1	144–160	8
Sarjana 2	180–194	12
Sarjana 3	230	16

All students following a degree course are given a Grade Point Average (GPA) on completion of their studies and must achieve a certain score in order to qualify for a degree. For an S1 the minimum requirement is 2.0, for S2: 2.5 and for S3: 3.0. The grading is on a scale of 1–4 and D–A:

A – 4   Excellent
B – 3   Good
C – 2   Fair/Pass
D – 1   Poor

SCHOOL EDUCATION

State schools, religious schools and private schools (*Sekolah Swasta*) operate side by side with the core curriculum controlled by the Ministry of Education. Schools are organized in three levels: primary (basic); junior secondary and senior secondary.

Primary (Basic Education)

Until 1994

This was a six-year course from age six or seven. Children were promoted from one year to the next depending on performance. In some cases, therefore, pupils were required to repeat a year. Those successful in the examination at the end of the primary cycle proceeded to junior secondary level.

Indonesia

From 1994

In July 1994 the government of Indonesia has instituted a nine year universal basic education programme. While the physical and institutional distinctions between primary and junior secondary schools remain there is now an integrated curriculum which covers years one to nine. Basic education is thus defined to cover education provided in both primary and junior secondary schools. The immediate aim is to increase the number of children continuing their schooling beyond primary level. The goal of nine years compulsory schooling for six to fifteen-year-olds is still some way in the future.

The 1994 curriculum has been designed to assist the introduction of more active learning approaches, but didactic teaching methods predominate in most schools.

There are still tests for promotion each year. Those successful in the examination of the basic cycle may proceed to senior secondary level.

Secondary

Until 1994

Junior secondary (*Sekolah Menengah Tingkat Pertama* – SMTP)

This cycle covered three years. Pupils attended general academic schools (*Sekolah Menengah Pertama* – SMP). Those successful in the examination at the end of this cycle proceeded to senior secondary level.

Before and after 1994

Senior secondary (*Sekolah Menengah Tingkat Atas* – SMTA)

This cycle also covers three years. There are several types of school:

Sekolah Menengah Atas (SMA) (Senior Secondary)

Before 1994

These schools offered a continuation of the academic course taken at the SMP schools at junior secondary level. After a common first year, students specialized in physical sciences, biological sciences, social studies, cultural studies or 'special' studies, for the remaining two years, although there was also a core programme which ran throughout the three years and was shared by the five streams. The curriculum was broader than **GCSE** studies in Britain. At the end of the course pupils took the **Ijazah SMA** (senior secondary leaving certificate).

There was a common curriculum consisting of Bahasa Indonesia (Indonesian language), *Pancasila* (state philosophy) and religion, in which pupils had to obtain not less than 6 on the marking scale 1–10. In other subjects 5 was the minimum pass-mark, except in the pupils chosen subject group (A1, A2, A3 or A4) in which the pass-mark was also 6.

A1: physics, mathematics, chemistry
A2: biology, mathematics, chemistry
A3: economics, English, geography, mathematics
A4: history, English, geography, foreign language.

From 1994

The Senior secondary school year runs for 240 days and is divided into three sessions. In the third year of senior secondary education students are streamed into three disciplines:

- Life Sciences (IPA)
- Social Sciences (IPS)
- Languages (Bahasa)

The streaming is meant to effectively determine which university departments the students may apply to upon completion of their study. The curriculum is broader than **GCSE** studies in Britain.

The SMA EBTANAS is taken in the final semester of the senior high school and covers most subjects taught during the three years with particular emphasis on the later semesters. Graduates of the senior high schools receive the STTB SMA. On the back of the certificate is a list of grades for all subjects tested in the EBTANAS as well as other subjects not tested under EBTANAS.

Technical and Vocational Secondary

Sekolah Menengah Ekonomi Atas (SMEA) offer commercial courses.

Sekolah Menengah Kesejahteraan Keluarga (SMKK) offer home economics.

Sekolah Teknik Menengah (STM) provide a three to four-year senior secondary course to train students up to the level of trade technician (i.e. above the tradesman level).

There are also agricultural secondary schools and vocational secondary schools, run by different ministries, e.g. legal schools, police schools, nursing schools and schools for junior pharmacists.

HIGHER EDUCATION

Students are admitted to state universities on the basis of a nation-wide examination called UMPTN (Entrance Examination to state universities). The UMPTN is given in three regions of the country, with equivalent forms of the test administered in each region. The UMPTN has two options: Social Sciences and Sciences. Secondary school graduates from physics and biology (IPA) streams can apply to any department; social science and humanities (IPS) graduates are restricted to non-science and non-technology fields.

Until 1981

Courses leading to the first qualification, the **Sarjana Muda**, were taken over three years, with a further two years, during which students wrote and presented a thesis, leading to the **Sarjana**. This latter qualification conferred the title of **Doctorandus** (Drs) for men, **Doctoranda** (Dra) for women, **Insinyur** (Ir) for technical subjects. Courses in certain subjects (e.g. medicine) were slightly longer. There was an intermediate qualification between the **Sarjana** and doctorate, the **Pasca Sarjana**. This was supposed to take two years' study after the **Sarjana** while a doctorate took a further two or three years.

Since 1981

The first degree S1

University faculties have now adopted the credit system to qualify for the award of a first degree. Under this system a minimum of 144 credits must be gained for the completion of the first degree – **Sarjana Satu (S1)**. **Sarjana Satu** degrees have been designed to be completed in four years in all subject areas. Where professional practice is involved (e.g. medicine, dentistry, veterinary science, pharmacy, engineering) an additional two to six semesters may be required.

The Magister S2

The **Magister** is awarded after a further two years of academic courses plus research. Some 36-50 credits beyond **S1** are required to graduate. Admission is competitive and requires a GPA of between 2.50 and 2.75 in the **S1**, letters of recommendation and sometimes a prequalification test. Some programmes require English proficiency for entry (TOFEL 400–450). Grading at this level is the same as at the undergraduate level.

The Doktor S3

The **Doktor** should take another six to ten semesters of research, but in practice there is little opportunity to continue direct from a **Magister** course to a **Doktor** in the minimum theoretical time. Most awards are given to established, mature academics and other researchers. Applicants must have an **S2** with a GPA of at least 3.25 to be admitted. Forty to fifty-three credits are required to graduate, twelve of which are research credits.

There are five main types of institution:

Universities

These offer courses leading to the award of **Sarjana, Magister, Doktor (S1, S2** and **S3)** and various diplomas. Only the top ten state institutions offer postgraduate courses. The many private universities award degrees to **S1** level only. These are either fully recognized by the Ministry of Education and Culture or the private degree is converted into a recognized degree by taking a supplementary Ministry examination (see below).

Technical institutes

There are three of these institutes which have the same standing as universities: the Bandung Institute of Technology (ITB), the Bogor Institute of Agriculture (IPA) and the Institute of Technology Surabaya (ITS).

Institut Keguruan dan Ilmu Pendidikan (IKIP) (Institutes of Teacher Training and Education Sciences)

There are ten of these institutions which rank as universities with full degree-granting status. Their function is to train teachers for the junior and senior secondary schools. It is likely that IKIPs may take on a greater role in the training of primary school teachers. See also **TEACHER EDUCATION**.

Polytechnics

Polytechnics are state institutions representing a major new government initiative. They were established to increase opportunities for practical training in technical fields. There are twenty five state polytechnics offering two, three and four years' professional non-degree programmes that lead to **Diploma II**, **DIII** and **DIV**, with the number in the title indicating the number of years studied.

Admission is based on a national examination called the Polytechnic Entrance Examination. Specialized programmes may have their own screening tests. The curriculum is composed of 45–80 per cent practical work or training and 20–45 per cent theory.

Akademi and Sekolah Tinggi

Single-faculty academies which offer diploma/certificate technician-level courses and which may be either state or private institutions. Recognition of their awards is normally subject to the control of the Directorate General of Higher Education.

The word *akademi* in Indonesian has a precise meaning. It denotes an institution of higher education giving specific vocational training. The majority of academies are attached to and run as part of government departments with the specific purpose of training their specialist staff. Several government departments have their own academies and award their own qualifications, for example the Armed Force Academies. In such cases, the Directorate General of Higher Education is not always able to exercise complete supervision.

Institut Agama Islam Negeri (IAIN) – these Islamic institutes are state bodies which have the same rank as universities and IKIPs. Their prime function is to train Islamic religious teachers. They come under the Ministry of Religious Affairs.

The Open University has been established providing instruction through printed materials and radio and television. It offers **S1 Sarjana** degree courses and non-degree diploma courses in several subjects. The Open University admits anyone who has graduated from secondary school regardless of the year of graduation. There is no entrance examination and the degree is equivalent to those of other state tertiary institutions.

Private Tertiary Institutions

These have increased in number and it is believed that in 1993 there were more than 1000 institutions. They range in quality from excellent to deplorable and in size from large multifaculty university to small single-subject institutions. The Directorate of Private Universities, within the Directorate General of Higher Education (DGHE), has overall responsibility for the assessment, supervision and quality of all private institutions. The Directorate devolves day-to-day responsibility to seven regional bodies known as KOPERTIS (*Koordinasi Perguruan Tinggi Swasta*). The KOPERTIS play a crucial role in controlling and developing private universities, organizing state examinations and certifying all diploma and certificates. The best ten private institutions are considered to be equal to the top ten state institutions.

Students at private universities must take state university examinations unless the course has been granted *di samakan* (equalized) status by the DGHE. *Di samakan* status is awarded on a department or faculty level, not to the university as a whole. The words *di samakan* at Sarjana level appear on the final certificate.

The criteria used for recognition at faculty level starts with the status of *terdaftar* (registered) which simply acknowledges its existence. A great number of private universities are in this category. By meeting a series of conditions the faculty may move to *diakui* (acknowledged) status and finally to *disamakan* (equalized) status. Institutions with registered or acknowledged status must present their students for examinations conducted by the state universities. A certificate of equivalence will be issued by the regional KOPERTIS to successful candidates.

TEACHER EDUCATION

Primary

Until 1988 teachers for this level were trained at the <u>Teacher Training College</u> which offered a three-year course at senior secondary level. The training of primary school teachers is currently under review and is likely to be at IKIP level in future.

Junior secondary

Training is at post-secondary level on two-year courses at IKIPs leading to the award of a diploma.

Senior secondary

Teachers for this level are trained at post-secondary level on four-and-a-half year courses at the IKIPs, leading to the award of the **Sarjana**.

Technical secondary

Faculties for technical teacher training (FKIT) exist at several IKIPs, awarding diploma and **Sarjana** qualifications.

NB: Where there is no IKIP the universities may have a Faculty of Education (FKIP) handling teacher training.

Iran

The Islamic Republic, established in 1979, has pursued an aggressive desecularization of the education system at all levels. Although there have been no significant structural or administrative reforms to the system of the former regime, there have been great changes in curriculum and personnel. In the early 1980s the curriculum and textbooks were rewritten. This affected the humanities and social sciences in particular, but mathematics and the natural sciences were little changed. There was a comprehensive turnover of officials, administrators and teachers at this time. Higher education institutions were closed between 1980 and 1983.

After 1983, a huge demand for higher education led to a restructuring of this sector. Reforms included the establishment of over three hundred new courses at the postgraduate level, the rationalization of existing higher education institutions and the opening of new ones, and the granting of permission for private institutions to operate once again in 1987.

Religion has a prominent role both as a subject and in the life of educational institutions.

School education is segregated for males and females.

In principal, education is compulsory for eight years, covering the primary sector and the guidance cycle of secondary education. However, in practice the guidance cycle (three years) is not at present compulsory.

The medium of instruction at all levels is Farsi (Persian). However, at the higher education level, courses in English are available at <u>Shiraz University</u> and the <u>College of Petroleum</u>.

Until 1987, private, foreign and co-educational schools were prohibited as they operated counter to official Islamic principles. An exception to this rule were schools of recognized religious minorities. However, the instruction in these schools had to follow the government curriculum and the medium of instruction had to be Farsi. Recent developments have however led to private schools and higher education being allowed to operate once again.

EVALUATION IN BRITAIN

School

Diplom-Metevaseth/National High School Diploma – generally considered comparable to GCSE standard (grades A, B and C) on a subject-for-subject basis when marks of at least 50 per cent are obtained in subjects which can be taken in the GCSE examinations (with the exception of English language).

Further

Fogh-Diplom or Kar dani – generally considered comparable to BTEC National Diploma / N/SVQ level 3 / Advanced GNVQ/GSVQ standard; may be considered to satisfy the general entrance requirements of British higher education institutions.

Higher

Licence or **Kar shenasi** – generally considered comparable to a standard between GCE Advanced and British Bachelor degree; may be given advanced standing by British higher education institutions.

Fogh-Licence or **Kashenasi-arshad** – generally considered comparable to British Bachelor degree standard.

MARKING SYSTEMS

School

In Primary and Guidance Schools the grading scale is 1–20, with ten as the minimum passing average.

In Secondary Schools the scale is 1–20, with 10 as the minimum passing average. One subject grade below 10 (but not 0) is allowed if the general average is 10. Two subject grades below 10 (but not 0) are allowed if the general average is 12.

Higher

Institutions use either the 1–20 scale (as at secondary level) or a form of letter grading similar to the following: A, B, C, D (marginal), F (fail), N (incomplete). A few institutions use a 0–4 grade point scale.

SCHOOL EDUCATION

Pre-Primary

Private institutions are available for one year for children from the age of five to six.

Primary (*Debestan*)

Primary education covers five years beginning at age six. At the end of the fifth year pupils take a national examination; success in this entitles a student to proceed to the guidance cycle of secondary education. Failure after two attempts results in the student leaving the formal education system.

Secondary

This can cover up to seven years divided into two cycles. The curriculum for the three-year guidance cycle (*Doreh-e rahanamaii*) is general and uniform for all schools, and is designed to prepare pupils for either academic or vocational studies. On completion of this cycle, students take a national examination, the **Certificate of General Education**. Those who pass are eligible to continue their education in one of the four branches of the four-year cycle of intermediate (secondary) education, subject to the student's ability and interests, and the needs of the country. A student who wishes to follow a course of study other than the one considered most suitable is required to pass a special entrance examination.

The four branches of intermediate secondary education (*Dabirestan*) are academic, industrial, rural and agricultural, and services. The first three years of the academic branch cover a generalized curriculum, while the final year offers specialization in: literature and the arts, natural science, physics and mathematics or social science and economics. This has traditionally been the most popular stream.

On completion of this four-year cycle, students take the **Emtahan-Sol-Shishum-dabiristan** examination (the secondary school-leaving examination). Successful candidates are awarded the **Diplom-Metevaseth** or **National High School Diploma**. Those who wish to go to university must also sit a competitive examination or **Concours** – the **Emtahan-Vordy-Sartasari**. A national ranking of the calculated score of all the candidates is published.

Vocational/technical secondary

Students tending towards vocational/technical secondary education follow either a four-year technical course or a two-year vocational or agricultural course. The four-year course aims to produce lower grade technicians (higher grade technicians are trained at the post-secondary institutes of technology), and leads to the **Second Class Technicians Certificate**, whilst the two-year course aims to produce skilled workers and farmers, and results in the award of a **Trade Certificate**. The services branch is intended for students wishing to enter the civil or public services (including, for example, banking, insurance, accountancy, etc.)

The four year course comprises a common core curriculum, with specialization beginning either in year one, or after one or two years of general courses. Each branch is further sub-divided into specializations (e.g. the technical branch offers sub-branches in mechanics, woodwork, electronics, building and construction etc.).

FURTHER EDUCATION

Institutes of Technology, higher education institutions and some universities offer a two or three year post-secondary school course leading to the qualification of **Kar-dani** (first class technician's certificate). An entrance examination is conducted to determine admissions. Before 1980, this qualification was invariably of two years' duration only and was known as the **Fogh-Diplom.**

HIGHER EDUCATION

Until 1947, the University of Tehran was the only higher education establishment in Iran. Rapid expansion of this sector after the Second World War led to the establishment of a large number of provincial universities and other higher education institutions. Over two hundred higher education institutions were in existence by 1979, but the post revolutionary period saw the reduction in their numbers and a corresponding reduction in student enrolment. The last ten years have however seen a reversal of this trend, with increases in the number of institutions and student enrolment. The latest figures (1989) indicate that there are over one hundred higher education institutions in Iran. Of these, thirty are universities.

Since the establishment of the Islamic Republic, a number of institutions have changed their names. Many have been closed: all higher education institutions were closed between 1980–3. Since this time, many new fields of study have been approved by the Ministry of Education, particularly at the postgraduate level, private institutions have been established, and restructuring of the higher education sector has resulted in many amalgamations and the establishment of many new institutions. The qualification system has also been restructured.

Although the **Concours** examination is the main determinant of access to higher education, a complex formula of other factors also applies. In addition to the candidate's ranking, each department and degree course is also ranked; each academic programme will accept the highest 'numbered' applicant. In addition, each subject is accorded a male:female ratio of students; some fields are completely segregated e.g. gynaecology is reserved for women and veterinary medicine for men. Some twenty per cent of the places are allocated to war veterans or close relatives of martyrs, twenty per cent to members of the Islamic citizen volunteer paramilitary force, and the remaining sixty per cent are allocated according to a combined merit/locality factor with fifteen per cent of the places going to the highest 'numbered' students residing in each of four groups; large cities, medium-size cities, towns, villages. There is intense competition for university places.

The first degree course normally lasts four years leading to the **Licence** or **Kar-shenasi**. Courses follow the semester and credit system and students tend to specialize less than they would in Britain. Under the credit system, the **Licence/Kar-shenasi** requires 140 semester hours, of which at least 60 must be in a major field.

The postgraduate qualification of **Fogh-Licence** or **Kashenasi-arshad** generally requires an additional two years of study above the **Licence/Kar-shenasi**.

There is also an integrated professional qualification at the postgraduate level, the **Karshenasi-arshad payvasteh**, which is of six years' duration and is offered in dentistry, medicine, pharmacy and veterinary medicine as a first degree. Prior to 1980 the first degree in these fields was a **Doctorate**.

Programmes leading to a **Doctorate** in the arts or sciences usually require three years of study above the **Fogh-Licence/Kashenasi-arshad**. Before 1980 the **Doctorate** required two years' study beyond the **Fogh-Licence**, or three years post **Licence** in fields where a **Fogh-Licence** was not available.

TEACHER EDUCATION

Primary

Girls who have completed the first cycle of secondary school enter Normal Schools for a two-year course aimed at training teachers for rural areas.

Graduates of the second cycle of secondary schools follow a one-year course at one of the teacher training centres.

Secondary

There are two main types of course available at teacher training colleges:

A four-year course leading to the qualification of **Licence** or **Kardani** (taken in two stages of two years each and open to students who have completed a full course of secondary education). The first two-year stage prepares teachers for the first cycle of secondary education. Students who complete the second two years receive the **Licence** and are eligible to teach in the second cycle of secondary education.

A one-year course open to holders of the university **Licence** or **Kardani** to train teachers for both cycles of secondary education. The first of these colleges was the National Teacher's College of Tehran (now the Teacher Training University); it has been followed by the establishment of similar colleges within other universities.

Regional teacher training colleges train teachers for the guidance cycle of secondary education. These colleges run two-year courses for students who complete their secondary education and pass an entrance examination. The students may specialize in one of four fields: science and mathematics, Persian and social studies, foreign languages, and pre-vocational courses.

Vocational/technical secondary

The Vocational Teachers' Training College admits students who have completed academic or technical secondary education. The four-year course is in two two-year stages leading to a **Licence**. The first stage trains teachers for vocational schools, the second stage for technical schools. Teachers for secondary business schools are trained in the College of Business.

Iraq

The text in this chapter regarding the education system in Iraq, reflects the situation up until 1992, as this is the most current information available to UK NARIC.

The education system is highly centralized, all levels of school education coming under direct control of the Ministry of Education. Tertiary education is under the control of the Ministry of Research and Higher Education. There is a rigid system of examinations; continuous assessment is not practised.

Free education is available at all stages. Since 1988, however, a number of private (fee-paying) institutes of higher education have opened. The syllabuses and examinations are still monitored by the Ministry of Research and Higher Education.

The medium of instruction is generally Arabic, with Kurdish also taught in Kurdish areas.

The academic year runs from September to June, divided into two semesters.

EVALUATION IN BRITAIN

School

Sixth Form Baccalauréat – generally considered comparable to GCSE standard (grades A, B and C) on a subject-for-subject basis when a minimum overall mark of 60 per cent has been obtained, with the exception of English language. Students with very good results may be considered for admission to access/bridging courses.

Further

Diploma/Technician Diploma – generally considered comparable to BTEC National Diploma / N/SVQ level 3 / Advanced GNVQ/GSVQ standard if the grades of very good or excellent have been obtained.

Higher

Bachelor degree – generally considered comparable to a standard between GCE Advanced and British Bachelor degree; may be considered for advanced standing by British higher education institutions. Exceptionally, students with very high grades may be considered for admission to postgraduate study.

Teaching

Diploma – may be considered to satisfy the general entrance requirements of universities and polytechnics.

Iraq

MARKING SYSTEM

School

The **Baccalauréat** is graded on a percentage scale, with a pass-mark of 50. It usually contains six subjects and 500+ is considered a high score.

Further

Diploma courses (in Technical Institutes) are graded on a percentage scale:

90+ per cent	excellent
80–89	very good
70–79	good
60–69	medium
50–59	pass
below 50	fail

Higher

Degrees – percentage scale:

90–100 per cent	distinction/excellent
80–89	very good
65–79	good
50–64	fair/pass
below 50	poor/fail

Al-Hikma University used the American system of letter grades

SCHOOL EDUCATION

Pre-primary

Optional kindergartens are available for children aged between four and six years.

Primary

This covers six years from age six. The curriculum includes Arabic, arithmetic and social studies. Promotion from class to class is based on examinations culminating in the **Certificate of Primary Studies**, also known as the **Primary Baccalauréat.**

Secondary

Secondary education is divided into two three-year cycles, intermediate and preparatory.

Intermediate

This lasts three years, from age 12–14, and all pupils follow a common curriculum. The course culminates in a general examination, held by the government. **Third-Form Baccalauréat** (or **Certificate of Intermediate Studies**) is awarded. Promotion to a higher class is based on passing the end-of-year examinations (pass-mark 50 per cent). Depending on the standard of pass-marks in any given year, students with the highest pass-marks have a choice of science, arts or vocational secondary schools, and those with the lowest pass-mark go to vocational schools.

Preparatory

Before 1966–7 this involved two years' study, leading to the examinations for the **Baccalauréat**. It now covers three years, from ages 15–17. In the general academic schools a degree of specialization is introduced: students choose scientific or literary studies culminating in the **Sixth-Form Baccalauréat** examination in the appropriate section. This is the basic qualification for university courses. Students who fail two subjects or less in the June examinations may resit in September; if more than two are failed in June or any subject is failed in September, the year must be repeated.

Vocational secondary

There are four types of vocational secondary school:

agricultural
industrial
veterinary
commercial.

For admission to any of these three-year courses pupils must hold the **Third-Form Baccalauréat**. All courses lead to a **Vocational Baccalauréat** in a particular speciality.

Holders of **Sixth-Form Baccalauréat Science** have a choice of all universities (depending on grades); **Sixth-Form Baccalauréat Arts** holders can choose from arts degree courses only, while the top ten per cent of vocational school graduates can gain acceptance to a degree course only in the subject they have studied at vocational school.

FURTHER EDUCATION

In 1992 there were thirty Technical Institutes, with new ones being established, specializing in administrative, technical, agricultural and medical subjects (governed by the National Foundation of Technical Institutes). Courses normally last two years, with six weeks' practical training each summer, leading to a **Diploma of Technician in (specialized field)**, e.g. Diploma of Technician in Computer Technology.

HIGHER EDUCATION

Competition is keenest for entry to **Bachelor degree** courses in the faculties of medicine, architecture, engineering and science; however, steps have been taken to limit the number of students admitted to courses in the humanities. Students are centrally allocated to university places by the Ministry of Higher Education and the field of study is determined by the mark obtained in the **Sixth Form Baccalauréat**. University colleges of medicine normally require a percentage mark in the mid-nineties. Most first-degree courses last four years (five for architecture, dentistry and pharmacy; six for medicine).

Examinations are held at the end of each year, but there are also internal monthly and/or mid-year examinations which contribute approximately 40 per cent to the final marks.

Tuition is mainly in Arabic, with usually at least one subject in English.

Of the ten state universities, the largest and oldest is the University of Baghdad, established in 1956, reorganized as a state university in 1958. It became independent in 1963. Originally it incorporated thirteen separate colleges and institutions, established between 1908 and 1955. In 1967, the Universities of Basrah and Mosul (formerly colleges of the University of Baghdad) were established as separate universities, each originally with six faculties. The College of Engineering Technology of the University of Baghdad was merged with the College of Technology of the University of Al-Mustansiriyah in 1975 to become the independent University of Technology. Al-Mustansiriyah University in Baghdad was founded in 1963 and at first ran evening classes leading to degrees; it became a state university in 1974. The University of Salahuddin (formerly Sulaimaniyah University) opened in 1968 in the Kurdish homeland as a state institution and moved to Erbil in 1981. Al-Hikma University, a private university run by the American Jesuit Fathers, was incorporated into the University of Baghdad in l970. New state universities have been opened in Anbar, Kufa, Tikrit and Qadissiyah.

Bachelor degrees are also awarded by Al-Bakr University (a military college in Baghdad), by Basrah Naval College (also military) and by Baghdad Police College.

Three new independent colleges have also opened in Baghdad – the Saddam College of Law, the Saddam College of Engineering and the Saddam Medical College. They are elite institutions reporting directly to the president, and taking the top fifty students each year.

The syllabus and standard are equivalent in all these institutions.

Postgraduate diploma programmes are offered mainly in the field of medicine.

Master degree programmes are available in a variety of subjects, mostly arts, but also mathematics, physics and medicine. They require two years of study, one by tuition, one by research.

Higher Diploma programmes were mainly offered prior to 1983. They were one to three-year graduate programmes, and those who performed well were permitted to use these courses to meet coursework requirements for **Master degree** programmes. Since 1983 **Higher Diplomas** have been offered mainly in medical fields and admission usually requires a **Bachelor degree** in the same field. A grade average of at least 65 per cent is required. In competitive fields the grade average required is much higher. Some specialized institutes such as the Foreign Service Institute of the Ministry of Foreign Affairs also offer a two-year postgraduate **Higher Diploma**.

Doctorates (PhD) require three years of study beyond the **Master's degree**, with one year of coursework and two years of thesis preparation. Courses are available in economics, agricultural education, plant protection, Arabic, geography, history, educational psychology, philosophy of education, some engineering disciplines, biology, chemistry and mathematics.

TEACHER EDUCATION

Primary

Primary school teachers take a five-year course, after secondary intermediate school, at one of the teacher training institutes, leading to a **Diploma**.

Secondary

Secondary school teachers are trained at colleges of education, the constituent colleges of the <u>Universities of Baghdad, Mosul, Basrah, Al-Mustansiriyah</u> and <u>Salahuddin</u>. They offer a four-year **Bachelor of Arts** course for prospective secondary teachers.

Ireland

Education was compulsory from the age of six to fourteen until 1972, when it became six to fifteen.

The medium of instruction in post-primary schools is English and Irish.

EVALUATION IN BRITAIN

School

Junior Certificate – generally considered to be below GCSE standard.

Leaving Certificate – passes at ordinary/standard level grades A–C are generally considered comparable to GCSE, while passes at higher/honours level grades A–C are considered comparable to a standard between GCSE and GCE Advanced (e.g. Scottish Higher grade). Some higher education institutions will accept very good passes in five subjects at higher level as satisfying their general entrance requirements, others may specify that these passes should be at honours standard.

National Certificate (of the National Council for Educational Awards – NCEA) – generally considered comparable to BTEC National Diploma / N/SVQ level 3 / Advanced GNVQ/GSVQ standard.

National Diploma (of the National Council for Educational Awards – NCEA) – generally considered comparable to BTEC Higher National Diploma / N/SVQ level 4 standard.

Higher

General degree – generally considered comparable to British Bachelor (Ordinary) degree standard.

Bachelor Honours degree – generally considered comparable to British Bachelor (Honours) degree standard.

Master's degree – generally considered comparable to British taught Master's degree standard.

Ireland

MARKING SYSTEMS

School

Junior and Leaving Certificate:

A	85–100 per cent	(Applies to subjects taken at both
B	70–84	higher and ordinary levels.)
C	55–69	
D	40–54	
E	25–39	
F	10–24	
No grade	less than 10	

Leaving Certificate (from 1992)

Individual subject grade		Points scale (Higher)	Points scale (Ordinary)	Bonus points*
A1	90–100 per cent	100	60	40
A2	85–89	90	50	35
B1	80–84	85	45	30
B2	75–79	80	40	25
B3	70–74	75	35	20
C1	65–69	70	30	15
C2	60–64	65	25	10
C3	55–59	60	20	5
D1	50–54	55	15	
D2	45–49	50	10	
D3	40–44	45	5	
E	25–39			
F	10–24			
No grade	0–9			

Before 1975 a candidate had to achieve grade D to pass in a subject and to achieve this grade in at least five subjects to qualify for the award of the **Leaving Certificate**. Since 1985, each candidate has been issued with a certificate showing the grades awarded at the examination. Thus the terms 'pass' and 'fail' no longer apply.

University Entrance – points system

The best six results in one **Leaving certificate** are counted for points computation. Only one sitting will be taken into consideration. The maximum possible points score is 600.

* Bonus points for **Leaving certificate** higher level mathematics are awarded by University College, Dublin and the University of Limerick. The Dublin Institute of Technology also awards bonus points for mathematics and a number of science subjects for specific degree courses.

Matriculation examination – the marking system varies between institutions:

University of Dublin, Trinity College

Subjects are graded A, B, C, D, E, F and these grades are equivalent to those used in the **Leaving Certificate**. In the mathematics examination the results are expressed in three grades:

O	credit
P	pass
F	fail

National University of Ireland

A	75–100 per cent
B	60–74
C	45–59
D	35–44
Pass	35
E	25–34
F	20–24
No grade	below 20

Higher

NCEA **national certificates and diplomas**:

Distinction	70 per cent
Merit	60 per cent
Pass	40 per cent

A **Bachelor degree** may be conferred as either a **General (Pass) degree** or an **Honours degree**. A **BA (Special)** is a combination of one subject at Honours level and one subject at general degree level.

Bachelor (Honours) degrees are classified as follows:

First Class Honours
Second Class Honours, grade I
Second Class Honours, grade II
Third Class Honours

An undifferentiated Second Class Honours grade is awarded in some degrees.

Pass or **General** degrees may be awarded with Credit or Distinction.

SCHOOL EDUCATION

Primary

Children may be admitted at age four, and schooling normally covers eight years.

There is no formal entrance test for secondary level, although individual schools may set an entrance examination.

Secondary

This covers five to six years divided into a junior cycle of three to four years, and a senior cycle of two years. On completion of the junior cycle, pupils take the **Junior Certificate** examination. Students normally take Irish, English and mathematics (at either higher or lower level), history and geography; they then choose not less than two subjects from Latin, Greek, classical studies, Hebrew studies, French, German, Spanish, Italian, science, home economics, music and musicianship, art, woodwork, metalwork, mechanical drawing and commerce. Civics is also studied in the lower cycle but not examined. Pupils may take the examination after three years' secondary education, provided they are at least fourteen years of age by 1 January in the year they are taking the examination. The **Junior Certificate** examination replaced the **Intermediate Certificate** examination in 1992.

Following the **Junior Certificate**, students have the option, in an increasing number of schools, to enter a transition year before commencing the senior cycle.

Pupils generally take the **Leaving Certificate** examination after a further two to three years' study. There are two syllabuses per subject: higher/honours and ordinary/standard level. The higher papers cover the same ground as those for the ordinary course, but in greater depth and detail. Pupils normally take six to nine subjects; they also study religious instruction and are taught physical education. Irish is not a compulsory examination subject for the **Junior** or **Leaving Certificate**; if a candidate fails to pass Irish in either of these examinations it no longer means failure of the overall examination. It is, however, compulsory to study it.

The **Senior Certificate** is a less common examination, taken by a small number of students instead of the leaving certificate, often by people not considering continuing into third level education. It is less academic than the **Leaving Certificate** and is not recognized in Ireland for entry to higher education.

In place of (or in addition to) the **Leaving Certificate** examination pupils may take the **Matriculation examination**. It is quite common for pupils to take both examinations; both represent the same level of attainment. However, the **Matriculation examination** of the National University of Ireland has been abolished since 1993.

To have obtained the **Matriculation Certificate** of the National University of Ireland, students had to pass six subjects which had to include Irish, English, a third language, mathematics (for science, medicine, etc.) and three other subjects of the programme for the **Matriculation examination**. Candidates not required to present in Irish had to present in an alternative subject, to a total of six, according to faculty groupings.

Specific subjects may be required for entry to different faculties.

The University of Dublin, Trinity College **Matriculation examination** is in the following subjects only: biblical studies, geology, and Russian. The examination does not qualify for admission to courses for primary degrees.

The matriculation requirements of the University of Dublin, Trinity College, based on the results of the **Leaving Certificate**, are a pass in English, a pass in mathematics and a pass in a language other than English, or a pass in Latin and a pass in another non-linguistic subject, and a pass in two further subjects; three of the five subjects must be passed at grade C, higher level.

For matriculation in the National University of Ireland on the basis of the **Leaving Certificate** the minimum requirement is a pass in two acceptable subjects at grade C, higher level and a pass in four other subjects at grade D, ordinary level. The passes must include the subjects specified for the faculties. Students may also matriculate on the joint results of the **Matriculation** and **Leaving Certificate** examinations.

If GCE examinations are presented, the general and specific faculty requirements must be satisfied, and at least two of the subjects must have been obtained at grade C, GCE Advanced.

For candidates presenting for Matriculation in the University of Dublin, Trinity College on the results of the GCE examination, the requirements are: pass in English language, pass in mathematics and pass in a language other than English, or a pass in Latin and a non-linguistic subject, and a pass in three further subjects. At least two of the five subjects (not including English language) must have been obtained at grade C, GCE Advanced.

Technical and vocational secondary

Vocational schools provide full-time post-primary courses with emphasis on practical or vocational subjects. Pupils aged thirteen to sixteen follow courses lasting two years for the award of the **Junior Certificate** (before 1992 this was known as the **Day Group Certificate**). Some of these schools also provide courses, lasting two years, leading to the award of the **Leaving Certificate**.

FAS, the Industrial Training Authority, lays down rules for school/ college attendance for apprentices. Junior and senior trade certificate courses are available for apprentices on day or block-release at the Regional Technical Colleges (RTC). These colleges also offer courses for the **Leaving Certificate** in technical and commercial fields, in addition to a wide range of third-level programmes. FAS has an agreement on joint certification with City and Guilds, and many vocational schools and centres offer courses leading to City and Guilds certificates.

Agricultural colleges offer courses lasting one to two years for prospective farmers, normally with an entrance level based on the **Junior Certificate**.

HIGHER AND FURTHER EDUCATION

University education

The main entrance requirement for higher education is the **Leaving Certificate**, taken by most pupils at seventeen or eighteen. Due to competition for places, a person possessing such a certificate is not guaranteed a place at university. Places are allocated in order of merit on the basis of leaving certificate grades. This order is established on the basis of a points score. For details see **MARKING SYSTEMS** above. In general, prospective undergraduate students are accepted on the basis of this system and are not interviewed by the college in question.

Higher education in Ireland is funded to a significant degree by the state. A number of administrative bodies with co-ordinating and planning functions exist. In practice, however, each institution has a degree of autonomy, especially in relation to academic matters.

The level of autonomy varies not only between the different groups of institutions, but also from college to college within any single group. Overall, however, the concept of college autonomy is recognized by the state and the development of the higher education system carried out in a spirit of co-operation between the two partners.

Courses of higher education are provided at over forty institutions.

At the constituent colleges of the National University there are three types of **Bachelor degree**: **General degrees**, **Honours degrees** and **BA (Special)**, obtained on completion of three or four years' study. However, for veterinary medicine, architecture and dentistry, the first qualification is obtained on completion of a five-year course. Degree courses in medicine take six years.

A **Master's degree** can be awarded after a minimum of one year of study following the **Bachelor degree**. Some taught courses are available at **Master's degree** level. It is also possible to obtain this degree following a period of research.

At Trinity College, students may obtain a **Bachelor (Honours) degree** on completion of four years' study. Courses in medicine and dentistry are longer. After a further three years and payment of a fee, graduates with the **Bachelor degree** in arts may be conferred with a **Master of Arts degree**. Earned **Master's degrees** require research/courses for specified periods of study.

The award of the **Doctorate (PhD)** is made on completion of at least two years' original research after the award of the **Bachelor degree**.

A number of bodies have been established, each with a specific role or function in the administration of higher education.

These bodies are:

The Department of Education

The Department of Education has overall responsibility for the administration of public education and the formation of policy. Most state subsidization of universities and other third-level educational colleges is channelled through this Department.

The Higher Education Authority (HEA)

The HEA is a statutory body with both executive and advisory functions in relation to the support and development of higher education by the state.

The advisory powers of the HEA apply throughout the whole of the third-level sector. Its funding role is limited to the universities and specifically designated institutions.

The Central Applications Office/Central Application Service (CAO/CAS)

The CAO/CAS provides a centralized applications and admission service for the universities, the regional technical colleges, the Dublin Institute of Technology, Limerick College of Art, Commerce and Technology and the colleges of art (except the National College of Art and Design).

Admission is based on the attainment of minimum academic standards in second-level education. The standard for each course is set by the colleges themselves. The processing system is designed to offer applicants the highest preference course to which they are entitled.

Until 1989 there were three universities: the National University of Ireland (NUI), the University of Dublin and the Pontifical University of Ireland. The National University has three constituent colleges (University College Dublin, University College Cork and University College Galway). St. Patrick's College, Maynooth is a recognized college of the National University of Ireland. It offers NUI degree courses in arts and science subjects. The Pontifical University of Ireland, which is located on the same campus, is outside the system of state-funded third-level education. Maynooth College is also the national seminary for priests of the Roman Catholic Church. Trinity College is the only college of the University of Dublin.

There were two National Institutes for Higher Education (NIHE), at Limerick and Dublin. NIHE Limerick admitted its first students in 1972 while NIHE Dublin admitted its first students in 1980. These two institutes became respectively the University of Limerick and Dublin City University in 1989.

Non-university education

The bodies below are concerned with non-university higher education and vocational education.

Vocational Education Committees (VECs)

VECs are responsible for the administration of technical and continuing education within particular regions. They are also responsible for the administration of state grants to:

- Regional Technical Colleges (RTCs);

- Dublin Institute of Technology;

- Other specified colleges (e.g. Limerick College of Art, Commerce and Technology).

The National Council for Educational Awards (NCEA)

The NCEA was established in 1972, and is the body which validates the majority of courses available in the National Institutes for Higher Education, the National College of Arts and Design and the Regional Technical Colleges and it confers many of their certificates, diplomas and degrees. It also validates a wide number of courses in other third-level colleges which operate primarily under the aegis of the local VEC.

The NCEA awards the one-year **National Certificate** (which is a post-**Leaving Certificate** course), the **National Certificate** (which follows a two-year, full-time course after the **Leaving Certificate**) and the **National Diploma** (which is either a one-year post-**National Certificate** course or a three-year post-**Leaving Certificate** course).

There are eleven RTCs located throughout the country and like the former NIHEs they represent a major new development in the provision of higher technical/technological education over the past twenty years. These colleges provide a comprehensive range of courses from second-level craft/apprenticeship programmes right through to two-year certificate, three-year diploma and four-year degree programmes in the applied fields of engineering, science and business studies and some postgraduate courses. In addition, these colleges play an important role in providing for recurrent educational needs by way of part-time and evening courses.

Most courses outside the universities and recognized colleges are validated by the National Council for Educational Awards (NCEA), established in 1972 to grant recognition to courses of higher education outside the university system. Institutions whose courses are in the main validated by the Council include the National Institutes, Thomond College (until 1991 when this college became part of the University of Limerick, and is now part of the faculty of education of that university), RTCs and Dublin Institute of Technology (DIT) colleges. There are, in all, thirty-one designated institutions to which the NCEA Act applies.

The six colleges of the Dublin Institute of Technology (DIT) and other colleges within the vocational sector provide education which is oriented towards vocational and professional needs. The provision of part-time third-level evening courses is an important part of their work.

TEACHER EDUCATION

Primary

The qualification for recognition as a primary teacher is a two-year diploma (NT) awarded before 1976, or the **Bachelor of Education (BEd) degree** of the National University of Ireland or of the University of Dublin. The **BEd** is a three-year course. In the National University of Ireland, the **BEd degree** may be awarded with Honours. In the University of Dublin, Trinity College, an Honours degree requires a fourth year of study wholly within Trinity College Department of Education.

Secondary

Graduates take a one-year university course leading to a **Higher Diploma in Education**. Training for teachers of specialized subjects is also available in four-year degree programmes at The University of Limerick (before 1991 these were awarded by the former Thomond College of Education, Limerick), and at colleges of home economics.

Teachers of home economics pursue a four-year **Bachelor of Education (Home Economics) degree** course while art teachers pursue a degree or diploma course at a recognized college followed by a one-year post-diploma/degree course. Teachers of music may train in the universities or at colleges of music.

Israel

The Ministry of Education and Culture is responsible for education in state schools, both secular and religious. In addition, operating independently, there are ultra-orthodox Agudat Yisrael schools, Arab schools and Druze schools.

Education is compulsory and free for ten years from age five to fifteen; and optional but free, from age fifteen to eighteen.

The languages of instruction are Hebrew at Jewish educational institutions and Arabic at Arab educational institutions.

The school and teacher training college academic year runs from September to June and the university academic year from November to July. Schools have three terms. Most higher-level institutions have a two-semester system.

EVALUATION IN BRITAIN

School

Bagrut (Matriculation) or **Mechina** (university preparatory) – may be considered to satisfy the general entrance requirements of British higher education institutions. In the Bagrut, grades of seven or above in six subjects should be obtained.

Further

Handassai (Licensed Practical Engineer) – generally considered to be between BTEC National Diploma / N/SVQ level 3 / Advanced GNVQ/GSVQ and BTEC Higher National Diploma / N/SVQ level 4 standard.

Higher

Bachelor degree – generally considered comparable to British Bachelor degree standard.

Master's degree – generally considered comparable to British MPhil degree.

MARKING SYSTEMS

School

Bagrut subjects may be taken at different levels, these being denoted by a system of units: 1, 2 or 3 study units denote subjects studied at a lower level; 4 or 5 study units denote an advanced subject, studied in greater depth. A student may choose to be examined on a lower level (2 or 3 units) or on a higher level (4 or 5 units) in any of the subjects. Two levels of examination exist in every subject.

The **Bagrut** examinations contain three principal components: A, compulsory core; B, elective; and C, additional elective.

A   Compulsory core subjects

These are:

subject	number of units
Hebrew grammar	1 unit
Hebrew composition	1 unit
Hebrew literature	2 units
history	2 units
mathematics	3 units
Bible	2 units
civics	1 unit
English	3 units (but 4 for university entrance)

B   Elective subjects

The pupil must choose at least one from among the elective subjects which may cover the same area as A or extend to other subject areas. Each subject is marked out of 10, with 6 is the minimum pass-mark. The compulsory core and compulsory selection examinations constitute at least 18 units of study.

C   Additional elective subjects

The pupil has the option of being examined in additional subjects in order to complete the compulsory 21 units or of continuing, up to a maximum of 32 units.

Higher

The grading scales at universities may use letters, numbers or words. Usually the numerical scale is 0–100, with the pass-mark at 50, 55 or 60.

SCHOOL EDUCATION

Before 1968, the system was based on a two-tier structure, consisting of eight years' primary and four years' secondary education. In 1968, a new pattern was introduced, involving six years' primary and six years' secondary (three years' lower secondary (middle school) and three years' upper secondary). Implementation of the new system is still in progress.

Throughout the school system there are four types of schools: state-secular (attended by the majority); state-religious; independent – mainly ultra orthodox; independent – Arab and Druze.

Pre-primary

Although not compulsory most children aged three and four attend kindergarten. At age five one year of pre-primary education is compulsory.

Primary

Although the majority of pupils now follow the six-year primary cycle, many still follow the pre-reform eight-year system. English is a compulsory subject from year 5 and, in Arab and Druze schools, Hebrew is studied from year 3.

Secondary

The reforms introduced in 1968 divided the secondary sector into two cycles: three-year lower secondary (middle school) and three-year upper secondary. Some schools are still operating the old four-year secondary cycle.

Most children transfer to local or regional lower secondary school from the primary sector. There is no external examination or certificate at the end of the lower secondary cycle but there is an internal school assessment.

At upper secondary level there are the four categories of school, as mentioned above, but a choice of either general academic-orientated or technical/vocational or agricultural school is also available.

General academic-orientated education is designed primarily to prepare students for higher education. The programme leads to the award of the **Bagrut** certificate.

Technical/vocational education is divided into three streams according to academic ability. The most able follow a course with a higher proportion of general education leading to the **Bagrut**. The two lower streams have a higher proportion of technical/vocational training, leading to a **Final Diploma**.

Secondary level training programmes are also organized by a non-governmental body, ORT, through its technical/vocational schools. ORT also includes several colleges which provide courses leading either to the **Bagrut**, or to the **Handassai** (licensed practical engineer) or to the **Technai** (licensed technician) qualification. In the near future ORT will be empowered to award academic degrees.

Agricultural schools provide general as well as agricultural education. Schools offering this type of education include a network of rural agricultural schools, usually residential, as well as those run by Kibbutzim. Pupils are eligible to take the **Bagrut**.

To pass the **Bagrut**, a pupil must accumulate 21 points in six subjects. These must include Hebrew, history, mathematics, Bible studies and English. A minimum grade of 6 must be obtained in each subject. To enter higher education a student would need a **Bagrut** score considerably above the pass-mark.

Entry to higher education also requires that the student pass the standard **Psychometric Test** which is the same for all universities.

Students who are not awarded the **Bagrut** examination may be awarded a final certificate showing that they have completed post-primary (or secondary) studies.

Religious schools

There is a separate religious education structure, within the state system. Religious schools are under the authority of the Religious Education Department of the Ministry of Education and Culture. They offer the same basic curriculum as the state schools but, in elective courses, religious subjects predominate.

Kibbutz schools

These form part of the state system and their programmes offer courses leading to the **Bagrut**.

Schools situated on the West Bank, including East Jerusalem, and in the Gaza Strip are the responsibility of the Palestinian National Authority.

FURTHER EDUCATION

Courses are available at technical and regional colleges. They offer two-year courses for students who have completed twelve years of education and hold a **Bagrut** certificate, although some colleges have more flexible entrance requirements. At the end of the first year (year 13) students are awarded the qualification **Technai** (licensed technician) and at the end of the second year (year 14), the qualification **Handassai** (licensed practical engineer). Students sit for external examinations in order to obtain these qualifications. In all, eleven different courses are available, leading to the **Handassai** qualification. In the course of the **Handassai** programme, students spend one year in industry and are required to submit a thesis based on their work experience. Courses may be taken on a part-time basis over a longer period. The **Handassai** qualification is awarded jointly by the Ministry of Labour and Welfare and by the Ministry of Education and Culture.

ORT offers a range of programmes, including post-secondary technical training, retraining for adults, special education for those with learning difficulties, and vocational courses.

There is an extensive network of evening classes available, offering vocational and recreational subjects. The Jewish Agency and other bodies organize courses in Hebrew for new immigrants.

HIGHER EDUCATION

Before embarking on a course of higher education, most Israeli women spend thirty-two months, and men three years, doing their military service.

The basic requirements for admission to higher education are the **Bagrut**, the **Psychometric Test**, proficiency in Hebrew and, in some cases, a personal interview.

The **Psychometric Test**, administered nationally, is used by institutions of higher education, in conjunction with **Bagrut** results, to determine eligibility for admission. It is a multi-choice test and may be taken in various languages, apart from Hebrew (Arabic, English, French, Russian and Spanish).

Students who do not meet the admission requirements may take a one-year preparatory course offered by the universities and leading to the **Mechina** (university preparation) qualification.

The first degree is the **Bachelor degree** which normally lasts three years, except in the case of subjects such as engineering, architecture, law, medicine, veterinary medicine and dentistry which take longer to complete.

The **Master's degrees** require an additional two years of study and **Doctoral** programmes, a minimum of two further years.

The structure of universities is similar to the USA and the credit system is used.

TEACHER EDUCATION

Prospective teachers are trained either at teacher-training colleges or at university faculties of education.

Primary and lower-secondary (middle school)

Students may take a three-year post-**Bagrut** course, either at a teacher training college or at an institution of higher education, leading to the title of **Qualified Teacher** or **Senior Qualified Teacher.**

Upper-secondary

The Ministry of Education and Culture requires all Upper-secondary school teachers to be graduates. Students can obtain a **BEd degree** from a teacher training college or from a university, studied over a four year period, and this will enable them to teach all grades. Alternatively, they may obtain a **Bachelor degree** in any field from a university, followed by a one (or two) year Teachers' Certificate from a School of Education of a university.

In-service

There are extensive opportunities for in-service teacher training, and teachers are encouraged to take advantage of the courses available. There are also full-time courses leading to certification for unqualified teachers.

Italy

The Ministero della Publica Istruzione (MPI – the Ministry of Education) and the Ministero delle Università e della Ricerca Scientifica e Tecnologica (MURST – the Ministry of Research and Higher Education) are responsible for formal education in schools and in universities respectively. There is no non-university higher education. Vocational education, outside technical secondary schools (under the MPI), is mainly the responsibility of the regions, and is notoriously difficult to keep track of – partly because of the decentralized organization, partly because there is no central examinations authority, and partly because advanced FE falls between the two main ministries (Ministero della Publica Instruzione and Ministero della Levoro).

Education is compulsory between the ages of 6 and 14. The medium of instruction is Italian.

The last main university reform act, which among other things introduced the PhD degree, was in 1980. A supplementary law in 1990 updated university ordinances and introduced a new degree qualification, the **diploma universitario**. There is currently a bill on university autonomy going through Parliament – it is at present in committee stage. Meanwhile, the Budget legislation for 1994 introduced a new, and for universities, revolutionary, method of financing, in which funds are allocated under three main headings instead of the previous detailed list. Furthermore, baseline funding from 1995 onwards is to be made dependent on teaching efficiency and research productivity measures yet to be defined. It remains to be seen how much of this last provision will actually be implemented, but the juggernaut of university administrative reform, as of civil service reform generally, is beginning to roll.

Apart from the introduction of the **diploma universitario**, the main change in recent years to the face of university education has been the growth of small satellite centres (the so-called *sedi distaccate*) offering a handful of Laura and diploma courses in towns other than main university centres. There has also been legislation introducing the concept of a personal tutor into what many students feel to be a depersonalized teaching environment, and introducing a compulsory test in a foreign language as a condition of awarding the degree.

EVALUATION IN BRITAIN

School

Diploma di Licenza della Scuola Media – generally considered to be below GCSE standard.

Diploma di Qualifica Professionale – generally considered comparable to the City and Guilds of London Institute Certificate Part II.

Diploma di Maturità Classica/Scientifica/Tecnica/Linguistica/Professionale/ Magistrale/Artistica – may be considered to satisfy the general entrance requirements of British higher education institutions. Because of the large number of compulsory subjects, individual subjects cannot be compared with GCE Advanced on a subject-for-subject basis. The more technical diplomas are considered comparable to BTEC National Diploma / N/SVQ level 3 / Advanced GNVQ/GSVQ standard.

Higher

Diploma Universitario (two to three-year university course) – generally considered to be between British GCE Advanced level and Bachelor (Ordinary) degree standard.

Diploma di Laurea – generally considered comparable to British Bachelor (Honours) degree standard, although the course lasts longer than in the UK. Graduates are entitled **Dottore**.

MARKING SYSTEMS

School

Until 1968

Marking was on a scale 0–10 (maximum); 6 was the minimum pass grade.

Since 1969

A variety of marking systems has been adopted, as follows:

In the primary school, at the end of each year, a global assessment is made. In the lower secondary school the final assessment is expressed in four grades:

sufficiente	pass
buono	good
distinto	distinction
ottimo	excellent

In the upper secondary school-leaving examination (**Maturità**) final marks are on a scale 0–60 (maximum); 36 is the minimum pass grade. For school work marking is on a scale of 0–10 with 6 as the pass-mark.

Higher

The final standard of degree is shown as the aggregate of the individual marks out of 110. Sometimes the degree is awarded *con lode/cum laude* and, exceptionally, *con lode e pubblicazione* which implies publication of the thesis. These two can be taken as marks of distinction. Marking of individual examinations taken during the degree course is on a scale of 0–30 with 18 as the pass-mark. For the specialist diplomas there is a marking scale of 0–70, 42 being the qualifying grade.

SCHOOL EDUCATION

Pre-primary (*Istruzione del Grado Preparatorio*)

Facilities are available for children from age three. State nursery schools (*Scuola Materna Statale*) were formally established in 1968 from already existing pre-primary schools.

Primary (*Istruzione Elementare*)

This covers five years from age six, divided into a two-year lower cycle followed by a three-year upper cycle. The curriculum includes Italian, a foreign language, mathematics, science, history, geography, social studies, religion, music and gymnastics.

At the end of the five years pupils take a final examination to obtain the **Licenza Elementare** (Primary School Diploma) which admits them to secondary school.

Secondary

Italy is about to introduce sweeping reforms in secondary schools (new curriculum and reorganization). The distinction between *liceo* and *istituto* is to be abolished and all secondary schools will be known as *licei* (there will be 17 types of *licei*). The idea is to do away with the early specialization which characterizes the current system, so the new-look schools will not be specialist. From 14 to 16 all pupils would study a common core curriculum (already being piloted in 260 schools). From 16, three courses (Italian, history and PE) would be identical in all *liceo*, while other subjects in common (such as modern language) would be treated differently. Piloting of this second stage began late in 1992. Real specialization would only come in at the age of 19. The new curriculum – introducing new subjects such as earth sciences, more space for computer studies, technology and languages – and reorganization document presuppose the raising of the school-leaving age to 16.

Secondary education presently covers eight years, divided into three years' lower secondary, followed by five years' upper secondary.

Lower

Until 1963, pupils could attend either a *Scuola Media* or *Scuola d'Avviamento Professionale* (more vocationally oriented studies); in that year the two types of institution were combined to form the *Scuola Media Unica*. Compulsory subjects in the curriculum are religious instruction, Italian, history and civics, geography, mathematics, nature study and elementary science, a foreign language, art education, handiwork and physical education; Latin was compulsory until 1977; music was compulsory for only the first year but now replaces Latin as a compulsory subject for the full cycle. However, students who wish to enter the classical branch of academic upper secondary school must have studied Latin.

Pupils obtain the **Diploma di Licenza della Scuola Media** (or before 1962 the **Diploma di Licenza di Avviamento Industriale/Professionale**) on completion of the cycle and after passing the final examination.

Upper

The upper secondary courses consist of classical, scientific, artistic, foriegn languages, technical, vocational and teacher training options. The classical and scientific options are purely academic, intended for pupils wishing to go on to university.

Classical secondary school/*Liceo Classico* – a five-year course divided into a two-year course at *Ginnasio* and three year *Liceo*, with emphasis on the humanities, but with science subjects in the second cycle:

two-year *Ginnasio* – Italian, Latin, Greek, a foreign language, history and civics, geography, mathematics, religious instruction, physical education;

three-year *Liceo* – Italian, Latin, Greek, history and civics, philosophy, natural science, chemistry, geography, mathematics, physics, art, history, religious instruction, physical education.

Scientific secondary school/*Liceo Scientifico* – more specialized preparation for those wishing to study science at university. The course lasts five years and includes Italian, Latin, a foreign language and literature, history and civics, philosophy, natural science, chemistry, geography, physics, mathematics, drawing, religious instruction, physical education.

On completion of the five-year course, pupils take the examinations for the **Maturità** in one of these two specializations (**Maturità Classica** or **Maturità Scientifica**), which allows automatic entry to all faculties of Italian universities. Students admitted to the **Maturitá** examinations are tested on six subjects, two written and four oral. The general organization is as follows:

Written examinations:

1st day – Italian (compulsory for all students): candidates are requested to write an essay on a given theme within a fixed time. Themes are determined at national level, four for each type of upper secondary school (USE) institution (1st: Italian literature and civilization; 2nd: world history; 3rd: topical subject; 4th: topic related to the specialization of each USE). The titles are officially announced on the exam morning and each student may therefore choose one of four.

2nd day – the test varies according to the type of USE institution, as it must be about one of its subjects of specialization; in the case of classical or modern language institutes, the test may consist of a translation from a classical or modern language into Italian (or vice-versa), in the case of scientific institutes it will involve the solution of maths/physics problems. The test is carried out within a fixed time.

Oral examinations

Under the supervision of the whole examiners' board, each candidate is interviewed by the teachers of the four disciplines determined by the Ministry, in the following order:

I)   Italian literature and civilization
II)   discipline chosen by the candidate
III & IV)   the remaining two disciplines, at the board's discretion.

The oral interview also includes some discussion about the student's written work.

When expressing their final evaluation, examiners must primarily take into account the examinees' general competence and maturity; then, they also consider the students' knowledge of the exam subjects, and finally, their previous study performance (e.g. the grades obtained in the last year assessment) as well as any other information made available to the board.

Each examiner disposes of ten marks, from one to ten, six being the minimum passing grade. The sum of all the marks attributed to each student corresponds to the final grade quoted in his/her **diploma di Maturitá**. Therefore, as each examining board is made up of six members, the examinees' performance is ultimately evaluated in sixtieths, according to a scale where 36/60 and 60/60 are the minimum and the maximum pass grades respectively.

As state examination certificates, **Maturitá** diplomas are issued by the Ministry of Education. In addition to the name of the Ministry, each diploma mentions the type of

USE institution attended by the student and/or the study course followed together with the final **Maturitá** mark (results obtained in the exam subjects are not quoted).

The law states that any citizen who is aged 18 years or over and gives evidence of having completed compulsory education may apply to take the **Maturitá** examination. Besides, candidates who have no previous educational qualifications whatever may also take the **Maturitá** examination, provided they are at least 23 years old.

Technical secondary

The full five-year technical upper secondary course is offered by the *Istituti Tecnici*. There are institutes and schools covering industry, commerce, business, draughtmanship, travel, agriculture, navigation, aeronautics, schools for foreign language correspondents and technical institutes for girls. About half of all those taking the **Maturità** attend these institutes.

The five years are divided into a two-year general course followed by three years' specialization (or four years' in the case of special courses in agriculture). On completion of the course pupils take the examinations for the **Diploma di Maturità Tecnica** with the appropriate suffix, e.g. **Industriale**. This allows entry to industry with the title *Perito*. Until the mid-1960s pupils could not proceed to university holding only this qualification, but since 1969 it has given access to all university faculties.

Vocational secondary

This is given in the *Istituti Professionali* (vocational training schools). Pupils must complete *Scuola Media* to gain entry but pupils without the certificate from that cycle, the **Diploma di Licenza della Scuola Media,** may be accepted on passing an entrance examination. The two or three-year courses (depending on the subject) lead to the **Diploma di Qualifica Professionale**. They are more practical than those of the technical secondary schools and aim to produce skilled workers for industries of importance to the economy. They cover the following fields of study: industrial, commercial, agricultural, hotel and catering, secretarial, food sciences, cinema and TV. There are also girls' schools. In 1969 experimental post-qualifying courses (*Corsi Sperimentali Post-qualifica*) were established in some of the *Istituti Professionali* offering a two-year course following on from the first course (i.e. from the **Diploma di Qualifica Professionale**). Thus, a total of five years leads to the **Diploma di Maturità Professionale** needed for university entry. (Despite being called experimental these courses are now fully established.)

The Liceo Artistico offers foundation courses for further studies at an Academy of Fine Art or at a university. Pupils are admitted for a four-year course on completion of lower secondary education. After the first two years the course is divided into two sections: one specialization enables the pupil to pursue artistic studies later at an Academy of Fine Art, and the other enables the pupil to enrol in the Faculty of Architecture (only) of a university; pupils wishing to enrol in other faculties must complete a further year of study. The final examination leads to the **Diploma di Maturità Artistica**.

The Istituto d'Arte provides training courses for craftsmen and awards the **Diploma di Maestro d'Arte** following a three-year cycle. A further two years at this school can lead to the **Diploma di Maturità d'Arte Applicata** (Diploma of Applied Arts).

The Liceo Linguistico provides language training and the music conservatories train musicians.

HIGHER EDUCATION

There are about 60 universities in Italy; most are State institutions with the normal range of teaching and research, but there are some private universities (*università libere*) recognized by the State, together with some specialized university-level institutions teaching a restricted range of subjects – for example the Instituto Navale in Naples. There are three Politecnici – institutions teaching engineering and architecture only – they are in Bari, Milan and Turin. As well as university courses in art, drama, and music, there are specialist Academies and Conservatories offering a professional training in these areas.

Universities can legally confer four degrees: the **Diploma universitario** (DU); **Diploma di Laurea**; **Diploma di Specializzazione** and **Dottorato di Ricerca** (PhD). There is no equivalent of the Open University in Italy, but some institutions do offer DUs by distance teaching. As might be expected in a country with a long and distinguished university tradition, institutions vary markedly in character; the universities of Bologna and Pavia have been teaching for more than 900 years, while the University of Teramo opened its doors in 1993. The University 'La Sapienza' in Rome has over 170,000 registered students, while the University of Molise at Campobasso has 3,000. Some are on splendid green field sites with purpose-built premises, others are in cramped city centre buildings.

With very few exceptions (e.g. dentistry), all students holding the **Diploma di Maturità** are entitled to enter a degree course of their choice – the concept of a '*numero chiuso*' is still politically unacceptable. However in recent years there has been a growing tendency to introduce 'entrance tests' and other devices to reduce the number of entrants to a more manageable figure, and though such methods are open to legal challenge, over 200 degree courses are now estimated to operate some kind of '*numero programmato*'. Most of the overcrowding for which Italian universities are famous occurs in the first year; by the later years of most courses except for the most fashionable, staff-student ratios are down to UK proportions. The DUs since their inception have restricted student numbers, usually to 100 per course.

Diploma universitario – this qualification was introduced in 1990 in an attempt to reduce crowding in degree courses, to provide a more vocationally-oriented type of education and to have something to set alongside other EU short-cycle higher education courses. The qualification is gradually replacing the so-called *scuole diretti a fini speciali* (sub-**laurea** courses mainly confined to paramedical subjects). Over 200 DU courses have now started up, but in some subjects, notably business studies, there are only a few courses available so far. The first degree holders emerged in 1994, but the 'market value' of the qualification with potential employers has yet to be established. The professional institutions (such as the Consiglio Nazionale degli Ingegneri, the equivalent of the Engineering Council) have yet to incorporate the DU into their registration systems.

The DU course lasts two or three years, depending on subject – the two-year degrees are usually in areas with four-year **laurea** courses, the three-year degrees in subjects with five-year laurea courses. In some technology courses one of the three years is spent in industry, though in general the tendency is for DUs to resemble short degree courses in content; this is partly to ensure that people with a DU can go on to a **laurea** course without having to start again from scratch.

Diploma di Laurea – the second degree. Courses last for either four years (in broad terms business studies, law, performing arts, humanities, languages, education, physics, mathematics, sociology) or five years (agriculture, architecture, engineering, veterinary medicine, chemistry, biology) and consist of between twenty-two and thirty modules.

Medicine is a six-year course. The first two years of some five-year courses (the so-called *biennio propadeutico*) are often composed of foundation or balancing studies in mathematics, statistics and science. There are no sandwich or part-time courses as such, but neither is there any obligation to complete all the modules within a set period – consequently a fair number of students complete their courses while working; many never get round to completing them, and the low graduation rate (about 30 per cent of the intake) is a matter for widespread concern. At the end of the degree course students have to defend a thesis – the work varies between a modest literature search and a fully-fledged (and occasionally publishable) research project. Most examinations, and the thesis, are examined orally, but some faculties require written tests as well. Holders of the **laurea** are entitled to the appellation '**Dottore**'.

Most students go to the university nearest their home, and live at home whilst studying. Student facilities, especially residences and sport facilities, on campus are therefore rather sparse. Many lecturers, too, live in a town (usually their home town) well removed from the city in which they hold their teaching post, and go to the university for two or three days a week. Consequently, social life does not revolve round the campus.

Diploma di specializzazione – there are very few master's degrees as such in Italy, and these are mainly in business studies and run by private consortia. These and other postgraduate qualifications are not legally recognized (this is no reflection on their quality; it merely means that no law has been passed regulating their contents). The State-recognized form of postgraduate course is the **Diploma di Specializzazione**; the course lasts a minimum of two years and is intended as a form of professional training. The vast majority of these courses are in the various medical specialties, where they lead to official recognition as a specialist, but there is quite a range of options available, from viticulture and oenology through ecclesiastical and canon law to reinforced concrete construction.

Dottorato di ricerca – the PhD in Italy was established by the 1980 university reform law, but the first enrolments came only in 1984. The annual number of places available has risen steadily but is still only about 4,000 a year; consequently there are probably only about 12,000 Italian-trained PhDs altogether. The PhD itself is very similar to the British one, in that it is not course-based and lasts for three years, at the end of which the student has to defend a thesis (in front of a large and formidable committee). PhD places are allocated to university departments by MURST, who fill them by open competition. Compared with the UK, a smaller proportion of places goes to science and engineering subjects. Students are encouraged to spend up to a year at a laboratory abroad (for which their grant is increased by 50 per cent), but there are negligible opportunities to do an industry-based PhD.

Professional formation – Italy has over thirty regulated professions, ranging from agro-forestry technician to actuary. Accession to each is regulated by the *Ministero di Grazia e Giustizia*, working through national and regional Councils. Candidates are admitted to the Register, or *Albo*, via a State examination. Most regulated professions are at graduate level, and only *Laureati* are eligible to take this **Esame di Stato**. Since there is rarely any requirement for periods of supervised training or practice, it is possible, indeed usual, to take the **Esame di Stato** soon after graduating.

TEACHER EDUCATION

Admission to permanent teaching employment at all levels is by competitive state examination (**Concorso**). There are two type of **Concorso** examination: the **Concorso Abilitante/Concorso di Abilitazione** which provides teachers who may have been employed as supply teachers for some time with a recognized teaching qualification;

and the **Concorso a Cattedra** which enables practising teachers and graduates to compete for permanent teaching positions.

Pre-primary/kindergarten

A three-year course (two years theory, one year methodology) at a *Scuola Magistrale* (after completion of the **Licenza Media**) leads to the **Diploma di Abilitazione all'Insegnamento nelle Scuole del Grado Preparatorio/nelle Scuole Materne**.

Primary

A four-year upper secondary course at one of the *Istituti Magistrali* leads to the **Diploma di Abilitazione Magistrale**.

Under the reform law of November 1990 – which has yet to be implemented – teachers' education and training at primary level is to be achieved through a specific **Laurea** course. The **Laurea** thus becomes the only qualification entitling access to the state competitive examination for the assignment of permanent teaching posts in primary schools. The passing of the examination will entitle to work as regular teacher even if the scores obtained are insufficient for the assignment of a permanent teaching post.

Secondary

There was no formal pre-service training before 1990, but teachers were university graduates.

The 1990 reform law defines the setting up of proper postgraduate *Scuole di specializzazione* (SS) within the universities for the training of qualified teachers at secondary level. Studies will last one to two years, ending in a final State examination organized by the SS itself. The courses will include various disciplinary areas and combine the study of teaching methodologies related to the different disciplines with practical training to be carried out in secondary schools. The final diploma will enable its holders to teach one or more disciplines at secondary level (same validity as the old **abilitazione**) and give admission to the competitive state examinations organized at national level for the assignment of permanent teaching posts in state secondary schools.

There is well-developed in-service training based in the University Education Departments (*Dipartimento di Pedagogia*) and the network of IRRSAE (*Istituto Regionale di Ricerca Sperimentazione e Aggiornamento Educativi*). Diplomas or certificates for in-service teacher-training programmes are not normally released.

Teachers of physical education in schools are trained in *Istituti Superiori di Educazione Fisica* (ISEF). Admission is by means of a public competition based on previous qualifications as well as written and oral examinations; the **Maturità** is required. ISEF courses last three years and combine theoretical education and practical training. The final diploma examination includes the discussion of a written thesis.

HIGHER EDUCATION INSTITUTIONS

STATE UNIVERSITIES

* Università degli studi di Ancona
* Università degli studi di Bari
* Università degli studi della Basilicata
* Libera Università degli Studi di Bergamo
* Università degli studi di Bologna
* Università degli studi di Brescia
* Università degli studi di Cagliari
* Università degli studi della Calabria
* Università degli studi di Camerino
* Università degli studi di Cassino
* Università degli studi di Catania
* Università degli studi 'G.D'Annunzio' di Chieti
* Università degli studi di Ferrara
* Università degli studi di Firenze
* Università degli studi di Genova
* Università degli studi de L'Aquila
* Università degli studi di Lecce
* Università degli studi di Macerata
* Università degli studi di Messina
* Università degli studi di Milano
* Università degli studi di Modena
* Università degli studi del Molise
* Università degli studi 'Federico II' di Napoli
* II Università degli studi di Napoli
* Università degli studi di Padova
* Università degli studi di Palermo
* Università degli studi di Parma
* Università degli studi di Pavia
* Università degli studi di Perugia
* Università degli studi di Pisa
* Università degli studi di Reggio Calabria
* Università degli studi di Roma I 'La Sapienza'
* Università degli studi di Roma II 'Tor Vergata'
* Università degli studi di Salerno
* Università degli studi di Sassari
* Università degli studi di Siena
* Università degli studi di Torino
* Università degli studi di Trento
* Università degli studi di Trieste
* Università degli studi della Tuscia
* Università degli studi di Udine
* Università degli studi di Venezia
* Università degli studi di Verona

STATE TECHNICAL UNIVERSITIES

* Politecnico di Bari
* Politecnico di Milano
* Politecnico di Torino

NON-STATE UNIVERSITIES LEGALLY RECOGNIZED BY MURST

* Università degli Studi di Urbino
* Libera Università Internazionale degli Studi Sociali di Roma
* Libera Università 'Maria SS Assunta' di Roma
* Università Cattolica del Sacro Cuore di Milano
* Università Commerciale 'Luigi Bocconi' di Milano

UNIVERSITY INSTITUTES

* Istituto Universario di Lingue Moderne di Milano
* Istituto Universario di Magistero 'Suor O Benincasa' di Napoli
* Libero Istituto Universario 'Campus bio-medico' (Roma)
* Libero Istituto Universario 'Carlo Cattaneo' (Castellanza)
* Istituto Universario Navale di Napoli
* Istituto Universitario Orientale di Napoli
* Istituto Universitario di Architettura di Venezia
* Scuola Normale Superiore di Pisa
* Scuola Superiore di Studi Universitari e di Perfezionamento 'S Anna' di Pisa
* Scuola Internazionale Superiore di Studi Avanzati di Trieste
* Università Italiana per Stranieri di Perugia
* Università di Lingua e Cultura Italiana per Stranieri di Siena

Qualifications from the University of San Marino Republic are recognized in Italy.

Jamaica

The education system is centralized. The Ministry of Education determines the curricula in all state schools.

The medium of instruction is English.

The academic year comprises three terms and runs from September to June.

EVALUATION IN BRITAIN

School

Jamaica School Certificate –   ) generally considered to be
Secondary School Certificate –   ) below GCSE standard.

Caribbean Examinations Council Secondary Education Certificate – grades 1 and 2 at the general proficiency generally considered comparable to GCSE standard (grades A, B or C) on a subject-for-subject basis.

GCE A level – generally equated to GCE Advanced taken in Britain.

Further

Diploma (from the College of Arts, Science and Technology) – may be considered to satisfy the general entrance requirements of British higher education institutions.

Higher

Associate degree – may be considered to satisfy the general entrance requirements of British higher education institutions.

Bachelor degree (from the University of the West Indies) – generally considered comparable to British Bachelor degree standard; students with good grades may be considered for admission to postgraduate study.

MARKING SYSTEMS

School

Caribbean Examinations Council Secondary Education Certificate: two schemes are available in the subject examinations; the general proficiency scheme and the basic proficiency scheme.

There is no pass/fail mark.

Five grades are awarded, defined as follows:

1 comprehensive working knowledge of the syllabus

2 working knowledge of most aspects of the syllabus

3 working knowledge of some aspects of the syllabus

4 limited knowledge of a few aspects of the syllabus

5 insufficient evidence on which to base a judgement.

GCE A levels – see Appendix 2.

Higher

Bachelor (Honours) degrees are awarded with the following classifications:

Class I
Class II upper division
Class II lower division

If the performance has been insufficient for Honours, the degree is awarded as a Pass.

SCHOOL EDUCATION

Pre-primary

There are a few public and private schools which offer two and three-year courses for children aged four to six. Basic schools, run by community and religious bodies, receive government assistance and provide pre-school instruction.

Primary

This covers six years from age six (grades 1 to 6).

At the end of this cycle pupils sit the **Common Entrance Examination** which forms the basis of selection for secondary education.

Secondary

This covers five years (grades 7 to 11) with an additional two years (grades 12 to 13) for those wishing to proceed to higher education.

The results of the **Common Entrance Examination** mainly determine which type of school a pupil attends.

High schools are the most selective providing a programme of a maximum of seven years leading to the **Caribbean Examinations Council Secondary Education Certificate** (CSEC) after five years (grade 11) and **GCE A levels** after a further two years (grade 13). (For further information on the Caribbean Examinations Council see Appendix 4.)

New secondary schools provide a five-year course. Pupils usually transfer from their local primary school. After four years pupils may take the **Jamaica School Certificate** (grade 10) and the course usually culminates in the **Secondary School Certificate** (grade 11).

Comprehensive schools are a mixture of the two schools mentioned above.

Pupils can take the 13+ **Common Entrance Examination** to a technical high school and follow a four-year course (grades 8 to 11).

Pupils at high, technical and comprehensive schools usually sit the CSEC general proficiency scheme whereas students at new secondary schools take the basic proficiency.

Community colleges have been developed to provide an alternative to sixth forms in high schools and to provide further education. They aim to prepare students not only for university entrance but also for work. Students are admitted from all the different types of secondary schools. Courses are offered in business (including secretarial studies), pre-nursing, etc. These colleges also act as evening institutes and non-formal education centres.

Technical secondary

Technical secondary education in technical high schools consists of four years (grades 8 to 11). The first two years are general, specialization occurring in grades 10 to 11. Admission is normally on the basis of the 13+ **Common Entrance Examination** but students may also transfer from high schools. Courses are also offered part-time and lead to **GCE**, Royal Society of Arts, City and Guilds of London Institute, Pitman qualifications and other similar examinations. (For further information on GCE examinations see Appendix 2.)

Apart from the vocational education programmes offered in technical high schools and most secondary schools, vocational training is offered in vocational schools and trade centres which provide courses lasting one to two years depending on the trade or level of skill required. These courses prepare students for employment.

In 1983, the Human Employment and Resource Training Programme (HEART) established academies for skill training in the areas of resort, agricultural, commercial, business, garment making and cosmetology skills.

FURTHER EDUCATION

This is offered mainly at the institutions listed below and at community colleges. Admission is usually on the basis of completion of grade 11.

The Jamaica School of Agriculture (JSA) offered **Diplomas** (two years) and **Associate degrees** (three years). It also trained specialist agricultural teachers. The JSA went out of existence in the early eighties. It has been replaced by:

The College of Agriculture (COA) which offers an Associate of Science (ASc) degree (3 years). Since September 1994, the College has been amalgamated with the Passley Gardens Teachers' College under the new name College of Agriculture, Science and Education (CASE).

The College of Arts, Science and Technology (CAST) offers courses of one to five years on a full-time, part-time day release or evening basis culminating in college **Certificate** (two years), **Diploma** (three years) or professional qualifications, including degrees and the training of teachers for technical and vocational schools. Entrance requirements vary according to course but full-time students must pass the **College Entrance Examination** or possess the required number of CSEC or **GCE O level** passes.

The Edna Manley School of Visual and Performing Arts (formerly The Cultural Training Centre) comprises the National Schools of Art, Dance, Drama and Music. The courses are two to three-year full-time and also part-time. Those trained as teachers in these areas are recognized as trained specialist teachers in their respective fields.

HIGHER EDUCATION

Jamaica is affiliated to the University of the West Indies (UWI), a regional institution with campuses in Jamaica, Barbados and Trinidad.

There are currently three private institutions which offer certain degree programmes which are recognized and accredited by the University Council of Jamaica. They are:

The Jamaica Theological Seminary, which offers a four-year Bachelor of Theology course.

The Caribbean Graduate School of Theology, which provides a master's degree programme in Theology.

The West Indies College, which offers associate and bachelor degree programmes in Biological Sciences and Business Studies.

There are two levels of admission to first degree courses. Students with the **Caribbean Examinations Council Secondary Education Certificate** (CSEC) or **GCSE** level equivalent take a preliminary year's study. Direct entry to degree courses is based on **GCE A level** or equivalent.

Associate degrees are usually of two years' duration beyond CXC/GCE O levels. They represent the first two years of a four-year degree and are broadly similar to the United States programme. Some universities accept the Associate degree for matriculation purposes while others regard it as the first year of a three-year Bachelor programme.

Bachelor degrees normally take three years.

Higher degrees and certificate and diploma courses are also available.

For further information see Appendix 10.

TEACHER EDUCATION

Entrance to teacher training colleges which train teachers mainly for primary and the new secondary schools, is generally based on completion of grade 11 (post-CSEC). The courses are normally three years. Upgrading courses are available for practising teachers and for those who do not meet the normal entrance requirements.

Training for teachers of specialized subjects takes place in teacher training departments within institutions such as the College of Arts, Science and Technology, the College of Agriculture and the Edna Manley School of Visual and Performing Arts.

Degree-level training is offered in the School of Education at the University of the West Indies. Graduate teachers are usually employed in high schools.

Japan

Japan's pre-War education system was characterized by strong centralized government control and by adherence to Confucianist attitudes, such as the ideal of the disciple following faithfully in the footsteps of his scholarly seniors, respect for learning and deference to authority. After the Second World War, under the American occupation, the system underwent a radical change, with the Fundamental Law of Education (1947) setting forth educational principles on the basis of pacifism and democracy. The new Constitution of Japan (1946) guaranteed compulsory education for nine years. Within the framework of democratization it was decided that authority should be transferred to locally elected boards of education, and that teachers should be free to form unions and take part in political activities as citizens.

The election of local boards was abolished in 1955. Since then the Ministry of Education has required more stringent adherence to centrally compiled curriculum guidelines, and the authorization of textbooks has become increasingly strict. The employment of teachers is, however, controlled by prefectural boards of education.

The private sector is numerically significant at upper secondary level (twenty-eight per cent in 1987) and at higher education level (see below).

In 1987, the University Council was inaugurated as an advisory body to consider the reform of higher education. As a result of recommendations, the Ministry of Education has revised University regulations and introduced a system of self-evaluation. Universities now enjoy a degree of autonomy in setting their curriculum, and evaluation of their work.

The academic year runs from April to March, and children enter school in the April after their sixth birthday. Schools employ a trimester system: from April to mid-July, from September to late December and from January to late March. Colleges and universities generally employ a two-term semester system: from April to September and September to March.

The language of instruction at all levels is Japanese.

The Ministry of Education, Science and Culture (*Monbusho*) is responsible for education at all levels.

EVALUATION IN BRITAIN

School

Chugakko Sotsugyo Shomeisho (Lower Secondary School Leaving Certificate) – generally considered to be below GCSE standard.

Kotogakko Sotsugyo Shomeisho (Upper Secondary School Leaving Certificate) – generally considered comparable to GCSE standard (grades A, B and C) on a subject-for-subject basis, with the exception of English language.

Higher

Bachelor degree – generally considered comparable to a standard between GCE Advanced and British Bachelor degree; may be given advanced standing by British higher education institutions. Candidates from prestigious institutions may be considered for admission to postgraduate study. For further information enquirers should contact the National Academic Recognition Information Centre.

MARKING SYSTEMS

School

Elementary School

Grading is on a 3-point scale

Secondary

Grading is on a scale of 5 (maximum) to 1 (fail) with 2 as the pass-mark:

5	maximum
4	
3	
2	minimum pass-mark
1	fail

Higher

A variety of grading systems is used, but the most common is the percentage scale with 60 per cent as the pass-mark:

A	80–100 per cent
B	70–79
C	60–69
F (fail)	0–59

SCHOOL EDUCATION

At all levels the curriculum is set by the Ministry of Education, and Ministry authorized textbooks must always be used.

Pre-elementary

There are two types of institutions at this level: kindergartens (*Yochien*) and day nurseries (*Hoikuen*), falling under the jurisdiction of the Ministry of Education, Science and Culture and the Ministry of Health and Welfare respectively.

Kindergartens admit children aged three, four or five to three, two and one-year courses respectively. The aim of the curriculum is to develop such qualities as self-reliance and awareness of the needs of others as well as encouraging intellectual creativity through play and other activities. Some 58.2 per cent (May 1993) of kindergartens are private.

Day nurseries accept children from shortly after birth until they enter elementary school. From the age of three they should also receive guidance and instruction comparable to that given in kindergartens.

Elementary

All children are obliged to attend a six-year course of elementary education. The percentage enrolment in private schools is only 0.7 per cent, but there is considerable competition to enter one of the small number of prestigious private schools, usually attached to a private university foundation, where entry virtually guarantees entry to the next cycle right up to university.

The majority of teachers teach a wide variety of subjects, with specialist teachers for certain subjects e.g. music, physical education and home economics. The school day begins at 08.30 and increases from four forty minute classes on a weekday and three on a Saturday for first-grade pupils, to five to six classes on a weekday and four on a Saturday for sixth-grade pupils. There have recently been moves towards the introduction of a five-day school week. School lunches are provided, after which children have meetings with their homeroom teacher, clean the classroom and school premises and, in higher grades, take part in supervised club activities. The average number of pupils in a class is thirty.

Reports giving a grading in each subject are provided at the end of each term, and the **leaving certificate**, provided on completion of elementary school, gives access to the lower secondary education cycle.

Lower secondary

Lower secondary education is compulsory for three years. Entrance to public lower secondary schools is by allocation of the local education board, but entrance to private or national schools is by examination. The percentage enrolment in private schools is only 4.7 per cent, but, as in the case of elementary schools, there is intense competition to enter prestigious lower secondary schools, with a relatively high percentage of elementary school pupils in higher grades attending special examination-preparation schools. A number of private schools offer six years of continuous education, covering the lower secondary and higher secondary cycles. The average number of pupils per class is 40.

A total of 1,050 class hours per grade are expected to be completed at all grades; required hours for individual subjects are specified in detail. Additional hours may be provided in some private schools e.g. for subjects not specified in the national curriculum. In the second and third year of lower secondary schools, attendance at *Juku* (private examination preparation schools) is common. (It is estimated that 67 per cent (1993 figures) of all pupils in the third year of lower secondary schools attend such *Juku*, normally for between two and four hours on weekday evenings and Saturdays with regular mock examinations on Sundays.)

Graded reports are provided at the end of each term, and pupils who complete this cycle satisfactorily are awarded the **Chugakko Sotsugyo Shomeisho (Lower Secondary School Leaving Certificate)**. Approximately ninety-six per cent of all lower secondary school leavers go on to higher grade schools and about two per cent enter employment.

Upper secondary

There is approximately thirty per cent enrolment in private schools, including many of the most prestigious ones; there are also seventeen national schools (0.3 per cent). Entrance to upper secondary schools is by examination or selection; in the case of local schools, examinations are set by the local education board, while private schools set their own examinations.

Full-time courses last three years, while part-time and correspondence courses last four years or more. Of all pupils attending upper secondary schools about 4 per cent attend part-time or take correspondence courses. In terms of subjects, upper secondary schools offer general and vocational courses; about fifty-seven per cent of courses are general academic, while vocational courses include engineering, agricultural and commercial courses.

In 1988 a new type of school called 'credit-system upper secondary school' was inaugurated. This new type of school is intended to offer people a unique type of part-time or correspondence course so that they may pursue their upper secondary studies at any time in accordance with their own needs. Credit requirements vary according to the type of course on which the student is enrolled and according to the type of university course he or she plans to follow.

As in the case of lower secondary schools, there is a high rate of attendance at *Juku* for preparation for university entrance examinations.

Acquisition of the required credits leads to the **Kotogakko Sotsugyo Shomeisho (Upper Secondary School Leaving Certificate)**.

The *Daiken*, an alternative route to higher education, was introduced in 1951 to give students who had not completed High School a second chance to get into university. It is feared that students see it as an alternative and so deliberately drop out of high school. It may be particularly appealing to those not wanting to study all the subjects dictated by the high school curriculum, or who have difficulty in conforming to the rigidity of the school system.

With a view to helping improve university entrance examinations, the *Monbusho* has introduced a new national examination administered by the **National Centre for University Entrance Examination**. Its main purpose is to assess the level of the applicant's basic academic achievements. The examinations are set by the National Centre.

FURTHER EDUCATION

Special training schools *(Senshugakko)*

The category of special training schools was inaugurated in 1976. They represent largely a response by the private sector to meeting educational and training needs. Of a total of 3,151 schools, 851 provide courses for lower secondary school graduates and 2,581 more advanced courses (there is an overlap). Some 88.8 per cent of all schools are in the private sector. Vocational courses last for at least one year and range from dressmaking and design to automobile engineering, electronics and computer programming.

Miscellaneous schools

This category, overwhelmingly (97.3 per cent) in the private sector, comprises 3,918 institutions, including a large number of schools offering tuition in English language, the abacus, etc, which do not meet the criteria laid down for special training schools.

From 1985, students who have completed an upper secondary course of a special training school may be granted a university entrance qualification, if the course is of three years or more and satisfies certain requirements.

Vocational training institutions (under Ministry of Labour auspices)

Operating under the control of the Employment Promotion Corporation, a statutory corporation under the jurisdiction of the Ministry of Labour, are eleven vocational training colleges offering two-year vocational courses to upper secondary school graduates. The Institute of Vocational Training, operating under the same auspices, offers four-year instructor training courses. A nation-wide network of prefectural vocational training colleges also offers a wide variety of vocational training courses, mainly for upper secondary school graduates and older students.

Colleges of Technology

Spanning both the secondary and higher education range are colleges of technology, offering five-year courses to students who have completed the lower secondary education cycle. In the first three years students take general subjects comparable to the upper secondary curriculum; the proportion of technological subjects is steadily increased as students move into higher grades. There are currently sixty-two colleges of technology. The percentage of female students increased from 2.0 per cent in 1980 to 4.9 per cent in 1987. Approximately 89 per cent of graduates enter employment, while 9.5 per cent proceed to higher level courses; graduates are eligible either to enter, through a special examination system, the third year of a four-year university course or to apply for a place at one of the two National Universities of Technology.

HIGHER EDUCATION

Universities

There are 474 (as of 1987) universities (95 national, 37 local and 342 private) offering four-year courses leading to the award of a **Bachelor degree**. Some 288 universities also offer **Master's degree** courses, and 198 of these also offer **doctoral** courses. Since 1979, applicants to national and public universities have had to sit the **Unified First Stage Examination** before sitting entrance examinations of the individual institutions. All universities set their own individual entrance examinations, generally subdivided by faculty. The predominant pattern of courses is for the first two years to be largely in the field of general education, with specialist courses mainly in the final two years. There are a total of 507 universities, out of which 313 offer postgraduate education (90 offer only master's courses, 233 offer doctorates).

Junior colleges

As of 1991 there were 593 junior colleges, offering mainly two-year and, in some cases, three-year courses to upper secondary school-leavers. They aim at conducting teaching and research in depth in specialized areas and at developing in students the abilities required for vocational or practical jobs. Some 90.8 per cent of students are female. Every institution sets its own individual entrance examination. About 81.0 per cent of junior college graduates enter employment, while 3.3 per cent go on to higher level courses.

The minimum credit requirement for graduation from a university is 124 (36 for general education, 8 for foreign languages, 4 for physical education and 76 for professional education). Students must obtain 64 credits in the first two years of general education which is followed by four years' professional training. For medicine and dentistry there is a 64 credit minimum for the six-year course. In two-year junior colleges the minimum credit requirement is 62 and for three-year junior colleges, 93. One credit can comprise either one one-hour lecture class per week for fifteen weeks with two hours' preparation or one two-hour seminar class per week for fifteen weeks with one hour's preparation or three laboratory hours per week.

TEACHER EDUCATION

Teachers employed in national schools are national public officials, and those in prefectural and municipal schools are local public officials. Most elementary school teachers are trained on four-year courses at national universities, although some are trained at private universities and junior colleges. Lower secondary school teachers have mainly followed a four-year undergraduate course, while upper secondary school teachers are required to take both undergraduate and postgraduate courses. Teacher appointments are made by either the prefectural or the municipal board of education depending on the type of school concerned. Public school teachers are given permanent tenure after six months' probationary service. Credit requirements are as for academic higher education courses and are awarded on the same basis.

ADULT EDUCATION

'Social Education' (non-formal education for adults and youths).

The *Monbusho* facilitates (and in some cases provides financial assistance) various community programmes 'for increasing the solidarity of community people, as well as to programs for contributing to enabling old people to feel alive'. It has also been endevouring to expand upper secondary school extension programmes, so that quality resources in universities and upper secondary schools may be utilized for social education, 'and diverse learning opportunities may be offered to citizens.'

ADDITIONAL INFORMATION:

1991: <u>Yomiuri Tokyo Junior College of Science & Engineering</u> and <u>Nippon Electronics Engineering College</u> are recognized by the governor of Japan <u>not</u> the Ministry of Education. High school graduation is the entry requirement, and both offer two-year engineering programmes that lead to the qualifications required to take the licensing examination to engineers in Japan.

THES 24 April 1992: Japan's most prestigious university is <u>Tokyo University</u>. <u>Waseda University</u> and <u>Keio University</u> (both private) are also prestigious.
<u>The University of the Air</u> – Open University. Bachelor degrees awarded after at least four years of study and 124 credits. Registration is open to high school graduates.

Jordan

The Official Gazette of the Hashemite Kingdom of Jordan, issue number 3958, April 2, 1994 published the Law # 3 for the year 1994 entitled the Law of Education in Jordan. This chapter will discuss education in Jordan as it is presented in this law.

Education in Jordan comprises three educational cycles. Kindergarten for two years, basic education for consequent ten years and secondary education for two years. Basic education is free and compulsory, secondary education is free but not compulsory.

The Ministry of Education is responsible for basic and secondary education and the Ministry of Higher Education and the Council for Higher Education for post-secondary education.

There are a number of private sector schools. These are either institutions which have to be licensed by the Ministry of Education and follow an approved curriculum leading to Ministry examination or foreign institutions which are schools teaching mainly non-Jordanians preparing them for foreign examinations.

The medium of instruction is Arabic, but English is the medium at most scientific and technological faculties in the universities.

The academic year runs from August to May in schools and September to June in the Higher Education level, both are divided into two semesters.

EVALUATION IN BRITAIN

School

Tawjihi: (General Secondary Education Certificate) – generally considered comparable to GCSE standard (grades A, B and C) on a subject for subject basis , with the exception of English language when a minimum overall mark of 60 per cent is obtained. Students with good results are qualified to undertake GCE A levels or access/bridging courses.

Higher

Bachelor degree – generally considered comparable to British Bachelor degree standard. Students with good grades and certain level of English language proficiency may be considered for admission to postgraduate study by British higher education institutions.

MARKING SYSTEMS

School

Tawjihi: each subject taken, in whichever stream, has a minimum pass-mark and a maximum score. A percentage average is calculated. For the scientific stream, the percentage average equals ten per cent of the sum of scores in Arabic, English, mathematics, physics, and the highest two scores from the remaining three subjects. The pass-mark score is 50 per cent. For the various vocational education streams, this average is the sum of scores obtained, divided by ten.

Higher

Percentage scale. Pass level: 50, and Cumulative average: 60. For theses: pass/fail

SCHOOL EDUCATION (*Al-Ta'leem Al-Madrase'*)

Pre-primary (*Riyadh Al-Atfaal*)

There are a number of kindergarten licensed by the Ministry of Education (private sector). Children are accepted for up to two years normally from age four to six.

Primary and Preparatory (Basic) (*Al-Asase'*)

Basic education covers ten years from age six to sixteen (grades 1–10). This level of education is maintained by Ministry of Education, private sector, UNRWA, and other government departments such as Ministry of Defence and Ministry of Social Welfare. The curriculum covers Islamic education, Arabic, English, mathematics, social science, physical science, art education, vocational training and physical education.

Secondary (*Al-Thanawe'*)

This is not compulsory and comprises the two years covering grades 11 and 12 between the ages of seventeen and eighteen. There are two types of secondary education, comprehensive secondary and applied secondary.

Comprehensive secondary education is further divided as follows:

> Academic schools provide a broad book-based education, and students are either placed in 'scientific stream' or the 'literary stream'. Common subjects in both streams are: Arabic, English, Islamic education, mathematics and science.

> Vocational schools link academic and vocational education by including more vocational subjects than academic schools. A student can choose to study in any of these five streams: industrial, business, agriculture, nursing and hotel management.

> All students who finish grade twelve sit for the **Tawjihi** examination in the various streams.

Applied secondary education concentrates on training students to become skilled workers in various crafts and industrial specializations. Training is both theoretical and practical, and lead to a school diploma, and students are not eligible to sit the **Tawjihi**.

Admission to secondary schools in the public sector is conditioned to the bylaws that the Minister of Education issues depending on the recommendations of the Board of Education.

FURTHER EDUCATION

Continuing Education (*Al-Taleem Al-Mustamer'*)

Non-formal Education is offered at all public universities and community colleges. Courses are in fields related to industry, computer science, agricultural industries, typing foreign languages, etc.. Applicants must hold the **Tawjihi** (General Secondary School Certificate). Courses last between one week and four months, and students receive certificate of attendance or achievement.

Community Colleges (*Kullia't Al-Mujtama'*)

Non-University-level post secondary education is offered at community colleges, access to which is limited to holders of **Tawjihi**. There are fifty-eight public and private community colleges. Some are controlled by the Ministry of Higher Education, and some by other ministries and government departments, the United Nations Relief and Workers Agency for Palestine refugees in Near East (UNRWA), and the private sector. Community colleges follow the credit-hour system, offering two-year courses in programmes which include art and sciences, education, engineering, agriculture, paramedical sciences, administration and finance, computer science, hotel management, applied arts, air traffic control services and social work. At the end of the two-year course students are awarded an intermediate diploma, for which they qualify after passing the comprehensive examination (**Al-Shame**).

In order to ensure educational quality and guarantee minimum standards in terms of academic facilities and programmes in community colleges, a system of evaluation (general and professional accreditation) has been introduced by the Ministry of Higher Education. Most of the community colleges have obtained both general as well as professional accreditation by now. All students have to sit for a comprehensive exam.

This accreditation procedure made possible the implementation of a bridging system between community colleges and universities. This enables the best students of the accredited community colleges to continue their higher education at the Jordanian universities. The first community college students who benefited from this system were accepted in the academic year 1992/1993.

HIGHER EDUCATION (*Al-Taleem Al- A'lee*)

Access to Higher Education:

Access to Higher Education is open to holders of the General Secondary School Certificate (**Tawjihi**), who pass the state examination after twelve years of schooling (10 years of basic education and 2 years of secondary education). Certificates from other countries are also acceptable if deemed equivalent. Certain programmes at Higher Education Institutions may require students to be holders of a general secondary school certificate in the scientific stream.

For university studies, applications from Jordanian candidates go before the 'Co-ordination Committee for Student Admission to Jordanian Universities'.

All universities and university-level institutions follow the credit-hour system. All offer **Bachelor** degrees, and some offer **Master's** and **Doctorate** degrees.

The **Bachelor degree** is usually earned after four to six academic years, depending on the discipline. The degree of **Doctor of Medicine** (MD) is awarded after a six-year course followed by a one-year internship.

The **Master's degree** requires two to four years after the **Bachelor degree**, while the **Doctorate degree** requires three to five years after the **Master's degree**.

A **Diploma in Education** requires a one-year course after the **Bachelor degree**, while a **High Diploma** requires two years after a **Bachelor degree**.

Counselling and advisory services are available to foreign university students.

Higher Education has developed along two separate lines, with traditional universities on the one hand, and non-university-level institutions (community colleges) on the other hand. All post-secondary education is supervised by the Ministry of Higher Education and the Council of Higher Education.

In 1989 the Council of Higher Education agreed upon the first policy document authorizing the establishment of private universities. Consequently there are two types of universities in Jordan, public and private.

The public universities are:

The University of Jordan: was established in Amman in 1962 and comprises fourteen faculties and nine affiliated centres.

Yarmouk University: was established in Irbid in 1976 and comprises seven faculties, two affiliated centres and one institute. One of the faculties is Hijjawi College of Technology which used to offer a three-year course of non-university level post secondary education. Now it offers four-year courses, see Hijjawi College of Technology.

University of Science and Technology: was part of Yarmouk University until 1986, when it became an independent university. It comprises eight faculties and one centre.

Mu'tah University: was established in Al-Karak in 1980. It has two separate divisions, civilian and military, and comprises six faculties.

Amman University College of Applied Engineering: used to be a two-year technical college only, but in 1989 it added a four-year programme in applied engineering culminating in the award of a **Bachelor degree** in applied engineering.

Hijjawi College of Technology: affiliated to Yarmouk University, offers a four-year course in engineering subjects leading to a **Bachelor degree** in applied engineering.

Al Zarga University: very recently a Royal Decree was issued calling for the establishment of a new public university, named Zarqa University.

The private universities are:

Amman National University: it was established in 1990 and comprises eighteen departments.

Al-Zaitunah University: was established in 1990 and comprises ten departments.

Jordan University for Women: was established in 1991 and comprises twenty-one departments.

<u>Philadelphia University</u>: was established 1991 and comprises twelve departments.

<u>Applied Science University</u>: was established in 1991 and comprises fourteen departments.

<u>Al-Isra University</u>: was established in 1991 and comprises seventeen departments.

<u>Al-Zarga Private University</u>: was established in 1991 and comprises five departments.

<u>Princess Sumaya University College for Technology</u>: was established in 1991. It offers a four-year course leading to the award of **Bachelor degree** in computer science or applied engineering.

<u>Irbid National University</u>: was established in 1991 and comprises nine departments.

<u>A'l al-Beit University for Arts and Sciences</u>: established 1992. The University Board of Trustees comprises Muslim scholars from Arab and Islamic countries headed by His Royal Highness Prince Hassan Bin Talal.

In addition there is one academy, the <u>Jordan Academy of Music</u> (Higher Institute of Music): this was established in 1989. It offers four different programmes leading to a **Bachelor degree** in music.

There are six more private universities that have been provisionally licensed and are still under construction.

TEACHER EDUCATION (*Ta'heel Al'Mu'alimeen*)

Primary and Preparatory (Basic) (*Al-Alsas'*)

A two-year post-**Tawjihi** course, with a minimum of 75 credit hours, leading to a **Diploma in Education.**

Secondary (*Al'Thanawe'*)

Teachers must be graduates and undertake a two-year **Postgraduate Diploma** course.

As a result of the new educational development plan, the conditions for teaching at any public or private school have changed. Basic-compulsory-school teachers must hold a **Bachelor degree**, secondary-school teachers must hold a **Bachelor degree** plus an educational qualification lasting not less than one year after the **Bachelor degree**.

On the other hand, higher-education teachers must hold a **Doctorate degree** (PhD); in some cases a **Master's degree** is sufficient.

The <u>Higher College for the Certification of Teachers</u> was established in 1988 in order to provide educational opportunities for in-service school teachers only to raise their qualifications to a university degree. In-service school teachers, who are holders of intermediate diplomas are awarded a **Bachelor degree** after having successfully completed 70 credit hours over seven semesters.

However, this job has been assigned as of academic year 1992/1993 to different public universities, which in turn will continue to upgrade the qualifications of the in-service school teachers who do not hold a **Bachelor degree.** Consequently, the <u>Higher College for the Certification of Teachers</u> does not exist any more.

Additional information

Statistics:

Kindergarten educational cycle:

| For entire population: | 28,751 | Male students |
| | 23,697 | Female students |

| Total: | **52,448** | Students |

Basic educational cycle:

| For entire population: | 396,120 | Male students |
| | 361,388 | Female students |

| Total: | **757,508** | Students |

Secondary educational cycle:

| For entire population: | 188,038 | Male students |
| | 204,548 | Female students |

| Total: | **392,586** | Students |

Summary for kindergarten + Basic + Secondary educational cycles:

| For entire population: | 612,909 | Male students |
| | 589,633 | Female students |

| Total: | **1,202,542** | Students |

Grand total of students enrolled in higher education for scientific degrees for the year 1993/1994 is (86,389). These are distributed as follows:

Males:

Bachelor degree:	55,830
Postgraduate diploma:	635
Master's degree:	4,043
Doctorate degree:	134

| Total: | **60,642** |

Females:

Bachelor degree:	24,504
Postgraduate diploma:	146
Master's degree:	1,078
Doctorate degree:	19

| Total: | **25,747** |

Number of students enrolled in the higher education institutions for the year 1992/1993 were 120,449. These were divided into 88,506 students in higher education institutions inside Jordan while the other 31,943 students were studying in higher education institutions outside Jordan.

Kazakhstan

Kazakhstan became an autonomous Soviet Socialist Republic in 1925, and a constituent republic of the Soviet Union in 1936. It became a member of the Commonwealth of Independent States in December 1991. The development of education until 1990 reflected central Soviet policy. For information on this period, please see the **Russian Federation** chapter.

Since independence, reforms in different fields of public life in Kazakhstan have proceeded at very different paces; in education, the lack of a powerful centre and the severe lack of funding have held back the developments proposed by a reformist Ministry. Education is strongly affected by government moves towards establishing a true political and cultural identity for the country, but many proposals for far-reaching change are put forward and fade away; the quality of education is felt to be declining, due to lack of funds and as teachers leave the profession due to low wages.

To a great extent, the system which applies in 1995 is based on the enduring features of the Soviet education system, with isolated amendments brought about by individual regions or institutions; these generally run contrary to education law, but the new free market in education and economic factors prevail.

Kazakh is the official language, with Russian as the language of inter-ethnic communication. The Kazakh and Russian populations of the country each number around 40 per cent, and there are many minority groups (German, Korean, Uighur, Ukrainian, Greek). Schools in the cities were mostly Russian-medium, with the village schools Kazakh-medium and a small percentage of minority-language-medium schools. This balance is changing, partly under Ministry policy to increase the number of Kazakh-medium schools, partly as the result of the emigration of many Russian teachers. However, this shift is hindered by a shortage of texts in Kazakh, and some resistance to Kazakh-medium teaching which does not allow access to the still privileged code of Russian. There are different curricula for Kazakh and Russian-medium schools, and separate streams in higher education, with the Russian curriculum expecting more of the student. This is expected to change, and proposals for integrating the curriculum are well received but not backed by funding, training or materials.

The school year runs from September to the end of May for primary schools, September to mid-June for secondary schools, and September to the end of June for tertiary institutions.

EVALUATION IN BRITAIN

School

Svidetel'stvo/o Srednem Obrazovanii (Certificate of Secondary Education)
at grade 10 – generally considered to be below GCSE standard.
at grade 11 – generally considered comparable to GCSE standard (grades A, B and C) on a subject-for-subject basis, with the exception of English language.

Higher

Diplom ob Okanchanii Vyssheg(v)o Uchebnog(v)o Zavedeniya (Diploma Specialist) – generally considered comparable to a standard between GCE Advanced and British Bachelor degree; may be given advanced standing by British higher education institutions. Candidates from prestigious institutions may be considered for admission to postgraduate study. Enquirers should contact the National Academic Recognition Information Centre for further information.

MARKING SYSTEM

School and Higher

Marking is on a 1–5 scale

5	excellent
4	good
3	satisfactory
2	unsatisfactory
1	totally unsatisfactory

SCHOOL EDUCATION

Pre-school provision

There were some 8,000 pre-school establishments in operation in 1993, but this number is declining rapidly. State funding has recently been withdrawn from pre-school care, and expensive private kindergartens are opening in the capital.

General school education

Primary (compulsory)
Grades 1 to 4 inclusive, starting at the age of six

'Incomplete' secondary (compulsory)
Grades 5 to 9

'Complete' secondary (non-compulsory)
Grades 10 to 11

At the end of grade 10 or 11 pupils take the **Svidetel'stvo/o Srednem Obrazovanii** (Certificate of Secondary Education).

Vocational training

There are two to three-year courses for those who have finished grade 9 ('incomplete' secondary). They constitute a variant of the 'sandwich-course' concept with 60 per cent of the time allocated to study, the rest spent on industrial placement. Successful completion of such a course is also regarded as an alternative way of completing secondary education. There are approximately 450 such vocational training establishments in Kazakhstan.

Secondary specialized education

This is open both to those with 'incomplete' and those with 'complete' secondary schooling. For the former, courses last three to four years, for the latter two to three years. On offer are courses in about 450 defined skills (plans exist to reduce this to 50 or so professional areas). There are 257 secondary specialized institutions. These courses lead to the **Diplom o Srednem Spetsialnom Obrazovanii** (Diploma of Specialized Secondary Education).

HIGHER EDUCATION

A new law on Higher Education was passed in November 1993 which allowed for considerable liberalization within higher education, the establishment of non-state institutions and the granting of much greater institutional autonomy. However, there is opposition within the Supreme Soviet which constrains the Ministry, and the public sector is concerned about the success of private institutions.

The law does not allow for the restructuring of the degree structure (**Diploma, Candidateship, Doctorate**) but there is a general move among the rectors of many higher education institutions towards establishing a system parallel to the shorter, more intensive degree pattern common in the West, with a three-year undergraduate degree followed by a two-year Master's course. Some institutions already run Master's courses, particularly in business fields (e.g. MBAs), with support from Western aid agencies.

First degree

Courses are offered in universities, polytechnics (specializing in engineering, science and technology), academies, conservatoires, etc. (68 institutions in all).

Admission is on the basis of success in a competitive entrance examination and possession of the **Svidetel'stvo/o Srednem Obrazovanii** (Certificate of Secondary Education) or the equivalent from a vocational training or secondary specialist institution. The entrance examination is specific to each institution. In some, the entrance examination has been redesigned and is now modelled on the American SAT. The Ministry intends to implement this type of test at all institutions. Once again, there is resistance to this move.

The first degree (**Diplom ob Okanchanii Vyssheg(v)o Uchebnog (v)o Zavedeniya**: Diploma Specialist) is generally awarded at the end of a five-year course.

Higher degrees

Full-time postgraduate studies (*Aspirantura*) leading to the qualification of **Kandidat nauk** (candidate of sciences) normally last three years. The **Doktoratura** (doctorate) is more concerned with original research.

ADULT CONTINUING EDUCATION

Many higher education institutions have specialist departments responsible for running professional updating courses. In addition, distance education techniques are widely practised.

Kenya

Kenya has implemented a highly centralized system of education since its independence in 1963.

In 1967 it co-operated with Tanzania and Uganda to form the East African Examinations Council (EAEC) to administer (at first with the University of Cambridge Local Examinations Syndicate, and from 1974 independently) the school examinations. However, Kenya withdrew from the EAEC in 1980 and has established its own Examinations Council (Kenya National Examinations Council) offering essentially the same examinations.

A new system of education, known as the 8–4–4 system, was introduced in 1985. Under this system, eight years of primary schooling are followed by four years of secondary schooling and a four-year programme leading to a first degree. This scheme replaces one which was based on the English pattern culminating in A levels and a three-year first degree course.

There are a number of private (religious and Harambee) schools; Harambee schools are self-help schools which have been created solely by voluntary contributions and are maintained by fees and donations.

Primary education is nominally free and compulsory.

The medium of instruction is English, but Swahili was used until 1970 in primary standards 1–4.

The academic year runs from: October to July at university; September to July in primary teachers' colleges and sub-degree secondary teacher education, and from January to December in primary and secondary schools.

EVALUATION IN BRITAIN

School

Kenya Junior Secondary Education (KJSE)	generally considered to be below GCSE standard
Cambridge Overseas School Certificate (COSC)	grades 1–6 generally equated to GCSE
East African Certificate of Education (EACE)	Comparable to GCSE on a subject-for-subject basis
Kenya Certificate of Education (KCE) (up to 1988)	

461

Kenyan Certificate of Secondary Education (KCSE) (from 1989)	If passed at grade C or above, generally considered although comparable to GCSE, some subjects may be of a higher standard
Cambridge Overseas Higher School Certificate (COHSC)	Grades A–E are generally equated to GCE Advanced standard
East African Advanced Certificate of Education (EAACE) **Kenya Advanced Certificate of Education** (KACE) (up to 1988)	Grades A–E are generally equated to GCE Advanced standard

Higher

Bachelor degree – generally considered comparable to British Bachelor degree standard.

MARKING SYSTEMS

School

Kenya Certificate of Primary Education (KCPE) – taken after eight years of primary education and examined for the first time in November 1985 – replaced **Kenya Preliminary Examination** (KPE) and **Certificate of Primary Education** (CPE). Seven major subject areas are examined; they are graded A–E.

Kenya Junior School Certificate (KJSE) was graded A–E.

Kenya Certificate of Education (KCE) was graded 1 (maximum) – 9 (fail).

1–2	very good
3–6	credit pass
7–8	pass
9	fail

The certificate also showed a classification in one of four divisions, which reflected overall examination performance, and is not important in ascertaining a pupil's performance in individual subjects.

Division 1: 6–23 points – pass in six or more subjects, including humanities (group II), a mathematical subject (group IV) and a science subject (group V); pass with credit in at least four subjects, including one language (group I or group III) and a high general standard, as judged by aggregate performance in the six best subjects.

Division 2: 24–33 points – pass in six or more subjects, including a language from either group I or group III; pass with credit in at least four subjects and a good general standard as judged by aggregate performance in the six best subjects.

Division 3: 34–45 points – pass in at least six subjects with credit in at least one of them; or pass in five subjects with credit in at least two of them and a satisfactory standard, as judged by the aggregate performance in the six best subjects.

Division 4: 46–51 points – at least one pass with credit in any one subject; or at least two passes at grade 7 in any two subjects; or at least three passes at grade 8 in any three subjects.

For groupings of subjects see **SCHOOL EDUCATION** below

Kenyan Certificate of Secondary Education (KCSE) – taken after four years of secondary education and examined for the first time in 1989. Students are required to take a minimum of eight subjects in order to be awarded the certificate. In the KCSE candidates are graded on a twelve-point scale as follows:

A   )   distinction/very good
A-   )

B+   )
B   )   credit/good
B-   )

C+   )
C   )   average
C-   )

D+   )
D   )   fair
D-   )

E   poor

Certificates are awarded to all candidates who take a minimum of eight subjects selected according to the entry requirements. (English Language and Literature and Kiswahili language and literature are compulsory and count as one subject only.) The certificate awarded shows achievement in each subject using the grades above. The certificate also shows an average grade determined by taking the mean achievement in the eight subjects chosen as follows:

The three subjects from group I
The best two subjects from group II
The best subject from group III
The best subject in groups IV and V
To make the eighth subject, the best subject is chosen from the remaining subjects in groups II, III, IV and V.

There are slightly different arrangements for visually handicapped students.

Kenya Advanced Certificate of Education (KACE) was taken (before 1989) two years after KCE:

Graded Principal passes A level and Subsidiary General Paper.

A   6
B   5
C   4
D   3
E   2
0   1 (Subsidiary pass not Principal pass)

Kenya

Higher

Bachelor degrees are classified:

First Class Honours
Second Class Honours (upper division)
Second Class Honours (lower division)
Pass

SCHOOL EDUCATION

Pre-primary

There is relatively little government provision. However, the government is streamlining pre-primary education through the recent establishment of National and District Centres for Early Childhood Education (NACECE and DICECE). Most pre-school education in urban centres is still provided by the private sector.

Primary

Before 1963 this covered eight years.

From 1964 to 1984 it covered seven years (standards I–VII) from age six.

Until 1967, pupils took the **Kenya Preliminary Examination** (KPE) on completion of standard VII; from 1968 to 1987 pupils took examinations for the **Certificate of Primary Education** (CPE).

From 1985, with the implementation of the new 8–4–4 education system, (eight years' primary, four years' secondary and four years' higher education), students complete eight years of primary education, at the end of which they take the **Kenya Certificate of Primary Education**. In this examination there are seven papers: mathematics; science/agriculture; English; Kiswahili; civics/geography/history; arts and crafts; and home science/business education.

Pupils may proceed to secondary school depending on the results of these examinations; those who do not qualify for secondary education will have been equipped for craft training. This is a major aim of the 8–4–4 system.

Lower Secondary

To obtain the **Kenya Junior Secondary School Certificate** pupils had to pass in at least five of seven subjects and have at least one pass in each of three groups of subjects.

Secondary

The introduction of the 8–4–4 education system has led to tremendous changes in the secondary school curriculum. This is in line with the need for a broad-based curriculum that prepares students for self-reliance, vocational training and further education.

In 1985 courses commenced leading to students taking the **Kenyan Certificate of Secondary Education** after four years of secondary education. In 1990, the first KCSE students entered university to begin four years of study for a general degree. From 1990 there was no form 5 or 6.

Kenya

The **Kenyan Certificate of Secondary Education** is administered by the Kenya National Examinations Council.

Subject groupings

Group I : English; Kiswahili; mathematics (compulsory subjects)

Group II : biology; physics; chemistry; physical science; biological science

Group III : history and government; geography; Islamic religious education; Christian religious education; social education and ethics; Hindu religious education

Group IV : home science; art and design; agriculture; woodwork; metalwork; building construction; power mechanics; electricity; drawing and design; aviation technology

Group V : French; German; Arabic; music; accounting; commerce; economics; typewriting with office practice

Candidates are required to take:

All three subjects in group I

EITHER any two subjects from biology, physics and chemistry
OR both physical and biological sciences

At least one subject from group III

EITHER at least one subject from group IV and one from group V
OR at least one subject from either group IV or V and at least one subject from either group II or III.

Brief history of the examination system in secondary schools

Until 1985, secondary education lasted for six years, covering four years' lower secondary followed by two years' upper secondary.

Until 1968, on completion of form 4, pupils took an externally set examination known as the **Joint Examination for the School Certificate and General Certificate of Education of the University of Cambridge**. The certificate was awarded in divisions I, II or III, reflecting overall performance.

From 1968–70, the **East African Certificate of Education** was administered by the University of Cambridge in collaboration with the newly established East African Examinations Council. Pupils had to take English language and between five and eight other subjects. Those who achieved, at the same examination, a pass with credit (grade 6 or better), two passes (grade 7) or three passes (grade 8) were awarded an **East African Certificate of Education** which incorporated a **General Certificate of Education**. The certificate was awarded in divisions (except for candidates from schools which had been categorized as entry category II; this would be indicated on the certificate).

From 1971–73, the **Joint Examination for the East African Certificate of Education and School Certificate** was administered by the University of Cambridge in collaboration with the East African Examinations Council.

From 1974–80, the East African Examinations Council took sole control of the examinations for the **East African Certificate of Education**.

From November 1980, the first examinations for the **Kenya Certificate of Education** were held and were based on the same syllabuses as those in use under the East African Examinations Council. Pupils took a maximum of nine subjects. The curriculum of forms 1–4 covered mathematics, physics, chemistry, biology, Kiswahili, English, French, history, geography, religious instruction, physical education, art, music, home science, agricultural science, industrial education and business education.

Upper secondary education covered forms 5 and 6. There were two streams in form 6 – arts and science. On completion of form 6, pupils took examinations (usually in three subjects) plus a general paper. Until 1974, pupils took the **Cambridge Overseas Higher School Certificate** (COHSC) examinations; from 1974 to 1980, the **East African Advanced Certificate of Education** (EAACE); and from 1980, they took the **Kenya Advanced Certificate of Education** (KACE).

Since 1985, on completion of four years of secondary education, students have studied the **Kenyan Certificate of Secondary Education** (KCSE). The first KCSE examination was taken in 1989.

Technical education

There are nineteen Technical Training Institutes (TTI), formerly known as technical secondary schools. These offer courses which consist of a group of basic general and scientific subjects, together with options in engineering, building, catering, tailoring or business studies. Until 1989, these subjects were examined in the **Kenya Certificate of Education** and the skill level demanded was equivalent to a Grade III trade test.

Classes covered forms 1 to 4. Form 5 and 6 pupils were accepted for pure science subjects in physics, mathematics, chemistry and biology.

Students who completed four years of secondary technical education could enter the polytechnics for the **Ordinary Diploma** in various options, or Harambee Institutes of Technology for craft courses.

Since 1989, technical education subjects have been taken in the **Kenyan Certificate of Secondary Education** in the Group IV alternative.

Craft training centres

Craft training centres, also known as youth polytechnics, provide low-level artisan training, largely for those in rural areas who have completed primary education. On completion of the two year training, they sit **Artisan** examinations and may also sit the Government **trade test III**.

On passing the government trade test, students may take up an apprenticeship or begin craft training at the technical training institutes.

FURTHER EDUCATION

Institutes of technology (previously known as Harambee Institutes of Technology)

These institutes have been set up through local and provincial initiatives and they provide training for school leavers with the **Kenya Certificate of Secondary Education**, equipping them for employment in medium and large-scale industry. There are eighteen institutes registered with the Ministry of Education, and eleven offer examinable courses. The Government, through the Ministry of Technical Training and

Technology, provides some financial assistance as well as soliciting aid from willing donors to establish such institutions.

Courses last between two and four years and cover subjects such as construction, engineering, business studies, textiles, agriculture, accountancy, home management etc.

Polytechnics

At present there are three polytechnics: the Kenya Polytechnic in Nairobi, the Mombassa Polytechnic and the Moi Eldoret Polytechnic.

The polytechnics offer a wide range of technical and business courses. Until recently, these courses were offered at **Ordinary Diploma, Technician,** and **Higher Diploma** level. Most courses taken at the polytechnics are examined by the Kenya National Examinations Council. The Kenya Accountants and Secretaries Examination Board examines professional courses leading to qualifications such as **Chartered Public Accountant** and **Chartered Public Secretary**.

Recent changes in technical education in Kenya have resulted in the introduction of the Technical Education programme (TEP). Technician, Ordinary Diploma and Higher Diploma courses are being phased out. Technical courses will be offered at **Artisan, Craft** and **Diploma** levels.

HIGHER EDUCATION

The entry requirement for all universities for the 8–4–4 students is a minimum average grade of C+. The first group of students to apply to university under the new system began higher education in 1990.

There are four universities: the University of Nairobi, Kenyatta University, Moi University at Eldoret and Egerton University.

University of Nairobi

Known before independence as the Royal Technical College of East Africa, and the Royal College of Nairobi – later became a constituent College of the University of East Africa as University College Nairobi; attained full independent status through an Act of Parliament in 1970 as the University of Nairobi.

Before 1990, the entrance requirement for a **Bachelor degree** was a minimum of five Ordinary level passes in the **Kenya Certificate of Education** and two Principal passes in the **Kenya Advanced Certificate of Education**.

Bachelor degrees with Honours (there are no Ordinary degrees) are generally obtained four years after entering with KCSE, including those in law and engineering; veterinary medicine takes five years, and architecture and medicine six years.

Master's degrees in architecture, humanities, law, commerce, science, engineering, medicine and education take between one and three years' further study after the **Bachelor degree**.

Holders of a **Master's degree** take a minimum of two years' research to obtain a **PhD**.

The University institutes offer postgraduate degrees through research, except the Institute of Adult Studies which runs a one-year **Diploma in Adult Education** course and the Institute of Computer Science which offers a one-year (four-term) **Diploma in Computer Science** course. The School of Journalism awards a **Postgraduate Diploma in Mass Communications**.

Kenyatta University

From 1978 to 1985, Kenyatta University College was a constituent college of the University of Nairobi, incorporating the University's Faculty of Education.

In September 1985, it achieved independent status as a university. Its major function is the training of teachers, largely for the secondary sector, at undergraduate, diploma and postgraduate levels.

Most students at Kenyatta University read for a **Bachelor of Education (BEd)**. One third of the time is spent on educational studies, and the rest on the two subjects they will teach at **Kenyan Certificate of Secondary Education** level.

Before 1990, the entry requirement for this three-year course was a minimum of two principal passes in the **Kenya Advanced Certificate of Education**.

The University also offers a two-year **Master's degree** and a one-year **Postgraduate Diploma in Education**.

Technical subjects are offered at the Jomo Kenyatta University College of Agriculture and Technology (JKUCAT) which is a constituent college of Kenyatta University. This college is about to achieve independent status; it only awaits legal formalities.

Moi University

Moi University opened in September 1984 with the transfer of the Department of Forestry from the University of Nairobi, now called the Faculty of Forestry Resources and Wildlife Management. More faculties have since opened, with a concentration on scientific and technological subjects.

Egerton University

Egerton College was established in 1939 as an Agricultural School. In 1986 it underwent a major change and attained university college status through an Act of Parliament. It has now gained full university status. The University offers diploma and degree programmes in a range of agricultural topics.

TEACHER EDUCATION

Primary

There are twenty primary teachers' colleges. All students admitted to teacher training colleges hold the **Kenyan Certificate of Secondary Education** and have completed four years of secondary education. The teacher training course lasts two years, at the end of which students are awarded a **P1**, **P2** or **P3** certificate, depending on their success in centrally set examinations.

Secondary

Kenya Technical Teachers College

This college was established with Canadian aid in 1978 to train technical teachers at

Diploma level. It offers a one-year course for the technically experienced and a three-year course for those with no technical background. Teachers are trained for teaching technical, industrial and business studies in secondary schools, technical training institutes and institutes of technology.

Kenya Science Teachers College

This college trains science teachers for secondary schools. Before 1983, it admitted students with the **Kenya Certificate of Education** for a three-year course leading to an **S1** qualification and those with the **Kenya Advanced Certificate of Education** for a two-year course leading to a **Teaching Diploma**. The college was established with Swedish aid in 1966 and is now staffed entirely by Kenyans.

There is one other diploma teacher training college; Kagumo.

Kisii college, which used to train diploma teachers and offer postgraduate teaching diplomas has recently been elevated to a university college.

Kenyatta University is a major teacher training institution (see **HIGHER EDUCATION**).

Agricultural training institutes

Embu Institute of Agriculture; Bukura Institute of Agriculture; and the Animal Health and Training Institute at Kabete run two year **Certificate** courses. Training is designed to produce a middle-level work force and to provide teachers for schools and farmers' training institutes. The minimum entry requirement for all courses is the **Kenyan Certificate of Secondary Education**. **Diploma** courses in agriculture are offered by some of the Institutes of Technology.

Kuwait

The education system is highly centralized, including central control of the curriculum at school level in both government and private schools. All Arab schools must prepare pupils for the Ministry-run examinations and use textbooks chosen by the Ministry. In foreign schools, Arabic language and religion must be taught. State primary and secondary education is free; the fees for higher education are nominal.

The Iraqi occupation was accompanied by a systematic attempt to destroy the Kuwaiti education system. There was wholesale looting of equipment. The Kuwait Institute for Scientific Research was attacked by troops.

Schools had reopened in August 1991 followed by post-secondary institutions in October 1991. The equivalent of two years of instruction was offered in the first year with teaching supplemented by parent/teacher groups. It has been difficult to re-establish teaching in engineering, light health and the medical sciences. Teachers have been recruited from foreign countries, notably the USA.

The University of Kuwait is now again fully operational.

Schools have been re-equipped with computers (computers were first introduced in Kuwaiti schools in 1986, as part of the Government's first drive towards computer literacy).

Private English-medium schools prepare students for British **GCSE/IGCSE, GCE AS Level** and **A level** examinations.

Compulsory education is from age six for eight years.

The medium of instruction is Arabic, although English is used in the Faculties of Science, Engineering, Medicine and Graduate Studies at Kuwait University. English is compulsory at school from the beginning of the elementary stage to the end of the secondary cycle.

The academic year runs from September/October to June and consists of two semesters.

EVALUATION IN BRITAIN

School

Shahadat-al-thanawia-al-a'ama (General Secondary School Certificate) – generally considered comparable to GCSE standard (grades A, B, C and D) on a subject-for-subject basis, when a minimum overall mark of 60 per cent has been obtained, with the exception of English language. Students with very good results may be considered for admission to access/bridging courses.

Further

Diploma in Applied Business Studies/Diploma in Applied Technology – generally considered comparable to BTEC National Diploma / N/SVQ level 3 / Advanced GNVQ/GSVQ standard; may be considered to satisfy the general entrance requirements of British higher education institutions.

Higher

Bachelor degree – generally considered comparable to a standard between GCE Advanced and British Bachelor degree; may be given advanced standing by British higher education institutions. Exceptionally students with very high grades may be considered for admission to postgraduate study.

MARKING SYSTEMS

School

This varies according to subject; minimum and maximum marks are noted on the transcript. The column headed '2nd session' on a transcript of marks refers to marks obtained in examinations which have been retaken.

Higher

Until September 1975

90–100 per cent distinction/excellent

(first-class honours if the grade of distinction was obtained in the final year and no yearly grade was below very good; second-class honours if the grade of distinction was obtained in the final year and no yearly grade was below good)

80–89 per cent very good

(second-class honours if the grade of very good was obtained in the final year, and no yearly grade was below good)

70–79 per cent	good
60–69	pass
below 60	fail

From September 1975 to September 1986

The grade determination was based 50 per cent on the semester's work and 50 per cent on the final examination.

A	9	excellent
A-	8	excellent
B+	7	very good
B	6	very good
B-	5	very good
C+	4	good
C	3	good
D+	2	pass
D	1	pass
F		fail

Since September 1987

Course grades

Distinction denoted by 'A' and divided into two categories:

A	4 points (grade-point average)
A	3.67 points

Very good denoted by 'B' and divided into three categories:

B+	3.33 points
B	3 points
B-	2.67 points

Good denoted by 'C' and divided into three categories:

C+	2.33 points
C	2.00 points
C-	1.67 points

Pass denoted by 'D' and divided into two categories:

D+	1.33 points
D	1.00 point

Weak (fail) denoted by 'F':

F	0.00 points

SCHOOL EDUCATION

Pre-primary

There is an increasing interest in nursery education.

Primary

This lasts four years from age six. The curriculum includes Islamic religion, Arabic, music, arithmetic, elementary science, drawing, physical education and (for girls) needlework. English as a subject was introduced in 1993.

Intermediate

This also lasts four years. The curriculum includes Arabic language and history, social studies (including geography), science (including physics, chemistry and biology), physical education, Islamic religion, mathematics and English as a foreign language. Practical studies (e.g. woodwork, home economics, metalwork, and needlework) are optional. Those who achieve 50 per cent plus in Arabic and religious studies and 40 per cent plus in the other academic subjects, go on to the secondary cycle. Assessment is school based and consists of formal examinations and continuous assessment. Pupils obtain the **Intermediate School Certificate**.

Secondary

This also lasts four years. Pupils continue with the same subjects as at the intermediate school for the first two years, specializing in literature (arts) or science for the final two years. Literature streams study French as a foreign language in addition to English. In the **Shahadat-al-thanawia-al-a'ama (General Secondary School Certificate)** subjects are marked on a percentage basis and various averages on the whole examination are specified as part of the entry requirements to tertiary education. A student who fails to achieve the minimum pass-mark in up to two subjects in any year, can retake in September. If three or more examinations are failed, the whole year has to be repeated.

Thirty-three (1994 figure) secondary schools follow a unit-credit system. Students may take various combinations of compulsory and optional subjects and eventually graduate on the basis of credits earned.

Vocational

Technical, vocational and adult education courses are controlled by the Public Authority for Applied Education and Training.

A Telecommunications Training Institute, was established in 1966.

The Vocational Training Centre, was established in 1971 to provide accelerated artisan training for intermediate school-leavers. Courses consist of six months' general studies followed by one year of studies in auto/diesel, machine-shop-fitting, air-conditioning/refrigeration, welding/sheet metal or heavy/light electricity, or two years' study of radio/television or instrumentation.

FURTHER EDUCATION

This consists of two-and-a-half year courses at the following institutes:

Kuwait Institute of Applied Technology, established in 1968 to train technicians in mechanics, construction, electricity, electronics and chemical technology. The qualification obtained is the **Diploma in Applied Technology**.

Kuwait Business Institute, established in 1975 to train middle-level executives in courses leading to a **Diploma in Applied Business Studies**.

Health Institute, established in 1974 to train nurses and allied health technicians. The qualification obtained is the **Major in General Nursing**.

Kuwait Business School for Girls.

All the institutes teach and assess students through the unit-credit system, and courses/semesters may be repeated up to a maximum enrolment period of eight semesters (four years).

HIGHER EDUCATION

The University of Kuwait was founded in 1966 with Colleges of Science, Art and Education and a residential University College for Women. Colleges of Law and

Sharia'a (Islamic Law) and of Commerce, Economics and Political Science were added in 1967, the College of Engineering and Petroleum in 1975 and the College of Medicine in 1976. The College of Higher Education (Graduate Studies) was established in 1977, and the College of Education was separated from Arts and began its own degree courses in 1981. The College of Medicine uses a system of assessment involving external examiners.

No specific entrance requirement is stated in the University Catalogue, which reads:

'The University Council, at the end of every academic year and in view of proposals submitted by the various Colleges, decides on the number of students to be enrolled from among Kuwaitis, Arab citizens and foreigners who have obtained their secondary school certificate or its equivalent.

'Names of those students accepted in each College will be announced. The distribution of students among the academic departments will be according to the capacity of each department, the student's choice and the marks obtained in the subjects recommended for each department.'

In practice, a Kuwaiti student with less than 70 per cent in the **Shahadat-al- thanawia-al-a'ama** is unlikely to qualify for admission to a major faculty. Under the quota system, non-Kuwaiti students would need a score of approximately 95 per cent to enter any faculty.

The unit-credit system for courses has been followed since 1975 in all departments.

Bachelor degrees normally take four years for all departments, except engineering (five years) and medicine (seven years).

Credits required for graduation (departments' requirements vary) are:

Faculties of Law and Commerce, Economics and Political Science	120
Faculties of Arts, Education and Science	126
Faculties of Engineering	144 (excluding the orientation and petroleum semester)
Faculty of Medicine	122
Faculty of Allied Health	120 for radiological sciences 121 for the other disciplines
Faculty of Graduate Studies	30 credits (including 9 for the thesis)

The study load is usually 15 to 19 credit-hours per semester with a possible 6 in the summer session. The minimum and maximum periods for graduation are 7 and 14 semesters respectively. The system considers students with the following credit-hours:

less than 30	first academic year
30–60	second academic year
61–90	third academic year
91–131	fourth academic year
132+	fifth academic year

To obtain the **Bachelor degree** a student must complete the specified number of credit hours and pass the required courses. In addition, the cumulative average and course average in the major subjects must not be less than 3 points.

A student whose grade-point average falls below 3 at the end of a semester, is put on probation for up to 2 semesters and dismissed if the grade-point average is not raised to 3 within two consecutive semesters.

A **Master's degree** (two years' full-time or up to four years' part-time) is available in course-plus-thesis form for chemistry, mathematics and physics. Other **Master's** programmes are in preparation. There is no **PhD**.

TEACHER EDUCATION

Primary/intermediate

A four-year post-secondary degree course at the College of Basic Education.

Secondary

Teachers are graduates. The Faculty of Arts of Kuwait University has courses leading to the **General Diploma in Education** and **Special Diploma in Education** in addition to the **BA** for students who want a teaching degree.

The Faculty of Education of Kuwait University began its undergraduate teaching programme in 1981, offering four-year courses leading to teaching degrees at all levels of general education (kindergarten to secondary), with majors in each subject in the intermediate and secondary school curriculum.

Laos

Since 1975, when the Laos People's Democratic Republic (LPDR) was established, the education system has grown rapidly with expansion in enrolment at all levels. The promotion of the Lao language has been a major goal of education during this period. The education system is developing in all areas, but the emphasis is still on specific technical training programmes.

There are four major language groups and a number of regional languages. There is limited use of western languages, with French the most used. Fluency in English language is limited.

The education system is relatively underdeveloped and lacking in trained teachers, adequate buildings and resources. There is now a reasonably extensive network of primary and secondary schools, but all operate at very basic levels. The government has committed itself to the goal of universal primary education by the year 2000.

At Sisavangvong University, Lao and French are the media of instruction.

EVALUATION IN BRITAIN

School

Baccalauréat – generally considered comparable to GCSE standard.

Higher

Diploma – generally considered comparable to a standard between GCE Advanced and British Bachelor degree; may be given advanced standing by British higher education institutions.

SCHOOL EDUCATION

School education comprises three years' pre-school education, five years' primary education (grades 1–5), four years' junior secondary school (grades 6–9) and two years' senior secondary (grades 10–11). There is a **Brevet d'Etudes du Premier Cycle** following lower secondary education. The **Baccalauréat**, taken at the end of the upper secondary cycle, admits to higher education.

TECHNICAL EDUCATION

Since 1975, there has been a proliferation of technical training schemes sponsored by different ministries, particularly those covering transport, agriculture, health and education.

HIGHER EDUCATION

Sisavangvong University was founded in 1958 and consisted of the Institute of Law and Administration, the School of Medicine, the Institute of Buddhist Studies and the School of Teacher Training. However, higher education is now offered in constituent institutions, sponsored by individual ministries, namely: the Faculty of Education; Faculty of Art; Faculty of Agriculture, Forestry and Irrigation; a Technical College; the Pali Institute and the Sanskrit Institute.

The newly-created National Polytechnic Institute is being developed by a World Bank/ Swiss government project and offers a five year course (teaching is in Lao with English as the preferred second language).

The Pedagogical University (formerly Dong Dok Teachers College) offers a four-year course and the Medical Sciences University offers five-year courses in pharmacy and dentistry, and a **Doctorate of Medicine**, lasting six years.

There are regional technical colleges in Luang, Pradang, Savannaket and Champasak.

TEACHER EDUCATION

The recruitment of teachers is undertaken at two levels, by provincial authorities for primary schools and by the Ministry of Education for secondary schools and tertiary institutions. Student teachers for primary schools are selected from those at least fifteen years old who have completed primary education; they take a three-year training course. For lower secondary teaching, lower secondary school-leavers are selected for a three-year training course at a teacher training college. Upper secondary teachers are selected from **Baccalauréat** holders and train for four years at the Pedagogical University in Vientiane.

Latvia

For more details of the situation before 1991, please see the **Russian Federation** chapter.

The three Baltic States became parts of the Tsarist Empire only in the eighteenth century. Before that they had for centuries been an area in which educational ideas and institutions from Western and Central Europe tended to prevail (influenced by German, Polish and Swedish educational traditions).

In the nineteenth century a Baltic tradition emerged, with strong attachment to national culture and a struggle for education in the mother tongue.

The Baltic States enjoyed two decades of independent political existence in the inter-war period 1918–40. Incorporated into the Soviet Union in 1940, they again saw their chance to become independent in the light of *glasnost*. Latvia declared independence on 21 August 1991, following the unsuccessful coup in Moscow.

During the period of Soviet rule, most children attended kindergartens, and the full period of secondary education lasted eleven years in Latvian schools and ten years in Russian schools. Higher education was standardized at five years, and led to the qualification of **diploma specialist**. However even at the end of the Soviet period (1986), the duration of secondary schooling was changed from eleven to twelve years in Latvian schools and ten to eleven years in Russian schools. This became twelve years in all schools after 1991.

One of the most serious problems facing the development of education policies is the language of instruction at all levels, due to mass migration into the region from other parts of the USSR over the last decades. In Latvia only about 52 per cent are Latvian by birth.

Compulsory education lasts for nine years (four years primary and five years lower secondary). A universal school starting age of six is gradually being introduced, so that compulsory education ends at age fifteen.

All citizens have equal rights to education, which is free.

The education system is currently regulated by the 1991 Education Act. This was one of the first laws adopted after Latvia's re-establishment as an independent country. Broadly, it introduced flexibility and student choice at school level and the autonomy of higher education institutions. These changes were very positive compared to the strict state regulation experienced under Soviet rule. However, no state regulation of higher education is provided for under the act, and the free choice of subjects at school level has been criticized. As a result, a new Education Act is currently being prepared and adoption is foreseen in 1995.

The school year runs from the beginning of September to the end of May.

The 1991 Education Act included a proposal for using Latvian, Russian and English as languages of instruction, but it only offers a guarantee of teaching in Latvian.

EVALUATION IN BRITAIN

School

Atestats par visparejo videjo izglitibu (attestation of general secondary education) – generally considered to be slightly above GCSE standard, with the exception of English language.

Diploms par arodpamatizglitibu (diploma of basic vocational education) – generally considered to be below GCSE standard.

Diploms par videjo arodizglitibu (diploma of secondary vocational education) – generally considered to be comparable to GCSE standard.

Diploms par augstako arodizglitibu (diploma of higher vocational education)/ **Tehnikum (T) diploma** – generally considered to be comparable to BTEC National Diploma / N/SVQ level 3 / Advanced GNVQ/GSVQ standard.

Higher

Bakalaurs – considered to be between GCE A level and British Bachelor degree standard.

Magistrs – considered comparable to British Bachelor degree standard. Applicants with high marks may be considered for admission to taught Master's degree courses.

Doktors – considered comparable to British PhD standard.

MARKING SYSTEMS

Secondary

The **attestation of general secondary education** is accompanied by a list of marks. This should contain marks in at least twelve subjects i.e. five compulsory and at least seven elective, from which at least two must be marked as *profilkurss* (advanced). Others are marked as *pamatkurss* (basic course).

Two marking systems exist in parallel. The traditional system has been a five-grade system used at all levels. However, Latvia's secondary education system is currently switching to a ten-grade system:

5-grade system:

5	*teicami*	excellent
4	*labi*	good
3	*apmierinosi/*	sufficient/
	viduveji	fair
2	*neapmierinosi*	insufficient
1	*loti vaji*	extremely weak

10–grade system:

	Latvian	English	Equivalent in 5-grade system
10	*izcili*	with distinction	more than 5
9	*teicami*	excellent	more than 5
8	*loti labi*	very good	5
7	*labi*	good	4
6	*gandriz labi*	almost good	3+ 4–
5	*viduveji*	fair	3
4	*gandriz viduveji*	almost fair	2+3–
3–1	*neapmierinosi*	insufficient	1+2–

The minimum pass-mark in the 5-grade system is three, and in the 10-grade system, four.

SCHOOL EDUCATION

Pre-school education

The family is seen as the most important element in pre-school education; the state, therefore, financially supports families that are raising children. The number of kindergartens has therefore dropped from 1,123 in 1991 to 624 in 1994.

General education

Children attend school from the age of six or seven.

There are three main stages: elementary (*sakumskola*) lasting four years, basic (*pamatskola*) for five years and secondary. Compulsory education covers the primary and basic stages (nine years in total), and is uniform throughout the country.

There is almost an even split between schools using Latvian as the medium of instruction and those using Russian. There is also a developing network of schools for national minorities, for example, Jewish, Estonian, gypsy and Polish.

Subjects taught at primary school include Latvian, mathematics, physical education, music, visual art, handicraft and nature, with a foreign language being introduced in grade three. At basic school a second foreign language is introduced as well as, at various stages, history, geography, biology, physics and chemistry. A third foreign language, computer studies and the study of society are added at secondary school, whilst some of the subjects introduced earlier are dropped; there is also an element of choice. The foreign languages taught are English, German and Russian.

Non-compulsory secondary education

The main choices after completing the nine years' compulsory education are general secondary education, vocational secondary or specialist secondary education.

General secondary

This is aimed at pupils wishing to enter higher education. There are two types of general secondary school: *vidusskola* (general secondary) and *gimmazija* (gymnasium). The latter is a slightly more prestigious secondary school, usually specializing in a given group of subjects, e.g. mathematics, chemistry and biology, languages, etc.

There are slight differences between the two types of school: in a *gymnasium*, the elective subjects available may be predicted by the character of the school rather than the free choice of the pupil. *Gymnasiums* may also set admission requirements whereas a general secondary school is obliged to admit any student in its catchment area who has successfully completed elementary school.

All institutions of general secondary education share the same set of five compulsory subjects : Latvian language and literature; mathematics; a foreign language; history and physical education. All other subjects are elective. Seven must be chosen from a list of subjects recognized by the Ministry of Education and Science.

There are two levels of programme in every subject : basic (*pamatkurss*) and advanced (*profilkurss*). Every student must choose at least two subjects at advanced level. In most schools not all subjects are offered at advanced level.

Courses lead to the award of a **Atestats par visparejo videjo izglitibu** (literally, attestation of general secondary education).

Vocational education

There are four types of vocational education, as follows:

Vocational elementary schools (*arodpamatskola*) conduct training in basic low skill vocational areas. Admission is on the basis of nine-year education but this may be incomplete. Programmes last two years and result in the award of a **diploms par arodpamatizglitibu** – diploma of basic vocational education.

Vocational secondary schools (*arodvidusskola*) provide a slightly higher level of training. Courses last three years based on successful completion of nine-year compulsory education. Courses lead to the **diploms par videjo arodizglitibu** – diploma of secondary vocational education.

More advanced vocational training is offered in two types of school. The *arodskola* (vocational school) offer a one or two-year course of higher vocational education, with admission based on completed secondary education (this means students already have the prerequisite qualifications for admission to higher education). The final qualification is a **diploms par augstako arodizglitibu** – diploma of higher vocational education.

The final type of vocational school, vocational gymnasium (*arodgimnazija)*, offers a four-year course. Vocational gymnasiums are the only type of vocational schools which provide general secondary education in parallel with vocational training and thus are unique in that their diplomas admit holders to higher education. The indicators to look for to determine if a diploma is of this category are: duration of studies – four years; the name of the school – *arodgimnazija*; and, since 1993, the words *iegustot visparejo videjo izglitibu* (achieving general secondary education) have been included to prevent confusion.

All the above institutions issue the same kind of diplomas – diplomas of vocational education. They can be recognized by the letters AVS (from *arod vidus skola* – vocational secondary school). The addition of the letter I (AVSI) indicates distinction (from *izciliba*).

Secondary specialized education

Secondary specialized education trains people for middle management in such fields as technology, medicine, the arts etc., and is provided in *tehnikums* or *koledza*. The latter were formed from institutions with a variety of names such as *muzikas vidusskola* (music secondary school); *makslas vidusskola* (art secondary school) or *medicinas skola* (nursing school).

Specialized secondary education takes four to five years after completion of the nine-year basic school. In addition, all the schools in this sector provide general secondary education, and therefore their diplomas allow admission to higher education. The courses may also be completed in a shorter period by those who have already completed general secondary education. In this case, the two or three years studied may be considered tertiary or post-secondary education, a possibility which is currently being debated in Latvia. The final qualification from these institutions is a diploma, with the letter T (*tehnikums*) or TI (with distinction).

HIGHER EDUCATION

In principle, access to higher education is automatic for all holders of general education certificates. However, because of the free choice of elective subjects at secondary level, institutions set their own requirements regarding the subjects which have to be offered as part of the secondary diploma for particular higher education programmes. Access may be by examination, by ranking of secondary diplomas or by interview, or a combination of these methods.

There are seventeen state recognized higher education institutions, which enjoy autonomy in the preparation of study programmes. However, a quality assessment process resulting in state accreditation of all study programmes is currently under development.

Private institutions, which are allowed to operate under the 1991 Education Act, have a licence for beginning higher education activities, but in most cases their diplomas are not yet accredited (most were only granted licences in 1993).

The language of instruction is mainly Latvian by law. Therefore knowledge of Latvian is also tested where the applicant has not received secondary education in this language.

Institutions of higher education provide academic and/or professional higher education.

Academic higher education (*Akademiska augstaka izglitiba*)

The first cycle leads to the award of a **Bakalaurs** (Bachelor degree), which includes the preparation of a thesis. The duration of studies varies between three and four-and-a-half years. This is seen as an intermediate qualification but is treated as completed higher education if four or more years are studied.

The second cycle leads to the award of **Magistrs** (Master's degree), is a terminal qualification of higher education, and also involves presentation of a thesis. The total duration of a **Magistrs** is five to seven years.

In some areas (such as medicine) **Magistrs** and **Bakalaurs** are not awarded. The following qualifications are considered equal to **Magistrs**: **arsts** (physician); **stomatologs** (dentist) and **farmaceits** (pharmacist).

Doctoral studies are available at both higher education institutions and research institutes. There are two levels of doctoral degree; **doktors** and **habilitets doktors**. A **doktors** degree is awarded three to four years after completion of the **Magistrs**, following the public defence of a thesis. The **habilitets doktors** is awarded after the defence of a thesis which is usually a short summary of several scientific publications.

Doctoral degrees are awarded by one of two councils:

promocijas padome (promotion council) awarding the **doktors** only, and *habilitacijas padome* awarding both doctoral degrees.

Higher professional education (*Profesionala augstaka izglitiba*)

Programmes of professional studies can take place independent of academic studies, parallel to or after them.

Non-university higher education institutions offer programmes of at least four years' duration leading to professional qualifications.

Universities offer one or two-year professional qualifications after completion of the **bakalaurs**.

TEACHER EDUCATION

The professional qualification of *skolotajs* (teacher) may be awarded as follows:

to those who have taken courses in teacher training parallel to their academic studies (**bakalaurs** and **magistrs**);

to those who have taken a professional teacher training programme after secondary school;

to those who have taken a postgraduate teacher training course.

The qualification is often given to teach specific subjects (listed on certificate) and may also specify certain grades of school (e.g. mathematics, grades 1–4).

Lebanon

There are three kinds of school: public, private tuition-free, and private fee-based. Private tuition-free education is available only at the pre-primary and primary levels, and schools in this category are most often sponsored by religious and philanthropic institutions. The National Ministry of Education and Fine Arts regulates curricula for all primary and secondary schools (public and private), and administers all official external examinations.

The school system is based on the French system.

Five years of primary education is compulsory by law.

The languages of instruction are Arabic and French or Arabic and English in state and private schools.

The academic year runs from October to June, divided into two semesters.

EVALUATION IN BRITAIN

School

Baccalauréat I – generally considered to be below GCSE standard.

Baccalauréat II/(from 1991) **Baccalauréat** – generally considered comparable to GCSE standard (grades A, B and C) on a subject-for-subject basis (with the exception of English language), provided candidates have an overall mark of at least 11.

Higher

Bachelor degree/Licence – generally considered comparable to a standard between GCE Advanced and British Bachelor degree; may be given advanced standing by British higher education institutions. Candidates from prestigious institutions may be considered for admission to postgraduate study.

MARKING SYSTEMS

School

The grading system is usually based on a scale of 1–20 with a minimum pass-mark of 10. Some private schools using a 0–100 or A–F scale.

18–20	excellent
15–17	very good
12–14	good
10–11	pass
0–9	fail

Higher

The <u>American University of Beirut</u> and <u>Beirut Arab University</u> use the following scale:

90–100 per cent	A	excellent
80–89	B	good
70–79	C	fair
60–69	D	weak
0– 59	F	fail

<u>Beirut University College</u> uses the grade-point average (1–4).

Institutions of higher education which follow the French system, which include the <u>Lebanese University</u> and the <u>Holy Spirit University</u>, use the 1–20 scale.

SCHOOL EDUCATION

Pre-primary

This lasts three years from age three to five: nursery, kindergarten I and kindergarten II.

Primary

This lasts five years from age six to eleven (grades 1 to 5).

Intermediate

This covers four years (grades 6 to 9) designed to prepare students for the official **Brevet** examination.

Secondary

This is a three-year academic course designed to prepare students for the **Baccalauréat II**. Three branches are available: scientific, literary or technical.

Vocational study is a three-year practical course after obtaining the official **Brevet diploma**. The vocational branch for such trades as business, tourism, electronics, advertising, nursing and mechanics, leading to the **Baccalauréat Technique II**.

There is a programme for prospective primary and intermediate school teachers leading to a **Teaching Diploma** after obtaining the **Baccalauréat II**.

The academic branch leading to the preliminary official examinations in English and Arabic literature taken after two years of the three-year cycle (year 11) and the **Baccalauréat II** at the end of the third year (year 12) until 1990.

Since 1991 there has been only one **Baccalauréat** at the end of secondary education.

Technical and vocational

There is no technical or vocational education in general schools. The Directorate of Technical Education runs separate technical and vocational schools. Agricultural colleges are run by the Ministry of Agriculture. There are numerous private schools offering vocational training but the qualifications they award are not officially recognized. The government examinations are the only recognized technical qualifications. Both private and state technical and vocational schools are authorized to issue Attestations only (stating that students have attended and successfully completed courses). The official certificates are awarded by the Ministry of Education (Directorate of Technical Education) to students who take the official government examinations.

Technical education is provided at upper secondary level; the **Baccalauréat Technique II** is awarded to students completing a three-year course. Before 1980, the **Baccalauréat Technique I** was taken after two years' study following the **Brevet Professionnel** and the **Baccalauréat Technique II** after a further two years. The **Technicien Supérieur** is awarded to students who are at least twenty years old and have completed two years of training post-**Baccalauréat Technique II**.

Holders of the **Baccalauréat II** can obtain the **Baccalauréat Technique II** upon completion of two years of training, and the **Technicien Supérieur** upon completion of three years of training.

HIGHER EDUCATION

There are sixteen colleges and universities; all but the Lebanese University are privately owned and run.

The entry requirement for higher education is the **Baccalauréat** (before 1991 the **Baccalauréat II**) and in some cases an entrance examination.

Some institutions offer short courses (two to three years) leading to professional qualifications. Where longer studies are involved, the first stage leads, after three to five years' study, to the **Licence, Bachelor degree** or **Maîtrise** (in science) or **Diploma**, depending on the institution attended. In medicine the first degree and professional qualification is the **Doctorat**; it is awarded after seven years' study.

The second stage involves more specialized work and leads to the **Maîtrise** (in non-scientific subjects), the **Master's degree** at the American University, the **Diplôme d'Etudes Supérieures**, the **Attestation d'Etudes Approfondies** (engineering), the **Doctorat de Troisième Cycle** or the **Doctorat d'Université**.

The third stage involves writing a thesis, followed by the award of a **Doctorate**.

The Lebanese University offers a four to five-year **Licence** course. Teaching is in Arabic, French or English, depending on the faculty.

The Beirut Arab University operates on a charter from the University of Alexandria (Egypt), with which it collaborates closely. It offers a four-year degree course. Arabic is the medium of instruction except in the Departments of English and Architecture where courses are in English.

The American University of Beirut is affiliated to New York State University. Entrance requirements are satisfied by the **Baccalauréat (II)**, an English-language test and the **AUB Scientific-Quantitative General Test**. The University offers a four-year **Bachelor degree** and postgraduate courses (based on the credit system). The medium of instruction is English.

The Université St Joseph is administered by the Society of Jesus and has strong links with the University of Lyon. French is the primary language of instruction. Qualifications awarded include two-year diplomas, the **Licence, Maîtrise**, higher diplomas and **Doctoral degrees**.

Holy Spirit University of Kaslik was founded as a Maronite seminary in 1808; in 1962 it was recognized by the Lebanese Ministry of Education. Its curriculum has expanded slowly to include subjects other than theology. French is the primary language of instruction, although English is becoming increasingly important.

The most important degree colleges include: Beirut University College (originally for women, affiliated to New York State University and offering American-type courses up to **Bachelor degree** level), the Armenian Haigazian College (an English-medium institute offering **Bachelor degrees**), and the Centre d'Etudes Supérieures (affiliated to the University of Lyon and offering a four-year **Licence**).

The University of Luwayzeh, the University of Balamand and the Institute of Islamic Studies: all these institutions follow a four-year programme leading to a **Bachelor degree** or **Licence**. The Institute of Islamic Studies also grants an **MA in Islamic Studies**.

TEACHER EDUCATION

Primary

Prospective primary school teachers take a three-year diploma course after the **Baccalauréat II** leading to the teacher-training diploma (since 1991).

Secondary

The Faculty of Education at the Lebanese University offers five-year courses for prospective secondary school teachers leading to the **Certificat d'Aptitude Pedagogique de l'Enseignement Secondaire** (CAPES). A **Postgraduate diploma in Education** is offered by the American University of Beirut. A **Bachelor degree in Education** is offered by Beirut University College. There is no provision for teaching practice during the diploma courses.

Lesotho

Lesotho, an independent constitutional monarchy since 1966, lies within the economic zone dominated by the Republic of South Africa.

There are approximately 179 secondary schools and 1,198 primary schools in Lesotho. Educational facilities are limited, particularly at the tertiary level, and no sector is compulsory. Most schools are run by church missions or are private with only a minority under government control.

Twenty per cent of secondary and primary school teachers are considered to be unqualified. Thirty-one per cent of the secondary school teachers are expatriate. Eighty-six per cent of primary schools are controlled by one of the churches. The primary and secondary school enrolments are 361,144 and 46,572 respectively (1992 figures, Bureau of Statistics Maseru).

Lesotho was closely connected with Botswana and Swaziland until it established its own university in 1975; the links are now more informal.

Machabeng High School in Maseru is government aided and its system of education is British. It offers **International General Certificate of Secondary Education** and **International Baccalaureate** courses. Pupils are taught by teachers from a variety of overseas countries.

English is the medium of instruction and examination after the first four years of primary education.

The university academic year runs from mid-August to mid-May whilst the school year runs from January to November.

EVALUATION IN BRITAIN

School

Cambridge Overseas School Certificate/GCE O level – grades 1–6 generally equated to GCSE standard (grades A, B and C) on a subject-for-subject basis.

Higher

Bachelor degree –

Part 1 (i.e. the first two years) of a degree course at the National University of Lesotho may be considered to satisfy the general entrance requirements of British higher education institutions.

Part 2 (i.e. the remaining two years) of a degree course is generally considered comparable to a standard between GCE Advanced and British Bachelor degree; may be given advanced standing in British higher education institutions.

MARKING SYSTEMS

School

Cambridge Overseas School Certificate/GCE O level is graded 1 (maximum) to 9 as follows:

1	excellent
2	good
3–6	credit
7–8	pass
9	fail

Higher

Until 1967

A	pass with distinction
B	pass
C	fail

Since 1967

Part 1 and Part 2 examinations are classified:

80 per cent +	A	excellent
70–79	B	very good
60–69	C	good
50–59	D	pass
40–49	E	fail (but can take supplementary examination)
below 40	F	complete fail

The degrees are classified:

First class	A	average
Second class first division	B	average
Second class second division	C	average
Pass	D	average
Fail	E, F	average

SCHOOL EDUCATION

Primary

This covers seven years, leading to the **Primary School Leaving Certificate**. Sesotho is the medium of instruction for the first four years, with English being used for the remaining three years.

Secondary

Pupils who pass the **Primary School Leaving Certificate** are eligible to enter secondary school, although places are limited.

Pupils may enter either a junior secondary school which offers three years of secondary schooling up to the level of the **Junior Certificate of Secondary Education**, or a high school which offers five years to the level of the **Cambridge Overseas School Certificate**. The examination for the **Junior Certificate** is set and marked by the examinations council of Lesotho. Compulsory subjects are English, Sesotho, mathematics, science and development studies. The medium of instruction is English.

Technical and vocational secondary

Various home economics and crafts schools and former training centres offer courses for standard-7 leavers.

Two trade schools offer two or three-year diploma and certificate courses for holders of the **Junior Certificate**.

FURTHER EDUCATION

The National Health Training Centre (1989), Maseru, Nursing School of Roma and the Seventh Day Adventist School, Mapoteng are registered for nursing training and offer courses for holders of either the **Junior Certificate** or **Cambridge Overseas School Certificate**. Scott Hospital, Morija offers training but is unregistered.

The Agricultural College offers two-and-a-half-year courses in agriculture, agricultural engineering and rural domestic economy for holders of the **Junior Certificate**. These courses lead to the **Certificate in Agriculture** and the **Certificate in Home Economics**. It recently introduced a two-year **Diploma** course in agriculture for holders of the **Cambridge Overseas School Certificate**.

The Lesotho Institute of Public Administration provides basic training for civil servants. Senior civil servants attend courses at the Institute of Development Management.

Lerotholi Polytechnic consists of a Technical Institute, a Technician Training Institute and a Commercial Training Institute, all of which accept school leavers with the **Cambridge Overseas School Certificate**. **Junior Certificate school** leavers are only accepted for the bricklaying, carpentry and plumbing courses at the Technical Institute. The Polytechnic offers three-year courses in building trades, mechanical, civil and electrical engineering and courses of varying length in typing, bookkeeping, accounting and business studies, the former leading to the qualifications of the City and Guilds of London Institute and the latter being similar to Royal Society of Arts (RSA) courses. There is also a German project on the training of automobile mechanics.

HIGHER EDUCATION

The country's only university was originally founded at Roma as the Pius XII College in 1945 and covered Lesotho and the neighbouring states of Botswana and Swaziland. The administration of the college was assumed by the Missionary Oblates of Mary Immaculate, who established a link with the University of South Africa. The status of the College was then changed by royal charter to the University of Basutoland, Bechuanaland Protectorate and Swaziland (UBBS). When these territories became independent the institution became, in 1966, the University of Botswana, Lesotho and Swaziland on a campus at Roma in Lesotho. The first degrees were conferred in 1967. In 1970 it was decided to decentralize the university and establish separate campuses in Botswana and Swaziland. In 1975 the campus at Roma became the National University of Lesotho (NUL).

The entrance requirement for degree courses at the <u>University of Botswana, Lesotho and Swaziland</u> and now the <u>National University of Lesotho</u> is the **Cambridge Overseas School Certificate** (1st or 2nd division) with credit in English language and mathematics. The university has six faculties, namely education, law, science, social studies, humanities and postgraduate studies. In these faculties the following degrees are offered: **BA**, **BComm**, **BSc**, **LLB**, **BAEd**, **BScEd**, and **BEd**. These courses last four years and are divided into two two-year parts. The faculty for postgraduate studies offers the following programmes: **MSc**, **MA** and **MEd**. These courses last two years and may also be obtained by research.

There are no facilities for training engineers or doctors.

TEACHER EDUCATION

Primary

The **Primary Teachers' Certificate** (PTC) is obtained after three years' study at the <u>National Teachers Training College</u> (NTTC) established in Maseru in 1975. The entrance requirement is the **Junior Certificate**, although in practice the **Cambridge Overseas School Certificate** would probably be required.

The **Advanced Primary Teachers' Certificate** (APTC), intended to train headteachers of primary schools, is also obtained after three years' study. The entrance requirement is the **Cambridge Overseas School Certificate**.

Secondary

The **Secondary Teachers' Certificate** (STC), intended for those who have been trained as non-specialist teachers for the junior classes of secondary schools, is obtained after three years' study for those holding the **Cambridge Overseas School Certificate**.

A two-year in-service course for practising teachers leads to the **Lesotho In-Service Education for Teachers Certificate** (LIET). It is recognized in Lesotho only for salary purposes, not as raising a person's academic standard to any significant extent.

The **Bachelor of Education degree** obtained after four years' study at the University qualifies teachers for higher secondary classes. Experienced teachers who already hold the **Primary Teachers' Certificate** may obtain the degree after only two years' study.

All students obtaining a degree at the University get a **Concurrent Certificate of Education** (CCE).

There is also the **Postgraduate Certificate in Education** (PCE) which is a one-year graduate certificate.

Liberia

The following chapter regarding the education system in Liberia is based on information obtained from the 3rd edition of this Guide, published in 1991, as NARIC has been unable to obtain more recent information.

The curriculum and syllabuses at school level are controlled by the Ministry of Education. The system of higher education is modelled on the American system.

The medium of instruction from primary level is English.

The academic year runs from March to December.

EVALUATION IN BRITAIN

School

Senior High School Certificate – generally considered comparable to GCSE standard (grades A, B and C) on a subject-for-subject basis.

Higher

Bachelor degree – generally considered comparable to a standard between GCE Advanced and British Bachelor degree; may be considered for advanced standing by British higher education institutions.

MARKING SYSTEMS

School

Marking is on a percentage scale, the pass-mark being 70 per cent.

Higher

A	90–100
B	80–89
C	70–79
D	60–69
F	fail

SCHOOL EDUCATION

Elementary

This covers six years from age six (grades 1 to 6). From 1961 to 1973 pupils took the

National Examination at the end of grade 6, but this has now been abolished. Promotion to secondary school is now automatic.

Secondary

This covers six years and is divided into two three-year cycles. The first cycle (grades 7 to 9) is the guidance cycle taken by all pupils. During the second cycle (grades 10 to 12) pupils may specialize.

In 1961, the Ministry of Education instituted the **National Examination** to be taken at the end of grades 6, 9 and 12 (now only 9 and 12) as a uniform means of comparing secondary school pupils. The examination is taken in four basic subject areas: mathematics, science, social studies and language. At the end of grade 9 it leads to the **Junior High School Certificate** and at the end of grade 12 to the **Senior High School Certificate**. In awarding these certificates some account is taken of marks obtained for course work.

Technical secondary

The Booker Washington Institute and the Liberian-Swedish Vocational Training Centre offer a variety of courses for holders of the **Junior High School Certificate**.

HIGHER EDUCATION

There are three institutions of higher education: the University of Liberia in Monrovia, Cuttington University College (private and linked to the Episcopalian Church) and William V.S. Tubman College of Technology in Cape Palmas. Entrance to degree courses is on the basis of results in the **Senior High School Certificate** plus an entrance examination in English and mathematics.

Bachelor degrees normally last four years, the first two years being spent on general studies and the liberal arts, and the last two on specialization. Degrees in law require three years of specialization.

Medical degrees take seven years: three years in natural sciences and four years in medical studies.
English and mathematics are compulsory during the first two years of the **Bachelor degree**.

There are no facilities for postgraduate study.

TEACHER EDUCATION

Primary

A three-year upper secondary course at a teacher training institute leads to a **Lower Primary Teacher's Certificate/Grade C Teaching Certificate**.

Secondary

Teachers are graduates; they may do a **BSc in Education** (at William Tubman Teachers College, but awarded by the University of Liberia) or undertake a two-year course leading to a **Grade A Teaching Certificate** if they already hold a degree in another subject.

Libya

Education is compulsory to age fifteen.

The medium of instruction is mainly Arabic, although English is sometimes used at higher education level.

The academic year runs from October to June.

EVALUATION IN BRITAIN

School

General Secondary Certificate – generally considered comparable to GCSE standard (grades A, B and C) on a subject-for-subject basis (with the exception of English language) where marks of at least 50 per cent have been obtained in subjects which can be taken in the GCSE examinations.

Higher

Bachelor degree – generally considered comparable to a standard between GCE Advanced and British Bachelor degree. Holders of a Bachelor degree need at least a qualifying year for admission to a taught Master's degree course.

Master's degree – generally considered comparable to British Bachelor degree standard.

MARKING SYSTEMS

School

For every subject the minimum and maximum marks are shown on the certificate. In the literary branch of the secondary school, the maximum mark is 260, the pass-mark being 130. In the natural science branch the maximum is 330, and the minimum pass-mark is 165.

Higher

Marking is on a percentage scale, with 50 per cent as the minimum pass-mark. There are slight variations in the grading system from one institution to another.

SCHOOL EDUCATION

Primary

This covers six years and pupils are tested annually.

Secondary

This covers six years divided into a three-year preparatory/intermediate cycle and a three-year secondary cycle. The curriculum for the first cycle covers religious education, Arabic, English, mathematics, science and health, art, agricultural education and home management, physical education, music.

The first year of the secondary cycle is common for all pupils and covers religious education, Arabic, English, French, history, geography, physics, chemistry, biology, mathematics, art, physical education and military education. Pupils may then specialize in the literary or science branches. The literary branch covers history, geography, philosophy, sociology; the scientific branch covers physics, chemistry, biology and mathematics; the common subjects to both branches are: religious education, Arabic, English, French, physical education and military education. On completion of this cycle, pupils take the examinations for the **General Secondary Certificate**.

Technical secondary

This is offered at two levels:

Lower – a four-year course for pupils who have completed primary education only, leading to a lower certificate.

Upper – a four-year course for pupils who have completed intermediate education, leading to a higher certificate.

In both cases the four-year course consists of two years' general education followed by specialization in a particular field in the last two years.

The courses are offered by schools and specialist institutions.

The Institute of Petroleum in Tobruk was established in 1971 and trains skilled technicians on two-year courses for pupils who have completed intermediate education.

Many trainees and employees within the oil companies take courses leading to qualifications of City and Guilds of London Institute.

HIGHER EDUCATION

There are five universities: Al Fateh University (Tripoli), Al-Arab Medical University, Bright Star University of Technology, University of Garyounis (founded in 1955 as the University of Libya) and Sebha University. The Higher College of Technology was established in 1961 and has since become the faculty of engineering at the Al Fateh University, offering five-year courses in engineering and technological fields, leading to a professional qualification and a **Bachelor of Science degree**. The first year is common for all students. The University of Garyounis also has a campus at Beida, sometimes referred to as the Islamic University, founded in 1971 as a specialist religious institution which also controls its own primary and secondary schools. There are also colleges of technology at Brak, Hun and Bani Walid.

A four-year course leads to a **Bachelor degree** and a further two years to a **Master's degree**. A **Doctorate** may be awarded after a further two years of research.

TEACHER EDUCATION

Until the late 1960s teachers were mostly trained on completion of only six years' primary education.

Primary/Preparatory/Intermediate

Is by means of a three-year higher education course at teacher training institutes.

Secondary

Is by means of a four-year higher education course at the faculty of education at <u>Al Fateh University</u>.

Liechtenstein

Liechtenstein's education system is characterized by the teaching traditions and school systems of the German speaking countries. The two neighbouring countries, Switzerland and Austria, exercise the most immediate influence on the Principality. The types of school and educational terminology are therefore largely the same as other German speaking countries. Differences exist only in the detail of the organization and development of the school system. The majority of Liechtenstein's teachers are trained in Switzerland.

The small size of the country prevents the state from offering a complete education system within its own borders, therefore a number of treaties have been signed with foreign ministries and regional authorities to ensure that places are available at schools and institutes of higher education in neighbouring countries. School authorities and teachers are members of Swiss cantonal and intercantonal associations. Liechtenstein has observer status in the Eastern Switzerland Regional Conference of Directors of Education and is represented at the Swiss Conference of Directors of Education. Only very recently has a non-university higher education system been set up in the Principality.

Liechtenstein also has ties with Austria in the field of education. Some 40 per cent of Liechtenstein students attend college in Austria. In 1976, Liechtenstein and Austria signed an agreement on the equivalence of qualifications.

The Government is responsible for all levels of education, both public and private, and provides financial support for the establishment and running costs of private schools. In some cases, the state also sponsors foreign educational establishments and meets the cost of tuition for Liechtenstein students who attend such schools.

Education at all levels is free and is compulsory for nine years (primary and secondary education) from the ages of seven to fifteen.

At school level, the academic year starts in the spring, and lasts for forty weeks. Since the academic year 1992/93, there have been no lessons on Saturdays in any type of school in Liechtenstein.

At the Liechtenstein Technical College the academic year runs from the second week of October to the end of September, while at the International Academy for Philosophy courses run from the first week of October to the end of June.

The medium of instruction is German.

EVALUATION IN BRITAIN

Matura certificate (Type B or Type E) – satisfies the general entrance requirements of British higher education institutions.

Further

From <u>Liechtenstein Technical College</u>:

Dipl Ing (FH) or **Dipl Arch (FH)** – comparable to British Bachelor degree standard.

Higher

From the <u>International Academy for Philosophy</u>:

Mag Phil – comparable to British Bachelor (Honours) degree standard.

Doctor of Philosophy – comparable to British PhD degree.

MARKING SYSTEM

School

1–6 (maximum) with 4 as the pass-mark.

SCHOOL EDUCATION

Pre-primary

Children from the age of five may attend kindergarten. The two years of kindergarten are optional.

There are special classes for children who at the age of six need extra help in learning German as a foreign language, at which attendance is compulsory. There is also speech therapy and a special kindergarten for handicapped children.

Primary

From the age of seven, pupils attend primary school (*Primarschule*). Primary school education lasts for five years. Normally, the primary school teacher teaches all the timetabled subjects. The first two years concentrate on language training, mathematics, art and music. Interdisciplinary subjects and the natural sciences are introduced in later years. Progress is based on adequate performance in German and mathematics.

There is one school kindergarten (*Schulkindergarten*), for children who have to attend school but who (at age six) have not attained the required standard. This takes the form of an additional year of preparatory education. It is also possible for a child to enrol on an introductory class (*Einfuhrungsklasse*), in which the first year syllabus is covered in two years.

There is one private primary school, the <u>Waldorf School</u>.

Secondary

There are three types of secondary school, lower (*Oberschule*), intermediate (*Realschule*), and higher (*Gymnasium*). Secondary schooling is divided into two stages; the *Oberschule* and *Realschule* cover the first stage only (grades six to nine), whilst the

Gymnasium covers stages one and two (grades six to thirteen). There are opportunities for students from the *Realschule* to transfer to a *Gymnasium* to study for a **Matura** (see below).

Admission to an appropriate secondary school is on the basis of tests in German and mathematics (40 per cent) and teacher recommendation (60 per cent). There are quotas for each type of school.

The *Oberschule* offers a vocational type of training. Obligatory subjects include German; mathematics; science; history/social studies; geography; business studies; English; domestic science; handicrafts; technical drawing; religion; music; art; typewriting and vocational studies. Optional subjects include French, word processing and information science. A lower secondary school **certificate** is issued to those who successfully complete the four-year programme. After one year at *Oberschule* (grade six) it is possible to transfer to grade six at a *Realschule*.

The *Realschule* prepares pupils for professional and further education. It covers the compulsory subjects of religion, German, French, mathematics, history, geography, biology, physics/chemistry, design, music, handicrafts, domestic science and art. From year seven, optional subjects can be studied, which may include English, Italian, information science, typewriting etc.

In years seven to nine, pupils may follow one of two streams in the *Realschule*:

A stream – for more academically able pupils, who will later go on into either further education or training for a technical or commercial profession.

B stream – less academically demanding, for pupils who will continue their education in the industrial and commercial sectors.

After the first year at *Realschule*, it is possible to be recommended for transfer to the second year of a *Gymnasium*. Also, after the third and fourth years, pupils may be recommended for transfer to second stage secondary education at a *Gymnasium* to study for a **Type E Matura Certificate** (see below).

On completion of the ninth year, pupils may continue for an optional tenth year. This is primarily in preparation for careers in the paramedical, social and teaching fields (especially kindergarten teachers).

The *Gymnasium* is the only type of school which covers both stages of secondary education and prepares pupils for higher education. Pupils study for the **Matura Certificate**, which is recognized for university entrance in Switzerland and Austria, as well as at the University of Tubingen in Germany. The examination is taken after thirteen years of schooling. There are two types of **Matura**: **Type B** and **Type E**. Both follow the curriculum set for the Swiss maturity examination. The *Gymnasium* course lasts from years six to thirteen, comprising a first stage of three years (grades six to eight), followed by five years of study directed towards a **Type B** or **Type E Matura** (grades nine to thirteen).

Entrance to the *Gymnasium* is possible via a number of routes and at a number of stages: direct entry from primary school (covering stages one and two of secondary education); from grade eight or nine of *Realschule* onto a **Type E** course (second stage – grades nine to thirteen); or direct transfer to year seven after completion of grade six at *Realschule*.

Those who entered a *Gymnasium* directly from *Primarschule* may choose to study for **Type B** or **Type E Matura** at grade nine.

Subjects studied are similar in both types of **Matura**. The only difference is that Latin features in **Type B**, while in **Type E** this is replaced by economics, business administration and accounting. The full list of subjects is as follows: German; mathematics; French, Latin (**Type B**); history; geography; biology; religion; art; music; nature (a combination of the sciences and geography) from year nine; and the business subjects mentioned above (**Type E**).

The **Matura** examination consists of written examinations in German, Latin (**Type B**); French; mathematics and English and oral examinations in German, Latin (**Type B**), French, mathematics, one of the optional science subjects and history or English. The **Type E** examinations are identical except that Latin is replaced by written and oral examinations in economics and sciences.

FURTHER EDUCATION

Vocational training is offered to graduates of *Oberschule* and *Realschule*. This takes the form of the dual training or apprenticeship system. Depending on the trade chosen, the period of training lasts from one to four years. Theoretical training takes place at vocational schools in Switzerland.

There is also the opportunity for those who wish to continue their education at a technical college after completion of vocational training to take extra classes at special evening schools. This form of training is known as a preparatory course – technical college/professional school entrance.

HIGHER EDUCATION

This sector has only been in existence in Liechtenstein since 1992.

Technical Colleges

The technical colleges include the Lichtensteinische Ingenieurschule/LIS (Liechtenstein Technical College) at Vaduz and the Interstaatliche Ingenieurschule Neu-Technikum Buchs/ NTB (Inter State Technical College) in Switzerland which is sponsored by two Swiss Cantons, the Austrian State of Vorarlberg and Liechtenstein.

Liechtenstein Technical College offers diploma courses of a vocational nature lasting eight terms in architecture, civil engineering, mechanical engineering and economics. There is a mid-course examination, and the course ends with a final examination and a thesis. Graduates are awarded one of two titles: **Dipl Ing (FH) or Dipl Arch (FH).**

Postgraduate courses are also offered lasting three terms in process automation, ecological engineering, ecology and industrial engineering. These courses result in a certificate awarded by the Conference of the Heads of the Swiss Technical Colleges. Specified professional activity is obligatory during these courses.

The International Academy for Philosophy in Schaan is the only university level institute in Liechtenstein. A **Magister Philosphiae** (Mag Phil) is awarded to graduates who have completed a five-year course. Examinations and a thesis mark the half-way point and end of this qualification.

Graduates from this programme may study for a doctoral degree for which a thesis must be submitted. The academic degree of **Doctor of Philosophy** is awarded on completion.

Lithuania

For details of the situation before 1991, please see the **Russian Federation** chapter.

The three Baltic States became part of the Tsarist Empire only in the eighteenth century. Before that they had for centuries been an area in which educational ideas and institutions paramount in Western and Central Europe tended markedly to prevail.

Education at that time was influenced by German, Polish and Swedish educational traditions, but in the nineteenth century a Baltic tradition emerged, with strong attachment to national culture, and a struggle for education in the mother tongue.

The Baltic States enjoyed two decades of independent political existence in the inter-war period, 1918–40. Incorporated into the Soviet Union in 1940, they again saw their chance to become independent in the light of *glasnost*. Lithuania declared independence on 11 March 1991.

Education is compulsory for ten years (ages six to sixteen), made up of four years' primary and six years' lower secondary.

The language of instruction is Lithuanian at all levels, except in national minority schools where the students' native language is used until sufficient fluency in Lithuanian is attained.

Recent educational reform in Lithuania can be broadly divided into four periods:

Phase I (up to March 1990)

The concept of the national school was established; Lithuanian teachers, scientists and artists began to create new curricula and textbooks based on national culture; the foundations of educational reform were drawn up.

Phase II (after the establishment of the Lithuanian State)

Administrative structures were reorganized; restructuring of vocational schools was implemented; higher education was reorganized; the restructuring was given legal basis in law.

Phase III (present phase)

A uniform and permanent Lithuanian education system has been created.

Phase IV (1998 – 2005)

The results of reform will be evaluated and analysed; the structure, curricula and textbooks will be revised and expanded.

EVALUATION IN BRITAIN

School

Secondary School Diploma – generally considered to be between GCSE and GCE Advanced level standard, with the exception of English language; students with good results may be considered for admission to undergraduate courses.

Higher

Bakalauras (Bachelor degree) – generally considered comparable to British Bachelor (Ordinary) degree standard.

Magistras (Master's degree) – generally considered comparable to British Bachelor (Honours) degree standard.

Daktaras (Doctorate) – generally considered comparable to British PhD standard.

MARKING SYSTEMS

NARIC has no information on the current marking systems in Lithuania.

SCHOOL EDUCATION

Children attend school from the age of six. Education is offered by primary, general secondary schools, *gymnasiums*, youth schools, vocational schools and special education schools. The Ministry of Culture and Education approves the curriculum at all levels.

Pre-school education

The family is seen as the most important element in pre-school education. Formal pre-schools do however exist, with nurseries available for infants up to three, and kindergartens which cater for children from ages four or five to age six. Pre-school education is not compulsory.

Primary

Primary education covers grades 1 to 4. Additional classes are also available for children aged five or six who have not attended kindergarten.

Secondary

Basic secondary education covers grades 5 to 10. Specialization is introduced in grade 7. At grades 9 and 10, compulsory subjects are supplemented by electives; subjects are also offered at two levels, Basic (B) and Advanced (A) at this stage. Upon completion of the tenth grade a certificate is issued which lists completed subjects and their evaluation at A or B level.

The non-compulsory upper secondary cycle covers grades 11 and 12. Schools at this level can offer a specialized programme such as one concentrating on liberal arts, natural sciences, technical subjects, economic subjects, etc. The cycle culminates in a series of five to seven examinations. Required subjects are the native language and literature, mathematics, a foreign language and one examination pass from each elective block: humanities, sciences and social sciences. Students choose whether to sit

A or B level in each subject. Success results in the award of a government-approved **Secondary School Diploma**. All such diplomas, whether from a secondary school, *gymnasium* or vocational school, give access to universities, colleges or higher vocational schools. If a student does not pass the examinations, a **Graduation Certificate** is awarded which allows access to higher vocational schools and some college programmes.

At a *gymnasium*, courses are offered at an advanced level, covering grades 9 to 12. Programmes in the humanities, natural sciences or technical/commercial subjects as well as a broader curriculum covering all subjects are offered. To graduate, the student must pass the standard secondary school graduation examinations.

National minority pre-schools and general education schools exist at all levels. These schools provide a general education based on the relevant national culture, with some subjects taught in the minority language. At the same time, the schools assist with the students' integration into Lithuanian culture and society. A mixture of Lithuanian and approved foreign language textbooks are used. Lithuanian is taught at all levels and a minimum level of fluency is required for students to continue their education.

Vocational secondary

Youth schools offer a basic vocational as well as general education. The education is at a lower level than general schools. Usually the youth school is attended for only one or two years. After this period, a student can re-enter a general education or vocational school. Youth schools are often affiliated to a vocational school.

Vocational schools provide training for work in the public and private sectors, in addition to a general secondary education. Vocational training begins after compulsory education has been completed (grade 10).

The main vocational programme lasts two or three years and is geared to those sixteen and over, who have completed basic school. Students receive vocational training and have the option of studying the general education required for them to apply to comparable schools of higher education. There are special programmes for students who have not completed basic school, offering basic general education programmes in addition to vocational training to allow students to 'catch up'. A minimum age of fifteen applies for enrolment on these programmes.

FURTHER EDUCATION

State-run and private colleges offer theoretical and practical training. The length of study is between two and four years, depending on the particular speciality. Courses consist of general subjects as well as core professional and special subjects. The general and core subjects are relatively uniform in all colleges. Colleges may offer **Bachelor degree** programmes.

HIGHER EDUCATION

There are state-run and private, university and non-university higher education establishments in Lithuania. The status of an institution is largely determined by the relationship between the general education and professional training it offers and the scale of research. The academic status of both state-run and private institutions is determined by the state. Fundamental scientific research is conducted in the universities, while applied research is predominant in non-university higher education establishments.

Private higher education is strongly state regulated. The granting of professional degrees by private institutions is decided by the state.

There is also a distinction between traditional and specialized universities. Traditional universities concentrate on the arts and natural sciences, while technical universities lay emphasis on engineering and related disciplines.

Entry to higher education is not limited; therefore possession of a **Secondary School Diploma** allows access to the first level of university study. Where there are more applicants than places, entrance examinations are organized.

University study comprises three levels, leading to the degrees of **Bachelor**, **Master** and **Doctor**. Studies at non-university institutes may be at any of these levels. **Bachelor** or **Master** courses can therefore be either independent programmes or components of higher level courses.

Bachelor degrees last up to four years. Programmes encompass general theory, speciality theory and practical subject modules. The programme may lead in addition to a professional qualification. The passing of state examinations is required if the profession in question is state regulated.

Master's degrees consist of more in-depth theory and special subject modules, as well as interdisciplinary courses. University **Master's** courses offer a broad spectrum of theory modules and interdisciplinary courses. Non-university **Master's** programmes have a narrower professional orientation. Studies last up to three years. Completion of the programme includes the preparation of a thesis. A professional title may also be granted, with regulated professions requiring a pass in a state examination.

Doctoral programmes are completed in no more than five years. There is a higher research qualification, the **Habilituotas daktaras**, awarded by institutes of science and research.

TEACHER EDUCATION

All teaching qualifications have to meet the following requirements:

The qualification level has to match state requirements; one year of practical teaching experience and additional theory courses must be completed; and the teaching establishments must have been granted the right to train teachers by the Ministry of Education and Culture.

The final qualification for teachers at all levels is a **Diploma** which states the speciality and the academic degree level.

Pre-school, primary and basic secondary

Teachers are trained in pedagogical colleges, which may be associated with universities. Admission is by means of a **Secondary School Diploma**. Studies last three or four years. Courses culminate in state examinations.

Secondary

A **Bachelor degree** lasting four or five years is the second level of teacher training.

Master's degrees confer the right to teach in *gymnasiums* and colleges. Admission is on the basis of a **Bachelor's degree** and at least one year of teaching experience.

Higher

A **Doctorate** is required for lecturers at this level.

NON-FORMAL ADULT EDUCATION

There is a large adult education sector in Lithuania, consisting of general and professional training at various levels, including special programmes at college and university. Instruction is offered at special adult schools, learning centres, open universities etc. and at adult education departments in universities and colleges. A national module system ensures a student's study is recognized and allows for the possibility of transfer to the formal education system.

Luxembourg

During the 1960s, a number of Acts were passed which affected almost every field of education. Under an Act of 1969, degrees and diplomas obtained at foreign universities are recognized in Luxembourg as there is no institution offering a full course of higher education.

The medium of instruction is Luxembourgeois at pre-primary and early primary level: it is soon to be replaced by German. French is taught intensively as a foreign language throughout the primary course. At secondary level, German and French are taught throughout. In the upper forms, French becomes the medium of instruction for most subjects, but German continues to be used for some.

Luxembourg is the only country in the EU to have introduced two years of compulsory education in pre-primary schools for all four-year-olds (such pre-school education may not, by law, involve formal teaching). Compulsory education in the usual sense of the word covers nine years, including six years of primary education.

The academic year runs from mid-September to mid-July.

EVALUATION IN BRITAIN

School

Diplôme de Fin d'Etudes Secondaires – may be considered to satisfy the general entrance requirements of British higher education institutions.

Further

Diplôme d'Ingénieur-Technicien – generally compared to BTEC Higher National Diploma standard / N/SVQ level 4.

Higher

Certificat d'Etudes – generally considered comparable to a standard between GCE Advanced and British Bachelor degree; may be given advanced standing by British higher education institutions.

MARKING SYSTEMS

School

On a scale of 1–60 (maximum)

Until 1970

55–60	*distingué*	excellent
45–54	*grand*	good
30–44	*satisfaisant*	satisfactory
20–29	*insuffisant*	unsatisfactory
10–19	*faible*	weak
01–09	*très faible*	very weak

Since 1971

50–60	*très bien*	very good
40–49	*bien*	good
30–39	*satisfaisant*	satisfactory
20–29	*insuffisant*	unsatisfactory
10–19	*mauvais*	bad
01–09	*très mauvais*	very bad

SCHOOL EDUCATION

Pre-primary

Some facilities are available for children aged four to six in kindergartens (*Jardins d'Enfants*). There is a compulsory two-year course before primary school.

Primary (*Premier Cycle de l'Enseignement Primaire*)

This lasts six years. The curriculum covers religious instruction, Luxembourgeois, French, German, arithmetic, national history, geography, study of local environment, natural science, drawing, music, and physical education.

Until 1994

Upper primary (*Deuxième Cycle de l'Enseignement Primaire/Classes Complémentaires*)

This covers three years for pupils who do not wish to proceed to secondary education but who must stay at school for a minimum of nine years. In addition to general subjects, the curriculum covers metalwork and woodwork for boys, home economics for girls, and includes some practical training. On completion, students obtain the **Certificat de Fin d'Etudes Primaires**.

Since 1994

Technical Education

To insure a better professional qualification of all pupils, a preparatory curriculum has been created. It is fully integrated in the structure of technical education.

The preparatory curriculum is characterized by a systematic individualization of teaching and training. It pursues two objectives:

1. to give all pupils a chance to catch up, as much as possible, with eventual deficits on a cognitive, social and affective level (formative objective)

2. to help a maximum of pupils attain a professional qualification (qualificative objective)

The educational system of the preparatory curriculum is organized in the form of learning modules. Such an organization will help to emphasize the competences and the affinities of the pupils by allowing them to progress according to their own pace and needs, but not necessarily in a uniform or synchronous way.

Further primary (*Enseignement Primaire Supérieur* – until 1965)

This also covered three years for pupils not wishing to proceed to some form of secondary schooling. It was more academic than the *classes complémentaires*, and the pupil was required to pass an entrance examination. These schools have been closing down since 1965 and have been replaced by intermediate schools (see below).

Intermediate

A five-year intermediate course was introduced in 1965 which was divided into two cycles of three and two years respectively, the first cycle replacing the further primary courses. These courses are taken at the newly created *Collèges d'Enseignement Moyen*. The curriculum of the first cycle covers religious instruction, German, French, English (from the beginning of the second year), arithmetic, algebra, geometry, history, geography, natural science, civics, art, music, physical education and commercial practice. In the second cycle, pupils may specialize in the biological and social sciences (biology, anatomy and chemistry), commerce (bookkeeping, data-processing and typing), or technical studies (mathematics, physics and technical drawing). On completion of the course, pupils take examinations, in all subjects studied, for the **Certificat de Fin d'Etudes Moyennes**.

Secondary (*l'Enseignement Secondaire*)

Academic secondary school covers seven years.

Before 1970, secondary education was divided into one branch for boys (classical or modern) and one for girls. There is now one system which lasts seven years and is divided into two cycles of three and four years respectively. Classes are numbered in descending order. Pupils must pass entrance examinations in German, French and arithmetic. The curriculum in the first year (*Classe d'Orientation*) is identical with the curriculum of the first year of the intermediate and technical schools. At the beginning of the second year (sixth class), pupils may specialize either in the classical branch (including the study of Latin) or in the modern branch (including the study of English). In the second cycle, pupils in the classical branch may specialize further in Latin and languages or Latin and sciences (with the option of taking: mathematics, sciences, economics or arts); pupils in the modern branch may specialize in modern languages (they must study a fourth modern language) or modern languages and sciences (with the option of: mathematics, sciences, economics or arts). The entrance examination to the second cycle (**Examen de Passage**) was abolished in 1974.

At the end of the upper cycle, pupils take the **Examen de Fin d'Etudes Secondaires** in the language in which each subject was taught in the last year of the second cycle. Most pupils take examinations in French, German, English, philosophy and history. Pupils who specialize in mathematics or science are required to take only two modern languages. Depending on the specialization, pupils also take three to five subjects from: Greek, Latin, geography, political economics, another modern language, mathematics, physics, chemistry, biology and economic science. Success in these examinations leads to the award of the **Certificat/Diplôme de Fin d'Etudes Secondaires**. The examinations may be retaken twice.

Technical secondary

Until 1979

The Trade and Crafts School (*Ecole des Arts et Métiers*) ran a four-year course for pupils who had completed two years of complementary classes. Pupils could specialize in building, mechanics, electrotechnics and industrial machine tools.

The technical schools offered a five-year course for those who had completed primary school and who wished to become skilled workers or technicians. The course was divided into a two-year cycle (*d'Orientation et d'Observation*), followed by three years of specialization (*Formation Professionnelle*), leading to the **Certificat d'Aptitude Professionnelle** (CAP). From 1970/1–9 pupils were able to follow a further two-year cycle leading to the technicians' certificate **Diplôme de Technicien**.

Since 1979

Under the new system technical secondary school is divided into three cycles:

Cycle Inférieur

This is a three-year course, following the sixth grade of primary school. The curriculum may be adapted according to the ability and needs of the individual. Pupils receive a certificate which confirms that they have completed compulsory education.

Cycle Moyen

This normally lasts two to three years and includes vocational training (*Régime Professionnel*) and technical courses (*Régime de la formation de Technicien*). Vocational courses are mainly apprenticeships and pupils normally study for two years and take one year of practical training. The qualification obtained on completion of the course is the **Certificat d'Aptitude Technique et Professionnelle** (CATP).

Cycle Supérieur

This lasts two years and leads to the following qualifications: **Diplôme de Fin d'Etudes Secondaires Techniques** (in sciences, administration and technological subjects), the **Diplôme de Technicien** (in agriculture, geology, chemistry, electrotechnics, mechanics and hotel business). These qualifications enable students to pursue their studies at a higher level in Luxembourg and abroad or to begin work.

Vocational secondary (see **Technical secondary**, *Cycle Moyen*)

On completion of compulsory schooling, apprenticeships in craft subjects last two to two-and-a-half years or three years in small and medium enterprises and industry. They lead to the **Certificat d'Aptitude Technique Professionnelle** (CATP). The **Certificat d'Initiation Technique et Professionnelle** (CITP) is divided into two degrees where the courses are based on a modular system and adapted to the particular skill of the pupils. It may lead to the CATP after the final degree.

Full-time courses are available in business management, secretarial skills, retailing, hotel and catering, agriculture and paramedical professions. Courses last two to three years (five years for the paramedical professions) for pupils aged approximately fourteen.

FURTHER EDUCATION

Until 1979

On completion of five years' intermediate secondary/technical studies, pupils could take a four-year course leading to a **Higher Technician Diploma (Ingénieur Technicien)** at the Ecole Technique. The course was divided into a one-year preparatory course, followed by three years' specialization in civil engineering, mechanics and electrotechnics. Before 1970, this course could be taken by holders of the **Trade and Crafts School Leaving Certificate** or on completion of four years' secondary education.

Since 1979

The Grand-Ducal regulation concerning the establishment of the Institut Supérieur de Technologie (IST) came into effect in September 1979. The IST, which replaces the Ecole Technique, is divided into four technical subject areas: mechanics, electrical engineering, civil engineering and computer science. Students with the following qualifications are admitted to IST: the **Certificat de Fin d'Etudes Secondaires** and the **Certificat de Fin d'Etudes Secondaires Techniques**. The studies at the IST last three years and lead to the **Diplôme d'Ingénieur-Technicien (Higher Technician Diploma)**. This diploma usually allows students to enter professional life; but they may also continue their studies at a foreign university.

HIGHER EDUCATION

There is no university in Luxembourg, only the Centre Universitaire established in 1969. This offers a one-year course (*Cours Universitaires*, formerly called *Cours Supérieurs*) and leads to one of the following qualifications depending on the student's chosen specialization:

Certificat d'Etudes Littéraires et de Sciences Humaines
Certificat d'Etudes Scientifiques
Certificat d'Etudes Juridiques et Economiques

These certificates give access to the second year of courses at all Austrian, French, Belgian, most German, and some Scottish universities.

Before 1983–4, at the Department of Law and Economics (*Département de Droit et des Sciences Economiques*) of the Centre Universitaire de Luxembourg, students could take a two-year course in applied economics and law (*Cycle Court d'Etudes Universitaires Pratiques d'Economie et de Droit*, EUPED), which prepared them for professional life. In 1984, this was replaced by a short (two-year) course offering two distinct sections: computer studies for management and management studies, the latter with the two following sections: banking and trading or business control and management.

The Centre Universitaire also offers postgraduate professional training (*Cours Complémentaires*) in subjects such as teaching and law for Luxembourg nationals. Although no qualification is obtained, Luxembourg students must attend to qualify for certain professions (solicitors, lawyers, teachers).

TEACHER EDUCATION

Primary

On completion of secondary school students follow a three-year course at the <u>Institut Supérieur d'Etudes et de Recherches Pédagogiques</u> (ISERP), which replaces the old <u>Institut Pédagogique</u>, to obtain the **Certificat d'Aptitude Pédagogique** (which replaces the old **Brevet d'Aptitude Pédagogique**). All students have the same curriculum during their first year. In the second and third years they must choose between two sections: pre-primary teacher or primary teacher.

Secondary

Luxembourg teachers can teach in any of the seven years of secondary education and there is no difference between lower and upper secondary teachers.

Teachers of general academic subjects attend their first year course at the <u>Centre Universitaire de Luxembourg</u>; they can complete their degree course in corresponding subjects at a foreign university (three years). Foreign-language teachers must hold a degree from the country where the language concerned is spoken.

Students who take other subjects (religion, art, music, etc.) are trained entirely at foreign universities (four years).

After completion of their degree courses, all future teachers must attend a three-year postgraduate professional training (*Stage Pédagogique*) in Luxembourg and pass a final examination.

Training at the <u>Centre Universitaire de Luxembourg</u> is not necessary for teachers of technical subjects; they attend a three-year course at a university or other institution of higher education abroad, followed by a three-year *Stage Pédagogique* in Luxembourg.

In view of the large number of teachers on the employment market, the Ministry of Education organizes special examinations (**Concours de Recrutement**) from time to time. Only teachers who have passed such an examination can be assured of a permanent posting in the education sector.

The final grade accorded to a teacher includes an assessment of the **Concours de Recrutement**, of the **Examen de Fin d'Etudes Secondaires** and of any studies taken at the <u>Centre Universitaire</u> (the latter being compulsory for teachers of foreign languages and science only).

Macao

Macao is a Chinese territory under Portuguese administration.

Education is free for the first nine years in government-administered schools.

The media of instruction at school level are Portuguese and Chinese and, in higher education, mainly English, although Chinese and Portuguese are used for some courses.

The academic year runs from September to June divided into two semesters.

EVALUATION IN BRITAIN

School

Cambridge Overseas School Certificate (COSC)/**GCE O level** – grades 1–6 generally equated to GCSE standard (grades A, B and C) on a subject-for-subject basis. Grades 7 and 8 may be equated to GCSE standard grades D and E. (For further information see Appendix 2.)

Cambridge Overseas Higher School Certificate (COHSC)/**GCE Advanced** – grades A–E generally equated grade-for-grade to GCE Advanced. (For further information see Appendix 2.)

Further (before 1991)

From the former <u>Polytechnic College of the University of East Asia</u>:

Diploma – generally considered comparable to BTEC National Diploma / N/SVQ level 3 / Advanced GNVQ/GSVQ standard; may be considered to satisfy the general entrance requirements of British higher education institutions.

Higher Diploma – generally considered comparable to a standard between BTEC National Diploma / N/SVQ level 3 / Advanced GNVQ/GSVQ, and BTEC Higher National Diploma / N/SVQ level 4.

Higher

From the former <u>Open College of the University of East Asia</u>:

First year level, English School of Undergraduate Studies – 64 credits may be considered to satisfy the general entrance requirements of the British higher education institutions.

Bachelor degree/Licenciatura – generally considered comparable to British Bachelor (Ordinary) degree standard; students with high grades may be considered for admission to taught Master's programme.

Master's degree – generally considered comparable to British Bachelor (Honours) degree standard.

MARKING SYSTEM

School

Cambridge Overseas Certificates and **GCE** examinations – see Appendix 2.

School and Higher

The <u>Centre for Pre-University Studies</u> and the <u>University of Macao</u> use a grade point average system for all courses as follows:

A	Superior	4.0
A-		3.7
B+		3.3
B	Good	3.0
B-		2.7
C+		2.3
C	Average	2.0
C-		1.7
D+		1.3
D	Pass	1.0
F	Fail	

All courses carry a credit rating in units. These units are earned as long as a grade of D or above is obtained. GPA is calculated by dividing the total number of weighted grade points by the total number of credit units attempted.

The <u>University of Macao</u> grades **Bachelor degrees** as follows:

Cumulative GPA of 3.70 to 4.00	First class honours
Cumulative GPA of 3.20 to 3.69	Second class upper honours
Cumulative GPA of 2.50 to 3.19	Second class lower honours
Cumulative GPA of 2.00 to 2.49	Third class honours

SCHOOL EDUCATION

Schools are classified as *Oficial* or public, *Oficializado* or semi-public and *Privado* or private which follow the language and curricular categories of Portuguese, Portuguese/Chinese and Chinese respectively. The great majority of pupils attend private schools.

This makes Macao's education system varied and complex.

The main sectors of school education are organized as follows:

State schools tend to follow the Portuguese pattern (primary six years, secondary four years, two years matriculation); schools funded by religious bodies follow the pattern of Anglo-Chinese schools in Hong Kong (six years primary, five years secondary, two years for A levels); other schools follow the Taiwanese system similar to the American format (six years primary, six years secondary, followed by an entrance examination for universities in Taiwan); yet others follow the Chinese pattern (five years primary, five years secondary, followed by China's national university entrance examination).

Pre-primary

This pre-school period can cover up to three years.

Primary

This covers four years followed by two years pre-secondary.

Secondary

This cycle normally covers up to six years. Macao does not have system-wide examinations.

The Centre for Pre-University Studies of the University of Macao offers a one year pre-university study programme. This provides form five and equivalent graduates with the opportunity to complete six years of secondary school education. The medium of instruction is primarily English. Graduates of the programme are eligible to sit for the University of Macao admission examination. They may also be entered for **GCSE** and **A level** subjects. On completion of the programme, a certificate of graduation is awarded.

Admission to the programme is based on successful completion of five years secondary education in Macao, good school reports and the headmaster's recommendation. Alternatively, grade E or higher in five subjects including English in the **Hong Kong Certificate of Education Examination** (HKCEE) or equivalent are accepted.

The curriculum is based around one of three subject clusters: the business and humanities cluster, sciences and mathematics cluster and the languages cluster.

Students who do not have the required level of English (mainly those from mainland China and Macao Chinese-medium schools) sit an English placement test to determine how fast they can progress, and if they need to first enrol on the Centre's one year intensive English Programme.

The English programme can be taken as a terminal qualification, for which a Certificate of Completion is awarded to successful candidates. Admission requirements are slightly lower than for the pre-university programme described above, namely four HKCEE passes at grade E or above.

FURTHER EDUCATION (Before 1991)

The former Junior College of the University of East Asia offered the following programmes:

A two-year **Associate degree** course which prepared students for transfer to the second year of the former University College of the University of East Asia;

An intensive one-year course which prepared students for admission to the University College of the University of East Asia. An essential feature of this course was an intensive six-week preparatory period in July/August mainly to raise the standard of students' English.

Admission requirements for both the above courses were satisfactory completion of grade twelve of school education together with five passes in the **Hong Kong Certificate of Education Examination** (HKCEE) or a combination of passes in the HKCEE, the **Hong Kong Higher Level** and the **Hong Kong Advanced-level Examination**.

The former Polytechnic College of the University of East Asia offered the following programmes:

Diploma and **Higher Diploma** courses in computer studies and hotel management: **Diploma** courses lasted two years and **Higher Diplomas** a further year.

Admission to the **Hotel Management Diploma** was completion of grade twelve of school education together with passes in the HKCEE or the **Hong Kong Higher Level Examination** or the **Hong Kong Advanced-level Examination** or a combination of passes in the three examinations.

All the above institutions ceased to exist in 1991. Their functions have been absorbed by the Centre for Pre-University Studies of the University of Macao.

HIGHER EDUCATION

There is one institution of higher education, the University of Macao, which was created from the former University of East Asia (UEA) in 1991. The University of East Asia was founded in 1981 as a privately funded institution. In 1988 it was purchased by the government, and the new University of Macao was created by Decree on 4th February 1991. Its first charter was approved on 3rd February 1992.

The University of Macao offers **Bachelor degrees** lasting four years. Admission is on the basis of the university's admission examinations. In order to sit for this examination, students must have completed form six or equivalent. Individual faculties may have additional requirements.

The medium of instruction for programmes in law, Portuguese language, and translation and interpretation is Portuguese; it is Chinese in the fields of Chinese public administration, education and Chinese language. For all other programmes the medium of instruction is English.

Exemption is given from the admission examinations for certain combinations of **Hong Kong Higher Level Examinations** and, **Hong Kong Advanced Level Examinations** and **GCSE/GCE A levels**.

TEACHER EDUCATION

There is very little teacher training available. The majority of primary teachers are untrained. A course at the University of Macao provides in-service training.

Macao

Most secondary teachers in private schools have degrees, mainly from higher education institutions in China and Taiwan, with some from the Philippines. Teachers with degrees from China teach in secular private schools and those with degrees from Taiwan and the Philippines, in Church-related schools.

Some teachers have been trained through a correspondence teaching programme provided by the South China Normal University in Guangzhou, China.

Former Yugoslav Republic of Macedonia

At the time of writing (March 1994), Slovenia, Croatia and the former Yugoslav Republic of Macedonia have become independent states, while the war in Bosnia-Herzegovina has resulted in a cessation of formal schooling (although some schooling continues as far as feasible).

Compulsory education covers the period of basic education; that is, eight years between ages seven and fifteen.

The medium of instruction is Macedonian.

The academic year runs from September/October to June.

EVALUATION IN BRITAIN

School

Matura (before 1980 from the *Gimnazija*/academic upper secondary course)/
Secondary School Leaving Diploma (before 1980 from a technical secondary school) – may be considered to satisfy the general entrance requirements of British higher education institutions.

Secondary School Leaving Diploma (obtained since 1980) – generally considered comparable to BTEC National Diploma / N/SVQ level 3 / Advanced GNVQ/GSVQ and may be considered to satisfy the general entrance requirements of British higher education institutions.

Higher

Vise Obrazovanje (first-level degree obtained on completion of a two- to three-year course) – generally considered comparable to a standard between GCE Advanced and British Bachelor degree; may be given advanced standing by British higher education institutions.

Visoko Obrazovanja (second-level degree obtained on completion of a four- to six-year course) – generally considered comparable to British Bachelor (Ordinary) degree standard.

Magistar – generally considered comparable to British Master's degree standard.

Doktor nauka – generally considered comparable to British PhD standard.

MARKING SYSTEMS

School

Marking is on the scale 1–5 (maximum), with 2 as the minimum pass-mark.

Higher

Marking is on the scale 5–10 (maximum), with 6 as the minimum pass-mark.

SCHOOL EDUCATION

Pre-primary

Facilities are available in crèches (*detski jasli*) for children up to age three and kinder-gartens (*detski gradinki*) for children aged three to six/seven and (*zabaviste*) for children aged six for pre-elementary education i.e. preparation for entering primary school.

Primary

This period of schooling (at *Osnovno uciliste*) covers eight years from age six/seven. The period is divided into two distinct stages: classes 1–4 (covering five to six subjects, with teaching being carried out by one teacher) and 5–8 (covering ten to fourteen subjects, with teaching being carried out by subject teachers). Classes are unstreamed and based on the comprehensive system. Pupils begin studying foreign languages in the fifth year and may usually choose between English, Russian, German and French. However, in some primary schools pupils begin studying one foreign language in the third year and, in the fifth year, take a second foreign language as well.

The pupils' results from the primary school and selective entrance tests decide whether they can enter the secondary school of their choice.

Secondary

Pupils can choose between general high school (*Gimnazija*), vocational schools (*Ucilista za zanimanja*), technical schools (*Tehnicki ucilista*) and art secondary school (*Umetnicko uciliste*).

The academic cycle covers four years at a *Gimnazija*, of which the first year is common to all pupils. After that they can choose to specialize in science/mathematics or humanities/social studies and languages. The final examination is the **Matura**. In the second half of the fourth year, pupils are supposed to choose one subject they are most interested in, write a project (*maturska tema*) on a particular topic and defend it, and pass a written examination in their mother tongue and literature.

The technical and other vocational schools educate technicians for different professions: medical, financial and other professional staff with secondary education. For instance, medical secondary school (*Sredno medicinsko uciliste*) includes the following branches: medical nurses (*medicinski sestri*); obstetric nurses (*akuserki*); laboratory technicians (*laboratoriski tehnicari*); pharmaceutical technicians (*farmacevtski tehnican*), etc.

In some schools, e.g. construction, agriculture, building mechanization, there are programmes of shorter duration (from several months to three years of training) for different occupations and crafts.

The art secondary school programme lasts four years. Entry is by entrance examination. The first-year programme combines general (academic) subjects and vocational courses of relevance to the arts field. In subsequent years, pupils specialize in either applied arts or fine and performance arts. Art education from the secondary level onwards is also available in colleges.

Entry to higher education is on the basis of the **Secondary Leaving Diploma**, plus entrance examinations (two to three subjects) depending on the educational programme of the faculty concerned.

HIGHER EDUCATION

Higher education is offered at two levels, in two types of institutions: colleges offer short courses of two years' duration, whereas university faculties and institutes offer courses lasting from four to six years.

First-year entrants are taken on for both regular and irregular study programmes in both types of institution. Both types of institution have the right to set their own admission criteria. Generally speaking, applications are welcome from both general and vocational school graduates, but the latter will in practice only be considered for admission to courses which relate to their specialization at the secondary level. Admission to higher education courses is, in any case, competitive.

Upon successful completion of higher education courses at faculties/institutes, students are awarded a diploma with professional title – e.g. engineer, lawyer, teacher, at the lower (college) level; graduate engineer, graduate lawyer, graduate teacher at the higher (faculty/institute) level. The exact duration of studies leading to higher level diplomas depends on the type of faculty.

Some of the Faculties in Macedonia:

> Faculty of Architecture – 4–year studies
> Electro-mechanical Faculty – 5–year studies
> Technological-metallurgical Faculty – 5–year studies
> Faculty of Civil Engineering – 4–year studies
> Faculty of Medicine – 6–year studies
> Faculty of Stomatology – 6–year studies
> Faculty of Agriculture – 4–year studies
> Faculty of Economics – 4–year studies
> Faculty of Law – 4–year studies
> Faculty of Philosophy, History, Pedagogy, etc.
> Faculty of Philology, Macedonian language and literature,
> English etc.
> Faculty for Physical Culture
> Faculty for Musical Art
> Faculty for Theatrical Art
> Faculty of Sciences: Biology, Chemistry, Geography, Mathematics
> Faculty for Tourism, etc.

Specialization, postgraduate and doctoral studies

Each graduate student has the opportunity to specialize in relevant professional fields – e.g. surgery, obstetrics, engineering. Such specialization requires one to five years of practical training.

Postgraduate courses are available. Two years' study followed by research and the writing of a thesis approved by a mentor and publicly defended leads to the award of the academic degree of **Magister** (Master of Science/Master of Arts). A Doctor of Science/Doctor of Philosophy (**Doktor na nauiki**) degree may be obtained after a further approved period of research and the defence of a doctoral dissertation.

The Workers University (*Rabutniski Univerzitet*) offers a great variety of courses for additional education. It does not award degrees but offers special courses leading to a particular qualification.

TEACHER EDUCATION

Primary

Teachers are trained in *Vise skole* (further education establishments) for two years.

Secondary

Teachers are university graduates. Courses last four years.

Madagascar

The following chapter regarding the education system in Madagascar is based on information obtained from the 3rd edition of this Guide, published in 1991, as NARIC has been unable to obtain more recent information.

In 1958 Madagascar was renamed the Malagasy Republic and became an autonomous state within the French community. It gained full independence in June 1960 as the Democratic Republic of Madagascar, comprising the large island of Madagascar and five small island dependencies.

The educational system retains a great deal of French influence and is based on the French pattern, with central control.

In theory, education has been compulsory from the age of six to fifteen since 1959, but in practice this cannot be enforced owing to a shortage of facilities.

The medium of instruction is French and sometimes Malagasy, although English is taught as a subject from the first year of secondary education.

The school year runs from September to July and the academic year from October to July.

EVALUATION IN BRITAIN

School

Baccalauréat de l'Enseignement du Second Degré – generally considered comparable to GCSE standard (grades A, B and C) on a subject-for-subject basis, with the exception of English language.

Higher

DUEL/DUES – may be considered to satisfy the general entrance requirements of British higher education institutions.

Licence – generally considered comparable to a standard between GCE Advanced and British Bachelor degree; may be given advanced standing in British higher education institutions.

Maîtrise – generally considered comparable to British Bachelor degree standard.

MARKING SYSTEM

School and Higher

Subjects are marked on a scale of 0–20 (maximum), 10 being the minimum pass-mark.

16–20	*très bien*	very good
14-15	*bien*	good
12-13	*assez bien*	fair
10-11	*passable*	pass

SCHOOL EDUCATION

Primary

This covers six years from the age of six, divided into three two-year cycles:

> *cours préparatoires*
> *cours élémentaires*
> *cours moyens*

On conclusion of the third cycle, pupils take the examination for the **Certificat d'Etudes Primaires Elémentaires** (CEPE). The medium of instruction during the first two-year cycle is often Malagasy.

Secondary

This covers seven years, divided into a four-year and a three-year cycle. On completion of the four-year cycle of *Enseignement Long* pupils obtain the **Brevet d'Etudes du Premier Cycle** (BEPC). The school years are numbered in descending order i.e. the first year is *Classe Sixième* the second year is *Classe Cinquième*, etc. On completion of the *Classe Première* (i.e. the second year of the three-year upper cycle) pupils take a qualifying examination for entry to the *Classe Terminale* (i.e. third and final year of this cycle). On completion of the *Classe Terminale* pupils take the examinations for the **Baccalauréat de l'Enseignement du Second Degré**. This may be one of three types:

Série	A	– *philosophie-lettres*
	C	– *mathématiques et sciences physiques*
	D	– *mathématiques et sciences naturelles*

depending on the specialization taken by the pupil during the three-year upper secondary cycle.

Enseignement Court: Pupils not wishing to proceed eventually to university may take only the four-year lower secondary course, covering classes 6–3. On conclusion of this cycle pupils obtain the **Brevet Elémentaire**.

The four-year lower secondary cycle may be taken at *Colléges d'Enseignement Général*, but the three-year upper secondary cycle may only be taken at *Lycées*.

Technical secondary

On conclusion of primary education pupils may go on to take a course of technical secondary education. After the four-year lower secondary course pupils obtain the **Brevet d'Etudes Industrielles/Commerciales** (depending on the specialization taken). After the three-year upper secondary course pupils take the examinations for the

Baccalauréat de l'Enseignement Technique in *Série* B, E, F or G.

FURTHER EDUCATION

A three-year course of post-secondary education leads to the **Brevet de Technicien**.

HIGHER EDUCATION

There are six universities. The University of Madagascar, which was established in Antananarivo in 1955 as the Institut des Hautes Etudes and became a university in 1961, was reorganized in 1976 as a decentralized institution with six regional centres. Each of these centres acquired the status of an independent university in 1988, so there are now six universities:

1. Université d' Antananarivo
2. Université d' Antsiranana
3. Université de Fianarantsoa
4. Université de Toamasina
5. Université de Mahajanga
6. Université de Toliara

Each university is independent with its own *'recteur'* (V/C) and awards its own degrees.

The entrance requirement for degree courses is the **Baccalauréat**. There is a two-year broad-based multidisciplinary course common to all students wishing to study letters, science and agriculture. Students have to obtain a minimum number of credit units at the end of each year and then obtain the **Diplôme Universitaire d'Etudes Littéraires** (DUEL) or the **Diplôme Universitaire d'Etudes Scientifiques** (DUES). A year of specialization leads to the **Licence,** and a further year to the **Maîtrise**. If students then successfully present a short thesis they are awarded the **Maîtrise d'Enseignement**.

The **Diplôme d'Etudes Approfondies** (DEA) may be obtained one year after the **Maîtrise**, and the **Diplôme d'Etudes Supérieures** (DES) two years after the **Maîtrise**. Presentation of a thesis then leads to the **Doctorat de Troisième Cycle**.

Law – Students wishing to study law may enter the university without the **Baccalauréat** and after two years obtain the **Capacité en Droit**. This is not a degree, but with this qualification students may apply to study for the **Licence** degree, which takes four years.

Medicine – At the end of the first year students obtain the **Certificat Préparatoire aux Etudes Médicales** (DPEM). The full course leading to the qualification of **Doctorat de Médécin** lasts seven years, plus one year of hospital practice.

Engineering – A two-year programme beyond the **Baccalauréat** leads to the **Diplôme Universitaire de Techniciens Supérieurs en Informatique** (DUTSI) or to the **Diplôme Universitaire d'Etudes Technologiques** (DUET). The **Diplôme d'Ingénieur** requires a further two years after the DUTSI/DUET.

TEACHER EDUCATION

1972–80

Primary·

Pupils with the **Brevet d'Etudes du Premier Cycle** (BEPC) took a course at a *Centre Pédagogique*.

Secondary

To teach at the *Colléges d'Enseignement Général* (i.e. lower secondary) students took a two-year course at an *Institut Pédagogique* from the level of the **Baccalauréat**.

The **Brevet d'Etudes du Premier Cycle** (BEPC) and three years at a teacher training college also allowed students to teach at the lower secondary level.

The **Baccalauréat** and a five-year university degree course with a postgraduate course at a teacher training college allow students to teach at the upper secondary level.

Since 1990

After streamlining in 1990, five regional and two national centres were created for national teacher training.

Malawi

Before independence in 1964, Malawi was known as Nyasaland. Its educational system was closely modelled on the British pattern. However, it possessed few secondary schools and no institutions of higher education. Since independence, the country has expanded its educational facilities. The University of Malawi was established in 1964.

The medium of instruction is Chichewa and English at primary school and English in all secondary and tertiary education institutes.

Education is not compulsory and attendance depends on the parents' ability to pay. Fees charged are for tuition and books.

The school year runs from October to August.

EVALUATION IN BRITAIN

School

Malawi School Certificate of Education (MSCE) **Cambridge Overseas School Certificate** (COSC)	grades 1–6 are generally equated to GCSE standard (grades A, B and C) on a subject-for-subject basis.

Cambridge Overseas Higher School Certificate (COHSC) – generally equated to GCE Advanced standard.

Higher

Bachelor degree – generally considered comparable to a standard between GCE Advanced and British Bachelor degree; may be given advanced standing by British higher education institutions.

Teaching

Bachelor of Education – may be considered for admission to taught Master's degree courses.

MARKING SYSTEMS

School

The **Malawi Certificate of Education** is graded as follows:

1, 2	pass with distinction
3, 4, 5, 6	pass with credit
7, 8	pass
9	fail

For further details of the **Cambridge Overseas School Certificate** (COSC) and **Cambridge Overseas Higher School Certificate** (COHSC) see Appendix 2.

From 1971 to 1981, certificates were issued only to candidates who fulfilled certain requirements concerning groups of subjects passed. From 1982 onwards the **Malawi School Certificate of Education** has been issued to candidates who meet the grouping requirements at one sitting, and the **Malawi General Certificate of Education** to candidates who obtain a pass with credit in one or more subjects but fail to fulfil the grouping requirements.

Higher

Students are assessed throughout the academic year and sit termly and yearly examinations. Course work may constitute up to forty per cent of the final result. Students are generally obliged to pass in all subjects. The grading system is as follows:

75 – 100	distinction
70 – 74	marginal distinction
60 – 69	bare distinction
50 – 59	pass
40 – 49	bare pass
35 – 39	marginal failure
0 – 34	undoubted failure

SCHOOL EDUCATION

Primary

Primary education lasts eight years. The recommended age to start primary education is five years. At the end of standard VIII pupils take the **Primary School Leaving Certificate** (PSLC). Secondary school places are available only for the top fourteen per cent of those who take the PSLC.

Secondary

Secondary education lasts four years. At the end of the second year pupils take the **Junior Certificate of Education Examination** (JCE)/**Junior Secondary School Certificate**. This gives access to certain jobs, some types of non-formal education and the apprenticeship scheme. Successful pupils may also enter form III.

At the end of form IV pupils take the **Malawi School Certificate of Education** (MSCE). Before 1972, most pupils took the **Cambridge Overseas School Certificate**, while a few took the GCE examinations of the Associated Examining Board. From 1972 to 1981, MCE certificates were issued jointly by the Malawi Certificate Examination and Testing Board in Malawi and by the Associated Examining Board in the UK, which was providing professional aid for the development of the Board in Malawi. Since 1982, certificates have been issued in the name of the Malawi Certificate Examination and Testing Board only, but the Associated Examining Board continues to monitor standards. The Kamuzu Academy, Kasungu, and one school in Blantyre offer facilities for children who obtain good results in the MSCE to sit for the **Cambridge Overseas Higher School Certificate**. Holders of this Certificate are admitted to the University of Malawi with one year of advanced standing.

FURTHER EDUCATION

Technical

Various facilities exist for craft and vocational training. Primary and junior-secondary school graduates undergo training at trade training centres for various trade certificates, City and Guilds of London Institute examinations and internal diplomas.

Joint examination arrangements exist between the Malawi Government and City and Guilds for specific vocational areas. Successful candidates receive joint City and Guilds/ Malawi Ministry of Education and Culture certificates. Within this arrangement the first examinations to be conducted entirely by the Malawi Government were held in 1989.

At a higher level the Malawi Polytechnic, one of the constituent colleges of the University of Malawi, offers technician training courses to students who hold the **Junior Secondary School Certificate**. Employed people may upgrade their skills at evening classes. Most of these courses would be below GCSE standard. Students can take preparatory courses for the **Junior Secondary School Certificate** and the **Malawi School Certificate of Education**.

Agricultural

The Ministry of Agriculture runs two-year courses.

HIGHER EDUCATION

The University of Malawi, founded in 1964, is composed of four colleges:

Bunda College of Agriculture at Lilongwe, Chancellor College at Zomba, Malawi Polytechnic at Blantyre, Kamuzu College of Nursing at Lilongwe and Blantyre. Admission is based on the **Malawi School Certificate of Education**, with six credit passes. Mature candidates take a special entrance examination or attend interviews. The University offers three-year DiplomA level courses and four-year General Degree courses. Students can stay on for a fifth Honours year. Bunda College offers a five-year degree in agriculture and Malawi Polytechnic a five-year degree in engineering.

TEACHING EDUCATION

Primary

There are two types of teacher training college: for T3 teachers (junior primary) and T2 teachers (senior primary). T2 colleges admit students with the **Malawi School Certificate of Education**. T3 colleges admit students with the **Junior Certificate of Education**. These colleges run two-year courses at the end of which students obtain the **T2** or **T3 Teachers Certificate**.

The <u>Malawi Institute of Education</u> was established as an in-service training college and curriculum development centre to provide teacher upgrading. 'Introduction courses' based at the centre are intended to give school-leavers the basic skills to act as 'assistant' or 'pupil' teachers.

Secondary

Secondary teacher training is provided at the Faculty of Education at <u>Chancellor College</u>. It offers a four-year educational programme, followed by the fifth year which consists of professional studies and teaching practice. The course leads to the degree of **Bachelor of Education** (BEd)

The **University Certificate of Education** is a one-year course currently offered for graduate teachers with one or more years' teaching experience, which is due to be integrated with the fifth year of the BEd programme.

ADULT EDUCATION

<u>Malawi Polytechnic</u> supervises evening class courses at <u>Lilongwe Technical School</u>. Many courses are aimed at assisting community development.

The Ministry of Agriculture and Natural Resources runs short courses (one to twelve days) for farmers to encourage better agricultural practice.

The Ministries of Agriculture, Community Development, Education and Health provide home economics training at village level.

Plans which existed for the establishment of a rural education centre in each district to provide the basis for various kinds of adult education programmes have recently been implemented.

Malaysia

Owing to the diversity of races, cultures and languages in Malaysia, the government imposes strict control over all areas of education with the aim of fostering Malaysian unity.

No sector of education is compulsory.

In 1956, the *Razak Report* recommended the establishment of a national system of education in which the national language(s) would be the medium of instruction, and a national system was then established by the Education Ordinance of 1957. Until 1967, under the terms of the Federal Constitution, English and Malay were the joint national languages; however, under the National Language Act of 1967, Bahasa Malaysia became the official language and medium of instruction at all levels, although in 1993, the Prime Minister confirmed that the English Language could be used alongside Bahasa Malaysia for the teaching of certain science subjects at undergraduate level and for any subjects at postgraduate level.

The school year normally runs from December to October and the university year from July to March.

EVALUATION IN BRITAIN

School

Penilaian Menengah Rendah (PMR) – generally considered to be below GCSE standard.

Certificate of Unified Examination of the Malaysian Independent Chinese Secondary Schools System (MICSS) – grades A and B (1 to 6) may be considered comparable to GCSE standard (grades A, B and C) on a subject-for-subject basis, with the exception of English language.

Sijil Pelajaran Malaysia (SPM)/**Sijil Pelajaran Malaysia Vokesyenal** (SPMV)/ – grades 1 to 6 generally considered comparable to GCSE standard (grades A, B and C) on a subject-for-subject basis, with the exception of English language.

Sijil Tinggi Persekolahan Malaysia (STPM) – principal level passes are generally considered comparable to GCE Advanced standard on a subject-for-subject basis; may be considered to satisfy the general entrance requirements of British higher education institutions.

Further

Polytechnic Technician Certificate – generally considered to approach BTEC National Diploma / N/SVQ level 3 / Advanced GNVQ/GSVQ standard.

Polytechnic Diploma (from Government-funded polytechnics) (3 year post-SPM/SPVM) awarded after a three-year course – may be considered to satisfy the general entrance requirements of British higher education institutions.

Institut Teknologi MARA Diploma (3 year post-SPM) – generally considered to be slightly above BTEC National Diploma / N/SVQ level 3 / Advanced GNVQ/GSVQ standard, but below BTEC Higher National Diploma / N/SVQ level 4 standard. Some British universities grant one year's advanced standing (second year entry) on to appropriate undergraduate degree programmes where ITM diploma holders have a CGPA of 2.8 or better.

Tunku Abdul Rahman College Certificate (2 year post-SPM) – generally considered to be slightly above BTEC National Diploma / N/SVQ level 3 / Advanced GNVQ/GSVQ standard.

Institut Teknologi MARA Diploma (3 year post-STPM)/**Tunku Abdul Rahman College Diploma** (3 year post-STPM) – generally considered to be slightly above BTEC Higher National Diploma / N/SVQ level 4 standard; could be considered for advanced standing on to appropriate undergraduate programmes.

Higher

Bachelor degree – generally considered comparable to British Bachelor degree standard.

MARKING SYSTEMS

School

Sijil Pelajaran Malaysia (SPM) is graded on a scale of 1 (maximum) to 9.

1		
2	*cemerlang*	distinction
3		
4		
5		
6	*kepujian*	credit
7	*lulus*	pass
8		
9	*gagal*	fail

Certificate of Unified Examinations (MICSS)

A1/A2	distinction
B3/B4/B5/B6	credit
C7/C8	pass
F9	fail

Cambridge Overseas School Certificate and **Cambridge Overseas Higher School Certificate** – see Appendix 2.

Sijil Tinggi Persekolahan Malaysia (STPM) is graded (like GCE Advanced) on a scale A–E.

A
B
C   principal pass
D
E

R   subsidiary (GCSE) pass

G   fail (*gagal*)

Further

MARA Institute of Technology Diploma is marked on a four-point cumulative grade system used by all campuses:

A	4	excellent
B	3.99–3.0	good
C	2.99–2.0	average
D	1.99–1.0	weak
E	0.99–0.0	fail
X	absent with permission or incomplete with permission	
Y	absent without permission.	

Each course earns a specified number of credits, depending on the work involved. Academic achievement is measured by grade points. On the 0–5 point scale, each credit-hour with A earns 4 grade points, B earns 3, C earns 2, D earns 1 and E earns none. The student's grade-point average (GPA) is calculated by dividing the total number of grade points (reached by multiplying the grade point for each course by the credit-hours of the course and then totalling them all) by the total number of credit-hours of enrolment. Students must normally maintain a minimum GPA of 2.0 to remain in good academic standing.

The cumulative grade-point average is the sum total of credit points obtained for all semesters divided by the total number of credit hours attempted for all semesters.

Polytechnics

Marks are awarded on the following basis in each subject studied at the end of each year of study:

A,B,C,D	*lulus*	pass
E	*gagal*	fail
K	*dikecualikan*	exempted

Higher

Degrees are awarded with Honours and the following classifications:

class 1
class 2   division i
              division ii
class 3

Students whose achievement is insufficient for Honours may be awarded Pass degrees.

All universities now follow the semester system, and each student is graded in each subject taken at the end of each semester, using the same grade system as <u>MARA Institute of Technology</u>.

SCHOOL EDUCATION

Primary

This begins at age six and continues for six years (standards 1 to 6). There is a national syllabus in each subject. Pupils are promoted automatically at the end of each year, but a national assessment examination, the **Ujian Percapaian Sekolah Rendah** (UPSR), is held at the end of standard 6.

English as a medium of instruction was finally phased out of primary schools in 1975. The former English-medium schools converted to Malay-medium, but Chinese (Mandarin) and Tamil schools remain. Students from Chinese and Tamil schools have to spend a year in the 'remove class' before entering lower secondary level to prepare them for study in Bahasa Malaysia. English is taught as a compulsory second language in all schools.

Pupils proceed automatically to secondary schooling at the end of standard 6.

Secondary

This covers a possible seven years, divided into three stages:

lower (forms I–III)
upper (forms IV and V)
lower and upper sixth forms.

Lower secondary

This covers three years (forms I to III). Schools offer pupils the opportunity to study subjects in at least one vocational area (commerce, agricultural science, domestic science or industrial arts) in addition to general subjects. At the end of form III pupils take the Malay medium PMR – **Penilaian Menengah Rendah** – formerly the English-medium Lower Certificate Examination (LCE) and known until 1993 as the **Sijil Rendah Pelajaran** (SRP).

Upper secondary

This covers two years (forms IV and V). There is selective entry to this cycle depending on results in the PMR. Pupils with the best results are offered places in academic schools, in either arts or science streams, while those with lower grades attend technical or vocational schools. Vocational schools are, however, enjoying increasing popularity among abler students. The great majority of pupils are enrolled in academic schools with less than ten per cent in technical and vocational schools. At the end of this cycle pupils take the Malay-medium **Sijil Pelajaran Malaysia** (SPM) which has replaced the English-medium Malaysia Certificate of Education (MCE). Both the MCE and SPM were drawn up by the University of Cambridge Local Examinations Syndicate (UCLES). Since 1978, however, responsibility has been given to the new Malaysian Examinations Syndicate, and Cambridge involvement is now minimal. A new English-language syllabus emphasizing communication skills has been introduced. This syllabus, known previously as English 122 and now as English 322, is not recognized outside Malaysia. Students can still take the Cambridge English-language **O level** (previously English 121, now English 1119) as an additional subject, and many opt to do so, particularly those who wish to study overseas. (For further information on this examination see Appendix 2.)

Technical/vocational secondary

Pupils not obtaining high enough marks in the PMR or not wishing to proceed to an academic school attend a vocational, agricultural or technical school for two years. These schools provide a general education with the opportunity to choose at least one vocational course in engineering, commerce, home economics or agriculture. Courses culminate in the **Sijil Pelajaran Malaysia Vokesyenal** (SPMV), the Malaysian Vocational Education Certificate.

This Certificate is equivalent to SPM for purposes of employment in government. Holders of the SPVM may be accepted for a polytechnic diploma course in Malaysia, if they have good grades.

Sixth forms/pre-university

There is selective entry to sixth forms based on the results of the SPM. At the end of the second year pupils take the Malay-medium **Sijil Tinggi Persekolahan Malaysia** (STPM), usually in four subjects plus a general paper (*Kertes Am*). This examination has replaced the English-medium **Cambridge Overseas Higher School Certificate**.

Pre-university courses are post-SPM courses offered by universities as an alternative access route to science-based degree programmes to that provided by the sixth forms.

The Malaysian Independent Chinese Secondary Schools System (MICSS) schools are the largest group of private secondary institutions. They offer a six-year programme leading to the internal **MICSS Unified Examination**. The main medium of instruction is Chinese though English and Bahasa Malaysia are compulsory subjects. The **Certificate** of the MICSS is accepted for university admission purposes in Taiwan, China and Singapore. It is not recognized in Malaysia, and students often take the SPM as well, unless they intend to continue their education overseas.

FURTHER EDUCATION

There are a number of institutions offering certificates, diplomas and professional qualifications. These include:

MARA Institute of Technology (Institut Teknologi MARA) (ITM)

The Institute, established in 1965, provides training for Malays. It has campuses throughout the country including Sabah and Sarawak. A wide variety of subjects is offered including engineering, accountancy, law, management, architecture, computing, art and design and library science. Most courses are three years post-SPM level leading to an internally assessed diploma. There are also three-year post-STPM level internal diploma courses. These are regarded by the government and local professional bodies as equivalent to first degrees. A range of courses for external, including British, professional examinations are offered for students with STPM. The school of library science offers a three-year diploma for students with STPM.

Tunku Abdul Rahman College (TARC)

Founded in 1969 the College is jointly funded by private sources and the government. The vast majority of its students are Chinese. It offers pre-university studies, two-year post-SPM certificate courses, three-year post-STPM diploma courses and courses leading to external, including British, professional qualifications.

Polytechnics

Polytechnics come under the Technical and Vocational Education Division of the Ministry of Education. They offer technical training and the vast majority of their students are Malays. They offer two-year post-SPM/SPMV certificate courses and three year diploma courses.

A growing number of institutions in the public and private sectors offer courses leading to a variety of external qualifications, particularly in business and commerce, electrical engineering, computer programming and information processing. Such qualifications include those awarded by the City and Guilds of London Institute, the Business and Technician Education Council, the London Chamber of Commerce and Industry, Pitman Examinations Institute, the Institute of Data Processing Management etc.

HIGHER EDUCATION

This is offered mainly by seven national universities and the independent International Islamic University. Entry to first degree courses is usually based on STPM results, although some students are accepted through the universities pre-degree programmes. **Bachelor degree** courses normally last three to four years except for those in medicine and architecture which take five to six years.

Postgraduate facilities are available leading to postgraduate diplomas, **Master's degrees** and **PhDs**.

A new university has been established in Kuching, the state capital of Sarawak. This university (the first in Sarawak) will also have a medical faculty at Sarawak general hospital in Kuching, and a branch campus at Bintulu.

The government has announced plans to establish a new university in Sabah as well as three more universities in Peninsula Malaysia – one in Ipoh (Perak) based on the branch campus of Universiti Sains Malaysia situated there, one concentrating on teacher education and an Open University.

THE PRIVATE SECTOR

This has expanded rapidly since 1990, with many new private colleges being established, teaching in the English medium and offering a wide range of courses leading to professional qualifications and overseas degrees through twinning arrangements with foreign universities. At present the government insists that part of all undergraduate degree courses are studied overseas although a revision of the Universities and Colleges Acts is likely to occur in late 1994 which would allow the establishment of branch campuses of overseas universities in Malaysia teaching full undergraduate degrees in English. Full taught **Master's degrees** (especially MBAs) are already offered at many private colleges.

TEACHER EDUCATION

Primary/lower secondary

Training is by means of a two-and-a-half-year post-SPM course at a teacher training college leading to a **Teaching Certificate**.

Upper secondary/sixth forms

Training is by means of a one-year postgraduate course leading to a **Diploma in Education**.

Mali

The medium of instruction is French.

The academic year runs from October to June.

EVALUATION IN BRITAIN

School

Baccalauréat and **(Technical) Baccalauréat** – is generally considered comparable to GCSE standard (grades A, B and C) on a subject-for-subject basis, with the exception of English language.

Further

Diploma – four-year courses from <u>Ecole National d'Ingénieurs</u>, <u>Institut Polytechnic Rural</u> and <u>Ecole Nationale d'Administration</u> generally considered comparable to BTEC Higher National Diploma / N/SVQ level 4.

Diplôme de Technicien Supérieur/Sciences Appliquées – generally considered comparable to a BTEC Higher National Diploma / N/SVQ level 4.

Teaching

Diplôme de l'Ecole Normale Supérieure – generally considered comparable to British Bachelor degree standard.

MARKING SYSTEMS

School

Baccalauréat (both options) and school education is graded on a scale of 0–20 (maximum), with 10 as the minimum pass-mark.

16–20	*très bien*	very good
14–15	*bien*	good
12–13	*assez bien*	quite good/fair
10–11	*passable*	satisfactory/pass
8–9	*médiocre*	mediocre
6–7	*faible*	weak
3–5	*très faible*	very weak
0–2	*nul*	zero

Higher

Generally the same grading system as above, except that the pass-mark is 12.

Ecole Nationale d'Ingénieurs

0–5 (maximum), with 3 as the minimum pass-mark.

SCHOOL EDUCATION

Primary

Primary education *(enseignement fondamental)* covers nine years. This is divided into two cycles of six years (classes 1 to 6) and three years (classes 7 to 9). On completion of class 6, pupils sit for a test introduced in 1970 which determines whether they continue into the general academic or vocational streams of the second cycle of primary education or terminate their education. Pupils are awarded the **Certificat de Fin d'Etudes du Premier Cycle de l'Enseignement Fondamental** (CFEPCF).

Pupils who successfully complete the full nine years of *Enseignement Fondamental* receive the **Diplôme d'Etudes Fondamentales** (DEF).

According to the results of the **Diplôme d'Etudes Fondamentales** and certain other factors, students are streamed into academic, technical, agricultural, or teacher training institutions; they may also leave.

Secondary

Academic

This covers three years (classes 10 to 12). This cycle is known as *Enseignement Secondaire.*

In class 10, pupils are divided into an arts stream (*10e Lettres*) and a science stream (*10e Sciences*). Arts stream subjects are: French language; French and Negro-African literature; English; German or Russian or Arabic; history; geography; and some minor subjects. In the final two years of the secondary cycle (classes 11 and 12), pupils may opt for one of the following specializations culminating in the corresponding **Baccalauréat**:

sciences humaines (SH)	social sciences
langues littérature (LL)	modern languages
sciences biologiques (SB)	biological sciences
sciences exactes (SE)	physical sciences

Four major subjects are studied in each stream, depending on the specialization, but French, English and mathematics are common to all specializations.

On completion of class 12, pupils sit for the **Mali Baccalauréat.** There are two types of **Baccalauréat**: the **Baccalauréat Option Malienne** and the **Baccalauréat Option Enrangére,** which is intended for foreigners and for Malian children who have had a large part of their education outside Mali. It is taken in one of four specializations (series).

A	*lettres et langues*	literature/languages
B	*sciences économiques*	economics and social sciences
C	*mathématiques et physiques*	mathematics and physical sciences
D	*mathématiques et sciences de la nature*	mathematics and natural sciences

Technical/vocational

As an alternative to the academic schools, students may enter the <u>Lycée Technique</u> which prepares them for the technical **Baccalauréat** in one of three fields:

Mathématiques techniques et industrie (MTI)
Mathématiques techniques et génie civil (MTGC)
Mathématiques techniques et économie (MTE).

Holders of the **Diplôme d'Etudes Fondamentales** may also attend a *Centre de Formation Professionnelle* where two-year courses lead to the qualification of **Certificat d'Aptitude Professionnelle** (CAP).

The technical *Lycées* no longer offer technician-training programmes. These are offered instead by the <u>Ecole Centrale pour l'Industrie, le Commerce et l'Administration</u>. Courses take four years and lead to the qualification of **Brevet de Technicien**.

Holders of the **Baccalauréat** may attend the <u>Ecole des Hautes Etudes Pratiques</u> for two years; there they receive the qualification of **Diplôme de Technicien Supérieur** in business studies, accountancy or as bilingual secretaries (French/English).

There is also an agricultural *Lycée* which offers three to four-year courses.

HIGHER EDUCATION

Mali has no university. Post-secondary education is continued at eleven institutes of higher education, according to specialization.

– <u>Ecole Normale Supérieure</u> (see **TEACHER EDUCATION**)
– <u>Ecole Nationale d'Ingénieurs</u> (1963)
– <u>Ecole Nationale de Medicine et de Pharmacie</u> (1968)
– <u>Institut Polytechnique Rural de Katibougou</u> (1966)
– <u>Ecole des Hautes Etudes Pratiques</u> (EHEP)
– <u>Ecole Nationale des Postes et Télécommunications</u> (1969)
– <u>Institut d'Ophtalmology Tropicale de l'Afrique</u>
– <u>Institut Marchoux</u> (leprosy)
– <u>Institut Supérieur pour la Formation et la Recherche Appliquée</u>

Students entering the <u>Ecole Normale Supérieure</u> (see also **TEACHER EDUCATION**) choose to specialize in a number of subjects. Because most of those who complete the course formerly entered the teaching profession all students undertake some teacher training.

The <u>Ecole Nationale d'Ingénieurs</u>, formerly known as the <u>Ecole Technique Supériéure</u>, was created in 1939 and offers four-year courses in electro-mechanical engineering, civil engineering, geology and topography for holders of the **Baccalauréat** in a science or the technical **Baccalauréat**. Successful graduates are awarded the **Diplôme d'Ingénieur** in the appropriate field.

The <u>Institut Polytechnique Rural de Katibougou</u> offers courses in agriculture, stockraising, forestry, and veterinary medicine and animal husbandry. Entrance is by competitive examination for holders of the **Baccalauréat**. Students can follow a two-year programme leading to the **Diplôme de Technicien Supérieur** or a **Sciences Appliquées**. A further three years beyond the **Diplôme d'Ingénieur** leads to the **Diplôme de Docteur-Ingénieur ès Sciences**.

The medical school, the <u>Ecole Nationale de Medicine et de Pharmacie</u>, offers a five-year course for holders of the **Baccalauréat**. It is affiliated to the <u>Faculty of Medicine, Marseille University, France</u>. On completion of the course, students must do one practice year before being awarded the **Diplôme de Docteur en Médecine/Pharmacie**.

The <u>Ecole des Hautes Etudes Pratiques</u> offers two-year courses in secretarial work, accountancy and business management.

The <u>Ecole Nationale d'Administration</u> provides four-year courses to train senior administrators for government service, in economics, public administration and management/legal science.

The <u>Institut Supérieur pour la Formation et la Reserche Appliquée</u> provides postgraduate programmes: entrance is based on possession of a **Bacc + 4 yrs Diplôme**. Two years of study lead to the **Diplôme d'Etudes Approfondies** (DEA); three years of study followed by a thesis to the **Doctorat Malien**.

TEACHER EDUCATION

Primary

Teacher training for teachers of the first six classes takes place at regional *Instituts Pedagogiques d'Enseignement General* (IPEGs). The course runs for four years (full-time) for holders of the **Diplome d'Etudes Fondamentales** and consists of general education, pedagogy, child psychology and teaching practice. Before 1969 this was a one-year course.

Training for teachers of classes 7 to 9 takes place in the *Ecoles Normales Secondaires* which run two-year courses for holders of the **Baccalauréat**. Students specialize in one of four areas: French; history and geography; mathematics; physics and chemistry; natural sciences, agriculture and animal husbandry; languages (English); art and music.

Secondary

Intending teachers of classes 10 to 12 attend the <u>Ecole Normale Supérieure</u>, which runs four-year courses for holders of the **Baccalauréat** who have passed an entrance examination. Graduates of the course receive a **Diplôme de l'Ecole Normale Supérieure**. Mature students who are already **Enseignement Fondamental** teachers may gain entry by way of a competitive entrance examination, the **Concours Professionnel d'Entrée.**

Malta

Education is governed by the Education Act (1988), which is the latest in a series of such acts and is the responsibility of the Minister of Education.

The state provides free education in all its schools, from kindergarten (at three years old), through to university or further education institutions, with the law requiring at least one primary school in each town or village. A number of licensed private schools also exist, providing education from kindergarten level (generally at three years old) to university entrance examinations. The state provides a subsidy to licensed secondary schools and sixth form colleges, which offer free education; private schools at other levels are fee-paying.

The Director General of Education is charged by law with the duty to publish and enforce a National Minimum Curriculum at all levels of the education system. State schools are centrally organized, and all students follow a common curriculum using centrally selected textbooks, but teachers can exercise considerable freedom in their choice of teaching methodologies.

Education is compulsory between the ages of five and sixteen, but kindergarten provision is available for children aged three years and over, and post-sixteen education is also available for suitably qualified students most of whom receive training grants from the state. Enrolment between the compulsory ages is nearly a hundred per cent, and over forty per cent of students receive some form of post-sixteen education.

In all state institutions, the academic year starts in mid-September and ends in mid-July, with holiday periods at Christmas and Easter. Private schools and the University normally have a slightly different academic year.

All schools teach the Maltese and English languages.

At the University and post-secondary schools, instruction is carried out in English.

EVALUATION IN BRITAIN

School

Matriculation (M) / Secondary Education Certificate – generally considered comparable to GCSE standard.

Intermediate Examination (IM) – generally considered comparable to Advanced Supplementary level.

Advanced Matriculation (AM) – generally considered comparable to GCE Advanced standard; may be considered to satisfy the general entrance requirements of British higher education institutions.

Higher

General degree – generally considered comparable to British Bachelor (Ordinary) degree standard.

Honours degree – generally considered comparable to British Bachelor (Honours) degree standard.

Master's degree – considered comparable to a British Master's degree.

MARKING SYSTEMS

School

GCE examinations, and all other UK examinations taken in Malta, are marked as in Britain.

The **Matriculation** and **Secondary Education Certificate** examinations offered by the University of Malta are marked as follows on a seven point scale: grades 1 (maximum) – 7 signifying a pass and Un – Unclassified. **Advanced** and **Intermediate Matriculation** examinations are marked on a six point scale; grades A (maximum) – E signifying pass and Un–Unclassified.

Further

Certificates issued on completion of the following courses at specialized training centres are recognized by the University of Malta as equivalent to GCE Advanced standard: secretarial studies; industrial electronics; architects' assistant and draughtsmen.

Higher

First degrees are classified as follows:

General degrees: first division, second division (upper), second division (lower), third division/pass.

Honours degrees: first class, second class (upper), second class (lower), third class/pass.

SCHOOL EDUCATION

Primary

Primary schooling is divided into two cycles of three years each from age five, with children attending the primary school in their town or village. In the first cycle, children are unstreamed; national examinations at the end of each year of the second cycle generally determine promotion and/or educational stream.

The primary curriculum includes: Maltese, English, mathematics, religious instruction, social studies, geography, history, science, physical education, art and handicrafts, music and singing.

Primary education is the responsibility of a Director of Education, who is also responsible for special education (for children with various types of disabilities and/or behavioural problems).

No formal certification of primary education exists.

Secondary

There are two types of secondary education: junior lyceums, entry into which depends on success at a national qualifying examination, and area secondary schools catering for the rest of primary school leavers except the weakest students. Both types of secondary school offer a five-year course, divided into a two-year orientation cycle followed by a three-year cycle of specialization.

In the first cycle, students in both types of school follow a common curriculum in Maltese, English, a foreign language, religious education, mathematics, integrated science, history, geography, social studies, physical education, craft (boys), home economics (girls), needlework (girls). In the second cycle, students follow a common core together with two or three optional subjects. The common core consists of Maltese, English, a foreign language, religious education, mathematics, physics, social studies and physical education. A broad selection of optional subjects or electives is available.

Students in secondary school are usually streamed by ability within the first cycle but through electives within the second. They are assessed by means of school-based, half-yearly examinations and by national examinations annually. Careers guidance is available in all schools.

At the end of their secondary education, students take **GCE/IGCSE Ordinary level** examinations of British Boards or the **Secondary Education Certificate** examinations. There are four state-run upper lyceums and three private sixth forms which prepare students for university entrance. Entrance into the upper lyceums and sixth forms requires passes in six **GCE O level** subjects (including Maltese, English, mathematics and physics). Students are paid a training grant (roughly one-third of the national minimum wage) and are provided with work experience for one month each year, with an extension of one month at the student's request.

Upper lyceum and sixth form courses prepare students for **GCE Advanced** examinations of British boards or the **Advanced Matriculation** examination (AM) of the University of Malta. A wide range of subjects are available.

Technical secondary

At the end of the first secondary cycle, students can opt to continue their education in trade schools, which offer technical education at craft level with a heavy vocational bias. Trade school courses are offered in a wide range of trades and last three or four years. The first year, designed on the module system, prepares students for specialized trade training from the second year.

Students in trade schools are assessed by means of school-based, half-yearly examinations and national examinations annually. The results of the assessment are used to help guide students in their choice of trade. A school-leaving certificate is issued by the head of the school.

Students who successfully finish their trade education can enrol in the Extended Skills Training Scheme, which provides an apprenticeship scheme on a block-release basis.

Planned reform of university entrance qualifications

From October 1997, the new **Matriculation Certificate** will be the main entry qualification at the University of Malta, replacing the current requirements of three **A levels** or **Advanced Matriculation** and five **O levels** or **Secondary Education Certificate**.

Under the revised structure, subjects will be offered at advanced and intermediate levels, and will be allocated into groups. Two subjects will be taken at advanced level and three at intermediate.

The overall grade of the **Matriculation Certificate** will be based on the performance in the five subjects taken and in Systems of Knowledge. The certificate will be awarded to candidates who obtain a pass in at least one of the subjects from each of three groups and in Systems of Knowledge. It will indicate an overall grade given as A–C. This **Matriculation Certificate** will satisfy the general entrance requirements of the University of Malta as from October 1996.

The level and syllabi of the new Advanced level will be identical to the present **Advanced Matriculation**.

FURTHER EDUCATION

There are two technical institutes: one specializes in electrical and telecommunications engineering and the other in mechanical and automobile engineering. Entry is generally dependent on successful completion of secondary education, with some courses requiring passes in a number of **GCE O levels** or **Secondary Education Certificate** examinations, (usually English, mathematics and physics). The institutes offer courses at both craft and technician level, leading to City and Guilds of London Institute examinations.

In addition, there are a number of specialized training centres, offering a broad range of vocational training in industrial electronics, precision engineering and tool-making, heavy plant maintenance, art and design, nursing and health care, hairdressing and beauty therapy, hotel management and catering and secretarial studies. Entry is dependent on successful completion of secondary education, but actual entry requirements vary with the type of course applied for. Each training centre issues its own certificate, but some students may enter for British examinations when this is considered appropriate or necessary.

HIGHER EDUCATION

The University of Malta is an autonomous institution mainly funded through a government subvention. There are ten main faculties: theology; law; medicine and surgery (including pharmacy); dental surgery; arts; science; education; economics, management and accounts; electrical and mechanical engineering; architecture and civil engineering. There are also a number of institutes, mostly interdisciplinary, in which the university seeks to concentrate its strengths. These include the institutes of agriculture, forensic studies, gerontology, health care, social welfare and youth studies.

Entry into degree courses requires three **Advanced level** passes (or the equivalent), two of which must be at grade C or higher, together with a number of **GCE O levels** or **Secondary Education Certificate** examinations (generally five). Students are prepared for **General** (three-year) and **Honours** (four-year) degrees.

The Faculty of Law at the University of Malta has restructured its Law studies, and in 1993 began offering a three-year course leading to a BA degree in Law and Humanistic studies, successful completion of which enables the student to progress onto a three year postgraduate course leading to the **Doctorate of Law** (LLD). This qualification is considered as a professional Doctorate equivalent to an academic degree at Master's level.

Students can prepare for **Master's** and **Doctorate** degrees, usually by research and submission of a thesis. The Faculties of Law and of Medicine and Surgery offer doctorate courses, the period of study in medicine being five years, in law six years. In addition postgraduate studies lead to MPhil and PhD degrees on a similar basis to British research qualifications. External examiners are involved in the moderation of final examinations.

TEACHER EDUCATION

Primary and secondary

The Education Act (1988) formally recognized teaching as a profession, and a warrant issued by the Minister of Education is a necessary prerequisite to employment in both state and private schools. Temporary warrants are also issued, valid for one year renewable annually.

The minimum professional qualifications for teachers are a **Bachelor of Education** (BEd) degree of the University of Malta or a **Master's** (or higher) **degree** of a recognized university. Regulations permit the issuing of a permanent warrant to teachers who had completed a professional teacher training course at a Maltese College of Education before 1988.

The **BEd degree** of the University of Malta requires students to major in a specific curriculum area (e.g. mathematics) or a particular age group (e.g. early and middle years), together with educational studies. The University also offers a course leading to the award of a **Postgraduate Certificate in Education** (PGCE).

The teaching complement of the Department of Education consists of teachers (university graduates with either a BEd, MEd or PGCE), instructors (in trade subjects but also in other curriculum areas/age groups when a shortage of professional staff exists) and kindergarten assistants. Instructors and kindergarten assistants receive in-service training organized by the Department in conjunction with the Faculty of Education.

In-service training for all other teachers is also organized on a regular basis, often with the participation of overseas specialists.

Mauritania

Mauritania, once a French colony, became independent in 1960. Formal education was introduced in Mauritania by the French in 1905. Since independence the Ministry of Education has implemented various reforms to the education system. Both public (government) and private schools operate in Mauritania.

In 1963 a national policy of bilingualism was introduced in schools. French and Arabic became the media of instruction. However, since then, Arabic has been given greater prominence in the education system. In the first two years of primary (*fondamental*) school, Arabic is taught to all Mauritanian pupils. From the third year Arab children have Arabic as the medium of instruction whereas Pulaar, Sooninke and Wolof children have the choice between Arabic and French.

There is no compulsory period of education.

The academic year runs from October to June.

EVALUATION IN BRITAIN

School

Brevet d'Etudes du Premier Cycle – generally considered to be below GCSE standard.

Diplôme de Bachelier de l'Enseignement du Second Degré (Baccalauréat) – generally considered to be above GCSE standard; may be considered for admission to access/bridging courses.

Higher

Maîtrise – generally considered comparable to British Bachelor degree standard.

Diplôme d'Etudes Universitaires Générales (DEUG) – may be considered to satisfy the general entrance requirements of British higher education institutions.

Teaching

CAPES – generally considered comparable to British Bachelor degree standard.

MARKING SYSTEM

School and Higher

Marking is on scale of 0 – 20 (maximum) with 10 as the pass-mark.

16 – 20	*très bien*	very good
14 – 15	*bien*	good
12 – 13	*assez bien*	fairly good
10 – 11	*passable*	pass
0 – 9	*échec*	fail

Candidates with 9/20 may be passed by the examination committee or board if term/year work and attendance are good.

SCHOOL EDUCATION

Pre-primary

The facilities for pre-primary education are very limited.

Primary

Primary education (*Ecole Fondamentale*) lasts six years, theoretically from age six, but owing to limited facilities, some children may not start school until age eight. It leads to the **Certificat d'Etudes Primaires** (CEP).

Secondary

Secondary school lasts six years and is divided into three years' lower secondary (*Collège*) – first cycle, and three years' upper secondary (*Lycée*) – second cycle. The years are numbered from first to sixth. There is a special entrance examination (**Concours d'Entrée en 1ère Année Secondaire et Technique**) akin to the former 11-plus examination in the United Kingdom.

Lower

This cycle leads to the **Brevet d'Etudes du Premier Cycle** (BEPC).

At the end of this cycle students are passed according to their yearly work average (10/20 or above required).

Upper

According to their performance in the different subjects, successful students are streamed from the fourth year into one of the following specializations:

A – arts/literature
C – mathematics, physics and chemistry
D – natural sciences

The second cycle ends in the **Baccalauréat de l'Enseignement du Second Degré** (Bac A; Bac C; Bac D).

HIGHER EDUCATION

There is one university, the Université de Nouakchott which opened in 1986. It has two faculties: the Faculty of Letters and Humanities and the Faculty of Law and Economics. Two years' university study lead to the **Diplôme d'Etudes Universitaires Générales** (DEUG); two more years lead to the **Maîtrise**. Postgraduate and doctoral diplomas are completed abroad.

There are five other institutions of higher education:

– the <u>Ecole Nationale d'Administration</u> (1966);

– the <u>Institut Supérieur Scientifique</u> (1986), offering courses in mathematics, physics, chemistry, biology and geology;

– the <u>Institut Supérieur des Sciences</u>, founded in 1970 as <u>Ecole Normale Supérieure</u>, which acquired its present title in 1986;

– the <u>Centre Supérieur d'Enseignement Technique</u>, founded in 1981 and offering courses in mechanical and electrical engineering;

– the <u>Ecole Nationale de Formation et de Vulgarisation Agricole</u>.

TEACHER EDUCATION

Primary

Holders of the BEPC undertake a three-year course at one of the *Ecoles Normales des Instituteurs* (ENI). Holders of the **Baccalauréat** diploma undertake a one-year course. Both courses lead to the **Diplôme de Fin d'Etudes Normales** (DFEN). There is an entrance examination for both courses.

Successful teacher trainees become primary school teachers (*Instituteurs*).

Secondary

Since 1971 the <u>Ecole Normale Supérieure</u> (ENS) has trained first and second-cycle teachers. In 1983 the <u>Centre de Formation des Professeurs du Premier Cycle</u> (CFPPC) was created specially for the training of first-cycle teachers, the ENS taking care of the second-cycle training course.

Finally, with the suppression of the first-cycle training in Mauritania in 1986, the CFPPC became the new ENS.

The following are allowed to sit for the entrance examination at the ENS:

a – for a two-year course:

first-cycle teachers from the field (with not less than three years of experience);

holders of the DEUG or an equivalent diploma;

b – for a one-year course (mainly pedagogical):

holders of the **Maîtrise** or an equivalent diploma.

The end-of-course examination leads to the **Certificat d'Aptitude de Professeur de l'Enseignement Secondaire** (CAPES).

Mauritius

Since the Education (Amendment) Act 1991, there is now a compulsory period of schooling for children from 5 to 12 years old.

The medium of instruction is officially English, but French and Creole are used at some institutions.

The academic year at schools lasts from January to November and at the University from September to July.

EVALUATION IN BRITAIN

School

Overseas School Certificate (University of Cambridge Local Examination Syndicate) and **GCE O level** (Associated Examining Board, University of London School Examinations Board, University of Oxford Delegacy of Local Examinations) – generally equated to GCSE standard. For details of grading see Appendix 2.

Overseas Higher School Certificate (University of Cambridge Local Examinations Sydicate) and **GCE A level** (Associated Examining Board, University of Oxford Delegacy of Local Examinations, University of London School Examinations Board) – generally equated grade-for-grade to subjects at GCE Advanced standard. For further information see Appendix 2.

Brevet de Technicien – generally considered comparable to City and Guilds of London Institute (C & G) Certificate Part II.

Brevet d'Aptitude Professionelle – generally considered comparable to C&G Certificate Part III.

Higher

Bachelor degrees – generally considered comparable to British Bachelor degree standard. Students with good grades may be considered for admission to taught postgraduate courses.

MARKING SYSTEMS

School

Overseas School Certificates and **GCE examinations**: See Appendix 2.

Cambridge Overseas Higher School Certificate is graded:

A–E	pass
S	subsidiary pass
F	fail

Higher

Bachelor degrees are classified:

class I
class II division i
class II division ii
class III or pass.

SCHOOL EDUCATION

Pre-primary

There are just over 700 private registered pre-primary units and 100 pre-primary classes attached to government primary schools.

Primary

This covers six years for children from age five.

The curriculum covers English, French, mathematics, science, geography, hygiene, civics, physical education, creative arts, environment and music. On completion of standard 6, pupils take the examinations for the **Certificate of Primary Education**. This certifies successful completion of primary education and determines the placement of pupils at secondary schools. Until 1979, pupils took the **Primary School Leaving Certificate**.

Secondary

This covers a possible seven years: forms I to V leading to the examinations for the **Cambridge Overseas School Certificate/GCE O level**, followed by two years in form VI leading to the examinations for the **Cambridge Overseas Higher School Certificate/GCE A level.**

Technical secondary

The Technical Institute was established in 1959. It offered pupils the opportunity to specialize from the third year in either a commercial stream (including shorthand, typing and accountancy) leading to the examinations of the Royal Society of Arts, or a technical stream (including general science, technical drawing, metalwork and woodwork). Compulsory subjects for each stream were English, French and mathematics. In 1965, the Technical Institute merged with a government secondary school to form the John Kennedy College offering three streams: science, commercial and technical.

The Lycée Polytechnique Sir Guy Forget was set up in January 1982 to train students from form III at technician or craft level. Technical courses last four years and lead to the **Brevet de Technicien**, while craft courses last three years and lead to the **Brevet d'Aptitude Professionelle**.

The Mahatma Gandhi Institute was set up in 1970 as a joint venture of the Government of India and the Government of Mauritius as a centre of studies of Indian culture and traditions and to promote education and culture in general. It has courses leading to diplomas and degrees in languages, music and dance and fine arts. It runs teacher training courses with the Mauritius Institute of Education and **Bachelor of Arts degree** in Hindi with the University of Mauritius.

The Industrial and Vocational Training Board (IVTB) is a parastatal organization established by Act of Parliament in 1988. It became operational in 1989 and is funded by a grant from government and a levy paid by the employers. The purpose of the board is to promote training at all levels, in all sectors and by any suitable means. It has identified the needs for training and has started courses since 1989 in the following sectors/occupational skills: agro-industry agriculture, bakery, building construction, clothing industry, electronics, footwear and leather craft, fashion and design, furniture making, hotel and catering, information technology, jewellery, plastics industry, precision engineering, tool and dye making and printing.

Since January 1993, all Industrial Trade Training Centres (ITTCs) are operating under the aegis of the IVTB.

FURTHER EDUCATION

Courses are available in paramedical subjects (e.g. nursing, medical laboratory technology, and engineering) leading to the **Ordinary Technicians Diploma** (OTD) after two to three years' post-**GCE O level** study.

HIGHER EDUCATION

There is one university, the University of Mauritius, established in 1965. It has five schools; agriculture, engineering, law and management, social studies and humanities, and science. The normal entrance requirement for degree courses is a minimum of two **GCE A levels**.

Courses leading to **Bachelor of Arts/Science** degrees with Honours last three years; those leading to **Bachelor of Technology** degrees with Honours last four years. The University also offers two, three and four-year post-**GCE O level** and **A level** courses leading to certificates and diplomas in a variety of fields.

The **Master of Philosophy** is awarded after a minimum of two years' postgraduate study and the **Doctorate** (PhD) after a minimum of three years.

There are postgraduate degrees awarded in all the faculties.

TEACHER EDUCATION

The Mauritius Institute of Education provides various training courses.

Primary

A two-year course or a three-year part-time course from the level of the **Cambridge Overseas School Certificate/GCE O level** or **Cambridge Overseas Higher School Certificate/GCE A level** leads to a **Teacher's Diploma**. A two-year part-time course leads to a **Teacher's Certificate**.

Secondary

Teachers should hold a university degree or a non-graduate professional qualification for teaching but not all do.

The Institute runs a one-year full-time/two-year part-time **Postgraduate Certificate in Education** and a two-year part-time **Certificate in Educational Administration**.

Mexico

Since 1989, the Mexican education system has undergone considerable reforms with changes to the constitution and the formulation of a new law for education. These seek to define the role of public education, re-examine the administration system of education and look again at curricula contents from nursery school to higher education and indigenous and technical education.

Education in Mexico has traditionally been centralized by the federal government, through the Ministry of Education (SEP). So, by 1992 the federal government had direct control of more than 117,000 schools, offering services to approximately 16 million students at all levels (around 65 per cent of total enrolment, the rest being through the private sector) and had more than 650,000 teachers and administrators. As a result of this growth, the SEP recognized that the whole system was not as efficient and productive as it could be and concluded that decentralization of the system was needed to devote more resources to priority areas such as the process of learning and teacher training.

The new education law of 1991 establishes, among other things, the following:

- Abolition of the law that prevented the Church and religious organizations to own or administer schools, although education is still secular.

- Mandatory education for all children including one year's nursery school, six years' primary school and three years' secondary school with no age limit.

- Primary and secondary education to be free within the public sector.

- The relative responsibilities of central and local government in education services.

- The aims, objectives, financial inputs and assessment of education.

- Regulation of education offered by the private sector.

- An increase in resources to support education at State and local level.

- The principle of equity within education by taking the responsibility of initiating compensatory programmes when necessary.

- The creation of councils with 'social' (parents, teachers, administrators and alumni) participation.

All these reforms have been taking place at all levels in both public and private sectors. However, higher education institutions, more specifically universities, because of their relative autonomy, are responsible for their own measures based on the general guidelines and reforms given by the Ministry of Education.

EVALUATION IN BRITAIN

School

Bachillerato – generally considered comparable to GCSE standard (grades A, B and C) on a subject-for-subject basis, with the exception of English language.

Higher

Licenciado/Professional title – generally considered comparable to British Bachelor degree standard if awarded after four or more years of study.

MARKING SYSTEMS

School

Marking is on a percentage scale, with 60 per cent as the pass-mark; or on a scale of 0–10 (highest), with 6 as the minimum pass-mark.

Higher

Institutions of higher education commonly grade on the following scale:

10	MB	(maximum)
9		
8	B	
7		
6	S	(minimum pass-mark)
5	NA	(fail)
4		
3		
2		
1		(minimum mark)

PRIMARY AND SECONDARY EDUCATION

Primary

All children have to attend primary and secondary schools by law. Primary school covers six years from age six and leads to the **Primary Certificate**. Traditionally, the education system has been centralized having a uniform curricula throughout the country. However, in recent years a process of decentralization has been taking place, with the purpose of allowing each of the 32 States the autonomy to define its own curricula based on its needs, as an addition to a mandatory centralized uniform section of the curricula.

Decentralization is also taking place at administrative level, delegating to the State government the responsibility of administering and operating the system, labour contracts and financial resources. Federal government will only be responsible for the definition of general norms, evaluation and assessment and the distribution of resources.

All private schools follow the same regulations but, in general, they offer a wide range of additional courses such as another foreign language (English, French, German etc), more hours in almost all subjects and more sophisticated sports and cultural activities.

One of the most difficult problems Mexican education has been facing for many years is rural and indigenous education. Mexico is such a large country with an enormous geographical dispersion in population (there are more than 60,000 communities with less than 100 inhabitants), with very difficult access and lack of communication infrastructure. There are very few schools in some rural areas and primary schools have a shortage of teachers. Around 10,000 schools have only one teacher covering all six grades in classrooms ranging between 25 and 50 children. Current policy is to increase the number of teachers within these schools.

In 1992, Nursery schools had an enrolment of 2,791,550 (11 per cent of the total in education) and Primary schools 14,396,993 (57.2 per cent of the total).

Secondary and Preparatory

Secondary school covers six years generally running from age 12 to 18, and is divided into two three-year cycles, the first called secondary and the second preparatory (high school). The secondary cycle is the last mandatory education level established by law and it is the minimum requirement to have access to technical, industrial or further education. The preparatory cycle is compulsory for students wishing to obtain a first degree at a university.

Secondary education is regulated by the SEP for both public and private schools. Preparatory education (preparation for higher education), however, is regulated and accredited by the universities and other institutions of higher education. Most public universities, specifically State universities, also have their own preparatory schools, with a three year period after which, if students achieve a minimum average of 7 (scale 1 to 10), they may proceed automatically to first degree courses within the same institution. No private preparatory schools has automatic entry to any university.

The first two years of preparatory level are usually devoted to general studies, after which students specialize in either humanities, social sciences or sciences. On successful completion, students obtain the **Bachillerato** Certificate.

For both levels, secondary and preparatory schools, English as a foreign language is compulsory for all students. In 1992, secondary schools had an enrolment of 4,160,692 students (16.5 per cent of all educational levels) and preparatory schools of 1,725,294 (6.9 per cent).

FURTHER EDUCATION/VOCATIONAL QUALIFICATIONS

Instead of following secondary and preparatory education, students can opt for vocational training, this after primary school. In Mexico this is offered at two levels, one of which, the **Bachillerato Tecnológico,** allows the student to re-enter mainstream education at university level if he/she wishes. This cycle lasts 6 years and leads to the **Bachillerato Tecnológico Diploma**.

Alternatively, after three years in secondary school, students can opt for technical schools whose objectives include the formation of technicians, of advanced craft supervisors and of higher technicians for industry and services. This is the National College for Professional Technical Education or CONALEP. CONALEP has approximately 240 campuses around the country and offers a wide range of programmes in six areas: fishing, industry, administration, agriculture, health and tourism.

Recent changes in Mexico's socio-economic situation and productive needs have persuaded CONALEP to go beyond its traditional role as a provider of courses at the technical level. It now also offers upgrading and specialized courses for ex-students and validates on-the-job training.

Regular programmes for technicians last approximately three years after secondary studies. The upgrading courses, offered exclusively to alumni from CONALEP or those with the **Bachillerato** in technology, range from 20 to 80 hours. The specialized courses, which are also for alumni from CONALEP, have a duration between 300 and 600 hours. Finally, CONALEP offers, in co-ordination with the industrial sector, courses for workers in different areas to update their knowledge and upgrade their skills.

HIGHER EDUCATION

Higher education in Mexico is organized in three different subsystems: universities, polytechnics or technological institutes and normal schools (teachers' colleges).

Universities

In Mexico there are 37 public universities or research centres and 39 private universities. In 1992, the total student enrolment, at both undergraduate and graduate levels, was 909,321 students, of which 748,435 were at public universities and 160,886 in the private sector. Graduate enrolment was 33,122 in both public and private sector, of which 87 per cent was from the public universities. The highest enrolment in undergraduate programmes was in social and administrative sciences (49.2 per cent) followed by engineering and technology (32 per cent) and health sciences (10 per cent).

The entrance requirement is the **Bachillerato** Certificate with a minimum average determined by each institution or success in an admission exam. Admission exams are designed, administered and operated by each one of the universities, so a student may have to take several.

Bachelor degrees have an average length of four years, with the exception of some, such as medicine, dentistry, architecture, that are longer. Degrees are obtained by gaining a stated number of credits and the successful presentation of a thesis.

Postgraduate programmes include **Master's**, which have an average length of two years after completion of the first degree, and **PhDs** which take two or three years after the **Master's**.

Private institutions of higher education may be incorporated with a state or federal university or obtain semi-autonomous status and thus be entitled to award their own degrees and use their own curricula. This status and accreditation have to be given by the Ministry of Education.

Technological Institutions

These institutions offer first degrees in both science and social sciences and specialized courses for technicians. Mexico has 110 technological institutions, including the National Polytechnic, all with public funds. The total enrolment in 1992 was 187,200 (14 per cent of the total enrolment in higher education).

TEACHER EDUCATION (Normal Schools)

Since 1985 teacher training has been considered to be part of the higher education system. In the past it was considered equivalent to senior high school.

The entrance requirement is the **Bachillerato** Certificate. Courses at first degree level have a duration of four years, and qualify students to teach either at primary or secondary level. In 1992, the number of teachers' colleges was 215 with public funds and 107 private schools. The total enrolment was 107,030, of which 73.8 per cent were from the public sector.

Mongolia

The following chapter regarding the education system in Mongolia is based on information obtained for the 3rd edition of this Guide, published in 1991, as NARIC has been unable to obtain more recent information.

Education has historically been modelled on the system in the USSR, but is now in a period of transition owing to political change. Eight years' primary and secondary education is compulsory, and 'complete' secondary education lasts for a further two, sometimes three, years. Higher education is centred on the capital, Ulan-Bator, apart from a teachers' training institute in the western provincial town of Khovd. Students leave Mongolia in substantial numbers to pursue courses of higher education at universities and institutes in the Soviet Union and Eastern Europe. As far as language study is concerned, there has been a shift of emphasis away from the study of Russian, so that the five special schools which formerly used Russian as the principal medium of instruction, will offer English, Japanese and Chinese in addition.

EVALUATION IN BRITAIN

School

School Leaving Certificate – generally considered to be below GCSE standard.

Higher

Diploma – may be considered to satisfy the general entrance requirements of British higher education institutions.

MARKING SYSTEM

Marking is on a scale 1–5, with three (average) as the pass-mark. The other grades are 5 (excellent), 4 (good) and 2 (poor), grade 1 not being awarded. A record of such grades is kept for each student, and the system continues into courses of higher education.

SCHOOL EDUCATION

Pre-primary

The Ministry of Health provides day-long nursery schooling for children under three years of age whose parents are in full employment. The service is free of charge, as are all medical services in Mongolia. Parents who choose to do so may send children between the ages of three and seven to kindergartens. A small fee is charged.

Primary and secondary

Children begin three years' primary education at the age of seven in joint primary and secondary schools. Secondary education is at present divided between junior schools (grades 4 to 8 of the system) and senior schools (grades 9 to 10/11).

It is possible for pupils to leave school at the 'incomplete' secondary stage after grade 8 to start work or to study at vocational training schools. A full range of subjects is taught, including Mongolian language and literature, with Russian as the second language until the academic year 1995–6. It is then planned that pupils will be able to choose between English and Russian as their second language. From the academic year 1991–2, the traditional Mongolian script was re-introduced and the Cyrillic alphabet employed only in Russian language texts. Minor subjects include computer studies, domestic science and education for family life.

Certificates are awarded on graduation from the primary stage, after the eighth grade, and on leaving school (**School Leaving Certificate**). Each pupil will also have a record of grades for all major subjects throughout their school career.

A degree of decentralization is being introduced, with some control of the curriculum passing to the schools themselves. Specialized study circles are organized throughout the country on a volunteer basis where demand exists for studies unavailable within the school curriculum.

HIGHER EDUCATION

Admission to the University and institutes of higher education is decided on the basis of the **School Leaving Certificate**, the students' recorded grades, and a special examination for entrance to higher education conducted in subjects relevant to the intended course of study.

In addition to the <u>Mongolian State University</u>, the capital has higher institutes of agriculture, medicine, foreign languages, arts and teacher-training, a polytechnic and a military institute.

Students study in two, three or five-year programmes, leading to the award of a **Diploma**. The first stage of postgraduate study (*Aspirantur*) leads to the writing of a thesis under the direct direction of a supervisor. On the basis of the thesis, and examination and published work the title **Candidate of Science** may be awarded, after a minimum three-year period of research. Doctoral degrees are granted on the basis of more extensive publication and a more developed thesis.

Morocco

The French protectorate covered most of the territory and lasted from 1912 to 1956; the Spanish protectorates in the north and south were renounced in 1956 and 1958: Ifni was surrendered in 1969, but Spanish enclaves have been retained at Ceuta and Melilla. The status of the (previously Spanish) Western Sahara awaits confirmation by UN Referendum.

The education system was originally modelled on that of France. Private schools exist alongside government schools.

In theory, education is compulsory between ages seven and fourteen; in practice, particularly in rural areas, many children do not attend for the whole of this period. Education is free in state schools.

In state primary schools the medium of instruction is Arabic. French is taught as a second language from grade three.

In private primary schools some subjects are taught in Arabic and some in French (on a fifty/fifty basis). English as a foreign language is taking off in a few private primary schools in main cities.

In both state and private secondary schools the mediums of instruction are Arabic and French. English/or another European language is taught from secondary grade four (i.e. for three years) in state secondary schools.

For schools and universities, the academic year begins on 15 September, ends on 30 June and is made up of three terms. For the final three years of secondary education, examinations counting for the **Baccalauréat** are held twice a year, in February and in June.

EVALUATION IN BRITAIN

School

Certificat d'Enseignement Secondaire – generally considered to be below GCSE standard.

Baccalauréat – generally considered comparable to a standard between GCSE and GCE Advanced. A British higher education institution may require GCE Advanced in addition or may accept the **Baccalauréat** provided an overall average mark of *bien* or above is achieved.

Higher

Diplôme d'Etudes Universitaires Générales (DEUG)/**Diplôme d'Etudes**

Universitaires Technologie (DEUT) – generally considered comparable to a standard between GCE Advanced and British Bachelor degree; may be given advanced standing in British higher education institutions.

Licence – generally considered comparable to British Bachelor (Ordinary) degree standard.

Magister – generally considered comparable to British Bachelor (Honours) degree standard.

MARKING SYSTEMS

School

Marking is on a scale of 0–20 (maximum) with 10 as the pass-mark.

16–20	*très bien*	very good
14–15	*bien*	good
12–13	*assez bien*	fairly good
10–11	*passable*	pass
0–9	*insuffisant*	fail

Candidates with 9/20 may be passed by the examination committee.

If *mention* on a certificate is blank, this means the mark is *passable*.

Higher

As for school.

Candidates with 9/20 will be considered by the Examination Board, who may pass them if term work and attendance are good.

SCHOOL EDUCATION

Nursery education

From age three to six Islamic education is introduced with basic subjects and will continue through primary and secondary schools.

State primary

Now called *Premier Cycle de l'Enseignement Fondamental*. This covers six years from age six to twelve (see Introduction)

State secondary

Access to secondary education is based on success in an examination in all subjects (*Examen Normalisé*) at age 12.

The secondary stage lasts six years and is in two parts:

Deuxième Cycle de l'Enseignement Fondamental (junior secondary) This covers a three-year period normally spent in a *Collège*. At the end of this cycle students who are not proceeding to upper secondary school take the **Certificat d'Enseignement Secondaire** (CES).

Enseignement Secondaire (senior secondary)

The senior secondary consists of three years' study, usually spent at a *Lycée*. At the end of the *Enseignement secondaire*, students take one of the following:

Baccalauréat in arts/economics/mathematics/sciences – on the basis of six termly assessments in the three years of senior secondary education. Students who fail the **Baccalauréat** may follow a two year preparatory course called *Capacité en Droit*. Success in this examination will only allow entry into the Faculty of Law.

Baccalauréat Lettres Originelles – awarded in Arabic studies after six years secondary education in *Instituts d'Enseignement Originel* (Institutes of Theology). These provide secondary education in Arabic only with emphasis on religious education.

Baccalauréat Technique – for those specializing in accountancy, commerce, hotel work, or various branches of engineering and technology.

Baccalauréat de l'Enseignement du Second Degré (French Baccalauréat) – awarded to students of French cultural missions.

International Baccalaureate – open to students of American schools in particular and to all students in general.

Private secondary

Several Moroccan private schools provide bilingual Arabic/French secondary education (just as in state secondary schools). All secondary education is supervised by the Ministry of Education.

French and Spanish cultural missions provide mainly French/Spanish secondary education. Arabic being compulsory as first foreign language for locals but offered as option to nationals of the mission. Up to half of students in French missions are Moroccan nationals.

The three American schools cater for the international English-speaking community although between a third to a half of students are Moroccan nationals.

Vocational

Various state or private schools offer vocational courses open to **Certificat d'Enseignement Secondaire** holders, leading to vocational qualifications. Students may go on to higher vocational schools or institutes and obtain higher vocational qualifications.

HIGHER EDUCATION

Higher education in Morocco is offered by the following institutions:

– Universities
– *Etablissements de la Formation des Cadres* (Professional Training Institutions)
– Vocational Training Institutions

Universities

There are 46 *facultés*, 7 *Ecoles Supérieures de Technologie* and 1 *Ecole de Traduction et Interpretariat* (translation/interpreting) grouped into 13 universities. The **Baccalauréat** satisfies university entrance requirements except for the Faculty of

Medicine and Pharmacy the Faculty of Dentistry, Higher Schools of Technology, and the School for Translation and Interpreting.

The medium of instruction is either Arabic or French. University education is organized as follows:

The *Premier Cycle:* Two years university study leads to the **Certificat Universitaire d'Etudes Littéraires** (CUEL) in Arts and Humanities or to the **Certificat Universitaire d'Etudes Scientifiques** (CUES) in Sciences, and Economics.

The *Deuxième Cycle:* a further two years leads to the **Licence**.

The *Troisième Cycle:* (in two stages)

– The **Diplome d'Etudes Supérieures** known simply as the DES is awarded after two to three-years' taught course including a research thesis following the **Licence**.

– The **Doctorat d'Etat**, the highest university degree, takes at least five years to complete after the DES. The period of research varies on average between seven to ten years.

Access to Faculties of Medicine, Pharmacy and Dentistry are highly selective. Seven years' study leads to the award of a **Doctorat in Medicine**, Six years' study leads to a **Doctorat in Pharmacy**, five years' study to a **Doctorat in Dentistry**.

New *Facultés des Sciences et Techniques* opened in Sept/Oct 1994. They offer a **Diplome d'Etudes Universitaires Générales** (DEUG) in Applied Sciences or a **Diplome d'Etudes Universitaires de Technologie** (DEUT) after two years' study. A further two years leads to the award of **Maîtrise**.

A new private university, Al Akhawayn in Ifrane opened in September 1994. The primary language of instruction is English. For the academic year 1994–95, AUI offers 3 undergraduate and 4 Graduate US-based programmes:

Bachelor of Business Administration
Bachelor of Science in General Engineering
Bachelor of Science in Social Sciences
Master of Arts with a major in Humanities
Master of Business Administration
Master of Science with a major in Computer Science
PhD with a major in Humanities

Professional Training Institutions

Besides universities, there are other types of higher education institutions called *Etablissements de Formation des Cadres* (Executives Training Institutions). There are 28 of these institutions divided into three broad fields of study:

1. Science/Technology
2. Law/Economics/Administration/Social Sciences
3. Teacher Training

Access to some of these institutions is by entrance examination. Eight *Grandes Ecoles d'Ingénieurs* (Engineering Schools) recruit students from *classes préparatoires* (preparatory course) following a selective common entry exam in *Mathématiques Spéciales*. The two year preparatory course can be followed in selected secondary schools.

Awards from these *Grandes Ecoles* are **Ingénieur d'Etat** (after five years) then **Doctorat d'Etat** (a further three to four years) in engineering, agriculture, a **Diplome/Diplome Supérieur** in Business (after four years), a **Diplome d'Architecte** after six years' study.

Vocational

There are more than 1,200 private and public vocational training institutions offering around 200 subjects. Vocational courses cover at least two years. Various government ministries, public and private offices offer vocational courses too.

TEACHER EDUCATION

Primary

Since 1982, the regional *Centres de Formation des Instituteures* have admitted both **Certificat Universitaires d'Etudes Littéraires** (CUEL) or **Licence** holders for a one-year training course in some subjects. **Baccalauréat** holders (plus entry examination) require a two years' training course in different subjects. Admission of **Baccalauréat** holders to teacher training courses varies from year to year depending on the specific demand for teachers.

Secondary

Junior secondary (*Deuxième Cycle de l'Enseignement Fondamental*) teachers are trained in *Centres Pédagogiques Regionaux*, where they follow a two-year course. The entry requirement is the **Baccalauréat**.

Senior secondary (*Enseignement Secondaire*) teachers are trained in one of the *Ecoles Normales Supérieures*, where they follow one to two-years' postgraduate course and obtain the **Diplome de Professeur de Deuxième Cycle**. Entry requirement is either a **Licence** in Arts or Sciences plus entry examination or a **junior secondary teaching diploma** plus entry examination.

The **Diplome de Professeur Agrégé** is awarded following a further two-years' study to *Professeurs de 2ème cycle* plus four years' teaching experience and an entrance examination.

Higher

Access to teaching posts in higher education is normally via the *Troisième cycle*.

Mozambique

Since independence the education system has changed considerably. From 1975 there was a rapid expansion in primary education, with changes made to course content at all levels. All educational establishments were nationalized. In 1981, the National Education System (NES), a unified system designed to meet the requirements of independent Mozambique, was approved and this has been gradually implemented since 1983.

Since 1976, university students have been required by decree to render as many years of public service (often teaching) as they have spent at university, after both **Bachelor** and **Licenciate** studies, before being awarded their degree.

Education is officially compulsory for seven years. Schools are racially mixed at all levels. The language of instruction is Portuguese.

The school year is divided into two semesters: February to June and July to December. The academic year is also divided into two semesters: August to December and February to August.

EVALUATION IN BRITAIN

School

Certificado de Habilitacoes Literarias (Secondary School Leaving Certificate) – generally considered comparable to GCSE standard (grades A, B and C) on a subject-for-subject basis, with the exception of English language.

Higher

Bacharelato – generally considered comparable to a standard between GCE Advanced and British Bachelor degree; may be given advanced standing by British higher education institutions.

Licenciatura – generally considered comparable to British Bachelor (Ordinary) degree standard but candidates with very high marks may be considered for admission to taught Master's degree courses.

MARKING SYSTEMS

School

The marking system used for the **Certificado de Habilitacoes Literarias** is generally 0–20 with ten as the pass-mark.

Higher

Bacharelato: pass, good, very good
Licenciatura: marked on a scale of 1–20

The University of Eduardo Mondlane regards 13 as being satisfactory.

SCHOOL EDUCATION

Pre-primary

Initiation classes in Portuguese begin at age five.

Primary

Under the NES there are seven years of primary education (classes 1 to 7). This is divided into two phases: Level 1 and Level 2. Children normally enter at the age of seven but may enter at up to ten years old.

Secondary

The objective of secondary education is to prepare students for further training. Less than 10 per cent of students from primary education progress to this level. Courses last approximately thirty-six weeks per year with about twenty-five teaching hours per week. Under the NES the best graduates of primary education progress to three years of secondary education. These are classes 8 to 10.

In the final year of secondary education students study mathematics, physics, chemistry, biology, Portuguese, geography, history, physical education and English. The course leads to the **Certificado de Habilitacoes Literarias** (Secondary School Leaving Certificate).

Adult education

Parallel to general education for young people there is a system of general education for adults (defined as being over fifteen). In the present system this comprises:

–   literacy campaigns
–   night classes in general education
–   night classes in technical education.

Under the NES adult education will be expanded.

TECHNICAL AND VOCATIONAL EDUCATION

The Ministry of Education, through the Secretary of State for Technical and Professional Education (SETEP), operates a system of technical schools and institutes. There are also about sixty institutions linked to various industries and other ministries which provide technical education. Most of the courses of the institutions run by SETEP have direct counterparts in the general education system.

Some of the industry-run institutions provide recognized courses at an accepted educational level. However, virtually all of them also provide short specialization courses which are not formally recognized by the Ministry of Education.

Elementary level

The technical schools lay great emphasis on basic-level training. This training is considered equivalent to secondary education and is provided in all provincial centres.

Medium level

Medium-level technical education courses are provided at the industrial institutes in Maput and Beira, at the Commercial Institute in Maputo and at the Agricultural Institute in Chimoio. The courses are three-year day or four-year evening courses. They are equivalent to pre-university education and give access to university education. Graduates of the technical courses are often referred to as *Engenheiros Tecnicos* (technician engineers) or *Technicos Medios* (middle level technicians).

HIGHER EDUCATION

There is one university: the Universidade Eduardo Mondlane (University of Eduardo Mondlane) in Maputo.

The entrance requirement is the **Certificado de Habilitacoes Literarias** and an entrance examination.

The first degree (**Bacharelato**) is a three-year course. The second degree (**Licenciatura**) is a two-year course. Only candidates achieving grades of 'good' or 'very good' in the **Bacharelato** may proceed to this level.

Licentiate degrees are offered in agriculture, veterinary sciences, engineering, architecture and medicine.

TEACHER EDUCATION

The teacher training system has been changing rapidly in response to the demands of the expanding education system.

After independence, teacher training concentrated on producing teachers for primary level schools. There are also higher level courses for teachers in general education, given at the education faculty of the university. Under the NES, teachers will attend four-year courses after graduating at least at the level at which they will teach. They will be qualified to middle-level technician or university-degree level.

University-level training is given at the Instituto Superior Pedagogico. Medium-level training is given at the Maputo Instituto Medio Pedagogico and at the Instituto Pedagogico Industrial in Nampula.

Myanmar

After the establishment in 1962 of the Revolutionary Government, the Higher Education Law of 1964 and the Basic Education Law of 1966 were promulgated and constitute the basis of educational legislation. The basic (primary and secondary) education cycle lasts eleven years and includes Kindergarten.

Education is not compulsory.

Burmese is the medium of instruction at all levels except in professional institutes (such as medicine and technology) where English is used.

EVALUATION IN BRITAIN

School

Basic Education High School Examination/Matriculation – generally considered comparable to GCSE standard (grades A, B and C) on a subject-for-subject basis, with the exception of English language.

Higher

Bachelor (Pass) degree – generally considered to be below British Bachelor (Ordinary) degree standard.

Bachelor (Honours) degree – generally considered comparable to British Bachelor (Ordinary) degree standard.

MARKING SYSTEM

School

Marking is on a percentage scale; a minimum average of 45 per cent is required for university entrance.

Higher

Since 1964–5 a percentage scale has been used. The minimum mark required for admission to the second, third and fourth years of courses is 50 per cent for major subjects and 40 per cent for minor ones.

SCHOOL EDUCATION

Primary and secondary

Since the early 1970s primary education has covered the first five years of education (Kindergarten + standards I–IV). Many children will previously have attended pre-schools from age three or four, and kindergarten at age five.

All schools are state-controlled except the *Phone Gyi Khaungs* or monastery schools run for young children by the clergy but these are to a certain extent dictated by government policy.

Middle schools cover standards V–VIII and high schools standards IX and X. At the end of middle school, the annual examination is now an internal examination conducted by school heads. At the end of standard X, students may take the **Basic Education High School Examination (Matriculation)**. Before 1980, according to their aggregate mark for all subjects, successful candidates were placed in merit order on the 'A' or 'B' lists. Those on the 'A' list could proceed to professional institutes, arts and science universities, degree colleges and colleges. Those on the 'B' list became, for example, primary teachers after professional training.

English is introduced in the first year of school i.e. the kindergarten and both English and Burmese are compulsory subjects in the **Matriculation** examination.

Technical secondary

The State Technical High School prepares students for admission to the post-secondary, government technical institutes and for employment in industry as apprentices.

A few trade schools (formerly called artisan training centres) provide two years of training for middle school leavers.

A number of agricultural schools provide training either at middle or high school level. There are also post-secondary state agricultural institutes.

FURTHER EDUCATION

The government technical institutes offer three-year courses in building construction; railway, highway and municipal technology; machine-tool design technology; diesel power and heavy equipment; electric power; electronics; and mining. Entry is post-**Matriculation** and is subject to success in an entrance examination.

The Agricultural Institute at Pyinmana offers post-secondary training for agricultural extension workers and for teachers of vocational agriculture in the high schools. Entrants must have passed the **Matriculation** and Regional College final examinations or be junior assistant teachers.

HIGHER EDUCATION

With the promulgation of the Union of Burma University Education Law in 1964, the new government undertook the reorganization of the universities and higher institutes of learning. The reorganization decentralized the University of Yangon and the University of Mandalay and transformed many of their component parts into separate institutions. The University for Adult Education achieved degree-granting status as the Workers' College, Yangon. Admission is on the basis of **Matriculation** results, but, depending on performance in this examination, students are admitted to either their first, second or third choice of institution.

The **Bachelor (Pass) degree** is now obtained on successful completion of a four-year course and the **Bachelor (Honours)** after a five-year course. Streaming is carried out after the second year.

The most notable changes in higher education took place with the enactment of the University Education Law of 1964. This was later replaced by the University Education Law of 1973.

At present (April 1994), there are over 31 higher education institutions under the Ministry of Education. There are six arts and science universities – Yangon, Mandalay, Mawlamyine, Taunggyi, Dagon and the University of Distance Education, Yangon, affiliated degree colleges number eight and the colleges number ten.

There are seven professional institutes. They are Yangon Institute of Technology; Mandalay Institute of Technology; Institute of Economics, Yangon; Yangon Institute of Education; Institute of Animal Husbandry and Veterinary Science; Institute of Computer Science and Technology, Yangon.

In addition, there are other professional universities and institutes under various ministries – the Institute of Agriculture, the Institute of Forestry, the four Institutes of Medicine, the Institute of Dental Medicine, the Institute of Nursing, the Institute of Paramedical Science, the Institute of Pharmacy, the University of the Development of National Races and the University of Culture.

TEACHER EDUCATION

Primary

Primary teachers must be holders of a relevant degree. They are given a one-month induction-cum-orientation teacher training course. After a number of years primary teachers attend a certificate course at a teacher training school.

Middle school

Only graduates are appointed as middle school teachers. Their induction is similar to that of primary teachers. Middle school teachers attend a one-year certificate course at a teacher-training college.

High school

Teachers are trained at the Institute of Education, Yangon (formerly the Faculty of Education at Rangoon University) and the Institute of Education, Mandalay. At present these institutions offer only the **Bachelor of Education (BEd)** degree which is for one academic year. The Institute of Education offers a two year **BEd** course by distance learning.

Namibia

Namibia is an independent republic within the Commonwealth, with a multi-party parliament elected by universal suffrage and a constitution which enshrines human rights. The government is formed by the ruling party, the South-West Africa People's Organization (SWAPO). Namibia is a member of the Southern African Customs Union and the Southern African Development Co-ordination Conference.

Namibia became independent from South Africa in March 1990 after a long period of guerrilla conflict and domestic political turmoil gave way to a transition to democracy supervised by the United Nations. Between 1915 and 1989, the country had been ruled by South Africa, under a League of Nations mandate from 1920, but, for most of the post-Second World War period, in defiance of the United Nations and, later, World Court rulings.

The official language of independent Namibia is English, but all Namibian languages, indigenous and otherwise, receive constitutional protection. A small minority of the population speak English as a mother tongue. The major languages of the black population are Kwanyama, Ndonga, Nama-Damara and Herero. The small coloured and Rehoboth communities, most whites and some blacks speak Afrikaans as their mother tongue. During South African rule, the country was officially bilingual in Afrikaans and English, but Afrikaans was the official language of preference. German is spoken by the small German community but understood more widely.

Until independence, the education system was strongly influenced by South Africa, which imposed its policy of ethnic differentiation through ten ethnically based, separate education systems and a Department of National Education. Education is now organized through six regions. The structure of the Ministry of Education and Culture has been re-shaped and is awaiting Cabinet approval for re-structuring to be put in place. It is expected that much of the professional educational input will be through the National Institute for Educational Development which will move to Okhandja in 1994. Educational opportunity and quality, reflected in expenditure per capita, was heavily skewed in favour of the white minority and to the disadvantage of the black majority. It is estimated that 60–70 per cent of the adult population of Namibia is illiterate. The government of independent Namibia, through the Ministry of Education and Culture, is committed to erase ethnic differentiation in educational policy and provision and construct a new, unitary system of education which is capable of fulfilling the country's constitutional promise of education for all.

EVALUATION IN BRITAIN

School

Cambridge School Certificate (CSC)/**Cambridge Overseas School Certificate** (COSC)/**GCE O level** – grades 1–6 are generally equated to GCSE standard (grades A, B and C).

Cambridge Overseas Higher School Certificate (COHSC)/**GCE A level** – generally equated to GCE Advanced standard.

Senior Certificate

The overall standard of the **Senior Certificate** (issued by the South African Joint Matriculation Board), showing the matriculation standard in English language (higher grade) and four other subjects, if it gives matriculation endorsement (previously called matriculation exemption), is generally considered to compare to a standard between GCSE and GCE Advanced level.

Matriculation endorsement requires passes in four subjects at the 'higher' grade and two at the 'standard' grade in the Senior Certificate.

On a subject-for-subject basis, subjects passed at the marks of A–E at 'higher' grade would generally be compared to GCSE. Subjects awarded an F are unlikely to be accorded GCSE status.

Higher grade passes in five subjects (a minimum of three Bs and two Cs) may be considered to satisfy the general entrance requirements of British higher education institutions.

Some institutions in Britain are willing to consider students holding only one of these certificates, with good performance in higher grade subjects, for entrance to a Bachelor degree course, but most would require at least successful completion of the first year of a South African degree course or, alternatively, GCE Advanced.

MARKING SYSTEM

School

Details of the CSC, COSC and COHSC marking systems are given in Appendix 2.

SCHOOL EDUCATION

Until independence, Namibia was subject to the influence of South African curricula and, at the senior secondary level, to the **Senior Certificate** (and **Matriculation Exemption**) examinations of the Cape Province Education Department. The official policy is to retain the inherited assessment arrangements until a National Assessment Authority is in place and has established a new system of qualifications. It has already been decided to adopt the **International General Certificate of Secondary Education** (IGCSE) in place of the **Cape Senior Certificate,** and the Ministry of Education and Culture is working with the Cambridge Examinations Syndicate to introduce the IGCSE in 1995.

The former system has been restructured into a seven-year primary cycle (grades 1 to 7), a three-year junior secondary cycle (grades 8 to 10), and a two-year senior secondary cycle (grades 11 to 12). In 1990, enrolment at each level was as follows:

Primary	353,100
Junior secondary	72,882
Senior secondary	19,220

The educational pyramid is obviously steep and characterized by high levels of wastage. Historically, very few black students have annually achieved the **South African Matriculation Exemption**.

FURTHER AND HIGHER EDUCATION

The President of Namibia appointed an international Commission on Higher Education under the chairmanship of Professor John D Turner of the University of Manchester to advise the government on all aspects of post-secondary higher education policy and development. The Commission reported in 1991.

In October 1992, the new University of Namibia was established with its main premises at the site of the former Windhoek College of Education and its city premises at the site of the former Academy. The Technicon and the College for Out-of-School Training (COST) are also based at the former Academy premises. Both institutions are under the jurisdiction of the university until the proposed Polytechnic is created and until the future of Distance Education is settled between the university and the Ministry of Education and Culture.

The University of Namibia will eventually have up to seven faculties (social and economic sciences, law, arts and humanities, education, natural sciences, agriculture and natural resources and medical and health sciences); four centres (computer, language, distance education and multi-disciplinary research centres); a School of Media Studies and an Institute of Administration and Management. The university will offer certificates, diplomas, advanced diplomas, degrees and postgraduate diplomas.

The Technicon organizes its students in 'curriculum groups', offering certificates or diplomas in management and administration, accounting and information systems, agriculture and nature conservation and secretarial training.

COST has a commerce and general section and a technical section, offering certificate-level courses only.

Very little other formal higher education exists within the country. Two small agricultural colleges, Neudamm near Windhoek and Tsumis Park near Rehoboth, offer diploma programmes.

Technical institutes at Okararara, Rundu and Valombola offer four-year programmes in woodwork, metalwork, construction and automechanics, and there are technical schools in Windhoek and Katima Mulilo. The combined enrolment is around 800. Existing capacity is under-utilized at present, and the government has received expert advice from ILO and SIDA missions on how vocational education could be developed on a national basis under a coherent national policy.

TEACHER EDUCATION

Since Independence, the Windhoek College of Education, formerly for whites only, and the Khomasdal Teachers' College, formerly for 'coloureds' were amalgamated. The college is open to all and has actively engaged in-service education. Primary teacher education is also undertaken at Ongwediva Teachers' College and at centres in Rundu and Katima Mulilo. There are also active resource centres around the country, including Rundu, Tsumeb, Otjiwarango, Swakopmund and Windhoek. The future development of teacher education has been studied by teams from UNESCO and SIDA and a large conference, sponsored by UNESCO, is planned for the summer of 1994. A high proportion of the existing teaching force of 15,280 (1993 figures) is either under-qualified (5,000) or has no professional training (7,000).

ADULT EDUCATION

The Ministry of Education and Culture gives high priority to adult and non-formal education and has established a division under the leadership of an under-secretary to formulate policy in this area. Before independence, the field was largely occupied by non-governmental organizations, particularly the churches. New partnerships between the independent government and NGOs are being forged in order to develop a structure of policy making and a variety of delivery systems to respond to the massive needs of the illiterate general population, and special categories such as the returnees from exile abroad, women in development, the wage employed, unemployed youth, and aspirants for further and higher education whose schooling had been prematurely ended.

Nepal

The Ministry of Education was first established in 1951, but comparatively little attention and resources were allocated to education until recently. In 1971, the government drew up the National Educational System Plan for a uniform system of education over the whole country. Some modifications to the Plan have been implemented, such as the introduction of the Basic Needs programme to provide universal primary education for children aged six to ten. At present the Plan is under review and further modifications are expected.

The Ministry of Education is responsible for the national curriculum in primary and secondary schools. <u>Tribhuvan University</u> is responsible for the curriculum at college and Bachelor degree level.

Education is not compulsory, due mainly to inadequate facilities.

At school level, Nepali is the medium of instruction but English may be used where schools have staff who are qualified to do so. English as a subject is compulsory in all schools from grade 4 in the primary school. College level education can be either in Nepali or English but postgraduate study is usually in English.

The academic year for schools begins in February and ends in December. The higher education academic year normally begins in August/September and ends in May.

EVALUATION IN BRITAIN

School

School Leaving Certificate (SLC) – generally considered to be below GCSE standard.

Higher

Proficiency Certificate – generally considered comparable to GCSE standard (grades A, B and C) on a subject-for-subject basis, with the exception of English language.

Bachelor degree – may be considered to satisfy the general entrance requirements of British higher education institutions.

Master's degree – generally considered comparable to British Bachelor (Ordinary) degree standard. Exceptionally, students with very high grades may be considered for admission to postgraduate study.

MARKING SYSTEM

School

The **School Leaving Certificate** (SLC) is a group certificate examination with subjects organized into compulsory, vocational and optional groupings. Students must present seven subjects: three compulsory, one vocational and three optional. The pass-mark on each paper is 32 per cent and students must pass all papers to obtain a certificate.

Division I	60 per cent and above
Division II	45 to 59
Division III	32 to 45

Higher

First Division	60 per cent and above
Second Division	45 to 59
Third Division	33 to 44

SCHOOL EDUCATION

Primary

The primary cycle covers five years (grades 1–5) from age six.

Secondary

This covers five years, divided into two years' lower secondary and three years' upper secondary/high school. In lower secondary, the teaching of Nepali is given priority; in upper secondary, English, Nepali, mathematics and vocational education are given most weight. At the end of this cycle (grade 10) students take the examinations for the **School Leaving Certificate** (SLC).

The National School, Budhanilkantha, offers **Cambridge Overseas Certificate** examinations. (For further information see Appendix 2.)

Plans are being discussed to integrate the plus 2 (grades 11 and 12) in the school system and the new structure will be secondary (grades 6 to 10) and higher secondary (grades 11 to 12).

Vocational

Vocational education at school level remains just one of the compulsory subjects taught, without the specific objective of providing skill training. A separate scheme of nine rural and urban technical schools (and six more planned) is being developed. The main intake will be at grade 10 (SLC pass). The type of training offered will include training certificates, **Technical School Leaving Certificate** for grade 10-pass students who have followed courses of two years' duration and a **Technician Certificate** for grade 10-pass students who have followed courses of three years' duration.

FURTHER EDUCATION

The current programme includes general literacy classes for adults and functional literacy programmes when skills such as agriculture, health and income-generating activities are introduced.

HIGHER EDUCATION

In 1971 <u>Tribhuvan University</u> was made the sole controller and manager of higher education in Nepal and was authorized to establish its own regulations. All existing colleges became part of the one national university. The exceptions are the Sanskrit colleges which merged to form <u>Mahendra Sanskrit University</u>. There are five technical institutes within <u>Tribhuvan University</u> (medicine, engineering, science, agriculture and forestry), four research centres and four faculties. Each institute or faculty has a number of campuses located in various parts of the country.

The entry qualification for undergraduate courses is the **School Leaving Certificate**. Courses leading to a **Bachelor degree** are taken in two parts; after two years' study students take the **Proficiency Certificate** (previously known as the **Intermediate Examination**), and after a further two years (three years for law and agriculture and four years for engineering, forestry and medicine) the examinations for the **Bachelor degree** (previously referred to as the diploma).

The **Master's degree** may be taken after a further two years.

A **PhD** may be obtained after a further three years.

TEACHER EDUCATION

In 1971, the existing <u>College of Education</u> was absorbed by <u>Tribhuvan University</u> as the Institute (now Faculty) of Education. Both the Faculty of Education and the Ministry of Education run a variety of teacher training pre-service and in-service courses for the primary, secondary and tertiary education sectors.

Primary

Women's Teacher Training Programme. A non-credit ten-month programme for girls to train as primary school teachers.

Secondary

Lower secondary:

A two-year post SLC course leading to the **Proficiency Certificate**.

Secondary:

A two-year course at post-**Proficiency Certificate** level or a one-year post-**BA** or **BSc** leading to **Bachelor in Education**.

Tertiary

A two-year course at post-**Bachelor** level leading to a **Master's in Education** for staff of education campuses.

Netherlands

Several education acts have changed the system at all levels since the mid-1950s. One of the most far-reaching was the Secondary Education Act of 1963 (also called the Mammoth Law), which came into force in August 1968. Its main purpose is to integrate the various types of secondary education. In 1986, two new higher education acts were introduced, the Higher Professional Education Act (WHBO) and the (renewed) University Education Act (WWO). These were superseded on 1 August 1993 by the new Higher Education and Research Act (WHW).

Until 1969 education was compulsory for eight years, beginning no later than age seven. The Compulsory Education Law of 1969 increased this to nine years, from age six to fifteen, and in 1975 it was extended to ten years, starting at age six. In 1985 the school-starting age was lowered to five years, thereby increasing compulsory education to eleven years.

The medium of instruction is Dutch, except in the international institutions where it is mainly English. English is introduced in the fifth year of primary education.

The academic year runs from August/September to June.

Abbreviations

bc	baccalaureus
dr	doctor
drs	doctorandus
HAO	*Hoger Agrarisch Onderwijs*
HAVO	*Hoger Algemeen Voortgezet Onderwijs*
HBO	*Hoger Beroepsonderwijs*
HBS	*Hogere Burgerschool* (before 1968)
HEO	*Hoger Economisch Onderwijs*
HGO	*Hoger Gezondheidszorgonderwijs*
HKO	*Hoger Kunstonderwijs*
HPO	*Hoger Pedagogisch Onderwijs*
HSAO	*Hoger Sociaal Agogisch Onderwijs*
HTO	*Hoger Technisch Onderwijs*
ing	ingenieur
ir	ingenieur
LAVO	*Lager Algemeen Voortgezet Onderwijs* (obsolete)
LBO	*Lager Beroepsonderwijs* (before 1992) (obsolete)
LEAO	*Lager Economisch en Administratief Onderwijs*
LLO	*Lager Landbouw Onderwijs*
LO	*Lager Onderwijs*
LTS	*Lagere Technische School*
MAVO	*Middelbaar Algemeen Voortgezet Onderwijs*
MBO	*Middelbaar Beroepsonderwijs*
MDGO	*Middelbaar Dienstverlenings-, Gezondheids – en Gezondheidszorgonderwijs*

MEO	*Middelbaar Economisch Onderwijs*
MLO	*Middelbaar Laboratorium Onderwijs/Landbouw Onderwijs*
MLNO	*Middelbaar- Landbouw en Natuurlijke Omgeving*
MMS	*Middelbare Meisjes School* (before 1968) (obsolete)
MO	*Middelbaar Onderwijs*
mr	**meester** – Law graduates only
MTO	*Middelbaar Technisch Onderwijs*
MTS	*Middelbare Technische School*
MULO	*Meer Uitgebreid Lager Onderwijs* (before 1968) (obsolete)
PA	*Pedagogische Academie* (obsolete)
PABO	*Pedagogische Academie voor het Basis Onderwijs*
ULO	*Uitgebreid Lager Onderwijs* (before 1968) (obsolete)
ULO	*Universitaire Lerarenopleiding* (since 1986)
VBO	*Voorbereidend Beroepsonderwijs*
VWO	*Voorbereidend Wetenschappelijk Onderwijs*
WO	*Wetenschappelijke Onderwijs*
WHBO	*Wet op het Hoger Beroepsonderwijs*
WHW	*Wet op het Hoger Onderwijs en Wetenschappelijk Onderzoek*
WWO	*Wet op het Wetenschappelijk Onderwijs*

EVALUATION IN BRITAIN

School

MAVO/MULO certificate – generally considered to be below GCSE standard.

MEO/HAVO certificate – generally considered comparable to GCSE standard (grades A, B and C), with the exception of English language.

VWO (**Gymnasium A/B** and **Atheneum A/B**) **diplomas** – satisfies the general entrance requirements of British higher education institutions.

Higher

Kandidaats (Intermediate exam done under the old system) – generally considered to be below British Bachelor degree standard.

Doctoraal (confers title of either drs, mr or ir) – generally considered comparable to British Bachelor (Honours) degree standard, although the course lasts longer than in the UK.

HBO diploma – constitutes a professionally oriented first degree; generally considered comparable to a standard above that of BTEC Higher National Diploma / N/SVQ level 4. Some institutions compare it to a UK first degree, some others require a minimum 65 per cent. In some circumstances it may be considered for admission to a taught Master's degree course.

MARKING SYSTEMS

School and Higher

10	*uitmuntend*	excellent
9	*zeer goed*	very good
8	*goed*	good
7	*ruim voldoende*	very satisfactory

6	*voldoende*	pass
5	*bijna voldoende*	almost satisfactory
4	*onvoldoende*	unsatisfactory
3	*zeer onvoldoende*	very unsatisfactory
2	*slecht*	poor
1	*zeer slecht*	very poor

Note: Although a 4 is unsatisfactory and a 5 not a full pass, school pupils are allowed a maximum of one 4 <u>or</u> two 5s on their leaving certificate, provided these are compensated for by high marks in other subjects.

SCHOOL EDUCATION

Pre-primary and primary (*Basisonderwijs*)

With the Primary Education Act (*Wet op het Basisonderwijs*) of 1985, pre-primary and primary education were integrated into one system of education for children of four to twelve years old. Education becomes compulsory one month after the child has reached the age of five, but children may enter school when they are four years old. *Basisonderwijs* therefore comprises eight years of education.

It offers a common curriculum which includes reading, writing, arithmetic, Dutch, geography, history, nature study, social relations, communicative skills, art, music, handicrafts and physical education.

Secondary

Until 1968

For pupils who wished to continue their education, but not to university entrance level, advanced primary education (*Uitgebreid Lager Onderwijs* – ULO) was offered in three to four-year courses after the six-year primary course. The leaving qualification of these courses was the **MULO-A** or **MULO-B certificate**, with which pupils could either leave school or proceed to intermediate vocational secondary education.

For pupils who wished to take a course in general education with the eventual aim of attending higher education, there were two types of school: the *Gymnasium* and the *Hogere Burgerschool*.

The *Gymnasium* offered (and still does) a six-year course. During the final two years pupils could specialize in Section A, with the emphasis on Greek and Latin, or Section B, with the emphasis on mathematics and science. The leaving certificate obtained on successful completion of the full six-year course entitled the holder to admission to university.

The *Hogere Burgerschool* (HBS) offered five-year courses. After the first three years, pupils could specialize in Section A, with the emphasis on economic and social studies and languages, or Section B, with the emphasis on mathematics and science. The **HBS-A certificate** gave admission to a limited number of university programmes: the **HBS-B certificate** gave admission to all programmes (except theology and classical studies). The last examinations for the *Hogere Burgerschool* were taken in 1973.

The *Middelbare Meisjesschool* (MMS) offered secondary education for girls only. It had a five-year course with a curriculum that on the whole was comparable to that of the **HBS-A**.

Since 1968

The 1963 Secondary Education Act, implemented in 1968, led to the following changes:

The **LAVO certificate** could be issued to pupils who completed two years of secondary education.

The **MAVO certificate** replaced the **ULO** and **MULO certificate**.

The **VWO**, or pre-university education, replaced the former *Gymnasium* and **HBS-B.**

The **HAVO** replaced the **HBS-A** and **MMS**.

An essential feature of the educational reforms was to integrate the various forms of secondary education. A common transition year or transition period of two years (*Brugklas/Brugperiode*) was introduced for all pupils entering general secondary education.

The first two years at secondary schools for lower vocational training culminated in the award of the **LAVO certificate**. This type of education and diploma has become obsolete with the introduction of the *basisvorming* (see below).

The **MAVO certificate** is obtained after a four-year course, including the common transition year. Examinations are held in six subjects and can be taken at a (lower) C level or (higher) D level. The certificate can admit the holder to the fourth year of the HAVO schools or to intermediate vocational secondary education.

The **HAVO certificate** is awarded on completion of a five-year course of general secondary education, including the transition year. For the last two years, pupils prepare for an examination in six subjects, which must include Dutch and at least one foreign language. The certificate gives admission to Higher Professional Education (HBO – see below).

The **VWO certificate** is obtained after six years of pre-university education, including the transition year. During the last two years, pupils prepare for an examination in seven subjects. The **VWO certificate** gives admission to universities as well as to HBO.

There are three types of VWO certificate: the **Gymnasium certificate**, the **Atheneum certificate**, and the unified **VWO certificate**. Of these, the *Gymnasium* and *Atheneum* are further divided into A and B streams.

In *Gymnasium* and *Atheneum*, five of the seven examination subjects are compulsory; for the unified **VWO certificate** only two (at some schools three) subjects are compulsory.

The *Gymnasium* teaches Latin and Greek during the whole six-year course. From the fourth or fifth year, pupils specialize in stream A, concentrating on the classics, or stream B, concentrating on mathematics and science.

The *Atheneum* does not include Greek or Latin, and there is greater emphasis on modern languages, history, geography, law and economics. From the fourth year the *Atheneum* divides into an A stream, concentrating on economics and social science and a B stream, concentrating on mathematics and science.

The *Lyceum* was a school offering both the *Gymnasium* and the *Atheneum* programmes, with the first year of the curriculum in common. This type of school no longer exists.

In the undivided **VWO certificate** (*ongedeeld* **VWO**) pupils initially study ten subjects – reduced in the fifth and sixth years to seven, which must include Dutch and one foreign language, and it is these which are tested in the final examination.

The **MAVO, HAVO** and **VWO certificates** show marks obtained in the state-regulated written examination and the oral and/or written examination set by the school.

Basic Education Act 1993 (*Basisvorming*)

Another important development in secondary education was the introduction of the *basisvorming* in 1993. *Basisvorming*, or basic education, provides general education in a fixed set of compulsory subjects during the first three years at all schools offering general or vocational education. These subjects include the subjects of the transitional period. The *basisvorming* is compulsory at all schools but schools may adapt the content to the level of their students. Students receive an average of thirty-two hours of instruction per week.

Basisvorming covers technology, computer science, home economics, Dutch, English, French or German, mathematics, science, the arts, biology, economics, history, geography and one optional subject (*vrije ruimte*) chosen by the school.

Vocational (*Beroepsonderwijs*)

Until 1992

Training could be divided into various levels as follows:

Lager Beroepsonderwijs (LBO)	–	lower vocational (same level as MAVO) training
Middelbaar Beroeps- onderwijs (MBO)	–	intermediate technical training
Hoger Beroepsonderwijs (HBO)	–	higher professional education

Specialization was available in various fields. The four main fields were: technology; health and social services; economics and administration; and agriculture.

Schools or sectors of education were referred to by an abbreviation which combines level and field of study, e.g. LTS (*Lagere Technische School* – Lower Technical School), MEAO (*Middelbaar Economisch Administratief Onderwijs* – Intermediate Economic and Administrative Education) and so on.

All LBO programmes took four years and gave admission to MBO courses. Most MBO programmes took four years, the third year usually being a practical year. **MBO certificates** gave admission to HBO. HBO is subsumed under higher education.

Technology:

The LTS used to offer mainly three-year courses, but these were increased to four years. Pupils entered directly from primary school for what was essentially basic trade-training. On completion of the course, they could take up an apprenticeship or begin work in a factory.

The MTS offered four-year courses which included a year of practical training in industry, mostly in engineering. Entrance to these was with the **LTS** or **MAVO certificates**.

Health and social services:

Training in nursing, health care and related fields, as well as the social services was offered at intermediate and not at lower level. As there may be considerable overlap between courses in these two sectors, they were grouped together. Most courses were connected within specific but widely different occupations.

From 1984 onwards all courses in these fields at intermediate level were brought together in schools of MDGO (*Middelbaar Dienstverlenings-, Gezondheids- en Gezondheidszorg Onderwijs*).

Economics and administration:

This was offered at lower (LEAO) and intermediate (MEAO) levels. MEAO programmes took three years.

Agriculture:

This was offered at lower (LLO) and intermediate (MLO) levels.

Since 1992

Vocational secondary education is given at two different levels, preparatory and intermediate. In addition, there is an apprenticeship system which runs parallel to the intermediate level system.

These levels are now as follows:

Voorbereidend beroeps-onderwijs (VBO)	–	preparatory vocational education (replaces LBO)
Middelbaar Beroeps-onderwijs (MBO)	–	intermediate vocational secondary education (revised, new structure)
Hoger Beroepsonderwijs (HBO)	–	higher professional education (also revised) Described under **HIGHER EDUCATION** below.

Preparatory vocational education (*voorbereidend beroepsonderwijs, VBO*)

Preparatory vocational education is the lower of the two existing forms of secondary vocational education, previously called LBO (see above). The major difference between LBO and VBO is the increased number of general education subjects, added in compliance with the *basisvorming*. VBO offers basic training in a particular vocation, and graduates can choose either to enter the work force upon completion of the programme or to continue their training in intermediate vocational secondary level education (MBO see below). All VBO programmes last a total of four years after completion of primary education.

Intermediate vocational secondary education (*Middelbaar Beroepsonderwijs*, MBO)

Intermediate vocational secondary education is currently (1994) at the end of a major reorganization process which has been taking place since the beginning of the 1990s. Part of this reform was a large-scale merging process that has reduced the number of schools from 400 at the end of the 1980s to 140 in 1990, and the organization of educational programmes into 4 sectors: technology (MTO), economics (MEO), health and human services (MDGO) and agriculture and the natural environment (MLNO).

Under the new structure there are four types of MBO programmes: orientation programmes, short programmes (2 years), intermediate programmes (3–4 years) and long programmes (3–4 years). The first three types are mostly work-related and do not give admission to HBO. Long programmes (*Lange Opleidingen*) contain more theory, students receive instruction in a broader range of subjects, and therefore these programmes are suitable for admission to HBO.

In addition, graduates of both intermediate and long MBO programmes are qualified to enter the workforce in their particular vocation.

The entry requirements to the intermediate and long programmes are either a **VBO** or **MAVO diploma**.

Apprentice training (*Leerlingwezen*)

As an alternative to MBO, school leavers who have had ten years of education may enter the *leerlingwezen*. This is a system of part-time vocational education, alongside formal apprentice training. Practical training is provided by the company that employs the apprentice, while theory is supplied at regional training colleges. Content and level of training programmes, as well as examinations, are co-ordinated by professional bodies that are responsible for vocational education in their fields.

The *leerlingwezen* is divided into three levels: primary (*primair*), advanced (*voortgezet*) and tertiary (*tertiair*). Primary programmes normally take two years, advanced and tertiary programmes take two years or less.

HIGHER EDUCATION

In 1986, two new higher education acts were introduced: the Higher Professional Education Act (WHBO – *Wet op het Hoger Beroepsonderwijs*) and the (renewed) University Education Act (WWO – *Wet op het Wetenschappelijk Onderwijs*).

The 1993 Higher Education and Research Act (WHW) supersedes the WHBO, the WWO and many other regulations. It increases the autonomy of higher education institutions by redistributing powers between central government and institutions, and improves administrative co-ordination. This Act gives far more control over study programmes to institutions, and introduces *studiepunten* (study points) or credits for study programmes. One credit represents 40 hours of study, which includes contact hours, practicals, practical training and independent work. The WHW operates on the principle that the workload for full-time students is 40 hours per week, and that the academic year lasts a total of 42 weeks. Most initial study programmes comprise 168 credits; exceptions are initial programmes in certain professional (primarily medical) fields, requiring 210 or 252 credits.

University education, provided by universities, and higher professional education, provided by *Hogescholen*, are now the two main streams in Dutch higher education. The Open University and the international education arrangements are two alternatives.

Higher Professional Education (HBO – *Hoger Beroepsonderwijs*)

Hogescholen were created in 1986 by the gradual merger, since 1983, of smaller HBO institutes. They offer four-year degree programmes, concentrating on applied studies, which are almost always closely associated with a particular profession. The third year is practical training under supervision, accounted for in a training report which is a requirement for graduation. Programmes of study are divided into seven sectors: technology (HTO), administration (HEO), health (HGO), fine arts (HKO), education (HPO), agriculture (HAO), social services (HSAO).

Admission is with the **HAVO** or **MBO certificates**. Course requirements are set for particular programmes. As with the university programmes, the first examination takes place at the end of the first year, which is called the **propaedeuse**. The **HBO propaedeuse** gives admission to the first year of a university programme. The **HBO diploma** gives exemptions from university study at the discretion of the university. In some fields, universities offer a shortened **Doctoraal** programme (see below) of two years which is open to HBO graduates only. In all fields HBO graduates may apply for admission to post-*doctoraal* programmes, such as those leading to a **doctorate**.

Graduates in technology and agriculture are awarded the title **ingenieur**, abbreviated **ing**; in other sectors the title is that of **baccalaureus**, abbreviated **bc**. Under the WHW, all graduates have the right to use the title of **bachelor**. *Hogescholen* are therefore empowered to issue statements, in the English language, defining the status of the *hogeschool* as a polytechnic and the title as a **bachelor** degree.

HBO graduates can go on to postgraduate programmes.

University Education (WO – *Wetenschappelijke Onderwijs*).

The **VWO certificate** or the **HBO Propaedeuse certificate** are the entrance requirements for courses of higher education at universities and institutions of comparable level. In theory, all students holding either of these qualifications have the right to a university place, and this has led to overcrowding. Since 1972, a system of *numerus clausus* (limited admission) has operated in the form of a lottery. The fields of study to which this applies and the number of places available are determined each year.

In 1982 a new university education structure was introduced; the old structure has now been phased out.

Courses under the old structure were normally taken in two stages, the first leading to the **Kandidaats examen** and the second to the **Doctoraal**. The **Kandidaats examen** was usually taken after three years (in some subjects after two or four years). It was not recognized as a professional qualification. In some subject areas the **Kandidaats examen** was preceded by a preliminary examination, **Propaedeutisch examen** taken after one year. The **Doctoraal** normally required two years' study after the **Kandidaats**. Under the old structure, students were allowed to resit any examinations and indeed to delay taking the examinations until they considered they were ready to do so.

Since 1982, university programmes have had a nominal course duration of four years with a *propaedeutisch* programme of one year, followed by a *doctoraal* programme of three years. Students are allowed a maximum registration period of five years to complete their studies. For the *propaedeuse* they are allowed a maximum of two years; if they fail to pass the **Propaedeuse examen** in that time, they are requested to leave university. For the *doctoraal* they may take as long as is left of the six years minus the time they used up for the *propaedeuse*. Statistics indicate that, on average, students take four-and-a-half to five years to meet the requirements for the **Doctoraal examen**. Many students then prefer to stay on at university, using the registration time that is left to take additional subjects.

The termination of university study both under the old and the new structure is the **Doctoraal examen**, which confers the title of **doctorandus**, **meester** (in law) or **ingenieur** (in technology and agriculture); the respective abbreviations, **drs**, **mr**, and **ir** may be used before the holder's name. These qualifications give the holder the legal right to practise a profession, except in dentistry (*tandarts*), veterinary science (*dierenarts*), pharmacy and medicine (*arts*), and teaching where a practical period of one or two years, culminating in a final examination, is required before entry to these professions. Under the WHW, all university graduates have the right to use the title of **master**.

Following the **Doctoraal examen**, students may prepare a dissertation after full-time research lasting a minimum of four years; successful admission and public defence of the dissertation leads to the qualification of **doctor (dr)**.

At present there are thirteen universities, fully subsidized by the state. In addition, there are eight institutions offering courses of university-level education: six theological universities, one university of humanistic studies and the Netherlands business school (Nijenrode). In 1982 Nijenrode was given university status and in 1986 was renamed the Nijenrode Universiteit voor Bedrijfskunde. These eight universities operate independently of, but are approved by, the Ministry of Education and Science, and they may award degrees that are equivalent to those of other universities.

The Open University – (OU – *Open Universiteit*)

The Open University first admitted students in 1984. There is no specific entry requirement, but every candidate is interviewed intensively and must be at least eighteen years old. Students choose the length of course that they wish to follow and can work towards a university or **HBO degree**, or an Open University qualification.

TEACHER EDUCATION

Pre-primary/nursery (*Kleuteronderwijs*)

Before 1984, courses were divided into two parts at nursery teacher training colleges (*Opleiding tot Kleuterleidster*).

Part 1 took three years and led to the qualification of **Kleuterleidster Akte A** (Nursery School Teacher's Certificate).

Part 2 took one year and led to the qualification of **Hoofdleidster Akte B** (Nursery School Head Teacher's Certificate).

For admission to Part 1, the **MAVO certificate** was required. The **HAVO** or **VWO diploma** gave exemption from the first year. The Primary School Teacher's Certificate (see below) gave exemption from the first two years.

For courses since 1984 see the following section.

Primary

Until 1968

Training for prospective primary school teachers was at three levels, in *Kweekscholen*. The first level lasted two years from the entrance standard of the **MULO certificate** or completion of three years of MMS, HBS or *Gymnasium*. This phase covered general education as in the ordinary secondary schools but did not lead to any particular qualification.

The second level lasted two years and led to the Primary School Teacher's Certificate (**Akte van Bekwaamheid als Onderwijzer**).

The third level lasted one year and led to the certificate of a fully qualified primary school teacher eligible to become head of a primary school <u>and</u> teach general subjects in ULO schools (**Akte van Bekwaamheid als Volledig Bevoegd Onderwijzer**).

1968–72

Training was divided into two parts, the entrance level to the first part being the **HAVO certificate** or Pre-Primary School Teacher's Certificate.

Part 1 lasted two years and led to the qualification of Primary School Teacher's Certificate (**Akte van Bekwaamheid als Onderwijzer**).

Part 2 lasted one year and was optional, leading to the qualification which made the holder eligible to become a head teacher (**Akte van Bekwaamheid als Volledig Bevoegd Onderwijzer**).

1972-84

The Part 2 course, available from 1968–72, became compulsory. The old *Kweekscholen* became *Pedagogische Academien* and a three-year course was devised with only one final examination, leading to the full qualification of primary school teacher, eligible to become head teacher (**Akte van Bekwaamheid als Volledig Bevoegd Onderwijzer**) and to teach several subjects at LAVO, MAVO and LBO schools.

Integrated pre-primary/primary (since 1984)

In 1984 the new *Pedagogische Academie voor het Basisonderwijs* (PABO) was introduced to replace training for pre-primary/nursery and primary school teachers. Due to this integration, teacher training programmes were extended by one year to form four year PABO programmes and, with effect from 1986, graduates were awarded the title of bachelor degrees (**baccalaureus**). This title was also granted to graduates of the four year PABO before 1986, retrospectively. The entrance requirement is the **HAVO certificate**.

Secondary

Since 1989, teaching qualifications for secondary education have been of two types. The first grade qualification (**eerstegraads bevoegdheid**) qualifies for teaching at all levels of secondary education and HBO. The second grade qualification (**tweedegraads bevoegdheid**) qualifies for teaching in vocational schools, MAVO schools and the first three forms of HAVO and VWO schools.

Before 1989, there was also a third grade qualification (**derdegraads bevoegdheid**), qualifying to teach in MAVO and LBO only; the latter has been abolished and replaced by a restricted second grade qualification (**beperkte tweedegraads bevoegdheid**).

Before 1968, these three grade qualifications did not exist as such but went by the name of full qualification (**volledige bevoegdheid**) and restricted qualification (**beperkte bevoegdheid**).

Until 1986

A first-grade qualification could be obtained through a university degree after an additional examination in theory and practice of education, or through the **MO-B certificate**.

There were several different types of non-university teacher training qualifications, the most important of which were the **LO certificates** (**Lager Onderwijs Akte**), the **MO certificates** (**Middelbaar Onderwijs Akte**) and the **NLO certificates** (**Nieuwe Lerarenopleiding**).

Courses leading to the **LO certificate**, also known as C-courses, took two years part-time. They gave a restricted (third grade) qualification for the subject studied. The **MO certificates** were divided into two levels. The first level consisted of a four-year part-time course from the level of **MULO** (later **HAVO**), leading to the **MO-A certificate**. This gave a restricted (second grade) qualification entitling the holder to teach in nursery teacher training schools, vocational schools and the lower forms of general secondary schools. To teach in primary teacher training institutes, students had to hold the **MO-A certificate** in two subjects.

The second level was a three- to four-year part-time course from the **MO-B certificate**. This gave a full (first grade) qualification, entitling holders to teach at all levels of secondary schools and pursue their studies at university.

In 1970 teacher training courses was extended by the implementation of full-time programmes at teacher training institutes linked to universities, the New Secondary School Teacher Training Colleges (*Nieuwe Lerarenopleidingen*), which are a new form of HBO.

All students at the *Nieuwe Lerarenopleidingen* were required to take two subjects, studied as part of a four-year full-time course, in which educational theory and practice were also studied. Practical training was given much attention, but its provision differed from one institute to another. After the four-year course a student obtained a third-grade qualification in these two subjects. The student could then choose to follow an additional course for six months in one subject, to obtain a second-grade qualification in that subject. Holders of the second-grade teacher qualification could enter university at a level determined at the discretion of the university concerned.

Since 1986

The university reforms of 1982 also affected teacher training at universities. Teacher training was taken out of the *doctoraal* programme and extended to a one-year course which is open to university and HBO graduates only. The course (*Universitaire Lerarenopleiding*, ULO) is the responsibility of the university, which is also the authority which awards the diploma. Admission is selective: university graduates must already have taken a preparatory course of two months during their *doctoraal* programme and must have obtained high marks. HBO graduates are admitted if they had high marks or have proved to be successful teachers.

A university or **HBO degree** in combination with the diploma of the university teacher training course gives a first-grade qualification.

LO and MO courses have been phased out. The third grade qualification has been abolished.

INTERNATIONAL EDUCATION

Since 1950, a number of institutions have existed alongside the formal university system offering international post-secondary and postgraduate courses. The medium of instruction is usually English, and the courses have been set up primarily for students from developing countries. The courses are normally short (between four weeks and two years) and offered in science and technology; medical sciences; media, communication and transport; agriculture; social sciences; European studies and culture; management and business. Entrance requirements vary, but in most cases a bachelor degree or equivalent is required for admission.

New Zealand

Until 1989 New Zealand's education system was largely under the administration of the Department of Education. Universities were autonomous institutions. Polytechnics, community colleges and colleges of education had their own councils but were under the control of the Department of Education. There were a number of separate national statutory bodies established for specific functions, such as the Board of Studies (for administering **School** and **Sixth form Certificates**), the Universities Entrance Board, the Trades Certification Board and the Authority for Advanced Vocational Awards.

Under the Education Act 1989 and the Education Amendment Act 1990, the centralized functions carried out by the Department of Education were devolved to schools and state agencies as follows:

The Ministry of Education is responsible for providing education policy advice to Government, for overseeing the implementation of approved policies, and for ensuring optimum use of resources allocated to education.

The New Zealand Qualifications Authority co-ordinates all qualifications in post–compulsory education and training; it sets and reviews standards, has the responsibility that New Zealand qualifications are recognized overseas and that overseas qualifications are recognized in New Zealand, and it administers national secondary and tertiary examinations.

The Education Review Office audits and reviews the performance of all registered schools and licensed early childhood centres.

The Teachers Registration Board registers teachers and monitors standards in teaching.

Boards of trustees, whose members include parent and staff representatives, now manage state primary and secondary schools. Secondary school boards may also have a student representative. The boards of trustees must ensure that the school has a written charter, approved by the Ministry of Education.

Elected Councils administer each university, polytechnic and college of education.

Although primary education is only compulsory from six years of age, nearly all New Zealand children start formal schooling on their fifth birthday and receive eight years of primary education. Secondary schooling starts at age 13, and is compulsory until 16.

English is the medium of instruction in nearly all New Zealand education institutions. However, in response to community demand, a significant number of early childhood centres, and a growing number of schools also provide instruction in Maori or Pacific Island languages. In 1987, Maori was formally recognized as an official language of New Zealand. In 1994, Maori is the medium of instruction in nearly 800 *Khoanga reo* (language nests) and some twenty schools known as *Kura Kaupapa*. Nearly 200 Pacific Island language nests provide opportunities for young children to have their pre-school education in one or more Pacific Island languages. Under the New Zealand curriculum framework all children have the opportunity to develop and use their own language as part of their schooling, and to acquire knowledge of Maori language and culture.

EVALUATION IN BRITAIN

School

School Certificate (awarded on completion of form 5) – generally considered to be below GCSE standard.

Matriculation

The following qualifications may be compared to approximately GCSE standard (grades A, B and C).

Sixth Form Certificate (awarded on completion of form 6).

University Entrance (awarded on completion of form 6, until 1986).

The following qualifications may be generally considered to be above GCSE standard:

Higher School Certificate (awarded on completion of form 7) – generally considered comparable to approximately one year above GCSE standard.

University Entrance, Bursaries and Scholarship Examination – may be compared to GCE Advanced standard overall, but not on a subject-for-subject basis, if aggregate marks of at least 250 are scored; satisfies the general entrance requirements of British higher education institutions, provided a score of at least 250 has been obtained.

University Junior Scholarship/Entrance Scholarship Examination prior to 1990 – may be compared to GCE Advanced standard on a subject-for-subject basis; satisfies the entrance requirements of British higher education institutions.

Technical

New Zealand Technicians Certificate – generally considered comparable to the City and Guilds Certificate Part III.

New Zealand Certificate (in various subjects) – generally considered comparable to BTEC Higher National Diploma / N/SVQ level 4.

Higher

Bachelor degree (three years) – generally considered comparable to British Bachelor (Ordinary) degree standard.

Bachelor (Honours) degree (four years) – generally considered comparable to British Bachelor (Honours) degree standard.

Master's degree – generally considered comparable to British taught Master's degree standard.

MARKING SYSTEMS

School

School Certificate

Until 1962: no grades.

1962–8: marks of over 50 per cent were needed in four subjects including English.

1969–86: success in one or more subjects, represented by grades A, B or C, as follows:

A = 80–100 per cent
B = 65–79
C = 50–64
Below 50 per cent was a fail.

1986 – 1991:			Since 1992:		
A1	–	80–100 per cent	A	–	80–100 per cent
A2	–	68–79 per cent	B	–	65–79 per cent
B1	–	56–67 per cent	C	–	50–64 per cent
B2	–	45–55 per cent	D	–	30–49 per cent
C1	–	31–44 per cent	E	–	1–29 per cent
C2	–	16–30 per cent			
D	–	0–15 per cent			

Sixth Form Certificate

1969–73   Five grades A–E

From 1974 awarded in nine grades (1–9) for all subjects entered:

Grade 1 and 2	–	excellent level of achievement
Grade 3	–	high level of achievement
Grade 4	–	very satisfactory level of achievement
Grade 5	–	satisfactory level of achievement
Grade 6 and 7	–	adequate level of achievement
Grade 8 and 9	–	low level of achievement

University Entrance Examination (until 1986)

Before 1986, university entrance was based on the **University Entrance Examination (UEE)**, which could be gained by accreditation (internally assessed) or by external examination. It was most often achieved by students at the end of the fourth year of secondary education. The marking scale for each subject taken in the examination was 0–100. The **UEE** was awarded when the total marks were 200 or better in at least four subjects. Most students however were accredited, and thus did not take the examination.

If a student obtained passes in only one, two or three subjects, or did not include English, a credit by examination was granted for each subject in which 50 or more marks were obtained.

University Entrance, Bursaries and Scholarships

Marks are on a scale of 0–100 per paper. Students may gain an **A Bursary** by aggregating 300 or more marks over four or five subjects, a **B Bursary** with 250–299 marks over four or five subjects, or the basic entrance qualification by obtaining three subjects at grade C:

A Grade	66–100 per cent
B Grade	55–65 per cent
C Grade	46–55 per cent
D Grade	30–45 per cent
E Grade	0–29 per cent

Higher

Universities

A+	high first
A	clear first
A–	bare first
B+	high second
B	clear second
B–	bare second
C+	sound pass
C	pass
C–	marginal pass
D	failure; reasonable chance of passing repeat course
E	failure

Classification for an **Honours Bachelor degree:**

First class	A
Second class (Division I)	A–/B
Second class (Division II)	B/B–
Third class	C+

Polytechnics

Either of these grading systems may be used:

A+	85–100 per cent	A	pass with credit
A	80–85	B	good pass
A–	75–79	C	pass
B+	70–74	D	marginal fail
B	65–69	E/F	fail
B–	60–64		
C+	55–59		
C	50–54		
D	45–49		
E	40–44		
F	0–39		

Colleges of Education

Each college uses its own grading system. The most common is the use of grades A to E, where A, B or C are passing grades, and D or E fail grades.

SCHOOL EDUCATION

Primary

This usually commences at age five, at the discretion of parents, but is not compulsory until age six. After the first two years of infant classes, children complete standards 1,

2, 3 and 4. The remaining two years are usually completed at an intermediate school, but if no such school is available, forms 1 and 2 are provided at the primary school.

Secondary

Secondary schooling starts at form 3, typically at age 13, and is available to form 8. Schooling is compulsory until age 16.

During the first two years of secondary schooling, students follow the national curriculum and also select from a number of optional subjects such as a second language, economics, home economics, or workshop technology. In form 5 students are encouraged to take a more specialized programme of study while maintaining a balanced curriculum. For the final two or three years, students are able to choose from a wide range of courses which lead to further study, training or work opportunities.

Secondary School Qualifications

There are currently four national qualifications for senior secondary school students: **School Certificate, Sixth form Certificate, Higher School Certificate** and **University Entrance, Bursaries and Scholarships Examinations**. All are administered by the New Zealand Qualifications Authority.

The **School Certificate** is usually taken at age 15 in the third year of secondary education. Any number of subjects may be taken (usually five or six). The certificate is awarded in single subjects. Assessment can be internal, external or a combination of both.

The **Sixth form Certificate** is awarded on a single subject basis to students who have completed a course of one year beyond **School Certificate** level. It is a nationally moderated, internally assessed qualification, with no public examination. A maximum of six subjects must be taken, which must include English. Schools are allocated an overall distribution of grades, and are then free to credit individual students with a grade for each subject taken, on a scale of 1 (highest) to 9.

Sixth form certificates are recognized for entry to polytechnics and colleges of education and, to a lesser extent, universities. It is planned that this qualification will be phased out when the National Qualifications Framework (see **Future Directions** below) is fully implemented in schools.

The **Higher School Certificate** is awarded after five years of secondary education, including an advanced course of one year beyond the **Sixth form Certificate** in at least three subjects. The qualification is awarded by schools. The **Higher School Certificate** has no examination, and no subject or grade appears on the certificate. It is planned that the **Higher School Certificate** will also be phased out under the National Qualifications Framework.

University Entrance, Bursaries and Scholarships are the final school examinations, usually taken in form 7. These national examinations have been the recognized method of entry to tertiary study since 1986. Assessment for all subjects, other than art and physical education, is by external examination.

Students enter from 1 to 6 subjects. A minimum of four subjects is required for the award of a bursary or scholarship. Until 1993, the minimum required for entry to university was four Ds or 160 marks in four subjects; since 1993, this has changed to three Cs plus the **Higher School certificate**.

A Bursaries are gained by students who achieve an aggregate of 300 marks or more and **B Bursaries** by those achieving between 250 and 299 marks in their best five subjects. Bursary awards may provide priority entry into selective universities and in some cases exemptions from first year university courses.

Future Directions

National Qualifications Framework

At the time of writing (June 1994) New Zealand is moving towards a new National Qualifications Framework. By 1997 it is envisaged that all nationally approved post-compulsory qualifications will come under the umbrella of the new framework.

The National Qualifications Framework is intended to ensure consistent approach to all New Zealand Qualifications in academic and vocational areas. All achievement objectives leading to national qualifications will be translated into unit standards and assigned to eight levels, where level 1 will be broadly equivalent to form 5 and level 8 represents advanced postgraduate qualifications.

The unit standards will contribute to one of three new national qualifications: a **National certificate** for levels 1 to 4; a **National Diploma** for levels 5 to 7 (which includes a first degree) and postgraduate degrees/diplomas represented by level 8. Prior learning, workplace assessment and Maori specific qualifications will be recognized.

Progress has already been made: over 170 standard setting bodies have been established, and seven national certificates and diplomas have been registered under the framework.

From 1997 it is planned that the **Sixth Form Certificate** and **Higher School Certificate** will be phased out and the **National Certificate** will be the sole national qualification for senior secondary school students. **School Certificate** and **University Entrance, Bursaries and Scholarships** will remain as optional examinations.

Entrance to University

Since 1993, students can be qualified to enter university in New Zealand in the following ways:

with the **New Zealand University Entrance, Bursaries and Scholarships Examination**, studied over a period of one or more years, with grades of A, B or C in three subjects, provided that the candidate has also gained a **New Zealand Higher School certificate**

or, with the **New Zealand Bursary** at A or B level in the **New Zealand University Entrance, Bursaries and Scholarships qualification**.

In response to continuing growth in applications, universities are becoming more selective. Each has developed its own admission criteria, which vary on a course-by-course basis. Restrictions such as an **A Bursary** are specified as a prerequisite. These restrictions have been in place for many years at the two medical schools (Auckland and Otago).

Students under the age of 20 years who have gained **Sixth Form Certificate** in at least one subject, or its equivalent, and have not, in the year of application, entered examinations in more than two subjects of the **University Entrance, Bursaries and Scholarships Examinations**, may apply for **provisional entrance** to a specified course of study. On the satisfactory completion of one year of full-time study or its equivalent, a student with provisional entrance is deemed to have qualified for entrance to a university. These students undertake regular courses.

TECHNICAL AND VOCATIONAL EDUCATION

Technical and vocational education is provided by state-owned polytechnics, private training establishments, and other community education providers. These providers, along with secondary schools, also offer transition education and training for senior secondary students and the unemployed. This seeks to develop skills for employment and further training.

Polytechnics

Entry to a polytechnic can occur at a number of different levels. Course entry requirements may specify a minimum grade in one or more **School Certificate** or **Sixth Form Certificate** subjects, or other qualifications or work experience. Degree programmes usually require similar entry requirements as universities.

Polytechnics provide part-time and full-time professional, technical, vocational and community based courses of varying length. These include introductory studies, trade training, pre-apprenticeship courses (required in some trades) and some first degree courses.

The major qualifications for technical and vocational education are the **New Zealand Technicians Certificate**, the **New Zealand Certificate** and various trade certificates. It is planned that these qualifications will progressively be integrated into the new National Qualifications Framework.

Technicians Certificates comprise a combination of three stages of part-time study and compulsory employment.

The **New Zealand Certificate** consists of a longer period of training, and includes a minimum of five years part-time regular study at day-release and evening classes, together with three years of work experience.

The **New Zealand Diploma** is an advanced qualification for students who have completed a further year of training and work experience beyond **New Zealand Certificate** level, and is available only in a limited number of fields.

Trade Certificates generally require a minimum of three years of combined study and work experience. Successful performance in the third year course and examination, together with the required work experience, leads to the award of a **New Zealand Trade Certificate**.

Further study and experience may lead to the **Advanced Trade Certificate**.

Polytechnics also offer recognized national courses, such as the **National Certificate in Business Studies**.

Nursing education

A **Diploma of Nursing** is awarded to a student who has successfully completed a three-year full-time course. These courses are offered at fifteen polytechnics. Such students are then eligible to sit the registration examination and to be considered for registration with the Nursing Council of New Zealand.

Post-basic courses in nursing are offered at five polytechnics. These courses include courses in midwifery and the **Advanced Diploma of Nursing**.

Bachelor degrees in midwifery and health sciences are also available.

DISTANCE EDUCATION

The Correspondence School provides academic primary and secondary courses for children as well as adults who want a second chance to pass school examinations.

The Open Polytechnic, formerly the New Zealand Technical Correspondence Institute provides a full range of trades technician training by correspondence, linked with periodic face-to-face practical instruction. All polytechnics may now offer courses by distance education.

Massey University offers a range of degree and diploma courses by correspondence, including annual face-to-face short residential courses. The University of Otago complements the Massey University extramural programme by offering a number of courses through its 'teaching at a distance' teleconference network. The University of Waikato offers off-campus certificates at first-year undergraduate level in association with regional polytechnics.

The Advanced Studies for Teachers Unit at Palmerston North College provides professional courses for teachers to upgrade their **Trained Teachers' Certificate** to a **Diploma in Teaching**.

HIGHER EDUCATION

Prior to 1990 degrees were only offered by universities. Polytechnics, colleges of education and registered private training establishments may now also be accredited to offer approved degree courses.

The university system in New Zealand is considered to be very similar to that in Britain.

The University of New Zealand was the only such institution until 1961. The University had constituent colleges which were subsequently split into the autonomous Universities of Otago, Canterbury, Auckland and Victoria. Massey Agricultural College, set up jointly by Auckland and Victoria University Colleges had been set up in 1926, and what was to become the University of Waikato, was established as a branch of Auckland University College in 1955. In 1964 the number of universities increased to six, with the establishment of the University of Waikato and Massey University as full and autonomous universities. Lincoln College existed as an autonomous agricultural college which awarded University of Canterbury degrees until 1990 when Lincoln University was established as the seventh university.

All universities offer diploma, degree and postgraduate courses in most disciplines. Most also specialize in certain fields as described below:

The University of Auckland offers courses in architecture, planning, engineering, medicine and optometry. It also specializes in Pacific and Asian studies and languages.

The University of Waikato has developed a good reputation in science education, technology, management, Maori cultural studies, and teaching English as a second language.

From its establishment <u>Massey University</u> of Palmerston North has concentrated on studies in agriculture, horticulture, food technology and veterinary science.

<u>Victoria University of Wellington</u> is noted for architecture, public administration and policy and social work.

The <u>University of Canterbury</u> is internationally known for its schools of engineering and forestry.

<u>Lincoln University</u> offers specialized programmes in agriculture and horticulture. It is the only tertiary institution in New Zealand to offer degrees in landscape architecture and in parks and recreation management.

The <u>University of Otago</u> is the country's oldest university and has an established reputation for its work in medicine, dentistry and pharmacy. Physical education, consumer science and surveying are among its other specialized programmes.

Polytechnics provide degree programmes in areas such as architecture, accounting, design, technology, business, commerce and communication. Some have developed joint degree courses with universities. In recent years colleges of education have also offered joint degree courses with universities.

The type of degree most commonly awarded is the three-year **Pass degree**, requiring 8 or 9 'units' (a 'unit' being a year's work in a subject) in at least two subjects and study at all three levels or stages. Since 1973, the universities have laid more emphasis on smaller units of academic value e.g. credit points and continuous assessment.

On average, 21 papers or 108 credits are required for a **Pass degree**, gained not less than three years from matriculation. A system of credit transfer exists between the universities so that students can move from one to another.

Honours degrees last at least four years, except in the case of students, who, in the **Entrance Scholarships Examination**, are admitted to the second year of a course.

Some degrees, mainly professional in character, are preceded by an intermediate course of one year. Intermediate courses can usually be taken at any university.

Master's degrees comprise two years study beyond the **Bachelor degree**. They may be awarded with Honours or Distinction and may involve course work, a thesis or both.

The **PhD** takes the form of supervised research for a minimum of three years, and must be completed in six.

There are several private training establishments which provide higher education courses, for example, the <u>Asia Pacific International Institute</u> (Auckland) offers undergraduate and postgraduate degree courses in business and management subjects. <u>The International Pacific College</u> in Palmerston North offers diplomas and degrees in English and international studies. Bachelor degrees in Divinity are provided by the <u>Bible College of New Zealand</u>; and a Bachelor of Fine Art degree by the <u>Whitecliffe College of Art and Design</u>.

TEACHER EDUCATION

Introduction

Colleges of Education provide training for teachers leading to the award of a **Diploma**

of Teaching. A degree in education from a New Zealand university does not in itself lead to trained teacher status.

There are five colleges of education (situated in Auckland, Palmerston North, Wellington, Christchurch and Dundedin) and a School of Education at the University of Waikato. Wanganui Regional Community Polytechnic also offers a course leading to a **Diploma of Teaching** in bilingual education with an emphasis on Maori language and culture.

Prior to 1983, teachers who completed academic studies to the level of two thirds of a degree were eligible for the award of a **Diploma in Teaching** by the Department for Education. This diploma was recognized in both primary and secondary schools.

From 1986, the **Diploma of Teaching** awarded by colleges of education became the recognized professional qualification for teachers in New Zealand.

The minimum academic entry requirements for students under 20 seeking training in early childhood and primary teaching is the completion of 12 years of schooling and a score of 20 or less in the best five subjects of the **Sixth form Certificate** (with a mark of 5 or better in English). Applicants who are 20 years or over may be admitted on the basis of recent study or work experience. All applicants must undergo a selection process.

Applicants seeking a career in secondary teaching are expected to complete a university degree in their area of speciality.

Early Childhood Education

All colleges of education provide both a three-year **Diploma of Teaching (Early Childhood Education)** programme and conjoint **Diploma of teaching/Bachelor of Education degree** programmes. Prior to the late 1980s a two-year programme leading to the **New Zealand Free Kindergarten Union Diploma** was available.

A range of other certificates are awarded by organizations involved in early childhood education which have varying official recognition. A person holding one of these qualifications may not necessarily be deemed fully qualified, but may be given some recognition.

Primary

Prior to 1986, the recognized qualification for primary teachers was the **Trained Teachers Certificate** awarded by the Department of Education after completion of a training course and a period of probationary teaching. Until 1972, courses were of two years' duration followed by one year of probationary teaching. From 1972, three-year courses were introduced and the probationary teaching period extended to two years. It was also possible to complete an **External Trained Teachers Certificate** on a part-time basis by distance education. Special certificates were awarded in the fields of home economics, technical and commercial teaching.

The **Trained Teachers Certificate** continued to be awarded to primary teachers until 1989. From this date the Teacher Registration Board issued only **practising certificates**.

As from 1986, most students take a three years college programme (Division A) leading to a **Diploma of Teaching (Primary)**. However, it is increasingly expected that students pursuing primary teacher education will have spent a period at university. College courses may be shortened to two years for university graduates or for those who are part-way through degree courses on entry.

A four-year conjoint **Diploma of Teaching (primary)/Bachelor of Education** degree is now available at all colleges in association with the universities. This is likely to replace the three-year diploma courses in the near future.

Secondary

Two options are available for those wishing to qualify as secondary school teachers. Graduates take a one-year course (Division C). A four-year concurrent university or polytechnic degree/professional teacher training (Division B) programme is also available.

Professional updating for teachers

Colleges of Education are involved in offering a wide range of undergraduate and postgraduate courses. All colleges provide Advanced Studies for Teachers (AST) courses through which teachers (mainly primary) can obtain either the **Higher** or **Advanced diploma of teaching**. The Advanced Studies for Teachers units at Palmerston North College and Massey University cater for the continuing education of teachers through distance education.

Postgraduate teaching diplomas for teachers of students with special needs are available. For example, a postgraduate course for bilingual Maori/English teachers is available at the University of Waikato.

Nicaragua

The following chapter regarding the education system in Nicaragua is based on information obtained for the 3rd edition of this Guide, published in 1991, as NARIC has been unable to obtain more recent information.

The medium of instruction is Spanish.

The academic year runs from March to December.

EVALUATION IN BRITAIN

School

Bachillerato – generally considered comparable to GCSE standard (grades A, B and C) on a subject-for-subject basis, with the exception of English language.

Higher

Licenciado/Professional title – generally considered comparable to British Bachelor degree standard if awarded after four or more years of study.

MARKING SYSTEMS

School

Marking is on a percentage scale with a 60 per cent minimum pass-mark ('good').

The **Bachillerato** is only awarded if the grade 'good' is obtained.

Higher

Marking is on a percentage scale with a 70 per cent minimum pass-mark.

SCHOOL EDUCATION

Primary

This covers six years.

Secondary

This covers five years, culminating in the examination for the **Bachillerato** in sciences or in humanities.

FURTHER EDUCATION

The <u>Instituto Politécnico</u> is a private institution which awards professional qualifications after courses lasting two to three years.

HIGHER EDUCATION

The entrance requirement for degree courses is the **Bachillerato** and an entrance examination.

A first degree course leading to a **Licenciado** or **Professional title** (e.g. **Ingeniero**) normally takes a minimum of four years. Some subjects such as law and medicine take longer.

TEACHER EDUCATION

Primary

A five-year secondary level course on completion of primary education, consisting of three years' general education followed by two years' specialization, leads to the qualification of **Diploma de Maestro de Educacion Primaria**.

Secondary

Teachers are holders of the **Licenciado** in their specialist subject.

Niger

Niger gained independence in 1960. There is a strong French influence on the educational system.

The medium of instruction is French.

The academic year runs from October to June.

EVALUATION IN BRITAIN

School

Baccalauréat/Diplôme de Bachelier de l'Enseignement du Second Degré – generally considered comparable to GCSE standard (grades A, B and C) on a subject-for-subject basis, with the exception of English language.

Higher

Diplôme Universitaire d'Etudes Littéraires (DUEL), **Diplôme Universitaire d'Etudes Scientifiques** (DUES) – may be considered to satisfy the general entrance requirements of British higher education institutions.

Licence – generally considered comparable to a standard between GCE Advanced and British Bachelor degree.

Maîtrise – generally considered comparable to British Bachelor (Ordinary) degree standard but where very high marks have been achieved candidates may be considered for admission to postgraduate study.

MARKING SYSTEMS

School and Higher

Marking is on a scale of 0–20; the minimum pass-mark is 10.

16–20	*très bien*	very good
14–15	*bien*	good
12–13	*assez bien*	quite good
10–11	*passable*	average

Pupils scoring between 8 and 9.5 can pass on the basis of a successful oral examination for individual subjects. Borderline cases are judged according to school records (*livret scolaire*).

SCHOOL EDUCATION

Primary

This covers six years and leads to the **Certificat d'Etudes Primaires Elémentaires**.

Secondary

This covers seven years, divided into a four-year lower general cycle followed by a three-year upper cycle, during which pupils may specialize. Pupils successfully completing the four-year lower general cycle gain the **Brevet d'Etudes du Premier Cycle** and are admitted to the *lycée*. On completion of the three-year academic cycle, pupils take the examinations for the **Baccalauréat/Diplôme de Bachelier de l'Enseignement du Second Degré**. The **Baccalauréat** is available in a variety of series/options:

Series A (options A1–A5)	*philosophie-lettres*	philosophy and letters
Series B	*sciences économiques et sociales*	economic and social sciences (available since 1976 but abolished in 1984)
Series C	*sciences mathématiques et physiques*	mathematics and physical sciences
Series D	*sciences mathématiques et naturelles*	mathematics and natural sciences
Series E	*mathématiques*	mathematics

Until 1972 the examinations were administered by the University of Abidjan in the Côte d'Ivoire; since then they have been administered by the University of Niamey.

Technical secondary

On completion of a technical upper secondary course pupils take the examinations for the **Baccalauréat/Bachelier Technicien** in Series F or G:

F1	*construction mécanique*
F3	*electrotechnique*
F4	*genie civil*
G1	*administration technique*
G2	*business*

HIGHER EDUCATION

There are two universities: the Université de Niamey, established in 1971 as the Centre d'Enseignement Supérieur and upgraded to university status in 1973, and the Université Islamique du Niger à Say, established in 1986. The entrance requirement is the

Baccalauréat. Students who do not hold the **Baccalauréat** are required to take an entrance examination.

After two years' study students obtain the **Diplôme Universitaire d'Etudes Littéraires** (DUEL) in arts or the **Diplôme Universitaire d'Etudes Scientifiques** (DUES) in mathematics or sciences. A further year leads to the **Licence** and yet a further year to the **Maîtrise.**

In engineering, students obtain the **Diplôme d'Ingénieur des Techniques de l'Agriculture** or the **Diplôme d'Agronomie Générale** (DAG) after two years' study. A further two years after the DAG leads to the **Diplôme d'Ingénieur Agronome/ Diplôme d'Agronomie Approfondie.**

The **Doctorat en Médecine** takes six years.

Other post-secondary institutions include:

– the Ecole Nationale d'Administration;
– the Ecole Nationale de la Santé Publique;
– the Ecole des Cadres de l'Elevage;
– the Ecole Africaine de la Météorologie et de l'Aviation Civile;
– the Centre de Formation aux Techniques de l'Information.

TEACHER EDUCATION

Primary

The *Ecoles Normales* train teachers for primary schools. The short cycle (*cycle court*) requires the student to hold the **Brevet d'Etudes du Premier Cycle** (BEPC) and takes two years. The long cycle (*cycle long*) takes four years and gives the student **Bachelier** status and the opportunity to go to a *Faculté de Pédagogie* to become a CEG teacher.

Secondary

Teachers for first-cycle secondary schools are trained by the *Faculté de Pédagogie* of the University of Niamey. A two-year programme leads to a professional diploma, the **Diplôme d'Aptitude Pédagogique au Professorat des Collèges d'Enseignement Général (DAP/CEG)**. The faculty also trains inspectors for primary level only and advisers. Second-cycle teachers are trained at the faculties of the University. Training forms part of the **Licence** programmes.

Nigeria

In the early 1970s, the Federal Government formulated a new national policy on education, with the aim of providing universal primary education, expanding facilities at secondary level, and enabling the more even development of facilities throughout the country.

At present no cycle of education is compulsory.

The medium of instruction is usually the local language for the first three years of primary education. Thereafter English is used.

EVALUATION IN BRITAIN

School

West African School Certificate/GCE O level (up to 1989) – grades 1–6 generally equated to GCSE standard (grades A, B and C) on a subject-for-subject basis.

Senior School Certificate (since 1989) – grades 1–6 generally equated to GCSE standard (grades A, B and C) on a subject-for-subject basis.

West African GCE A level (up to 1989) – generally equated to GCE Advanced standard.

Further

National Diploma (ND) – generally considered comparable to BTEC National Diploma / N/SVQ level 3 / Advanced GNVQ/GSVQ standard; may be considered to satisfy the general entrance requirements of British higher education institutions, provided the course is of at least two years duration.

Higher National Diploma (HND) – generally considered comparable to BTEC Higher National Diploma / N/SVQ level 4 standard.

Higher

Bachelor degree – generally considered comparable to British Bachelor degree standard, depending on the awarding institution. (For further information contact the National Academic Recognition Information Centre.)

Teaching

Grade 3 Teacher's Certificate – generally considered to be below GCSE standard.

Grade 2 Teacher's Certificate – generally considered to be below GCSE standard.

Grade 1 Teacher's Certificate – generally considered to be comparable to GCSE standard.

Nigerian Certificate of Education – may be considered to approach GCE Advanced standard.

MARKING SYSTEMS

School

West African School Certificate/GCE O level		Senior School Certificate	
1	excellent	1	excellent
2	very good	2	very good
3	good	3	good
4–6	credit	4–6	good
7–8	pass	7–8	pass
9	fail	9	fail

West African GCE A level

A–E	pass
O	subsidiary pass
F	fail

Higher

Bachelor degrees

1st class	70–100 per cent
2nd class upper division	60–69
2nd class lower division	50–59
3rd class pass	40–49

SCHOOL EDUCATION

Pre-primary

Pre-primary education covers three years, from age three.

Primary

This is now being standardized to cover six years, from age six.

A school certificate is issued at the end of this cycle by headteachers; progress and certification is based on continuous overall assessment by teachers. Before 1992 **Primary School Leaving Certificate** was issued after success in a state administered examination.

The objectives of primary education include preparation for a broad-based education with emphasis on the attainment of permanent and functional literacy and numeracy and effective communication skills. Curriculum offerings include language study, integrated science, mathematics, social studies, cultural arts, health and physical education, religious instruction, agriculture and home economics.

Secondary

Secondary education is divided into junior and senior levels, each lasting three years. A common diversified curriculum is operated at the junior secondary level. At the senior level, there are three different types of school: senior secondary (academic); technical college (craft training) and teachers' colleges for primary teacher training.

The **Junior School Certificate** may be taken at the end of three years of junior secondary education, based on a continuous assessment method and end-of-course examination conducted by the appropriate Ministry of Education.

The **Senior School Certificate** may be taken at the end of the three year cycle, at the same stage as the former **West African GCE O level**. The **Senior School Certificate** replaced the **West African GCE O level** in 1989.

There is a core curriculum consisting of the six following compulsory subjects: English language; one Nigerian language; mathematics; one of physics, chemistry and biology; one of literature in English, history and geography; and agricultural science or a vocational subject. Additionally, students must offer three elective subjects not already offered as core subjects, but may drop one of these in the third year. To obtain the **Senior School Certificate** candidates must enter and sit a minimum of eight subjects (six core subjects plus two or three electives). However, the certificate is awarded on a single-subject basis.

Until 1989, students could stay on for a two-year course in the sixth form leading to the **West African GCE A level**. Under the new system, this option has disappeared and there is no school examination corresponding to the former **West African GCE A level**.

Technical secondary

Junior Craft Schools, Trade Centres and Technical Colleges offer a variety of courses, and admit students from either primary or junior secondary schools. Most courses lead to a City and Guilds qualification, usually Part I. The West African Examinations Council no longer administers examinations on behalf of City and Guilds; individual centres within Nigeria make entries for City and Guilds examinations directly.

Technical colleges belong in part to the upper secondary cycle, and in part to the lower segment of the tertiary education sector, and thus constitute crucial avenues in the provision of vocational training in Nigeria.

A two-tier system of nationally certified courses is offered, leading to the award of **Craft** and **Advanced Craft** certificates, which carry the rank of craftsman and mastercraftsman respectively. The craft level programme lasts three years after Junior Secondary School and is the equivalent of Senior Secondary School; the Advanced Craft programme requires two years pre-entry industrial work experience and ranks alongside lower tertiary programmes.

The system of certification is due to change from 1995. Nationally certified technical/commercial certificates will replace the City and Guilds qualifications. These certificates will be awarded by the National Business and Technical Examinations Board (NABTEB). At the lower level they will be called **National Technical/Business Certificates**, while at the advanced level **Advanced National Technical/Business Certificates** will be awarded.

FURTHER EDUCATION

In the late 1960s/early 1970s, ten polytechnics were established at: Auchi, Calabar, Enugu, Ibadan, Ilorin, Kaduna, Maiduguri, Makurdi, Port Harcourt and Yaba. Additional polytechnics have recently been established all over the country by federal and state governments. From 1979, these institutions offered a four-year course (including one year of practical training) from **West African GCE O level**, leading to the **Higher National Diploma**. Until that date, the colleges offered two-year post-**GCE O level Ordinary National Diplomas** and two-year **Higher Diplomas**. Many colleges still offer the two-stage diplomas in place of the **Higher National Diploma**. Entrance requirements are now the **Senior School Certificate**. The HND programme currently requires an additional one year work placement to be taken after the first two years.

All these programmes are accredited by the National Board for Technical Education to ensure consistency and high standards in both the federal and state colleges of technology and polytechnics. Admission is controlled by the Joint Admissions Matriculation Board (JAMB). Certificates are issued by the individual institutions.

The colleges also offer various certificates in technology which may be obtained after one, two or three years.

HIGHER EDUCATION

Until 1972, both federal and state governments were able to establish institutions of higher education and each region planned its own provision. In 1972, the federal government took over sole responsibility for higher education throughout Nigeria, in an attempt to develop more evenly the facilities for higher education throughout the country. In 1976, the campus of Ibadan University at Jos and the Calabar campus of the University of Nigeria became universities in their own right, and new universities were established at Sokoto and Maiduguri (upgraded and enlarged from the previously existing college of science and technology). Bayero College of Ahmadu Bello University became a university college, and university colleges were also established at Ilorin and Port Harcourt, but all three were immediately upgraded into full universities.

The usual entrance requirement to **Bachelor degree** courses at Nigerian universities has been five **West African GCE O level** and two **A level** passes. Since 1977, admission has been centrally arranged by the Joint Admissions and Matriculation Board (JAMB).

Students who obtained good grades in the **West African GCE O** and **A levels** qualified for 'direct entry' to a three-year degree course.

Students who held only the **West African GCE O level** or obtained only poor grades in the **West African GCE A level** were able to take entrance examinations conducted by individual universities until 1977. Students who passed these examinations were able to proceed to a one-year preliminary course, before embarking on the degree course.

When the JAMB was established, the responsibility for setting and administering the matriculation examination passed from the individual university to the Board. Between 1977 and 1989, the JAMB conducted a competitive entrance examination for admission to the preliminary course at university. The examination was in two parts:

Part 1 the use of English

Part 2 the candidate was required to answer questions in three subject areas related to the intended course of study.

The Ahmadu Bello University ran its own Interim Joint Matriculation Board Examination which admitted to the three year degree programme while also participating in JAMB.

The Universities of Benin and Nigeria incorporated the usual content of a preliminary course in their four-year degree courses and admitted students with **O level** qualifications.

Since the introduction of the **Senior School Certificate** there has been a shift from three to four-year degree courses with a corresponding loss of the additional years in the sixth form.

Courses leading to a **Bachelor degree** normally last four years, except for those in medicine and veterinary medicine (five years).

Students may take either a single-subject Honours degree course or combined Honours. In the former, students study three subjects in the first year, two in the second year and one in the third. In the combined Honours course students take three subjects in the first year and two subjects in both the second and third years. In the fourth year, single subject Honours students take one subject and combined-subject Honours students take at least two subjects.

Postgraduate facilities exist at most institutions with courses leading to certificates, diplomas and **Master's** and **doctorate degrees.**

TEACHER EDUCATION

Primary

Two years' post-primary study at a grade 3 teacher training college led to a **Grade 3 Certificate/Elementary Teacher's Certificate**. These colleges have been phased out.

Four years' (sometimes five in the North) post-primary study at a grade 2 teacher training college leads to a **Grade 2 Certificate/Higher Elementary Teacher's Certificate**. Holders of the old **Grade 3 Certificate** may take an upgrading course to become grade 2 teachers.

Secondary

Holders of the **Grade 2 Certificate** may also teach in lower secondary schools. Secondary level teachers are normally trained in universities (on a **BEd** course) or colleges of education (formerly advanced teachers' colleges). The entrance requirement for both types of college is the **West African GCE O level** or a **Grade 2 Certificate**. There used to be Grade 1 teachers' colleges which offered two-year courses during which students studied education and two teaching subjects and on successful completion obtained a **Grade 1 Certificate**. This qualified holders to teach in junior secondary schools. However, junior secondary teachers are now trained in colleges of education leading to the **Nigerian Certificate of Education**, which also qualifies them for university admission. Holders of the **Grade 2 Certificate** may be admitted to this course or to the one-year course leading to the **Associate Certificate in Education**.

Admission to Colleges of Education is conducted by the JAMB, and programmes are accredited by the National Commission for Colleges of Education. It is envisaged that the **Nigerian Certificate of Education** will eventually be the minimum qualification for teaching at primary level.

Nigeria

Technical

Technical Teachers' Colleges offer three-year courses in technical or commercial fields leading to the **Nigerian Certificate of Education (technical)** and a one-year diploma course for technical teachers already qualified in their subject.

Norway

The significant feature of the Norwegian education system has in the past been its centralization and control by the state of all aspects, including syllabuses and timetables. The aim remains to ensure equality of standards and of opportunity throughout the country. Various reforms have been introduced, mostly at the level of school education. Radical changes continue to result from moves during the 1980s towards decentralization of decision-making from the ministries to local authorities.

There are two languages – *Bokmål* and *Nynorsk*. Both are taught in schools, although *Bokmål* prevails.

The academic year runs from August to June.

EVALUATION IN BRITAIN

School

Avgangseksamen – generally considered comparable to GCSE (grades A, B and C) on a subject-for-subject basis, with the exception of English language.

Examen Artium (before 1981) – and **Vitnemål fra den Videregående Skole** (since 1982 replaces **Examen Artium** for general subjects and for administration and commerce) – may be considered to satisfy the general entrance requirements of British higher education institutions.

Higher

Ingenior (from *Ingenior høgskoler*) generally considered comparable to BTEC Higher National Diploma / N/SVQ level 4 standard.

Høgskole Kandidat (from *distriktshøgskoler)* generally considered comparable to BTEC Higher National Diploma / N/SVQ level 4 standard.

Candidatus Magisteri – generally considered comparable to British Bachelor (Honours) degree standard, although the course lasts longer than in the UK.

Candidatus Realium, Candidatus Philologiae – generally considered comparable to British MPhil degree standard.

Licentiatus, Doctor – generally considered comparable to British PhD degree standard.

MARKING SYSTEMS

School

Since 1968

Marking is on the scale 6 (maximum) to 0, with 2 as the pass-mark.

This system was first used in:

1969 for subjects finished in the first year of upper secondary school (*Gymnasium*);

1970 for subjects finished in the second year;

1971 for subjects finished in the third year.

Deltatt

Where the student has taken optional subjects but has chosen not to be given a mark in a particular subject, the word *deltatt* (has followed the teaching) appears instead of a mark.

Tekniske Høgskoler

Marking is on the scale:

1.0	(excellent, almost never awarded)
1.5	
2.0	
3.0	
3.5	(lowest passing average)
4.0	(lowest passing mark)
4.5	
5.0	
6.0.	

Distriktshøgskoler (regional colleges)

Marking is on the scale 1.0, 1.5, 2.0, 3.0, 3.5, 4.0; fail-marks are not recorded.

Higher

1.0–1.5	*laudabilis prae ceteris* (maximum)
1.6–2.5	*laudabilis*
2.6–3.2	*haud illaudabilis*
3.3–4.0	*non contemnendus* (lowest passing grade)

Only one decimal point is used when grading each subject, the final grade of a degree has two decimal places.

For general linguistics and general phonetics only 'passed' is used.

Teacher

Pedagogiske Høgskoler – 4 (maximum) to 1 (lowest passing grade).

SCHOOL EDUCATION

Kindergarten (*Barnehager*)

Facilities are available at this level for some children between the ages of three and six-and-a-half years. It is not compulsory.

Primary

Until 1959, primary schooling (*Folkeskole*) was compulsory for seven years from age seven. The 1959 Primary Schools Act established nine years of compulsory education (*Grunnskolen*) divided into six years' elementary (*Barneskole*) and three years' secondary (*Ungdomsskole*). By the academic year 1970–1 this increased period of compulsory education had been established more or less throughout the country.

The curriculum at *Barneskole* includes religious instruction, Norwegian, arithmetic, writing, arts, geography, history, music, handiwork, physical education, natural science, English (introduced in grade 4), social science, home economics, study of local history and folklore.

The introduction of compulsory schooling for six-year-olds will be introduced in 1997, which will bring the total length of compulsory education to ten years (ages six to sixteen).

Lower secondary

Until 1959

On completion of the seven-year primary course, pupils proceeded to the three-year course at a *Realskole*. The syllabus of the first and second years was the same as that of the first two years of the five-year *Gymnasium* course. The final certificate obtained on completion of the second year of the three-year course was the **Realskole-Eksamen**. Pupils could then stay on for an additional year or transfer to a *Gymnasium* (see below).

Since 1959

Under the system of nine years' compulsory education pupils proceed to a three-year course at an *Ungdomsskole* (comprehensive school) on completion of the elementary school. There is no entrance examination to these courses and no streaming.

At the end of the ninth year, pupils may exceptionally stay on for a tenth year to improve their marks or to consolidate their studies before starting work or beginning at the *Gymnasium/Videregående Skole*.

In grade 7 the curriculum includes Norwegian, mathematics, religious instruction, social studies, natural science, English, music, physical education, art and home economics. In grades 8 and 9 there is the possibility of specialization and a second foreign language may be taken. However, besides the obligatory subjects, certain topics must be covered: traffic training, alcohol, drugs, tobacco, environment, careers, school council, family life, consumer education, nutrition, first aid, dental health and sex education.

On completion of grade 9, the leaving examination is taken, **Avgangseksamen**, usually in four subjects, to include two from Norwegian, mathematics, English and science, which, together with teachers' assessments, produce a final mark (*vitnemål*).

Upper secondary

Until 1976

A three-year course was offered, generally culminating in the **Examen Artium**, for pupils who, until 1959, had completed two years of *Realskole*, and after that date for those who completed the course at *Ungdomsskole*. Pupils would already have studied English.

Before 1976, six *Linjer* (areas of specialization) were available, although not all may have been available in one school. These were:

Real-Linje	physics and mathematics
Latin-Linje	classical languages
Engelsk-Linje	modern languages (English as the main subject)
Norron-Linje	Norwegian history and language
Naturfag-Linje	biology and chemistry
Økonomisk-Linje	economics.

Regardless of the specialization taken, all pupils studied Norwegian, English, German, French, history and civics, geography, biology, chemistry with physiology, mathematics, physical training and singing. More time was devoted to particular subjects, depending on the specialization. Both official Norwegian languages were compulsory.

The final examination, the **Examen Artium**, consisted of written and oral tests in Norwegian, English, German, mathematics, physics (only the science line) and Latin (only the Latin line) and a series of oral examinations in other subjects. Pupils had to pass in all subjects to matriculate. The results were analysed by the Council of Secondary Education, to ensure that the grading was uniform in all parts of the country. The full examination could be gradually built up by sitting the necessary individual examinations over a longer period of time, and certain subjects could be examined in the penultimate year.

Handelsgymnasia (commercial secondary schools)

These offered a three-year course from completion of the second year of *Realskole* (before 1959) or the leaving examination of an *Ungdomsskole*. The course offered was similar to the *Økonomisk-Linje* of the *Gymnasia* (before 1976) and prepared the pupil for higher education.

Landsgymnasia

These were regional secondary schools offering a four-year course on completion of seven years' primary education and a six-month continuation course.

1976 – 1994

The 1974 New Curriculum Plan included a reform of the upper secondary school and introduced an all-round school system (i.e. combining academic upper secondary (*Gymnasium*) and vocational), the *Videregående Skole*. The new system was established formally from 1 January 1976 and fully operational from 1 August 1979. The *Videregående Skole* offered one to two-year basic courses (*grunnkurs*) and advanced courses (*videregåendekurs*). The general studies option normally lasted three years.

The upper secondary school curriculum comprised eight areas of study. Two were previously taken at the *Gymnasia:* the general option and the commercial and clerical option. The others were vocational: aesthetics, fishing and maritime studies, handicraft and industry, physical education, home economics and health and social subjects. The vocational areas of study were job oriented, whilst the general area of study led on to academic study.

Obligatory subjects in the general and commercial and clerical areas of study were:

Norwegian; English – language A; modern languages – language B (begun in the lower secondary school in addition to English) and language C (begun in the upper secondary school – usually French and German); social studies (i.e. geography, history/civics), mathematics, natural science, physical education and religious education.

In the second and third years of general studies, pupils specialized in one of four branches until 1990:

Natural science – based on two or more of physics, chemistry, biology, mathematics;

Social studies – based on two or more of law, history, mathematics, social studies, social economics, business administration and economics;

Language – based on two or more of linguistics, English, Latin, Old Norse, languages B and C (usually German and French);

Music (few schools) – based on theoretical and practical studies of music.

However, the separation into branches ceased to apply from 1990–1; all pupils have been able to choose subjects from two or more of the former branches from this date.

There were also optional subjects covering ten periods a year. (The number depends on how many periods were covered in the subjects in the chosen specialization in years two and three, and on the choice of the second foreign language.) These optional subjects could have been additional courses from the chosen specialization, fine or performing arts courses or vocational courses such as typing.

On completion of the three-year general area of study pupils took the examination for the **Vitnemål fra den Videregående Skole**/Certificate of Upper Secondary Education.

Folkehøgskoler (folk high schools)

These offer courses of general education lasting up to two years to students aged at least seventeen. No examinations are taken.

REFORM '94

A major reorganization of upper secondary education came into force in 1994. All young people between the ages of 16 and 19 now have a statutory right to upper secondary education. One of the main goals is to preserve a decentralized education system.

There is now a selection of thirteen foundation courses, followed by specialization at the advanced level (I and II).

The model for vocational training, leading to a craftsman or journeyman's certificate, is two years of school-based training, followed by up to two years of work-based training.

The **Vitnemål fra den Videregående Skole**/Certificate of Upper Secondary Education remains the general qualification for entry to higher education. The minimum requirements for this qualification are now as follows:

Completed three-year upper secondary education, including a foundation course and advanced level courses I and II, **or** a craft or journeyman's certificate, **and** a specified level of knowledge in the following subjects: Norwegian, English, social studies, mathematics and natural sciences/environmental studies.

The reform will thus ensure that applicants from all streams of upper secondary education should be able to qualify for higher education, and pupils who wish to qualify for higher education as well as gaining an occupational qualification will be able to do so.

Further to the aims of REFORM '94, universities and colleges may only set additional entry requirements if there are sound technical reasons for doing so.

Technical secondary

Until 1976

Technical schools (*Tekniske Skoler*) offered two-year courses, lengthened in the early 1960s to three years. The entrance requirement was the **Realskole-Eksamen** plus one year of practical experience, or the *Ungdomsskole* final examination and the corresponding practical experience. The qualification obtained, **Ingeniør** (technician) had the same standing as the **Examen Artium** and admitted to university. Students entering the course already holding the **Examen Artium** did not need the practical experience.

Today the qualification of **Ingeniør** is awarded only after a two to three-year post-secondary course.

The *Tekniske Fagskoler* were more practically based and their two-year course led to the qualification of **Tekniker**. They had the same academic requirements as the *Tekniske Skoler* but required two years' practical experience in addition.

Specialist vocational schools offered basic education and specialist training in a variety of fields through courses lasting between six months and three years. Most courses required, for admission, completion of the *Realskole* or *Ungdomsskole*.

Verkstedskoler offered basic vocational training before beginning an apprenticeship, lasting about one year, but sometimes up to three.

Laerlingskoler were part-time schools for apprentices.

Since 1976

The *Videregående Skoler* have offered courses at further education level in all areas.

REFORM '94 (see above) has reorganized technical and vocational upper secondary education.

There are no longer separate technical schools. However, *Tekniske Fagskoler* still exist, providing more advanced technical education for students who have completed their basic training and have work experience.

HIGHER EDUCATION

This is offered at a variety of institutions: universities and university-level national colleges, regional colleges (*Distrikthøgskoler*), teacher-training colleges (*Pedagogiske Høgskoler*) and advanced vocational institutions (of engineering, social services, music and advanced nursing.) Some of these institutions offer courses which in Britain would be classified as further education.

Recent reforms allow studies at regional colleges to be combined with educational programmes at other institutes of higher education. They can also provide the basic entry requirements for postgraduate study at universities and university colleges.

Entrance to higher education is based on **Vitnemål fra den Videregående Skole** (general studies or administration and commerce). Many university faculties now operate a system of *numerus clausus* (restricted entry).

There are four multi-faculty universities and six university colleges. The latter carry out research and offer university level instruction, both undergraduate and postgraduate.

The University of Tromsø is the newest university, founded in 1972 to provide an infrastructure of higher learning north of the Arctic Circle. The University of Trondheim was established in 1969 by bringing together three major educational and scientific institutions already in existence: Det Kongelige Norske Videnskabers Selskap (Royal Norwegian Society of Science), the Norges Laererhøgskole (State College for Teachers), and the Norges Tekniske Høgskole (Norwegian Institute of Technology). There is no strict time limit set for the completion of studies for a degree, and students present themselves for examination when they think they are ready. All students (except at Norges Tekniske Høgskole) must complete a preliminary course (normally about one semester), leading to the **Examen Philosophicum**. The average length of study for a final graduate degree is five to seven years and they are acquired by accumulating subjects at subsidiary (*grunnfag*), minor (*mellomfag*) and major (*hovedfag*) levels.

In the humanities faculty of the University of Oslo, in addition to the courses at *grunnfag*, *mellomfag* and *hovedfag* which are on average calculated to last respectively two, three and four semesters, there are now courses lasting half a semester (*halvsemesteremner*), one semester (*semesteremner*) and four semesters, the same length as *hovedfag*, but having a different structure and entitled *storfag*. The *storfag* can be used as a preparation for *hovedfag* but will probably be most important as a self-contained post-experience course.

Students of liberal arts, social sciences and natural sciences usually read for a **Candidatus Magisterii** (Cand Mag), the first university degree, which is obtained by accumulating subjects at the subsidiary and minor levels, usually after a minimum of three-and-a-half to four years. Higher degrees, awarded after two years' further study and research at the major *hovedfag* level, are the degrees of **Candidatus Philologiae** (Cand Philol), **Candidatus serum politicanum** and **Candidatus Realium** (Cand Real) in the humanities and sciences respectively.

Doctoral study programmes (**dr scient**, **dr art**, **dr Polit**, etc.) take three to four years of research based study. In addition to completing a doctoral thesis under supervision, the candidate has to undergo obligatory training in scientific method. There is also a general doctoral degree **doctor philosophiae** (**dr philos**) requiring no obligatory training but with very high requirements for the doctoral thesis. Dissertations of original research are examined by a committee of specialists after the candidate has defended the work in two public lectures.

Engineering graduates of the <u>Norwegian Institute of Technology</u> obtain the qualification of **Sivilingeniør** after approximately four-and-a-half years. (Note the difference between this and the qualification of **Ingeniør**, obtained before 1976 after a course of technical secondary education and since then after a three-year post **Examen Artium** course.)

Law:

The **Candidatus Juris** (Cand Juris) is obtained after a course of five to six years, leading on to courses for the **Licentiatus Juris** and **Doctor Juris**.

Medicine:

The **Candidatus Mediciniae** (Cand Med) is obtained after a course of six to seven years, leading on to the course for the **Doctor Mediciniae**.

Dental science normally takes four years; veterinary science takes six to six-and-a-half years.

Architecture:

The <u>Oslo School of Architecture</u>, the <u>Bergen School of Architecture</u> and the <u>University of Trondheim</u> offers a five-year course leading to the qualification of **Arkitekt**.

Agriculture:

The <u>State College of Agriculture (Norges Landbrukshøgskole)</u> offers a five-year course leading to the qualification of **Candidatus Agric** (Cand Agric).

Engineering:

There are twelve colleges of engineering (*Ingeniørhøgskoler*) which offer two- and three-year full-time courses from the level of the **Examen Artium**, leading to the status of **Ingeniør**.

Adult Education *Folkeuniversitet* (FU)

This is the national body into which *Friundervisningen's* (adult education) branches are grouped. The oldest organization was founded in Oslo in 1864 to encourage university students to teach working-class adults. There are over 300 local branches of the *Folkeuniversitet*, which offer academic and vocational courses.

District Colleges *Distriktshøgskoler*

There are also a number of district colleges (*Distriktshøgskoler*), the first of which was created in 1969. These provide courses of higher education of shorter duration than those offered by the universities, often vocational or based on the particular needs of the region and built on an interdisciplinary approach. Courses last one to three years from the level of the **Examen Artium**. Students are awarded the qualification of **Høgskole Kandidat** after courses lasting two years. Courses are generally broader and more innovative than those of the non-university colleges of engineering, social work, etc.

Some *Distriktshøgskoler* teach courses which the universities have validated and recognized as being *grunnfag* and (in fewer cases) *mellomfag* levels. Recent developments have led the *Distriktshøgskoler* (and the other advanced vocational institutions) to award the degree of **Candidatus Magisterii** to those who accumulate the appropriate number of subjects at *grunnfag* and *mellomfag* levels.

From August 1994 these institutions came under a reorganization programme. All institutions in the college sector will be termed *Høgskolen* and will be gradually concentrated into a lesser number of college centres. The aim is that they will then have a common regulation structure, and be on par with the university sector.

TEACHER EDUCATION

Until 1973

Folkeskole, Barneskole, Ungdomsskole – prospective teachers took a four-year course at a *Laererskole* on completion of *Realskole/Grunnskole* or a two-year course if they entered with the **Examen Artium**. Both courses led to the status of **Laerer**.

Since 1973

The new Law on Teacher Education (1973) changed the name of the *Laererskoler* to *Pedagogiske Høgskoler*, and these now offer a three-year course from the level of the **Examen Artium**. This has, since 1992, been extended to four years.

The title of **Adjunkt** is obtained either by a further one year of approved study in the case of a **Laerer**, or in the case of university graduates holding a lower degree (e.g. Cand Mag), by completing a six-month course covering educational theory and teaching practice at a *Pedagogisk Seminar*.

Lektors, the majority of whom work in *Videregående Skoler*, have either obtained a higher university degree and taken the six-month course at the *Pedagogisk Seminar* or have completed approved studies at *hovedfag* level (see **HIGHER EDUCATION**) lasting a minimum of two years after the award of **Adjunkt** and three years after receiving the title **Laerer**.

Oman

Until 1970, there were very few facilities for Western education. Since then, there has been considerable development, and it is believed that 90 per cent of children, male and female, start primary school. The drop-out rate still gives cause for concern but the general picture is one of continuing progress, especially in rural areas. The birth rate is estimated at over four per cent, which means that half of Oman's population is of school age. Government attention is turning increasingly to the role of education in training for employment, as part of its overall policy of reducing dependence on expatriates.

The Ministry of Education and Youth is responsible for general education including teacher training and the University. The Gulf Co-operation Council, of which Oman is a member, is attempting to harmonize curricula in some subjects and promote transferability of qualifications among member states. Most technical and vocational education is handled by the Ministry of Labour and Vocational Training.

There are several private schools in Oman, usually taking a mixture of Omani and expatriate pupils. A few offer **GCSE, BTEC First Certificate**, American High School credits or the **International Baccalaureate**.

Education at government schools is free but not compulsory.

The medium of instruction in schools is Arabic; the teaching of English begins in the fourth year of primary education. In further and higher education institutions English is normally the medium of instruction in the sciences, Arabic in the arts.

The academic year runs from September to June, with a short break around February.

EVALUATION IN BRITAIN

School

Thanawiya amma (Secondary School Leaving Certificate) – generally considered comparable to GCSE standard (grades A, B and C) on a subject-for-subject basis when a minimum overall mark of 80 per cent has been obtained, with the exception of English language. Students with very good results may be considered for admission to access/bridging courses.

Higher

Bachelor degree – may be considered to satisfy the general entrance requirements of British higher education institutions. Exceptionally, students with very high grades may be given advanced standing.

MARKING SYSTEM

School

Thanawiya amma (Secondary School Leaving Certificate) is marked on a percentage scale. As a general rule it can be assumed that 65 per cent is the mean score and is also the minimum mark for progression to higher education.

Higher

The university runs on the American system of credits gained over ten semesters.

SCHOOL EDUCATION

Primary

This cycle covers six years, generally from age six. Students sit examinations at the end of each year on the results of which they qualify for promotion to the next year. This system extends through to the end of the preparatory level. About one-third of primary schools are mixed.

Preparatory

The preparatory cycle covers three years at the end of which is a national examination, the **Preparatory Certificate**. The results of this examination determine whether a student proceeds into the academic stream at secondary school, attends a job-oriented institute or goes straight into employment. The curriculum includes religion, Arabic, English, mathematics, history and geography, general science and health, arts and crafts, and sports.

Secondary

The secondary cycle covers three years with specialization in the arts or the sciences in the second and third years. The course leads to the **Thanawiya amma (Secondary School Leaving Certificate)** on which pupils' prospects of continuing their education depends. There are no mixed secondary schools.

Technical and vocational secondary

Instead of going to a general secondary school at the end of preparatory level, pupils can attend one of the following specialist schools:

Commercial School (one for boys and one for girls)

Secondary Technical School (one for boys, at Sohar)

It offers technology-based courses in electrical, mechanical and automotive engineering. Most pupils expect to go on to higher education.

Agricultural Institute (one for boys, at Nizwa)

This is a diploma-awarding institute run by the Ministry of Education and Youth. There are proposals to upgrade the institute to post-secondary status.

Vocational Training Institutes (eleven institutions)

These institutes, run by the Ministry of Labour and Vocational Training, teach craft-level skills within the areas of electrical, mechanical, automotive, construction and business/commercial occupations. English is taught as a job-related skill.

The institutes offer courses leading to the qualifications of the City and Guilds of London Institute.

Other vocational training

A number of public and private-sector employers and the armed forces have training centres which give specialized training to their own employees.

In addition to conventional schooling, there is a large adult literacy and education programme in which people can bring themselves up to **Thanawiya amma** standard as mature students.

FURTHER EDUCATION

Oman Technical Industrial College (OTIC)

OTIC offers a two-year course leading to a **Diploma** which is based on the UK **BTEC National Certificate/Diploma** curricula. The entry level is a pass in the **Thanawiya amma**, though the College is able to select its 250 entrants per year from 750 applicants, and thus the actual mark is usually higher than the minimum. The subjects covered are mechanical and electrical engineering, construction, laboratory science, computing and business studies. The last is taught in Arabic, the rest in English. Male and female students work together. Two periods of six weeks' industrial attachment form part of the course. Most students are expected to go into employment, but a few have joined the University, with exemption from its foundation course.

Institute of Health Sciences

This is run by the Ministry of Health for potential employees. It teaches three-year courses in nursing, medical laboratory sciences, radiography and physiotherapy. For all except nursing, where either science or arts is acceptable, entrants need a pass in the science stream of the **Thanawiya amma**. The course includes practical attachments in the neighbouring hospital.

HIGHER EDUCATION

In September 1986, Oman opened its first higher education institution, Sultan Qaboos University. On opening, the University had five faculties, Agriculture, Medicine, Engineering, Science and Education/Islamic Studies. A Faculty of Humanities was added the following year. The language of instruction is English in the first four; for their first eighteen months, students in these faculties follow a foundation course in science and English language before transferring to their parent faculty. Entry level is theoretically 65 per cent overall in the **Thanawiya amma** with some faculties specifying minimum levels in key subjects. However, the competition for places is such that the effective minimum in 1993 was over 80 per cent, and at least 90–95 per cent is needed for entry to the Faculty of Medicine. **Bachelor degree** courses vary in length from four years for agriculture to seven years for medicine.

TEACHER EDUCATION

There are six 'intermediate' teacher training colleges – one each for men and women in the capital area and in Salalah, one for men in Sur and one for women in Rustaq. They were upgraded in 1984 to post-secondary colleges and run two-year courses for prospective primary teachers.

Pakistan

Although there is a Federal Ministry of Education, each province (Punjab, Sind, North West Frontier and Baluchistan) has its own education administration.

Education is compulsory up to grade 10 but in practice there is a high drop-out rate.

Urdu is the official medium of instruction at primary and secondary level although there may be some teaching in the local language. At the intermediate stage and in higher education, in addition to Urdu, English is also used as a medium of instruction, particularly in the sciences.

The academic year normally runs from September to June but there is some variation to this.

EVALUATION IN BRITAIN

School

Secondary School Certificate/Matriculation – generally considered to be below GCSE standard.

Intermediate/Higher Secondary School Certificate – generally considered comparable to GCSE standard (grades A, B and C) if marks of over 50 per cent have been obtained, regardless of the pass-mark in each subject, with the exception of English language.

Diploma of Faculty of Arts/Science (FA/FSc) – generally considered comparable to GCSE standard (grades A, B and C) on a subject-for-subject basis.

Higher

Bachelor of Arts/Science/Commerce (Pass) – generally considered to approach GCE Advanced standard.

Bachelor of Arts/Science/Commerce (Honours) – may be considered to satisfy the general entrance requirements of British higher education institutions.

Bachelor of Engineering/Science in Engineering – generally considered comparable to British Bachelor (Ordinary) degree standard but exceptionally students with very high grades may be considered for admission to postgraduate study.

Master's degree – generally considered comparable to British Bachelor (Ordinary) degree standard but exceptionally students with very high grades may be considered for admission to postgraduate study.

Master of Engineering/Science in Engineering – generally considered comparable to British Bachelor (Honours) degree standard.

MARKING SYSTEMS

School

	A-1	80–100 per cent	Outstanding
Secondary School Certificate)	A	70–79	Excellent
Matriculation)	B	60–69	Very good
Higher Secondary Certificate)	C	50–59	Good
Intermediate Certificate)	D	40–49	Satisfactory
	E	33–39	Pass
	F	32 and below	Fail

All Boards have the same grades.

Higher

Until 1977, **Bachelor degrees** were marked as the school sector above.

Most universities now operate the following marking system, although some use grade points.

Division I	60 per cent+
Division II	45–59.9
Division III	33–44.9
Fail	below 33

Alternatively some universities may use:

A	Excellent
B	Good
C	Satisfactory
D	Average

SCHOOL EDUCATION

Pre-primary

Private kindergartens and nurseries are available in the larger cities.

Primary

Primary education covers grades 1 to 5, normally from age five.

Secondary

This sector is divided into three cycles: three years' middle school (grades 6 to 8), two years' secondary (grades 9 and 10) and two years' higher secondary (or intermediate) (grades 11 and 12). On completion of the second cycle (grade 10) students take the **Secondary School Certificate** or **Matriculation** examination, an external examination conducted by the six Boards of Intermediate and Secondary Education. Pupils are examined in nine subjects: Urdu, English, Pakistan and Islamic Studies, Islamiyat, a vocational subject, and either four science subjects or four general subjects (including general science and general mathematics or home economics). This stage marks the end of compulsory education.

Pupils may study for a further two years (grades 11 and 12), specializing in science or arts. At the end of this period pupils take the examinations for the **Intermediate Certificate** or **Higher Secondary School Certificate**. These consist of papers in Urdu, Islamiyat and English with either four science or four subjects from a social sciences/general group. The **Intermediate Certificate** may be taken at a college offering full higher education facilities and may in certain circumstances form the first two years of a four-year degree course.

The **Secondary School Certificate** is an adequate entry qualification for the two-year course leading to the **Diploma of Faculty of Arts/Science** (FA/FSc) at a university/degree college.

Students may also take the **Cambridge Overseas Examinations**: after eleven years, the **School Certificate** and after a further two years, the **Higher School Certificate**. (For further information see Appendix 2.)

Technical secondary

Vocational secondary schools provide courses at secondary level (grades 9 and 10) leading to **the Secondary School Certificate** in technical subjects.

FURTHER EDUCATION

Polytechnics, technical and commercial institutes offer a variety of courses mainly at post-**Secondary School Certificate** level. The institutes provide mainly one and two-year courses leading to certificates and diplomas and the polytechnics mainly provide three-year diploma courses. Examinations are conducted by the provincial Boards of Technical Education.

HIGHER EDUCATION

The **Intermediate** or **Higher Secondary School Certificate** is the normal entry requirement for first degree courses.

Some institutions are affiliating institutions, i.e. the affiliated colleges depend on the university to which they are attached for their courses, examinations and approval and award of qualifications. Affiliated colleges normally only provide courses leading to Pass or Ordinary degrees, whereas universities offer courses leading to Honours degrees.

Bachelor of Arts, Science and Commerce: Pass degrees are normally obtained after a two-year course, and Honours degrees after three years. First degrees in engineering take four years' study and medicine five years.

A **Master's degree** requires two years' study after a Pass degree and one year after a Bachelor (Honours) degree.

The **BEd** requires one year of study beyond a **Bachelor degree** in arts or science.

The **LLB (Bachelor of Law)** is a postgraduate qualification and entry to the two-year course is by **Bachelor degree** in any other subject.

TEACHER EDUCATION

Primary

Training is by means of a one-year post-**Secondary School Certificate** course leading to a **Primary Teaching Certificate**.

Middle School

Training is by means of a one-year post-**Intermediate/Higher Secondary School Certificate** course leading to a **Certificate in Teaching**.

Secondary

Training is by means of a one-year postgraduate course leading to a **BEd degree**.

Panama

The American system of education is dominant. The Ministry of Education determines curricula and teaching methods (i.e. the system is centralized).

A draft Education Act modifying the system has been on the table since 1987 but has not yet been promulgated.

Education is free, universal and compulsory between ages six and fifteen.

The medium of instruction is Spanish.

The academic year runs straight through for nine months, generally March to December, with a short break in mid-August. Starting dates are established annually by the Ministry and are subject to fluctuation as a result of external factors.

EVALUATION IN BRITAIN

School

Bachillerato – generally considered comparable to GCSE standard (Grades A, B and C) on a subject-for-subject basis, with the exception of English language.

High School Graduation Diploma – generally considered comparable to GCSE standard (see chapter on the USA).

Higher

Licenciado/Professional title – generally considered comparable to British Bachelor degree standard if awarded after four or more years of study.

MARKING SYSTEMS

School

Marks are usually given on a scale 1–5, the top mark being 5 and minimum pass-mark 3.

Higher

Marks are given on a percentage basis, the minimum pass-mark being 61 per cent.

A	100–91 per cent	*sobresaliente*	excellent
B	90–81	*bueno*	good
C	80–71	*regular*	average
D	70–61	*minima de promocion*	lowest passing grade
F	60– 0	*fracasado*	fail

SCHOOL EDUCATION

Private schools play an important role in secondary education where there are a number of established, particularly Catholic, institutions. There are also a number of private primary schools.

Primary

This lasts six years, though few of the rural primary schools offer the full course.

Secondary

This is divided into two cycles. The first cycle (*Ciclo Comun*) covers three years of general education. The second cycle (*Ciclo Academico*) consists of three years of more specialized study. The last two years of this cycle lead to the **Bachillerato de Ciencias** or **de Letras** (often taken as joint *Letras y ciencias*) or **de Comerico**.

Some private schools have an 'American Style' of education with courses taught in English. The education the students receive is structured to enable them to join US American colleges or US higher education institutions without the usual transition problems from one education environment to another. Courses lead to the **High School Graduation Diploma**.

FURTHER EDUCATION

The Department of Literacy and Adult Education offers adult education courses. The Institute for Training and Utilization of Human Resources offers comprehensive training courses for adults.

HIGHER EDUCATION

Higher education is offered by the following seven universities:

Florida State University Panama
Nova University
Universidad del Istmo
Universidad Interamericana de Educación a Distancia
Universidad Latina de Costa Rica
Universidad Latinoamericana de Ciencias y Technologia
Universidad Santa Maria la Antigua

The **Bachillerato de Ciencias** and success in a university entrance examination gives access to the science faculties. The **Bachillerato de Letras** and success in the university entrance examination gives access to the arts faculty. The **Bachillerato de Letras** allows admission to all other faculties. The **Bachillerato de Comercio** allows admission to business administration, economics and related studies.

A first degree course leading to a **Licenciado** or a **Professional title** normally takes four to five years. A further two years lead to a **Master of Arts** or **Master of Science** degree.

It is not possible to continue to a **PhD**.

TEACHER EDUCATION

Primary

Primary school teachers are trained in *Escuelas Normales* at secondary level. Students enter the course after completing the first cycle of secondary education. The three-year training leads to the award of **Certificado de Maestro Normal** (equivalent to the **Bachillerato**). The certificate gives access to the same university faculties as a **Bachillerato de Letras**.

Secondary school teachers must hold a degree.

Papua New Guinea

The education system is extensively decentralized with important powers being vested in provincial Educational Boards.

Education is not compulsory.

The medium of instruction is English.

The school year runs from January to December, the university year from February to November.

EVALUATION IN BRITAIN

School

Secondary School Leaving Certificate – generally considered to be below GCSE standard.

Higher School Certificate – generally considered to be comparable to GCSE standard on a subject-for-subject basis.

Higher

Bachelor (Pass) degree – generally considered comparable to British Bachelor (Ordinary) degree standard.

Bachelor (Honours) degree – generally considered comparable to British Bachelor (Honours) degree standard.

MARKING SYSTEM

Higher

Bachelor (Honours) degrees are classified:

Class I
Class II   division A
Class II   division B
Class III

SCHOOL EDUCATION

Primary

This lasts six years, normally from age seven. Primary schools are now called community schools and cover grades 1–6.

Secondary

This lasts a possible six years. Students are selected from the results of national grade 6 examinations. Grades 7–10 are undertaken in provincial high schools, culminating in the **Secondary School Leaving Certificate**. Selected pupils may then proceed to grades 11 and 12 at national high schools, which culminate in the **Higher School Certificate**. This latter qualification is the entrance qualification for university degree courses.

FURTHER EDUCATION

There are nine technical colleges, many vocational centres run mainly by church organizations and various specialized institutions which offer courses of varying length.

HIGHER EDUCATION

The University of Papua New Guinea was established in 1965 by the Australian government. The normal entrance qualification is the **Higher School Certificate**. Most students then follow a foundation course of one year.

The university offers four-year **Bachelor degree** courses in arts, sciences and education, with an additional year for **Honours**, and five-year degree courses in medicine and law. The university has adopted a credit system for the arts and science degrees: each course runs for half or a full academic year, and progress towards a degree is achieved by accumulating passes in credit courses until the required number of credit points is obtained. Credit points are valued at 3, 4 and 6 points for courses, e.g. the Education Department runs four-year courses of 3, 4 and 6 points, culminating in 90 credit points, and two-year in-service **BEd** courses of 3, 4 and 6 points, culminating in 48 credit points.

The University of Technology was founded in 1973 and offers various degree and diploma courses. Some degree courses start as two-year diploma courses followed by a further two years for a degree, i.e. accountancy, business studies, surveying, cartography and land management. Some degree courses last four years, i.e. forestry and engineering, and some five years, i.e. applied chemistry, mineral technology and food technology. There are also diploma courses aimed at the technician level, i.e. a five-year diploma in applied physics.

Postgraduate courses are available at both universities leading to postgraduate diplomas, **Master's degrees** and **PhDs.**

TEACHER EDUCATION

Primary

There are eleven community teachers' colleges, which run a two-year course to train primary school teachers. The minimum entrance requirement is now completion of grade 10.

Secondary

Teachers are trained at <u>Goroka Teachers College</u> (now part of the <u>University of Papua New Guinea</u>) in a three-year diploma course, following a minimum of four years' secondary education, or at the <u>University of Papua New Guinea</u> where they can obtain a **Bachelor of Education** degree after four years' study, or a **BA** or **BSc** plus **Postgraduate Diploma in Education** after five years of study.

Paraguay

Education is free, universal and compulsory from the age of seven for six years to the end of primary school.

The medium of instruction is Spanish.

The school year runs from March to November.

EVALUATION IN BRITAIN

School

Bachillerato – generally considered comparable to GCSE standard (grades A, B and C) on a subject-for-subject basis, with the exception of English language.

Higher

Licenciado and **Professional title** – generally considered comparable to British Bachelor degree standard if awarded after four or more years of study.

MARKING SYSTEMS

School

Two grading systems are used in secondary schools: 1–5 (the new system) and 0–10 (the old system).

5	10	*sobresaliente*	excellent
4	9	*muy bueno*	very good
	8		
3	7	*bueno*	good
	6		
2	5	*suficiente*	average
	4	*regular*	
1	3	*aceptable*	failed
	2	*no aprobado*	
	1	*aplazado*	
0	0	*insuficiente*	(given only in cases of cheating)

Higher

Grading is on a scale of 1–5.

5	*sobresaliente*	excellent
4	*distinguido*	very good
3	*bueno*	good
2	*regular*	average
1	*reprobado*	fail

SCHOOL EDUCATION

Pre-primary

This is not compulsory. It is divided into two cycles, the first being for children between three to five years known as *Jardin de Infantes* and the second for children aged six known as *Pre-Escolar*.

Primary

This lasts six years.

Secondary

This lasts six years and is divided into two three-year cycles, the first being a general course known as *Ciclo Básico* and the second a specialized course known as *Ciclo Bachillerato*.

Students who have completed *Ciclo Básico* may choose to enter either a vocational course or an academic/technical course.

Secondary school courses lead to the **Bachillerato**. This satisfies matriculation requirements. In 1973 a law was passed to introduce curriculum reform to secondary education, the aim being to prepare graduates for employment as well as higher education.

Other specialized schools offer **Bachillerato** courses i.e. the <u>Military School</u>, the <u>Police School</u> and the <u>Telecommunications School</u>.

The diversified cycle has been divided into different tracks.

Old system:

Science and letters	*Bachiller en Ciencas y Letras*
Commerce	*Bachiller Comercial*
Normal school	*Profesor de Enseñanza Primaria* (Primary School Teacher)

New system:

Humanities and science	*Bachiller en Humanidades y Ciencia*
Technical – industrial	*Bachiller en Industria Técnica*
Agricultural	*Bachiller Agrónomo*
Commercial	*Bachiller Comercial*

Vocational

One main centre for vocational training operates under the Ministry of Education: the Escuela Técnica Vocacional 'Presidente Carlos Antonio López'. It provides vocational training for adults who have completed primary school and offers courses which last up to three years. Examinations are graded on a 0–10 scale. Students who successfully complete a course with an average of six or above are awarded a diploma. Students with an average below six receive a certificate of attendance.

Technical

Courses lead to the **Bachillerato en Industria Técnica,** which satisfies university matriculation requirements.

The Escuela de Técnicas Industriales (School of Industrial Techniques) offers a six-year course divided into two cycles: the *Ciclo Básico* and the *Ciclo Profesional*. Graduation from the Escuela de Técnicas Industriales is not recognized for university admission.

Other technical courses are offered at a variety of schools run by different ministries.

Agricultural

Before the new reforms, agricultural education at secondary level was offered at the Colegio Nacional de Agricultura. After a four-year course students are awarded a **Certificado de Agrónomo** (agronomist). Graduates are eligible to enter the Faculties of Agriculture and Veterinary Science.

HIGHER EDUCATION

Paraguay has three institutions of higher education: the Universidad de Asunción – under state control; the Universidad Católica 'Nuestra Senora de la Asunción' – under private control; the Instituto Superior de Educacion (higher education institute) – under state control.

The entrance requirement to these three institutions is the **Bachillerato** in humanities or science.

The first degree course normally lasts four to five years leading to the award of **Licenciado** or **Professional title**.

TEACHER EDUCATION

From 1972 teacher education changed from secondary school level to post-secondary level. The entrance requirement for all teacher training courses is a **Bachillerato** in humanities or science.

Pre-Primary

A two-year course leading to the qualification of **Profesor de Enseñanza Pre-Primaria**.

Paraguay

Primary

A two-year course leading to the qualification of **Profesor de Enseñanza Primaria**.

Secondary

A four-year course leading to the qualification of **Profesor de Enseñanza Secundaria**. Teaching diplomas are not recognized as equivalent to university degrees in Paraguay, although the entrance requirement and course duration are similar.

Peru

The educational system in Peru is governed by the General Education Law of 1982, issued during the government of President Fernando Belaunde Terry.

The state controls more than two thirds of basic education and a large part of higher education. However, there are also many private educational centres and universities that are invariably well organized and academically excellent.

Primary and secondary education is compulsory, and begins at age six.

The medium of instruction is Spanish. However, in communities that have a native language, primary education is initiated in the native language with a gradual introduction of Spanish.

The academic year runs from March to December, with a fifteen-day break in July.

EVALUATION IN BRITAIN

School

Certificado de Educación Secundaria Común Completa – generally considered comparable to GCSE standard (grades A, B and C) on a subject-for-subject basis, with the exception of English language.

Higher

Licenciado/Professional title – generally considered comparable to British Bachelor degree standard if awarded after four or more years of study.

MARKING SYSTEM

School and Higher

Marking is on a scale 0–20 (maximum), 11 being the minimum pass-mark. There is no classification of degrees.

SCHOOL EDUCATION

Primary

This lasts six years from age six. Prior to this there is an obligatory one-year transition class between kindergarten or family and formal primary education. If pupils receive an overall average mark of eleven or more, and achieve passes in Spanish and mathematics, they pass automatically into the next grade. If the average is sufficient but passes are not obtained in language and maths, another chance is given in March in which at least one of these two subjects must be passed; failure at this stage means repeating the year. In practice there are few failures. To pass from primary to secondary education pupils need to have a record certifying that all courses have been completed.

Secondary

This covers five years divided into two cycles, the first covering two years of general studies and the second covering three years of specialization. In the second cycle, pupils choose from agricultural, craft, commerce, industry and academic branches. All branches are considered equivalent for further and higher education purposes.

Academic secondary

In the academic branch, pupils may choose between the arts or science section. Pupils who fail more than four subjects in their annual examinations must repeat the whole year. On successful completion of the second cycle, pupils obtain the **Certificado de Educación Secundaria Común Completa** (not the **Bachillerato**, as with most other Latin American countries). Subjects studied include: Spanish language and literature, history (and history of Peru), geography, religion, mathematics, chemistry, biology, physics, art and physical education.

Although pupils may take the university entrance examination directly after their final examinations at secondary school, many first undertake a one-year course of study (*Curso Preparatario*), often at a private school (*Academia*). Recently some universities have been offering the option of pre-university preparatory studies.

Technical secondary

On successful completion of the second cycle of secondary education in the agricultural, commercial or industrial branch, pupils obtain the **Diploma de Aptitud Profesional**.

HIGHER EDUCATION

Higher education is offered in two sectors – university and non-university.

Non-university higher education

This sector offers various alternatives conducted at higher institutes. Admission requires a completed secondary education certificate and a pass in an entrance examination which is not always competitive. The duration of studies in this sector is a minimum of four semesters. Studies can lead to a professional title, a technical diploma or a competent technician certificate.

Higher Education Schools

These schools generally offer studies with a duration of eight semesters. Among the subjects offered are: nursing; journalism; social studies, and art subjects.

Superior Technological Institutes

These institutes offer professional training lasting six semesters in specialized professions such as : computing; nursing; accountancy; administration, etc., and the following industrial careers: agriculture; mechanics; electrical engineering, etc. About half of these institutes are in the private sector (mainly in metropolitan Lima) and half are run by the state (mainly in rural areas).

The qualifications obtained are terminal; they do not admit the holder to university in Peru.

University education

Students wishing to enter a course of higher education at one of the thirty-one state universities or twenty-seven private institutions (*Datos Grade*) must hold the **Certificado de Educación Secundaria Común Completa** and pass the competitive entrance examination. Students may only apply for one faculty of one institution at a time.

Some universities provide general studies facilities. Students need to obtain a particular number of credits to enter the faculty for their specialization.

The period of specialization is three to five years, and leads to the **Bachillerato** (bachelor degree). This is granted automatically on completing university studies. Successful submission of a thesis, which normally takes six months to a year, leads to a **Licenciado** (or a **Professional title**). Most courses leading to the **Licenciado** take about five years in total. In law and medicine the professional qualification is obtained three and five years, respectively, after the award of the **Bachillerato**.

Some universities grant a **Master's degree** after students have obtained the **Bachillerato**, taken additional subjects and successfully presented a thesis, while some award the **Doctorado** on successful submission of a thesis at least two years after obtaining the **Licenciado/Professional title**.

TEACHER EDUCATION

Primary

A three-year upper secondary course on completion of the two-year lower secondary course leads to the title of **Maestro Normal**.

Secondary

Teachers at this level (*Profesores*) must have completed a five-year course at a higher teacher training institute (see non-university higher education) or at university.

Philippines

The Department of Education, headed by the Secretary, has overall responsibility for education. The Department is responsible for determining curricula. Two notable features of the system are the predominance of central government support at primary level and the large-scale involvement of the private sector in further and higher education. These private institutions have to obtain specific authorization from the Board of Higher Education before they can grant certificates, diplomas or degrees.

Education is compulsory from age seven to twelve which covers the six grades of primary education.

A bilingual education policy has been in effect since 1974. In schools, English is used for teaching science and mathematics and Tagalog-based Filipino for all other subjects. The medium of instruction in college and university courses is generally English.

The academic year runs from June to March, consisting of two semesters, with a short break in October.

EVALUATION IN BRITAIN

School

High School Diploma – generally considered to be below GCSE standard.

Higher

Bachelor degree – may be considered to satisfy the general entrance requirements of British higher education institutions.

A minimum of 124 units is required for the award of a **Bachelor degree**, but the total is usually 144 to 164. One unit accounts for about 18 hours of tuition.

Candidates from prestigious institutions may be given advanced standing by British higher education institutions (usually no more than second year entry). For further information enquirers should contact the National Academic Recognition Information Centre.

Master's degree – generally considered comparable to a standard approaching British Bachelor degree (Honours standard if awarded by a prestigious institution, Ordinary standard from elsewhere).

MARKING SYSTEM

Marking systems vary from institution to institution. A, B and C grades and percentages are found at all levels.

Higher

The University of the Philippines and some other institutions use:

1	excellent
1.25, 1.5, 1.75	very good
2.0, 2.5	good
3.0	fair
4.0	conditional fail
5.0	fail

Marks are sometimes expressed:

A	1.00	97–100 per cent or	A	4.0	97–100 per cent
A–	1.25	94–96	A–	3.5	93–96
B+	1.50	91–93	B	3.0	89–92
B	1.75	88–90	B–	2.5	85–88
B–	2.00	85–87	C+	2.0	80–84
C+	2.50	80–84	C	1.5	75–79
C	3.00	75–79	C–	1.0	70–74
D	4.00	failed	F	0.0	69 and below

SCHOOL EDUCATION

Primary

This lasts six years in government schools from age seven to twelve. Private schools start a year earlier. Progression is by passing the final examinations at the end of each year. A diploma or certificate is awarded on completion of this cycle.

Secondary

Secondary education usually lasts four years. Compulsory subjects include English, Filipino, science, social studies, mathematics, practical arts, Youth Development Training (YDT) and Citizens Army Training (CAT). The cycle culminates in the examinations for the **High School Diploma**. The **National Secondary Aptitude test** is also taken at this time, and is used for university admission purposes.

FURTHER EDUCATION

This takes place largely in community colleges offering one-year post-secondary courses in advertising, bookkeeping, clerical studies, co-operatives, food services, general office practice, office management, skills development, retail merchandising, secretarial studies, etc.

Colleges of agriculture offer one-year certificate courses in farm mechanics.

HIGHER EDUCATION

Entrance to universities and other institutions offering courses of higher education is dependent on (a) possession of a **High School Diploma,** (b) results of the **National Secondary Aptitude Test,** (c) for elite institutions, a pass in the university's own entrance examination. The University of the Philippines, for example, also requires a satisfactory score in their **UP College Admissions Test** (UPCAT). In the private higher education sector there is the **College Scholastic Aptitude Tests (CSAT)**, administered by the Fund for Assistance to Private Education (FAPE).

The **National College Entrance Examination** (NCEE) has recently been abolished. It was held for the first time in November 1973. From the school year 1974–5, any student seeking admission to any post-secondary academic or professional degree course requiring a minimum of four years' study at any institution (regardless of whether private or public) had to pass this examination. The examination was a general scholastic aptitude test to regulate the entry of high school graduates to college. A cut-off score equivalent to 50 per cent was required for a **Bachelor degree**; individual institutions required higher cut-off scores for their courses. The NCEE was considered by many not to be discriminative enough.

In 1994, the NCEE was replaced by the **National Secondary Aptitude Test**, taken in the fourth year of high school.

In most institutions it is possible to obtain an **Associate degree/certificate** after the first two years of a course. Junior colleges only offer courses lasting two years.

In general, **Bachelor degree** courses last four years full-time. Pharmacy, engineering, architecture and music courses generally last five years; dentistry and veterinary medicine six years.

A law degree often takes up to eight years to obtain. Students must already have obtained a **Bachelor degree** in another subject before beginning the course in law.

In medical studies students must first obtain a **Bachelor degree** in another relevant subject before beginning a three-year course in medicine, followed by one-year of clinical clerkship, one year internship and three to five years' residency (for specialization).

The qualification of **Graduate Nurse** and **Bachelor of Science in Nursing** (BSN) is obtained after two years' pre-nursing study at a college or university followed by two years' study in a hospital school of nursing. Before 1976 the course consisted of one-year pre-nursing study plus three years of study in a hospital school of nursing.

A variety of courses in philosophy and theology are offered by Catholic and Protestant seminaries.

Master's degrees normally require a further two years (in architecture five), with a further three (minimum) for a **PhD.**

TEACHER EDUCATION

Teachers at any stage must be university graduates, having completed one of the following courses:

BSc in Elementary Education (171 units)
BSc in Industrial Education (172–180 units) to prepare vocational and industrial teachers for trade schools
BSc in Education (185 units) to teach in secondary schools.

Poland

Education is supervised centrally by the Ministry of National Education at school and higher education level. The Polish government has recently acknowledged that many aspects of the system will need modernizing over the next few years in order to satisfy the needs of a changing economy, areas to be singled out for special attention will include changes to the curriculum such as the introduction of experimental curricula, changes to the training required for some professions, adapting the experience of other countries in the training of workers and technicians, in-service training for teachers, stressing the environmental approach in training and teaching for the free-market economy. Three new Higher Education Acts (the Act on School Education, the Act of Higher Education and the Act on Academic Title and Academic degrees) came into force in September 1990. They define the basis for the functioning of universities, the degree of their autonomy and central supervision, describe internal organization of universities and competencies of university self-government organs, contain the rules for employment of academic teachers, and define the rights and duties of students.

The Teacher's Charter, which defines the rights and obligations of teachers, was established in 1982 (it has since been modified a number of times).

Public universities are funded from the state budget allocated by the Minister of National Education.

Primary education is compulsory from the calendar year in which a person becomes seven until the end of primary school (which usually lasts 8 years).

The medium of instruction is Polish.

The school academic year runs from September to June.

EVALUATION IN BRITAIN

School

Matura/Swiadectwo Dojrzalosci – satisfies the general entrance requirements of British higher education institutions.

Swiadectwo Ukonczenia Diploma (from a *Technikum* or *Liceum Zawodowe*) – generally considered comparable to BTEC National Diploma / N/SVQ level 3 / Advanced GNVQ/GSVQ standard.

Higher

Licencjat / Inzynier – generally considered comparable to BTEC Higher National Diploma / NVQ Level 4 standard.

Magister/Magisterium Lekarz – generally considered comparable to British Bachelor

(Honours) degree standard, although the course lasts longer than in UK.

Doktor – generally considered comparable to British PhD standard.

MARKING SYSTEMS

Higher (and school until 1991)

6	*celujący*	excellent
5	*bardzo dobry*	very good
4	*dobry*	good
3	*dostateczny*	satisfactory/pass
2	*niedostateczny*	unsatisfactory/fail

Grade 6 (excellent) was not used before 1992.

School (since 1992)

6	*celujący*	excellent
5	*bardzo dobry*	very good
4	*dobry*	good
3	*dostateczny*	satisfactory
2	*miezny*	mediocre
1	*niedostateczny*	unsatisfactory

SCHOOL EDUCATION

There is optional pre-school/kindergarten for children aged three to five. Children aged six can follow a one-year preparatory course.

Primary

Education is compulsory for eight years from the age of seven until the end of primary school. The present system consists of an eight-year course at primary school (*Szkola Podstawowa*). These schools offer a general curriculum in the following subjects: Polish language and literature, civics, history, modern languages, mathematics, biology, geography, physics, chemistry, music, arts, the environment, technology, computing and physical education. There are no set curricula as such; instead, there are only minimum curriculum requirements. In terms of textbooks, teachers can use any books they wish, as long as they have been recognized by the Ministry of National Education. Therefore different textbooks may be used to teach the same subject at the same school. Teachers are given considerable flexibility in the way they teach and attempts have been made in recent years to encourage individual creativity and to break away from passive learning. On completion of grade 8 pupils obtain a certificate which is necessary for admission to secondary education.

Secondary

About ninety-six per cent of primary school-leavers continue their education, almost thirty per cent of them at general secondary schools (*Liceum Ogolnoksztalcace*) and thirty per cent at technical/vocational secondary schools (*Technikum* and *Liceum Zawodowe*), both of which prepare pupils for admission to higher education. At general secondary schools the course lasts four years, at technical/vocational secondary schools four to five years. The general secondary school perpetuates the Central European academic tradition of the *Gymnasium*. Compulsory subjects during the first three years are Polish language and literature, two foreign languages, history, mathematics, physics with astronomy, physical education and social education, chemistry, geography, biology with hygiene and environmental studies; art and technology/computing are compulsory for the first two years. Optional subjects include another West European language and Latin. In the fourth year some specialization is introduced.

There are a number of schools which concentrate particularly on such subjects as mathematics and approximately forty where at least some of the teaching is in English, French, German or Spanish.

All courses culminate in the matriculation examination (**Egzamin Dojrzalosci**). It is taken in three to four subjects: written examinations in Polish language and literature and a second subject chosen from history, Latin, biology with hygiene and environmental studies, mathematics, a modern language, chemistry and physics with astronomy; oral examinations in Polish language and literature or a modern language; and a third subject chosen from a second modern language, Latin, Greek, history, geography, biology with hygiene and environmental studies, mathematics, chemistry, physics with astronomy, computing, psychology, educational studies and social studies. (The subject chosen for the second written examination might be chosen also for oral examination.) Teachers' gradings, based on continuous assessment, for the other subjects taken in the secondary education courses are included on **Swiadectwo Dojrzalosci**. Pupils may retake the part they failed within two years. After two years **Swiadectwo Dojrzalosci** can still be obtained but only after successfully retaking all examinations. The *Technikum* and *Liceum Zawodowe* courses are similar, but with more emphasis on vocational subjects. The examination leading to **Swiadectwo Dojrzalosci** taken at a *Technikum* and a *Liceum Zawodowe* differs from the one taken at a *Liceum Ogolnoksztalcace* in the oral examinations which in the former are taken in Polish language and literature and a second subject is chosen from history, geography, mathematics, physics, chemistry, computing and social studies. Additionally vocational studies are taken as part of the examinations leading to the completion of this schooling.

In schools in which a minority language and literature are taught, this is additionally examined, both in a written and oral form, at the **Swiadectwo Dojrzalosci** level.

There are twenty-four countrywide competitions, known as *Olimpiada*, both in specific subjects and interdisciplinary, open to all secondary school students. Each consists of a written and oral examination in a specific subject. Winners are given preferential treatment upon applying to a higher education institution of their choice. The winners of competitions in biology, chemistry, physics, mathematics, computer studies and Russian language and literature take part in international competitions.

The school system was reformed in 1978 in an attempt to create a common level of education for all. The revised system consisted of a ten-year school course (and one compulsory year of kindergarten), intended to cover the same ground educationally as the previous 8 + 4 system. The **Matura** examination was taken at the end of the tenth year. Those wishing to proceed to higher education then attended a two-year course in the intended specialism at a further school. The subject groupings available at further schools were: physical sciences and technology; medical sciences, biology and agriculture; social sciences and humanities and others. Winners of the *Olympiads* were able to go direct to university, bypassing these two-year courses. This system operated for only two years; it was abandoned in 1980 and the previous 8 + 4 system was reinstated.

FURTHER EDUCATION

There are three-year basic (vocational) schools (*Szkola Zasadnicza*), following on from the eight years' compulsory education, which are often attached to industrial enterprises to enable students to obtain practical experience. Some time is spent on civics, mathematics, physics, environmental studies, Polish language and literature, history and a foreign language. On completion of this basic vocational course students receive the Certificate of Completion of Basic School (**Swiadectwo Ukonczenia Szkoly Zasadniczej**). The Certificate of Completion of Basic School does not entitle the student to sit the examination leading to **Swiadectwo Dojrzalosci**. However it gives the possibility of continuing studies at a *Technikum* using the foundations acquired in the Basic School. Once the studies have been completed, the examination for **Swiadectwo Dojrzalosci** can be taken.

HIGHER EDUCATION

As prescribed by the new Higher Education Act, the general requirement for admission to study at public and private universities is the **Swiadectwo Dojrzalosci**. Unlike the previous regulations, the Act does not provide for uniform admission rules or procedures at all universities; they may introduce competitive entrance exams or hold interviews. Admission rules and procedures are defined by the university Senate on the motion of boards of study.

After three or four years of successful study, Polish universities and other higher education institutions grant the **Licencjat** degree (humanities, sciences, social studies, economics, physical education, leisure and tourism, physical rehabilitation/therapy, pharmacy, medical laboratory science, nursing) or **Inzynier** (engineering and technology, agriculture, economics). After completing between four and five years and defending a research thesis (*Praca Magisterska*) the degree of **Magister** is granted. This could include the subject title, eg. **Magister Inzynier**. Duration of medical studies is six years and the studies end with the diploma of **Lekarz** (physician). Studies can also lead to the diplomas of **Lekarz stomatolog** (dentistry) and **Lekarz weterynarii** (veterinary surgeon) which last five years.

Higher education institutions tend to specialize more than their British counterparts. Hence the universities (*Uniwersytet*) do not normally have departments of engineering, applied science and architecture as these subjects are taught by the technical universities (*Politechnika*). The universities cover the pure sciences, social science, languages and humanities, although, in practice, some pure science research is conducted at technical universities and vice versa. In the academic year 1994/95 there were 89 public schools of university type, among them 12 universities. There were the technical universities as well as engineering schools, one mining and metallurgy academy, agricultural academies, academies of economics and theological academies, higher teacher education schools, medical academies (supervised by the Ministry of Health and Social Welfare), merchant marine academies (under the Ministry of Transport and Maritime Economy), fine arts academies, music academies, schools of theatre studies and a school of film and TV studies (under the Ministry of Culture) and physical education academies (supervised by the State Sports and Tourism Administration).

There are two levels of doctoral degree. The lower degree of **Doktor (dr)**, which involves the presentation of a dissertation, is taken after graduating by those who wish to develop a research capability. Most doctorates are completed after six or seven years (students also teach (full-time)), eight years being the maximum period allowed. On average, only six per cent of those who hold the **Magister** go on to obtain a doctorate.

In fine and performing arts (music included) the qualification equivalent to **Doctor** is the **First Degree of Qualifications**. The higher degree (**Doktor Habilitowany – dr hab**) is awarded on submission of a considerable volume of original post-doctoral research, published as a thesis for the degree. It is the Polish counterpart of the German **Habilitation** and is necessary for any university teacher who wishes to become an academic professor. In fine and performing arts the qualification equivalent to **Doktor habilitowany** is the **Second Degree Qualification**.

In addition to the 89 state schools of university type registered with the Ministry of National Education there are 63 registered non-state HEIs. On the whole, the latter are small institutions, employing a small teaching staff and granting graduates the title of **Licencjat**. In the academic year 1993/94 only three of them were authorized to award the **Magister** degree.

The Central School of Planning and Statistics, Warsaw, the largest and oldest school of economics in Poland, has links with LSE and similar colleges in other countries.

TEACHER EDUCATION

Pre-school/kindergarten and primary

Until 1994 teachers at these levels were educated in Teacher Schools (*Studium Nauczycielskie*). They could take either a two-year post-**Swiadectwo Dojrzalosci** course or a six-year course for those who had only completed eight years of primary education. The latter courses were discontinued in 1992. In 1990 new types of 3-year teacher training courses were established. The Teacher Schools were replaced with two types of colleges: Teacher Colleges (*Kolegium Nauczycielskie*) under local educational authorities (*Kuratorium*) and supervised by the Ministry of National Education, and Teacher Training Colleges (*Kolegium Nauczycielskie*) functioning within the academic structure and awarding their graduates with the **Licencjat** degree.

Those who complete the Teacher Colleges under a local educational authority obtain the certificate of completion from the school (**Dyplom Ukonczenia** of a given Teacher College).

Graduates of three to four-year university courses leading to the **Licencjat** degree can also teach at these levels provided they complete courses on pedagogy. Graduates of Higher Teacher Education Schools (*Wyzsza Szkola Pedagogiczna*) may also obtain the **Licencjat** degree.

Secondary/all levels

Specialised Foreign Language Teacher Training Colleges functioning within the academic structure provide three-year courses for teachers of English, German and French. The graduates receive the **Licencjat** degree.

Universities and Higher Teacher Education Schools (*Wyzsza Szkola Pedagogiczna*) train teachers for primary and secondary schools on five-year courses, the graduates of which are awarded the **Magister** degree.

Teacher training for teachers of vocational subjects at technical/vocational schools is carried out in higher education institutions of engineering, agriculture, economics, etc., with pedagogy, psychology and methodology of teaching as compulsory subjects.

The teacher training system is an open one.

Portugal

The Minister of Education is responsible for all state institutions of higher education (universities and polytechnics) and supervises the private sector at this level.

In the 1970s steps were taken to implement the principle of self-government by the state universities. This principle was embodied in a general law, *Lei de Bases do Sistema Educativo* (LBSE) – law 46/86, dated 14 October 1986, and was afterwards set down in the University Autonomy Law (*Lei da Autonomia Universitária*) – law 108/88, dated 24 September 1988. Under this law, the principle of academic freedom governs state universities.

Pedagogic autonomy implies the right: to create, suspend and cancel courses; to define educational methods; to award degrees and diplomas; to grant equivalence and recognition to foreign higher education degrees and academic qualifications. Scientific autonomy gives the universities the right to carry out research and all other scientific and cultural activities as well as to take part in joint activities with other public or private, national or foreign institutions. Polytechnics must submit their curricula to the Minister of Education.

Foreign students are admitted to Portuguese institutions of higher education if they have a qualification equivalent to the twelfth year of schooling and have met the three requirements established under Decree-law 289/92, dated 3 September 1992 (described under '**secondary education**' below).

There is direct access under specific conditions for candidates from Portuguese speaking countries, who are covered by specific bilateral agreements.

The Statute of the Private Higher Education Institution (*Estatuto do Ensino Superior Particular e Cooperativo*) was recently approved and published in the Official Journal by means of the Decree-law 16/94, dated 22 January 1994 (this revoked the former Decree-law 271/89, dated 19 August 1989). It contains the principles of organization for private higher education institutions including procedures for their creation, conditions for the establishment of institutions, creation of courses and the recognition of corresponding degrees and diplomas. It also defines the supervision role of the state in the quality of teaching offered and the options for financial support.

Private higher education institutions are not allowed to operate without the recognition of the Ministry of Education. Access to this type of institution is regulated by the same procedures as those for state higher education institutions.

The medium of instruction is Portuguese. The academic year is divided into three terms. At primary and secondary schools classes begin in the second week of September and end in June/July. Generally, at higher education institutions, courses begin in October. Courses of study can be organized on the basis of years or semesters (two per academic year).

EVALUATION IN BRITAIN

School

Certificado de fim de Estudos Secundários (previously **Certidáo do Décimo Segundo Ano**) – considered to satisfy the general entrance requirements of British higher education institutions provided an overall mark of at least 14 has been obtained.

Higher

Bacharel – constitutes a professionally oriented first degree; generally considered comparable to a standard above that of BTEC Higher National Diploma / N/SVQ level 4.

Licenciado – generally considered comparable to British Bachelor (Honours) degree standard, although the course lasts longer than in the UK.

Mestra – generally considered comparable to taught Master's degree standard.

Doutor – generally considered comparable to British PhD standard.

MARKING SYSTEMS

School

Since 1974

In preparatory and lower secondary schools marking is on a scale of 0–5 with 3 as the minimum pass-mark.

In upper secondary schools there is a scale of 0–20, with 10 as the minimum pass-mark, as follows:

10–13	*suficiente*	satisfactory
14–17	*bom*	good
18–20	*muito bom*	very good

Higher

Marking is on a scale of 0–20, with 10 as the minimum pass-mark, as follows:

14–15	*bom*	good
16–17	*bom com distinção*	good with distinction
18–19	*muito bom com distinção*	very good with distinction
20	*muito bom com distinção e louvor*	very good with distinction and honours

SCHOOL EDUCATION

Since 1988

Pre-primary

Education is available, but not compulsory, for children aged three to six.

Basic education

Before 1986 there were six years of compulsory basic education for children between the ages of 6 and 12 (four years' primary and two years' preparatory). Students who completed basic education were awarded the **Certidão do segundo ano do Ensino Preparatório.**

Since 1986 there have been nine years of compulsory basic education, between the ages of six and fifteen. This is divided into three cycles (four years, two years and three years respectively).

Secondary education

This now lasts three years.

Before 1986 it lasted six years, consisting of the General Unified Course (seventh, eighth and ninth years), which led to the **Certidão do Curso do Ensino Unificado**, and the complementary course (tenth and eleventh years of schooling). Subjects included Portuguese, philosophy, a foreign language and physical education. On completion of the eleventh year pupils obtained the **Certidão do Curso Complementar.**

Before 1986 the twelfth year of schooling (the pre-university year) was initially designed for students intending to enter university. It offered two curricular options: academic and vocational. The academic option developed into five courses according to the area of studies attended in the tenth and eleventh years of schooling. These were mathematics with science, mathematics with arts, philosophy with arts, literature with languages and drawing with science. It prepared students for admission to university higher education. The vocational option provided information and training in a wide range of technological areas. It offered a great variety of more specifically oriented courses and prepared students for entry to polytechnic institutions. On completion of the twelfth year, a **Certidão do Décimo Segundo Ano** was obtained which ensured access to higher education or employment.

From 1989 the **Certificado de fim de Estudos Secundários** was awarded on successful completion of the twelfth year.

According to the law, the system of access in force since 1989/90 should be evaluated three years after its implementation. This evaluation led to the revision of the previous model of access and to the elaboration and publication of the Decree-law 289/92, dated 3 September 1992, which establishes the new conditions for access to higher education. Students must sit for 1) the '**prova de aferição**' (counter test) corresponding to the student's secondary course; 2) the '**provas específicas**' (specific examinations) in accordance with the higher education course the student wishes to attend; 3) and have fulfilled the prerequisites for the higher education course they wish to attend, if required.

VOCATIONAL EDUCATION

The *Escolas Profissionais* (Professional Schools) were created in 1989 by the Decree-law 26/89, dated 21 January. These schools are a result of a joint action of the Ministry of Education and the Ministry of Employment as well as industry and employers. Although separate from mainstream education, this system maintains a close link with it.

After successful completion of a three year course, an academic certificate is awarded which certifies the completion of secondary school education and a professional certificate (III level). This enables the student either to pursue studies in higher education, or to exercise the profession.

The courses offered by these schools may vary from one to three years depending on the entrance qualification of the candidate.

FURTHER EDUCATION

Evening courses are intended for students over fourteen and include:

the *Curso Geral Nocturno* (evening general course) – is equivalent to the ninth year of schooling and confers the **Certidão do Curso Geral Nocturno**;

the *Curso Complementar Nocturno* (evening complementary course) – enables the student to enrol in the twelfth year of schooling.

Technical and vocational education is at present being developed. It offers pupils courses of professional training on completion of the ninth year of schooling. Two kinds of course may be followed, the one-year technical course with a six-month training period and the three-year technical/professional course leading either to employment or to higher education.

HIGHER EDUCATION

Higher education is offered by the universities and by a number of state and private institutions. There are traditional universities in Lisbon (University of Lisbon and Technical University of Lisbon), Coimbra and Oporto. The new universities established since 1973 are the New University in Lisbon and those of Minho, Algarve, Aveiro, Évora, the Azores, Beira Interior, Madeira and Trás-os-Montes e Alto Douro.

University studies lead to the **Licenciado** after a four-to six-year course (arts and humanities, four years; law, social sciences, natural sciences, technology, pharmacy, agriculture and husbandry, environmental sciences and physical education, five years; medicine and dentistry, six years). Most holders are called **doutor** by tradition and use the initials **dr**.

Holders of a **Licenciado** can become University lecturers. If they want to pursue an academic career they must obtain a **Master's degree** within three years of being contracted. Prior to that they are *Assistentes Estagiários*. After successfully completing the **Master's degree** they become *Assistentes*.

The **Mestrado** is a postgraduate qualification open to holders of a **Licenciado** degree, with a minimum pass-mark of 14 on a scale of 0–20. The degree of **Mestre** is awarded after a two year course. A dissertation must be presented within two years after the completion of the academic course. The degree of **Mestre** is certified by a *Carta Magistral*.

The **Doutor** degree is open to holders of a **Licenciado** degree with a minimum pass-mark of 16 on a scale of 0–20, or to holders of a **Mestra** degree. There are no specialized courses leading to a **Doutor degree**. This degree is only awarded by the universities.

No period of time is defined by law during which the candidate must prepare for the **Doutoramento** (doctorate examinations). The preparatory work usually takes between five and six years in the humanities, and from three to four years for subjects in technology and the exact sciences.

Holders of a **Doutor** degree can move forward in the academic career and become *Professor Adjunto*, *Professor Associado*, *Professor Coordenador* and *Professor Catedrático*. Promotion to the posts of *Professor Associado*, *Professor Coordenador* and *Professor Catedrático* is subject to the successful completion of specific examinations.

The **Agregação** is open only to holders of the **Doutor** degree; it requires a high capacity for research and special pedagogical competence in a specific field of knowledge. It is awarded after passing specific examinations.

Non-university higher education (Polytechnic education)

This is provided mainly in the polytechnic institutes which offer three-year courses leading to a **Bacharel** degree. At present, these institutions offer courses in the following fields: education, agriculture, engineering and technology, management and accountancy, administration, music, dance, cinema and theatre.

Holders of the **Bacharel** degree may attend two-year courses, offered by these institutions, leading to the **Diploma de Estudos Superiores Especializados** (DESE) – Diploma of Specialized Higher Studies. This Diploma is equivalent to a university **Licenciado** degree.

Higher schools of fine arts are integrated in the universities. The Faculdade de Belas-Artes de Lisboa is integrated in the Universidade de Lisboa, and the Faculdade de Belas-Artes do Porto is integrated in the Universidade do Porto. They award the following degrees:

Diploma do ciclo básico – lasting for three years and equivalent to the **Bacharel** degree;

Diploma do ciclo especial – lasting for two years after the **Diploma do ciclo básico**, and equivalent to a **Licenciado** degree.

Private higher education

The development of private higher education institutions took place after 1986, and the number of them is still increasing. The *Estatuto do Ensino Superior Particular e Cooperativo* (Statute of Private and Cooperative Higher Education) was recently approved and published by the Decree-law 16/94, dated 22 January 1994. This statute states the conditions for the creation of private institutions as well as of courses, and the recognition of corresponding degrees and diplomas. It also defines the supervision role of the state in the quality of teaching offered and the options for financial support.

Diplomas and degrees awarded by these institutions have the same value and recognition, academically and professionally, as those from public institutions.

The Universidade Catolica Portuguesa (UCP – Portuguese Catholic University) occupies a special place within the higher education system in Portugal, since it is a legal and economic entity instituted by decree of the Holy See and recognized by the State of Portugal. Within this legal and institutional framework the UCP does not need permission from the government to set up or recognize schools, courses or other units. It simply informs government departments of the schools and courses in operation.

TEACHER EDUCATION

Basic education

Training courses for educators (pre-school education) and for teachers of the first and second cycles of basic education, take place at *Escolas Superiores de Educação* (Higher Schools of Education). These institutions are integrated in the Institutos Polytécnicos (polytechnics) as well as in *Centros Integrados de Formação de Professores* (CIFOPs) – Integrated Centres for Teacher Training – at the universities of Évora, Aveiro, Minho, the Azores and Trás-os-Montes e Alto Douro. The Portuguese *Universidade Aberta* (Open University) also administers teacher training programmes.

Courses offered at these institutions last between three and four years and include educational theory, teaching methodology and periods of teaching practice. Courses for teachers of the first cycle of basic education, lead to the award of the **Bacharel** degree.

Courses for teachers of the second cycle of basic education last four years. These include practical training and students usually specialize in two subject areas (sometimes in one or three). Courses lead to the award of the **Licenciado** degree.

Secondary education

Teachers of the third cycle of basic education and of secondary education receive their training at universities. Initial training includes, besides the scientific and educational sciences, a paid period of one year practical training.

According to the issuing institution, degrees vary in title as follows:

Licenciado em Ensino (5 years);

Licenciado Ramo de Formação Educacional (5–6 years).

Pedagogical training is integrated into the university study course.

Holders of a **Licenciado** degree who wish to acquire professional qualifications in order to become teachers, may have their pedagogical training either on the job under the supervision of a more senior teacher, or by obtaining the necessary pedagogical training in an adequate course.

Higher education

Teachers at this level receive no formal professional training, but there are minimum qualifications laid down for each category.

Puerto Rico

There is a strong American influence on the education system, as shown by the use of the credit-unit system at both school and higher education levels, although no examinations are set or marked by examining bodies in the United States of America.

The medium of instruction is Spanish apart from the faculties of dentistry and medicine at the University of Puerto Rico where it is English.

The academic year runs from August to May.

EVALUATION IN BRITAIN

School

High School Graduation Diploma – generally considered comparable to GCSE standard (grades A, B and C) on a subject-for-subject basis, with the exception of English language.

Higher

Associate degree – may be considered to satisfy the general entrance requirements of British higher education institutions.

Bachelor degree – the five Puerto Rican universities are accredited in the United States of America. They are generally middle-ranking institutions. See the United States of America chapter for further information.

Master's degree – see United States of America chapter.

MARKING SYSTEMS

School

A credit-unit system is used. Pupils must earn 20 units at grades 9–12 to graduate.

Higher

A credit-unit system is used; it is usually explained on the transcript of marks.

SCHOOL EDUCATION

Primary

This covers seven years. In September 1995 all students will begin schooling in Kindergarten.

Secondary

This covers six years divided into two three-year cycles. In the second cycle, pupils can specialize in general/academic or technical subjects. Regardless of the specialization all pupils take mathematics, English, Spanish, natural science and the social sciences. On completion of this period, pupils take the examinations for the **High School Graduation Diploma**.

FURTHER EDUCATION

There are five technical colleges established in the 1960s which were originally intended to offer two-year courses only. However, they now offer **Certificate**, two-year **Associate degree** and transitional courses for those going on to degree courses at university.

HIGHER EDUCATION

There are five universities: the <u>University of Puerto Rico</u>, the <u>Bayamon Central University</u>, the <u>Catholic University of Puerto Rico</u>, the <u>Inter-American University of Puerto Rico</u> and the <u>University of the Sacred Heart</u>.

Entrance to degree courses is on the basis of the **High School Graduation Diploma** and an entrance examination.

The institutions are run on the American pattern of a credit-unit system. An **Associate degree** can be obtained in some fields after two years. **Bachelor degrees** take three to six years, the average being four. **Master's degrees** take a further one to two years. Honours courses may be taken by academically more able students.

Law – students have to hold a **Bachelor degree** in another subject before beginning this course.

Medicine and dentistry – students have to undertake three years' preparatory study before beginning the degree course.

TEACHER EDUCATION

Teacher training is at higher education level; students may take a four-year **Bachelor degree** course or higher qualification. All teacher certification requires at least a **Bachelor's degree**.

Qatar

The modern education system dates from 1956. It is free at all levels for Qataris (but not non-Qataris) of both sexes. The primary stage is in theory compulsory.

English is introduced as a subject at the fifth grade of primary level and continues through to the end of secondary education.

The academic year is divided into two terms and runs from September/October until the end of May with a break in January/February.

EVALUATION IN BRITAIN

School

Thanawaya Aam Qatari (Qatari General Secondary Education Certificate) – generally considered comparable to GCSE standard (grades A, B and C) on a subject-for-subject basis (with the exception of English language), when a minimum overall mark of 70 per cent has been obtained. Students with very good results may be considered for admission to access/bridging courses.

Higher

BA/BSc – may be considered to satisfy the general entrance requirements of British higher education institutions. Exceptionally, students with very high grades may be considered for advanced standing by British higher education institutions.

MARKING SYSTEM

School

The **Thanawaya Aam** is marked on a percentage scale.

Higher

The University operates the standard North American credit system.

SCHOOL EDUCATION

Primary

Primary schools normally enrol children at age six for a six-year course, grades 1 to 6. The school year is divided into two terms. There are two examinations in each grade, one taken in the middle of the year and one at the end of the school year.

Preparatory

This is a three-year course which covers grades 7 to 9 at the end of which pupils take a promotion examination administered by the Ministry of Education.

Secondary

This three-year course covers grades 10 to 12 with the final two years divided into scientific and literary streams. At the end of grade 12 pupils take the **Thanawaya Aam** examination.

Technical/vocational secondary

Vocational training is available for boys at preparatory and secondary levels in a six-year course at the vocational school.

Special vocational courses are available for adults to enable them to find employment. A two-year course at the preparatory level allows adults with primary education to compress the usual three years into two by emphasizing the vocational subject matter and placing less stress on Arabic, religion and social studies than in the normal vocational curriculum.

A regional vocational training centre was established in Doha in 1970 to train Qataris and nationals of other Gulf countries in a variety of vocational, technical and clerical skills for employment in various industries during a two-year course in building, mechanical and electrical trades. A number of courses leading to City and Guilds of London Institute qualifications are also taught.

HIGHER EDUCATION

The University of Qatar was founded as twin Faculties of Education (male and female) in 1973. It acquired university status in 1977. It has seven faculties: education, humanities and social science, science, sharia law and Islamic studies, engineering, administration and economics, technology, and the following associated institutes: Educational Research Centre, Documentation and Humanities Research Centre, Scientific and Applied Research Centre and the Research Centre for Sirra and Sunni Studies.

For entry to a first degree course a 65 per cent pass in the literary stream, and 60 per cent pass in the scientific stream of the **Thanawaya Aam** is required.

Except in the Faculties of Administration and Economics and of Engineering, all students must first pass a four-year **Bachelor of Education** course. Students who succeed in this examination may continue for a fifth year, leading to a **BA** or **BSc degree**.

English is the medium of instruction only in the English Department, the Engineering Faculty and the English-language methodology course offered by the English Language Unit of the University: all students must earn between eight and ten service English credit hours.

TEACHER EDUCATION

Teacher training for all stages is conducted by the <u>Faculty of Education of Qatar University</u>. The courses available are: **BA in Primary Education, General Diploma in Education** and a **Special Diploma in Education**.

Romania

The Ministry of Education (*Ministerul Invătămăntului*) is responsible for the implementation of the education policy of the State.

Following the December 1989 Revolution, an interim Education Decree (dated May 1990) provided the legal framework for the organization of school education in 1990–1. The government has since approved decisions concerning the development of the education system on an annual basis.

From 1969 to 1989, compulsory education was for ten years (ages six to sixteen). The May 1990 Decree reduced this to eight years. At present (1994) education is compulsory for all pupils up to the age of sixteen.

Public education is free; private instruction will be covered by a future Education Act.

The medium of instruction is Romanian. Use of mother tongue at all levels of education is ensured to each nationality within the country.

The academic year is thirty-four to thirty-eight weeks (varying according to level of education), from October to July.

EVALUATION IN BRITAIN

School

Diploma de Baccalaureat – may be considered to satisfy the general entrance requirements of British higher education institutions, provided high marks have been obtained.

Higher

Diploma de Licenta – generally considered comparable to British Bachelor (Ordinary) degree standard; students with high grades may be considered for admission to postgraduate study.

MARKING SYSTEM

Marking is on a scale of 1–10, with 5 as the minimum pass-mark, except for the higher education graduation examination in which 6 is the minimum pass-mark.

SCHOOL EDUCATION

Pre-school (*Invatamintul Pre-scolar*)

Facilities are available in crèches (*Crese*) for children aged one to three years and in nursery schools (*Gradinite de Copii*) for children aged three to six years.

Before 1991

Primary and middle

The eight-year basic education (*Scoala Generala*) was composed of four years' elementary (forms I–IV), beginning at age six or seven, plus four years' middle school at *Gymnasium* (forms V–VIII). Schools at this stage were unstreamed. To develop students' abilities, groups with additional music, fine arts and choreography programmes could be organized. Promotion to the next grade was by continuous assessment.

Secondary

Pupils attended either Day High School (*Liceul*) or vocational school. *Liceul* comprised two levels, each lasting two years: lower (forms nine and ten) and upper (forms eleven and twelve, eventually thirteen). Form thirteen consisted of evening classes only and led to the **Bacalaureat** examinations. High school evening classes were organized only at the upper level and lasted three years.

Admission to form nine depended on successful completion of form eight. Lower high school was an integral part of ten-year compulsory education started in elementary and middle school. It provided training in a trade which enabled students to take jobs as probationers, to enrol in vocational school, or to enter upper high school.

Admission to upper high school was by entrance examination.

The syllabuses were differentiated by high school type and specialization. They were centrally controlled for every specialization and contained basic scientific disciplines, humanities, social sciences and specialized disciplines.

There were high schools for industrial, military, agricultural/industrial training, forestry, economics, medical studies, and for mathematics and physics, natural sciences, philology and history, pedagogy, arts, computer science, sport and theology.

High school studies ended with a school-leaving examination (**Examen de Bacalaureat**). Candidates who passed received a **Diploma de Bacalaureat** (School Leaving Diploma) which entitled them to sit the entrance examination for any higher education establishment or to take a job.

After 1991

The lack of resources in schools is considered by some to have resulted in a lowering of overall standards, despite twelve years of schooling.

The reform of 1991 introduced four years' primary education (grades I–IV), five years' lower secondary education (in *Gymnasium*) leading to the **Certificate of Compulsory Education** (grades V–VIII), and three years' non-compulsory upper secondary education (in *Lyceum*) culminating in the **Diploma de Bacalaureat**. Upper secondary education is now divided into science, technical and humanities streams (covers grades IX–XII or XIII).

Lower-secondary education is organized on both a full time and extramural basis. Special schools exist at both primary and lower secondary level in subjects such as fine arts (e.g. music, dance) and sports. There are also schools offering intensive foreign language training and alternative systems (e.g. Freinet, Montessori, Waldorf etc.)

Upper Secondary Schools

Upper secondary education is provided in the form of ful-time, evening or extramural studies. It is carried out in many types of school: academic; industrial; agricultural; forestry; economic; computer science; metrology; fine arts; pedagogical; sports; military and theological secondary schools.

Academic schools provide for grades IX–XII (full-time and extramural courses) and grades IX–XIII (evening courses) in both arts and science disciplines. Pedagogical schools provide full-time courses for grades IX–XIII.

Admission to secondary education (grade IX) is by a competitive entrance examination for pupils who have completed lower secondary education. On completing the final grade at all types of secondary school pupils can sit for the **Baccalaureate** exam. Irrespective of the type of secondary school, holders of the **Baccalaureate** diploma have the right to take the entrance examinations for post secondary schools or higher education establishments.

In the other types of school listed above, school leavers are, in addition to the **Baccalaureate,** awarded a diploma for their vocational training.

Vocational and Apprenticeship training

Vocational schools train for the basic trades of the national economy. Admission is by competitive entrance examination taken by lower secondary school leavers. The course culminates in a school-leaving examination; pupils who pass are awarded a diploma which carries a right to practice in the trade.

Complementary and apprenticeship training is organized for VIII grade leavers who have not registered in a secondary or vocational school. These students earn a diploma for the vocational training, and are also able to continue their studies in secondary education, provided they pass supplementary examinations.

There are also Technical Foreman schools which provide one-and-a-half or two-year training.

FURTHER EDUCATION

Post secondary specialized schools provide both full-time and evening courses, and are aimed at academic school leavers who wish to undertake additional, vocational training. They grant a diploma which entitles holders to practice their chosen vocation.

HIGHER EDUCATION

For all state higher education institutions in Romania, the appropriate ministry determines general curricula, criteria for admission, the requirement for the awarding of degrees, and is responsible for the appointment of academic staff and for the number of research and administrative staff.

Higher education (*Invatamintul Superior*) is provided in universities, institutes, polytechnics and academies, offering courses lasting four to six years (long cycle) or a shorter cycle of higher education lasting three years at university colleges.

Many private universities have been established since the revolution.

The distinction between universities, polytechnics, institutes and academies is one of fields of study (the polytechnics are normally entirely engineering or other vocationally-oriented institutions). Academic standards are similar.

Teaching and research in clinical medicine, in most subjects allied to medicine and in veterinary science takes place predominantly in some twenty professional institutes grouped under the Academy of Sciences, but also in universities.

Admission to higher education is by competitive entrance examination (**Examen de Admitere**) open to those holding a school-leaving certificate (**Diploma de Bacalaureat**). Evening and extramural courses may be attended only by people in employment.

Studies in university colleges (*Colegii Universitaire*) last three years and lead to the **Diploma de absolvire**.

The University courses for the **Licenta** last four to five years; evening and extramural studies last one year longer. Studies end in a graduation paper (**Examen de Diploma**). Those who pass are awarded the **Diploma de Licenta** (Graduation Diploma).

Courses in engineering last five years and lead to the **Diploma de Inginer**; courses in architecture and medicine last six years and lead to the **Diploma de Architect** and **Diploma de Doctor-medic** respectively.

Further studies of one to two years (*Studii aprofundate*) after the **Diploma de Licenta** lead to the award of a Master's style diploma.

Postgraduate courses are available in all fields (economics, science, technology and humanities) for graduates of a higher education establishment who have completed (at least) university studies. These postgraduate courses last from two months to two years and are organized by higher education establishments, usually on an extramural basis. Graduation is through examinations and defence of a graduation paper. In medicine, courses last three years and lead to the title of **Specialist MD**.

The doctoral (**Doktorat**) degree is the highest form of specialist training in various branches of science, technology and humanities. It is organized by higher education establishments, academies of sciences and central research institutions. Courses last three years full-time, four years part-time.

The title of **Doctor-Docent in Stiinte** may be awarded after a long period of research.

TEACHER EDUCATION

School

Nursery school teachers (*Educatoare*) and primary teachers (*Invatatori*) are trained for two to three years in colleges (*Colegii*).

High school and middle-school teachers (*Profesori*) graduate from and take the diploma examination in a higher education establishment (four or five-year course). At the same time, they must also pass the **Diploma de Absolvire** from a Pedagogical Seminar, which lasts two years.

Vocational school teachers graduate from and take the diploma examination in a higher education establishment lasting at least four years, or in a school for middle-grade engineers. In common with high school teachers, they must also pass the **Diploma de Absolvire.**

Higher

Higher education teaching staff are either assistant lecturers (*Asistenti*), lecturers/senior lecturers (*Lectori*), readers (*Conferentiari*) or professors (*Profesori*) who graduate from and take the diploma examination in a higher education establishment lasting at least four years. They too must pass the **Diploma de Absolvire**.

The positions of reader and professor require a doctoral degree.

Russian Federation

All former republics of the Soviet Union are covered in this chapter for the period until they became independent in 1991. See separate chapters on the developments post-1991 in AZERBAIJAN, BELARUS, ESTONIA, KAZAKHSTAN, LATVIA, LITHUANIA and the UKRAINE. NARIC has been unable to obtain up-to-date post-independence information on the other former Soviet States of Armenia, Georgia, Kyrgyzstan, Moldova, Tajikistan, Turkmenistan or Uzbekistan.

The former Soviet government with its ministerial structure has in practice been taken over, with some reduction in numbers and changes of function. The Russian Soviet Federative Socialist Republic in December 1991 became a founding member of the Commonwealth of Independent States and adopted the title 'Russian Federation' (RF).

Whereas the main features of the state education system were, in the past, central control and uniformity throughout the Union, the situation since 1990 has been one of rapid devolution of responsibilities, with individual republican ministries and, to an ever-increasing extent, even individual institutions being granted, or simply taking, control. Alongside change and experimentation, however, there remains a large element of inertia, as well as a more conscious resistance to change on the part of conservative forces in the educational establishment.

Since the death of Stalin there has been a history of fitful and often contradictory reform in state education. The main events are:

In 1958 a law called for a strengthening of links between schools and the world of work. The aim of the so-called 'Khrushchev reforms' was to give vocational training to all. Compulsory schooling increased from seven to eight years. Full (non-compulsory) secondary schooling increased from ten to eleven years;

During the period 1964–70, revision of some of the changes brought in under the 'Khrushchev reforms' was carried out, including less emphasis on vocational training in secondary schools; measures for the further improvement of the general secondary schools and for more emphasis on intensive learning in primary schools were included. The length of the latter was reduced from four to three years.

The desire to ensure ten years' schooling for *all* young people was regularly expressed; in 1975 it was stated that all seven-year-olds now at school would receive ten years of education. If this ideal was never achieved one hundred per cent, by the 1980s it had very largely been accomplished, at least in urban areas.

In 1984 a major attempt to reform the whole system from primary school to higher education took place. The school starting age was to be brought down to six (politically a very sensitive issue in Russia where parents widely believe 'school is no place for six-year-olds'), all young people were to receive vocational education at school if not in vocational colleges, curricula were to be considerably reformed and content reduced. Unfortunately, decisions were taken before *perestroika* went into full swing; thus while children were to be taught to 'think for themselves', at the same time 'children must be made into convinced communists'. The internal contradictions, the lack of facilities for vocational training, the lack of will to come to grips with curricular problems and many other failings led very soon to disillusionment with the '1984' measures.

Meanwhile, from the early 1980s, reforming progressive educators had been attracting the greatest of public interest in their experimental 'child-centred' schools. Certain leading figures in Soviet education, including ministers of education, gave considerable support to moves for reform.

The very first decree of Yeltsin as President of the RF in 1991 was devoted to education. Inability to live up to financial promises made in this decree has caused disappointment. A new Law on Education has more recently been adopted. There has been a retreat from the ideal of compulsory education for eleven years; children may leave school at fifteen. Private fee-paying schools are now permitted. Massive attempts at decentralizing the system and placing all sorts of financial, methodological and curricular responsibilities on republics, local areas and individual schools are taking place. A 1994 Law of the RF is entitled 'On degovernmentalization and demonopolization in the educational sphere'. These clumsy words express a clear desire to free the system and liberate local and private initiative.

Linguistic and ethnic minorities

The language map of the RF is immensely complex. Nineteen per cent of the population is ethnically non-Russian. Depending on how a 'language' is defined, about 120 different languages are spoken on the territory of the RF. The medium of instruction is a difficult cultural and political issue. Russian, of course, dominates, and is available everywhere. Instruction takes place in 66 other languages (1990 figure), but in the case of very many of these languages such instruction will continue for one or two years only. In secondary, and especially higher education, Russian is the almost inevitable choice.

Hitherto, the school year has run from September to the end of May for primary schools, September to mid-June for secondary schools, and September to the end of June for tertiary institutions.

EVALUATION IN BRITAIN

School

Attestat o srednem obrazovanii (Certificate of Secondary Education) (also known colloquially as **Attestat zrelosti**):

at grade 10 – generally considered to be below GCSE standard
at grade 11 – generally considered comparable to GCSE standard (grades A, B and C) on a subject-for-subject basis, with the exception of English language.

Diplom ob okanchanii proftekhuchilishcha (Diploma of Completed Vocational-Technical Education) – generally considered comparable to City and Guilds Certificate Part I.

Diplom ob okanchanii srednego spetsial'nogo uchebnogo zavedeniya (Diploma of Completed Specialized Secondary Education) – generally considered comparable to BTEC National Diploma / N/SVQ level 3 / Advanced GNVQ/GSVQ standard.

Higher

Diplom ob okanchanii vysshego uchebnogo zavedeniya (Diploma Specialist) –
generally considered comparable to a standard between GCE Advanced and British
Bachelor degree; may be given advanced standing by British higher education
institutions. Candidates from prestigious institutions may be considered for admission
to postgraduate study. Enquirers should contact the National Academic Recognition
Information Centre for further information.

MARKING SYSTEM

Marking is on a 1–5 scale at all levels of the education system

5	excellent	
4	good	
3	satisfactory	(a pass, but regarded as something of an insult: feel of 'C minus')
2	unsatisfactory	(a failure)
1	totally unsatisfactory	(not usually awarded: a disastrous failure)

SCHOOL EDUCATION

Pre-school provision

In 1988, 58 per cent of the age-group (three months to six to seven years) were enrolled
in pre-school establishments such as nurseries *(detskie sady)*, and day-care centres
(detskie iasli). This provision is now greatly reduced for reasons of finance.

General school education

Elementary education *(nachalnoe obrazovanie)* is compulsory and lasts from grades 1
to 4 inclusive, starting theoretically at the age of six. Only 30 per cent of the age-group
do in fact start at six, and two-thirds of them do not attend school, going instead to
school-type classes in pre-school institutions.

'Incomplete' secondary education *(nepol'noe obshchee srednee obrazovanie)* is also
compulsory and lasts from grades 5 to 9.

Upper secondary education (complete secondary, *polnoe srednee obrazovanie*) is now
non-compulsory and lasts from grades 10 to 11.

In the late 1980s, full ('complete') secondary education was theoretically increased to
eleven years. Resistance from parents, disagreement between teachers and educators on
the subject and shortcomings in material provision all mean that very few children (30
per cent of the age cohort) in fact are receiving eleven years even now. The current
structure, then, ideally appears as follows:

Primary school	Grades 1–4
'Incomplete' secondary	Grades 5–9
General secondary	Grades 10–11

In recent years a strong desire for devolution and local decision-making has emerged.
The central authorities are encouraging this by legislation and administrative action.
The curriculum was until very recently tightly controlled by the centre, but now local

authorities and even individual schools have considerable freedom and flexibility to establish their own curricula and syllabuses in many subjects.

Innovation and experiment by national and local educational bodies and by voluntary associations is encouraged. A small private sector (less than one per cent of children at school) is developing in the larger urban centres with governmental support. If this seems to imply fragmentation, Russia sees it as 'diversity' and seeks actively to dismantle the remains of state monopoly.

School examinations are held at age fifteen in Russian/native language and mathematics. Written and oral methods of testing are used. At the age of seventeen the leaving examinations are taken – **Attestat o srednem obrazovanii** (Certificate of Secondary Education). Not all subjects studied are tested. The traditional Russian stress on oral testing is here very obvious. This is not a single-subject examination like GCSE; all subjects taken must be passed.

Vocational training in the PTUs (*Professional'no-tekhnicheskie uchilishcha)* **or SPTUs** (*Srednie* etc.)

There are two to three-year courses for those who have finished grade 9 ('incomplete' secondary). Sixty per cent of the time is allocated to study, the rest spent on industrial placement. The **SPTUs** (S stands for 'secondary') gave students a certificate of complete general secondary education, though at a less advanced level than that achieved in the general schools. There are approximately 4,300 such vocational training establishments and about two million students.

The **Diplom ob okanchanii proftekhuchilishcha** (Diploma of Completed Vocational-Technical Education) is the diploma/certificate received by students of the vocational-technical colleges. Holders of these certificates will have trained for moderately skilled jobs in industry or public services.

Secondary specialized education

This is open both to those with 'incomplete' and those with 'complete' secondary schooling. For the former, courses last three to four years, for the latter two to three years. There are 2,600 secondary specialized institutions and about 2.3 million students.

The **Diplom ob okanchanii srednego spetsial'nogo uchebnogo zavedeniya** (Diploma of Completed Specialized Secondary Education) is awarded on completion. Holders of this diploma/certificate have received a higher level of training than the above, and include skilled workers in industry and young professionals such as nursery nurses (in Russian terms: 'kindergarten upbringers'), paramedics and the like.

HIGHER EDUCATION

Undergraduate level

Over 2.8 million students enrol in institutions at this level every year: universities, institutes, polytechnic institutions (specializing in engineering, science and technology), academies, conservatoires, etc. (514 institutions in all). The term *Vuz* (an abbreviation for Higher Education Establishment) is used as the generic term for all such; the institutions with the highest prestige are called universities.

Admission is on the basis of success in a competitive entrance examination and possession of the school-leaving examination (see below).

The first degree (not called a 'degree', but a **diplom**) is generally awarded at the end of a five-year course. Curricula and teaching methods are currently under review, but traditionalist attitudes will doubtless disappear slowly (see **Diplom . . .** below)

Higher education

Diplom ob okanchanii vysshego uchebnogo zavedeniya (Diploma Specialist) – as explained above, Russian undergraduates usually study for five years after leaving school at seventeen. There is no central authority responsible for the quality of the education offered, and the qualifications issued vary markedly. The concept of an 'external examiner' to ensure comparability of standards is not understood in Russia. It is important to understand that the nature of the courses differs markedly from the practice in Western universities. While there are some slight moves towards reform, Russian undergraduates spend most of their time taking notes in lectures. Small group discussion, seminars, independent reading and writing and meaningful debate are extremely limited in scope.

Since the revolution of the early 1990s many Russian universities and higher education institutions have been intending to replace the **diplom** with Western style bachelor and master's degrees (**bakalavr** and **magistr**). In most universities limited progress has been made in this respect.

Higher degrees

Full-time postgraduate studies (*aspirantura*) leading to the qualification of **kandidat nauk** (candidate of sciences) normally last three years and include original research and publication. The *doktorantura* (degree entitled **doktor nauk**) is, in British terms, a higher doctorate.

The further degree of **kandidat**, is often considered roughly equivalent to the PhD, and some Russian *kandidaty* style themselves 'Dr' when abroad.

ADULT CONTINUING EDUCATION

Many higher education institutions have specialist departments responsible for running professional updating courses. These are developing academic programmes in the field of psychology of adult learning, and they are establishing links between such departments and their counterparts in the United Kingdom and North America. In addition, distance education techniques are widely practised. The development of open university and college systems is taking place, based on Western experience and example. The non-formal sector is particularly active. The All-Union Society of Knowledge (*Znanie*) is now considerably reduced in influence. The old political programmes have virtually disappeared, to be replaced by intense activity in the field of independently provided courses for the general public, especially where these have a vocational orientation: foreign language courses are a good example.

Professional and learned societies, especially in engineering and the applied sciences, are increasingly active in monitoring and providing adult continuing education. Independent trade unions and the emergence of an open labour market have led to the development of parallel worker and trade union education, which is very different from the heavily politicized 'education' provided formerly in this context.

APPENDIX

There are 28 academies of various specialities:

15 technical engineering and technological;
4 financial and economic;
5 teaching the humanities;
2 agricultural and veterinary;
1 medical;
1 Jewish.

Under the jurisdiction of the State Committee for Higher Education of the Russian Federation there are 220 higher educational institutions; under the Ministry of Education there are 96 institutions; the Ministry of Agriculture – 62; the Ministry of Culture – 41; Health Care Ministry – 47; other ministries and departments – 69 institutions.

A third (138) of the higher education institutions in Russia are in the Central and North-Western economic regions. 87 are concentrated near Moscow, and 42 near St Petersburg. There are fewer institutions located within the Northern region (15), the Volga-Vyatsky region (22) and Chernozemny region (26).

The distribution of higher school institutions over the economic regions of Russia

Economic Regions	Number of Higher Ed Inst. 1992/93 acad. year	Number of Students (thousand)		
		1990/1991 acad. yr.	1991/1992 acad. yr.	1992/1993 acad. yr.
Russian Federation (total)	535	2,825.5	2,762.8	2,638
Northern	15	58.8	59.0	58.1
North-Western	47	266.1	255.5	238.8
Central	136	797.4	765.0	724.1
Volga-Vyatsky	22	133.8	131.8	127.4
Central-Chernozemny	26	123.9	123.0	119.8
Volga-River	59	300.7	297.5	286.1
North-Caucasian	51	250.5	249.2	241.3
Uralsky	57	303.7	298.1	288.5
West-Siberian	55	287.7	284.5	270.6
East-Siberian	32	164.7	161.6	155.4
Far-Eastern	32	122.4	122.4	115.8
Kaliningradsky region	3	15.8	15.2	12.1

In addition to state institutions in the Russian Federation, there are now 200 non-state educational institutions offering different levels of vocational training; 141 of these have been given a licence. The proportion of licensed non-state educational institutions is 26.3 per cent of state ones. About 80 per cent of the former are situated in Moscow and the Moscow region.

Rwanda

The following chapter regarding the education system in Rwanda is based on information obtained from the 3rd edition of this Guide, published in 1991, as NARIC has been unable to obtain more recent information.

This chapter covers the period since independence in 1962. Before then the territory was the Belgian-administered trust territory of Rwanda-Urundi.

Education is compulsory in theory until age fifteen but few children actually stay on until then. Since 1964–5 children have been able to begin their schooling at age six.

EVALUATION IN BRITAIN

School

Certificat des Humanités – generally considered comparable to GCSE standard (grades A, B and C) on a subject-for-subject basis, with the exception of English language.

Higher

Licence – generally considered comparable to a standard between GCE Advanced and British Bachelor degree; may be given advanced standing by British higher education institutions.

Agrégation de l'Enseignement Secondaire Supérieur – generally considered comparable to British Bachelor degree standard.

MARKING SYSTEM

School

90 per cent	*plus grande distinction*
80	*grande distinction*
70	*distinction*
50–69	*satisfaction*

Higher

As above.

SCHOOL EDUCATION

Primary

This covers six years divided into two cycles. The *Premier Cycle* (literacy cycle) lasts four years during which teaching is in Kinyarwanda and is intended to give children a basic knowledge of arithmetic, geography, history, civics, religion and reading. On completion of this cycle pupils take an examination, success in which gives admission to the *Deuxième Cycle*. This lasts two years, teaching is in French, and it culminates in examinations in French, arithmetic and civics, success in which gives access to secondary school. Pupils who are not able to enter an academic secondary school (as there is only a limited number of places, a high passing score is set) may stay at primary school for a seventh year (*Septième Complémentaire*) during which home economics and farming methods are taught.

Secondary

This covers six years divided into two three-year cycles:

1st cycle – *Tronc Commun d'Orientation*
2nd cycle – in modern or classical humanities (*Sections Moyennes Générales*).

On successful completion of the second cycle pupils are awarded the **Certificat des Humanités**.

There are also junior seminaries where many boys take courses based on Greek and Latin.

Technical secondary

There is a variety of two-year courses to train aides in crafts and trades for pupils who have completed two to three years of academic secondary, although pupils could also enter directly from primary school.

The Official Trade School (Ecole Officielle de Métiers) in Kicukiro, Kigali, offers a four-year post-primary course in carpentry, cabinet-making, mechanics, automechanics, electricity and welding.

The Groupe Scolaire in Butare (established in 1929 by the Roman Catholic Order of the Brothers of Charity) offers four-year courses for students to train as medical, agricultural and veterinary assistants, business administrators or nurses.

HIGHER EDUCATION

The National University of Rwanda was established at Butare in 1963. Admission to degree courses is based on successful completion of the second three-year cycle of academic secondary education.

The first stage of higher education normally lasts two years and leads to the title of **Bachelier**: **Bachelier ès Sciences, ès Lettres**, etc. (depending on the subject). A further two years lead to the **Licence**.

In engineering, the **Baccalauréat /Diplóme de Bachelier** takes three years and a further two years lead to the professional title of **Ingénieur.**

In medicine the qualification of **Doctor** is obtained after a seven-year course – one year of general studies in the Faculty of Science and two years' general study in the Faculty of Medicine, followed by four years' specialization.

Other post-secondary institutions are:

–   the Université Adventiste d'Afrique Centrale, founded in 1984;

–   the Institut Africain et Mauricien de Statistiques et d'Economie Appliquée, offering a three-year programme leading to the **Diplôme d'Ingénieur des Travaux Statistiques (ITS)**;

–   the Institut Supérieur des Finances Publiques, founded in 1986;

–   the Ecole Supérieure de Gestion et d'Informatique (Institut Fidèle), founded in 1985 and offering a two-year diploma course.

TEACHER EDUCATION

Ecoles de Moniteurs Auxiliaires (for boys) and *Ecoles de Monitrices Auxiliaires* (for girls) offer two-year post-primary courses to train aides for primary school teachers.

Ecoles Normales Inférieures train primary school teachers on five-year post-primary courses (the first three years cover the same ground as the first cycle of general secondary education and are followed by two years' pedagogical training).

Ecoles Normales Moyennes used to train teachers for the first cycle of general secondary education on a seven-year post-primary course (five years' general secondary followed by two years' teacher training).

The Institut Pedagogique National provides teacher training in conjunction with the University's faculties of letters and science. Students who successfully complete the three-year course culminating in the **Agrégation de l'Enseignement Secondaire Inférieur** may teach in the lower secondary cycle. Students who successfully complete the five-year course culminating in the **Agregation de l'Enseignement Secondaire Supérieur,** may teach in the upper secondary cycle.

Saudi Arabia

Educational administration, facilities and instruction are completely separate for men and women. Private schools follow the state schools curriculum but sometimes add more subjects and courses. There are a number of international schools modelled on the British or American systems.

Education is free and voluntary at all levels.

Arabic is the medium of instruction, except in most of the faculties of science and medicine, where some tuition is in English.

The academic year runs from September to June.

EVALUATION IN BRITAIN

School

Tawjihiyah (General Secondary Education Certificate) – generally considered comparable to GCSE standard (grades A, B and C) on a subject-for-subject basis, with the exception of English language, when a minimum overall mark of 60 per cent has been obtained. Students with very good results may be considered for admission to access/bridging courses.

Higher

Bachelor degree – generally considered comparable to a standard between GCE Advanced and British Bachelor degree; may be given advanced standing by British higher education institutions. Exceptionally, students with very high grades may be considered for admission to postgraduate study.

MARKING SYSTEM

School

Tawjihiyah

On a percentage scale; the minimum pass-mark in each subject is 50 per cent. Final certificate scores are converted to descriptive grades as follows:

90–100 per cent	excellent
75–89	very good
60–74	good
50–59	pass
0–49	fail

Higher

Universities grade first degrees using one of the following systems:

1	excellent	A	90–100 per cent	4.0
2	very good	B	80–89	3.0
3	good	C	70–79	2.0
4	pass	D	60–69	1.0
5	poor (fail)	F		0.0

The <u>College of Engineering</u> operates a grading scale of 1–100 with 50 as the minimum pass-mark.

SCHOOL EDUCATION

Although male and female pupils are strictly segregated, they follow a basic curriculum and a 6-3-3 pattern of education. At primary and intermediate schools, both sexes follow the same curriculum. Physical education is not offered by all girls schools. The same yearly examinations are taken by both sexes.

Primary

This covers a six-year cycle between ages six and twelve. At the end of each year, students take examinations. Success in every subject is essential for promotion to the next grade. If a student fails a subject that particular subject or course must be retaken after the summer holidays. Failure on this occasion means that the pupil must repeat the entire year. At the end of the sixth-year examination, successful students are awarded the **General Elementary School Certificate**. This grants access to the intermediate school.

Intermediate

This covers a three-year cycle between ages twelve and fifteen and prepares students for general secondary education or technical education. Students take yearly examinations. At the end of the ninth year, those who pass the final examination are awarded the **Intermediate School Certificate**. This grants access to secondary education (a grade of 65 per cent or more is required).

Secondary

This is also a three-year cycle. Students can choose between general secondary and technical schools.

General

This is the main type of secondary school. In the first year students share a common curriculum. At the end of this year, they are divided into the scientific and literary streams for the final two years. A student scoring 60 per cent in all the first-year subjects may choose between the scientific and literary streams. A student scoring less than 60 per cent must opt for the literary stream. The course culminates in the **Tawjihiyah (General Secondary Education Certificate)**, the marks for which are a combination of classroom performance (30 per cent) and the final examination (70 per cent).

Technical

All technical and vocational training is handled by the General Organization for Technical Education and Vocational Training (GOTEVOT) operating under a council of members of different government agencies and chaired by the Ministry of Labour and Social Affairs.

Technical education at secondary level includes three types of schools – vocational (technical), commercial and agricultural. An **Intermediate School Certificate** is required for entry. The courses lead to the **Secondary Vocational School Diploma**, the **Secondary Commercial School Diploma** and the **Secondary Agricultural School Diploma**. The grading system in these schools is the same as in the general secondary schools.

FURTHER EDUCATION

Vocational training centres offer a range of courses lasting between twelve and eighteen months. Students must have completed five to six years of primary education. Courses include both theoretical and practical instruction. On satisfactory completion of the course students are awarded the **Vocational Training Certificate**.

Post-secondary technical and vocational education is provided by Higher Institutes and the Technical College offering three-year programmes leading to certificates and diplomas.

A number of institutions offer courses leading to the awards, at different levels, of the City and Guilds of London Institute.

HIGHER EDUCATION

There are two kinds of establishment offering higher education: the traditional Islamic Colleges and the more Western-styled Colleges.

Admission to higher education is based on success in the **Tawjihiyah** examinations. Some faculties also require students to pass their entrance examination. Part-time students are accepted.

The normal length of a **Bachelor degree** course is four years, apart from pharmacy and medicine (four years plus hospital training) and engineering and veterinary medicine (five years). Every course represents a certain number of hours, credits or points generally corresponding to the number of class-hours offered each week. The average student takes approximately 30–35 credits during the academic year; undergraduates must complete a minimum of 120 credits to graduate.

Women are admitted to university on the same terms as men, but their studies are completely segregated. They have separate facilities, are admitted to classes at different times from the men or attend classes broadcast over closed-circuit television.

Master's degrees normally take two years' study following a first degree.

PhDs normally take a minimum of three years following a **Master's degree**.

TEACHER EDUCATION

Primary

Until 1974

Intermediate school graduates could take a three-year (previously two-year) training course at secondary level training institutions to enable them to teach in primary schools.

Since 1974

Teachers must now have the **Tawjihiyah (General Secondary Education Certificate)**, since the Intermediate Teacher Training Institutes were upgraded to Secondary Teacher Training Institutes. To persuade more women to become primary school teachers, the Girls' Education Administration offers three-month post-secondary courses. There are also Junior Colleges offering two-year courses for women leading to a **Certificate of Education** enabling them to teach at primary and intermediate schools.

Intermediate and secondary

Men

A **Bachelor of Education** degree at university. Graduates who did not study education in their degree course are generally sent abroad to follow one-year teaching courses.

Women

There are seven Colleges of Education for girls providing four-year courses leading to a **BA** or **BSc in Education**. Graduates are qualified to teach in secondary schools. Three of these colleges (Jeddah, Riyadh and Dammam) provide postgraduate training for women interested in specialization.

Science and mathematics

The Ministry of Education has established 18 Teachers Colleges for training and retraining science and mathematics teachers for work in intermediate schools. Trainees must be graduates of the Teacher Training Institutes or holders of the **Tawjihiyah**. A preliminary remedial science course is followed by a three-year course which leads to a **Teacher Proficiency Certificate**.

Fine arts and physical education

There are separate fine arts institutes for men and women. Only men are allowed to teach physical education. Women can enter the fine arts institutes on the basis of the **General Elementary School Certificate**.

HIGHER EDUCATION INSTITUTIONS

There are seven universities and eleven girls colleges.

Universities

There are two Islamic universities: Imam Mohammed Bin Saud Islamic University and the Islamic University in Madinah. Imam Mohammed, whose student body is primarily Saudi, provides training for Islamic specialists. Women students may register, but only for correspondence courses. The <u>Islamic University</u> is an international Islamic institution established by royal decree in 1961 to provide training to promote the Islamic faith. It accepts Muslim students – males only – from all over the world.

<u>King Abdulaziz University</u> – founded as a private institution in 1967, it became a public university in 1971. The second largest university in the Kingdom.

<u>King Fahd University of Petroleum and Minerals</u> – provides advanced training in science and engineering to serve the petroleum and minerals industries in the Kingdom. All instruction is in English and students take a preparatory year before entering one of the undergraduate colleges.

<u>King Faisal University</u> – founded in 1975, it has two campuses: one in Dammam, which houses the College of Medicine and Medical Sciences and the College of Architecture and Planning; and one in Al Hasa, where the Colleges of Administration and Planning, Agriculture and Food Science, Education, and Veterinary Medicine are located.

<u>King Saud University</u> – the oldest and largest in the Kingdom, founded in 1957 by royal decree. Previously known as the <u>University of Riyadh</u>. In addition to the main campus in Riyadh, the university has branches in Abha and Qaseem.

<u>Umm Al-Qura University</u> – established in 1981, incorporating existing faculties of the <u>King Abdul Aziz University</u>.

Girls Colleges

Seven of the eleven girls colleges are Colleges of Education (see above). There are also two Colleges of Arts (one in Riyadh and one in Dammam), one College of Science in Dammam, and one College of Social Work in Riyadh.

Senegal

Formerly a French colony, Senegal became a member of the French Community in 1958. It was a part, together with Sudan, of the Federation of Mali from January 1959 to August 1960. On 20 August 1960, it became a fully independent state known as the Republic of Senegal.

There remains a strong French influence on the educational system. In 1985, according to the conclusions of the *Commission Nationale de Réforme de l'Education et de la Formation*, a new code was established, although it remains open to continual reinterpretation. Since then, there have been various revisions, the most recent one, dated 30/1/91, being the *Loi 91-22 d'Orientation de l'Education nationale*.

There is no compulsory period of education.

The medium of instruction is French.

The academic year runs from October to July.

Education is free for all.

EVALUATION IN BRITAIN

School

Diplôme de Bachelier de l'Enseignement du Second Degré/Baccalauréat (*mention Assez Bien*) – generally considered to be slightly above GCSE standard.

Higher

Diplôme Universitaire d'Etudes Littéraires (DUEL), **Diplôme Universitaire d'Etudes Scientifiques** (DUES), **Diplôme d'Etudes Universitaires Générales** (DEUG) – may be considered to satisfy the general entrance requirements of British higher education institutions.

Diplôme Universitaire de Technologie (DUT) – generally considered comparable to BTEC Higher National Diploma / N/SVQ level 4 standard and may be considered to satisfy the entrance requirements for the third year of a first degree course when curriculae are similar.

Licence – generally considered comparable to British Bachelor (Ordinary) degree standard when marks are good.

Maîtrise – generally considered comparable to British Bachelor (Ordinary or Honours) degree, and may be considered for admission to postgraduate study when very high marks have been achieved, or candidates have professional experience.

MARKING SYSTEM

School and Higher

Marking is on a scale 0–20 (maximum); 10 is the minimum pass-mark.

16–20	*très bien*	very good
14–15	*bien*	good
12–13	*assez bien*	quite good
10–11	*passable*	average

SCHOOL EDUCATION

Enseignement Fondamental

Pre-primary

Very limited facilities, with 173 schools (private 64.67 per cent). National enrolment, 1.6 per cent; girls, 49.4 per cent in 1992.

Primary

This covers six years, from age six, leading to the **Certificat d'Etudes Primaires Elémentaires** (CEPE). The years are numbered from *Douzième* (12th) to *Septième* (7th).

726,000 pupils; national enrolment 55.8 per cent; rural 35.3 per cent; girls 47.1 per cent.

Secondary

There is a special entrance examination, akin to the former 11-plus examination in the UK (22,000 candidates in 1992). Secondary education lasts seven years, divided into four years' lower secondary and three years' upper secondary. The years are numbered in reverse order i.e. the first year is *Classe de Sixième* and the seventh year *Classe de Terminale*.

Middle

This cycle, also called *moyen* can be studied at a *Collège d'Enseignement Général* (CEG), or a *Collège d'Enseignement Moyen* (CEM), which offer lower secondary education only, or a *Lycée*. The cycle ends in the examinations for the **Brevet de Fin d'Etudes Moyennes** (BFEM). Successful pupils may choose whether to proceed to a *Centre de Formation Professionnelle* or a *Lycée d'Enseignement Général* or *Technique* for upper secondary education.

Enrolment: 280 colleges (private sector 35.7 per cent); 140,000 pupils (ps 25.8 per cent); national rate 21.2 per cent.

Upper General

The three-year academic course ends in the examinations for the **Diplôme de Bachelier de l'Enseignement du Second Degré/Baccalauréat** (the examination in French literature, **Épreuve Anticipée de Français**, ends the second year), which may be taken in one of seven series, depending on the specialization taken in the last two years:

A   *philosophie-lettres* (sub-options A2, A3)
B   *économique et social*
C   *mathématiques et sciences physiques*
D   *mathématiques et sciences de la nature*
E, F, G (see below)

Enrolment: 60 institutions (private sector 46.7 per cent); 45,000 pupils (ps 12.5 per cent); national rate 10.7 per cent, girls 32.7 per cent.

Vocational secondary

Before the **Baccalauréat**, facilities are very limited since there is only one *Centre de Formation Professionnelle* in each region, which offer only one or two specialities.

Hardly any of those who fail at the BFEM may undertake three-year courses leading to the qualification of **Certificat d'Aptitude Professionnelle** (CAP). This is the terminal qualification in this track.

Holders of BFEM may undertake:

a two-year course leading to a **Brevet d'Etudes Professionnelles** (BEP). Some of them with professional experience take a supplementary one-year course leading to a **Brevet Professionnel** (BP)

or

a three-year course leading to the **Brevet de Technicien du Développement Rural** (BTDR), **Brevet de Technicien de l'Industrie** (BTI) or **de Maintenance Hospitalière** (BTMH). These diplomas are recognized as equivalent to the **Baccalauréat** but are not accepted in higher institutions

or

a three-year course in a *Lycée* leading to the **Baccalauréat Technique/Diplôme de Bachelier Technicien** in one of the following options:

E   *mathématiques et technique*
F1   *fabrication mécanique*
F2   *électronique*
F3   *mécanique auto*
F6   *biochimie*
F7   *biologie*
G2   *techniques quantitatives de gestion*

Enrolment: 7 institutions; 7,571 pupils; 33.5 per cent girls.

HIGHER EDUCATION

The **Baccalauréat** is the entrance requirement for degree courses at university. Holders of **Baccalauréat E** must take a bridging Course in physics, before embarking on a DUT.

There are two universities, the Université Cheikh Anta Diop in Dakar, established in 1959 and a second established in 1989, the Université de Saint Louis in Saint Louis. There are also *Grandes Ecoles* and *Instituts*, entry to which involves a special examination, which are similar to those in France and offer specialized courses. 23,000 students were registered in 1992.

At the university all students take a multidisciplinary course for two years, leading to the **Diplôme Universitaire d'Etudes Littéraires** (DUEL), **Diplôme Universitaire d'Etudes Scientifiques** (DUES), **Diplôme d'Etudes Juridiques Générales** (DEJG), or **Diplôme d'Etudes Economiques Générales** (DEEG), depending on the student's specialization.

A further year of specialization leads to the **Licence d'Enseignement** or **de Recherche**.

Students holding the **Licence** may undertake a one-year postgraduate course leading to the **Maîtrise**. In law and economics, there is no **Licence**; the **Maîtrise** is obtained two years after the **DEJG/DEEG**.

One year's research following the **Maîtrise** leads to the **Diplôme d'Etudes Approfondies** (DEA); a further two years to the **Doctorat de Troisième Cycle** and many more years to the **Doctorat d'Etat**. These qualifications are necessary to teach in higher education.

Holders of **Licence** or **Maîtrise**, well-known and well published in their discipline, may obtain a **Doctorat d'Université sur Travaux** through presentation of their books and articles to a selection committee.

Medicine: the first qualification is the **Doctorat d'Etat en Médecine** obtained after seven years.

Pharmacy and dentistry: the first qualifications, obtained after five years, are the **Diplôme de Pharmacien** and **Doctorat d'Etat en Chirurgie Dentaire** respectively.

Schooling enrolment: – Dakar: 20,500 students (female 25.2 per cent); arts 36.78 per cent (28.5 per cent of them are female); sciences 15.9 per cent (f. 10 per cent); social sc. 30.7 per cent (f. 26.54 per cent); medicine/pharmacy 12.6 per cent (f. 37.5 per cent); Institutes and Grandes Ecoles 1,220 students (f. 23.8 per cent) –Saint Louis: 1,500 students (f. 23.8 per cent).

TEACHER EDUCATION

Primary

Teachers (*Instituteurs*): Holders of the **Baccalauréat** undertake a four-year course at the *Ecoles Normales Régionales*, leading to the **Certificat d'Aptitude Pédagogique** (CAP).

Assistant teachers (*Instituteurs-adjoints*) who hold the **BFEM** and have professional experience may undertake a one-year course at the *Centre de Formation Pédagogique*, leading to the same diploma (CAP).

Number of primary teachers: 13,340 (26.9 per cent women)

Secondary

Teachers are trained at the Ecole Normale Supérieure (ENS):

Lower

Teachers for the *Collèges d'Enseignement Moyen* embark on a one-year course after the **Licence**, leading to the **Certificat d'Aptitude à l'Enseignement Moyen** (CAEM); or on a two-year course after the **Baccalauréat**, leading to the **Certificat d'Aptitude à l'Enseignement des Collèges d'Enseignement Moyen** (CAECEM).

Number of teachers: 2,867 (15.2 per cent women)

Upper

Holders of a **Maîtrise** take a two-year course leading to a **Certificat d'Aptitude à l'Enseignement Secondaire**.

Vocational trainers take at the Ecole Normale Supérieure de l'Enseignement Professionnel et Technique (ENSPT), a four-year (for *Collèges d'Enseignement Moyen*) or a five-year course (for *Lycées* and *Centres de Formation Professionnelle*) after the **Baccalauréat**, or a two-year course after the **Licence** (i.e. *psychologues Conseillers*).

Teachers in music, arts and sports take five-year courses in specialized *Ecole Nationales*.

Number of teachers: 2,507 (12.4 per cent women)

Higher

Since 1960, *aggrégations* have been delivered by, and teachers appointed with the agreement of an African Board, the *Conseil Africain et Malgache pour l'Enseignement Supérieur* (CAMES).

There are four main grades of teachers:

Assistant: has undertaken a **Doctorat de Troisième Cycle**.

Maître Assistant: holds a **Doctorat de Troisième Cycle**, and is listed on the *Liste d'Aptitude* of the CAMES.

Maître de Conférence: holds a **Doctorat d'Etat**, is listed on the *Liste d'Aptitude* and has seven years of teaching experience.

Professeur titulaire: justifies three years as *Maître de Conférence*, has presented a *Rapport Pédagogique*, has supervised many **Doctorats** and researches, and been listed on the *Liste d'Aptitude*.

In law, economics, medicine, dentistry, pharmacy and veterinary sciences, the *aggrégation* is necessary.

Number of teachers and professors: Dakar 965 (12.9 per cent women)
Saint Louis 44 (3 women)

Seychelles

Seychelles has undergone considerable changes, with respect to the political character of the country, in recent years. Multi-party democracy has been adopted, a new constitution was approved by referendum in 1992, and a new government was elected in July 1993, for a period of five years.

One consequence of these changes was that the Cultural Affairs Section was combined with the Ministry of Education.

The present system of education has existed since the late 1970s, although there was a major educational review in 1991. The Ministry of Education deals with all aspects of the education system.

Education is compulsory from age five to fourteen.

The medium of instruction is Creole for the first four years of primary. It then changes to English, but in some subjects Creole may be used as well.

EVALUATION IN BRITAIN

School

Cambridge Overseas School Certificate – grades 1–6 are equated to GCSE (grades A, B and C). (For further information see Appendix 2.)

Cambridge Overseas Higher School Certificate – passes at grades A–E are equated to GCE Advanced. (For further information see Appendix 2.)

Seychelles National Certificate of Education (1982–4) – not generally recognized in Britain.

MARKING SYSTEM

School

Cambridge Overseas Certificates: see Appendix 2.

SCHOOL EDUCATION

Pre-primary

Pre-school education is carried out from age three to five, although attendance is voluntary.

Primary (P1 – P6)

This lasts for six years from age five. The curriculum includes Creole, English, French, mathematics, science, social sciences, art and craft, music, social education and religion and physical education. There is a national attainment test at the end of year six.

Secondary (S1 – S4; NYS)

The secondary cycle is divided into two stages:

Secondary 1 – Secondary 4 (S1 – S4)

Secondary schooling is carried out for four years, from age 11 to 14 years. This stage is compulsory. There is a national attainment test at the end of the fourth year.

National Youth Service (NYS)

This is a voluntary one-year residential system of education following on directly from S4, offering academic and pre-vocational studies as well as a programme of social and cultural activities. There is a national attainment test at the end of the year. **UCLES General Certificate of Education – Ordinary Level** is taken by promising pupils.

FURTHER EDUCATION

Courses are available at the <u>Seychelles Polytechnic</u> for those who have completed the eleventh year of schooling, or equivalent, and who have satisfied all other criteria for entry onto the course. The Polytechnic, founded in 1983, provides academic and vocational courses, including those leading to **Cambridge International General Certificate of Secondary Education**, **UCLES General Certificate of Education – Ordinary and Advanced Level**, **City and Guilds** and **Royal Society of Arts** examinations, as well as nationally awarded certificates and diplomas.

HIGHER EDUCATION

There are no institutions of higher education. Generally, those wishing to continue their education do so at overseas institutions.

TEACHER EDUCATION

In-service courses are organized in vacations and occasionally on a day-release basis during term time.

Primary

Primary teachers train for four years, post 11th year of schooling, to gain a Diploma 1 in Education (the minimum teaching qualification at this level). These teachers may progress onto a one-year Diploma 2 in Education course and then be selected for a two-year **Bachelor of Education** (BEd) degree course at an overseas institution.

Secondary

Students who have two passes at **General Certificate of Education – Advanced level** may take a further two-year course leading to a Diploma 2 in Education (the minimum teaching qualification at secondary level). These teachers may progress onto a two-year BEd course at an overseas institution.

Sierra Leone

There is no compulsory period of education.

The medium of instruction is English.

The academic year runs from September/October to July.

Education is free in government primary classes 1–6.

EVALUATION IN BRITAIN

School

West African School Certificate (WASC)/GCE O level/ Cambridge Overseas School Certificate (COSC)	grades 1–6 are generally equated to GCSE standard (grades A, B, and C) on a subject-for-subject basis.
Senior School Certificate	generally considered comparable to GCSE standard (grades A, B and C) on a subject-for-subject basis. Some subjects may be of a higher standard.
West African Higher School Certificate (WAHSC)/GCE A level/ Cambridge Overseas Higher School Certificate (COHSC)	generally equated to GCE Advanced standard.

Higher

Bachelor degree – general degrees are generally considered comparable to British Bachelor (Ordinary) degree standard. Honours degrees are generally considered comparable to British Bachelor (Honours) degree standard.

Master's degree – may be considered comparable to a British Master's degree.

MARKING SYSTEMS

School

West African School Certificate/ GCE O level/ Cambridge Overseas School Certificate	graded 1 (maximum) to 9 (fail)
West African Higher School Certificate/ Cambridge Overseas Higher School Certificate GCE A level	graded A, B, C, D, E, O (subsidiary pass), F (fail)

Higher

Njala University College	Fourah Bay College		Class of degrees
			Honours degrees
A 5 excellent	A 70–100 per cent		Class I
B 4 good	B+ 60–69		Class II (upper and lower)
C 3 fair	B 50–59		Class III
D 2 bare pass	C+ 45-49		
F 1 fail	C 40–44		Pass degrees
	D 35–39	fail	Division I, II, III
	E below 35	fail	General degrees

SCHOOL EDUCATION

Pre-primary

Limited facilities available.

Primary

This covers six years from age six. In the new 6-3-3-4 system of education, this period of education is not intended to be terminal like in the old system but to prepare the child for further education.

The curriculum covers: language arts; mathematics; science; social studies; physical/health education; practical/creative arts; religious education; pre-vocational subjects i.e. home economics, agriculture etc; and indigenous language. The local language is often the medium of instruction in at least the first two years, even though the official medium is English.

On completion of the six years pupils take the **National Primary School Examination (NPSE)** set by the West African Examination Council. This new examination includes a general knowledge paper which was not formerly part of the selective entrance examination.

Continuous assessment is part of the primary school system. It is a method by which the pupil's overall progress and performance in class is continuously assessed within the duration of the course. The assessment includes class tests, assignments (home work), projects, practical skills and end of term examinations.

The **National Primary School Examinations (NPSE)** is not a pass or fail examination. Its purpose is to give an indication as to the pupil's ability or capability.

Secondary

The new 6-3-3-4 education system divides secondary education into two levels of equal duration – three years of junior secondary and three years of senior secondary, either of which can be terminal.

The subjects offered at the junior secondary are: mathematics; language arts; integrated science; social studies; French; agriculture; religious and moral education; physical and health education; and one major Sierra Leone language (Mende, Temne, Krio or Limba). There are electives which include pre-vocational and non-vocational subjects. The pre-vocational subjects are: local crafts; introductory technology; home economics; business studies and electronics.

Pupils are assessed in each class of the junior secondary school by a system of continuous assessment. At the end of JSS3 pupils may take the **Basic Education Certificate Examination (BECE)**. The result of this is used for placement into senior secondary schools, community education centres, trade centres and vocational institutes.

To enter senior secondary school, a student must possess:

(i)   A grade 6 pass or higher in at least 6 core subjects plus,
(ii)   A grade 6 pass or higher in at least two electives, one of which must be pre-vocational.

At the senior secondary level the following core subjects are offered in addition to three elective subjects, not already offered as core subjects: English language; mathematics; one Sierra Leonean language (Mende, Temne, Limba and Krio); science i.e. physics, chemistry, biology, general integrated science; Sierra Leone studies; and one vocational subject or technical subject or agriculture.

On completion of the three years of senior secondary school, students will take the **Senior School Certificate Examination.** The examination will be administered by the West African Examination Council who will continue to control the **Higher School Leaving Certificate Examination** in the English speaking West African sub-region.

Technical Education

At present there are two technical institutes (Kenema and Freetown) offering a variety of courses leading to qualifications of the City and Guilds of London Institute and to **BTEC National** and **Higher National Diplomas** (in building and engineering). Freetown Technical Institute also offers London Chamber of Commerce and Industry Examination in commercial subjects and qualifications of the Royal Society of Arts Secretarial courses.

Two trade centres offer three-year lower-level courses in various fields from the end of the third year of primary school.

HIGHER EDUCATION

The <u>University of Sierra Leone</u> consists of three colleges – <u>Fourah Bay</u>, <u>Njala</u> and the <u>College of Medicine and Allied Health Sciences</u>. In 1960 <u>Fourah Bay College</u> became <u>University College of Sierra Leone</u> and, in 1966, it became a constituent college of the <u>University of Sierra Leone</u> along with <u>Njala University College</u> (opened 1964); at this point it reverted to the title <u>Fourah Bay College</u>. Until 1967, the university awarded degrees by the <u>University of Durham</u>. In 1988, the <u>College of Medicine and Allied Health Sciences</u> became a constituent part of the <u>University of Sierra Leone</u>.

The entrance requirement to **Bachelor degree** courses is normally five O levels; general degrees take four years, honours degrees five years. With good A levels, the degree courses can be reduced by one year, students starting in year two. With poor A level results students start on a par with O level entrants.

A one-year course on completion of an Honours degree may lead to a **Master's degree**, but this is not available in all departments.

A minimum of three years' research after the **Bachelor degree** leads to a **PhD**.

The University also offers a large number of certificates and diplomas. The most common are:

Postgraduate Diploma in Education
Postgraduate Diploma in Library Studies
Certificate and Diploma in Adult Education
Diploma in African Studies
Certificate and Diploma in Library Studies
Certificate in Science Education

TEACHER EDUCATION

Primary

A three-year course is offered at a teacher training college.

Holders of three **GCE O level** passes may take a three-year course to gain a **Teaching Certificate**. Holders of four GCE O level passes may take a three-year course to gain a **Higher Teaching Certificate**. Students may also pursue studies leading to the **Advanced Teaching Certificate**.

Secondary

Lower

A three-year course starting with four **GCE O levels** leads to a **Higher Teachers' Certificate** at <u>Milton Margai Teachers College</u>. This compares to the **West African Higher School Certificate** (WAHSC) and allows holders to enrol for **Bachelor degrees**.

Upper

Students take a four-year **Bachelor of Education** degree course at <u>Njala University College</u> or a one-year **Postgraduate Diploma in education** after a **Bachelor of Arts/Science degree** course at <u>Fourah Bay College</u>.

In 1972 the <u>Institute of Education</u> became a constituent institution of the University.

Singapore

The Singapore education system is geared towards providing at least ten years of general education for all children. This comprises six years of primary education and four years of secondary education. In addition to the ten years of general education, pupils can undergo technical-vocational, pre-university and tertiary courses after secondary school.

Pupils learn at least two languages, English and their mother tongue in school. The mother tongue, which can be Chinese, Malay or Tamil, is given prominence, as is English, the medium of instruction and language of administration, commerce and technology in Singapore.

Besides the emphasis on language learning, pupils are also streamed at various stages of the system to place them in the course best suited to their abilities.

The academic year is divided into four terms (two semesters) from January to November.

EVALUATION IN BRITAIN

School

Singapore/Cambridge GCE N level – generally considered to be below GCSE standard.

Singapore/Cambridge GCE O level – grades 1–6 generally equated to GCSE standard (grades A, B and C) on a subject-for-subject basis.

Singapore/Cambridge GCE A level – generally equated to GCE Advanced standard on a subject-for-subject basis.

Certificate in Business Studies (Vocational and Industrial Training Board) – generally considered comparable to BTEC National Diploma / N/SVQ level 3 / Advanced GNVQ/GSVQ standard if the grade of distinction is achieved.

Industrial Technician Certificate (Vocational and Industrial Training Board) – generally considered comparable to the Final Technician Certificate of the City and Guilds of London Institute and to BTEC National Diploma / N/SVQ level 3 / Advanced GNVQ/GSVQ standard if the grade of distinction is achieved.

Further

Diploma (from the polytechnics, two or three years full-time) – may be considered comparable to a standard between BTEC National Diploma / N/SVQ level 3 / Advanced GNVQ/GSVQ, and BTEC Higher National Diploma / N/SVQ Level 4; may be considered to satisfy the general entrance requirements of British higher education institutions; students with high grades may be considered for advanced standing.

Diploma (from the <u>Centre for Computer Studies</u> at the <u>Ngee Ann Polytechnic</u>) – generally considered to satisfy the general entrance requirements of British higher education institutions; students may be considered, on an individual basis, for second year entry.

Diploma (from <u>French-Singapore Institute</u>, <u>German-Singapore Institute</u> and <u>Japan-Singapore Institute of Software Technology</u>) – may be considered to satisfy the general entrance requirements of British higher education institutions; students with very good results may be given advanced standing. Exceptionally, diploma holders from the <u>Japan-Singapore Institute of Software Technology</u> with relevant work experience may be considered for admission to taught Master's degree courses.

Advanced diploma (from the polytechnics) – generally considered comparable to a standard between GCE Advanced and British Bachelor degree; may be given advanced standing by British higher education institutions.

Some holders of the **Advanced Diploma** in computer studies awarded by <u>Ngee Ann Polytechnic</u> have been admitted on an individual basis, for entry to an MSc course.

Higher

Bachelor degree – generally considered comparable to British Bachelor degree standard; and is acceptable for entry to postgraduate study.

MARKING SYSTEMS

School

Singapore/Cambridge GCE O level   ) see Appendix 2.
Singapore/Cambridge GCE A level   )

Further

<u>Singapore/Ngee Ann/Temasek/Nanyang Polytechnic</u>

distinction	Dist (for top 5 per cent)	
excellent	A	80–100 per cent
credit	B	70–79
good	C	60–69
pass	D	50–59
subsidiary pass	E*	
fail	F	

* (Applicable to Singapore and Temasek Polytechnic only)

Students who possess diplomas from the polytechnics and who have achieved an appropriate standard are often admitted directly into the second year of undergraduate courses by British universities. Each case is assessed on its own merits and account is taken of the grades achieved and the local and proposed course of study to be taken at the institution. The advanced diplomas offered by the polytechnics in certain subjects to students with post-diploma working experience has been recognized by some British universities as a sufficient pre-qualification for postgraduate study.

Singapore

Japan-Singapore Institute of Software Technology

Dist   awarded only on recommendation
A   80–100 per cent
B   70–79
C   60–69
D   50–59
Fail   below 50

Higher

Honours degrees are classified as follows:

class I
class II division i
class II division ii
class III

Hons (I or II) are awarded for the degrees of **BEng, BAcc, BSc** (Building), **BSc** (Estate Management) and the **LLB.**

Hons (unclassified) are awarded for degrees of **BArch, BDS,** and **MBBS.**

SCHOOL EDUCATION

Primary

At primary level, which lasts six years from age six, pupils undergo a four-year foundation stage (from Primary One to Primary Four) and a two-year orientation stage (from Primary Five to Primary Six). Pupils are streamed according to their abilities and orientation at the end of Primary Four. The first stream is for the academically able and linguistically talented pupils who take both English and the mother tongue, that is Higher Chinese, Higher Malay of Higher Tamil. The majority of the pupils are streamed into the second stream where they learn English and the mother tongue, that is Chinese, Malay or Tamil. The third stream is for less able pupils who take English and either Basic Chinese, Basic Malay or Basic Tamil. The fourth stream involves the learning of the mother tongue (either Higher Chinese, Higher Malay or Higher Tamil) and Basic English.

There is regular assessment of pupils to enable lateral movement to take place between the streams. Pupils sit a national placement examination called the **Primary School-Leaving Examination** (PSLE) at the end of Primary Six. The examination assesses their suitability for secondary education and pupils are placed in an appropriate secondary school course to suit their learning ability.

Secondary

This is divided into four or five years' secondary and two years' higher secondary (or pre-university). Subjects taught at secondary level include English, a second language, mathematics, science, literature, history, geography, art and craft, music, physical education, civics, current affairs and moral education. At the end of the second year, English, a second language, mathematics and science remain as 'core' subjects with the other subjects being studied on an optional basis.

There are three streams in the secondary school:

(a)   Special course – this stream consists of the top students (about ten per cent) based on the PSLE results. They complete the **Singapore/Cambridge GCE O level** course in four years and study English and their mother tongue at the same level i.e. as first languages. They become effectively bilingual.

(b)   Express course – this stream consists of those students (about forty-five per cent) who will be expected to pass **GCE O level** successfully with at least three **GCE O level** passes at the end of the four-year course. They study English as a first language and their mother tongue as a second language.

(c)   Normal course – this stream consists of those students (about forty-five per cent) most of whom will take **GCE O level** in five years rather than four years as with the express course. Within the Normal course, pupils have the option of taking either the Normal (Academic) course or the Normal (Technical) course, both of which lead to the **GCE N (Normal) level** examination at the end of four years. They can also sit the **GCE O level** examination at the end of the fifth year, depending on their **GCE N level** results.

At higher secondary (pre-university level) courses lead to the **Singapore/Cambridge GCE A level** examination. The subjects studied reflect the secondary curriculum. In addition, all pupils have to sit an English language general paper. Students with the best **GCE O level** results follow a two-year course at a junior college. Other students follow a three-year course at one of the four pre-university institutes.

The **Singapore/Cambridge GCE O level** examination was established in 1971. The examination is conducted by the University of Cambridge Local Examinations Syndicate (UCLES) in conjunction with the Singapore Ministry of Education; the Cambridge Syndicate is the examining authority for subjects examined in the medium of English, and the Ministry of Education is the examining authority for subjects examined in Chinese, Tamil or Malay. A pass in a second language is needed to obtain the certificate. (For further information see Appendix 2.)

Technical secondary

Some schools provide four-year courses offering specialization in woodwork, metalwork, mechanics and technical drawing, with the possibility of taking examinations at the end of the course for the **GCE O level** or **N levels**.

One secondary commercial school prepares pupils for the London Chamber of Commerce examinations.

TECHNICAL-VOCATIONAL EDUCATION

The Institute of Technical Education (ITE), was set up in 1992 to take over the functions of the Vocational and Industrial Training Board (VITB) to upgrade vocational training. The ITE provides full-time institutional training and apprenticeship courses for school leavers and offers part-time Continuing Education and Training (CET) programmes for adults already in employment.

The training available includes a two-year full-time post-**GCE O level** course leading to an **Industrial Technician Certificate**, a two-year full-time post **GCE O level** course leading to a **Certificate in Business Studies**, two and one-year post **GCE O/N level** **National Trade Certificate** courses, as well as, courses leading to City and Guilds of London Institute qualifications.

FURTHER EDUCATION

Singapore Polytechnic, Ngee Ann Polytechnic, Temasek Polytechnic and Nanyang Polytechnic were established to provide middle-level technical training. They offer a wide range of certificate, diploma and advanced diploma courses in various fields of engineering, science, mass communications, marketing, graphic, product and interior design, computer studies, nursing, radiography, information technology, business and maritime studies. The main courses available are three-year post-**GCE O level** or two-year post-**GCE A level Diplomas** and two-year part-time **Advanced Diplomas** for holders of a polytechnic diploma and relevant work experience. Some courses are also available on a part-time basis.

The French-Singapore Institute (FSI), the German-Singapore Institute (GSI) and the Japan-Singapore Technical Institute (JSTI) which were established as joint ventures between Singapore and the respective governments were taken under the umbrella of the Nanyang Polytechnic's School of Engineering and School of Information Technology in 1993.

The Japan-Singapore Institute of Software Technology (JSIST), which became an autonomous institute within Singapore Polytechnic in 1987, offers a two-year post-**GCE A level Diploma** course and a one-year **Advanced Diploma** for holders of the **JSIST Diploma** and relevant work experience.

La Salle College and Nanyang Academy of Fine Art are private, non-profit making institutions providing training in various branches of the fine arts and music. La Salle offers a three-year or four-year post-**GCE O level Associateship** course and a four-year post-**GCE A level Licenciate Diploma**. Nanyang also offers a four-year post-**GCE A level Diploma.**

HIGHER EDUCATION

The National University of Singapore (NUS) and Nanyang Technological University (NTU) provide degree level education. The NUS was established in 1980 through the merger of the University of Singapore and Nanyang University and, in 1981, Nanyang Technical Institute (NTI) was established as a second university level institution. There were close academic links between NTI and NUS, as part of which, NTI graduates received degrees from NUS. In 1991, NTI was reconstituted and renamed Nanyang Technological University, awarding its own degrees.

Admission to first degree courses is on the basis of **GCE A** and **O level** results. **Bachelor (Pass or Pass with Merit) degrees** are normally obtained after three years' study and **Honours degrees** after four years. A direct Honours degree in three rather than four years was introduced in 1982 in parallel with existing courses. **Bachelor degrees** in dentistry, law, engineering, building and estate management take four years, architecture (excluding a year out for practical experience) and medicine take five years.

A new modular system which incorporates the American universities' credit system but with a prescribed core curriculum has been introduced in all the schools in NTU and in five faculties in NUS (Arts and Social Sciences, Business Administration, Engineering, Science, School of Building and Estate Management). This will enable some students to complete their degrees in less than the standard time.

Following a first degree, postgraduate diplomas are obtained after one or two years, a

Master's degree after a minimum of one year and a **Doctorate** after a minimum of two further years.

The Singapore Open University Degree Programme (OUDP), which started its first intake of students in January 1994 offers part-time degree programmes in mathematics, English literature and computer science awarded by the UK Open University.

The Management Development Institute of Singapore (MDIS) offers professionally-oriented certificates and diplomas at various levels (including postgraduate diplomas). Their awards are recognized by British educational and professional bodies such as BTEC, the Association of Business Executives (ABE), etc.

TEACHER EDUCATION

The National Institute of Education (NIE), an institute of the Nanyang Technological University is the only tertiary level institution providing both pre- and in-service teacher education.

Pre-service courses include a two-year **Diploma in Education** or **Diploma in Physical Education**, or a four-year **Bachelor of Arts** or **Bachelor of Science degree** with a **Diploma in Education** or **Diploma in Education (Physical Education)** for non-graduates. There is also a one-year **Postgraduate Diploma in Education**, or a two-year **Postgraduate Diploma in Education (Physical Education)** for graduates.

Further training is provided for practising teachers through in-service courses.

NIE also offers postgraduate courses leading to a **Master's degree in Education** and a PhD for those who are interested in educational research.

Slovakia

In 1992 the Czech and Slovak Federation was dissolved and each republic became independent. In both republics, which used to form the Czech and Slovak Federative Republic, the same radical higher education reform (known as Act 172) was passed in 1990. In higher education most of the decisions affecting institutions are now devolved to the institutions from the central ministries; these include the authority to establish curricula, to regulate student numbers, to impose specific admission requirements and to create new faculties.

Education is compulsory between the ages of six and fifteen.

The medium of instruction is Slovak. In some areas, tuition up to secondary level may be available in Hungarian, Polish or Ukrainian.

The academic year is from September to August, although the normal academic year ends on 30 June. Students in higher education are entitled to only four weeks' summer vacation, as examinations also take place in July and August. Higher education institutions have two, fifteen-week terms, followed by examination periods.

EVALUATION IN BRITAIN

School

Maturitná skúska/Maturita – may be considered to satisfy the general entrance requirements of British higher education institutions.

Higher

Bakalár – generally considered comparable to British Bachelor (Ordinary) degree standard.

Magister/Inzinier (formerly **Absolvent Vysoke Skoly)/Professional title** – generally considered comparable to British Bachelor (Honours) degree standard.

PhDr – may be compared to a British PhD degree but requires evaluation on a case-by-case basis.

Candidate of Science – generally considered comparable to British PhD degree standard.

DrSc – generally considered comparable to British DLit/DSc degree standard.

MARKING SYSTEMS

School

1	*výborný*	excellent
2	*chválitebný*	very good
3	*dobrý*	good
4	*dostatocný*	pass
5	*nedostatocný*	fail

Higher

výborne	excellent
veľmi dobre	good
dobre	pass
nevyhovel	fail

SCHOOL EDUCATION

Pre-primary

Facilities are available in crèches (*Jasle*) for children aged one to three and in nurseries (*Materská škola*) for children aged four to six.

Basic

The system consists of a nine-year primary and lower secondary course of so-called basic education (*Základná škola*) which is compulsory. This is followed by a four-year upper secondary course; grade 9 is voluntary. Basic education is divided into lower and upper cycles and the compulsory subjects are the mother tongue (Slovak, or, in some areas, Hungarian, Polish, Ukrainian, German), history, geography, mathematics, civics, general science, physical education, art, music and work training. Some specialization is possible from grade 5 and progress to each grade is made by continuous assessment.

Secondary

Higher secondary education (*Stredoškolské vzdelanie*) can be taken in a general secondary school (*Gymnázium*), a secondary vocational school, or a specialized secondary school. All courses last four years and culminate in the matriculation examination, **Vysvedčenie o Maturitnej skúske** or **Maturita**. In general, secondary school students specialize in either science, humanities or mathematics, but spend most of their time on the general core subjects of Czech/Slovak language and literature, one modern language, mathematics, history, geography, physics, chemistry, biology, physical education and, since 1987, information science and computer technology. There are a number of bilingual secondary schools (English, German, Spanish, French, Italian) and English is likely to be taught more and more widely, at the expense of Russian. The **Maturita** examinations are normally taken in only four subjects: Slovak, one modern language, mathematics and one optional subject, or two optional subjects if mathematics is not selected by the student. The **Maturita** following the vocational secondary course of vocational training and general education, involves Slovak, technical subjects and an oral exam in one optional subject.

Secondary vocational schools (*Stredné odborné učilištia*) run by major industrial concerns, offer courses of two to four years for pupils who have eight years' basic education. The courses contain an element of general education and train pupils to become skilled workers. The graduates who have completed four year courses with the school-leaving examination (**Maturitná Skúska**) may apply to universities.

FURTHER EDUCATION

Specialist institutions such as language schools, people's schools of art or shorthand institutes cater for people wishing to acquire new skills. At a language school, for example, students may eventually take the **Štátna skúške** (State Examination) which brings them to almost the same level as a university graduate.

Factories and other work organizations provide courses related to their own interests, while local 'houses of culture' (*Dom kultúry*) and many private institutions offer classes in mainly non-academic pastimes and activities.

HIGHER EDUCATION

There are14 institutions of higher education, excluding military schools and their faculties (five universities, three technical institutes, one university of economy, two schools of performing art/music/drama and visual arts, one teacher training college, one college of agriculture, one college of transport and communications). The traditional oldest universities are: <u>Comenius University</u> in Bratislava and <u>Paval Jozef Šafárik University</u> in Košice. They offer courses in humanities, pure science, law and medicine.

Prior to the recent reform, entrance was on the basis of the **Maturita**, an entrance examination and the applicant's 'civic and normal character'. Admission quotas were determined annually by the State Planning Commission and the Ministry allocated places to institutions accordingly. Henceforth, the institutions can impose more specific, independent entrance requirements, although successful completion of secondary education confirmed by the **Maturita** remains the minimum requirement. The new, more selective entrance procedure ensures that the subject aptitude of candidates is more appropriately satisfied and should result in better qualified graduates and higher standards.

Before the recent reform, the period of the initial higher education course was four to six years, depending on the subject. This course led to the status of *Absolvent Vysokej skoly* (higher education graduate), on passing the **Štátna záverečná skúška**: this *Absolvent* was a status and not a formal degree. Graduates in humanities and sciences from the traditional universities (except medical graduates) did not add letters to their names. *Promovaný* ceased to be a formal degree in 1966. Graduates from higher technical education institutions and some other institutions of higher education, were, and still are, entitled to use the prefix **Ing (Inzinier)**, even if their course was not connected with engineering. However, the six-year course in medicine and the five-year course in dentistry led to the professional title **Doktor Medicíny** (MUDr); the five-year course in veterinary medicine to the professional title **Doktor Veterinárnej Medicíny** (MVDr); the five-year course in architecture to the professional title **Inžinier architekt** (IngArch) and the six-year course (from the Faculty of Visual Arts) to the professional title **Akademický Architekt** (AkadArch) Courses in sculpture and painting led respectively to the titles **Akad Sochár** and **Akad Maliar**. Graduates without a title used to be able to obtain the title **Doktor** by undergoing an additional, oral examination (**Examen Rigorosum/Rigorózna skúška**) which was taken at any time after graduation; no thesis has been required since 1980. The doctorates on offer were: **Doktor filozofie** in humanities (PhDr), **Doktor práv.** in law (JUDr) and **Doktor Prírodných Vied** in natural sciences (RNDr), **Doktor Pedagogiky** in education (PaedDr), **Doktor farmácie** in Pharmacy (PharmDr) and **Doktor sociálno-politických**

vied in social and political sciences (RSDr) In exceptional cases, the doctorate was awarded on graduation. At postgraduate level, the *Ašpirantúra* involving the preparation of a thesis and a minimum of three years' full-time or five years' part-time study used to lead to the **Candidatus Scientiarum/Kandidát Vied** (CSc). A further indeterminate period of research could have led to the Doctor of Science (**Doktor Vied**, DrSc).

Under the new law (Higher Education Act 172) the new degree titles of **Bakalár** (Bc) and **Magister** (Mgr) are being introduced. The former can be awarded to a student who has completed the 'comprehensive component' of a first-degree course after two or three years' study (short course). The latter is a formal degree award for those who were formerly just *Absolvent/Promovaný* (long course). The title **Inžinier** is equivalent to the **Magister**. The only doctorates awarded as first degrees will be those in medicine and veterinary medicine (**Doktor Medicíny** – MUDr and **Doktor Veterinárnej Medicíny** – MVDr) where only the 'long course' is available; all the others will become postgraduate qualifications requiring two or three years' study after the **Magister/Inžinier**, presentation of a thesis and the **Examen Rigorosum/Rigorózna skúška**. The degree awarded since 1990 is **Doktor** (Dr) or **Kandidát vied** (CSc).

TEACHER EDUCATION

Kindergarten

After finishing basic education teachers follow a four-year course or a two-year course for holders of the **Maturita**. There is also a five-year part-time course at university.

Primary (lower cycle)

Teachers follow a four-year course for holders of the **Maturita** at a pedagogical faculty or a Teachers Training College.

Primary (upper cycle) and secondary

Students of any faculty studying subjects taught at either of these levels normally have to include a pedagogical element as part of their first degree. They have to study two main subjects, e.g. English and Russian, whereas if they choose to follow the purely academic, non-pedagogical option, only one subject need be studied.

Alternatively, a student may be based at a university pedagogical faculty in which case the pedagogical content will be relatively greater and the academic content relatively smaller than if the student studied in the relevant subject faculty. Pedagogical qualifications may also be obtained by study at a university pedagogical faculty or an equivalent institution pedagogical department after the completion of first-degree studies containing no pedagogical element.

Slovenia

Compulsory education covers the period of basic education; that is eight years between ages seven and fifteen.

The medium of instruction is Slovene. There is also Italian in the coastal region for the Italian minority and bilingual Hungarian/Slovene in the region near the Hungarian border.

The academic year runs from September/October to June.

EVALUATION IN BRITAIN

School

Matura (before 1980 from the *Gimnazija*/academic upper secondary course)/ **Secondary School-Leaving Diploma** (before 1980 from a technical secondary school) – may be considered to satisfy the general entrance requirements of British higher education institutions.

Secondary School-Leaving Diploma (obtained since 1980) – generally considered comparable to British BTEC National Diploma / N/SVQ level 3 / Advanced GNVQ/GSVQ standard and may be considered to satisfy the general entrance requirements of British higher education institutions.

Higher

Vise Obrazovanje (first-level degree obtained on completion of a two to three-year course) – generally considered comparable to a standard between GCE Advanced and British Bachelor degree; may be given advanced standing by British higher education institutions.

Visoko Obrazovanja (second-level degree obtained on completion of a four to six-year course) – generally considered comparable to British Bachelor (Ordinary) degree standard.

Magistar – generally considered comparable to British Master's degree standard.

MARKING SYSTEM

Primary and secondary schools

Marking is on scale 1 – 5 (maximum), with 2 as a minimum pass-mark.

1   fail
2   satisfactory
3   good
4   very good
5   excellent

Higher education

1 – 10 (maximum). Most of the faculties use 5 – 10 scale. 5 is regarded as a fail and 6 as minimum pass.

SCHOOL EDUCATION

Pre-primary

Public pre-school institutions are part of the educational system. Institutions are organized in a unified system and include crèches (*otroske jasli*) for children aged between one and three, pre-school groups (*otroski vrtec*) for children aged between three and six, and groups of the preparatory programme for school (*mala sola*) for children aged between six and seven.

Primary

This period of schooling (at *osnovna sola*) covers eight years from age seven, but children may be admitted from age six. Primary school is divided into two four-year levels (4+4): primary lower (classes 1–4) and lower secondary level (classes 5–8). Classes are unstreamed and based on the comprehensive system. Pupils begin studying foreign languages in the fifth year and may usually choose between English and German.

Secondary

After successful completion of primary school, students can enrol in a secondary school, which prepares for further studies or employment. He/she can choose from one of the following types:

grammar school   (*gimnazija*)
technical school   (*tehnica sola, strokovna sola*)
vocational school   (*poklicna sola*)

Grammar school

The *gimnazija* curriculum is the most general educational programme in the secondary education system. It prepares students for higher education. The curriculum covers three basic areas: compulsory subjects, which covers 80 per cent of the schooling, courses for in-depth study of subject areas (as preparation for the **Matura** examination) and compulsory electives, which satisfy the aptitudes of individual students. This system allows students some specialization in their field of interest, e.g. science/mathematics, humanities/social studies or languages, choosing optional subjects for the final examination.

Technical school

Technical schools offer four and five-year study programmes. The curriculum consists of three basic areas: general subjects and theoretical disciplinary subjects, practical instructions and compulsory electives. In the third form students can choose either for preparation for the **Matura** examination, offering access to higher education, or preparation for final examination which leads to employment or studies at professional higher education institutions, with a different ratio between the general subjects and practical instruction.

Vocational education

Two and three-year vocational programmes are offered. Emphasis is placed on vocational-oriented theoretical subjects and practical instructions at schools and on the job. Education ends with a final examination. In the school year 1993/94, students who finished a vocational education could continue their education in the supplementary programme (3+2), which ends with the final examination of the same level as the examination at the end of technical school.

Completion of secondary schooling

For the completion of secondary school, students can choose between the final examination (**zakljucni izpit**) and the **Matura** school-leaving examination. They are offered as parallel alternative examinations at the end of a secondary school. Both are secondary school-leaving examinations and lead to the completion of secondary school. There is a difference: final examination leads to employment of studies at professional higher education institutions, **Matura** examination offers access to university studies.

The final examination is an internal examination consisting of two compulsory subjects (the mother tongue and mathematics or a foreign language) and two elective subjects. The elective part consists of two basic disciplinary subjects or a basic disciplinary subject and a paper, product or project and its presentation. Examination is prepared and administered by the school. Successful candidates receive a **Secondary School Leaving Certificate**.

In 1995 candidates sat the first external **Matura** school-leaving examination, which is composed of five subjects: three compulsory subjects (the mother tongue, mathematics and a foreign language); and two optional subjects (e.g. from natural sciences, social sciences, humanities, foreign languages, technical subjects, etc.).

Candidates can optionally take one or two subjects (these are mathematics, foreign languages or Latin) on higher level. From 1998 onward one subject on higher level will be compulsory. Candidates can also take more optional subjects than two.

Overall grade for the **Matura** examination is expressed in points as a sum of subject grades. For subjects taken at higher level, extra points are added:

to grades satisfactory (2) and good (3) one point is added;

to grade very good (4) two points are added;

to grade excellent (5) three points are added.

If a candidate passes **Matura** examination with more optional subjects as determined, for the overall grade only the best grades in the compulsory number of optional **Matura** subjects is taken into account. Maximum overall grade at the **Matura** examination is 31.

Matura examination is a state examination, administered by the National Examinations Centre (*Republiski izpitni center*), which prepares question papers and organizes the examination, marking and grading procedures. Certificates are issued by the secondary school. The National Examinations Centre issues separate certificates with detailed information on subjects, used in case of selection.

Changes in school legislation

The time between 1992 and 1994 was a period involving the preparation of conceptual and material conditions for developmental and education system changes, which will define the strategy of education carried out until the end of the decade, which will be fully realized only after the year 2000. The Higher Education Act was adopted in December 1993 and establishes a unified and academically autonomous university and makes provisions for the establishment of professional higher education institutions as a parallel system.

The proposal for new legislation regulating pre-school education, the entire pre-university education system and the field of adult education has won the approval of the government and was to be placed on the agenda of the Parliament in the autumn of 1994.

FURTHER EDUCATION

Until the Higher Education Act, further education was part of higher education, offering two to three-year courses. Parallel with the reorganization of universities, the professional higher education institution will be introduced (see higher education). **Secondary School Leaving Certificate** will be appropriate for entering this type of institution.

HIGHER EDUCATION

Entry to a course of higher education was until 1994 on the basis of the **Secondary School Leaving Certificate**, regardless of whether it was obtained on completion of an academic or technical course. Whereas the former would admit to all faculties, the vocational/technical diploma gave admission only to certain faculties. In those cases candidates or holders of qualifications from a professional school/apprenticeship had to sit differential examinations. A system of *numerus clausus*, (restricted entry) operates in some faculties. Admission to those institutions is based on a combination of criteria (**Secondary School Leaving Certificate**, entrance examinations, grades from secondary school).

From June 1995 entrance to higher education (*univerza*) has been limited to holders of **Matura** certificate. In case of *numerus clausus*, selection has been made on the basis of **Matura** results, grades from secondary school and in rare cases on the basis of grades in selected **Matura** subjects.

Higher education courses are offered by university faculties (*fakultet*) and art academies (*umetniske akademije*, e.g. art, music). Part of the old system were also two-year colleges (*visje sole*), offering courses in professional and technical education, and high schools (*visoke sole*) with courses of higher education. With the new Higher Education Act two-year colleges were abolished and professional higher education institutions introduced. The latter can join one of the universities and its members or, in contrast to faculties and art academies, decide to remain free-standing. It is also possible to establish a private higher education institution with appropriate accreditation.

Until 1959

There was only one degree, obtained after a course lasting four to six years (depending on the subject).

Since 1960

Within the organization of higher education, three stages for degrees can usually be identified:

First stage, covering two to three years, leading to Diploma of Higher Education (**visjesolska diploma** or **diploma visje sole**) with a professional title (*strokovni naziv*) e.g. engineer (*inzenir*), lawyer (*pravnik*), economist (*ekonomist*), etc.

Second stage, covering a further two or three years, a complete higher education course of four-and-a-half to six years, leads to Advanced Diploma of Higher Education (**visokosolska diploma, diploma visoke sole, univerzitetna diploma**) with a professional title (*strokovni naziv*), e.g. graduate engineer (*diplomirani inzenir*) graduate lawyer (*diplomirani pravnik*), doctor of medicine (*doktor medicine*), professor (*profesor*), academic painter (*academski slikar*), etc.

Third grade, postgraduate studies (**magisterij**), covering two-and-a-half years' study and research, lead to academic degree (*akademski naziv*) of Master of Science or Art (**magister**), which can be an intermediate degree leading to a doctorate. One-year specialization (*specializacija*) leads to the advanced specialist diploma (**specialist**).

A **Doctorate of Science (doktorat znanosti)** may be obtained after a further approved period of research and defence of a thesis. This leads to academic degree Doctor of Science (**doktor znanosti**).

TEACHER EDUCATION

Primary

Teachers are trained in Faculties of Pedagogy (*Pedagoska fakulteta*). Initial teacher training was prolonged in the last decade and is now carried out as a four-year university course for both teachers of lower and upper grades of primary school.

Secondary

Teachers are university graduates. Courses last at least four-and-a-half years. Teachers may also take postgraduate studies.

ADULT EDUCATION

Institutions offering adult education courses are:

People's Universities (*ljudske univerze*) – offering vocational and general education courses and courses for the completion of primary and secondary school studies;

regular schools of all levels – offer courses for adult education as well;

accredited and non-accredited education centres, special departments in companies and other institutions;

private educational institutions.

Solomon Islands

The following chapter regarding the education system in the Solomon Islands is based on information obtained from the 3rd edition of this Guide, published in 1991, as NARIC has been unable to obtain more recent information.

Education in the Solomon Islands is a Government responsibility; before 1946 this responsibility belonged to the Church.

There is no compulsory education.

There are over 100 Melanesian languages spoken. Pidgin English and English are in common use.

The academic year runs from January to November.

EVALUATION IN BRITAIN

School

Solomon Islands School Certificate – generally considered comparable to GCSE standard.

Pacific Senior Secondary Certificate – grades 1–5 generally considered comparable to GCSE standard (grades A, B and C) on a subject-for-subject basis.

Higher

Bachelor degrees (from the University of the South Pacific) – generally considered comparable to British Bachelor degree standard.

MARKING SYSTEM

School

Pacific Senior Secondary Certificate – students receive a single-digit grade that can range from 1 to 9 (based on their ranking) for each subject that they have taken. The highest achievement grade is 1, the lowest is 9. The idea of 'pass' or 'fail' is discouraged. Descriptors that are used at present in association with these grades are:

Grade	Descriptor
1	Excellent standard of achievement
2	Very high standard of achievement
3	High standard of achievement
4	Good standard of achievement
5	Satisfactory standard of achievement
6	Adequate standard of achievement
7	Some achievement
8	Lower level of achievement
9	Little level of achievement

Higher

Degrees from the University of the South Pacific are unclassified.

SCHOOL EDUCATION

This lasts six years, formerly seven years, covering standards 1 to 6. There is a preparatory year taken by most children entering standard 1.

Secondary

This lasts a maximum of five years.

Eight national secondary schools offer academic courses leading to the **Solomon Islands School Certificate** after five years.

There are twelve provincial secondary schools. The length of attendance at these schools is three years. The schools are situated in rural areas and are designed to promote self-sufficiency and contribute towards improvement in rural life. The schools grow much of their own food and the core curriculum of English and mathematics is allied to skills and occupations relevant to the area in which the school is situated.

During the third year, all secondary school students undergo a Form III Assessment which is English and is mathematics based. Completion of form III represents the end of school education for most students. Those leaving full-time education qualify for a **Form III Leaver's Certificate**. Students continuing education either transfer to a national secondary school for forms IV and V for an academic course leading to the **Solomon Islands School Certificate** or transfer to the Solomon Islands College of Higher Education.

The National Sixth Form is situated at King George VI School in Honiara and draws pupils from all national secondary schools. Betikma Adventist High School has a small sixth form intake of students from the Seventh Day Adventist faith. Sixth form courses lead to the **Pacific Senior Secondary Certificate** administered by the South Pacific Board for Educational Assessment (SPBEA). (For further information on the SPBEA see Appendix 8.)

There are also a number of church and independent schools.

FURTHER EDUCATION

Solomon Islands College of Higher Education (SICHE) is an autonomous institution which opened in 1984. It replaced four government training institutions and the first students were registered in 1985. The College has six schools: education and cultural studies, industrial development, finance and administration, nursing and paramedical studies, marine studies, and natural resources. The College accepts students with the **Form III Leaver's Certificate** or with the **Solomon Islands School Certificate**. Each student follows a one-year foundation programme and then a certificate or a diploma course.

HIGHER EDUCATION

Degree studies are available at the University of the South Pacific in Fiji, or at the University of Papua New Guinea.

The University of the South Pacific has campuses in Fiji and Western Samoa.

Admission to first degree courses is based on satisfactory completion of the University's one-year foundation programme or an equivalent qualification.

The normal length of **Bachelor degree** courses is three years except for medicine which takes four years.

Postgraduate certificates and diplomas, **Master's degrees** and **PhD** programmes are available in a number of areas.

For further information on the University of the South Pacific see Appendix 9 and on the University of Papua New Guinea see Papua New Guinea chapter.

TEACHER EDUCATION

Courses may be taken at the Solomon Islands College of Higher Education leading to the **Solomon Islands Teaching Certificate** for primary teachers, or a **Diploma of Education** for provincial and national secondary school teachers.

Courses are also available at degree level at the University of the South Pacific or the University of Papua New Guinea.

Somalia

The following chapter regarding the education system in Somalia is based on information obtained for the 3rd edition of this Guide, published in 1991, as NARIC has been unable to obtain more recent information.

Formerly two separate colonies (British and Italian), Somalia became independent in 1960.

Schools were nationalized in 1972 and education is now free. The national language is Somali, but Arabic is also in official use, and English and Italian are still widely spoken.

Education is officially compulsory to age fourteen.

A World Bank project to assist all aspects of education started in 1990.

EVALUATION IN BRITAIN

School

Secondary School Leaving Certificate – may be considered to approach GCSE standard.

Further

Diploma – the two-year diploma course following the Secondary School Leaving Certificate might be considered comparable to BTEC National Diploma / N/SVQ level 3 / Advanced GNVQ/GSVQ standard.

Higher

Laurea/Bachelor degree – generally considered comparable to a standard between GCE Advanced and British Bachelor degree.

Degrees from Lafole College are not considered to be of the same standard as those from the National University of Somalia.

MARKING SYSTEMS

School

The pass-mark in the **Secondary School Leaving Certificate** is 60 per cent.

Higher

In the faculties which follow the Italian system, all subjects are marked out of a possible maximum of 30 with 18 as the pass-mark.

The marks for each of the subjects which make up the degree course are shown on the certificate. Most of these marks, however, are clustered around the upper end of the scale and should be treated with caution as indicators of achievement.

SCHOOL EDUCATION

Throughout Somalia there is a grade 12 system (eight years' primary and four years' secondary) leading to the **Secondary School Leaving Certificate**. All main subjects (mathematics, geography, religion, home economics, Arabic, Somali and English) are taught. English is taught as a subject at secondary school level. The medium of instruction at both primary and secondary schools is Somali. Schools are in a poor condition with large class sizes and minimal resources. The Ministry of Education's Curriculum Development Centre is in the process of writing new materials for all grades. The textbooks for the primary grades 1 to 8 have been printed but are in short supply. Examinations for the end of primary and secondary education are set nationally by the National Examination Board. All other examinations, including grade promotion ones, are set by the class teachers.

Vocational secondary education

There are twelve technical/vocational secondary schools where subjects such as building, electrical/mechanical engineering, automechanics, commerce, marine and fisheries, telecommunications and agriculture can be studied. The medium of instruction at these schools is English even though English is not studied at primary level. Marine, Fisheries and Navigation College is a technical secondary college offering a four-year course. The technical/vocational schools curriculum is being revised.

HIGHER EDUCATION

The National University of Somalia was founded in 1954 and awarded university status in 1969. The university also houses Lafole College which was established in the 1960s and used to be affiliated to Michigan State University. It offers two-year intensive degree courses. The University also incorporates the Somali Institute of Development Administration and Management. All faculties of the university follow a three-term academic year with the exception of the Faculty of Journalism which operates a two-semester system.

The media of instruction are Somali, Arabic, Italian and English. All students undertake one term of language training and different faculties use different languages. The following faculties use Italian: basic science, industrial chemistry, geology, engineering, veterinary science, agriculture, medicine, economics and law. The following faculties use English: education, journalism (which may also be taught in Arabic) and technical teacher training. Political science is taught in Somali and Islamic studies are taught in Arabic.

Secondary school-leavers are admitted to the university after a two-year period of national service, selection being made on the basis of a competitive examination. Entry is very competitive with only about eleven per cent of school students going on to university. Overall standards tend to be rather low, mainly as a result of the lack of proper entry assessment and internal assessment procedures. This is due to the low attainment level required to pass the **Secondary School Leaving Certificate**. Standards tend to be a little higher in the sciences, applied sciences and medicine than in the arts and humanities. The four-year course leads to the **Laurea/Bachelor degree**. The Somali Institute of Development Administration and Management offers a four-year programme in public administration and management.

TEACHER EDUCATION

Primary

There is a primary teacher training institute where primary teachers are trained on a two-year course. Primary teachers are trained at secondary level, though a one-year intensive course for new primary teachers has been introduced at Halare College.

Secondary

Secondary school teachers are trained at the National University's Faculty of Education and the Institute of Technical Teacher Training runs three-year teacher training courses for secondary school teachers. The entrance requirement is the **Secondary School Leaving Certificate**. Teachers salaries are low and there are too few of them. The shortage is made up with untrained National Service teachers.

South Africa

The whole education system is undergoing major changes as the last vestiges of apartheid disappear after the first democratic General Election on 27 April 1994, building on the new 1993 Constitution. Post-election educational policy proposals are included in this chapter where possible. Many reforms are due to be implemented during 1995, and it remains to be seen how they are turned into reality, especially in rural communities.

Since the constitution of 1984 each 'Own' Affairs Section (the House of Assembly for Whites, the House of Delegates for Indians, and the House of Representatives for Coloureds) had its own Education Department, all known as the Department of Education and Culture, which dealt with the education of the specific race groups.

Black affairs, including black education, were not considered to be an 'Own' Affair. The Department of Education and Training continued to administer African education within the Republic of South Africa; each of the ten (four independent, six non-independent) homelands had its own education department and administered its own education.

The Department of National Education was considered a 'general' affair and dealt with matters which affected all racial groups; it set norms and standards for educational running costs, for salaries and conditions of employment of staff, for the professional registration of teachers, for syllabuses and examinations, and for the certification of qualifications.

As from the implementation of the present constitution, the development of general education policy is the domain of the Department of Education. Nine regional/ provincial education authorities came into being although the extent to which they will be involved in examinations was not known at the time of going to press.

In 1991, integrated schools run by the state were introduced for the first time, but only where the parent body voted to open such schools. The draft white paper on education and training, dated September 1994, enshrines the rights to equality in education, and the right to equal access to educational institutions for all citizens.

The academic year runs from January to November/December, but exact dates vary from province to province.

Compulsory education for white children used to be from age seven to sixteen; for coloured children from seven to sixteen; and for Indian children from seven to fifteen. Compulsory education for black children was gradually introduced into those schools where the Management Council requested it.

The latest educational policy proposals allow for the addition of one compulsory additional year of pre-primary education extending compulsory education for all citizens to ten years. This would cover ages five to fifteen, or until completion of standard seven.

The implementation of ten years compulsory schooling however, has not yet been implemented and will be phased in gradually starting in 1995. It will not be possible to implement in the short term due to the need to expand capacity in many rural areas. It is hoped however that in 1995, all children of age six can be enrolled in grade one. At present, it is also not possible to implement the proposed additional year of compulsory pre-primary education, which forms part of the ten years compulsory schooling for all citizens currently envisaged, due also to lack of teachers and facilities. However, the Ministry of Education is committed to this policy through the Early Childhood Development programme.

South Africa has eleven official languages: English, Afrikaans; isiNdebele; Sesotho sa Leboa; Sesotho; SiSwati; Xitsonga; Setswana; Tshivenda; isiXhosa and isiZulu. The medium of instruction at school/further education level is as follows:

> White – English or Afrikaans, depending on the mother tongue, but both subjects are compulsory;
> Black – the vernacular until standard 2, English/Afrikaans thereafter;
> Coloured – Afrikaans and English;
> Indian – English.

At the higher education level, English is used as the medium of instruction at the following universities: <u>Cape Town</u>, <u>Natal</u>, <u>Rhodes</u> and <u>Witwatersrand</u>; Afrikaans is used at the universities in <u>Orange Free State</u>, <u>Pretoria</u>, <u>Rand Afrikaans</u>, <u>Stellenbosch</u> and <u>Potche-stroom</u>. However, most Afrikaans medium universities offer tuition in English in addition to Afrikaans. In specialized courses at some of these universities, e.g. veterinary science at the <u>University of Pretoria</u>, and in certain postgraduate courses, English is the medium of instruction. At some universities too, students may write their undergraduate papers in English as well as dissertations for postgraduate degrees. <u>Port Elizabeth University</u> and the <u>University of South Africa</u> (UNISA) are bilingual.

EVALUATION IN BRITAIN

School

The overall standard of the **Senior Certificate** (issued by the South African Joint Matriculation Board), showing the matriculation standard in English language (higher grade) and four other subjects, <u>if it gives</u> matriculation endorsement (previously called matriculation exemption), is generally considered to compare to a standard between GCSE and GCE Advanced level.

Matriculation endorsement requires passes in four subjects at the 'higher' grade and two at the 'standard' grade in the Senior Certificate.

On a subject-for-subject basis, subjects passed at the marks of A–E at both the 'higher' and 'standard' grade would generally be compared to GCSE. Subjects awarded an F at either grade are unlikely to be accorded GCSE status.

Higher grade passes in five subjects (a minimum of three Bs and two Cs) may be considered to satisfy the general entrance requirements of British higher education institutions.

Some institutions in Britain are willing to consider students holding only one of these certificates for entrance to a Bachelor degree course, but others would require at least successful completion of the first year of a South African degree course or, alternatively, GCE Advanced.

Further (Pre-Tertiary)

National (Technical) Certificate (N training) (when all three parts are completed (N1, N2 and N3)) may be considered equivalent to the **Senior Certificate** if additional passes are gained in Afrikaans and English, for entry to **Technikon National Diploma** courses.

N1   comparable to City and Guilds Certificate Part I
N2   comparable to City and Guilds Certificate Part II
N3   comparable to C&G Part II possibly Part III
N4   comparable to C&G Part III (possibly slightly higher)
N5   comparable to a BTEC National Diploma / N/SVQ level 3 / Advanced
       GNVQ/GSVQ standard
N6   slightly above BTEC National Diploma / N/SVQ level 3 / Advanced
       GNVQ/GSVQ standard

All these qualifications, up to and including **National Diploma** (N6) are regarded as craft training.

Tertiary

Technikon National Certificate (T1) one year – generally considered comparable to BTEC National Certificate standard.

Technikon National Higher Certificate (T2) two year – generally considered comparable to BTEC National Diploma / N/SVQ level 3 / Advanced GNVQ/GSVQ standard.

Technikon National Diploma (T3) three year – generally considered comparable to BTEC Higher National Diploma / N/SVQ level 4 standard.

Technikon National Higher Diploma (T4) – generally considered comparable to a standard above BTEC Higher National Diploma / N/SVQ level 4.

Master's Diploma in Technology (T5) – generally considered comparable to British Bachelor (Ordinary) degree standard. To be phased out and replaced by the **Master's Degree in Technology** (see below).

Laureatus in Technology (T6) – generally considered comparable to British Bachelor (Honours) degree standard. Involves an extensive applied research project. To be phased out and replaced by the **Doctor's degree in Technology** (see below).

Higher

Bachelor (Ordinary) degree – 3 year. Generally considered comparable to British Bachelor (Ordinary) degree standard.

Bachelor (Honours) degree – 4 year. Generally considered comparable to British Bachelor (Honours) degree standard.

Technikon Degrees:

Bachelor Degree in Technology (BTech) – generally considered comparable to British Bachelor (Honours) degree.

Master's Degree in Technology (MTech) – generally considered comparable to British Master's degree.

Doctor's Degree in Technology (DTech) – generally considered comparable to British MPhil.

MARKING SYSTEMS

Senior Certificate/Matriculation

A	80–100 per cent	
B	70–79	for both standard and higher-grade
C	60–69	subjects in the **Matriculation** and
D	50–59	**Senior Certificates**
E	40–49	
F	33–39	

The pass-mark in all higher grade subjects is 40 per cent except in Afrikaans second language higher grade, and English second language higher grade. The pass-mark in all standard grade subjects is 33 per cent. The aggregate pass-mark for matriculation is 45 per cent; until 1960 it was 40 per cent.

Proposals for late 1995 will stipulate an average of 50 per cent in four HG subjects at a maximum of two sittings. See below for details.

Higher

Bachelor and **Bachelor (Honours) degrees** are classified at some (usually English-speaking universities):

1st class	75–100 per cent
2nd class division 1	70–74
2nd class division 2	60–69
3rd class	50–59
fail	below 50

Some universities only distinguish:

Distinction	75–100 per cent
Pass	50–74 per cent

SCHOOL EDUCATION

Pre-primary

This was considered a priority up to 1986 when government (DNE) began cutting support for pre-primary teaching posts. It is now considered a priority once again. One additional year of pre-primary education is proposed under the Early Childhood Development scheme. Implementation will be phased in from 1995.

Primary

Until 1967 this covered seven years for all children from age five, except those in the black sector who had to complete an extra year, learning English and Afrikaans. The system that followed covered six years for white and Indian children, seven years for black children. It consisted of grades one and two and standards one to five.

The curriculum covers English, Afrikaans, arithmetic, history, geography, nature study, hygiene, religious instruction, art and crafts, physical education and woodwork/homecraft.

Until the mid-1970s, students took tests for the **Primary School Leaving Examination Certificate** on completion of standard 6. In black schools, since 1976, examinations leading to the **Higher Primary Certificate** have been taken at the end of standard 1.

Secondary (standards six to ten)

Compulsory education in the newly proposed education system will terminate after ten years (age fifteen) followed by the non-compulsory senior secondary or further education.

The curriculum is centrally prescribed by national education policy. In standard six it covers the first and second languages, mathematics, history, geography, and general science; in standards 6/7 and 7/8, industrial arts/housecraft and an optional subject are added.

On completion of standard eight, pupils in black schools sat the external examinations for the **Junior Certificate**.

Standard 9 is not usually compared to GCSE as GCSE involves more school assessment.

Senior Secondary

In the senior secondary cycle of education, students may study subjects either at the higher, standard or lower grade.

Until 1976, only languages were offered with two levels of syllabus. In some education departments, they were designated as higher and lower, in others as A and B.

The following system is current, but proposals for change in late 1995 are set out below.

Examination subjects leading to the **Senior Certificate** (standards eight to ten) have been divided into six groups:

> English and Afrikaans (official languages)
> Mathematics
> Natural sciences
> Third languages
> Human sciences
> Additional subjects (e.g. commercial subjects and arts).

A first and second language must be passed for the award of the **Senior Certificate**.

Until September 1992, each examination authority had its own system of **Senior Certificate Examinations** but admission to university was controlled by the Joint Matriculation Board, which represented all universities in the RSA, and it conducted its own **Matriculation Examination** for this purpose. **Senior Certificates** were recognized for university admission if they conformed to the requirements of the Joint Matriculation Board for Matriculation exemption.

It was not possible to accumulate passes for the **Matriculation Certificate**, but the whole examination could be retaken. The Joint Matriculation Board also granted partial exemption: a student who had passed two of the three higher grade subjects had five years to make up the deficient higher grade subject.

From 1992, the South African Certification Council (SAFCERT) has been responsible for certifying senior certificate outputs and those candidates satisfying the university admission requirements were given matriculation (university admission) endorsements.

In general, these require a candidate to:

1. Offer at least six and no more than seven subjects from the six groups.
2. Pass in at least five subjects in one sitting.
3. Attain an aggregate mark of at least 45.
4. Pass at the higher grade in at least three subjects from the first five groups with at least 40 per cent in each.
5. Pass in both Afrikaans and English, at least one at the higher grade (in the first language).
6. Offer at least one subject from each of four of the groups, provided no more than four languages are offered.

Students who do not meet the requirements for the **Senior Certificate** may retake some or all of the examinations, or have some of their higher grade marks converted into standard grade. Under certain conditions, students may retake one or more subjects at a supplementary examination, provided they have passed at least three subjects at a minimum of 40 per cent at the first sitting. They may not, however, use this opportunity to retake a standard grade subject as a higher grade, or a lower grade subject as a standard grade subject.

Universities may apply for matriculation exemption on the grounds of 'mature age' on behalf of candidates who have attained the age of 23.

New University Admission regulations (proposed to begin in November 1995)

New regulations have been drafted for university admission requirements. They are intended for implementation from November 1995, but at the time of going to press they were still awaiting ministerial approval.

The proposals are termed the amended matriculation endorsement requirements, and are as follows:

The holder of a **Senior Certificate** (consisting of at least five HG and SG subjects) must have obtained 40 per cent in one university tuition language HG (Afrikaans OR English) AND have passed three additional HG subjects with a minimum of 40 per cent in each AND have obtained at least 50 per cent average for four HG subjects at a maximum of two examination sittings.

This new requirement will reduce the compulsory languages for university admission from two to one even though the candidate is still required to offer a second language to qualify for a senior certificate. In addition, the average of four subjects instead of six is used, two sittings are allowed and subjects will be grouped in only two categories, replacing the current six.

It is however still possible for a specific university to stipulate more demanding entrance requirements, and this new policy represents a shift from admission requirements determined in general terms by the Matriculation Board towards the universities themselves deciding course specific requirements.

Technical secondary

At the secondary school level, technical education is available through technical centres, vocational schools and technical high schools.

The technical high schools offer a course leading to matriculation, by means of which entry to universities and technikons is available.

Vocational schools offer artisan training in courses lasting two to four years, plus a period of practical training. Trainees may then take a standardized government trade test, success in which awards full artisan status. Trainees usually enter technical courses on completion of standard 8. After a four-year course, a qualification may be gained which is considered comparable to the **Standard 10 Certificate**.

FURTHER EDUCATION

At the pre-tertiary and tertiary levels, there are technical colleges and technikons respectively (other types of institution have largely been phased out). For information on the new Technikon degree structure, see under **HIGHER EDUCATION** below.

An essential distinction should be made between apprentices (N courses), who are trained to become artisans mainly from standard seven level of education (referred to in this chapter as pre-tertiary), and technicians (T courses), whose training is based on a post-standard-10 level of education (referred to as tertiary).

Pre-Tertiary

Apprenticeship training for technicians is offered by technical colleges. The entrance requirement is standard six, seven or eight, depending on the trade. Apprentices study for the **National (Technical) Certificate** during their training, which consists of three parts, N1, N2 and N3, each part lasting one year. At least three subjects must be passed at each level. When part N3 is supplemented by passes in English and Afrikaans, it may be considered equivalent to the **Senior Certificate** for entry to tertiary level **National Certificate** courses. N4, N5 and N6 form the **National Diploma** (N) equivalent to T3.

Some technical colleges offer tertiary level training, but most training in technical colleges is at pre-**Senior Certificate** level. Training is offered through sandwich courses, part-time courses and short-release courses. While some one-year certificate courses still exist, the majority of programmes have the three-year **National Diploma** as the basic qualification.

The Department of National Education controls official courses offered at technical colleges; it draws up the syllabuses and is the examining body. Most of these institutions, however, also offer courses which are not controlled by the National Department of Education. The admission qualification for all courses offered by the technikons is the **Senior Certificate** or an equivalent qualification.

Tertiary

Tertiary courses are available at technikons and some technical colleges.

The credit system used below assigns a credit value to individual subject offerings. The credit value of each instructional unit is expressed to the third decimal place (e.g. 0.025). A complete instructional programme involving one year's full time study represents one credit. Courses are sequential, allowing a student to obtain a nationally recognized qualification after each successive year of tertiary study. Each year is also represented by a study level (I–VI) based on the number of years studied. Each course component has been assigned a level.

National Certificate (N Certificate)

A qualification with a duration of at least one year's tertiary education. Admission is on the basis of the **Senior Certificate** or equivalent. All components should be at least at level I, with a total credit value of 1.0, including experimental time where appropriate.

National Higher Certificate (NH Certificate)

A two year course, or one year after the **National certificate**. Requirements are the same as for the **National certificate**, plus an additional 1.0 credits, at least 0.5 of these at level II, including experimental time as appropriate.

National Diploma (NDip)

A three year (total) course, which may be studied for one year after the **NH Certificate**. The additional requirements are 1.0 credits, at least 0.5 of these at level III, including experimental time as appropriate.

National Higher Diploma (NHDip)

Four years total study leads to the **NHDip**. For this qualification, an additional 1.0 credit is required, with at least 0.5 from level IV, including experimental time as appropriate.

The sequential series of certificates is continued under **HIGHER EDUCATION** below.

HIGHER EDUCATION

Until 1992

Admission to courses leading to a **Bachelor degree** at South African universities was controlled by the Joint Matriculation Board, originally created as an examining body for the universities and responsible for setting the **Matriculation Examination**. Gradually it became responsible for co-ordinating the **Senior Certificate** examinations of the racially segregated education authorities.

The Joint Matriculation Board granted exemption from the **Matriculation Examination** to holders of a **Senior Certificate** with sufficient marks in a particular combination of subjects.

Since 1992

Admission to **Bachelor degree** courses is now under the jurisdiction of the Matriculation Board of the Committee of University Principals (CUP). See **SCHOOL EDUCATION** above.

The University of South Africa (UNISA) offers tuition by correspondence only, either in English or in Afrikaans, for **Bachelor degrees** and postgraduate qualifications. Course work is structured in modules, with students registering for papers in a unit/credit system, and a maximum of ten years is allowed to obtain a **Bachelor degree**, three years for postgraduate qualifications, an additional year for honours degrees, two further years for a master's degree and two years for a doctorate. The degrees are considered in South Africa to be equivalent in standard to those awarded by other universities.

With the exception of UNISA, many universities were organized on the basis of racial segregation.

However, since early 1986, the position was that all universities were free to admit students of all racial groups satisfying their admissions criteria without reference to the responsible minister.

Courses leading to the award of a **Bachelor degree** last three to six years, as follows:

humanities, commerce, science – three years; agriculture, law, engineering, pharmacy and education – four years; veterinary medicine and architecture – five years; dentistry – five-and-a-half years; medicine and theology – six years.

Students of the humanities, commerce and science, who are awarded a **Bachelor degree** after three years of study, are required to take an **Honours degree**, which can be awarded after a further year's study, before they can proceed to a **Master's degree**.

A **Master's degree** generally requires a minimum of one to two years' research after the award of an **Honours degree**.

A **Doctorate** requires a minimum of two years' research beyond the **Master's degree**.

The Technikons, tertiary educational institutions, are autonomous, subsidized by the Department of National Education, and they provide training at the post-**Senior Certificate** level; courses lead to a range of qualifications. All technikons use the same curriculum for a particular course. The statutory body, SERTEC (Certification Council for Technikons) is responsible for issuing the diplomas. SERTEC monitors standards by accreditation visits to each Technikon. Recent legislation allows Technikons to award undergraduate degrees with a minimum first degree duration of four years (**Bachelor of Technology**), as well as postgraduate courses (**Master of Technology** and **Doctor of Technology**). The **MTech** takes one year after the **BTech**, the **DTech** takes a further two years of study. This structure came into effect in January 1995. Course requirements are as follows:

The following qualifications follow on from the sequential National Diploma and certificate courses described under **FURTHER EDUCATION** above.

Bachelor Degree in Technology (BTech)

A qualification of at least one year's duration after the National Diploma. This comprises 1 credit, at least 0.5 of which must be at level IV. No experimental time may be included.

Master's Degree in Technology (MTech)

Obtained at least one year after the BTech, this is an advanced qualification comprising taught subjects and research, or solely research. The thesis must relate to an industry specific problem.

Doctorate in Technology (DTech)

A research based qualification of at least two years' duration. Comprises an advanced research project.

TEACHER EDUCATION

Teacher training can be taken in three ways; through the Department of Education, Arts and Science, through the provincial Education Departments, or at the universities and some technikons.

Degree-level courses for secondary school teachers are run by all universities; for admission, a **Matriculation Certificate** or a **Senior Certificate** with Matriculation exemption is required. It is also possible to do primary education at degree level.

Three- or four-year diploma courses, qualifying their holders to teach in primary schools, are run by provincial training colleges and certain universities. The general admissions requirement for diploma courses is a **Senior Certificate** with pass-marks in both official languages, one of which must be at the higher grade, with one other subject besides a language on the higher grade, and certain other specified subjects.

The **Higher Diploma in Education** is a post-graduate course, of one year's duration, or a four year post-Matriculation course and is considered comparable to a **Bachelor of Education**.

Black

All pre-standard-10 and two-year teacher training courses at teachers' colleges run by the Department of Education and Training were phased out in 1982; they have been replaced with a variety of three-year post-standard-10 primary and secondary school teachers' diplomas.

Teacher training is offered at the universities which previously had been for blacks; courses offered include four-year integrated education degrees for which a **Matriculation Certificate** or Matriculation exemption is the entry requirement.

Coloured

Primary and junior secondary school teachers are trained over a three-year course for which a **Senior Certificate** is the entry requirement.

The University of the Western Cape trains teachers at undergraduate and postgraduate levels for all academic secondary school subjects; the entry qualification is a **Matriculation Certificate** or Matriculation exemption.

Indian

Three-year courses leading to diplomas in primary and junior secondary education, for which a **Senior Certificate** is the entry requirement, are run by colleges of education and the University of Durban-Westville.

The University also offers a four-year integrated degree and a one-year postgraduate **Higher Diploma in Education** for secondary school teachers; a **Matriculation Certificate** or Matriculation exemption is the entry requirement to these courses.

South Korea

From 1910 to 1945 Korea was a Japanese colony. In 1945 the country was liberated by American and Soviet forces and subsequently divided into the Republic of Korea in the south and the Democratic People's Republic of Korea in the north. The system of education in the Republic of Korea has been influenced more recently by the USA. It was previously modelled on the Japanese education system.

There are many private institutions in both the school and higher education sectors.

Education is compulsory for nine years from age six to fifteen.

The medium of instruction is Korean. English is a compulsory subject at secondary school, and attempts are now being made to introduce it as an extra-curricular activity in primary schools as well.

The academic year runs from March to February.

EVALUATION IN BRITAIN

School

High School Diploma – generally considered comparable to GCSE standard (grades A, B and C) on a subject-for-subject basis, with the exception of English language.

Higher

Junior College Diploma – generally considered to satisfy the general entrance requirements of British higher education institutions.

Bachelor degree – generally considered comparable to a standard between GCE Advanced and British Bachelor degree; may be given advanced standing by British higher education institutions. Candidates from prestigious institutions may be considered for admission to postgraduate study. For further information enquirers should contact the National Academic Recognition Information Centre.

MARKING SYSTEMS

School

There are no uniform grades in Korean secondary schools. The marking system may be lettered:

A   pass
B   pass
C   pass
D   pass
E   fail

It should be noted that in practice Korean secondary schools rarely fail students, as this would stop them moving up to the next grade.

or numerical:

1 – 100 (maximum)

Higher

90–100 per cent	A
80–89	B
70–79	C
60–69	D
0–59	F

SCHOOL EDUCATION

Pre-primary

Facilities are available for three to five-year-olds.

Primary

This cycle covers six years (grades 1 to 6). Pupils concentrate on basic literacy and mathematical skills. The curriculum also covers moral education, Korean, social ethics, mathematics, natural science, physical education, music, fine arts and crafts. English may be taught in grades 4 to 6 as an optional course. A residential district-based random placement system assigns grade 6 children to a lower-secondary (i.e. middle) school.

Secondary

Lower secondary

This cycle lasts three years (grades 7 to 9) and is provided in lower secondary schools, known as middle schools. On successful completion of the course students receive a diploma.

The curriculum concentrates on Korean, English and mathematics, although twelve academic subjects (including electives) are covered altogether.

Upper secondary

This cycle covering three years (grades 10–12), is not compulsory and is provided in three different types of high school: academic (general); vocational and special purpose high schools (i.e. science, foreign language, art and athletic high schools). Admission to vocational and special purpose high schools is decided earlier than academic high schools, and is based on either each schools own entrance examination or locally standardized academic performance assessments.

Admission to academic high schools is determined by locally standardized tests and, once passed, the candidates are allocated to schools within their school district by a computer lottery system. The lottery system is however only practised in so called 'equalized areas'. In 'non equalized areas' high school candidates have to compete by taking a qualifying examination administered by the local district.

In academic high schools, during the final two years, students may choose to specialize in humanities or sciences. Studies are organized according to the credit system, each subject being allocated a number of units on successful completion. Students must accumulate at least 204 units for graduation.

Vocational high schools are divided into several categories: agricultural, technical, commercial, fishery and marine, and home economics. Vocational high schools offer students at least 82 units (around 40 per cent of total needed for graduation) of specialized subjects, as well as general academic subjects which should occupy another 40 per cent of the whole curriculum. In special purpose high schools the curriculum organization is similar to that of the vocational high school.

Students who successfully complete this cycle are awarded a **High School Diploma**.

FURTHER EDUCATION

Junior colleges

These offer programmes in a wide range of subjects including commerce, kindergarten education, engineering, technical subjects, agriculture, liberal arts and health and design, usually leading to a **diploma**. Courses are two years in length except for fisheries/marine colleges which offer an additional six-month course for navigation practice and the nursing programme which lasts three years.

Most of the programmes for training kindergarten teachers are provided at junior colleges. However recently the number of university educated kindergarten teachers has been increasing.

Miscellaneous schools

This category was established by the Ministry of Education to indicate institutions which are highly specialized and not broadly diversified in their academic programme. Miscellaneous schools may also include schools which do not fall into the category of college or university. As a rule, these schools lack a sufficient liberal arts core or basic general education programme to meet the standards for an accepted undergraduate or university programme. They are predominantly theological or single-purpose institutions.

Schools which have received Ministry of Education approval run courses of four years in length with students receiving a **diploma** on completion of their studies.

HIGHER EDUCATION

There are seven types of higher education institutions, which can be categorized as follows:

Colleges and universities offering four-year undergraduate programmes (six years for medical and dental colleges); graduate schools; teachers' colleges (see under

TEACHER EDUCATION); two or three year junior colleges; Correspondence University; miscellaneous schools; open colleges.

Colleges and universities

Entry is by entry examination together with the student's high school record, which must be given at least a 40 per cent weighting in this process. For the remaining 60 per cent, colleges and universities are free to use either the **Scholastic Ability Test for colleges**, a nationally standardized entrance examination or their own entrance examination, or from a combination of two or more of these tests.

Individual colleges can, in principal and in line with the above, select students solely on the basis of existing student records. In 1994, most universities and colleges opted for the combination of 40 per cent student record and 60 per cent of **Scholastic Ability Test for Colleges** scores. However, from 1995 at least 47 universities will use their individual entrance examination to make up 20 to 40 per cent of the admission scores.

First-degree courses normally last four years. The credit system is used for marking. Successful completion of 140 credit hours is required for the award of the **Bachelor degree**. A total of 180 credits are required in medicine and dentistry where courses last six years.

Graduate schools

Progression to postgraduate study is by graduation (accumulation of 140 credits) and an entrance examination.

Master's degrees are obtained by satisfactory completion of 24 credits over two or three years and the submission of a thesis. Students can sit for no more than 12 credits per year.

A **PhD** requires a further 36 credits (i.e. a total of 60 credits) over two or three years. A **PhD** candidate must also demonstrate fluency in English and one other foreign language, pass an oral examination and submit a doctoral dissertation.

Correspondence University

The Korea Air and Correspondent University started as an affiliated junior college to the Seoul National University in 1972. It now operates as an independent national institution and, as of 1992, offers a four-year university programme leading to a **Bachelor degree**.

Open colleges

These provide flexible two and four-year programmes in vocational/technical fields. Two-year courses lead to a **diploma**, four-year courses to a **Bachelor degree**.

TEACHER EDUCATION

Primary teacher training is carried out at specialized universities, whereas secondary teacher training is taught through faculties of education in four-year universities.

Primary

Thirteen national teachers' colleges provide four-year courses. Graduates receive a **Bachelor degree** and certification to teach in primary schools.

Secondary

Teachers' certificates for secondary schools are given to graduates of universities or four year colleges who have completed prescribed courses of study in education as part of their entire university of college course.

ADULT EDUCATION

There are a number of continuing education institutions mainly for adults who left school early. They provide part-time or evening courses varying from one or several months to two or three years in length. The schools include civic schools, higher civic schools, trade schools, senior higher trade schools and the Air and Correspondence High School.

Spain

The administration of education is currently being devolved to the seventeen autonomous communities that now constitute Spain. The extent and nature of Ministry of Education and Science control varies widely in these autonomous communities. Catalunya, Basque country, Galicia, Navarre, Andalucia, Valencia and the Canaries have full competence over educational matters. The others will follow shortly. The Ministry plans to maintain control of general policy, national inspectorate, recognition of qualifications and curriculum development in primary and secondary education.

In 1985 the LODE: *Ley Organica del Derecho a la Educación* (Right to Education Act) was passed under the new Socialist government. The LODE was the Ministry of Education and Science's statutory provision for the development of principles referring to educational matters laid down in the 1978 Constitution. LODE lays down certain rights and responsibilities for students, teachers, parents and government concerning education. It also sets out the general school categories and makes provision for each category – state schools, private schools, special agreement schools (private schools which are maintained with public funds and give free education) and non-maintained schools (private, no public funds, fee paying).

Until 1964, only six years of schooling were compulsory; since then compulsory education has been increased to eight years, starting at age six. There are now plans to make education compulsory up to the age of sixteen and to reform **Educación General Básica** (EGB) (higher) and **Bachillerato Unificado y Polivalente** (BUP) into a single programme with a later division (i.e. at sixteen) between academic and technical/vocational training. These plans have taken shape in the form of a 1990 reform, known as the LOGSE reform.

LOGSE involves wide ranging, politically sensitive reforms. As a result, its implementation has been delayed. Officially, the programme is about one year behind schedule. Currently, in 1994, implementation is patchy. It has certainly started at the primary level (*Educación Primaria*) and some autonomous communities have already started implementing the secondary level (*Secundaria Obligatoria* and **Bachillerato**) ahead of schedule, but in other parts of Spain there seem to be serious delays.

The main aims of LOGSE are: education to be compulsory from age six to sixteen (ten academic years) and the system of general education to be divided into three areas. These are infant education, up to age six; primary education, lasting six academic years from age six; and secondary education which will include statutory secondary education, **Bachillerato** studies and intermediate level vocational training.

Secondary education will be divided as follows: first cycle, leading to **Graduado en Educación Secundaria** at age 16, and second cycle, leading to the **Título de Bachillerato** at age 18.

The first holders of **Graduado en Educación Secundaria** are expected to come through the system in 1995, and holders of **Título de Bachillerato** in 1997.

Officially, LOGSE will be implemented one educational cycle at a time. This decision involves a delay of one year as compared to the original proposal. The reform of the second cycle of primary education will therefore be implemented in 93/4 and that of the third cycle in 94/5.

The academic year runs from October to July.

EVALUATION IN BRITAIN

Bachillerato Unificado y Polivalente (BUP) / **Graduado en Educación Secundaria** – generally considered comparable to GCSE (grades A, B and C) overall, and subject-for-subject, where marks of at least 6 have been obtained, with the exception of English language.

Curso de Orientación Universitaria (COU) / **Título de Bachillerato** – may be considered to satisfy the general entrance requirements of British higher education institutions, provided an average mark of 6 has been obtained.

Selectividad – may be considered to satisfy the general entrance requirements of British higher education institutions, provided an average mark of 6 has been obtained.

Licenciado, Título de Ingeniero, Título de Arquitecto – generally considered comparable to British Bachelor (Honours) degree standard, although the course lasts longer than in the UK.

Diplomado/Diplomatura – regarded as equivalent to DipHE.

Note : The **Diplomado** is a qualification gained on successful completion of the first university cycle, whereas the **Diplomatura** is received after a *Diplomatura* course such as *Magisterio* or tourism and is taken at an *Escuela Universitaria*, i.e. it is a terminal qualification and transfer to a degree course in Spain is via the appropriate bridging course. However, in practice these two qualifications are regarded as of a comparable level.

Formación Profesional (further education)

Primer Grado (first grade) would be regarded as below BTEC First Diploma / N/SVQ level 1 standard.

Segundo Grado (second grade) comparable to BTEC National Diploma / N/SVQ level 3 / Advanced GNVQ/GSVQ standard.

MARKING SYSTEMS

At BUP and COU levels, schools award marks internally out of ten as follows:

School

10	*sobresaliente (matricula de honor)*
8.5 – 9	*sobresaliente*
7 – 8.4	*notable*
6 – 6.9	*bien*
5 – 6	*suficiente*
Below 5	*insuficiente*

These marks are awarded for, on average, three internal assessments per year and then averaged. The resulting average is then translated into one of the above grades expressed in words. For example, a student obtaining 8, 6.5 and 6 has an average of 6.8, i.e. *bien*. This average expressed in words is the mark shown on the scholastic record. The *calificación global* or overall average for the year is the average of these marks calculated according to the following scale:

Mark		Abbreviation
sobresaliente	9	SB
notable	7.5	NT
bien	6.5	BI
suficiente	5.5	SF
insuficiente	< 5	IN/INSUF

Insuficiente does not count in calculating the average as students have to resit in September any failed subjects to pass the year in question and the average will then include the resit mark. Students may resit up to two subjects. Failure in more than two subjects or in the September resit leads to repeating a year.

The average for the year is then calculated by averaging the marks for the various subjects. For example; 3 *sobresaliente*, 2 *notable* and 2 *bien* marks = 3×9 (27) + 2×7.5 (15) + 2×6.5 (13) = 55/7 = 7.9.

Higher

10	*matricula de honor*	distinction with honour
9–9.9	*sobresaliente*	distinction
7–8.9	*notable*	very good
6–6.9	*aprobado*	good
5–5.9		satisfactory
below 5	*suspenso*	fail

Doctorate

Apto   Awarded by tribunal, before which the student has to defend a doctorate thesis.

No Apto   This is awarded when it is not satisfactory.

Cum Laude   An excellent marking for the thesis, which may be awarded by the tribunal.

SCHOOL EDUCATION

Primary

1970 – 1990/94

Educación General Básica (EGB: basic general education)

EGB was provided in *Centros de Educación General Básica*: state schools were called *Colegios Públicos*. The introduction of the revised system following the 1970

Education Act was begun in 1971–2 and completed in 1974–5.

The *Primera Etapa* (first stage) of EGB lasted five years, age six to eleven. The *Segunda Etapa* (second stage) lasted three years, to age fourteen. On satisfactory completion of the *Segunda Etapa*, pupils were awarded the title **Graduado Escolar** which gave access to upper secondary schools (*Centros de Bachillerato*). Pupils who failed to attain the required standard received the **Certificado de Escolaridad** (Certificate of Schooling) which gave access to vocational training centres.

Since 1981

The EGB structure was amended in 1981 to:

Inicial	Years 1 and 2
Medio	Years 3–5
Superior	Years 6–8

Secondary

1970 – 1990/94

Holders of the **Graduado Escolar** could be admitted to *Centros de Bachillerato* to follow a three-year course leading to the **Bachillerato Unificado y Polivalente** (BUP) or upper secondary school-leaving certificate obtained at age seventeen. The course included Spanish, a foreign language, social science, natural science, mathematics, art and music, religion and physical education. These subjects were compulsory. Pupils also studied one of industrial technology, agriculture, commerce and home economics.

Students were only admitted to each BUP year if they had passed the preceding one and if they were of the requisite age, although two failed subjects could be carried over (three failures necessitated repeating the year). The full BUP was awarded when all three years of the programme had been completed and passed.

BUP years one and two were standard for all students. BUP year three was a mixture of common subjects and options.

Curso de Orientación Universitaria (COU: university preparation course)

Pupils holding the **Bachillerato** could be admitted to the one-year COU (year 12). COU was streamed into science/technology, biosciences, social sciences and humanities/linguistic options. The Spanish language, a foreign language and philosophy were common to all streams. Within each stream two subjects were compulsory and students elected a further two subjects from a choice of four, for example, in science/technology stream, mathematics and physics were compulsory and students elected a further two subjects from chemistry, biology, geology and technical drawing. The choice of stream and options was also a factor in university entrance.

The COU was organized and supervised by a university but was taught in establishments of secondary education. Students were assessed by continuous assessment. The certificate was issued by the Ministry of Education and Science.

Holders of the **COU Certificate** were qualified for admission to university. They had completed twelve years of education, from age six to eighteen inclusive.

Selectividad

This is a university entrance examination set by each university. Candidates must have successfully completed COU. **Selectividad** consists of six tests. The mark obtained is added to the average for the BUP and COU marks and the result is divided by two to give a new overall average that will determine access to first-degree courses.

Vocational and technical secondary

Since 1970

The transition to the reformed system was completed by the academic year 1976–7.

Centros de Formación Profesional Industrial

Courses are provided at two grades. The first grade is described here. Grade two is for students of post-secondary level (see below: **FURTHER EDUCATION**).

Primer Grado, Iniciación Profesional (first grade)

This grade is open to holders of the **Graduado Escolar** certificate or the **Certificado de Escolaridad**, both obtained at age thirteen. The *Primer Grado* is a two-year full-time course, compulsory for pupils who are not continuing with academic study. The course consists of a six-month period of lessons called *Introduction to the world of work* followed by training in a trade or occupation such as agriculture, commerce, art, or catering.

Escuelas de Arte y Oficios Artísticos (art schools), *Escuelas de Cerámica*

These schools provide vocational training for pupils who have completed six years of school (at age eleven). The five-year full-time course is divided into two parts: the first three years provide a common course of general and vocational studies, while the last two years are devoted to one specialization. The final certificate is in a particular specialization (such as *Decoración y Arte Publicitario*: decoration and advertising art; or *Artes Aplicables al Libro*: book crafts or in art teaching).

Escuelas Periciales de Comercio (commercial schools)

Pupils aged fourteen who hold the **Graduado Escolar** or **Certificado de Escolaridad**, and have passed an entrance examination, can enter these institutions to follow a three-year full-time commercial course. Evening classes are also offered. The title granted on leaving is **Especialista Técnico en Administración** (within *Formación Profesional Segundo Grado* – see under **FURTHER EDUCATION**).

The national vocational training programme adopted in 1993 should make for better links between the various forms of vocational training organized by the Ministry of Education and the Ministry of Labour. These will enjoy equal recognition as from 1995 in the framework of a national system of vocational qualifications.

An overview of the LOGSE reforms (implementation began in 1993/94)

Statutory secondary education now lasts four years, divided into two two-year cycles. Successful completion will lead to the award of **Graduado en Educación Secundaria** which will allow the student to study further, either on an academic or vocational level.

Studies leading to the **Título de Bachillerato** will take a further two years. There will be different types of **Bachillerato** to allow for specialization in preparation for further study, again, either academic or at advanced vocational level, but there will also be a common core of subjects (physical education, philosophy, history, Castillian and the regional language and literature and a foreign language). To gain the **Título de Bachillerato** exams must be taken and passed in all subjects studied.

To enter university it will still be necessary to take an entrance examination, in addition to the **Bachillerato**.

Vocational Training

Anyone holding the **Graduado en Educación Secundaria** certificate may embark on vocational training at intermediate level; to take vocational training at advanced level it is necessary to hold the **Bachillerato**.

If a candidate over the age of twenty and without the established academic qualifications wishes to undertake vocational training, s/he can do so by passing an examination (regulated by the Education authorities) to demonstrate that s/he is sufficiently prepared to complete the course successfully.

The design and implementation of vocational training courses will be shaped by the concerns of industry, and the training will include work placements.

It is also possible to gain entry to university with the **Advanced Engineer** qualification, although the subject chosen will have to correspond to that studied at the advanced vocational training level.

CHANGES TO THE SPANISH EDUCATION SYSTEM AS A RESULT OF THE RECENT LOGSE REFORM

AGE	CURRENT SYSTEM	NEW SYSTEM
6	Start school *Educación General Básica*	Start school *Educación Primaria*
12	Start compulsory secondary education	
14	End compulsory education **Graduado Escolar** awarded to successful students and gives access to BUP course; Unsuccessful students receive **Certificado de Escolaridad** giving access to vocational training Start 3 year BUP course.	
16	*Secundaria*; gives access to academic study and vocational training Start 2 year **Bachillerato** course	End compulsory education **Graduado en Educación**
17	End BUP course (**Bachillerato Unificado y Polivalente***)* 1 year **Curso de Orientación Universitaria** (COU)	
18	End COU **Selectividad** – university entrance examination	End **Bachillerato – Título de Bachillerato** University entrance examination

FURTHER EDUCATION

Since 1970

Centros de Formación Profesional Industrial

The first grade is described above.

Segundo Grado, Nivel Medio (second grade, intermediate level) provides full-time courses of a maximum of three years for students who hold the **Bachillerato**, aged sixteen or seventeen, or for those who have completed the *Primer Grado* of *Formación Profesional Industrial* (also aged sixteen or seventeen). The course provides training relevant to employment in specific areas such as agriculture, commerce, administration.

HIGHER EDUCATION

Since 1970

Universidades (universities) and *Universidades Politecnicas* (polytechnic universities)

Polytechnic universities were formed where there were groups of *Escuelas Técnicas Superiores* (higher technical colleges) e.g. in Madrid, Barcelona, Valencia and Las Palmas. They incorporate the former *Escuelas de Formación Profesional, Tercer Grado* (schools of professional training, third grade) and *Escuelas Universitarias Técnicas* (university technical schools).

This sector also incorporates still existing *Escuelas Técnicas Superiores* of engineering and architecture, which are considered to have very high standards.

While most degree courses last five years, medicine, architecture and most engineering courses last between five-and-a-half and six years (including an end-of-course project for engineers and architects).

Courses are divided into three cycles:

Primer Ciclo, Ciclo Básico (First cycle, basic course)

Admission is still in 1994 on the basis of the BUP plus the COU certificate plus, in most cases, **Selectividad**. (People aged over twenty-five who do not have the **Bachillerato** can enter university on the basis of an entrance examination.)

The *Primer Ciclo* lasts three years and is devoted to the study of basic disciplines. On successful completion, students are awarded a **Diplomado**, and may continue to the *Segundo Ciclo* of university.

Primer Ciclo courses are taught not only in universities but also in *Colegios Universitarios* which offer no facilities beyond this level but enable students to go straight into *Segundo Ciclo* at the university to which the *Colegio* is affiliated.

Segundo Ciclo, Ciclo de Especialización (Second cycle, cycle of specialization)

To enter the *Segundo Ciclo*, a student must have completed the *Primer Ciclo* of a university or *Colegio Universitario*, or a bridging course after graduation from an *Escuela Universitaria, Escuela de Arquitectura Técnica* or *Escuela de Ingenieria Técnica*.

The *Segundo Ciclo* provides a two-year course of specialization. The degree awarded is the **Licenciado** in most fields, the **Título de Ingeniero** in engineering and the **Título de Arquitecto** in architecture. To obtain the **Título**, engineers and architects must complete an end-of-course project (*Proyecto Fin de Carrera*).

Tercer Ciclo, Ciclo de Especialización para la Investigacion y Docencia (Third cycle, specialization for research and teaching)

To enter the *Tercer Ciclo* a student must hold the **Licenciado** or **Título de Ingeniero/Arquitecto**. Students follow a number of special courses (*Cursos Monográficos de Doctorado*) during the first two years on which they are examined. They do research which may take a year or more after the first two years and have to defend a thesis before a tribunal to obtain the **Título de Doctorado** (PhD).

Escuelas Universitarias were envisaged as providing professional short courses of one cycle (under the Education Act of 1970) which has been modified by the University Reform Act, making it easier to go into second-cycle studies.

Entrance requirements for universities and polytechnic universities are the same, except that the **Curso de Orientación Universitaria** has a more technical emphasis for entry into the polytechnics.

The 1983 University Reform Act (LRU – *Ley de Reforma Universitaria*) made it possible for universities to become autonomous. Nevertheless, very few universities have so far exercised this right. Those which have done so have a great deal of flexibility within broad Ministry of Education guidelines, but the curricula for first-degree courses in the remainder are still laid down by the Ministry. Degrees in most universities are awarded by the Ministry of Education and Science but in the autonomous ones they are awarded by the Rector of the university in the name of the King of Spain.

Official postgraduate qualifications are limited to the **Tercer Ciclo** (doctorate). Nevertheless, many universities, public and private, are beginning to offer their own **Master's degrees** to meet an increasing demand from business and their own students.

The titles **Diplomado**, **Ingeniero Técnico** and **Arquitecto Técnico** are awarded to students successfully completing a three-year course at *Escuelas Universitarias, Escuelas de Ingeniera Técnica and Escuelas de Arquitectura Técnica* respectively. The corresponding course is similar – but not identical to the *Primer Ciclo* of degree courses – and the holders of these qualifications can only go on to the *Segundo Ciclo* after taking the appropriate bridging course. (i.e. these are terminal qualifications). *Colegios Universitarios*, however, do prepare *Primer Ciclo*, and successful students directly enter the university to which their *Colegio* is affiliated to begin the *Segundo Ciclo*.

Music, drama and dance studies

Conservatories offering music, drama and dance depend on the Ministry of Education and Science (or autonomous community where education powers have been devolved). The Ministry has a *Subdirección General de Enseñanzas Artísticas*. There are *Conservatorios Elementales, Conservatorios Profesionales* (which offer **Título de Grado Medio** previously also called **Grado Profesional**), *Conservatorios Superiores* (which offer **Título de Grado Medio** and **Título Superior**). Children can attend from age eight having passed an entrance examination. Children accepted by conservatories follow their normal education in state schools and do specific courses in the conservatories at the same time. They have to have completed the relevant EGB/BUP courses to obtain qualifications from the conservatories.

Fine arts degrees are studied at university in faculties of fine arts.

TEACHER EDUCATION

Since 1970

Primary and lower secondary

Escuelas Universitarias de Formación de Profesorado (primary and lower secondary – EGB – teacher training schools)

Since 1970, the former *Escuelas Superiores de Magisterio* have become *Escuelas Universitarias* (university schools). Admission requirements are as for any university course (see above). The teacher training course lasts three years and graduates are awarded the **Diploma de Profesor de Educación General Básica**, which qualifies them for pre-school and primary school teaching posts (children from four to thirteen), obtained after competitive examinations (*oposiciónes*).

Upper secondary

Teachers in upper secondary schools (*Centros de Bachillerato*) must hold a university degree (**Licenciado**) or equivalent. It is possible to combine pedagogic studies with a degree course; students who have not done this receive training at an *Instituto de Ciencias de la Educación* for the **Certificado de Aptitud Pedagógica** (CAP). *Licenciados* who can prove that they have already taught for at least two years are exempt from passing the CAP.

Centros de Formación Profesional

Teachers for both levels must have a first degree (**Licenciado, Ingeniero** or **Arquitecto**) or the **Diploma de Escuela Universitaria de Formación Profesional**.

Higher

Teachers in university schools (*Escuelas Universitarias*) must hold a **Licenciado** or equivalent; unless the degree course included pedagogic training, prospective teachers must attend an intensive course run by an *Instituto de Ciencias de la Educación*.

Since 1970, there have been fewer official categories of university teacher. These are:

Catedráticos Numerarios (professors who hold chairs) must have a doctorate plus pedagogic training.

Profesores Agregados (associate professors) have the same qualifications as *Catedraticos Numerarios*.

Profesores Adjuntos (assistant professors) must have a doctorate plus at least one year's experience as an *Ayudante* or of research with the Higher Scientific Research Council.

Visiting professors may also be appointed. Both *Profesores Adjuntos* and visiting professors are appointed to perform specific duties.

Profesores Ayudantes (assistant lecturers) must have at least a **Licenciado** or equivalent. They are appointed for one year with the possibility of renewal for a maximum of four successive years.

Extraordinary professors may be appointed for a limited time and very occasionally for an indefinite period. They can never receive civil servant status.

Only about ten per cent of university teaching staff have a permanent appointment.

ANDORRA

Andorra, a principality jointly administered between France and Spain, has not established a separate education system. Instead, students choose between the Spanish and French systems.

Sri Lanka

Education is the responsibility of the Ministry of Education and the Ministry of Higher Education.

Education is compulsory from age five to fourteen and free from kindergarten to university level in state institutions. There are also fee-levying private institutions up to university level.

At school level, Sinhala and Tamil are the media of instruction. English is taught as a second language from year IV but is not compulsory for Sri Lankan **GCE O levels**, nor for university entrance. At university level, Sinhala, Tamil and English are the media of instruction, depending largely on the subjects studied. Lectures in the arts and social sciences faculties are usually held in Sinhala and/or Tamil; medicine, engineering and architecture are generally taught in English; all the other subjects are initially taught in Sinhala and/or Tamil with an increasing use of English towards the end of the degree course. Answers for the university examinations may be written in Sinhala, Tamil or English.

The school year is divided into three terms starting in January; the university year runs from October to June.

EVALUATION IN BRITAIN

School

National Certificate of General Education (NCGE – introduced in 1975 and abolished in 1977) – generally considered to be below GCSE standard.

Sri Lankan General Certificate of Education (Ordinary level) – generally considered comparable to GCSE standard (grades A, B and C) on a subject-for-subject basis (with the exception of English language), provided that grades of distinction (D) and credit (C) are obtained.

Sri Lankan General Certificate of Education (Advanced level) – generally considered comparable to GCE Advanced standard grades A, B or C.

Higher

Bachelor General degree – generally considered comparable to British Bachelor (Ordinary) degree standard.

Bachelor Special degree – generally considered comparable to British Bachelor (Honours) degree standard.

MARKING SYSTEMS

School

Sri Lankan **GCE O levels** are graded as follows:

75–100 per cent	D	distinction
50–74	C	credit
35–49	S	pass
0–34	F	fail

Sri Lankan **GCE A levels** are graded as follows:

75–100 per cent	A	distinction
65–74	B	very good pass
55–64	C	credit
40–54	S	ordinary pass (simple pass)
0–39	F	fail

Higher

The grading system for first degrees is as follows:

75–100 per cent	A
55–74	B
40–54	C
30–39	D
0–29	E

Degrees are awarded according to class or division. The method of calculating the class or division can vary. A fairly typical pattern is given below:

First class: candidates must obtain an average of at least 70 per cent with A grades in at least half the papers and a minimum grade of C in the remaining papers.

Upper second: candidates must average at least 60 per cent with A or B grades in at least half the papers and a minimum grade of C in the remaining papers.

Lower second: candidates must average at least 55 per cent.

Pass: candidates must average 40 per cent or more with a minimum grade of C in all papers.

SCHOOL EDUCATION

1972–7

A new school system, introduced in 1972, aimed to provide a general education better suited to modern needs which would allow greater equality of opportunity. It was organized in three stages: primary (years I to V), junior secondary (years VI to IX) and senior secondary (years X to XI).

Two new examinations were introduced, the **National Certificate of General Education** (NCGE), taken at the end of junior secondary (year IX) and the **National Certificate of Higher Education** (NCHE), taken at the end of senior secondary (year XI).

The **National Certificate of General Education** was not an examination which candidates passed or failed; instead, each candidate received a certificate, indicating performance in the different subject areas on a five-point scale: a, b, c (pass), d and e. School assessment also contributed to the final grades.

The first NCGE examination was held in December 1975 and the second in 1976. The first NCHE examination was to have been held in April 1978. The old system (i.e. **GCE O** and **A level** examinations), which was to have been phased out in 1979, ran concurrently with the new system.

1977–84

The government elected in 1977 decided to revert to the **GCE O** and **A level** examinations, and the NCGE and NCHE examinations were cancelled. Candidates preparing for the NCHE examination sat for the 'Interim Syllabus' in 1979. Those who took the NCGE were allowed an extra year at school to sit **GCE O levels** if required.

Since January 1985

Primary

This covers a six-year course (years I–VI) with entry at five to six years.

Junior secondary

This covers two years (years VII and VIII) and is compulsory up to the school-leaving age of fourteen.

Senior secondary

This lasts three years from age fourteen (years IX–XI). At the end of year XI pupils sit for **Sri Lankan GCE O levels**. Students take the examination in eight subjects and must pass in six including mathematics and Sinhala or Tamil.

Pre-university

This course, sometimes known as post-secondary, lasts two years (years XII–XIII) from age seventeen. At the end of year XIII pupils sit for **Sri Lankan GCE A levels**. Students take four examinations and must pass in three to be considered for university admission.

In February 1986 a new national examination in English language was held, the **National Certificate in English** (NCE). The level is rather above that of **Sri Lankan GCE O level** and it is hoped the certificate will provide a language profile of use to employers.

FURTHER EDUCATION

Technical and vocational

There are eight polytechnical institutes and fourteen junior technical institutes providing three types of courses in engineering, commerce, business and crafts:

Certificate courses lasting up to two years. Most are post-**GCE O level** but some admit students on completion of year VIII or IX.

National Diploma courses lasting two or three years which may be post-**GCE O** or **A level**.

Higher National Diploma (HND) courses lasting four years full or part-time post-**GCE A level**.

A number of institutions offer courses leading to the awards, at different levels, of the City and Guilds of London Institute.

Youth work

Government-sponsored youth schemes include: agricultural projects designed for youth settlement, practical farm schools, young farmers' clubs and programmes of the Department of Small Industries. Some non-government organizations are involved in youth work, notably SARVODOYA, a national secular movement which runs youth farms and youth leadership courses.

Technical courses are provided at the Ministry of Labour's vocational training centres, at the Ministry of Education's Technical Units and by the National Apprenticeship Board.

Rural development

This work is organized by the Rural Development Department, which offers on-the-job training (through its network of rural development officers) and residential courses for officials of local groups.

HIGHER EDUCATION

Higher education in Sri Lanka is provided in three kinds of institutions, universities and affiliated university colleges, specialized private and state institutions and other private institutions. One per cent of places on any given course in the state universities (at least one place), is reserved for the admission of students with foreign qualifications.

The affiliated university colleges set up in 1991 in eight provinces will function with academic and administrative links with the traditional universities and are expected to develop eventually into autonomous higher education institutes. The colleges will conduct courses leading to a **diploma** in subjects such as: home science and nutrition, mathematical sciences, entrepreneurship and small business management, agriculture, English, accountancy and finance, hotel management, tourism and culture, travel and tourism and science with specialization in bio/physical science.

The Kotalawala Defence Academy and the Institute of Surveying and Mapping are the state higher education institutions which function as degree awarding institutes.

The Law College, Institute of Chartered Accountants, Chartered Institute of Management Accountants, Institute of Chemistry, Institute of Physics, Institution of Engineers and the Institute of Architecture are other state and private education institutions which conduct courses in professional fields.

At present there are nine full-fledged universities in Sri Lanka and nine institutes of higher education: five at postgraduate level and four at undergraduate level. In addition, the Buddhasravaka Dharmapitiya and the Pali and Buddhist University are higher education institutes set up by Acts of Parliament for the study of Buddhism. All universities conduct postgraduate courses leading to **MA/MSc**, **MPhil** and **PhD** and full time and part-time extension courses at diploma and certificate levels.

The Open University of Sri-Lanka was established in 1980 and is modelled on the British Open University. It does not have formal admission requirements and caters to the higher educational needs of those who do not get an opportunity to further their education in the formal education system. It is designed to enable those who are eighteen years or older to pursue a first or **Postgraduate degree** or **certificate** or **diploma** in their own time by means of distance learning.

Except for the Open University, the students are selected for admission to university on their performance at the **General Certificate of Education (GCE), Advanced level** examination. The minimum requirement for admission is a pass in four **GCE Advanced level** subjects or pass in three subjects with not less than 25 per cent in the fourth subject as long as an overall aggregate of 180 marks has been achieved.

Bachelor General degrees, in which students read three subjects throughout the course, require three years' study while **Bachelor Special degrees**, in which students specialize for most of the course in one subject e.g. agriculture, vet. science, engineering, architecture, dental science and law, require four years (except medicine which requires five years plus an additional internship period lasting one year).

Postgraduate diplomas usually require one year of study following a **Bachelor degree** and **Master's degrees** usually two years. A **Doctorate** normally requires two to three years' study beyond a **Master's degree**.

TEACHER EDUCATION

Until 1981, the minimum qualification for teacher training was **GCE O level** passes in four subjects. Since December 1981 the minimum entry qualification has been six **GCE O levels** and two **GCE A level** passes.

Primary

A three-year course (two years' course work and one year's practical in-service training) post-**GCE A level** at a general teacher training college leads to a **Trained Teacher's Certificate**.

Secondary

A three-year course (two years' course work and one year's practical in-service training) post-**A level**, specializing in the subject(s) to be taught at secondary level, at a teacher training college leads to a **Trained Teacher's Certificate**.

Sudan

The medium of instruction in most schools in Sudan is Arabic. English is a compulsory subject from primary five. There are some vernacular primary schools.

In theory, school years in Sudan run from August to April except for the eastern region and southern areas which have different calendars dependent on the weather (i.e. closures in the very hot season or as a result of too much rain). In practice there is some variation for other reasons as well.

EVALUATION IN BRITAIN

School

Sudan School Certificate (formerly called the **Secondary School Certificate** or **Higher Secondary School Certificate**) – generally considered comparable to GCSE standard on a subject-for-subject basis (with the exception of English language), provided that marks of at least 50 per cent are obtained in subjects which can be taken in the GCSE examinations.

Higher

Bachelor (Ordinary) degree – generally considered comparable to a standard between GCE Advanced and British Bachelor degree; may be given advanced standing by British higher education institutions.

Bachelor (Honours) degree – generally considered to approach British Bachelor degree standard. Students with degrees from prestigious universities may be considered for admission to postgraduate study.

MARKING SYSTEMS

School

The **Sudan School Certificate** can be awarded with distinction, credit or as a pass.

A percentage mark is also obtained from all subjects, four of which are core (Arabic, mathematics, English and religion (Islamic or Christian) and three optional. No certificate will be awarded if the candidate fails one of the core subjects.

Higher

The marking system for the third and fourth years of the general degrees at the University of Khartoum is as follows:

66–100	A	Div I
50–65	B	Div II
45–49	C	Div III
0–44	F	Fail

For the five-year Honours degree Division II is divided into upper and lower sections.

SCHOOL EDUCATION

Primary

This course of basic education lasts eight years (age 6–14).

Intermediate

This lasts three years (age 15–17).

Secondary

Academic

The academic secondary schools offer a common course which leads to the **Sudan School Certificate**. The Cambridge Overseas Examinations Syndicate was involved in administering the **Sudan School Certificate**. Formal collaboration ended in 1962, but the same pattern has followed although the 'Boxing' system has been replaced with percentage marks.

In the first and second years, pupils follow a common course, but in the third year they choose to enter literature (arts) or science streams.

Technical

The technical secondary schools grew out of the intermediate trade schools discontinued in 1967–8. They include industrial, commercial and agricultural schools. Courses last three years and the students specialize in technical subjects. On successful completion, students receive the **Sudan School Certificate** and may enter a technical university.

Vocational Training Centre

There is a Vocational Training Centre in Khartoum. It offers a primarily vocational two-year terminal post-basic course. Specialization includes: woodwork, metalwork, leatherwork, electrical work, furniture-making etc.

FURTHER EDUCATION

Facilities for learning outside of the formal education system exist.

The Sudan University of Science and Technology offers evening craft classes to primary school-leavers and a wide range of City and Guilds and NC-type courses, plus more specialist courses.

The Sudan Council of Churches provides vocational training courses and also has schemes especially geared to the needs of southern Sudan.

HIGHER EDUCATION

A student wishing to enter university must hold the **Sudan School Certificate** with passes in all seven subjects and with an average of at least 60 per cent (1994). Individual universities set minimum entrance marks; the University of Khartoum is the most difficult to enter with a minimum requirement of 68 per cent (83 per cent for the medical faculty).

The language of instruction is Arabic but there is still quite a lot of teaching in English, particularly in the medical faculties and in the private universities. English is a compulsory subject for all university students and no first degree can be awarded to a student who fails the English course. Four-year **Bachelor (General) degrees** and five-year **Bachelor (Honours) degrees** are offered by the established government universities (University of Khartoum, University of Gezira, University of Juba and the Islamic University of Omdurman).

University of Cairo (Khartoum branch) used to offer Cairo University degrees but now runs four-year courses of its own, mainly to part-time students.

Omdurman Ahlia University College and Ahfad University College for Women are private universities which offer four-year degree courses, diploma and certificate courses. Sudan University for Science Technology offers four-year degree courses in a variety of technical subjects as well as a **BTech**.

Since 1990 a further 17 government universities have been established, mostly in the provinces. At least 4 private tertiary institutions have also opened. They will offer as many diploma courses as degree courses.

TEACHER EDUCATION

Primary

Originally the primary teacher training institutes accepted intermediate school graduates for a four-year course. Most institutes operate under the new system which admits secondary school graduates for a one-year course.

There are plans for teaching to become an all graduate profession. To further this the old teacher training colleges are being linked to universities, particularly the new ones, and they will offer four-year **BEd degrees**.

Intermediate

There are three National Institutes for training intermediate school teachers: one for men at Bakht er Ruda; and two for women at Omdurman. There are also three regional Intermediate Teacher Training Institutes. Courses last two years and applicants are normally secondary school graduates with several years' teaching experience.

Intermediate education is being phased out and the Intermediate Teacher Training Institutes will be retitled Basic Teacher Education Institutes, linked to universities and offering four-year **BEd degrees**.

Secondary

Secondary school teachers are taught at the Faculties of Education of the Universities of Khartoum, Gezira and Juba. Graduates are awarded a **BEd degree**. There is also a special one-year course for unqualified teachers.

ISETI

The <u>In-Service and Educational Training Institute</u> (ISETI) was established with Unicef support. It provides service training for primary and secondary teachers. ISETI is based in Khartoum, with 17 regional branches.

Surinam

In 1975 Surinam, a former colony of the Netherlands, became independent. The education system is still largely based on that of the Netherlands, but is no longer an exact copy. Anglo-Saxon influences were prominent in higher education after the re-opening of the University of Surinam in 1983. There are numerous private institutions recognized by the state.

Education is compulsory from age seven to twelve.

The medium of instruction is Dutch.

EVALUATION IN BRITAIN

School

VWO Certificate – generally considered to be between GCSE and GCE Advanced standard.

Higher

Candidaatsexamen (until 1983) – generally considered comparable to a standard between GCE Advanced and British Bachelor degree.

Doctoraal Examen (until 1983) – generally considered comparable to British Bachelor degree standard.

Bachelor Degree (since 1983) – generally considered comparable to British Bachelor degree standard if awarded after four or more years of study.

Doctoraal Examen (since 1983) – generally considered comparable to British Bachelor (Honours) degree standard.

MARKING SYSTEM

School

10	*uitmuntend*	excellent
9	*zeer goed*	very good
8	*goed*	good
7	*ruim voldoende*	quite good
6	*voldoende*	satisfactory
5	*bijna voldoende*	not quite satisfactory
4	*onvoldoende*	unsatisfactory
3	*gering*	low
2	*slecht*	poor
1	*zeerslecht*	very poor

Higher

cum laude	with distinction
met genoegen	good
met goed gevolg	satisfactory

Sometimes the American style of marking is used (for further information see US chapter).

SCHOOL EDUCATION

Pre-primary (*Kleuterschool*)

There are limited facilities for children aged four to six.

Primary/elementary (*Gewoon Lager Onderwijs*/GLO)

This lasts for six years and the curriculum covers Dutch, history, geography, natural history, singing, drawing, needlework, reading, writing, arithmetic and physical education.

Extended elementary (*Uitgebreid Lager Onderwijs*/ULO)

Until 1975

This covered two years for children who had completed six years' primary education and were to have no further schooling. The curriculum was the same as in the primary school, with some commercial subjects in addition (e.g. bookkeeping). Extended elementary education was phased out in 1975.

General secondary

All children who wish to continue their education sit for a compulsory general achievement test, during the final year of primary education. This test is used mainly as a means to direct pupils to different schools at junior secondary level.

Junior (lower) secondary education (*voortgezet onderwijs op junioren niveau*)

MULO (*Meer Uitgebreid Lager Onderwijs*: more extended elementary education)

Nowadays this is the only form of general education at the lower secondary level. Pupils may specialize in section A (with an emphasis on commercial subjects) and section B (with mathematics and physics). Dutch, English, Spanish or German, geography, history, biology and drawing are compulsory subjects for both sections. Pupils obtain the diploma (**MULO-A** or **MULO-B**) after four years. They may sit for the entrance examination for higher secondary education (HAVO and VWO) after passing from the third to the fourth year or after the fourth year.

Senior (higher) secondary education (*voortgezet onderwijs op senioren niveau*)

The former types of higher secondary education were being phased out by the middle of the seventies and replaced by the HAVO and VWO (in conformity with changes in Dutch secondary education). These were the former AMS-A and AMS-B courses at the Algemene Middelbare School (AMS), the former *Atheneum* and *Gymnasium* courses at the *Lyceum* (all three-year courses after three or four years of MULO) and the former HBS courses (five years after primary school), which all gave admission to higher education.

After three or four years of the MULO course pupils may proceed to one of the following two courses, depending on the results of an entrance examination:

Hoger Algemeen Voortgezet Onderwijs (HAVO: upper general secondary education)

This is a two-year course. Compulsory subjects are Dutch and English. In addition, pupils must choose four other subjects from mathematics, physics, chemistry, biology, Spanish, French, German, geography, history and economics. Drawing/handicraft, physical education and civics are also studied in the first year, but dropped in the second year. On completion of the course, pupils must take an examination in these six subjects to obtain the **HAVO certificate**. This certificate gives admission to higher professional education and to the bridging year of the university (*schakeljaar/ propaedeuse* – this year is **not** part of the university course and should not be confused with the *propaedeuse* in the Netherlands).

Voorbereidend Wetenschappelijk Onderwijs (VWO: university preparatory education)

This is a three-year course of a more advanced level than that offered by HAVO. Compulsory subjects are Dutch and English. Pupils must choose five other subjects out of mathematics, physics, chemistry, biology, Spanish, French, German, geography, history, economics and sociology. During the first two years drawing, physical education, civics and sociology are also studied. The last year is concentrated on the seven subjects of the examination. On completion pupils obtain the **VWO certificate** and are eligible for university entrance.

There is one possibility to follow a six-year VWO course, after primary education.

Vocational secondary

Vocational secondary education is available at the lower secondary level (after primary education), and takes one of the following forms:

a three-year course in the field of home economics at the *Lager Nijverheids Onderwijs* (LNO) level;

a four-year technical course at the *Lager Technisch Onderwijs* (LTO) level

a four-year course at the *Lager Beroepsgericht Onderwijs* (*LBGO*) level. The programme of the first two years is of a general nature and common to all pupils. After these years pupils specialize in one of the following streams: a) domestic stream, b) technical stream, c) administrative-economic stream, d) agricultural stream.

At the upper secondary level, intermediate vocational education is available in the fields of technology and agriculture at the <u>Natuurtechnisch Instituut</u> (NATIN), lasting four years (until 1985: three years). The **MULO-B certificate** gives direct admission to the NATIN, the **LBGO** and **LTO certificates** only to a bridging year (*schakelklas NATIN*).

A business administration course (three years) and a secretarial training programme (two years) are offered at the <u>Surinaamse Middelbare Handelsschool</u> (MHS) or the <u>Instituut Middelbaar Economisch en Administratief Onderwijs</u> (IMEO, since 1982). The **MULO certificate** gives direct admission to these courses, the **LBGO certificate** to a bridging year (*schakelklas*).

Except for the secretarial training course, all the upper secondary intermediate vocational training courses give access to higher professional education and to the bridging year of the university (*propaedeuse/schakeljaar*).

Surinam

Higher Education

Until 1968, pupils wishing to go on to a course of higher education normally went to the Netherlands, except in the fields of law and medicine, for which facilities were available. In that year the <u>Universiteit van Suriname</u> (University of Surinam) was proclaimed. In addition to the faculties of law and medicine (created in 1968 and 1969 respectively), the faculties of economics and social sciences (1975), agricultural sciences (which in Surinam includes mining, geology, and the physical sciences) (1976) and engineering (1977) were created.

In the autumn of 1982 the university was closed (because of the political situation) and restructured. The institution was re-opened in October 1983 as the <u>Anton de Kom Universiteit van Suriname</u>. The number of faculties was reduced to three: the faculty of social sciences (including law, economy and business administration courses), faculty of technology (and agricultural sciences) and the faculty of medical sciences.

Until 1983

All courses, with the exception of the medical one, were five years in length and divided in two parts: two or three years to the **Candidaatsexamen**, followed by two or three years (depending on the duration of the **Candidaats**) to the **Doctoraal examen**. Upon completion of the course the title of *Doctorandus (drs)* was conferred; in the case of law studies the title of *Meester (mr)*.

An exception was (and is) the programme in medicine: two years' pre-medical and clinical work leads to the **Candidaatsexamen,** a further two years' clinical work leads to the **Doctoraal**. After a further two years of internship/training the **assistent-artsexamen** is taken and after one year the **artsexamen** (professional examination to be fully qualified).

Since 1983

In all faculties Bachelor degree programmes were introduced with a nominal course duration of four years in which a practical period was included. These programmes were made up of three stages: the B(achelor)I stage (first year), the BII stage (second and third year) and the BIII stage (fourth year) and were concluded with the **Bachelor of Science degree**.

The structure of the medical programme remained unchanged; the university course however is also concluded with the **Bachelor degree.**

Theoretically, students could proceed to a **Master's** programme after the **Bachelor degree**. In reality this programme was never implemented.

Since 1993 the title of *Doctorandus* was reintroduced by law. The bachelor programmes have neither been fundamentally restructured for this purpose nor is the nominal duration of the courses extended.

Entrance to the university is based on the **VWO certificate** or the *propaedeuse/schakeljaar.*

Higher professional education

Until 1983

Higher professional education was offered at the <u>University of Surinam</u> in four-year programmes, concluded with the diploma of **Licentiaat**. Admission to these programmes was based on the **HAVO certificate**.

These programmes have been phased out since 1983.

Since 1983

Higher professional education is offered at the <u>Academie voor Hoger Kunst- en Cultuuronderwijs</u> (AHKCO) in the field of arts, social work and journalism. The nominal duration of the programmes is four years; courses lead to the **Bachelor of Arts degree.**

The **HAVO certificate** gives admission to the AHKCO.

Teacher Education

Primary

Pre-primary teachers are trained at secondary level. Admission may be given on completion of two years' MULO. The course is concluded with the **certificate Onderwijzeres-A**, after a further year with the certificate of **Hoofdkleuterleidster**. Graduates may teach in kindergarten and in the first two years of primary education.

Primary school teachers are trained in a four-year programme. The first two years are aimed at general education, the last two years consist of professional and practical teacher training. Admission is based on the **MULO certificate**. A **HAVO certificate** gives admission to the second part (the third year) of the programme. The course is concluded with the **Akte van Volledig Bevoegd Onderwijzer/Hoofdakte.**

Secondary

Courses are offered at the <u>Instituut voor de Opleiding van Leraren</u> (IOL):

Lager Onderwijs (LO) Akte

This two-year part-time course leads to the **LO certificate**, which entitles to teach at lower (junior) secondary level. Admission is based on the **HAVO certificate**.

Middelbaar Onderwijs (MO) Akte

MO-A – a three-year part-time course from VWO, or two years from LO entitling to teach at lower (junior) and the first years of higher (senior) secondary level.
MO-B – a two-year part-time course from MO-A, entitling graduates to teach at any level of secondary school, at the institutions of primary teacher training and in higher professional education.

Swaziland

Swaziland is an independent monarchy. Independence was attained in 1968. Figures released in 1984 show that the total enrolment at primary and secondary schools was 87 per cent of the school-age population.

Swaziland has 534 primary schools, 91 junior secondary and 77 high schools (1992). It also has three teacher training colleges, one university, one college of technology and one institute of health sciences.

Primary education is officially compulsory and lasts for seven years from the age of six.

Swaziland was linked with Botswana and Lesotho until 1975 through the University of Botswana, Lesotho and Swaziland (UBLS) and the Examinations Council of the University, which was responsible for conducting the **Junior Certificate** and **Cambridge Overseas School Certificate** examinations throughout the three countries.

The school year consists of three terms: January to April, May to August and September to December. The academic year at the university runs from August to June, split into two semesters.

EVALUATION IN BRITAIN

School

Cambridge Overseas School Certificate (COSC) – grades 1–6 are generally equated to GCSE (grades A, B and C) on a subject-for-subject basis.

Higher

Part 1 (i.e. the first two years) of a degree course at the University of Swaziland – may be considered to satisfy the general entrance requirements of British higher education institutions.

Part 2 (i.e. the remaining two years) leading to **BA/BSc** – generally considered comparable to a standard between GCE Advanced and British Bachelor degree; may be given advanced standing by British higher education institutions. Exceptionally, students with high grades may be considered for admission to postgraduate study.

Master's degree – comparable to a standard approaching British Bachelor (Honours) degree level.

MARKING SYSTEMS

School

Swaziland takes **Cambridge Overseas School Certificate** (COSC) and this requires the student to pass six subjects including English at one sitting. The six subjects must also include one science and one humanities subject. The aggregate of the best six subjects is taken for the grading.

Individual subjects are marked as follows:

Percentage	Standard	Grade	GCSE equivalent
75–100 per cent	Very Good	1	A
65–74		2	A
60–64	Pass	3	B
55–59	with	4	B
50–54	Credit	5	C
45–49		6	C
40–44	Subject	7	D
35–39	pass	8	E
0–34	Fail	9	U

The aggregate is obtained from the addition of the number of points of the best six subjects on the following scale:

6–23 points   1st class pass
24–33 points   2nd class pass
34–43 points   3rd class pass
44 + points   4th class pass

Higher

Until 1967

A   pass with distinction
B   pass
C   fail

Since 1967

Examinations at the end of **Part 1** and **Part 2** are classified:

A   80–100 per cent   excellent
B   70–79   very good
C   60–69   good
D   50–59   pass
E   40–49   fail, but student can take a supplementary examination in the faculties of humanities and education only
F   below 39   complete fail

Bachelor degrees are classified:

1st class   B average
2nd class first division   C average
2nd class lower division   D average
pass   E, F average
fail

SCHOOL EDUCATION

Primary

This used to last for eight years, from age six, divided into two cycles of six years and two years respectively; it now lasts seven years covering standards 1–7 or grades 1 and 2 followed by standards I–V. On completion, pupils obtain the **Primary School Certificate.**

There is often a high incidence of pupils repeating grades.

Secondary

This covers up to five years, forms I–V. On successful completion of form III pupils obtain the **Junior Certificate** and on completion of form V the **Cambridge Overseas School Certificate** (COSE).

St. Marks High School in Mbabane prepares pupils for the **Cambridge Overseas Higher School Certificate** (COHSC) examination and Waterford Kamhlaba United World College for the **International Baccalaureate**.

TECHNICAL/FURTHER EDUCATION

Technical/vocational education is offered at the following institutions:

Swaziland College of Technology (SCOT) offers courses at craft, technician and diploma levels. Admission requirements vary between **Junior Certificate** and **O level**. Courses are certified locally and/or from overseas (e.g. Pitman, AAT., City and Guilds). Courses are structured over three or five years depending upon the type and subject and are designed so that students obtain commercial or industrial experience between each part of the course. All courses are designed to fit into the formal apprenticeship period.

The Vocational and Commercial Training Institute Matsapha (VOCTIM) is a vocational institution offering a variety of subjects at craft level spread over three or four year periods. The policy of this institution is to survey the needs of local industry and mount courses to satisfy these needs. The minimum entry qualification is the **Junior Certificate** but most VOCTIM students have form V level qualifications due to the competition for entry resulting from the large number of applications.

The institute certifies its own courses; however, an application has been made to City and Guilds for permission to operate certain of their courses.

Manzini Industrial Training Centre (MITC) was established to provide training for students who have not graduated from the regular school system and who do not have prerequisite academic admission requirements for other vocational training institutions. Programmes are provided in various trades for students aged between 18 and 25. Similar types of courses are offered by Nhlangano Agricultural Skills Training Centre (NASTC), which is a sister institute to MITC. Plans are underway to establish a third centre in the Lubombo region.

Mpaka High School offers vocational subjects to form IV and V students who have earned their **Junior Certificate**. The programmes are termed pre-vocational but the curriculum is at vocational level. Some courses are accredited by City and Guilds.

HIGHER EDUCATION

The University of Botswana, Lesotho and Swaziland (UBLS), which was established in 1964 at Roma in Lesotho, covered higher education in Swaziland. In 1966 the Swaziland Agricultural College became associated with the University and was renamed the Swaziland Agricultural College and University Centre (SACUC). In 1971 teaching for **Part 1** of the degree courses began at SACUC. A new campus of UBLS was opened in 1973 in Swaziland. Students then completed the first two years (i.e. **Part 1**) of their degree course there and transferred to the campus at Roma for the final two years (**Part 2**). Students now undertake the whole of their course at the campus in Swaziland. When Lesotho withdrew from the arrangement in 1975, Botswana and Swaziland continued their co-operation, and the university became the University of Botswana and Swaziland, with campuses at Gaborone (Botswana) and Kwaluseni (Swaziland). In July 1982 the two constituent colleges of the University of Botswana and Swaziland became the University of Swaziland and the University of Botswana.

Courses leading to the **BA** and **BSc** generally last four years, divided into two-year cycles, **Part 1** and **Part 2**. The normal entrance requirement is the **Cambridge Overseas School Certificate** with a pass in the first or second division, and with a credit in English language. Students holding two or more relevant passes at **GCE Advanced** standard or in the **Cambridge Overseas Higher School Certificate** may be admitted directly into the second year of the course.

There are no facilities for studying engineering, architecture, medicine, pharmacy, dentistry or veterinary medicine.

Courses are available leading to the award of an **MA, MSc** or **MEd**. A wide range of undergraduate certificate and diploma courses is also offered.

TEACHER EDUCATION

Primary

Until 1969 prospective primary teachers obtained the **Elementary Vernacular Certificate** after a period of study. This course was then discontinued and replaced by a three-year part-time upgrading course to bring teachers to the level of the **Primary Lower Certificate**. This upgrading course was discontinued in 1978.

The normal courses of study were the two-year course for the **Primary Lower Certificate,** for students who had completed forms I and II, and the two-year course leading on from the **Primary Lower Certificate** for the **Primary Higher Certificate** for those holding the **Junior Certificate**.

In the early 1970s, these two courses were condensed into a two-year course for the **Primary Teachers' Certificate** for holders of the **Junior Certificate**.

In 1987, the **Primary Teachers' Certificate** was upgraded to **Primary Teachers' Diploma**. The **Cambridge Overseas School Certificate** is now a prerequisite for admission. William Pitcher College, Nazarene College and Ngwane College all offer this course which now lasts three years.

(Beginning in 1994, the **Primary Teachers' Diploma** is gradually being phased out at the William Pitcher College.)

Secondary

A two-year course for holders of the **Cambridge Overseas School Certificate** leads to the **Secondary Teaching Certificate** obtained from the <u>William Pitcher Teacher Training College</u> which was established in 1962 for lower-secondary teachers. In 1987 this two-year **Secondary Teaching Certificate** was upgraded to the **Secondary Teachers' Diploma** and now lasts three years.

The <u>University of Swaziland</u> offers a **Postgraduate Certificate in Education,** which replaces the **Concurrent Diploma in Education (CAE).**

Sweden

Since the early 1950s, education reforms have been introduced at all levels. It is difficult to divide the system into the usual sectors of school (primary and secondary), further, higher and teacher, as the only clear divisions are comprehensive school and upper secondary (*Gymnasium*) and higher. The reforms give more emphasis to continuous assessment and the 'development of personality' than to examinations. The extreme centralization of the system has been altered since the end of the 1970s. Decision-making powers have increasingly been delegated to individual municipalities and schools, allowing greater scope for local curriculum development and teacher-pupil influence. The 1977 Higher Education Act decentralized decision-making powers and created a unified higher education system (*Hogskola*).

This decentralization has continued in the 1993 Higher Education Act under which the Government deregulated study programmes and only specified the length, goals and degree requirements for education.

Also the upper secondary school has undergone changes, including decentralization, an increase in length of study from two to three years during 1993–95, and a new structure of programmes are just some of these changes.

Education is compulsory for nine years from age seven.

English is compulsory from grades 3 or 4 to 9. English is the medium of instruction in some universities.

The academic year runs from mid-August/September to May/June.

EVALUATION IN BRITAIN

School

Slutbetyg fran Grundskola – generally considered comparable to GCSE standard if grades of 3 or above have been obtained, with the exception of English language.

Avgangsbetyg (previously **Studentexamen**) – may be considered to satisfy the general entrance requirements of British higher education institutions, provided applicants have completed three years at upper secondary school.

Slutbetyg (from the *Teknisk Linje*) – generally considered comparable to BTEC National Diploma / N/SVQ level 3 / Advanced GNVQ/GSVQ; may be considered to satisfy the general entrance requirements of British higher education institutions.

Higher

Hogskoleexamen (Diploma) may be given advanced standing by British higher education institutions.

Bachelor degree/Kandidatexamen – generally considered comparable to British Bachelor (Honours) degree standard.

Master's degree/Magisterexamen – generally considered comparable to British Master's degree standard.

MARKING SYSTEMS

School

Grundskola Certificate is graded 1–5 (maximum). The marks are relative, i.e. they refer to the average national level of achievement in each subject. There is no fail grade.

Avgangsbetyg is graded 1–5 (maximum). The marks are relative and there is no fail grade. A new goal and achievement marking system was implemented in 1994, the first students under the new system will complete their studies in 1997.

Higher

In most fields of education there is a three-level scale: fail, pass, pass with distinction, or a two-level scale: fail and pass. Law and engineering are exceptions with several fields.

Degrees are awarded on a points system. One point equals one week's successful study (called a *poang*), making 40 points per academic year. Minimum requirements are:

Hogskoleexamen (Diploma)	80 points
Bachelor degree/Kandidatexamen	120 points, including 60 in the major (10 for thesis)
Master's degree/Magisterexamen	160 points, including 80 in the major (20 for thesis)

The above are examples only: They are general degrees introduced in 1993. In addition there are around 40 professional degrees. Before 1993 there were around 100 different types of degree.

Teacher

Teaching certificates were before 1992 awarded with three grades in teaching skill:

3 (highest) earned by	15 per cent
2	25 per cent
1 (average)	60 per cent

Since 1982 only grades 'approved' or 'failed' have been awarded.

SCHOOL EDUCATION

Pre-primary/kindergarten

There are extensive facilities for day-care at this level available for children aged one to six, the last year being a compulsory year preparing for primary school.

Primary and secondary

Since 1962

In 1962 an Act of Parliament established the nine-year compulsory course of comprehensive education. The course at the *grundskolor* is divided into three stages, each of three years: junior (*Lagstadium*) covering grades 1–3, middle (*Mellanstadium*) covering grades 4–6 and senior (*Hogstadium*) covering grades 7–9; all three comprising *Grundskola*.

During grades 1–6 all pupils take the same subjects: Swedish, mathematics, music, physical education, religious instruction and local studies in grades 1–3; handicrafts and English are added in grade 3. In grades 4–6 drawing, civics, history, geography and nature study are added. In grades 7–9 there are common subjects (as in grades 4–6, physics, chemistry and biology being taken instead of nature study) and with the possibility of specialization.

There is no streaming in the comprehensive schools. There are no formal external examinations, and a pupil's performance is judged by continuous assessment, based partly on standardized tests which are centrally prepared and locally marked. The result is intended to be related to average performance throughout the country.

There is no final school-leaving examination; in their last term, pupils are given a leaving certificate which states their average mark per subject. The **Slutbetyg** is obtained on completion of the full nine years of comprehensive education.

Upper Secondary School (*Gymnasium*)

On completion of grade 9, there is selective entrance to the upper secondary school/ *Gymnasium*. This stage includes both academic programmes and a wide selection of two-year vocational programmes and special courses.

Three-year programmes are mainly preparatory for higher education. Apart from academic studies in general subjects, some of them include theoretical vocational subjects, such as business administration.

Four-year technical programmes conferring the qualification of upper secondary school engineering (or technology) graduate was abolished when the new two-year higher education technology degree was introduced.

Two-year vocational programmes have traditionally been either specifically vocational and included extensive practical training together with the relevant theory and some general subjects, or they have been predominantly theoretical (e.g. the economics, social and technical programmes). They may also, after complementary studies in specific subjects, qualify the student for higher education.

In compulsory school 97 per cent of pupils complete the final grade and 95 per cent continue their studies at upper secondary school. There are also 'mature applicants' who have either acquired varying degrees of work experience instead of coming straight from compulsory school or have attended school in another country. Consequently, upper secondary school graduates can be between 17 and 20 years old.

At this level 38 per cent of the students choose three and four-year programmes, 37 per cent vocational programmes and 5 per cent two-year theoretical programmes. About 20 per cent take special shorter courses, mostly vocational.

Foreign languages are compulsory in all academic programmes and optional in the vocational ones. Most students study English for 8–10 years.

In 1969 the final school-leaving examination **Studentexamen** was abolished and replaced by continuous assessment and national tests in major subjects. The final certificate is called **Avgangsbetyg** for which there are no specific requirements or general average subject mark targets required to complete studies.

There are few private upper secondary schools in Sweden. Those that exist are mainly boarding schools, but there are also state schools for various kinds of speciality, e.g. sport, music, art and mathematics. In state schools it is possible to study a variety of languages, e.g. Finnish, Russian, Spanish, Italian, and sometimes Chinese.

There are also upper secondary schools specifically for adult learners (*Komvux, kommunal vuxenutbilding*) which offer courses for students who want to change their specialization in order to apply for higher education in a field for which they would not otherwise be eligible.

Upper secondary schooling is currently in a process of change. All programmes will become three years in length, including the vocational ones. The present system is due to be replaced by a system with national programmes consisting of partly fixed subjects, partly free choices.

Outside the upper secondary school system, are the 'folk high schools' (*Folkhögskolan*). Most of these schools are subsidized by the state and run either by the counties or are attached to organizations. The schools have great freedom to decide their curricula, and special attention is paid to education in good citizenship. There are no formal examinations. In some cases, however, a university preparatory programme will be offered. In these cases they give eligibility to higher education.

HIGHER EDUCATION

1977–1993

After the 1977 Higher Education Act, most undergraduate education was organized into about a hundred general study programmes, established by parliament, which varied in length from one to five-and-a-half years. Each programme was designed to meet professional training requirements, and each may be classified within one of the following five professional training sectors: technical; administrative, economic and social welfare; medical and nursing; teaching; and cultural and informational.

There were also local study programmes. Like the general study programmes, these varied in length. The difference was that a local study programme was normally aimed at local needs and conditions. A third type of specialization was the individual study programme, intended to fulfil the wishes of one or more students for a particular educational programme. Both local and individual study programmes were established by the governing board of each institution of higher education.

1977 to present

There are also separate single-subject courses which are short-cycle study programmes designed to meet the need for further education or advanced professional training. Separate single-subject courses are also established by the governing board of each institution of higher education. For students in employment, single subject courses are often offered at evening classes on a part-time basis, or as distance learning courses. Part-time students usually take twice as long to complete their course as full-time students. Single subject courses have served one of the objectives of the 1977 reform:

to make higher education a forum for recurrent education. They also offer the opportunity for the student to compile his or her own degree profile. Students can decide whether they want to study for a full degree (**fil kand examen**) or to take courses leading to a certificate (**utbildningsbevis**).

The new Higher Education Act of 1993 established a more decentralized organization, which gives greater freedom for universities to set up study programmes and single subject courses, based on the new degree ordinance.

Degree and course requirements

Until 1993

Studies were carried out either in the form of *utbildningslinjer* (study programmes) or *fristaende kurser*, earlier *enstaka kurser* (single subject courses); either way these courses ended with the award of a degree. Sweden has a system of points (*poang*), where one term of successful full-time studies equals 20 points, one year 40 points (40 weeks). A major subject requirement is usually 60 points. Thus the minimum requirements for e.g. a **filosofie kandidatexamen** (**fil kand**) or **hogskoleexamen pa xx-linjen** are 120 points with a major in a single subject which would give eligibility for research education (doctoral studies) in the same field. The length of study programmes leading to such a **hogskoleexamen** or a **fil kand examen** has varied between three and four years, sometimes longer. Programmes leading to **ekonomexamen** (business administration and economics) and **socionmexamen** (social work) lasted three-and-a-half years. Other degrees in engineering, agriculture, law, psychology, medicine, dentistry etc. required up to five-and-a-half years. The years described are the nominal time, normally the students need more than three years to reach 120 points.

Since 1993

Students must obtain at least 120 points with at least 60 points in one subject and apply to their respective institution for the title of **Kandidat**. 160 points (with at least 80 points in one subject) are required for the title **Magister**. 180 points are required for the title **JurKand** and 140–160 points for the title of **TeolKand**.

Marks are given on a three-level scale: fail, pass and pass with distinction. Some fields of education use only a twO level scale: pass and fail, while others, like law and engineering, have several levels. On completion, the student receives a diploma (**utbildningsbevis**). When these studies have comprised a full study programme, the diploma indicates the name of the degree earned. Each includes the Swedish word *examen* (degree), regardless of the time required to complete the study programme. The name of the degree also indicates the field of studies or the occupation involved.

Admission to postgraduate study is based on completion of a study programme or a degree or single subject courses. The student must have at least 60 points in the subject to be studied at postgraduate level and must have taken advanced courses in this subject involving independent work and a major paper. The **Doktorsexamen** (doctorate) is obtained after a minimum of four years' full-time study in one subject and successful defence of a dissertation. The **Licentiatexamen** (**licentiate**) is a research degree obtained after two years' full-time study and a dissertation.

Within the system of higher education (*Högskola*) there are specialist colleges, notably those for social work, public administration, journalism, agriculture and forestry. These institutes have full university status:

Lulea University College and Institute of Technology
The Karolinska Institute, Stockholm (medicine and dentistry)
Royal Institute of Technology, Stockholm
Chalmers University of Technology, Göteborg (engineering and technology)
Handelshögskolan i Stockholm (Stockholm School of Economics)
Sveriges Lantbruksuniversitet (University of Agricultural Sciences), Uppsala.

TEACHER EDUCATION

1977–88

Teacher training was carried out within the universities or in *Högskola*. The basic
qualification for teaching at the junior and middle levels of comprehensive schools was
obtained after a two-and-a-half or three-year course. For teaching at the third stage of
the comprehensive school or at the *Gymnasieskolan* students followed integrated four
or four-and-a-half year programmes consisting of three or three-and-a-half years'
theoretical study and one year's teaching-method including teaching practice. The
curriculum was set up strictly following the Education Act regulations. At least three
subjects were studied for the comprehensive school and at least two for the *Gymnasium*
with at least 60 points in one subject. The combination of subjects was also regulated.
A one-year education course was available for those fulfilling the theoretical
requirements and wanting to teach at the third stage of comprehensive schools or
Gymnasium.

Since July 1988

Teacher training for the comprehensive school years 1–9 has been reformed. It is now a
basic common training for all teachers in the comprehensive schools with specialization
for grades 1–7 or 4–9 and for different subject areas. For grades 1–7 (140 points) the
specialist subject areas are mathematics/science or Swedish/social sciences. At some
training institutes, studies in an immigrant language as a first language, Swedish as a
second language or basic teaching of adults are available options. For grades 4–9
(140–180 points), the options are science, mathematics/science, social sciences,
Swedish/foreign language or a practical or aesthetical subject in combination with
another subject. The general requirement for entry to a teachers' college is the same as
for other university studies. Special requirements vary according to the subject area
chosen.

Teacher training for upper secondary school (*gymnasielararutbildning*, formerly
amneslararlinjen) is still based on a certain combination of subjects with a total of 160
to 200/220 points, 60 or 80 points in the main subjects and a 40 point education course.

Since 1993

It is now possible for upper secondary school teachers to have only one subject relevant
for school teaching, which must be at least 80 points out of the required 140 points of
academic subjects. Similar to the system of teacher training before 1977, it is also
possible for prospective teachers for both lower and upper secondary school to first
study academic subjects at the university and then a 40 point education course at the
Institute for Teacher Training.

Switzerland

Switzerland is a confederation of twenty-six cantons and half-cantons. School Education is primarily the responsibility of the individual cantons, so the system in operation for each area varies. Higher Education is the responsibility of the twenty six cantons jointly with the confederation. (It is suggested that enquirers contact the National Academic Recognition Information Centre regarding qualifications which do not seem to fit the general pattern outlined here.)

There is no federal ministry of education, but there are federal regulations for studies, training and certification in certain fields (medicine, veterinary medicine, dentistry, pharmacy, food chemistry, surveying, physical education teaching, and vocational continuation school or technical school teaching).

Nursing is a cantonal responsibility, but in 1976 all the cantons signed an agreement with the Swiss Red Cross (SRK), which has taken over the responsibility for most non-university health professions (nursing, midwifery, radiology assistant etc.). The SRK organizes and supervises the education; the diplomas which it confers are recognized by all the cantons in entire Switzerland. The SRK is also responsible for the recognition of foreign diplomas in the same field.

Vocational training (in industrial fields, handicrafts, commerce, banking and insurance, transportation, hotel management and restoration, service industries, agriculture and home economics) is under federal control to ensure that it is uniform and that the qualifications obtained are valid throughout Switzerland. There is also a **Federal Maturity Certificate,** and a system of **Federally recognized Cantonal Maturity Certificates,** all of which give admission to all institutions of higher education. The two Federal Institutes of Technology in Zürich and Lausanne, Eidgenossische Technische Hochschule Zurich (ETHZ) and Ecole Polytechniqe Federale Lausanne (EPFL) are also under federal control.

The Swiss Conference of the Heads of Cantonal Departments of Education, which co-ordinates school reform throughout Switzerland, approved the Educational Co-ordination Agreement in 1970. This was ratified by twenty-one of the twenty-six cantons. Under this agreement certain standards were established: uniformity of age of entry to school (six years); duration of compulsory schooling to be nine years; and the length of study to be undertaken by pupils who take the maturity examination (minimum twelve years, maximum thirteen). Vital differences remain, however, between the Italian, French and German-speaking cantons and between cantons within each of these linguistic regions. For example, entry to school in many cantons is at the age of seven.

Another recent initiative taken on at cantonal level by the Swiss Conference of the Heads of Cantonal Departments of Education, is the *inter-cantonal agreement on the recognition of diplomas.* Once implemented it will – within Switzerland – regulate the recognition of all cantonal certificates and diplomas as well as the comparable foreign certificates. Diplomas in the area of, for example: general secondary education; *gymnasium* and *liceé*; cantonal apprenticeships; teacher education of all levels;

education in social work; education in art, music theatre and design; education for librarians and documentalists; and adult education are included. The agreement stipulates also that co-operation between the federal government and the cantons is to be sought in the area of professional or academic maturity certificates and in international affairs.

There are international schools, particularly in the French-speaking region, which may offer the courses and qualifications offered by the national schools but are run predominantly on American or British lines and offer American or British qualifications.

There are a number of private institutions, both at school level and at further education level, especially in the area of hotel management and catering. Some of these enjoy federal recognition or recognition by one or more cantons.

Since 1970, the period of compulsory education has been nine years throughout Switzerland, with twelve or thirteen years leading to the **Maturity certificate**.

The media of instruction are principally German, French or Italian, depending on the language of the region. In the Romansch-speaking areas of the Grisons the medium of instruction in primary schools is Romansch. Pupils learn German as a foreign language from the fourth year, and their secondary schooling, with the exception of biology and music, is in German.

Since 1989, the school year has begun between August and October (after the summer holidays) all over Switzerland.

Cantons and half-cantons

Canton	Medium of instruction
Aargau	German
Appenzell is divided into the half-cantons of:	
Appenzell-Ausser Rhoden	German
Appenzell-Inner Rhoden	German
Basel (Basle) is divided into the half-cantons of:	
Basel-Landschaft (country)	German
Basel-Stadt (town)	German
Bern (Berne)	German, French in the Jura region
Fribourg (Freiburg)	French, German
Genève (Geneva)	French
Glarus	German
Graubünden (Grisons)	Romansch (at primary school), German (at secondary school), Italian
Jura	French
Luzern (Lucerne)	German

Neuchâtel	French
Schaffhausen	German
Schwyz	German
Solothurn	German
St Gallen	German
Thurgau	German
Ticino	Italian (rarely German)

Unterwalden is divided into the half-cantons of:

Nidwalden	German
Obwalden	German
Uri	German
Valais	French, German
Vaud	French
Zug	German
Zürich	German

EVALUATION IN BRITAIN

School

Federal Maturity Certificate/Maturitätszeugnis (German-speaking cantons)/**Certificat de Maturité** (French-speaking cantons, except Vaud)/**Baccalauréat** (Vaud)/**Attestato di Maturità** (Italian-speaking canton of Ticino) –

AND

the **Federally recognized Cantonal Maturity Certificate (Eidgenössisch anerkanntes kantonales Maturitätszeugnis/Certificat de matutité cantonal reconnu par la Confédération/Attestato di maturità cantonale riconosciuto dalla Confederazione)** –

may be considered to satisfy the general entrance requirements of British higher education institutions.

Cantonal Maturity Certificate (Kantonale Maturität/Maturité Cantonale/Maturità Cantonale) – **NOT RECOGNIZED FEDERALLY** – does not automatically satisfy the general entrance requirements of British higher education institutions; students may be considered on an individual basis.

Higher

Vordiplomprüfung I/Propédeutique I/Examen Préliminaire I – conferred after one full year of study (two semesters);

Vordiplomprüfung II/Zwischenprüfung/Propédeutique II/Examen Préliminaire II/Demi-Licence – conferred after two full years of study (four semesters) –

generally considered comparable to a standard between GCE Advanced and British Bachelor degree; may be given advanced standing by British higher education institutions.

Diplom/Diplôme; Lizentiat/Licence; Staatsdiplom/Diplôme d'Etat – generally considered comparable to British Bachelor (Honours) degree standard, although the course lasts longer than in the UK.

MARKING SYSTEMS

School and Higher

Different scales are used:

1–6 (maximum); minimum pass 4 (most frequently used)
1–10 (maximum); minimum pass 6
6–1 (maximum); minimum pass 3.

6	10	1	*sehr gut/très bien/*	very good
–	9	–	*molto bene*	
5	8	2	*gut/bien/bene*	good
–	7	–		
4	6	3	*genügend/suffisant/*	fair/pass
–	5	–	*sufficiente*	
3	4	4	*ungenügend/insuffisant/*	poor/fail
–	3	–	*insufficiente*	
2	2	5	*schlecht/schwach/sehr*	
			schwach/	fail
			mauvais/molto debole	
			(nullo)	
–	1	–		

The **Federal Maturity Examination** is marked out of 90 (using the 1–6 scale) with 58 as the pass-mark. Each of the eleven subjects taken carries a maximum mark of 6 (making a maximum possible total of 66), four of the eleven subjects carry double marks (maximum extra of 24), making a maximum possible total of 90. The four subjects which carry double marks are usually underlined on the certificate.

SCHOOL EDUCATION

The school system in years per canton:

	Primary (+ Lower Secondary)	Upper Secondary (NOT COMPULSORY)
Aargau	5 + 4	+ 4
Appenzell:		
Appenzell-Ausser Rhoden	6 + 3	+ 4
Appenzell-Inner Rhoden	6 + 3	+ 4
Basel (Basle):		
Basel-Landschaft (county)	5 + 4	+ 4
Basel-Stadt (town)	5 + 4	+ 4
Bern (Berne)	6 + 3	+ 4
Fribourg (Freiburg)	5 + 4	+ 4 (or 6+3 + 4)
Genève (Geneva)	6 + 3	+ 4
Glarus	6 + 3	+ 4
Graubünden (Grisons)	6 + 3	+ 4
Jura	6 + 3	+ 4
Luzern (Lucerne)	6 + 3	+ 4
Neuchâtel	5 + 4	+ 3
Schaffhausen	6 + 3	+ 4
Schwyz	6 + 3	+ 4
Solothurn	5 + 4	+ 4 (or 6+3 + 4)
St Gallen	6 + 3	+ 4
Thurgau	6 + 3	+ 4
Ticino	5 + 4	+ 4
Unterwalden:		
Nidwalden	6 + 3	+ 4
Obwalden	6 + 3	+ 4
Uri	6 + 3	+ 4
Valais	6 + 3	+ 4/5
Vaud	4 + 5	+ 3
Zug	6 + 3	+ 4
Zürich	6 + 3	+ 3

Pre-primary

About ninety per cent of children attend at least one year of pre-school education – *Kindergarten/Écoles Enfantines/Case dei Bambini*. Kindergarten is not compulsory.

Primary

The period of schooling varies according to the canton from four to six years for children from age six (sometimes seven). In cantons where primary education covers six years, this period is generally divided into a three-year lower and a three-year upper cycle. During the lower cycle (of the six-year course) or the full four or five-year course pupils study their mother tongue, reading, writing, arithmetic, physical education, singing and environmental studies and, in the upper cycle, art.

Lower secondary

This represents the second part of nine year compulsory education, and lasts between four and six years, depending on the canton and the length of primary education. This cycle is characterized as middle/lower secondary, and courses are taken at one of the following:

Realschule/Mittelschule/Progymnase/Sekundarschule/Collège Cantonal/Ecole Secondaire/Collège Moderne/Ginnasio/Sculoa Maggiore.

During this cycle and the upper cycle of the six-year primary course (in cantons where this exists) the study of the second national language is compulsory; in the French-speaking cantons it is German, in the German-speaking cantons French, and in Ticino it is French and German.

There are three types of lower secondary school: basic, intermediate and academic. For entrance to the last two types pupils must pass an entrance examination. The curriculum of the basic type covers: mother tongue, mathematics, elementary science, drawing, geography, history, industrial arts or domestic science, physical education, singing and writing. The intermediate lower secondary schools offer the same curriculum, but at a more advanced academic level. Pupils who complete the course at a basic or intermediate secondary school normally proceed to vocational school or general education continuation school or take up an apprenticeship. Pupils who complete a course at an academic lower secondary school can proceed to an academic upper secondary school *(Gymnasium).*

In a few cantons this cycle of education is called the *Cycle d'Orientation* and contains the various types of lower secondary (and upper primary) education in a course offered by a comprehensive school. This system operates in Geneva, Valais, Fribourg, Neuchâtel and Ticino.

Pupils do not normally obtain a qualification on completion of this cycle of education, but sometimes a **Certificat d'Etudes** or **Certificat Secondaire** is awarded. However, completion of a course at the intermediate level is a prerequisite for some professions (e.g. nurse, commercial secretary). In contrast, most of the students following the basic course can only qualify for less-demanding jobs in the same field (e.g. medical auxiliary, clerk).

Upper secondary

This lasts three to five years, or three to four years at a post-compulsory level, depending on the canton, and is undertaken at:

Gymnasium/Gymnase/Lyceum/Lyzeum/Lycée/Liceo/Istituto/Kollegium/Collège Classique.

Before the agreement of 1970, schools offered a grade fourteen, but this now only exists in the canton of Valais for pupils taking the specialization A or B. Under Swiss law all pupils preparing the maturity examination have to complete six years of preparatory (secondary) work.

Between 1973 and 1995 there has been the opportunity for pupils to specialize in one of five options (before that only options A, B and C were available):

A   Latin/Greek
B   Latin/modern languages
C   mathematics/science
D   modern languages
E   economic science.

Of the eleven subjects in the curriculum nine are compulsory throughout the cycle and the same for all pupils: two national languages (i.e. two of French, German or Italian), history, geography, mathematics, physics, chemistry, natural sciences and drawing or music. In the maturity examinations pupils must include, as a minimum, two national languages, mathematics and one of the specialist subjects of their option. These subjects and history must be studied during the final year. Specialist subjects per option are:

A   Latin and Greek
B   Latin and the third national language or English
C   descriptive geometry and the third national language or English
D   English and the third national language or Spanish or Russian
E   economic science and the third national language or English.

Depending on the canton, there may be additional compulsory subjects. In order to follow a course in the humanities students must either have studied Latin or must take a special Latin course.

On completion of this cycle, pupils may take the examinations for one of three maturity certificates:

Federal Maturity Certificate (Maturitätszeugnis/Certificat de Maturité/ Baccalauréat/Attestato di Maturità);

Federally recognized Cantonal Maturity Certificate; (Eidgenössisch anerkanntes kantonales Maturitätszeugnis/Certificat de matutité cantonal reconnu par la Confederation/Attestato di maturità cantonale riconosciuto dalla Confederazione);

Cantonal Maturity Certificate (Kantonale Maturität/Maturité Cantonale/ Maturità Cantonale).

The value of the first and second is the same. Students holding either of these certificates can study any subject at university without further examinations. The number of students who take the Federal Maturity is rather small; it is offered mainly in private schools.

Public schools (*lycee, college, Gymnasium, Kollegium* etc.) offer programmes which lead to the **Federally recognized Cantonal Maturity Certificate** in the majority of cases. Most Swiss students therefore earn this certificate.

Cantonal Maturity certificates which are not federally recognized are specialized (e.g. artistic type **M-Maturitat** conferred by Canton Basle or **Maturité artistique genevoise** conferred by Canton Geneva or pedagogical maturity certificates awarded by various Cantons) and have a rather restricted value within Switzerland. If they are accepted for entrance to university, not all subjects may be studied. They are designed as preparation for a specific vocation, and often Swiss universities decide whether to accept them on a case-by-case basis. Even within the issuing canton, recognition is not guaranteed. Only a small percentage of all students hold a **Cantonal Maturity Certificate** which is not Federally recognized.

Each canton has its own regulations for the cantonal examinations (not federally recognized), which follow the outline of the federal examinations, though sometimes they are a little less rigorous and the final marks include an element of continuous assessment. The cantonal examinations are usually offered in the same five subject options, but not all options may be available at all schools in each canton. In the French-speaking cantons pupils may receive both a **Federal Maturity Certificate** and the **Cantonal Maturity Certificate (Bachelier/Baccalauréat)**.

The **Federal Maturity Certificate** has as its main heading **Schweizerische Eidgenossenschaft/Confédération Suisse/Confederazione Svizzera** (Swiss Confederation), while the **Federally recognized Cantonal Maturity Certificate** is designated **Eidgenössisch anerkanntes kantonales Maturitätszeugnis/Certificat de matutité cantonal reconnu par la Confederation/Attestato di maturità cantonale riconosciuto dalla Confederazione**. All diplomas bearing one of these designations (regardless of the issuing body) and the words 'according to the ordinance of the Federal Council concerning the recognition of the *Maturité* certificate of 22 May 1968' are federally recognized and controlled and of the same standard. The **Cantonal Maturity Certificate** has the name of the canton as its heading.

In February 1995 the Federal Government and the cantons agreed on new regulations on the recognition of the Swiss Maturity Certificates. This agreement entered into force in August 1995, and the deadline for implementation is August 2003.

Importantly, the new regulations outlined below cover only the **Cantonal Maturity Certificates** which are federally recognized. It does not concern those few **Cantonal Maturity Certificates** which do not have federal recognition, nor **Federal Maturity Certificates** (in this case a revision is anticipated).

Before this agreement, the federal government had sole responsibility for the federal recognition of **Maturity Certificates**. The new regulations share this responsibility between the federal government and the cantons. A new Swiss Maturity Committee will be established which will have representatives from both sides, and will propose the recognition of **Maturity Certificates** they are presented with.

Maturity Certificates Types A–E have been abolished. Only one type of **Swiss Maturity Certificate** remains. Types A–E are replaced by a system of mandatory and optional subjects. The total number of subjects studied has been reduced from eleven to nine. Seven of these are compulsory subjects.

The final examination must be taken in five subjects (plus one other determined by the canton). In addition an independent research project must be completed.

Grading is on a scale from 0–6. Four is the minimum pass mark. There are also half grades (e.g. 5.5). In order to qualify for a **Maturity Certificate** the student must compensate for all grades below four. The students must not have more than three grades below four.

The minimum total duration of education remains twelve years. At least four years of upper secondary schooling must be spent on a programme preparing for the **Maturity** examination.

Vocational secondary

On completion of primary schooling and/or basic/intermediate secondary school pupils may opt for a full-time vocational secondary course or an apprenticeship (which includes part-time attendance at school).

Technical and vocational training is the responsibility of cantonal and local governments under the guidelines of Federal law. The Federal agency is the Federal Office for Industry, Crafts and Labour (*Bundesamt für Industrie, Arbeit und Gewerbe/Office Fédérale de l'Industrie, des Arts et Métiers et du Travail*).

Full-time vocational courses at schools are available in commerce and artistic fields. Courses normally last three to four years. At the full-time commercial schools (*Handelsschulen/Ecoles Supérieures de Commerce/Scuole di Commercio*) pupils may take the examinations for the **Handelsmatürität/Maturité Commerciale** as well as for the **Federal Certificate of Capability; (Fähigkeitszeugnis/Certificat de Capacité/Attestato di Capacità**) on completion of the four-year course.

Apprenticeships may be undertaken:

by in-service training with a firm/factory/office, with part-time attendance (minimum of one day per week) at a vocational continuation school (*Gewerbeschule/Gewerbliche Berufsschule/Ecole Professionnelle/Scuola Professionale*);

by in-service training, with general education given in a teaching workshop (*Lehrwerkstätte/Ecole de Métiers/Scuola Cantonale d'Arti e Mestiere*), such full-time schools being run by industries or the cantons to train apprentices for particular vocations;

or by in-service training, with general education given in a workshop school (*Werksschule/Ecole Atelier*), such schools usually being run by large companies to train future employees.

Training, normally lasting three to four years, from the minimum age of fifteen, is subject to federal regulations which determine the designation of the profession, length of apprenticeship and organization of examinations. On completion, pupils take a final examination (**Lehrabschlussprüfung/Examen de Fin d'Apprentissage/Esame di Fine Tirocino**) conducted by the cantonal authority. Success leads to the qualification of **Federal Certificate of Capability (Fähigkeitszeugnis/Certificat de Capacité/ Attestato di Capacità**) and the status of skilled worker. The certificate does not normally state the length of training, but it is usually possible to obtain a transcript of marks.

Since the 1970s, higher vocational schools (*Berufsmittelschulen/Ecoles Professionnelles Supérieures/Scuole Medie Professionali*) have been established. These offer academic instruction beyond the compulsory minimum. Pupils have to study two languages (their own plus a second national language or English) and contemporary history. They still only receive the **Federal Certificate of Capability**, although in certain circumstances a **Berufsmittelschuldiplom/Baccalauréat Technique** may be awarded.

There are also a few general education continuation upper secondary schools (*Diplommittelschule/Ecole de Culture Générale/Scuola Cultura Generale*) which offer two or three years of general subjects for pupils who have completed compulsory schooling. The diploma awarded is rarely accepted for university entrance, but since 1970 it has been recognized throughout Switzerland. It is often required by students wishing to start nursing school or other health professions.

FURTHER EDUCATION

Higher technical and commercial schools (*Höhere Technische Lehranstalt (HTL)/Ecole Technique Supérieure (ETS)/ Scuola Tecnica Superiore/Technikums und Höhere Wirtschaftsschulen*) offer courses lasting three or four years. For some courses, students are admitted directly on completion of compulsory schooling (i.e. nine years' study), whereas most students will have completed their apprenticeship or attended a craft school. Students have to sit an entrance examination in mathematics, drawing and their own national language. Students who have completed a course of academic upper secondary education have to undertake practical training before beginning the course proper. There are both day schools, where the length of study is three years, and evening schools (four years).

HIGHER EDUCATION

Courses are offered by eight universities, which are under cantonal legislation: three in the French-speaking cantons (Genève, Lausanne, Neuchâtel); four in the German-speaking cantons (Basel, Bern, Zürich, and the <u>University of St Gallen</u> – Luzern which offer courses in business administration, economics, law and social sciences); and one using both French and German for its medium of instruction (Fribourg). There is no university in the Italian-speaking region, although there are currently (1994) plans to establish one. There are two Federal Institutes of Technology (Zürich and Lausanne) and graduate schools specializing in law, business, economics and public administration (for example, St Gallen).

The **Federal Maturity Certificate** or the **Federally recognized Cantonal Maturity Certificate** (and, in some cases, the **Cantonal Maturity Certificate**) satisfies the admission requirement to degree courses. There is no *numerus clausus* for courses of higher education, except in medicine.

In general, the first degree, obtained after a minimum of four years, is the **Diplom/Licence/Lizentiat**. In pharmacy and architecture, courses last five years, including a one year internship in the field; in veterinary medicine and dentistry, five years; and in medicine, five to six years. In many courses students take an intermediate examination on general studies and basic work in their subject at the end of the first year: **Vordiplomprüfung I/Propédeutique I/Examen Prélimiaire I** and an intermediate examination at the end of the second year: **Vordiplomprüfung II/Zwischenprüfung/Propédeutique II/Examen Préliminaire II**. Both of these examinations give the student only the right to continue their studies. On some courses at the universities in the French-speaking cantons a **Demi-Licence** may be obtained after the first part of the course (two to three years).

Although a minimum period of study is stipulated for a degree, most students take longer. Students sometimes move from university to university during their studies. For courses in certain professional fields it is not possible for students to move to another university during their studies, as the courses are more structured.

At the Federal Institutes of Technology the first qualification **Staatsdiplom/Diplôme d'Etat** may be obtained after nine to ten semesters.

The qualification obtained on successful completion of a course of higher education does not automatically entitle the holders to practise their profession, e.g. medicine, law, architecture. They must pass a state examination officially set by their cantonal authorities; in medicine this is a federal examination.

To obtain a **Doctorate**, a doctoral thesis has to be written, defended and accepted by a professor. In many cases the thesis is written during the course of an assistantship, the duration of which is four to eight years.

Shorter postgraduate taught courses (often part-time) are also available, referred to variously as **Nachdiplomstudium/Postgraduiertenstudium/Etudes de troisième cycle**. No diplomas are conferred, but students receive *Zertifikat/Zertifikat NDS, DIS-Zertifikat/Ausweis/Certificat/Certificat de la DIS*.

TEACHER EDUCATION

The requirements for prospective teachers vary greatly from canton to canton, except for teachers at vocational continuation school or technical school teachers, where there are federal requirements. The following diploma is required: **Eidgenössisch diplomlerter (eidg dipl)/Berufsschullehrer/Diplôme fédéral de maître professionnel/Diploma federale di docente professionali.**

Primary

Except for the cantons of Genève, Basel, Jura, Neuchâtel, Aargau, Vaud, Zürich and Schaffhausen training is undertaken over four to five years at a *Lehrer(innen)seminar* (teacher training college)/*Ecole Normale/Scuola Magistrale*, after completing nine years of compulsory schooling. In the German-speaking cantons half of the *Lehrer(innen)seminar* are divided into two phases:

first phase – three or three-and-a-half years of secondary level general education

second phase – one-and-a-half or two years of full time pedagogical education and training.

The other half of the teacher training colleges are mono-phasic; secondary level general education and pedagogical training are intertwined during the whole four or five years.

For students holding the **Maturity Certificate,** full time training takes between one-and-a-half and three years. This training is undertaken either at a *Lehrer(innen)seminar* or at isolated teacher training institutions. These students may go straight into the second phase, described above.

In the cantons of Basel, Neuchâtel, Aargau, Jura, Vaud and Genève training is only open to holders of the **Maturity Certificate** (either federal or cantonal). The course lasts two years (full time) in the first five cantons and three years in Geneva. In the canton of Aargau, holders of the **Cantonal Maturity Certificate** enter the Höhere Pädagogische Lehranstalt (HPL) for a two-year course leading to the **Primarlehrerpatent**.

In the cantons of Aargau, Bern, Fribourg, Jura, Luzern, Thurgau and Ticino students with vocational training may undertake specialized studies at a *Lehrer(innen)seminar* lasting two to four years.

All these types of teacher training lead to the qualification of **Primarlehrerdiplom/ Patent/Fähigkeitszeugnis für Elementarlehrer/Lehrerpatent/Wahlfähigkeit als Lehrer/Certificat d'Aptitude à l'enseignement Primaire/Brevet d'enseignement Primaire/Patente di Maestro di Scuola Elementare.**

Secondary

This includes the training undertaken for the basic or intermediate cycle in those cantons where primary education lasts no longer than four to five years.

The distinction in training for lower and upper secondary school teachers is made in the German-speaking cantons, Ticino and Neuchâtel. There are no teacher training courses for prospective upper secondary school teachers in Ticino; students undertake studies in a foreign language – German or French.

Students holding the **Maturity Certificate** may undertake a university course lasting six to eight semesters (depending on the canton), leading to the qualification of **Mittellehrerdiplom/Sekundarlehrerpatent/Fachpatent/Bezirkslehrerpatent.**

Students who hold the primary teachers' certificate may either:

take a course at a teacher training college lasting one to eight semesters, leading to the qualification of **Bezirkslehrerpatent/Mittellehrerdiplom/Oberschullehrerdiplom/ Reallehrerdiplom/Sekundarlehrerpatent**;

or undertake a university course (as above).

In Neuchâtel, prospective teachers undertake a six-semester course from the entrance level of the **Maturity Certificate**, leading to the qualification of **Brevet pour l'enseignement du Degré Secondaire Inférieur**; if the prospective teacher already holds a **Licence** (university diploma), a two-semester course leads to the **Certificat d'Aptitude Pédagogique**.

In the German-speaking cantons the students must complete a degree course at university beyond their **Lizenziat** in order to acquire the diploma of an upper secondary teacher; **Diplom für das Höhere Lehramt/Gymnasiallehrerdiplom/Patent für das Höhere Lehramt/Oberlehrerdiplom**.

Teaching qualification by different school levels:

Primary school;

Primarlehrerdiplom
Brevet d'enseignement Primaire
Certificat d'Aptitude à l'enseignement Primaire
Patente di Maestro di Scuola Elementare

Secondary school (lower);

Mittellehrerdiplom
Sekundarlehrerpatent
Bezirkslehrerpatent
Oberschullehrerdiplom
Reallehrerdiplom
Brevet pour l'enseignement du Degré Secondaire Inférieur

Secondary school (upper);

Certificat d'Aptitude Pédagogique
Diplom für das Höhere Lehramt
Gymnasiallehrerdiplom
Patent für das Höhere Lehramt
Oberlehrerdiplom.

Syria

Education is universal, free and compulsory up to age fourteen (the end of the preparatory cycle).

The medium of instruction is Arabic but both French and English are taught as second languages in the preparatory and secondary cycles.

The school year runs from the first of September to mid June and the university year from the first of September till late June.

EVALUATION IN BRITAIN

School

Al Shahada Al Thanawiya/Baccalauréat (Secondary School Leaving Certificate) – generally considered comparable to GCSE standard (grades A, B and C) on a subject-for-subject basis, with the exception of English language, when a minimum overall mark of 60 per cent has been obtained. Students with very good results may be considered for admission to access/bridging courses.

Higher

Licence/Bachelor degree – generally considered comparable to a standard between GCE Advanced and British Bachelor degree; may be given advanced standing by British higher education institutions. Exceptionally, students with very high grades or who have taken a course lasting longer than four years (for example, engineering), may be considered for admission to postgraduate study.

MARKING SYSTEMS

School

Marks in the literary branch of the **Baccalauréat** are out of a maximum of 240; the minimum pass-mark is 102.

Marks in the scientific branch of the **Baccalauréat** are out of a maximum of 260; the minimum pass-mark is 104.

Higher

Marks are based on a percentage system; the minimum pass-mark is 50 per cent.

90–100 per cent	*martabet al Sharaf*	honours (rarely awarded)
80–89	*momtaz*	excellent
70–79	*jayed Jeddar*	very good
60–69	*jayed*	good
50–59	*makboul*	pass
0–49	*raseb*	fail

SCHOOL EDUCATION

Primary

This lasts for six years and children enter school at age six. During the first three years, pupils must repeat the year if they receive more than two unsatisfactory markings (*daief*) in reading, writing and arithmetic. In the fourth, fifth and sixth years, further subjects are studied. Pupils must repeat the year if they receive more than two unsatisfactory markings.

Preparatory/lower secondary

This lasts for three years. Pupils study a wider range of subjects. At the end of grade 9 pupils sit an examination for the **Preparatory School Leaving Certificate** known as **Al Kafa'a**. Maximum marks in the **Al Kafa'a** are 290; the minimum pass-mark is 122. Pupils must pass in Arabic to obtain the certificate. Pupils with scores of 180 and above proceed to ordinary schools, the rest go on to technical schools.

Secondary

This lasts three years and covers grades 10 to 12 (ages fifteen to seventeen). Students may enter either the general or technical branches, although entry is selective and based on the **Al Kafa'a** examination.

General

The first year is introductory. After this pupils enter one of two streams: literary or scientific. At the end of the three-year course, pupils sit for the **Secondary School Leaving Certificate** known as the **Baccalauréat** or **Al Shahada Al Thanawiya**, which is the only qualification which gives automatic access to higher education.

Technical

All technical secondary schools are run by the government. Technical secondary education is divided into two streams: industrial and commercial. At the end of the course pupils take the **Technical Baccalauréat**. This offers only limited opportunities in the field of further education, such as entry to the Institute of Technical Education in Aleppo.

Agriculture

The Ministry of Agriculture runs various secondary agricultural schools, two of which offer special training (one in veterinary science in Damascus, the other in farm machinery in Al-Hassaka).

Religious

Religious education in Islam is free and run by the Ministry of Religious Affairs (*Awkaf*). It provides a six-year course parallel to the preparatory and secondary cycles in the secular system.

UNRWA SCHOOLS

The United Nations Relief and Works Agency (UNRWA) runs over one hundred schools at primary and preparatory levels for Palestinian refugees. English is the only foreign language taught in these schools. UNRWA also provides teacher training at its Development Unit and runs a Vocational Training Centre at Mezzeh, Damascus for holders of the **Al Kafa'a** (**Preparatory School Leaving Certificate**) and the **Baccalauréat**.

HIGHER EDUCATION

University

There are four universities: Damascus University, Aleppo University, Tichreen University at Latakia and Al-Baath University at Homs.

Competition for university places is fierce, particularly for the prestigious faculties of medicine, dentistry, and engineering. Standards are consequently higher in those fields.

Licence/Bachelor degree courses last four to six years and the medium of instruction is Arabic.

Most faculties at the four Universities provide one-year **Postgraduate Diploma** courses and two-year **Master's** courses by instruction. Certain Faculties at Damascus and Aleppo Universities provide **PhD**s by research. Research is undertaken in many departments.

Intermediate

There are 95 Intermediate Institutes throughout the country. Study is for two years following the **Technical Baccalauréat**. Courses are more practical than theoretical. Intermediate Institutes are under the supervision of the Ministry of Higher Education for academic matters and other ministries for administration and finance. Courses lead to an **Associate degree** in the chosen field of study.

TEACHER EDUCATION

Primary

Training is by means of a two-year post-secondary course.

Preparatory/lower secondary

Holders of the **Baccalauréat** attend a two-year training course. Graduates may teach without special training.

Secondary

Graduate students study at university faculties of education. For subjects where there is a teacher shortage, preparatory school teachers are given two-year training at an intermediate institute.

Vocational

Holders of the **Technical Baccalauréat** follow a two-year course at an intermediate institute. A new teacher training institute for vocational teachers is being established.

Taiwan

The Ministry of Education formulates national policies for education at all levels. The system is highly centralized.

Education is free of tuition fees and compulsory for nine years from age six to fifteen. Incidental fees are charged.

There is a substantial private sector at all levels of education.

The medium of instruction is Mandarin Chinese.

The academic year consists of two eighteen-week semesters and runs from August to July.

EVALUATION IN BRITAIN

School

Senior High School Leaving Certificate – generally considered comparable to GCSE standard (grades A, B and C) on a subject-for-subject basis, with the exception of English language, but overall judged to be of a higher standard. Candidates may be considered for admission to access/bridging courses.

Further

Junior College Diploma – generally considered comparable to BTEC National Diploma / N/SVQ level 3 / Advanced GNVQ/GSVQ standard; may be considered to satisfy the general entrance requirements of British higher education institutions (candidates with very good results from prestigious institutions may approach BTEC Higher National Diploma / N/SVQ level 4 standard).

Holders of diplomas from junior colleges may be considered for direct admission to the first year of a degree course; candidates from prestigious junior colleges/departments within colleges may be considered for second year entry.

For further details on specific junior colleges and their departments enquirers should contact the National Academic Recognition Information Centre.

English Language Requirements

It is recommended that applicants should take one of the following examinations, all available in Taiwan:

The British Council's IELTS examination. A score of 5.5 should be the minimum requirement.

A TOEFL score of 450 or better is necessary for undergraduate study in the English-speaking area.

There are also registered examination centres in Taiwan of Pitman Examinations Institute and other ABB members where levels of tests acceptable for matriculation purposes by British higher education institutions may be sat.

Higher

Bachelor degree – generally considered comparable to a standard between GCE Advanced and British Bachelor degree; may be given advanced standing by British higher education institutions. Candidates from prestigious institutions may be considered for admission to postgraduate study.

Successful completion of the first year of degree studies at a Taiwanese university may also be considered for entry to the first year of the British Bachelor degree course, so long as there is curriculum compatibility. Completion of more than one year might justify second year entry.

It is certainly not necessary to demand the possession of a Taiwan first degree for first year entry in the UK.

For further information enquirers should contact the National Academic Recognition Information Centre.

MARKING SYSTEM

A percentage grading system is in use at all levels:

A   80–100 per cent
B   70–79
C   60–69
D   50–59

70 per cent is the minimum pass-mark in postgraduate courses and 60 per cent in undergraduate courses.

SCHOOL EDUCATION

Primary

This covers six years. A certificate is awarded on completion of the cycle.

Secondary

This also covers six years: three years' junior high school and three years' senior high school or senior vocational high school.

Junior high school

Junior high schools are intended both for terminal education and as preparation for further and higher education. The study of English is compulsory. Successful graduates receive a certificate and may proceed to senior secondary schools or five-year junior colleges.

Senior high school/senior vocational high school

Senior secondary education is offered by senior high schools and senior vocational high schools. Graduates of the junior high school take different entrance examinations for the two different types of school. The study of English is compulsory. Most students attend vocational high schools rather than high schools.

Senior high schools offer a more academic course. Students specialize in either natural sciences or social sciences. They attend either for three years full-time or for a four-year evening-class course. They are selected for one of these divisions on the basis of their performance in the **Senior High School Entrance Examination**.

Senior vocational high schools offer a more practical education. There are nine types of school: agriculture; agriculture and technology; commerce; home economics and commerce; marine technology; medicine and nursing; technology; technology and commerce; and technology and home economics. There are also a few Senior High Schools which offer a limited number of vocational courses. Students are required to follow an academic or vocational route. As at senior high school, students attend either during the day or in the evening. Students are selected on the basis of a **Senior Vocational High School Entrance Examination.**

Although it is possible to do so, most students do not proceed to a four-year college or university degree course, but continue their education on two-year Junior College Diploma courses or four-year Technical college/Polytechnic University courses.

At both types of high school at the end of the course successful students are awarded a **Senior High School Leaving Certificate**.

FURTHER EDUCATION

Junior colleges provide two different types of programme: five-year courses for graduates of Junior High Schools and two-year courses for graduates of Senior High and Senior Vocational High Schools. Admission is by entrance examination. All colleges specialize in particular subject areas. These areas are: agriculture; agriculture and technology; arts; commerce; foreign languages; home economics; hotel and catering; management; industrial and commercial management; marine technology; medicine and pharmacology; medical technology and nursing; nursing; physical education and technology; not to mention the police and military institutions of Junior College level. On successful completion of the course students are awarded a **diploma**.

HIGHER EDUCATION

Higher education is provided by four-year technical colleges/polytechnics and universities. To qualify as a university an institute must consist of three or more colleges or faculties.

Institutes of technology are operated by the government, and are designed to offer vocational school and junior college graduates a chance to receive advanced education specializing in technology. Admission is granted only for those who pass the entrance examination. The length of study is two years for junior college graduates and four years for senior vocational school graduates.

Admission to university undergraduate programmes

Admission is based on the results obtained in the **Universities and Colleges Joint Entrance Examination**. This examination is supervised by the Ministry of Education, and is regarded as difficult. Only about half those entering are generally successful.

The **Universities and Colleges Joint Entrance Examination** is split into four academic groups and the arts group:

Academic Group One:
humanities, business, law and social sciences and related subjects.

Academic Group Two:
engineering and science and related subjects.

Academic Group Three:
biology and medicine and related subjects.

Academic Group Four:
agricultural science and related subjects.

Arts Group:
arts and performing arts and related subjects.

It is important to note that institutions in Taiwan are obliged to accept students whose results meet their minimum entrance requirements. Taiwan institutions therefore have no say in selecting students, no interviews are held, and no consideration is given to work experience, enthusiasm, motivation or any other factor.

Most **Bachelor degree** courses last four years. The exceptions are medicine (seven years), dentistry (six years), veterinary medicine (five years) and education (five years). A total of 128 credits are required for a **Bachelor degree**.

Courses closely follow the US model involving education in breadth and credit accumulation.

Facilities in universities are good and can be compared with those found in many Western European countries; science and engineering laboratories are comparable to those in the UK and libraries are well-stocked.

Master's degrees normally involve two years' study following a **Bachelor degree**. A **Doctorate** requires a minimum of a further two years' study.

TEACHER EDUCATION

Admission to training courses is based on the **Universities and Colleges Joint Entrance Examination**.

Primary

Training is at post-secondary level. The five-year course at a normal (teachers') college includes one year of teaching practice.

Secondary

Training, at post-secondary level, consists of a five-year course at a university. This includes a year of teaching practice.

As of September 1989 normal schools and teacher education (Primary) junior normal colleges have been upgraded to normal colleges and will therefore accept students who have graduated at senior high school level or above.

Tanzania

This chapter covers the period from 1961, when Tanganyika became independent. In 1964, Zanzibar was united with the mainland and the country became known as Tanzania. Zanzibar, however, retained its own system of education. This chapter is, therefore, split into two sections, the first covering the mainland part of Tanzania and the second Zanzibar.

MAINLAND TANZANIA

There is central control of school curricula, and since 1973, the National Examinations Council of Tanzania has administered the main school examinations.

Education is compulsory from age seven for seven years (standards 1 to 7).

The medium of instruction is Swahili in primary schools and English in secondary schools, colleges and at university. Swahili is compulsory in secondary schools.

The academic year runs from:

October –   University of Dar-es-Salaam and most other further (and higher) education establishments.
January –   Sokoine University of Agriculture and primary and secondary schools.
July –   Advanced secondary schools and teacher colleges.

EVALUATION IN BRITAIN

School

Cambridge Overseas School Certificate (COSC); **East African Certificate of Education** (EACE) – grades 1–6 generally considered comparable to GCSE standard (grades A, B and C) on a subject-for-subject basis.

National Form IV Examination/Certificate of Secondary Education (CSE) – grades A, B and C generally considered comparable to GCSE standard (grades A, B and C), with the exception of English language.

Cambridge Overseas Higher School Certificate (COHSC); **East African Advanced Certificate of Education** (EAACE); grades A–E generally considered comparable to GCE Advanced standard on a subject-for-subject basis.

National Form VI Examination; Advanced Certificate of Secondary Education (ACSE) – may be considered to satisfy the general entrance requirements of British higher education institutions.

Further

Diploma in Electronics and Telecommunication Engineering from <u>DSM Technical College</u> – may be compared to British Bachelor degree standard if awarded with a grade of average or above.

Advanced Diploma – may be compared to BTEC Higher National Diploma / N/SVQ level 4 standard.

National Accountancy Diploma (NAD) – **part II** may be compared to A level standard.

Higher

Bachelor degree – generally considered comparable to British Bachelor degree standard.

MARKING SYSTEMS

School

Cambridge Overseas School Certificate (COSC) **East African Certificate of Education** (EACE)	these were graded 1 (maximum) – 9 (fail)

National Form IV Examination/Certificate of Secondary Education (CSE) – graded A–D and F, where F is a fail grade.

A candidate gets the **Certificate of Secondary Education** for achieving, at one sitting, a pass at grade D (minimum) in Kiswahili and a pass at grade A, B or C in any other subject. Candidates who fail to meet this requirement but obtain at least two passes at grade D in any two subjects will be awarded a statement of results.

Cambridge Overseas Higher School Certificate (COHSC) **East African Advanced Certificate of Education** (EAACE)	graded A, B, C, D, E, O or S (O and S were both subsidiary pass grades), F (fail).

National Form VI Examination/Advanced Certificate of Secondary Education (ACSE) is graded A, B, C, D, E (principal level), S (subsidiary pass), F (fail). A candidate obtains the certificate for achieving at least three subsidiary passes, two of which must be in subjects offered at principal level. Candidates who do not qualify but obtain at least one pass at subsidiary level in a subject offered at principal level, and a pass in a general paper, will be awarded a statement of results.

Higher

Degrees are classified:

1st class Honours
2nd class Honours (upper)
2nd class Honours (lower)
Pass

SCHOOL EDUCATION

Pre-primary

There is no state provision.

Primary

This covers seven years from age seven, divided into lower (covering grades 1 to 4) and upper (grades 5 to 7). It culminates in the **Primary Certificate Examination** (PCE).

Secondary

This covers six years, divided into four years' lower secondary followed by two years' upper secondary. From form II, pupils are streamed into arts or science. Since 1973, secondary education has been oriented towards vocational subjects and all schools are designated technical, agricultural, commercial or home economics.

Until 1969, pupils normally took the **Cambridge Overseas School Certificate** (COSC) and London **GCE O level** examinations at the end of form IV and the **Cambridge Overseas Higher School Certificate** (COHSC) and London **GCE A level** examinations at the end of form VI.

From 1970 to 1973, pupils took the **East African Certificate of Education** (EACE) examination at the end of form IV and the **East African Advanced Certificate of Education** (EAACE) examination at the end of form VI, both examinations being run by the East African Examinations Council.

However, in 1971, Tanzania announced that it was withdrawing from the East African Examinations Council and would run its own national examinations through the National Examinations Council of Tanzania. In the past, all form IV pupils sat an internally set examination, called the **Regional Form IV Examination**, in August. The results were used to select those pupils who would begin in form V the following January, as the results of the COSC or EACE were not available until March or later. This initial selection was subsequently changed in accordance with the COSC or EACE results, once these were known. With the development of the **National Form IV Examination**, taken in November, which was first set in 1974, the **Regional Form IV Examination** was scrapped. In the **National Form IV Examination** pupils took civics, Kiswahili, English language, mathematics, history, geography and biology and a maximum of three optional subjects. The **Certificate of Secondary Education** (CSE) has now replaced the **National Form IV Examination**.

Pupils take the **National Form VI Examination**, now called the **Advanced Certificate of Secondary Education** (ACSE), at the end of form VI.

Technical secondary

As indicated above, some secondary schools are technically biased, and although students in these, as in others, undertake a core of common subjects, the emphasis is on technical subjects. Students successfully completing the CSE may continue their studies at technical colleges which offer certificate and diploma level training.

Lower-level vocational training can be obtained at centres run by the National Vocational Training Division, offering full-time (four years) and part-time basic craft training.

FURTHER EDUCATION

There are over 300 institutions offering specialist training at post-form IV (or form VI) level, leading to **certificates** or **diplomas** at the semi-professional level in a wide variety of disciplines. The institutions are the responsibility of the relevant government ministry under which they fall e.g. Ministry of Agriculture and Livestock Development: Agricultural (MATIs) and Livestock (LITIs) Training Institutes; Ministry of Health and Social Welfare: Nurse Training Schools and Medical Assistants' Training Centres; and Ministry of Finance: Dar-es-Salaam School of Accountancy.

In addition, there are several training centres designed primarily for form VI leavers. These include the Institute of Finance Management, the National Institute of Transport, Ardhi Institute and the Institute of Development Management (now the Institute of Management Development). These offer three-year advanced diploma courses in subjects related to their speciality, and the qualification obtained is regarded as a near-degree equivalent and will allow entry into higher degrees in Tanzania.

The Institute of Development Management also offers **Master of Business Administration** (MBA) and **Master of Public Administration** (MPA) courses.

The **National Business Examination Certificate** is a two-year full-time course. It is set at 3 levels: Elementary, Intermediate and Advanced. The Advanced level is comparable to BTEC National Diploma standard, but is more practical.

The **Certificate in Medical Laboratory Technology** from Muhimbili Medical Centre (the teaching hospital of UDSM), is a three-year course. Entrance is from form IV with good passes in science.

The **Diploma in Medical Laboratory Technology** follows on from the certificate but entrance also requires two years' work experience. The course lasts one year.

The **Full Technician's Certificate** is a three-year full-time course offered by Arusha Technical College (founded with German aid in 1978). Entrance is from form IV of a technically biased school or form IV plus relevant experience. Completion would satisfy the entrance requirements of Tanzanian universities.

Advanced Diplomas are three years in duration, and are regarded as 'near-degree equivalents'. Entrance requirements are two passes in form VI exams or 5 O levels (including English and maths) and four years' experience.

HIGHER EDUCATION

There are three universities. The University of Dar-Es-Salaam, established in 1970, was originally founded in 1961 as the University College of Dar-Es-Salaam and became a constituent college of the University of East Africa in 1963. Sokoine University of Agriculture, located in Morogoro and founded in July 1984, was created from the former Faculty of Agriculture, Forestry and Veterinary Science of the University of Dar-es-Salaam.

The Open University of Tanzania was opened in 1993 and is located in Dar-es-Salaam.

Admission to degree courses is based on passes in the **Certificate of Secondary Education** plus passes in the **Advanced Certificate of Secondary Education**. Applicants must also complete six months of National Service training before beginning their university courses (this programme has however been suspended indefinitely). The academic requirements are two passes at principal level, one at subsidiary level in the ACSE and five passes in the CSE.

Applicants may also apply to university through the Mature Age Entry Examination Scheme.

Bachelor degree courses last four years. A further one to three years' study leads to a **Master's degree**. A minimum of a further two years' original research leads to a **PhD**.

TEACHER EDUCATION

Primary

The **Grade C Certificate** entitles the holder to teach in the first two grades of primary education. The course lasts three years from the end of grade seven.

The **Grade B Certificate** is obtained by promotion or by successfully completing a four-year course at a teacher training college after grade seven.

The **Grade A Certificate** is obtained on successful completion of a two-year course after the end of form IV and allows the holder to teach in all seven grades of primary education.

Secondary

Lower

A two-year diploma course at a teacher training college is required after passing the ACSE.

Upper

Teachers for this level should be graduates.

ZANZIBAR

Zanzibar and Tanganyika were united in 1964 to form the United Republic of Tanzania. Zanzibar, however, retained its own Ministry of Education and its own system of education, which has never been fully integrated into that of the mainland, although pupils take the **Tanzanian National Examinations**. For higher education courses students have to go to the universities on the mainland.

Education is free and compulsory for eleven years from age 6 (standards 1–8 and forms I–III).

Swahili is the medium of instruction for standards 1 to 8 and English for form I and above.

EVALUATION IN BRITAIN

See **MAINLAND TANZANIA**.

MARKING SYSTEMS

See **MAINLAND TANZANIA**.

SCHOOL EDUCATION

Nursery is optional from age three to six. There are government nursery schools in nine towns (five on Zanzibar, four on Pemba).

Primary

This lasts eight years (standards 1 to 8) and covers similar subjects to those studied on the mainland but includes Arabic and Islamic studies.

Secondary

This covers six years. At the end of form III, pupils take Zanzibar examinations to determine who continues to form IV. A number of different colleges offer the form–IV course leading to the **National Form IV Examinations/Certificate of Secondary Education** (CSE).

Lumumba and Fidel Castro secondary schools offer the form–IV course and the two-year course leading to the **National Form VI Examinations/Advanced Certificate of Secondary Education** (ACSE).

Technical

Technical secondary education is offered by Mikunguni Technical Secondary School up to form IV.

FURTHER EDUCATION

Karume Technical College offers the CSE and a three-year course leading to the **Full Technician's Certificate**.

HIGHER EDUCATION

There are no higher education institutions. Students have to go to the universities on the mainland. See **MAINLAND TANZANIA** section.

TEACHER EDUCATION

Nkrumah College offers a two-year teacher training course to post-form IV students which enables them to teach up to standard 8. A two-year in-service course is also available to untrained teachers already teaching at primary level. The College also offers a two-year course leading to the **Diploma in Education** for teachers already holding the **Primary Teacher's Certificate**.

The Institute of Kiswahili and Foreign Language teaches Swahili to foreign and local students. A diploma is offered to local post-form IV students after four years of study of Swahili and other academic arts subjects, including two foreign languages. The course also includes an education component and can lead to further study at the <u>University of Dar-es-Salaam</u> or employment in government posts. The Institute also conducts research into oral literature and the Swahili language and its dialects.

Thailand

Responsibility for the provision of education is divided between the Ministry of the Interior, the Ministry of Education and the Ministry of University Affairs. The Ministry of the Interior supervises primary education administered by local municipal authorities. The Ministry of Education has overall responsibility for all levels of non-university education – primary, secondary, further education and teacher training. It determines curricula; establishes educational standards; controls and supervises all related aspects of the national education system. The Ministry of University Affairs is in charge of the supervision and direction of higher education, both government and private at undergraduate and postgraduate levels. It also has responsibility for curriculum standardization; personnel management; budget proposals and allocations.

The National Education Policy of 1977 introduced changes which were implemented between 1978 and 1983. The Seventh National Education Development Plan (1992–1996) is currently being implemented.

Education is compulsory for the six years of primary education.

The medium of instruction is Thai in state schools and colleges and on most university courses, although an increasing number of 'international' degree programmes are available.

The non-university academic year runs from May to April and the university year from June to March.

EVALUATION IN BRITAIN

School

Mathayom Suksa 3 (MS3) (before 1984) and **Maw 3** (M3) (since 1984) – generally considered to be below GCSE standard.

Mathayom Suksa 5 (MS5) (before 1984) and **Maw 6** (M6) (since 1984) – generally considered comparable to GCSE standard (grades A, B and C) on a subject-for-subject basis, with the exception of English language.

Mathayom is the Thai name for 'secondary' and refers to the education level for children aged 13–18 (M – pronounced 'Maw' – 1–6). It is NOT the name for an examination, although examinations are given at M3 (i.e. the junior secondary exit point). **M3 and M6** exams are organised on a regional basis, so there are no country-wide standards.

Higher

Bachelor degree – generally considered to be below British Bachelor degree standard. Candidates from prestigious institutions may be considered for admission to postgraduate study. For further information enquirers should contact the National Academic Recognition Information Centre.

MARKING SYSTEMS

School

Mathayom Suksa 5 (MS5)

1960–75 – percentage system; pupils had to obtain at least 500 marks out of 1,000; English could account for up to 240.

Note: Mathayom Suska marking system:
0	0 –	49 per cent
1	50 –	59 per cent
2	60 –	69 per cent
3	70 –	79 per cent
4	80 –	100 per cent

1976–81

Under a credit system, pupils had to obtain 100 credits of which 34 had to be from the compulsory subjects. The remaining 66 credits allowed pupils to choose from elective subjects; a maximum of 40 credits for English could be chosen. (This system was still in use in some areas until 1983.)

Maw 6 (M6)

Since 1981 – the unit system was introduced (adopted from the American system of Carnegie Units). The first pupils to complete M6 on the unit system did so in 1984. Pupils are required to complete 75 units for graduation from M6; of these, 30 units must come from compulsory subjects, consisting of 15 units of core compulsory subjects (Thai, social studies, physical education) and 15 units of elective compulsory subjects (sciences; foundation of vocational education). The remaining 45 units are for free elective subjects.

Grades

Achievement levels are graded on a scale of 0–4, with 1 as the minimum pass-mark.

Grade point	Level of Achievement	Percentage estimate
4	excellent	80–100
3	good	70–79
2	fair	60–69
1	pass	50–59
0	fail	0–49

Further, higher and teacher education

Further education, university and teacher training levels use the credit system to assess students' academic performance. The number of credits required and the average and cumulative grade-points are published in the institutions' prospectuses.

The grading system used is as follows:

A	4.00	excellent
B+	3.50	very good
B	3.00	good
C+	2.50	fairly good
C	2.00	fair
D+	1.50	poor
D	1.00	very poor
F	0.00	fail

The pass grade is 2 at undergraduate level and 3 at postgraduate level.

From 1983 first class honours are awarded to students with a cumulative GPA of 3.75 and second class honours to those with between 3.5 and 3.74.

The two open universities (STOU and Ramkhamhaeng) have their own systems.

SCHOOL EDUCATION

Pre-primary

This is voluntary and is available for children aged three to five.

Primary

Until 1978

This covered seven years divided into two cycles from age six or seven: *lower prathom* (grades I–IV) and *upper prathom* (grades V–VII).

Since 1978

This is now a six-year cycle covering grades I–VI. On completion of this cycle pupils take the **Primary School Leaving Certificate**.

Secondary

Until 1978

This covered five years divided into two cycles, lower secondary (grades VIII to X/Mawsaw 1–3) leading to the **Mathayom Suksa 3** (MS3) examination and upper secondary (grades XI to XII/Mawsaw 4–5) leading to the final school-leaving examination, the **Mathayom Suksa 5** (MS5).

Since 1978

This now covers six years divided into two cycles, lower secondary (grades VII to IX, M 1–3) leading to the **Maw 3** (M3) examination and upper secondary (grades X to XII, M 4–6) leading to the final school-leaving examination, the **Maw 6** (M6). At upper secondary level students can choose between the general stream (sub-divided into science and arts) and the vocational stream.

The current National Education Development Plan aims to provide places for all eligible pupils for the lower secondary cycle by 1996. This cycle will then be compulsory.

There are a number of private secondary schools run by missionary societies and Chinese and Muslim groups.

School equivalency

The School Equivalency Programme offers a variety of courses for people who need equivalency certificates for employment purposes (i.e. to bring them up to a recognized grade in the school system). Instruction is provided at five levels which are compared as follows:

Level 1 – primary grades 1 and 2
Level 2 – primary grades 3 and 4
Level 3 – primary grades 5 and 6
Level 4 – lower secondary (M1–3)
Level 5 – upper secondary (M4–6).

FURTHER EDUCATION

In addition to general education, the Ministry of Education provides vocational and technical training through 279 colleges administered by the Department of Vocational Education and the Rajamangala Institute of Technology.

The Department of Vocational Education, founded in 1941, is responsible for vocational, post-school and continuing education at non-advanced level leading to qualifications up to certificate and diploma level (the equivalent of the second year of a degree course). There is a wide range of courses in five subject areas – trade and industry; commerce and business administration; home economics; arts and crafts and agriculture – available on a full-time and a part-time basis. This sector is expanding rapidly with new colleges opening every year.

Rajamangala Institute of Technology – RIT formerly The Institute of Technology and Vocational Education – ITVE, founded in 1975, is responsible for technical training at advanced non-degree and degree levels in subject areas which overlap with some of those offered by the colleges under the supervision of the Department of Vocational Education. The areas covered are agriculture, business administration, education, engineering technology, home economics, fine arts, music, drama and liberal arts. Training available includes a three-year post-M3 course leading to a **Certificate of Vocational Education**, a two-year post-M6 course leading to a **Higher Vocational Diploma**, and four-year **Bachelor Degree** courses. There are thirty-one RIT campuses throughout Thailand.

There are two types of private vocational schools/colleges: those which follow curricula designed by the ministry, and those which construct their own syllabuses; the ministry will not recognize the latter's qualifications, although some employers do.

HIGHER EDUCATION

Higher Education comes under the jurisdiction of the Ministry of University Affairs. It is provided by state and private universities and private colleges. The basic requirement for admission is the completion of twelve years of education and the **Maw 6** (M6) certificate. In addition, there is a national entrance examination for all state institutions (WEE – **Written Entrance Examination**); the pass rate is adjusted to fill the university places available. Some private universities and colleges have their own selection procedures and entrance examinations, but others use the WEE.

English is a compulsory subject for the first year of university study but not thereafter except in a few disciplines.

Bachelor degrees are normally obtained after four years' study, with five years for architecture, fine arts and pharmacy and six for medicine, dentistry and veterinary medicine.

Master's degrees normally require two years' study after a first degree. A **PhD** requires a further two to three years' study.

A credit system (comparable to that of the United States) was initiated in 1957 and is now more or less nationwide, 144 credits being required for the award of a **Bachelor degree**. Examinations are taken at the end of each semester and a cumulative grade-point average of not less than 2.00 is required to be able to continue the course.

There are two open universities which require only the **Maw 6** (M6) certificates for entry, with no entrance examination.

TEACHER EDUCATION

Teacher training colleges (*Rajabhat* Institutes) offer two and four-year courses. The two-year courses lead to an **Associate Degree** which entitles the holder to teach at the lower secondary level. The four-year course leads to a **BEd**. Certain colleges offer specialized courses (e.g. physical education, nursery teaching).

Teachers colleges also offer **Associate** and **Bachelor degrees** (BA or BSc) in Science and Liberal Arts. They come under the jurisdiction of the Ministry of Education.

Togo

Education in Togo is centrally administered by the Ministry of Education and the Ministry of Technical Education and Professional Training.

Education is compulsory to age sixteen, although in practice many children do not attend school.

The official medium of instruction is French although two local languages, Ewe and Kabiye, are being introduced into primary education. English is a compulsory subject throughout secondary education.

EVALUATION IN BRITAIN

School

Baccalauréat – generally considered comparable to GCSE standard (grades A, B and C) on a subject-for-subject basis, with the exception of English language.

Higher

Diplôme Universitaire d'Etudes Littéraires (DUEL), **Diplôme Universitaire d'Etudes Scientifiques** (DUES) – may be considered to satisfy the general entrance requirements of British higher education institutions.

Licence – generally considered comparable to a standard between GCE Advanced and British Bachelor degree; may be given advanced standing in British higher education institutions.

Maîtrise – generally considered comparable to British Bachelor (Ordinary) degree standard but where very high marks have been achieved candidates could be considered for admission to postgraduate study.

Teaching

CAPES – generally considered comparable to British Bachelor (Ordinary) degree standard.

MARKING SYSTEMS

School

The **Baccalauréat** is graded and specified in *mentions*:

très bien	very good
bien	good
assez bien	quite good
passable	average

Higher

Each faculty has its own system of examining, although grading is usually on a scale of 0–20 (maximum). Students are normally given the option of being evaluated on the basis of continuous assessment or by examination. Students whose performance is evaluated on the basis of continuous assessment and thereby pass or obtain an average of 10/20 in all major subjects during the academic year, are not required to take the written examinations in June. Those students who do not obtain a minimum pass in classwork during the year in all major subjects, or those who have not been graded in all subjects for any reason, sit for the formal examinations in June. The results in the major subjects are multiplied by a coefficient which varies from subject to subject. The grading system is as follows:

16–20	*très bien*	very good
14–16	*bien*	good
12–14	*assez bien*	quite good
10–12	*passable*	average

SCHOOL EDUCATION

Primary

Children begin school at age six or seven. Primary schooling lasts six years, at the end of which pupils are awarded a **Certificat de Fin d'Etudes du Premier Degré** (CEPD).

Secondary

Pupils are streamed at the end of primary schooling for entry to the first cycle of secondary education. This cycle of lower secondary education lasts four years (*6ème, 5ème, 4ème* and *3ème*) after which students take the examinations for the **Brevet d'Etudes du Premier Cycle**.

Students are then streamed again and oriented into vocational or training institutes or enter the university preparatory cycle at a *Lycée*. This second cycle lasts three years (*2ème, première* and *terminale*). The **Baccalauréat Probatoire** is taken on completion of the *première* year. On completion of this cycle pupils take the examinations for the **Baccalauréat** administered by the *Office du Baccalauréat de l'Enseignement du Second Degré*. The **Baccalauréat** can be taken in any of five options:

A	humanities and philosophy
B	economics
C	mathematics and physical sciences
D	applied sciences and mathematics
E	science and technology.

English is an obligatory subject in the **Baccalauréat**, and at this stage all students will have completed seven years of English study at school.

Students who do not pass the examinations at the first sitting in June may resit in September/October. A supplementary oral test may be taken after the written examinations.

The **Certificat de Fin d'Etudes Secondaires** is not the equivalent of the **Baccalauréat**, although it may be obtained at the same time. It represents class attendance in the last year of secondary school. If a student presents this, it often means that the student was not successful in passing the **Baccalauréat** examination.

Students may not be able to produce a transcript of marks for the **Baccalauréat** (the *livret scolaire*) as this is not generally given to the student but can be obtained direct from a school.

Technical secondary

On completion of the four-year cycle of lower secondary education, students may go on to a three-year cycle of technical secondary education culminating in the examinations for the **Baccalauréat Technicien** in option F (engineering and science) or G (business and commerce).

HIGHER EDUCATION

Until 1977, the university academic year ran from October to July; it now runs from October to June. It is rare for students to go straight through secondary school without repeating any year, and many students do not then go straight on to university. Most students do not begin their university studies until the age of about twenty-two. All students who pass the **Baccalauréat** have the right to enter university and study the subject of their choice, although there is a special entrance examination for those who do not hold the **Baccalauréat**.

Université du Benin

The Centre d'Enseignement Supérieur was established in 1962 with buildings in Dahomey and Togo under an agreement between the governments of the two countries and the government of France. In 1970 Dahomey decided to create its own national institution. The University of Benin was then established in Togo to replace the former Togolese part of the Centre. The university is French orientated and modelled on similar French institutions. In 1972 major reforms were put through affecting the curriculum and structure of courses.

The first cycle of two years' study leads in the science faculty to the **Diplôme Universitaire d'Etudes Scientifiques** (DUES) and in the arts faculty to the **Diplôme Universitaire d'Etudes Littéraires** (DUEL). A further year of study leads to the **Licence**.

The Institut National des Sciences de l'Education (INSE) has recently been created and offers compulsory courses to be taken throughout the three-year course leading to the **Licence**. Entry is generally based on the DUEL or DUES, although students from other faculties who have completed two years of undergraduate study are also admissible.

Ecole Nationale Supérieure d'Administration et des Carrières Juridiques

On completion of the first two-year cycle, students who have not performed outstandingly well in the earlier part of the course obtain the **Diplôme Universitaire de Techniques Juridiques** (DUTJ), which is generally a final qualification. Those students who are proceeding to the second two-year cycle do not normally obtain this qualification and go on to take the examinations for the **Licence**.

Ecole Supérieure de Techniques Economiques et de Gestion

A four-year course leads to the **Licence en Techniques de Commerce et Gestion** or the **Licence en Techniques Economiques**.

Ecole Supérieure de Mécanique Industrielle (ESMI)

This institution was established in 1972 to train engineers at two levels: **Ingénieur de Réalisation** and **Ingénieur de Conception**. The short cycle lasts three years and leads to the qualification of **Ingénieur de Réalisation** (advanced technician). Students wishing to obtain the **Diplôme d'Ingénieur de Conception** are usually streamed out of the second year of the short cycle and then proceed to a further three years of study.

Ecole Supérieure d'Agronomie (ESA)

This institute follows the same pattern of courses as the ESMI.

In 1975 the university began to offer postgraduate courses. In humanities, students on courses leading to the **Maîtrise** have first to hold a **Licence**. They then have to obtain a **Certificat de Maîtrise** and submit a short thesis. In science the **Maîtrise** is often obtained without candidates holding a **Licence**. The course takes one year from the **Licence** (humanities) or two years from the **DUES** (science). The **Diplôme d'Etudes Supérieures** (DES) or the **Diplôme d'Etudes Approfondies** (DEA) represents completion of a further one or two years of academic study beyond the **Maîtrise**. Persons holding the **Doctorat de Specialité de Troisième Cycle** will have completed one or two years' study beyond the DES or DEA.

The first degree in medicine is the **Doctorat** which requires seven years' study.

TEACHER EDUCATION

Primary

A three-year course at the upper secondary level can be taken at two teacher training colleges: Ecole Normale d'Instituteurs, Notse and ENI, Kara. The qualification awarded is the **Certificat d'Aptitude Pédagogique**.

Secondary

A three-year course at post-secondary level taken at a teacher-training college (*Ecole Normale Supérieure*) leads to a professional qualification and entitles the holder to teach at lower secondary level. A one-year course is open to practising teachers.

Teachers at the upper secondary level are trained in the school of arts where they obtain a **Licence d'Enseignement** and a **Certificat d'Aptitude au Professorat de l'Enseignement du Second Degré/Secondaire** (CAPES).

Higher

Teachers at this level must theoretically hold the **Doctorat du Troisième Cycle**. However, owing to a shortage of **Doctorats**, many university lecturers are temporary lecturers (*Vacataires*).

The *Agrégation de l'Enseignement du Second Degré* and the *Agrégation de l'Université* are certificates of outstanding proficiency in teaching and are obtained by examination before a committee. The *agrégation* is not in itself a degree and requires no specific course or research qualifications.

Tonga

Education is compulsory between the ages of six and fourteen.

The medium of instruction at primary level is Tongan, with English taught as a second language. At secondary level, English is the medium of instruction with Tongan taught as a subject.

The academic year runs from January to December.

EVALUATION IN BRITAIN

School

Until 1987

Higher Leaving Certificate –   ) generally considered to
New Zealand School Certificate –   ) be below GCSE standard.

New Zealand University Entrance Certificate – generally considered comparable to GCSE standard.

Since 1987

Tonga School Certificate – generally considered to be below GCSE standard.

Pacific Senior Secondary Certificate – generally considered comparable to GCSE standard.

Tonga National Form 7 – generally considered comparable to GCSE standard.

Higher

Bachelor degree (from the University of the South Pacific) – generally considered comparable to British Bachelor degree standard.

MARKING SYSTEMS

School

Pacific Senior Secondary Certificate – students receive a single-digit grade that can range from 1 to 9 (based on their ranking) for each subject that they have taken. The highest achievement grade is 1, the lowest is 9. The idea of 'pass' or 'fail' is discouraged. Descriptors that are used at present in association with these grades are:

Grade Descriptor

1   Excellent standard of achievement

2   Very high standard of achievement

3   High standard of achievement

4   Good standard of achievement

5   Satisfactory standard of achievement

6   Adequate standard of achievement

7   Some achievement

8   Lower level of achievement

9   Little level of achievement

New Zealand School   )
Certificate –   ) See chapter on
New Zealand University   ) New Zealand
Entrance Examination –   )

Higher

Degrees from the University of the South Pacific are unclassified.

SCHOOL EDUCATION

Primary

This covers six years, at the end of which pupils take the secondary entrance examination to all middle and secondary schools.

Secondary

Until 1987

This covered a possible six years. After four years pupils took the **Higher Leaving Certificate**. At some schools, after a further year, pupils took the **New Zealand School Certificate** and after an additional year (year six) the **New Zealand University Entrance Examination** leading to the **New Zealand University Entrance Certificate**.

Since 1987

This covers a possible seven years for most students and six for the most able. On completion of six years (or five for some), students take the **Tonga School Certificate**. Some schools go on to prepare pupils for the **Pacific Senior Secondary Certificate** in the seventh year (six for some), which is administered by the South Pacific Board for Educational Assessment (SPBEA). (For further information on the SPBEA see Appendix 8.) After the **Pacific Senior Secondary Certificate**, selected eligible students enter the *Tonga National Form 7* for a one-year course. This is administered by Tonga with professional assistance from the NZ Ministry of Education. Curriculum in this course is in line with the NZ Bursaries.

FURTHER EDUCATION

The Community Development and Training Centre (CDTC) co-ordinates all education and training at post-secondary level, as well as conducting formal and non-formal programmes for both non-government and government trainees in aviation, finance and management, trade training and testing, tourism, and computer training, among other things. CDTC incorporates under its umbrella:

The Institute of Science and Technology which offers a three-year block-training programme in general engineering, and in marine engineering and catering for ships for able-bodied seamen. The minimum entry qualification is the **Tonga School Certificate**. The Institute was formerly known as the Tonga Maritime Polytechnic Institute with a lower minimum entry level of the **Tonga Higher Leaving Certificate**.

The Institute's activities are planned to include: seamen and officer training, marine engineering, construction and civil engineering, electronics and communication, general engineering, marine studies and technology and agricultural science and technology.

The Tonga Teachers' Training College – for further details see **TEACHER EDUCATION**.

Distance Education and Research Centre – established in 1991, this centre administers programmes on adult education, satellite communication, computer and diploma courses.

The Ministry of Works' Trades Training Scheme, which offers a four-year trades certificate course in the following areas: carpentry and joinery; plumbing; automotive engineering; heavy plant; fitting and machining; welding and fabrication; panel beating and spray-painting; auto-electrical.

The minimum entry qualification was the **Tonga Higher Leaving Certificate** but it has been upgraded to the **Tonga School Certificate**.

CDTC is also loosely affiliated with these institutions:

Hango Agricultural College, a Methodist institution, which offers a two-year course in agriculture, for those intending to become farmers/farm managers. Minimum entry qualification is the **Tonga School Certificate** but candidates may be accepted without this.

St Joseph's Business College, a Roman Catholic institution, which offers a two-year secretarial course, which includes typing, shorthand, wordprocessing, audiotyping, accounting, filing, telex machining, and office practice.

The Queen Salote School of Nursing, which offers a three-year basic nursing course. Minimum entry qualification is the **Tonga School Certificate**. In addition, it also offers specialist courses from time to time in midwifery and public health nursing.

The Tupou Young Farmers' School for young farmers, another Methodist institution, which offers a one-year largely practical training programme. No entry qualification is required.

HIGHER EDUCATION

Degree courses are available at the <u>University of the South Pacific</u> which has campuses in Fiji and Western Samoa.

Admission to first degree courses is based on satisfactory completion of the University's one-year foundation programme or an equivalent form 7 secondary qualification.

The normal length of **Bachelor degree** courses is three years except for medicine which takes four years for a first degree.

Postgraduate certificates and diplomas, **Master's degree** and **PhD** programmes are available in a number of areas.

For further information on the <u>University of the South Pacific</u> see Appendix 9.

<u>Atenisi University</u> (secular, non-government) runs degree courses.

TEACHER EDUCATION

<u>The Tonga Teachers' Training College</u> offers a three-year integrated **Teaching Diploma** for primary and secondary school teachers. The minimum entry requirement is the **Pacific Senior School Certificate** or equivalent.

Trinidad and Tobago

The education system is based on the British model.

Compulsory education is from age six to twelve.

The medium of instruction at all levels is English.

The academic year runs from September to July.

EVALUATION IN BRITAIN

School

Caribbean Examinations Council Secondary Education Certificate (CSEC) – grades 1 and 2 at general proficiency generally considered comparable to GCSE standard (grades A, B or C) on a subject-for-subject basis.

GCE O and **A levels** – generally equated to GCSE and GCE Advanced examinations taken in Britain.

Higher

Bachelor degree (from the University of the West Indies) – generally considered comparable to British Bachelor degree standard; students with high grades may be considered for admission to taught Master's degree programme.

MARKING SYSTEMS

School

Caribbean Examinations Council Secondary Education Certificate (CSEC): two schemes are available in the subject examinations; the general proficiency scheme and the basic proficiency scheme.

There is no pass/fail-mark.

Five grades are awarded, defined as follows:

1   comprehensive working knowledge of the syllabus

2   working knowledge of most aspects of the syllabus

3   working knowledge of some aspects of the syllabus

4   limited knowledge of a few aspects of the syllabus

5   insufficient evidence on which to base a judgement.

GCE O and **A levels** – see Appendix 2.

Higher

Bachelor (Honours) degrees are awarded with the following classifications:

first class
second class upper division
second class lower division

If the performance has been insufficient for Honours, the degree is awarded as a Pass.

SCHOOL EDUCATION

Primary

This covers six years, generally from age five, culminating in the **Common Entrance Examination** (11+ examination), which is to be phased out as rapidly as the resources of the economy allow.

Secondary

This covers a possible seven years.

Pupils are placed in schools of their choice according to their performance in the **Common Entrance Examination**.

There are two types of secondary education, the traditional academic sector providing five-year or seven-year schools and the new system providing three-year junior secondary and two or four-year senior secondary schools. There are plans for these new system schools to be transformed into five to seven-year secondary comprehensive schools. New-type schools offer a more diversified curriculum than the academic courses provided by the traditional schools.

After five years, courses lead to the examinations for **Caribbean Examinations Council Secondary Education Certificate** (for further information see Appendix 4) and after a further two years to **GCE A level** examinations. (For further information see Appendix 2.)

Under the comprehensive system there is a common curriculum for the first three years: agriculture; arts and crafts; electives; English; general science; industrial arts or home economics; mathematics; music; physical education; religious instruction; social studies; and Spanish. In the final two years offered by the comprehensive schools, there are three streams: academic, pre-technician or craft. The core subjects for all three streams are: English; mathematics; science; social studies; and Spanish. In the academic stream, pupils take more courses in: mathematics; chemistry; physics; biology and English *or* language, arts (English, literature, Spanish and French) *or* social studies (history, geography, economics and English).

Technical and vocational courses are offered in: business studies; engineering; surveying; home economics; and graphic and applied arts. Craft-level courses do not require **Caribbean Examinations Council Secondary Education Certificate** (CSEC) for admission; they lead to the **National Craftsman Certificate** which is awarded by the National Examinations Council of the Ministry of Education.

TERTIARY EDUCATION

There are a number of institutions, both public and private, which provide a wide range of courses.

The John S Donaldson and San Fernando Technical Institutes offers technical and vocational courses in applied science and home economics, business education and management, computer studies, engineering, and technical teacher training. Technical courses offered lead to the **National Technician Certificate** awarded by the National Examinations Council.

The Trinidad and Tobago Hospitality Institute offers courses related to the training needs of the hospitality industry as well as appropriate training for the trades and middle management.

The Eastern Caribbean Institute of Agriculture and Forestry offers courses at the technical and sub-professional levels in the fields of agriculture, forestry and agricultural teacher training.

The National Institute of Higher Education Research Science and Technology (NIHERST)

There are four main teaching divisions within NIHERST which offer courses/programmes leading to the award of Associate Degree, Diploma or Certificate. The General Education Division provides courses to the other divisions in communication skills, the natural sciences including mathematics, the social sciences and the fine arts.

> The College of Health Sciences offers specialized training courses in the health care field including the radiological sciences, medical laboratory technology, environmental/occupational safety and health, continuing education courses in substance and drug abuse prevention, and peer counselling.

> The College of Nursing offers basic general nursing and psychiatric nursing programmes.

> The Information Technology College offers programmes/courses in the fields of information management, processing and technology, and short courses in the application of software packages and specialized areas.

> The School of Languages offers courses providing a facility in foreign languages (Spanish, French, German, Hindi, Portuguese) in order to transact foreign and official business, to engage academic pursuits, to undertake research and development and to pursue leisure and culture activities.

The Caribbean Union College (CUC) established in 1927 by the Seventh Day Adventists, is affiliated to the Andrews University in Michigan, USA and prepares students for Degree and Associate Degree programmes in a wide range of subjects in liberal and industrial arts, in business, and in education. CUC also offers secondary level courses leading to examinations for the **CSEC** and **GCE Advanced**.

Trinidad and Tobago is a contributing territory to the University of the West Indies which is a regional institution with campuses in Jamaica, Barbados and Trinidad.

There are two levels of admission to first degree courses. Students with the **Caribbean Examinations Council Secondary Education Certificate** or **GCSE**-level equivalents take a preliminary year's study. Direct entry to degree courses is based on **GCE A level**. **Bachelor degree** courses normally take three years. Higher degrees and certificate and diploma courses are also available. (For further information see Appendix 10.)

TEACHER EDUCATION

For primary and some secondary schools a two-year post-**Caribbean Examinations Council Secondary Education Certificate** leading to a **Teacher's Diploma**. Other secondary teachers are graduates.

Tunisia

Tunisia was a French protectorate from 1881 to 1956. The education system was originally modelled on the French pattern and is only now beginning to evolve into a more specifically Tunisian form.

Primary education is compulsory.

The medium of instruction in primary school is Arabic, with French taught as a foreign language in the last three years. At secondary school, the humanities are taught in Arabic and the sciences and mathematics in French. English is the most common second foreign language (the first being French); it is introduced in the fourth year. The medium of instruction at university is French, except for Islamic studies, where it is necessarily Arabic, and in departments of foreign languages, where the medium is usually the language studied.

The academic year runs from mid-October to the end of June.

EVALUATION IN BRITAIN

School

Baccalauréat – generally considered comparable to a standard between GCSE and GCE Advanced. British higher education institutions may require additional GCE Advanced passes or may accept the **Baccalauréat** provided an overall average mark of *assez bien* or *bien* is achieved.

Higher

Diplôme Universitaire d'Etudes Scientifiques (DUES), **Diplôme Universitaire d'Etudes Littéraires** (DUEL) – generally considered comparable to a standard between GCE Advanced and British Bachelor degree; may be given advanced standing by British higher education institutions.

Licence – generally considered comparable to British Bachelor (Ordinary) degree standard.

Maîtrise – generally considered comparable to British Bachelor (Honours) degree standard.

MARKING SYSTEM

School

Marks are on a scale of 0–20 (maximum); 10 is the pass-mark.

16–20	*très bien*	very good
14–15	*bien*	good
12–13	*assez bien*	fairly good
10–11	*passable*	pass
0– 9	*insuffisant*	fail

The overall result of the **Baccalauréat** is determined by a system of coefficients, varying between the main streams, applied to the subject scores.

Higher

The marking system used is as above. *Très bien* is rare.

SCHOOL EDUCATION

Primary

Primary education begins at six years of age and lasts six years, leading to a competitive secondary entrance examination which is being discontinued from 1994/95. The Sixth Development Plan (1982–7) established the extension of basic education to nine years and included an element of technical training and preparation for working life. *L'Ecole de base* started in October 1989 with the first grade and will reach its ninth grade in 1998/99.

Secondary

Secondary education lasts seven years with specialization over the last two years in *science mathématiques, sciences expérimentales, technique, économie et gestion* and *lettres*, all leading to a **Baccalauréat**.

HIGHER EDUCATION

Tunisian institutions of higher education are under the supervision of the Ministry of Higher Education or of the ministry most appropriate to their speciality (e.g. agriculture). All these institutions offer university-level qualifications. Since 1986, the institutions of higher education have been grouped into the Universities of Tunis I, II, III and the Universities of the Centre and the South. University-level study is divided into three cycles of two years each; it is necessary to complete both the first and second cycles to achieve the **Maîtrise, Licence** or **Diplôme d'Ingénieur**.

The commonest qualifications awarded are:

Diplôme Universitaire d'Etudes Scientifiques (DUES), **Diplôme Universitaire d'Etudes Littéraires** (DUEL)
after the first two-year cycle

Licence, Diplôme d'Ingénieur, Maîtrise
after the second cycle lasting occasionally one but usually two years

Diplôme d'Etudes	research degrees requiring
Approfondies	two years after the
Diplôme Supérieur	Licence/Maîtrise
Doctorat de Spécialité	after six or more years
Doctorat en Médecine	
Doctorat d'Etat	

In some disciplines there is also a Tunisian form of **Agrégation**, achieved by competitive examination and often required for teaching posts in higher education.

TEACHER EDUCATION

Primary

Prospective primary school teachers attend secondary-level *Ecoles Normales*.

Secondary

Secondary teachers are trained at the <u>Ecole Normale Supérieure</u> which is being phased out, or the <u>Ecole Normale Supérieure de l'Enseignement Technique</u>, which has a structure similar to that of the regular university faculties, including a postgraduate cycle.

Turkey

There is a centralized system of state education, according to the principles of Atatürk, which is provided for in the Basic Law of National Education. The Ministry of National Education prepares the curriculum, provides teachers and educational buildings and materials, and supervises and inspects schools at all levels. The Council for Higher Education (YÖK) has supervised and co-ordinated higher education since 1981 with a view to improving the quality of teaching and research.

The private sector is expanding, with the encouragement of the government, but is not significant numerically. Standards are high because of the competitive entrance examination.

Primary school education is compulsory from ages six to eleven.

The academic year runs from September or October until June, and is divided into two semesters with a two-week break in February.

Turkish is the medium of instruction at all levels in state schools. But there are 528 private secondary schools in some of which the medium of instruction is a foreign language (generally English). There are also selected state secondary schools (*Anadolu Lises*) which teach some courses in a foreign language, usually English. English is the medium of instruction at the Middle East Technical, Gaziantep, Bogaziçi, Bilkent and Koç universities.

Number of students in Turkish Education (1993 figures):

Primary school	6,908,986
Middle school	2,498,545
Secondary school (lycee and equivalent)	1,742,795
Higher education	854,950
Applicants for university exam	1,154,000
Available first year places at universities	210,000

Government is trying to create new education opportunities, at all levels, for the growing young population and brought changes into the education system. The recent developments are:

i)   The introduction of a new marking system to secondary schools since 92/93.

ii) Open lycees (*Açik Lise*): An opportunity to achieve a lycee diploma through open education system. Those who are graduates of a middle school but could not follow lycee-taught courses for various reasons will be eligible to apply. Students can be admitted in the mid-classes too.

iii) The number of universities has been increased to 56 in 1994 from 29 in 1992. There were 9 universities until 1972. Government has launched new scholarship programmes for the research assistants to take academic training at the foreign universities. These scholars will be then appointed as academics at the new universities.

iv) Night classes at the universities: additional places were created for the students who could not be placed after the university entrance exam because of the scarce places. Some courses are planned to be held after 4.00 p.m. at the existing universities. Students will achieve the original diploma of the university. Some universities started applying the system. But it created enormous problems in practice, the system is a matter of debate at the moment. The number of academic and administrative staff, budget and the infrastructure was not sufficient to go on with the system. Universities are waiting for the decision of Higher Education Council. The system may be abolished but the existing students will complete their degree programme. Tuition fees are much higher than the fees of day classes.

v) Additional places at Anadolu University: Government opened new faculties and increased the contingency of the Open Education Faculty of Anadolu University. Those who passed the 1st stage exam, took the 2nd stage exam but could not achieve a place due to lack of contingency will be eligible to apply and be placed according to their scores. 138,000 students applied and 72,000 of them were registered and started studying in January 1994. Education will be given in the form of taught courses, external study or open education. Students will make use of all Open Faculty facilities and TRT4 Channel of Turkish Radio Television which will enable them to follow the courses from other places of the country. The students will be awarded the degree of Anadolu University upon the completion of their study successfully. The faculties of the Anadolu University where the additional places were created are: economics, management, open education (with various subjects), literature, science, law, tourism and hotel management, physical education. The system is new and new changes may be introduced in future.

EVALUATION IN BRITAIN

School

Devlet Lise Diplomasi (State High School Diploma) and **Lise Bitirme Diplomasi** (Private High School Finishing Diploma) – generally considered to be at least GCSE standard. May be considered for admission to access/bridging courses.

For the above qualifications, students with an overall average of at least 8, or 4 under the new system, satisfy the general entrance requirements of some British higher education institutions.

Devlet Teknik Lise Diplomasi (State Technical four-year High School Diploma) and **Devlet Meslek Lise Diplomasi** (State Vocational or Trade High School Diploma) – have been considered to be of a similar standard to the State High School Diploma, but these diplomas may be less suitable as a preparation for academic study.

Higher

Lisans Diplomasi – generally considered comparable to British Bachelor (Ordinary) degree standard. Students with high marks could be considered for admission to postgraduate study.

Yüksek Lisans Diplomasi (**Master's degree**) – generally considered comparable to British Bachelor (Honours) degree standard; students with high marks may be considered for entry to PhD.

MARKING SYSTEMS

School

Primary school (six to eleven years): marking is on a scale of 1–5 (maximum), with 2 as the minimum pass-mark.

Middle school (twelve to foureen years): marking is on a scale of 1–5 (maximum), with 2 as the minimum pass-mark.

Secondary

Secondary school (fourteen to eighteen plus): before 1992 the marking system was on a scale of 1–10 (maximum) with 5 as the pass-mark.

A new system of marking was introduced in Turkish secondary schools since 1992/93. The new system involves a group of compulsory subjects and optional subjects. All examinations, homework and projects are considered over 100 total points. At the end of each term, points are converted into marks, then are indicated in letters. This system enables students to pass subjects rather than passing the classes as in the old system. Students are expected to complete their *lycee* education in a maximum five years.

Compulsory subjects:

i)   Students are obliged to take Turkish language and literature 1, history 1, maths 1, science 1, and foreign language 1 in the first semester.

ii)   The following subjects can be taken in any one of the 6 semesters:
      Turkish language and literature 2,3
      Religious studies 1,2,3
      Turkish Republic Revolutionary History and Atatürkism
      Geography 1,2
      Physical education 1,2
      Military science 1
      Mathematics 2
      History 2

iii) Philosophy 1,2 will be taken from 3rd semester onwards.

A student who is unsuccessful in any one of the above subjects can take those subjects in the following semesters. Those who fail after the repetition of a subject(s) can complete the required credits by taking other optional subjects.

Optional Subjects

Optional subjects can be taken in any semester. Students are given a second chance if they fail the first time. But if they are still unsuccessful a new subject has to be chosen. School Education Counsellors give guidance in choosing the optional courses. Principal subjects are: science, social sciences, fine arts, sports, Turkish-maths, foreign language, general knowledge.

Assessment

Assessment is through written, oral and applied examinations, homework projects and activities within and outside the classroom. The marking system is as follows:

Point	Mark	Letter value	Final Comment
85–100	5	A	very good
70–84	4	B	good
55–69	3	C	average
45–54	2	D	pass
0–44	1	E	fail

There are still schools operating under the old system where marking is on a scale of 1–10 (maximum) with 5 as the pass-mark:

9–10	very good
7–8	good
5–6	average
below 5	fail

Higher

Marking systems vary. Many universities use the numerical scales of 1–4, 1–5, 1–10 (maximum) or 1–10 (minimum). Some use letter grades A–F where A is the maximum. Some use the American grade-point average system.

The marking system for the degree is based on the whole course and usually graded as follows:

85–100	*pekiyi*	very good
65–84	*iyi*	good
50–64	*orta*	fair

SCHOOL EDUCATION

Pre-school education

Children from three to five can enter independent kindergartens or, at the age of five, nursery classes attached to primary schools. Such schooling is optional, and no diploma is awarded.

Primary and middle education (*Ilkokul/Ortaokul*)

The primary education is five years and is compulsory. It is taken between 6–11 years. A pupil can continue his primary education until 14 years of age. There are projects to extend the compulsory education to eight years.

The primary curriculum covers Turkish, mathematics, science, social studies, religious instruction, art, music, and physical education, for a total of 25 hours per week. In primary schools, pupils must satisfy teachers before moving up. Thereafter they must pass in every subject in the class examinations to go on to the following year.

The middle school curriculum covers the same subjects as primary school with the addition of history, geography, civics and a foreign language totalling 31–35 hours per week. The **Middle School** or **Basic Education Diploma** is awarded on completion of this stage.

Secondary school (*Lise*)

There are several types of schools and programmes, lasting three or four years. The school-leaving diploma (**Lise Diplomasi**) is awarded on completion of secondary education.

General high schools offer three-year curricula covering Turkish language and literature, psychology, philosophy, logic and sociology, history, geography, mathematics, biology, physics, chemistry, foreign language, religious education, physical training and elective courses, totalling 36 hours per week.

Science high schools (*Fen Lise*) offer similar three-year programmes, but with more emphasis on modern science and mathematics. In 1983/84 there were 3 such schools with 573 students. In 1992/93 the number rose to 18 with 3,870 students. The admission to these schools are by examination and are very competitive. 86,000 students applied for a total of 4,500 places at *Fen Lises* in 1994. The graduates of these schools generally achieve the highest scores at the university entrance exams.

Anatolian high schools (*Anadolu Lise*) – the equivalent of grammar schools – teach certain subjects such as science and mathematics in English, French or German, and programmes take three years. A language prep school exists prior to 3 year high school education. There is a very competitive entrance examination:

265,000 students applied in 1994 of which 30,456 were accepted to study. The numbers of Anatolian *Lises* increased to 384 in 1994 which was 193 in 1992/93. Graduates are generally very successful at the university entrance exam.

Technical high schools (*Teknik Lise*) offer four-year programmes to prepare students for employment or university entrance. Subjects include all those studied in the science section of the general *Lises*, plus technical courses such as electronics, technical drawing, and communications. Teaching covers forty hours per week.

Commercial high schools (*Ticaret Lise*) also offer three-year courses in accounting, economics, finance, law, typewriting, banking, hotel and tourism, etc.

Teknik and *Ticaret Lises* are the vocational and commercial equivalents to the *Anadolu Lises*.

Vocational high schools (*Meslek Lise*) offer three-year programmes in a wide range of industrial and other subjects. There are 2,396 such schools which offer education on 118 subjects. Admission is through an exam. 270,000 students applied in 1994, of which, 120,000 were accepted.

There are also a number of private schools which only the wealthy can afford. Entry to these schools is attained by the same type of competitive examinations set for *Anadolu Lises*. Academic standards are therefore high. Most of these schools are foreign (usually English) language medium schools.

Technical and vocational education

There is a recognized need to expand and improve this sector, to meet the increasing personnel demands of rapidly developing industries.

Secondary-level *Lises* described above offer three or four-year courses in vocational and technical subjects, taught alongside other more general studies. Graduates receive a qualification as craftsmen or technicians and could expect to take up jobs in industry as semi-skilled or skilled workers or junior technicians. Tertiary-level technical education is carried out at vocational higher schools run by the universities, through two-year programmes. Entrance is by examination and is open to holders of *Lise* diplomas. Curricula cover subjects such as Turkish language and literature, history and a foreign language as well as theoretical and practical work in a technical subject. Graduates of these schools are employed as higher technicians in industry.

In general, the practical content of technical and vocational courses in Turkey is less than for comparable courses in UK, with the emphasis on the acquisition of knowledge rather than skills, though this is gradually changing.

In the non-formal sector there is a nationwide network of training centres (TCs) operated by the Ministry of Education: Public TCs, Apprenticeship TCs, Adult Technical TCs, Commerce/Tourism TCs, Practical Trade Schools for Girls. The processes of skill testing and certification are being addressed by the ministry.

FURTHER EDUCATION

There are no Turkish counterparts to colleges of further education. The institutions described above fulfil some of the functions of the UK further education sector.

HIGHER EDUCATION

All tertiary institutions except military colleges and police academies were incorporated into the universities in 1982. There are 52 state universities and four private universities. Each university is fully autonomous and determines its own curricula and regulations. Almost all of the universities are multicampus institutions, with a main campus in an urban centre (usually a provincial capital) and one or more small satellite campuses.

All holders of a *Lise* diploma are entitled to take the two-part university central examination. The first part is a general examination; applicants passing this can enter two-year diploma or vocational courses or the Open Education Faculty of <u>Anadolu University</u>, by taking the entrance tests of individual institutions. The second part of the central examination covers specialist subjects. Applicants indicate a choice of courses and institutions on a selection form. Entry to the university is highly competitive, and of over one million applicants and reapplicants only about 22–25 per cent are accepted every year, 1,154,000 students applied for 210,000 first year degree programmes places in 1993. 1,250,000 students applied in 1994 for approximately 250,000 places at the universities (open education and external degree places are not included). For the most popular courses, only 1 per cent of the applicants can be accepted. Engineering (especially electronics, industrial), medicine, economics and business related courses are the most popular fields of study.

Pre-licentiate Diploma (Önlisans) courses take two years and are offered in technical or vocational subjects.

Bachelor or first degree (Lisans Diplomasi) courses take a minimum of four years. Dentistry, veterinary medicine, architecture courses last five years and medicine six years. In the universities where all teaching is in English – <u>Bogaziçi University</u>, <u>Bilkent University</u> and the <u>Middle East Technical University</u> – there is a one-year preparatory English course. Faculties and departments in other universities are teaching an increasing number of courses in English, particularly engineering and medicine. At some universities (e.g. <u>Ege</u>, <u>Gaziantep</u>, <u>Hacettepe</u>, <u>Marmara</u>, <u>Anadolu</u>, and <u>Istanbul</u>)

certain courses are taught in English and students are required to study English for one year before they take up their studies in a chosen field. English is the medium of instruction at the newly established KOÇ Private University and French is the medium of instruction at the Private Galatasaray University which is newly established too.

Master's degrees (Yüksek Lisans Diplomasi) are entered by examination, and last two years. The first year is a taught course assessed by examination, with the second year for preparation of a thesis.

The **Higher Engineer's Diploma (Yüksek Mühendis Diplomasi)** is the equivalent of a **Master's degree**. The **Engineer's Diploma (Mühendis Diplomasi)** is the equivalent of a **Bachelor degree**.

Doctorate programmes require candidates to have a **Master's degree**, and pass an examination. A PhD is awarded following a two-year instruction period and upon the completion of a doctoral thesis. The **Specialist degree (Uzmanlik)** awarded for disciplines of clinical medicine is equivalent to the **Doctorate**.

Assistant Professorship: any holder of a PhD who is affiliated with a department in a university can be appointed as assistant professor following an academic assessment of the candidate's scholarly publications. Requirements vary between universities e.g. Middle East Technical University requires an article at a reputable international publication and at least one year academic study abroad at a well known foreign university.

Professorship: the title of full professor is also conferred following an assessment of publications.

TEACHER EDUCATION

All teachers must take a course after graduating from *Lise*, whatever the level at which they intend to teach.

All primary, middle and secondary school teachers must complete a four-year degree programme at a university faculty of education and obtain a **Lisans Diplomasi** (Bachelor/First degree). Programmes include courses in the specialist subject, pedagogy and general certificate in order to teach at middle and high school level. Teachers Competency Examination which was held annually by the Ministry of Education and which all teacher candidates were required to take in the past was abolished in 91/92. Prior to 1982, two or three-year courses could be taken by *Lise* graduates at Teacher Training Institutions, but these have now been replaced by the universities.

In-service training of teachers takes place at summer and evening schools and at courses and seminars organized by the Ministry of Education.

HIGHER EDUCATION INSTITUTIONS

Old State Universities:

1. Akdeniz University (Antalya) – founded in 1982.

2. Anadolu University (Eskisekir) – founded in 1973. Incorporated the Academy of Economics and Commercial Sciences and the Academy of Engineering and Architecture in 1982. Some courses are taught in English.

3.	Ankara University (Ankara) – comprehensive university founded in 1946. The prestigious faculties are medicine, and political sciences.

4.	Atatürk University (Erzurum) – founded in 1957

5.	Boğaziçi University (Istanbul) formerly Robert College, a private institution run along American lines; established as a university in 1971. English is the language of instruction. Academic standing is calculated on the basis of Grade Point Average on a 0–4 scale.

6.	Cumhuriyet (Republic) University (Sivas) founded in 1974

7.	Çukurova University (Adana) – founded in 1969 as a College of Agriculture, became a university in 1973. Some courses are taught in English.

8.	Dicle University (Diyarbakir) – founded in 1974

9.	Dokuz Eylül University (İzmir) – founded in 1982 from twenty-four existing institutions; formerly known as (İzmir University. Some courses are taught in English.

10.	Ege University (İzmir) – founded in 1955

11.	Erciyes University (Kayseri) – founded in 1978

12.	Firat University (Elaziğ) – founded in 1975

13.	Gazi University (Ankara) – founded in 1982

14.	Gaziantep University (Gaziantep) – founded in 1987

15.	Hacettepe University (Ankara) – founded in 1967 but traces its history back to the Hospital and Medical School. Although other faculties and institutes have gradually been established, the university still centres around the Medical Complex. Uses both Turkish and English as language of instruction.

16.	İnönü University (Malatya) – founded in 1975

17.	İstanbul University (İstanbul) – the oldest university in Turkey; first established in the 15th Century, it acquired its present status in 1933. The University opened its first English-medium departments in 1987 in business, economics and medical faculties.

18.	İstanbul Technical University (İstanbul) – founded in 1944

19.	Karadeniz Technical University (Trabzon) – founded in 1955

20.	Marmara University (İstanbul) – founded in 1982

21.	Mimar Sinan University (İstanbul) – founded in 1982

22.	Ondokuz Mayis University (Samsun) – founded in 1975

23.	Middle East Technical University (Ankara) – established in 1959 with the objective of training Turkish and foreign students in scientific, technical and professional fields of study. English is the medium of instruction. Academic standing is calculated on the basis of Grade Point Average (GPA) on a 0–4 scale.

24. Selçuk University (Konya) – founded in 1975

25. Trakya University (Edirne) – established in 1982; formerly known as Edirne University

26. Uludağ University (Bursa) – founded in 1975

27. Yildiz University (İstanbul) – founded in 1982

28. Yüzüncü Yil University (Van) – founded in 1982

New State Universities (founded in 1992):

.1. Abant İzzet Baysal University (Bolu)

2. Adnan Mederes University (Aydin)

3. Afyon Kocatepe University (Afyon)

4. Balikesir University (Balikesir)

5. Celal Bayar University (Manisa)

6. Çanakkale 18 Mart University (Çanakkale)

7. Dumlupinar University (Kütahya)

8. Gaziosmanpaşa University (Tokat)

9. Gebze Higher Technical Institute (Gebze)

10. Harran University (Şanh Urfa)

11. İzmir Higher Technical Institute (İzmir)

12 Kafkas University (Kars)

13. K. Maraş Sütçü İmam University (K. Maraş)

14. Kirikkale University (Kirikkale)

15. Kocaeli University (Kocaeli)

16. Mersin University (Mersin)

17. Muğla University (Muğla)

18. Mustafa Kemal University (Hatay)

19. Niğde University (Niğde)

20. Pamukkale University (Denizli)

21. Sakarya University (Sakarya)

22. Süleyman Demirel University (Isparta)

23. <u>Zonguldak Karaelmas University</u> (Zonguldak)

24. <u>Osman Gazi University</u> (Eskişehir) founded in 1993 and used to be part of Anadolu University in Eskişehir

Private or Special Universities:

1. <u>Bilkent University</u> (Ankara) The first private university in Turkey, founded in 1984 through the joint efforts of the Hacettepe Foundations. The name Bilkent is an abbreviated form of 'Bilim Kenti' or 'City of Science' in Turkish. English is the medium of instruction, academic standing is calculated on the basis of Grade Point Average (GPA) on a 0–4 scale

2. <u>Koç University</u> (İstanbul) – founded in 1992. English is the medium of instruction

3. <u>Başkent University</u> (Ankara) – founded in 1993

4. <u>Galatasaray University</u> (İstanbul) – founded in 1993. French is the medium of instruction.

Uganda

Until 1972, pupils took the examinations of the University of Cambridge Local Examinations Syndicate. In 1967, the East African Examinations Council (EAEC) was established, with Kenya and Tanzania as co-members. Collaboration with the University of Cambridge Local Examinations Syndicate in the administration of the East African Certificate of Education (EACE) and the East African Advanced Certificate of Education (EAACE) continued until 1974. In 1971, Tanzania withdrew from the EAEC, and in 1980 Kenya withdrew. The Uganda National Examinations Board (NEB) then took over the conduct of all examinations previously run by the EAEC (from 1980) and also the **Primary Leaving Examination** formerly conducted by the Ugandan Ministry of Education and Sports.

There is no period of compulsory education.

The medium of instruction is English.

The school year runs from January to December, and the university year from October to September. University examinations are taken in June.

EVALUATION IN BRITAIN

School

Uganda Certificate of Education –	) grades 1–6 generally
Cambridge Overseas School	) equated to GCSE
Certificate –	) standard (grades A,
East African Certificate of	) B and C) on a subject-
Education –	) for-subject basis.

Uganda Advanced Certificate of	) grades A–E are
Education –	) generally equated
Cambridge Overseas Higher School	) to GCE Advanced
Certificate –	) standard.
East African Advanced Certificate	)
of Education –	)

Higher

Bachelor degree – generally considered comparable to British Bachelor degree standard.

MARKING SYSTEMS

School

Uganda Certificate of Education (UCE)	graded 1 (maximum) – 9 (fail) grades 1–2 = distinction grades 3–6 = credit grades 7–8 = pass grade 9 = fail
Cambridge Overseas School Certificate (COSC) **East African Certificate of Education (EACE)**	graded 1 (maximum) – 9 (fail)
Uganda Advanced Certificate of Education (UACE)	graded A–F (fail)

Most of the principal subjects offered at the **Uganda Advanced Certificate of Education** are examined by more than one paper. These are history, economics, literature in English, French, German, geography, biology, physics, chemistry and divinity. For example, economics is examined by two papers. A candidate's marks scored on each of the two papers are converted into grades using a numerical point scale i.e. –

1–2	– very good (distinction)
3–6	– credit pass
7–8	– pass grade
9	– fail

To arrive at a subject grade for the candidate in economics, the paper grades are added to give a numerical aggregate which may range from 2 to 18. The aggregate is then converted into letter grades according to the candidate's level of achievement.

Subject total aggregate	letter grade	description
2–5	A	very good
6–7	B	good
8–9	C	above average
10–11	D	average
12	E	lowest principal pass
13–16	O	subsidiary pass
17–18	F	fail grade

Cambridge Overseas Higher School Certificate (COHSC)	graded A–F (fail)
East African Advanced Certificate of Education (EAACE)	grades A–F (fail)

Higher

Bachelor degrees:

class I	Top Honours
class II i	Honours Upper
class II ii	Honours Lower
pass	General Pass
fail	

The University Senate, <u>Makerere University</u> has recently put up the pass-marks from 45 per cent to 50 per cent.

SCHOOL EDUCATION

Pre-primary

Pre-school education is available in all urban areas throughout Uganda. These schools are privately run and are not licensed by the Ministry of Education.

Primary

This consists of a seven-year course for children mainly aged six to fourteen years. At the end of seven years pupils sit for the national examination, the **Primary Leaving Examination** (PLE), which serves both as a terminal examination and a qualifying test for post-primary institutions. A Bill before Parliament, if it becomes law, will put up the primary education period to 8 years from 7 years.

The curriculum consists of religious education (both Christian and Islamic), languages (English and vernacular), handwriting, numbers (mathematics), science (nature and health), art and crafts, music, physical education and social studies.

Secondary

Until 1961, this covered six years plus two years in form 6.

Since 1961, it has covered four years (lower secondary) plus two years (upper secondary), S1–6. The curriculum covers English, general science, geography, history, home economics and needlework (girls), civics, metal science and woodwork (two of these three for boys), mathematics, physical education, religious instruction, singing, arts and crafts, languages, commerce and political education. Agriculture is compulsory in all secondary schools.

Until 1970, pupils could take the examinations for the **Cambridge Overseas School Certificate** (COSC) at the end of form 4 and for the **Cambridge Overseas Higher School Certificate** (COHSC) at the end of form 6.

From 1968 to 1980 pupils could take the examinations for the **East African Certificate of Education** (EACE) at the end of form 4 and, from 1969 to 1980, for the **East African Advanced Certificate of Education** (EAACE) at the end of form 6.

Since 1980 when the Uganda National Examinations Board took charge of all school examinations, pupils have taken the examinations for the **Uganda Certificate of Education** (UCE) at the end of form 4 and for the **Uganda Advanced Certificate of Education** (UACE) at the end of form 6. The Bill before Parliament proposes to reduce the UCE from 4 years to 3 years.

Technical secondary

Technical schools offer three-year full-time courses to pupils who successfully pass the **Primary Leaving Examination**. All technical schools offer full-time courses in the following subjects: carpentry and joinery, bricklaying and concrete practice, plumbing, pottery, electrical installation work, leather tanning and shoe-making, tailoring, motor vehicle maintenance, tropical agriculture. Students sit for the **Uganda Junior Technical Certificate** examination. Qualifying students who do very well may join the Technical Institutes.

FURTHER EDUCATION

Uganda College of Commerce, also known as National School of Business Studies, offers a two-year course in business studies for pupils holding the COSC/EACE/UCE. UACE holders may be given advanced standing, but will normally have to attend the full two years.

Technical Institutes offer two-year courses leading to the **Uganda Technical Institute Certificate**. Students are usually selected from secondary school-leavers who have obtained the **Uganda Certificate of Education** with credits in mathematics, physics and technical subjects.

UCE holders take craft 1, 2 and 3 courses.

UACE holders take technician 1, 2 and 3 courses. Holders of the Technician 3 can then go on to diploma level.

Technical Colleges offer two-year courses leading to the **Ordinary Technician's Diploma**. A further two-year course leads to the **Higher Technician's Diploma**. The intake base is students with UACE certificates with at least one principal pass in physics, and a subsidiary pass in mathematics, or vice versa.

Uganda Polytechnic, formerly Uganda Technical College, requires two passes at the UACE level, one principal pass and one subsidiary pass.

Ordinary Diploma in Electrical Engineering.

Requirements for entry are at least two principal passes in mathematics, chemistry or physics; and one subsidiary pass in any one of them.

The subjects/papers studied are: mathematics, electrical engineering drawing, electrical engineering science, mechanical engineering science, power production, electrical power, electronics and engineering drawing office practice.

This is a full-time, three-year course.

Marking system

Nine-point scale with grades 1 (maximum) to 9 (fail).

1–2 distinction	75–100 per cent
3–6 credit	40–74 per cent
7–8 pass	30–39 per cent

Higher Diploma in Electrical Engineering.

Requirements for entry are an **Ordinary Diploma** pass with grade passes 1–2 and 3–6. Students must also have completed one year's practical work experience. The subjects/papers studied are: mathematics, industrial organization and management, electrical measurements, central systems, power supply, machines and utilization, digital electronics, industrial electronics and communication systems.

This is a full-time, two-year course with the same marking scheme as the **Ordinary Diploma**.

HIGHER EDUCATION

Makerere University was founded in 1922 as a technical college, became a university college with a special relationship with the University of London in 1950, part of the University of East Africa in 1963 and an independent university in 1971.

Admission to degree courses was similar to that in Britain, a minimum of three UCEs and two UACEs but there is now a minimum of six UCEs plus one or two UACEs. The grades required are very high owing to intense competition for entry.

Courses leading to the award of a **Bachelor degree** in arts, science, agriculture and law last three years, with four years in veterinary science and technology and five years in medicine (with a minimum of one year's internship).

Two years' additional study are required for the **Master's degree** and a further two years in research for a **Doctorate**.

Certain certificate and diploma courses leading to various professional awards are also offered.

An International Islamic University for the whole of Africa was founded in Mbale. The University offers all disciplines except medicine, engineering, agriculture and law.

There is now established the Mbarara University of Science and Technology. The University offers only medicine.

The Uganda Martyrs University is a private university founded in September 1993 and offers courses similar to those offered by the Islamic University.

TEACHER EDUCATION

Primary

Lower: two-year course for pupils who have completed S4 (four years of secondary education) leading to the **Grade III Teachers Certificate**.

Upper: one-year course for holders of the COSC/EACE/UCE, leading to the **Grade IV Teachers Certificate**.

Secondary

The National Teachers' Colleges run two-year courses for holders of the COHSC/EAACE/UACE, leading to a **Grade V Teachers Certificate**. There is also a three-year upgrading course for grade IV teachers, leading to the **Grade V Teachers Certificate**. To teach in the sixth form, teachers must hold a **Bachelor of Education** degree.

Ukraine

The Ukrainian Soviet Socialist Republic was proclaimed in December 1917 and was finally established in December 1919. It became a constituent republic of the Soviet Union in 1922. The republic declared itself independent on 24 August 1991, a decision endorsed by a referendum later that year. The development of education until 1990 reflected central Soviet policy. For details of this period please see the **Russian Federation** chapter.

Ukrainian is the official language.

The Ministry of Education, which was formed in December 1991, is responsible for all levels of education. A number of higher education establishments are supervised by other ministries (e.g. Health Care, Agriculture and Food, Defence), but the educational standards are set by the Ministry of Education and are obligatory for all institutions.

Since 1992 there has been an accreditation system for all levels of educational institution. This involves three stages: licensing (registration), assessment and certification.

The 25 June 1991 Law on Education is the foundation for educational reforms.

The state national programme 'Education Ukraine in the 21st Century' approved in 1993 provides guidelines for reforming the education system by 2005. All the new legislation lays emphasis on the devolution of the education system, its continuity and its diversity in the context of the political and economic reforms in Ukraine.

The school year runs from September to the end of May for primary schools, September to mid-June for secondary schools, and September to the end of June for tertiary institutions.

Education is compulsory from the age of six or seven to fifteen.

EVALUATION IN BRITAIN

School

Atestat pro Povnu Zagal'nu Sersdniu Osvitu (Certificate of complete general secondary education)

at grade 10 – generally considered to be below GCSE standard
at grade 11 – generally considered comparable to GCSE standard (grades A, B and C) on a subject-for-subject basis, with the exception of English language
at grade 12 – generally considered to be slightly above GCSE standard.

Higher

Until 1990

Diplom ob Okanchanii Vyssheg(v)o Uchebnog(v)o Zavedeniya (Diploma Specialist) – generally considered comparable to a standard between GCE Advanced and British Bachelor degree; may be given advanced standing by British higher education institutions. Candidates from prestigious institutions may be considered for admission to postgraduate study. Enquirers should contact the National Academic Recognition Information Centre for further information.

Since 1991

Dyplom molodshogo spetsialista (junior specialist diploma) – generally considered comparable to BTEC National Diploma / N/SVQ level 3 / Advanced GNVQ/GSVQ standard.

Dyplom bakalavra (Bachelor degree) – generally considered comparable to British Bachelor (Ordinary) degree standard.

Dyplom spetsialista (specialist diploma) – generally considered comparable to British Bachelor (Honours) degree standard.

Dyplom magistra (Master's Degree) – generally considered comparable to British Bachelor (Honours) degree standard.

MARKING SYSTEM

School and Higher

Marking is on a 2–5 scale

5	excellent
4	good
3	satisfactory
2	unsatisfactory

Schools and higher education establishments may use other marking systems (e.g. 100 point scale) but these systems are subsidiary to the main 2–5 scale.

1993–5

The marking in the experimental school tests at grades 9, 11 and 12 and higher education entrance examinations were based on a 60 or 100-point scale.

SCHOOL EDUCATION

Pre-school provision

In 1993, there were more than 23,000 pre-school establishments such as nursery schools, day-care centres, kindergartens and children's homes. The age range for infants enrolled in these establishments is from one to six or seven years. About 43 per cent of the age group attended pre-school establishments in 1993.

General school education

Under the new legislation, secondary schooling is made up of three levels of school, each of which may be independent:

First level (compulsory), primary school
Grades 1 to 4 inclusive, starting at the age of six or seven.

Second level (compulsory)
Grades 5 to 9, until the age of fifteen.

Third level (non-compulsory) upper school
Grades 10 to 11 (in some school there is also a grade 12).

At the end of grade 9 pupils take examinations and those who are successful are granted the **Svidotstvo pro Nepovnu Seredniu Zagal'nu Osvitu** (Certificate of incomplete secondary education). After finishing grade 9, young people may go on to upper school, a vocational school or enter the job market. Fifty-three per cent of school leavers go on to upper school, at the end of which they sit for the **Atestat pro Povnu Zagal'nu Sersdniu Osvitu** (Certificate of complete general secondary education).

Since 1991 several new types of school have been set up: these include *gymnasiums*, *lyceums*, educational complexes, private schools, etc. The most prestigious schools have been accredited as *gymnasiums* or *lyceums*, and are usually specialized. They admit on a competitive basis and offer advanced training in their specialism (e.g. physical and mathematical *lyceums*, art *gymnasiums*, etc.). There are also schools of mixed type known as school-*gymnasium* or school-*lyceum* in which only the upper grades (level three) offer advanced level schooling.

Final testing was introduced as an experiment in 1993; final examinations in the eleventh and twelfth grades and entrance examinations at pedagogical institutes were established. In 1994, the experiment was extended to cover final examinations at ninth-grade secondary and entrance examinations at all higher education establishments in the Ukraine. Both these examinations results were used for determining entry to higher education institutions. However, the current state of constant change in educational policy was illustrated when the Ministry of Education cancelled final school testing for 1995.

Of over 21,000 full-time secondary schools in the Ukraine in 1993, 95 were *gymnasiums* and over a hundred were *lyceums*. There were 28 private schools.

The move towards autonomy has reached the school sector. Individual schools design their own working syllabus, based on ministry guidelines, and have direct control over about one quarter of the total teaching time.

Vocational training

Vocational schools (*proftekhuchylyshcha*) provide vocational training leading to the qualification of a skilled worker. In response to the needs of economic reform, vocational training is undergoing structural change.

In 1993, 250 vocational schools changed the nomenclature of this sector of training. A new type of vocational school, the higher vocational school was introduced. Students enter at age fifteen and the final qualification is known as the diploma of junior specialist (**Dyplom molodshogo spetsialista**). Around three quarters of all vocational schools provide three to four-year courses which offer complete secondary education along with vocational training.

HIGHER EDUCATION

There is currently some confusion within the Ukraine concerning the old and new structures of higher education, which exist simultaneously in 1995. For example, many students take the degree of **specialist**, but there is then uncertainty as to where the **Master's degree** and **candidate of sciences** come in. In 1995 standards are still being worked out for **Bachelor** and **Master's degrees** under the new structure.

First degree

Admission is on the basis of complete general secondary education and three or four entrance examinations.

Under new legislation, all higher education establishments are granted one of four types of accreditation by the Interdepartmental Accreditation Committee together with the Ministry of Education:

Level	Type of Institution	Type of Qualification
I	technical school vocational school	**Dyplom molodshogo spetsialista** (Junior Specialist Diploma)
II	colleges	**Dyplom bakalavra** (Bachelor Degree)
III	institutes	**Dyplom spetsialista** (Specialist Diploma)
IV	universities academies	**Dyplom magistra** (Master's Diploma)

Institutions with one level of accreditation may have rights to award qualifications of lower levels. The requirements for the qualifications listed above have been worked out over the period 1993–5 (but have not yet been finalized or properly implemented).

In 1993, there were 754 state-maintained higher educational establishments with accreditation at levels I and II, and 159 with levels III and IV. There are also a number of private institutions with varying levels of accreditation: five universities, two academies, 35 institutes, ten colleges and vocational schools.

The length of higher educational courses varies from four to six years.

Postgraduate education

Postgraduate education in 1995 is based on education/research programmes and includes the qualifications **Dyplom pro Prysudzhenia Naukovogo Stupenia Kandydata Nauk** (Diploma of candidate of sciences) and **Dyplom pro Prysudzhenia Naukovogo Stupenia Doktora Nauk** (Diploma of doctor of sciences). Each of these programmes lasts three years. The new degree of **Master** has been introduced but standards are still being developed.

Ukraine

Higher degrees are awarded by specialized academic boards on the basis of a publicly defended thesis and are confirmed by the High Certification Committee of Ukraine (*Vyshcha Atestatsiyna Komisioa*, VAK), set up in 1992.

United Arab Emirates

The United Arab Emirates (UAE) is the federation established out of the former Trucial States in December 1971 when the British withdrew from the Gulf. The federation consists of the seven emirates: Adu Dhabi, Dubai, Sharjah, Ajman, Umm al Qawain, Ras al Khaimah and Fujairah. The Federal Ministry of Education came into being in 1972. The Ministry of Higher Education and Scientific Research was established in 1992 and deals with education of at least one year beyond high school. It is now in the process of evaluating all institutions of higher education in the UAE for accreditation purposes. It is also responsible for scholarships.

The UAE follows a 6–6–3 (primary-intermediate-secondary) year school system. Male and female students in all sectors are segregated, usually in separate buildings, although some private schools teach pupils in separate classrooms or in split shifts.

The school year lasts from early September to mid-June and the university academic year lasts from late August to mid-June. There is a two-week mid-year break towards the end of January.

EVALUATION IN BRITAIN

School

Tawjihiyya (Secondary School Certificate) – generally considered comparable to GCSE standard (grades A, B and C) on a subject-for-subject basis, with the exception of English language, when a minimum overall mark of 70 per cent has been obtained. Students with very good results and a recognized international English language qualification may be considered for admission to access/bridging courses.

Higher

Bachelor degree – may be considered to satisfy the general entrance requirements of British higher education institutions. Students with very high grades may be given advanced standing.

MARKING SYSTEMS

School

The **Tawjihiyya** shows the name of the subject studied; alongside this are four columns of marks (maximum, minimum, score obtained and retake score). Subjects have different maximum or minimum scores, according to their weighting.

Higher

The University of the United Arab Emirates uses the following grading system:

90–100 per cent	A	4.0
85–89	B+	3.5
80–84	B	3.0
75–79	C+	2.5
70–74	C	2.0
65–69	D+	1.5
60–64	D	1.0
0–59	E	0

The semester and cumulative grade point averages are assigned the following designations:

Point average	Designation
3.6+	excellent
3–3.5	very good
2.5–2.9	good
2–2.4	pass
below 2	fail

SCHOOL EDUCATION

Primary

This is compulsory and lasts six years. English has now been introduced in the first year. Twice yearly examinations are held from the third year. Pupils must be successful in final examinations in order to enter the preparatory stage.

Preparatory

This intermediate stage covers the next three years with the same type of curriculum as that of the primary level.

Secondary

At this stage the system offers a three-year general, religious or vocational course.

General: the present system provides a general education with a choice between a scientific and an arts bias after the common first year. At the end of the twelfth year students take the examinations for the **Tawjihiyya** (Secondary School Certificate) set by the Ministry of Education Inspectorate.

Religious institutes: there are four traditional religious institutes which cover the same curriculum as mainstream secondary schools but teach five additional periods of Islamic studies.

Vocational schools: there are five institutions of technical education in the UAE offering the six years of intermediate and secondary education. They deal either with technical training, agriculture or commerce. They follow the same curriculum as other secondary schools but have a longer day and replace humanities with their vocational specialization.

HIGHER EDUCATION

Courses started at the United Arab Emirates University in 1977 in four faculties: arts, science, administrative and political science. The following faculties have been added since: Sharia and law, agriculture, engineering (including architecture) and health and medicine sciences. The language of instruction is Arabic in all faculties except engineering, science, health and medical science where the language of instruction is English. There is also a Department of Higher Education, a Department of Student Affairs and a Faculty of External Tutorial Studies which offers tuition to external students by means of centres in each Emirate.

The required grades in the **Tawjihiyya** for entry to the university are as follows:

Faculty	UAE nationals	GCC residents	expatriate	faculty children
arts	60	60	80	70
science	60	60	80	70
education	60	60	80	65
economics and management	70	70	80	75
Sharia and law	60	60	80	65
agriculture	60	60	80	65
engineering	65	65	90	85
health and medical sciences	80	–	–	-

For nationals, the **Tawjihiyya** should not be more than three years old, except for health and medical sciences (2 years). Some faculties may require students to undergo an interview. All students must satisfy the Basic University Education requirements.

The Basic University Education Centre offers a foundation programme aimed at developing core skills in Arabic, English, scientific research methodology and mathematics. There is strong emphasis on the use of computers and modern educational concepts. At the time of enrolment, the student is tested to establish deficiencies to be remedied through the centre. Since 1992, nationals with marks above 70 per cent with technical or vocational high school certificates in commerce, manufacturing or agriculture, have been allowed to join the BUE centre. Students with less than 60 per cent may be allowed to register subject to satisfactory BUE performance. To graduate, the following number of credit units are required:

college	number of units
arts	132
science	134–136
education	132
economics and management	132
Sharia and law	150
agriculture	136
engineering	170
health and medical sciences	7 years plus one year's residence after graduation

Postgraduate work now centres on a **Master's degree** in environmental sciences, offered by the College of Science, and a **Diploma** offered by the College of Education.

Higher Colleges of Technology

Established by the Federal government in 1988, the eight Higher Colleges of Technology offer UAE nationals three-year career programmes leading to the award of the **Higher Diploma** in various engineering technologies and business disciplines. New programmes began in communication arts (1994) and health sciences (1995). For most students, a foundation programme of usually one year's duration is essential before they can embark on their chosen career programme. The language of instruction is English and students must obtain a minimum of 5 on the IELTS test before they can be awarded the **Higher Diploma**. The colleges, with separate buildings for men and women, are located in Abu Dhabi, Al Ain, Dubai and Ras al Khaimah, are housed in modern buildings and are well equipped, resourced and staffed. In 1993 it was decreed by the Federal government that the **Higher Diploma** would be considered the equivalent of the UAE University **Bachelor's degree** for the purposes of employment. The entry requirements include a minimum of 60 per cent on the school-leaving certificate.

Dubai Medical College for Girls was set up in 1986 as a private college, but with full support from the Dubai government. The aims of the college are to produce intellectual graduate physicians who are scientifically, ethically, morally and spiritually strong; to offer the opportunity for UAE women to study medicine in their home country; to create qualified female Muslim physicians; and to extend to expatriate females the opportunity to study medicine in the UAE.

Applications are accepted in June and July each year and priority is given to UAE students. Candidates must hold **Tawjihiyya** with 80 per cent, or an equivalent qualification, and must attend an interview. Students accepted with a low standard of English must attend a supplementary summer English course at the college.

The college contains lecture rooms equipped with: visual aids; a dissecting room; library; separate laboratories for different medical subjects and departments; and a pathology museum. It is connected by computer with Al Ain University library. Students carry out their internship at hospitals belonging to Dubai Department of Health and Medical Services which offer up-to-date facilities for clinical education. The college also offers hostels for students, a mosque and a sports centre.

Graduates, of which there have been three batches to date, are now working as resident doctors in different Dubai government hospitals. Some have registered for FRCP in England, others for Arab or American Board examinations qualifying them for post-graduate studies or jobs in those countries.

Emirates Banking Training Institute (EBTI) is a national corporation for professional training and education, entrusted primarily with the preparation of qualified and competent UAE nationals who can successfully enter the banking and financial services sector and develop their careers to positions of responsibility and leadership. The EBTI acts as a medium for the development of national and other human resources already employed in the banking and financial services industry.

The institute offers a wide range of short training programmes in all the functional areas of banking and in some areas of insurance, as well as a one-year **Banking Diploma** for nationals. EBTI acts as a catalyst for interaction, exchange and innovation within the sector which it serves, by organizing conferences and symposia on current and relevant issues, and by undertaking to publish materials which deal with these issues and enhance bankers' and financial professionals' understanding of their profession.

EBTI also provides a link between the local financial community and the larger academic and professional community by building relations and entering into collaborative agreements with similar training institutions, with recognized professional bodies and with colleges and universities in the UAE and abroad.

Etisalat College of Engineering was set up by Etisalat, the UAE telecommunications corporation in 1989. It is a university-level college specializing in electronic engineering only. It currently offers a two-year BTEC HND leading on to a three-year full **BEng Honours** programme in Electronics and Communications Engineering. The degree programme is moderated by external examiners from Queen Mary and Westfield College and Bradford University. The programme itself was developed along the lines of the British system in collaboration with Bradford and Ilkley Community College and Bradford University. The college produced its first batch of graduates in June 1994.

The BTEC HND constitutes the foundation programme for the degree course and includes, where necessary, supplementary English language training. Candidates should have at least 70 per cent on the **Tawjihiyya** and are required to sit an entrance examination in English and mathematics.

Dubai Aviation College, which was set up in 1991 as a private institution, offers a number of BTEC National Diplomas as an alternative to the academic route of GCE Advanced or their equivalent. Diplomas offered include: business and finance; hotel and catering management; travel and tourism; electrical and electronic engineering; information technology applications and aerospace studies (aircraft engineering). All diplomas require two years of full-time study and combine classroom teaching with continuous assessments, examinations and work experience placements.

PRIVATE COLLEGES

There are a number of private institutions offering courses ranging from computer and business studies to languages and domestic science. Some have established links with overseas institutions in order to provide courses leading to the overseas qualifications. Links may take various forms: some provide full staffing and resourcing locally; others bring teaching staff from the overseas institution to deliver modules; others simply require a local agency for the provision of distance packages. At the moment the Ministry of Education has responsibility for monitoring these organizations. However, the whole question of the local delivery of overseas higher education qualifications is of serious concern at present and this sector may be transferred to the Ministry of Higher Education and Scientific Research and placed under close restriction.

NURSE TRAINING

There are four schools of nursing with a fifth under construction. These were set up in 1974 and it is planned in late 1994 to offer first degree and postgraduate programmes.

TEACHER EDUCATION

Until the establishment of the University in 1977, only two teacher training institutes existed at secondary level. On completion of training, teachers could teach only in the primary/preparatory cycle, as a university degree was required for teaching at a higher level.

United Arab Emirates

Teacher training has now become the responsibility of the Faculty of Education at the University, which concentrates on training secondary stage teachers, and of the Federal Ministry of Education, which concentrates on in-service training at that level and pre-service training for primary school teachers.

United States of America

The U.S. Department of Education does not regulate standards, oversee the establishment of institutions or provide accreditation. Public authority is constitutionally reserved to the states.

Accreditation is a voluntary, non-governmental process for educational institutions and professional programmes to assure an acceptable level of performance, integrity and quality. This recognition is given by institutional or professional associations which establish criteria for accreditation, arrange site visits, evaluate candidates and assign accreditation status. Institutional accreditation is granted by any one of the six regional bodies which operate in a specified geographical area or one of the accrediting commissions which cater to defined segments of higher education. For purposes of transfer credit, regional accreditation is the primary basis for consideration; however, decisions on transfer of credit are made by the individual admitting institutions. Regional accrediting associations are:

> Middle States Association of Colleges and Schools
> New England Association of Schools and Colleges
> North Central Association of Colleges and Schools
> North West Association of Schools and Colleges
> Southern Association of Colleges and Schools
> Western Association of Schools and Colleges.

Other institutional accrediting bodies for specialized areas include:

> American Association of Bible Colleges
> Association of Independent Colleges and Schools
> National Home Study Council
> Association of Theological Schools
> National Association of Trade and Technical Schools.

Professional accrediting bodies review degree courses in specific areas such as business or engineering.

In most states education is compulsory from age six to sixteen.

The school year runs from September to June.

EVALUATION IN BRITAIN

School

High School Graduation Diploma – generally considered comparable to GCSE standard (grades A, B and C) provided an average of at least C is obtained in subjects which have counterparts in the GCSE syllabus. Students who have completed an academic programme (college prep., indicated by a 'p' after the subject on the transcript; an 'h' indicates honours) exceeding the required units (sometimes called Carnegie Units), and who are considered eligible for admission to prestigious American colleges and universities, may be considered to satisfy the general entrance requirements of British higher education institutions.

Students who have not completed an academic high school programme normally need to have studied for one or two years at an accredited American college or university before satisfying the general entrance requirements. However, some British higher education institutions, will consider high school graduates whose qualifications include a good performance in the **Scholastic Aptitude Test** (SAT), usually not less than 500 in verbal and mathematical performance, plus **SAT II** (formerly **achievement tests**) in three subjects, or **Advanced Placement Tests**, in at least two, but preferably three or four subjects with marks of three and above.

Higher

Associate degree – may be considered to satisfy the general entrance requirements of British higher education institutions. Courses of a more vocational nature (**Associate of Applied Arts or Science**) may be considered comparable to the BTEC National Diploma / N/SVQ level 3 / Advanced GNVQ/GSVQ standard.

Bachelor degree – diversity is the key to American higher education with more than three thousand institutions offering post-secondary education. This means a uniform standard of **Bachelor degree** is impossible. Students who have attended a regionally accredited institution, have gained good grade-point averages (GPA – normally at least 3.0), both overall and in individual courses, have taken advanced-level courses in appropriate subjects, have accumulated sufficient credits in major courses (typically between 30 and 54), and have good academic references, may be considered for admission to postgraduate study. For further information enquirers should contact the National Academic Recognition Information Centre.

NARIC does not comment on institutions which are not regionally accredited.

Master's degree – in terms of specialization, the American Master's degree from prestigious colleges and universities is considered comparable to the British Bachelor (Honours) degree. Candidates who have followed academically rigorous programmes have reached a standard comparable to that of a British taught Master's degree.

MARKING SYSTEMS

School

The **High School Graduation Diploma** is awarded on the basis of continuous assessment, during which the student must obtain a minimum of 16 units over four years. To earn a unit the student must study a subject for a one-hour period per day per five-day week for thirty-six weeks, pass the prescribed tests and complete the prescribed written assignments. An increasing number of states and schools are raising minimum requirements to 18 or more units before a diploma can be awarded.

The grading system used is as follows:

A   excellent
B   good
C   average
D   pass
F   fail

Students entering higher education would generally need a minimum of grade C or better in the **High School Graduation Diploma**.

Higher

Institutions of higher education use the credit system. This means that each course earns a specified number of credits/units/hours depending on the work involved. The course grades or marks constitute the basis for evaluating the student's academic performance:

A	excellent	4.0
B	good	3.0
C	average	2.0
D	pass	1.0
F	fail	0

Students should maintain an average of C (a minimum grade-point average of 2.0) or better to remain in good academic standing.

Academic achievement is measured by grade points. On the 0–4 point scale, each credit hour with a grade of A earns 4 grade points, B earns 3, C earns 2, D earns 1, and F earns no grade points. The student's grade-point average (GPA) is calculated by multiplying the grade point for each course by the credit hours of the course and then dividing by the total number of credit hours of enrolment.

SCHOOL EDUCATION

Diagrams illustrating the education system in the United States of America may be obtained from the Fulbright Commission.

Elementary

Children normally enter grade 1 at age six, after an optional year at kindergarten, and attend elementary school for six years.

Middle

Some school districts include a middle school which may begin at grade 5 or 6 and generally include grades 7 and 8.

Secondary

Junior high school

Where no middle school exists, students normally attend junior high school for three years from grades 7 to 9.

Senior high

Students normally attend senior high school for three or four years (grades 9 or 10 to 12). By the beginning of grade 10, they must decide whether to take an academic course, a vocational course, or a general course, consisting of both options. All courses lead to the **High School Graduation Diploma**, awarded to students who have successfully completed 16 credits with an average of grade D or above.

Some school districts may follow an 8–4 year pattern, rather than the 6–3–3 or 5–3–4 patterns.

The units which make up a **High School Graduation Diploma** are recorded on a transcript, which will indicate the subject, number of credits (or units), and grades per term. If so instructed by the student, the school will send copies of transcripts to anyone who needs to see them. Students may choose to follow one of several programmes: general, academic, vocational or technical, university preparatory and honours (for example). A typical academic (college prep.) diploma might consist of four years for English and three years for mathematics (algebra I and II and geometry), with the remaining 8 or 9 units spread over foreign languages, social sciences and natural sciences.

Vocational High School – students will complete the general course and gain the **High School Graduation Diploma** as well as more vocationally-based courses, e.g. Diploma in Air Conditioning and Refrigeration.

HIGHER EDUCATION

Admissions procedures for higher education

In addition to a high school transcript, evidence of completion and references, most colleges and universities require scholastic achievement tests. The most frequently used are the **Scholastic Achievement Test** (SAT I) and the **American College Test** (ACT). Some institutions also require one to three achievement tests in specific subjects (called **Achievement tests** until 1994, **SAT II** from 1994/5).

Scholastic Achievement Test (SAT I)

This two-and-a-half-hour multiple-choice test consists of five thirty-minute timed sections, testing verbal and mathematical ability. The score reports show sub-scores for each section of the test, percentile ranks (to show how the student scores in relation to the other students taking the test) and scaled scores, which run from 200 to 800, in each section. Students often quote one total score by adding the two scaled scores together. Average scores of students seeking admission are 426 verbal and 471 mathematics.

700 +	exceptional
600 +	high
480–550	above average
420–480	average
200–420	below average

It should be noted that these scores are section scores, not combined verbal and quantitative.

Individual subject Achievement Tests – until 1994

These were one-hour, multiple-choice tests which measured knowledge in specific subjects. There was a choice of thirteen subjects and most colleges which require achievement tests asked for three. The scores ranged from 200 to 800.

SAT II – Since 1994

SAT II tests have now replaced the individual subject **Achievement Tests.** They take the same one hour format, but are now available in five general subject areas: English (writing, literature), history and social studies (American history and social studies, world history), mathematics, sciences and foreign languages.

Starting in May 1995, all SAT I and II scores, which are reported on the 200–800 scale, will be 'recentred'. This process will place the average SAT I score near 500, and will affect SAT II scores, which are linked to the SAT I scale. Recentring will not effect the relationship between tests taken after May 1995, but will effect comparisons between subject tests taken before and after this date.

Test of Standard Written English (TSWE)

The **Test of Standard Written English** (TSWE) is included in the **Scholastic Achievement Test** and examines knowledge of the mechanics of written English. This test is used by colleges for placement purposes. Scores are reported on a scale of 20–60.

American College Test (ACT)

This test examines a student's knowledge in English, mathematics, reading and science reasoning.

This multiple-choice examination changed its format in October 1989 and a composite (average) score of 24 would be comparable to a total SAT score of 1,000. Scores in each section range from 1–36.

The score range is from 1–33 in English, 1–36 in mathematics, 1–34 in social studies and 1–35 in natural sciences. The average of these scores is called the composite score. This test would be considered comparable to the SAT test and is often required by universities in the south of the US.

Advanced Placement Tests

These tests are set by the College Entrance Examination Board and offered annually to gifted high school students to demonstrate university-level achievement. In the examinations students answer essay questions, having followed a prescribed syllabus. The grading system used is on a 1–5 (maximum) scale. Students achieving a score of 3 may be given some credit. In 1990, the mean grade was 3.06, with 14.7 per cent achieving 5.

Essays ('free-response' sections) are graded by a national group, comprising school and university teachers, overseen by a chief reader. Multiple-choice questions are graded separately by the Educational Testing Service in Princeton, New Jersey. Many tests incorporate both formats. In 1986, the mean grade was 3.10, with 14.2 per cent achieving 5.

Some 43 per cent of secondary schools offer this course to 13 per cent of their university-bound students. The number of students sitting these exams has increased a great deal in the past few years. In 1983, 141,000 candidates sat for 189,000 **Advanced Placement Tests**; in 1990 this number had increased to 330,000 candidates taking 490,000 tests. Testing outside the United States has more than doubled in this time period, from 1,900 candidates taking 3,000 tests in 1983 to 6,300 candidates sitting for 9,600 examinations in 1990.

English proficiency tests

Students whose mother tongue is not English normally have to take the **Test of English as a Foreign Language** (TOEFL). This consists of a two-hour, multiple-choice test, involving listening comprehension, reading comprehension/vocabulary and structure/written expression. Scores range from 20 to 80. The overall score for the entire test ranges from 200 to 800. Most American universities and colleges require an overall score of 550+ at the undergraduate level.

General Educational Development (GED) tests

Adults who did not acquire a **High School Graduation Diploma** while at school, foreign students, etc. may take GED tests, which are set nation-wide and consist of five multiple-choice sections. These are designed to investigate correctness and effectiveness of expression, interpretation of reading materials in the social sciences and natural sciences, interpretation of literary materials and general mathematical ability. Students who achieve an average GED section score of 45 may be awarded a **High School Equivalency Diploma** by the State Department of Education concerned. Many American universities will accept the GED in lieu of the **High School Graduation Diploma**, provided average scores of 50 are obtained.

Higher Education Degrees

Associate degree

Community and junior colleges provide courses for vocational, technical and academic study, leading to an **Associate degree** after two years of study as well as shorter certificate courses. A 'terminal' **Associate of Applied Arts** or **Applied Sciences degree** tends to be vocational or technical training, while a 'transfer' programme provides the core curriculum in preparation for the final two years of a **Bachelor degree**. In most states, 'articulation' agreements exist, whereby a student who successfully completes a prescribed curriculum can automatically transfer to a state university to complete the final two years of a **Bachelor degree**. Many students also transfer to private colleges.

Community colleges are usually locally controlled and publicly financed for the benefit of the nearby population. This option is attractive to students because of the low fees for tuition and the ability to commute from home.

Bachelor degree

Degree courses are offered by universities and colleges. The terms 'universities' and 'colleges' are of equal academic standing, but colleges mainly award undergraduate qualifications. Liberal arts colleges (originally entitled liberal arts and sciences colleges) were founded to provide academic rather than professional education, although all now offer some professional courses. Training for some professions, e.g. medicine and law, is undertaken at postgraduate level only.

The **Bachelor degree** involves four years of academic study:

First year   – freshman
Second year   – sophomore
Third year   – junior
Fourth year   – senior

Courses taken in the first two years are referred to as 'lower division courses' and those in the last two years as 'upper division courses'.

The degree has three components: core courses (general education in various fields); the major field; and electives or options. During the first two years students take their core courses, introductory courses to their major fields and some electives. During the last two years they concentrate on courses in their major field and also take some electives which may complement or support the major.

A typical undergraduate enrols in four or five courses each term, representing 12–18 credit hours. The semester system, used by most colleges and universities, consists of two fourteen to eighteen-week terms each academic year. Normally, a student must complete 120 semester credit hours or eight semesters for a **Bachelor degree**, and maintain a minimum grade-point average of 2.00 to remain in good academic standing.

Honours degrees

Universities may offer various academic honours upon graduation. The terms *cum laude*, *magna cum laude* and *summa cum laude* indicate that the student is academically outstanding.

The term 'Honours programme' may indicate the submission of a special 'Honours' thesis.

Admission procedures to Graduate Schools

Graduate Record Examinations (GRE)

Many graduate and professional schools and fellowship sponsors require or recommend that their applicants submit scores on either the GRE general test, a subject test or both, to be used by admissions officers to supplement undergraduates' records and other indicators of students' potential for postgraduate study. The scores provide a common measure for comparing the qualifications of applicants who come from a variety of colleges and universities with different standards.

The GRE general test is a multiple choice examination administered by the Educational Testing Service and contains sections which measure verbal, quantitative and analytical abilities. It consists of seven thirty-minute sections. Six sections of the general test contribute to the test scores; one unidentified, separately-timed section has trial questions which are not included in the actual test scores. This section is used to evaluate questions for possible inclusion in subsequent test editions.

Graduate Management Admissions Test (GMAT)

The **Graduate Management Admissions Test** is designed to help graduate schools of business assess the qualifications of applicants for advanced study in business and management. It consists of nine separately timed sections, seven containing at least 15 multiple-choice questions and two separately timed 30–minute writing tasks. The GMAT measures general verbal, mathematical, and analytical writing skills that are developed over a long period of time and are associated with success in the first year of study at graduate schools of management. Scores on the test have two important characteristics: they are reliable measures of certain developed mental skills that have been found to be important in the study of management at graduate level and unlike undergraduate averages, which vary in their meaning according to the grading standards of each institution, GMAT scores are based on the same standard for all candidates.

Law School Admission Test (LSAT)

The **Law School Admission Test** is a half-day standardized test. It consists of four forty-five minute sections of multiple-choice questions and one thirty-minute writing sample. Only three of the four sections are scored, and each of the scored sections contains a different type of question. The fourth section is used to pre-test new test items or to equate new test forms. The LSAT score scale is 10–48 with 48 being the highest possible score. The test is designed to measure skills that are considered essential for success in law school. It provides a standard measure of academic aptitude common to all applicants.

Medical College Admission Test (MCAT)

This test is administered by the American College Testing Programme under the direction of the Association of American Medical Colleges. It is designed to measure general academic ability, general information and scientific knowledge.

Graduate degrees

The **Master's degree** is a taught degree and involves one to two years of full-time academic study beyond the **Bachelor degree**. A thesis is required in some cases and is often an option. This degree represents advanced subject specialization and, in some programmes, advanced professional specialization. In some subjects a thesis is an option, for which 6–12 credits are given.

The **Doctor of Philosophy degree** (PhD) usually involves four to seven years' study and research beyond the **Bachelor degree**. Candidates must complete graduate-level courses lasting up to two or three years, which culminate in a qualifying examination, and may include proficiency in one or two languages. Students then embark on their doctoral thesis.

Professional degrees

The study of medicine, law, education and dentistry is undertaken usually after completion of a **Bachelor degree**. To qualify for a **medical degree** (MD), four years of study including clinical work are necessary. Many qualified doctors then pursue further specialized study and a residency programme.

The first law degree is called the **Doctor of Jurisprudence** (JD). It requires three years of study.

Holders of professional degrees in dentistry, law and medicine must pass state examinations before beginning to practise in their profession.

TEACHER EDUCATION

Teacher education is offered exclusively at the higher education level by universities, state colleges, liberal arts colleges and special schools. The minimum requirement for teaching at elementary or secondary level in any of the fifty states is the **Bachelor degree**, while almost half the states require teachers to obtain a postgraduate degree within a given period.

In-service courses and workshops are available to serving teachers.

Licensing Tests are mandatory in 48 states, the idea is to reinforce teacher competence. They are administered by a private company Educational Testing Service. Although the tests are standardized each state sets its own pass-marks based on the need for teachers in a given year. Three separate processes are being instituted to improve and assess teacher competence. The ETS has developed a Praxis Series of assessments designed to test beginning teachers' knowledge of subject matter and pedagogy and performance skills. The Praxis is currently being pilot tested in some states. The Interstate New Teachers Assessment and Support Consortium (INTASC) is developing beginning (first year) teacher standards including generic skills and subject specific pedagogy. The

National Board for Professional Teaching Standards is developing thirty different types of expert teaching assessments, of which two are now being pilot tested. All of these assessments are voluntary.

ADULT EDUCATION

This sector has expanded more rapidly than any other during the last fifteen years. The motivation comes from two sources. The universities/colleges themselves wish to make economic use of their facilities outside normal academic terms, while, at the same time, state authorities have increased certification requirements in many fields, particularly health and education. The unit system which forms the basic structure of American higher education makes it flexible and easily adaptable to part-time study.

Most institutions offer part-time courses, specially designed for mature students, through weekend, evening and summer courses, but also through correspondence.

In addition to four-year degree-granting institutions, community colleges have always played an extensive part in adult education. Co-operation with industry to complement on-the-job-training, and distance learning, through the use of audio-visual equipment to link work-places with colleges, are fairly common.

Uruguay

The following chapter regarding the education system in Uruguay is based on information obtained from the 3rd edition of this Guide, published in 1991, as NARIC has been unable to obtain more recent information.

Education was compulsory for six years until 1972. This has now been extended to nine years.

The medium of instruction is Spanish.

The academic year runs from March to November.

EVALUATION IN BRITAIN

School

Bachillerato – generally considered comparable to GCSE standard (grades A, B and C) on a subject-for-subject basis, with the exception of English language.

Higher

Licenciado/Professional title – generally considered comparable to British Bachelor degree standard if awarded after four or more years of study.

MARKING SYSTEM

School and Higher

Marking is on the scale 1–6 (maximum), with 3 as the minimum pass-mark.

6	*sobresaliente* (S)	excellent
5	*muy bueno* (MB)	very good
4	*bueno* (B)	good
3	*bueno regular* (BR)	average
2	*regular* (R)	below average
1	*deficiente* (D)	bad

SCHOOL EDUCATION

Pre-primary

This is available from ages three to five.

Primary

This covers six years, from age six.

Secondary

Until 1978

This covered six years divided into a four-year lower cycle and a two-year higher cycle. Final-year pupils could specialize in law, agricultural science, architecture, economics, engineering or medical science. At the same time, a system co-existed of a four-year lower cycle, the fifth year allowing diversification to opt for biology, humanities or sciences and the sixth year allowing full specialization.

The Reform Plan introduced into a limited number of schools the pattern of six years divided into five years (again subdivided into three plus two) plus one year. This system is being phased out.

Since 1978

Under the Reform Plan of 1976 schools are now operating on the system of a three-year *Ciclo Basico* followed by a three-year *Ciclo Diversificado*. The curriculum of the *Ciclo Basico* covers Spanish, mathematics, French, biology, history, moral and civic education, geography, physical education, and manual arts. The first year of the *Ciclo Diversificado* is divided into two specializations: humanities and science; the second year into three: humanities, science and biology; the third into six: law, economics, architecture, engineering, agronomy and medicine. On completion of this cycle successful students leave with the **Bachillerato**.

A few schools also offer a *Ciclo Preparatorio*, specifically for university entrance.

Technical secondary

Until 1978 pupils could specialize in a technical field during the final two-year cycle of secondary education. The reforms of 1976 increased this to four years and holders of the **Bachillerato** from the *Ciclo Tecnico* may now go on to university. In the first year there are eight specializations, increasing to twelve in the final year.

HIGHER EDUCATION

There are three universities: the Universidad de la Republica (State University); the Universidad del Trabajo (Technical University of Uruguay); and the Universidad Catolica del Uruguay Damaso Antonio Larranaga (a private institution recognized by the Uruguayan authorities in 1985).

The first qualification obtained is the **Licenciado**, generally after a course lasting four years. Postgraduate courses lead to the **Doctorado**. The first qualification may be obtained after a course lasting seven years for medicine, five for dentistry and six for law and social science.

Three-year courses offer professional training in engineering, medicine and administration.

Taught postgraduate courses are available in economics, odontology, chemistry, veterinary science, psychology and medicine. There are no research facilities.

TEACHER EDUCATION

Primary

Until 1955

Teachers were trained on a seven-year course consisting of the four-year secondary course followed by three years' teacher training, leading to the qualification of **Maestro de Primer Grado,** with which teachers could teach children in grades 1 to 4. To teach grades 5 and 6, holders of this qualification had to pass an additional examination leading to the title of **Maestro de Segundo Grado.**

1955 to early 1970s

Teachers were trained on an eight-year course consisting of the four-year academic secondary course followed by four years' teacher training at an *Instituto Normal.* The course led to the qualification of **Maestro,** with which the holder could register in some university faculties.

Since the early 1970s

Teachers have been trained on a three-year post-secondary course leading to the title of **Maestro de Educacion Primaria**. The course was extended to four years from 1986.

Secondary

Teachers were trained at higher education level on a course lasting four years until 1979. From 1980 to 1984 the course lasted for three years; however, since 1985, the course has reverted to four years and leads to the title of *Profesor*.

Vanuatu

The following chapter regarding the education system in Vanuatu is based on information obtained from the 3rd edition of this Guide, published in 1991, as NARIC has been unable to obtain more recent information.

The Anglo-French condominium of the New Hebrides became the independent Republic of Vanuatu on 30 July 1980.

Before independence, dual French and English education systems were in operation. Since independence, the systems have been unified under one Ministry of Education, even though the media of instruction continue to be either French or English.
The national language, Bislama, is used as an official language along with French and English, but it is not used as a medium of instruction in the schools.

The country is developing a common curriculum for all schools at both the primary and the secondary level. Common examinations were introduced at year 10 in 1989 and will follow at tertiary level at a later date.

Education is not compulsory but is free at primary level.

EVALUATION IN BRITAIN

School

Year 10 Leaving Certificate – generally considered to be below GCSE standard.

Dossier/Baccalauréat – may approach GCSE standard.

Higher

Bachelor degrees (from the University of the South Pacific) – generally considered comparable to British Bachelor degree standard.

MARKING SYSTEM

School

International General Certificate of Secondary Education has a seven-point scale of grades: A, B, C, D, E, F and G. Grade A is awarded for the highest level of achievement; grade G indicates minimum satisfactory performance.

Higher

Degrees from the University of the South Pacific are unclassified.

SCHOOL EDUCATION

Primary

In both the English and the French systems this lasts six years.

At the end of the cycle, pupils take the **National Primary Education Examination**, the basis for selection for the secondary cycle. At present there are separate examinations in the two systems with a common certificate (printed in the two languages). It is planned to have a common curriculum and examination in the two languages in due course.

Secondary

Secondary education in both English and French-medium schools consists of two cycles of four years (years 7 to 10) and then three years (years 11 to 13).

In the first cycle, a common curriculum for both English and French medium was introduced in 1989. Pupils study a core curriculum of English, French, mathematics, social science, basic science and agriculture. On completion of these four years, students sit for the **Year 10 Leaving Certificate**.

In the second cycle, English-medium students take a two-year course leading to the **International General Certificate of Secondary Education** (IGCSE), an examination administered by the University of Cambridge Local Examinations Syndicate (UCLES). (For further information on the IGCSE see Appendix 2.)

Those successful in the IGCSE may continue into year 13 in preparation for tertiary education specializing in arts or science. An internal examination is set. However, a significant proportion (up to 30 per cent) of the more able students are offered scholarships to study in New Zealand for the **New Zealand University Entrance Examinations** and continue with higher education in New Zealand.

Under the French system, at the end of the two-year second cycle (or possibly after one year) students sit an internally set **dossier**. Some formal international recognition is being sought for this examination. Previously the examination was the **Baccalauréat**.

It is planned to have a common examination at the end of year 13. Its recognition will be negotiated with France and Britain, so that Vanuatu students have access to wider higher education overseas.

HIGHER EDUCATION

Students intending to pursue undergraduate studies may enrol at the University of the South Pacific which has campuses in Fiji and Western Samoa.

Admission to degree courses is based on satisfactory completion of the University's one-year foundation programme or an equivalent form 7 secondary qualification.

The normal length of **Bachelor degree** courses is three years except for medicine which takes four years for a first degree. Postgraduate certificates and diplomas, **Master's degrees** and **PhD** programmes are offered in a number of areas. (For further information on the University of the South Pacific see Appendix 9.)

Students who have followed the French system tend to go to mainland France for higher education studies.

TEACHER EDUCATION

Primary

There is now a common course for English and French-medium students at the Institute of Education's <u>Teacher Education Centre</u>.

The Centre offers a three-year **Certificate** course with the minimum entry requirement of a **Year 10 Leaving Certificate**. The course is two years' full-time study followed by a one-year supervised internship in school.

Secondary

There are no courses for secondary teachers in Vanuatu. Students are trained at the <u>University of the South Pacific</u> or in other overseas institutions.

Venezuela

The education system is highly centralized under the Ministry of Education.

Education is free and compulsory from ages seven to sixteen (grades 1 to 9).

The medium of instruction is Spanish.

The school year runs from September to July and the university year from January to December or in some cases from September to July.

EVALUATION IN BRITAIN

School

Bachillerato – generally considered comparable to GCSE standard (grades A, B and C) on a subject-for-subject basis, with the exception of English language.

Higher

Licenciado/Professional title – generally considered comparable to British Bachelor degree standard if awarded after four or more years of study.

MARKING SYSTEM

School

Most institutions of secondary education, in both the common and diversified cycles use yearly grades. Examinations are not nationally set but are designed by individual schools under the supervision of the Ministry of Education.

Grading is on a scale of 20 (maximum)–1, with 10 as the minimum pass-mark.

Each academic year is divided into three or more periods. A grade is given for each period. At the end of the year the grades for each period are averaged to form a *previa* grade. This makes up 60 per cent of the pupil's final mark. If an overall grade of 10 in the final examination and in the combination of the *previa* and the final examination is not obtained, the pupil must resit in September.

Higher

Examinations are graded on a 20 (maximum)–0 scale, with 10 as the minimum pass-mark. Two or more partial examinations are taken during each marking period. The average of all the partial examinations yields 40 per cent of the final grade and must be 10 per cent or above for the student to take the final examination.

Institutions of higher education differ in the grading scales they use. Some use both a percentage scale, others a 1–5 or a 1–9 scale:

9	91–100 per cent	*excelente*	excellent
8	81–90	*sobresaliente*	outstanding
7	71–80	*distinguido*	very good
6	61–70	*bueno*	good
5	50–60	*satisfactorio*	average
4	37–49	*deficiente*	failure
3	25–36	*deficiente*	
2	13–24	*muy deficiente*	
1	1–12	*muy deficiente*	

SCHOOL EDUCATION

Pre-primary

This is voluntary for children aged four to six. The Ministry of Education has been active in expanding the provision of places at this level.

Until 1981

Primary

This was free and compulsory from age seven to thirteen (grades 1 to 6). Promotion from one grade to another was based on the teacher's assessment and was generally automatic. In the last year pupils had to take an examination set by the teacher of the sixth grade. Successful pupils were awarded a **Certificado de Educacion Primaria** (Certificate of Primary Education) which granted access to secondary education.

Secondary

This lasted five to six years. It was made up of two cycles – a basic common cycle of three years followed by a diversified cycle of two or occasionally three years.

Basic common cycle

This covered three years providing a general course of education. Promotion from one year to the next was dependent on the average marks obtained during the year and on the results of the end-of-year examinations. Successful completion of the basic common cycle gave access to the diversified cycle. Students did not receive a certificate but graduated with a grade record.

Diversified cycle

In this cycle of two or three years pupils followed one of three specialized courses: academic, technical and normal.

All students followed basic subjects during the first year of this cycle. These were Spanish language and literature, mathematics, Venezuelan history and geography, English and physical education.

The academic course, followed by the vast majority, lasted two years and included science and humanities. Successful completion led to the award of the **Bachillerato**.

The technical course lasted three years and was subdivided into commercial, agricultural, industrial and social work. Successful completion led to the award of the **Bachillerato**.

The normal course lasted three years and provided teacher training for primary level teaching. Successful completion led to the award of the **Maestro**.

Since 1981

Basic primary

In 1981, basic primary education became free and compulsory from age seven to sixteen (grades 1 to 9). Final-year students take an examination set by the teacher of grade 9 and if successful are awarded a **Certificado de Educacion Basica** which grants access to secondary education.

Secondary

This lasts two or three years and is the diversified cycle, which remains the same as the pre-1981 diversified cycle.

Vocational

The Instituto Nacional de Cooperacion Educativa (INCE) was founded in 1959. It operates fifty-four centres throughout the country and mobile units servicing the rural areas. INCE provides free courses and course materials and assists students when necessary.

Apprenticeship programmes last up to three years. Apprentices must have completed primary school. Special courses are available for those who have not reached the required standard to begin their training programmes.

Full-time vocational training is available from age sixteen to twenty-six.

FURTHER EDUCATION

Institutos Universitarios de Tecnologia (university institutes of technology) provide post-secondary sub-degree training. They offer three-year courses leading to the award of **Tecnico Superior**.

Institutos Universitarios Politecnicos (university polytechnic institutes) provide post-secondary five-year degree courses focusing especially on engineering and on the practical/vocational side.

Colegios Universitarios (university colleges) provide post-secondary sub-degree training. They offer three-year courses leading to the award of **Técnico Superior**.

HIGHER EDUCATION

Entry to university is based on the **Bachillerato** (constituting 60 per cent of the marks and the **National Academic Aptitude Examination** (40 per cent).

First degree courses leading to the **Licenciado** or a **Professional title** normally lasts four to five years. Courses are usually organized on a credit system.

Postgraduate studies are of three types: **Master's** courses (**Maestria**), courses of **Especializacion** and **Doctoral** programmes.

TEACHER EDUCATION

Primary

Primary school teachers are trained within the secondary school system on a three-year course in normal (pedagogical) schools. In future, primary teacher training will be part of higher education although the courses may last only two years.

Secondary

Secondary school teachers are trained in *Institutos Pedagogicos* (teacher training institutes) and universities or junior colleges. The teacher training institutes operate outside the university system but are officially accorded equal status.

In-service training for teachers is offered at two special training centres – the Centro Interamericano de Educacion Rural and the Centro de Capitacion Docente El Macaro.

The Instituto de Mejoramiento de Profesores (literally the Institute for the Improvement of Teachers) offers correspondence courses to allow unqualified practising teachers to obtain the teacher's certificate.

ADULT EDUCATION

The Division of Adult Education is largely responsible for non-formal education, assisted by bodies such as INCE, IAN (Instituto Agrario Nacional) and the individual municipalities. Adults can now follow a shortened period of schooling (four years' primary and five years' secondary) at night school, ordinary school or through radio, television and correspondence courses. Various vocational adult courses are held in conjunction with primary school training.

Vietnam

The following chapter regarding the education system in Vietnam is based on information obtained from the 3rd edition of this Guide, published in 1991, as NARIC has been unable to obtain more recent information.

After the unification of the Democratic Republic of Vietnam (North Vietnam) and the Republic of Vietnam (South Vietnam) in April 1975, the new Socialist Republic of Vietnam reorganized the education system, abolishing school fees and nationalizing private schools. The new, unified system was inaugurated at the fourth congress of the Communist Party in December 1976. The 1980 constitution provided for free, compulsory education for all, but since 1989 free education has no longer been a right.

The first section of this chapter describes the present system and the second section the pre-1975 system in the Republic of Vietnam (South Vietnam).

Educational facilities were severely affected by the hostilities in the 1950s, late 1960s and 1970s. Many educational documents and certificates were lost or left behind during this time, and thus it may not be possible to obtain evidence of qualifications held. Between 1975 and 1986 the education system was subject to the general disruption following the unification of North Vietnam and South Vietnam. This means that certificates granted in this period may not represent officially sanctioned educational awards.

There was a strong French influence in the area from the beginning of this century, and until the late 1970s four almost separate educational systems existed: Vietnamese, Franco-Vietnamese, French, and 'foreign' (e.g. American, Chinese); the last three only in southern Vietnam.

Education is compulsory for children aged six to fifteen.

The medium of instruction is now Vietnamese.

The academic year runs from September to June.

EVALUATION IN BRITAIN

School

Tot Nghiep Pho Thong (Universal Graduation) – generally considered comparable to GCSE standard (grades A, B and C).

Higher

Tot Nghiep Dai Hoc Su Pham (Diploma) – generally considered comparable to a standard between GCE Advanced and British Bachelor degree; may be given advanced standing by British higher education institutions.

854

MARKING SYSTEM

School

There is a 10-point scale. General evaluation in term examinations is rated:

excellent
good
fair
bad

Pupils who fail may be allowed to resit. Pupils who achieve a mark of 5 or more (without any 3s) will automatically pass. Those who average 4–5 (without any 0s) and who have been rated 'excellent' or 'good' at school will also pass.

SCHOOL EDUCATION

Pre-primary

Crèches are available for infants from two months to three years old.

There are kindergartens for ages three to five. They are the responsibility of the Ministry of Education, but directly run by agricultural co-operatives, factories and state farms. Semi-boarding kindergartens are beginning to appear in rural areas.

Basic general

This level of education is compulsory. There are 9 grades for those aged six to fifteen, split into two levels. Level 1 runs from grade 1 to 5 and is taught by one class teacher. Level 2 runs from grade 6 to 9 and subjects are taught by subject teachers.

Secondary general

This covers grades 10 to 12 and prepares pupils for further education. The school year is divided into two terms of about four months each.

The syllabus at both basic general education schools and secondary general education schools includes: civic duties, ethics, history, geography, literature (Vietnamese and world), and a foreign language; mathematics, physics, chemistry and biology, drawing, music, physical culture, sport and basic military training. Pupils are also taught general skills for industry and agriculture.

Examinations are taken at the end of each term, and there are special examinations for the selection of majors, and entry examinations.

Basic general school examinations are the responsibility of the provincial education services. Secondary general school examinations are the responsibility of the Ministry of Education.

Study of work schools

This is run on an experimental basis. Pupils attend classes for four hours a day, and work three to four hours a day in factories or on state farms.

Complementary education

This began in 1945 and is open to all adults. There are two main types: in-service training for people who are studying whilst employed, and classes for adult literacy, basic mathematics, basic agricultural skills, and hygiene.

Since 1945, mass literacy has been an educational priority, together with replacing French by Vietnamese as the main medium of instruction.

Job training

There are now at least 360 schools set up to train pupils in technical skills. Entry is usually from basic general education schools, although 40 only accept secondary general school graduates. Training courses last one to three years.

HIGHER EDUCATION

Entry to university is based on an entrance examination set by each department.

The first qualification awarded is a **Diploma** usually after four or five years of study.

There are now ninety-five universities and other institutions of higher education in Vietnam. Many Vietnamese study at undergraduate and postgraduate level in the USSR, but there are contacts for the purposes of research collaboration with Japan and Australia as well.

There is a growth in post-university research centres in Vietnam, of which there are now some 150 following training initiatives by different ministries.

In 1989, Thang Long College – the first private institution – was opened in Hanoi.

TEACHER EDUCATION

Teacher training classes are run by the Ministry of Education for graduates of secondary schools. Four- to five-year courses are offered for teaching subjects at secondary school level.

Provincial and municipal administrations run three-year courses for graduates of secondary general schools to teach one main subject plus one subsidiary subject at a basic general education school (level 2).

Two-year courses are available to enable teachers to teach at basic general education schools (level 1).

Two-year courses exist for kindergarten teachers.

University training is provided to train teachers for teacher training schools.

All teacher training courses include four months of practical training. Follow-up training for teachers is also provided.

System pre-1975 in Republic of Vietnam (South Vietnam)

Primary education was compulsory, but in practice limited facilities prevented this in some areas.

The medium of instruction for general education varied according to the type of school:

Vietnamese schools – Vietnamese throughout;

Chinese schools – usually Mandarin, but required to teach six hours of Vietnamese per week;

French schools – French, but required to teach Vietnamese as a subject;

International schools (American and English) – English and Vietnamese.

At the higher education level French was used, but in the 1960s, Vietnamese gradually replaced French in the humanities.

EVALUATION IN BRITAIN

School

Baccalauréat Part II (before 1970) – generally considered comparable to GCSE standard (grades A, B and C) on a subject-for-subject basis.

SCHOOL EDUCATION

Primary

From age six, this covered five years. The curriculum included Vietnamese, moral education, civics, history, geography, science, and arithmetic. On conclusion of this cycle, pupils took the examination for the **Certificat d'Etudes Primaries** (CEP).

Secondary

This covered seven years. Admission was gained by the CEP and by success in a competitive entrance examination. From 1965 until 1975, there were four branches: general; technical and vocational; agricultural; and comprehensive. In the general branch, studies were divided into a four-year cycle followed by a three-year cycle. In the first cycle, pupils studied history, geography, French, English, Chinese, physics, chemistry, and mathematics, and could obtain the **Brevet d'Etudes du Premier Cycle** (BEP) on conclusion of this cycle.

Pupils could then chose which specialization they wished to take in the second cycle: experimental science, mathematics, modern literature, classical literature.

Until 1973, pupils took the national **Baccalauréat I/Bang Tu-Tai Nhut/Bang Tu-Tai Mot** on completion of year 11. Pupils had to obtain one of these qualifications to proceed to grade/year 12. The examinations were abolished in 1972–3. On completion of year 12, pupils took the examinations for the **Baccalauréat II/Bang Tu-Tai Hai** (until 1973) and for the **General Education Baccalauréat Diploma/Tu Tai Po Thong** (1974–5).

After 1965, the comprehensive branch was available in a limited number of 'model' schools established under American auspices, which operated the American high school system.

Pupils were also able to study for the Vietnamese **Baccalauréat** examinations by home study/correspondence.

A number of schools teaching through the medium of French operated on the French system until 1975. Examinations were set for the **Brevet d'Etudes du Premier Cycle**, and **Baccalauréats I** and **II** (the last two until approximately 1972; after that the **Baccalauréat de l'Enseignement Secondaire** was awarded), with papers and examiners being sent annually from France (administered by the *Service Culturel Français*).

Technical and vocational

Until 1973, admission to this branch was by a competitive examination at the end of grade 7 (i.e. five years' primary followed by two years of general technical education). The courses lasted five years, divided into two cycles of two and three years respectively. On completion of grade 11, pupils took the **Technical Baccalauréat I**, and at the end of grade 12, **Technical Baccalauréat II** examinations.

During 1973–5, admission to the course was on completion of grade 9, and it lasted three years. The **Technical Baccalauréat I** was abolished, but pupils could obtain the **Technical Baccalauréat** on successful completion of grade 12.

Agricultural

Until 1973, this lasted seven years, for pupils who were successful in an entrance examination at the end of grade 5. From 1973, the course lasted three years from completion of grade 9. On completion of grade 12, pupils did not take the examinations for the **Baccalauréat**, but if they met the course requirements they were awarded the **Agricultural Baccalauréat Diploma (Bang Tu-Tai Canh-Nong)**, and the status of **Agricultural Technician**.

FURTHER EDUCATION

Community colleges were established in 1972–3, offering two-year courses to train middle-level technicians. A few specialist institutions also offered courses at this level.

HIGHER EDUCATION

The University of Saigon was established in 1954, and the Universities of Can Tho and Hue in the 1960s. There were also private universities established by religious groups.

University admission was on the basis of the **Baccalauréat II/Bang Tu-Tai Hai** until 1972, when it was replaced by the general education **Baccalauréat Diploma/Tu-Tai Po Thong**. Some institutions also administered entrance examinations (**Thi Tuyen**).

Courses usually lasted four to five years, leading to the **Licence/Cu/Nhan/Professional qualification**:

architecture	six years
dentistry	five
law	three until 1964–5, then four
medicine	seven
pharmacy	five

A further two years' study led to the **Advanced Diploma of Higher Education (Bang Cao Hoc)**. A minimum of two years' further research led to the **Doctorate (Tien Si)**. At the <u>University of Saigon</u> the **Doctorat de Troisième Degré** could be obtained on successful completion of three years' research after the first university qualification, and the **Doctorat d'Etat** after five years.

West Bank and Gaza

This chapter covers the period since the Israeli occupation began in 1967. The system described is that of the West Bank, including East Jerusalem, and the Gaza Strip.

Primary and preparatory (lower secondary) education is compulsory.

The medium of instruction is Arabic, with the exception of a few private schools which prepare students for the **GCE** examinations.

The academic year runs from September to May.

EVALUATION IN BRITAIN

School

Tawjihi (General Secondary Education Certificate)/Al Thanaweya Al A'ama (General Secondary School Certificate) – generally considered comparable to GCSE standard (grades A, B and C) on a subject-for-subject basis (with the exception of English language), when a minimum overall mark of 60 per cent has been obtained. Students with very good results may be considered for admission to access/bridging courses.

Higher

Bachelor degree – generally considered comparable to a standard between GCE Advanced and British Bachelor degree; may be given advanced standing by British higher education institutions. Exceptionally, students with very high grades may be considered for admission to postgraduate study.

MARKING SYSTEMS

School

The system varies according to subject but is clearly marked on the certificate.

Higher

The grading system used is:

A	excellent	4.0
B	good	3.0
C	average	2.0
D	pass	1.0
E	fail	0

Students must normally maintain an average of C or better to remain in good academic standing.

SCHOOL EDUCATION

Up till now schools in the Gaza Strip have been following the Egyptian curriculum whereas schools in the West Bank have followed the Jordanian system. As the Palestinian National Authority has now taken over responsibility in the West Bank and Gaza it is expected that the curriculum will be revised soon.

Pre-primary

There are a large number of kindergartens run by non-government schools and private charitable organizations.

Primary/elementary

This covers six years from age six. The curriculum includes: Arabic, religion, arithmetic, civics, history, geography, science, drawing, embroidery (for girls), music and physical education. English is taught from grade 5 while in private schools it is taught from grade 1.

Preparatory/lower secondary

This covers three years (grades 7 to 9) and includes some vocational training. The curriculum includes: Arabic, religion, English, mathematics, social studies, science, art and physical education. Most boys' schools offer one vocational course namely book-keeping.

Secondary

This also covers three years. In the first year (grade 10) all pupils follow the same course. In grade 11, pupils are placed in either the arts or the science stream, depending on their performance in the previous year's work. The common curriculum includes: Arabic, religion, English, mathematics, drawing, vocational education and physical education, with those in the arts stream also taking general science, history, geography, economics and extra Arabic and those in the science stream taking biology, physics, chemistry and additional mathematics. On completion of grade 12 pupils on the West Bank take the examinations for the Jordanian **Tawjihi (General Secondary Education Certificate)** and those in Gaza the Egyptian **Al Thanaweya Al A'ama (General Secondary School Certificate)**.

In addition to the general academic education described above, three-year vocational/technical courses are available at a number of schools in the fields of agriculture, commerce and industry. Courses lead to the **Tawjihi**.

It is expected that a Palestinian **Tawjihi** will be held in the future instead of the Jordanian and Egyptian.

FURTHER EDUCATION

Hebron Technical Engineering College, previously known as Hebron Polytechnic, offers two-year courses leading to various technical diplomas, after the completion of 70 credit hours. There are a number of vocational training centres, run either by the government, private organizations or the United Nations Relief and Works Agency for Palestinian Refugees in the Near East (UNRWA). They provide two to three-year post-preparatory programmes leading to a trade certificate.

HIGHER EDUCATION

The universities were closed by military order in December 1987, and did not reopen until Spring 1992.

In 1967, there was no university education on the West Bank or in Gaza but since then, seven higher institutions have been opened or developed from lower level schools: Birzeit University, Bethlehem University, An Najah National University at Nablus, Hebron University, the Islamic University of Gaza, Al Quds University and Al Azhar University of Gaza.

Birzeit University was first founded in 1924 as a high school; in 1961 it became a junior college and in 1972 began offering **Bachelor degree** courses. Arabic is the official language, but English is the main medium of instruction. Courses are organized on the credit system.

Bethlehem University was established in 1973 with the administrative co-operation of the De La Salle Brothers and has links with Laval University in Canada and Dublin University. It is sponsored by the Vatican to serve the higher education needs of the Palestinians in the West Bank and Gaza. Courses are organized on the credit system. The media of instruction are Arabic and English.

An Najah National University began in 1965 as a college offering two-year teacher training courses. In 1977, it was inaugurated as a university and now offers courses at both undergraduate and postgraduate level. The media of instruction are Arabic and English.

Hebron University, founded in 1971 as Al Sharia College, became a university in 1980. It has four main faculties: arts, sciences, agriculture and Sharia. They are now in the process of establishing a Business School awarding BSc degrees in Business Administration.

The Islamic University of Gaza is a private university recognized by the Association of Arab Universities. It is run on Islamic fundamentalist principles.

Al Quds University consists of:

College of Islamic Studies, subjects taught include Koranic studies, legislation in Islam, Arabic language and English language;

College of Science and Technology, Abu Dies, established in 1981, which awards **BSc** in science and technology (135 credits required);

Arab College of Medical Professions established in 1979 as a nursing college. In 1980, a medical technology course was introduced and since then the college has become a degree-awarding institution;

Arts College for Women evolved from Dar Al Tifl College for Women and awards **BA degrees** in Arabic, English language and literature, social studies and a **Diploma in Education**.

Entrance to first degree courses is on the basis of the **Al Thanaweya Al A'ama/Tawjihi**. Courses normally last four years and lead to a **Bachelor degree**.

Al-Quds Open University (QOU) was established in 1990 but the launch was hampered during the Gulf War and the first students registered in 1992. Its courses are funded and accredited by the Council for Higher Education. Students enrol at six regional centres in the Territories (in Jerusalem, Bethlehem, Hebron, Nablus, Ramallah and Jenin). Centres have been opened in Gaza and Tolkarn. Work is prepared at home from textbooks and discussed at regular meetings with tutors in groups of up to 15 students. Students also carry out assignments and take examinations for each credit; they take between 3 and 18 credits by semesters and have to amass at least 130 credits to be awarded a degree. Undergraduate degrees and continuing education and training are offered in: land and rural development; home and family development; technology and applied science; management and education.

TEACHER EDUCATION

Primary/preparatory/lower secondary

Prospective teachers undertake a two-year post-secondary course at a teacher training institute.

Secondary

Teachers for this level are generally graduates and should have undertaken a **Graduate Teaching Diploma** at one of the universities.

UNITED NATIONS RELIEF AND WORKS AGENCY FOR PALESTINIAN REFUGEES IN THE NEAR EAST

The United Nations Relief and Works Agency for Palestinian Refugees in the Near East (UNRWA) operates an educational system for Palestinian refugees in the West Bank and Gaza as well as in Jordan, Lebanon and Syria.

UNRWA aims to provide a system of nine years' education (primary/elementary and preparatory) for registered refugees and their families.

UNRWA is not involved in secondary education but does provide post-preparatory vocational training and to a limited extent, post-secondary education and teacher training. Vocational and trade programmes are two to three years in length and are provided at UNRWA training centres. They cover a wide range of subjects including mechanics, engineering, building crafts, commercial studies and para-medical subjects.

Yemen

The two countries of the Yemen Arab Republic and the People's Democratic Republic of Yemen joined together as one country, Republic of Yemen, in 1990.

Two major events, the Gulf War and the recent civil war, have each had an impact on the education system. After the Gulf War many Yemeni nationals were forced to return from other Gulf countries, leading to severe overcrowding in the schools (especially in the tribal areas). The problem was compounded by the departure of many Egyptian teachers at the outbreak of hostilities, and a shortage of textbooks. In response to the situation mixed ability classes were introduced, taught in Arabic. One of the consequences of the recent civil war has been a serious delay in the development of the Yemeni education system and the introduction of planned reforms.

The development of education in Yemen has (until recent events) been rapid. At the time of the revolution against the Imamate in 1962, there were only four government secondary schools in the country. After the end of the civil war in 1970 there was a large increase in the provision of secondary schools, and by 1986 the number had risen to 164. Now there are approximately 200.

Schooling is based on a two level system, basic and secondary. The school curriculum was originally adopted from the Egyptian model, but is currently (and rapidly) being Yemenized.

The medium of instruction is Arabic except for certain courses at <u>Sana'a University</u>.

The academic year runs from September to June.

EVALUATION IN BRITAIN

School

Al Thanawiya (General Secondary Education Certificate) – generally considered comparable to GCSE standard (grades A, B and C) on a subject-for-subject basis (with the exception of English language), when a minimum overall mark of 70 per cent has been obtained. Students with very good results may be considered for admission to access/bridging courses.

Higher

Bachelor degree – may be considered to satisfy the general entrance requirements of British higher education institutions. Exceptionally, students with very high grades may be given advanced standing.

MARKING SYSTEMS

School

The **Al Thanawiya** is graded out of 700 as follows:

over 630	excellent
561–630	very good
491–560	good
421–490	fair
350–420	pass

Higher

University degrees are graded according to the following percentages:

88–100 per cent	excellent
78–87	very good
63–77	good
48–62	pass

SCHOOL EDUCATION

Basic

This covers nine years. Enrolment represents about ten per cent of the children of preparatory school age, of which about ten per cent are girls. On completion of the cycle students are awarded the **Intermediate School Certificate**.

Secondary

This covers three years. After a common first-year curriculum, students choose either the scientific or literary stream for the remaining two years. The **Al Thanawiya** (**General Secondary Education Certificate**) examination is taken at the end of the third year.

FURTHER EDUCATION

There are some technical secondary schools, three vocational training centres, a Veterinary Training School, a Health Manpower Training Institute and a few agricultural secondary schools. In addition, there are religious institutes concentrating on Islamic education. Plans are currently being implemented for a general strengthening of technical and vocational education and for the establishment of a polytechnic in Aden (funded by Germany).

HIGHER EDUCATION

Higher education is provided by the University of Sana'a, founded in 1970 and the University of Aden, founded in 1973. Admission is based on the **Al Thanawiya**. A score of at least 80 per cent is required for admission to the faculties of medicine and engineering. For the faculties of science, agriculture and commerce, the requirement is 65–70 per cent and for the faculties of law, education and arts around 50–60 per cent. Precise entry requirements may vary from year to year.

Bachelor degree courses normally last four years.

TEACHER EDUCATION

Basic Education

Teachers are trained at 14 Teacher Training Institutes, of which three are Women's TTIs. The course lasts two years.

Secondary

Teachers for secondary schools are trained in the faculty of education at <u>Sana'a University</u> and <u>Aden University</u>. The Sana's faculty was the 'mother college' of the University when it was established in 1970; for many years enrolment was low (approximately 10 per cent of the total student body), but there has been a substantial increase recently.

Federal Republic of Yugoslavia

At the time of writing (March 1994), Slovenia, Croatia and the Former Yugoslav Republic of Macedonia have become independent states, while the war in Bosnia-Herzegovina has resulted in a cessation of formal schooling (although some schooling continues as far as feasible). In the Federal Republic of Yugoslavia (Serbia and Montenegro) schooling continues as normal, moving to a reinstatement of the stronger academic tradition and higher relative standards.

Compulsory education covers the period of basic education; that is, eight years between ages seven and fifteen.

The medium of instruction is Serbian (there is also Albanian at the University of Priština and Hungarian at the University of Novi Sad).

The academic year runs from September/October to June.

EVALUATION IN BRITAIN

School

Matura (before 1980 from the *Gimnazija*/academic upper secondary course)/ **Secondary School Leaving Diploma** (before 1980 from a technical secondary school) – may be considered to satisfy the general entrance requirements of British higher education institutions.

Secondary School Leaving Diploma (obtained since 1980) – generally considered comparable to British BTEC National Diploma / N/SVQ level 3 / Advanced GNVQ/GSVQ and may be considered to satisfy the general entrance requirements of British higher education institutions.

Higher

Vise Obrazovanje (first-level degree obtained on completion of a two to three-year course) – generally considered comparable to a standard between GCE Advanced and British Bachelor degree; may be given advanced standing by British higher education institutions.

Visoko Obrazovanja (second-level degree obtained on completion of a four to six-year course) – generally considered comparable to British Bachelor (Ordinary) degree standard; students with high grades may be considered for admission to postgraduate study.

Magistar – generally considered comparable to British Master's degree standard.

Doktor nauka – generally considered comparable to British PhD standard.

MARKING SYSTEMS

School

Marking is on the scale 1–5 (maximum), with 2 as the minimum pass-mark.

Higher

Marking is on the scale 5–10 (maximum), with 6 as the minimum pass-mark.

SCHOOL EDUCATION

Pre-primary

Limited facilities are available in crèches (*Decje Jaslice*) for children to age three and kindergartens (*Decji Vrtici*) for children aged three to seven.

Primary

This period of schooling (at *Osnovna skole*) covers eight years from age seven. The period is divided into two distinct stages: classes 1–4 and 5–8. Classes are unstreamed and based on the comprehensive system. Pupils begin studying foreign languages in the fifth year and may usually choose between English, Russian, German and French. However, in Belgrade, as well as in some other towns, pupils begin studying one foreign language in the third year and, in the fifth year, take a second foreign language as well.

Secondary

Until 1980

Selective entrance tests decided what form of secondary education pupils could enter. The academic cycle covered four years at a *Gimnazija*, of which the first year was common to all pupils. They could then choose to specialize in science/mathematics or humanities/social studies and languages. The final examination was the **Matura**.

Technical secondary education covered a variety of fields. On completion of the four-year course, pupils took examinations for the **Matura** and a vocational qualification.

Vocational schools offered courses lasting three years, including a period of practical instruction. Apprentice schools offered training courses lasting two to three years, leading to the qualification of skilled worker.

Since 1980

All forms of secondary schooling now contain an element of vocational training and instruction. The course still covers four years, of which the first two covered a common-core syllabus until 1987. Compulsory subjects are the mother tongue and its literature, a foreign language, art, history, geography, mathematics, physics, chemistry, biology, physical and medical education, defence and initiation into production and technology. During the second cycle of two years (*Usemreno Obrazovanje* – 'directed' education) pupils may undertake some specialization. Admission is by competition. The vocational diploma obtained on completion of the second cycle is based on continuous assessment rather than examination. Since 1987, specialization has operated throughout secondary schooling, and there is no longer a common-core syllabus for the first two years.

FURTHER EDUCATION

There are many post-secondary schools (*Vise skole*) which offer two-year courses in professional and technical education.

HIGHER EDUCATION

Entry to a course of higher education is on the basis of a **Secondary School Leaving Certificate,** regardless of whether it was obtained on completion of an academic or technical course. Whereas the former will admit to all faculties, the vocational/technical diploma gives admission only to certain faculties. Holders of a qualification from a professional school/apprenticeship may have to sit entrance examinations. A system of *numerus clausus* (restricted entry) operates in some universities.

Higher education courses are offered by university faculties, specialist institutes (e.g. art academies), and high schools (*Visoke skole*).

Note: 'high' schools (*Visoke skole*) offer courses of higher education, whereas 'higher' schools (*Vise skole*) offer lower level courses. (See under **FURTHER EDUCATION.**)

Until 1959

There was only one degree, obtained after a course lasting four to six years (depending on the subject).

Since 1960

Within the organization of higher education, four types of 'degrees' can usually be identified:

covering two to three years, leading to the **Diplom Višeg Obrazovanje** (Diploma of Higher Education) with a professional title (*Struçni naziv*) – e.g. engineer (*Inženjer*), lawyer (*Pravnik*), teacher (*Nastavnik*) – not a full university degree.

covering four to six years, during which students specialize, leading to a **Diplom Visokog Obrazovanja** (Advanced Diploma of Higher Education) with a professional title (*Struçni naziv*) – e.g. graduate engineer (*Diplomirani inženjer*), graduate lawyer (*Diplomirani pravnik*), graduate teacher (*Profesor*) – full university degree.

postgraduate studies, covering two years' research and defence of a thesis, leading to the academic degree (**Akademski stepen**) of **Magistar**.

a **Doctorate of Science** may be obtained after a further approved period of research and defence of a thesis.

Workers' (*Radnicki*)/People's (*Narodni*) Universities (*Univerziteti*)

These offer a great variety of courses lasting from only two weeks to two years. They do not award degrees but offer special courses leading to a particular vocational qualification and are used mainly to remedy earlier deficiencies in a person's education; for example; by preparatory courses for adults wishing to enter a course of higher education.

TEACHER EDUCATION

Primary

Teachers are trained in *Vise skole* (further education establishments) for two years.

Secondary

Teachers are university graduates. Courses last four years.

ADULT EDUCATION

Basic schools for adults (*Osnovne skole za Odrasle*) offer the course of basic education (normally taken over eight years) over only four years. The certificate awarded at the end is of the same value as that awarded at the end of the normal eight-year course.

Secondary schools for adults (*Srednje skole za Odrasle*) offer the normal course of secondary education, but it may be undertaken through part-time study (e.g. in the evening), correspondence, or, in the case of workers, on full-time paid leave.

Zaire

The following chapter regarding the education system in Zaire is based on information obtained for the 3rd edition of this Guide, published in 1991, as NARIC has been unable to obtain more recent information.

This chapter covers the period since independence was gained in 1960. The area was previously occupied by Belgium as the Belgian Congo and became the Democratic Republic of the Congo in June 1960. The country became Zaire in 1971.

The medium of instruction is French.

The academic year runs from October to June.

EVALUATION IN BRITAIN

School

Diplôme d'Etat d'Etudes Secondaires du Cycle Long – generally considered comparable to GCSE standard.

Higher

Licence – generally considered comparable to a standard between GCE Advanced and British Bachelor degree; may be given advanced standing by British higher education institutions.

Licence d'Enseignement – generally considered comparable to British Bachelor degree standard.

MARKING SYSTEMS

School

Marking is on a percentage scale, the minimum pass-mark is 50 per cent.

For the **Diplôme d'Etat**, pupils must obtain at least 50 per cent in each subject. Course work accounts for 25 per cent of the final mark.

Higher

Marking is on a percentage basis.

90–100 per cent	*la plus grande distinction*
80–89	*grande distinction*
70–79	*distinction*
50–69	*satisfaction*
50	*minimum pass*

An attestation is given at the end of each year confirming whether a student has been successful and noting the *mention* (grade) obtained.

SCHOOL EDUCATION

Primary

This covers six years and is referred to as primary school. The classes are numbered 1 to 6.

The curriculum includes: French, arithmetic, moral and religious instruction, physical and natural sciences, history and geography, civic instruction, physical education, art, and African languages. Until 1961, primary education was taught in the vernacular.

A **Certificat d'Etudes Primaires** is awarded to pupils who do well in the **Examen de Fin de Cycle**.

Secondary

Pupils have to sit the **Examen Selectif,** which determines admission to secondary education.

Until 1986

There were two cycles, the lower lasting two years and the upper four years. The lower cycle, referred to as the *Cycle d'Orientation/Cycle Inférieur/CO*, covered general education. The curriculum included: French, mathematics, history, geography, science, technology, African sociology, civic instruction, and physical education. On completion of class 2, pupils took an examination and successful performance led to the **Brevet du Cycle d'Orientation**.

There were two types of course in the *Cycle Supérieur: Cycle Long and Cycle Court.*

Cycle Court – this consisted of technical secondary and professional training courses lasting two to three years and leading to the **Diplôme de Fin d'Etudes Secondaires** in technical fields and the **Brevet de Fin d'Etudes Secondaires** in professional areas.

Cycle Long – this lasted four years. Pupils could specialize in one of the following options: Greek – Latin – humanities/Latin – mathematics/Latin – science/modern science A or B/modern economics. The following subjects were common to all options – religion and civics, French, English, history, geography, and mathematics. Until 1967, pupils took school examinations and were awarded diplomas by the individual school at the end of class 6. In 1967, the **Examen d'Etat** was established as the final examination. In that year, pupils were awarded a **Diplôme de Fin d'Etudes Secondaires**, but from 1968–71 the final certificate awarded on successful performance in the **Examen d'Etat** was the **Diplôme d'Etat de l'Enseignement Secondaire**. Until 1970, if pupils obtained marks of no more than 40–50 per cent, they were awarded a **Certificat d'Etat**. Since 1972, the final certificate has been the **Diplôme d'Etat d'Etudes Secondaires du Cycle Long**.

Prior to 1976, pupils wishing to go on to higher education took the **Epreuve d'Orientation**, in which they had to obtain 45 per cent in their subject of specialization. The examination included tests in general subjects plus the desired subject of specialization and led to the **Certificat du Jury d'Enseignement Secondaire**. Pupils who failed this examination could undertake a preliminary year – *Propedeutique*.

Since 1986

Secondary education still lasts six years but is made up of one cycle only. Pupils choose their field of study at age 12 and there is no examination at age 14.

Students may enter a technical field of study from the age of 12 and either study that at *cycle court* level or at *cycle long* level. If they have taken a technical subject at *cycle long* level they will be eligible to apply for higher education.

The qualification awarded on successful completion of the *cycle long* – the **Diplôme d'Etat d'Etudes Secondaires du Cycle Long** – is the entry requirement for higher education whether at a university or a technical institute.

Homologation – legalization of a certificate by the *Commission d'Homologation*. The Commission ensures that the course of studies has followed the state teaching course or a course approved by the Ministry of Education. Before the introduction of the **Examen d'Etat** in 1967, the Commission also homologated the school diplomas issued by the individual schools.

FURTHER EDUCATION

There are technician/training institutions affiliated to the university e.g. Ecole Supérieur de Commerce. They offer three-year courses for students who have completed secondary school, and lead to the qualification of **Gradue**.

HIGHER EDUCATION

Between 1971 and 1981 there was one university, the National University of Zaire (UNAZA). The three existing universities were integrated into one institution following the 'nationalization' of education. Since 1981, there have been three state universities: Kinshasa, Lubumbashi and Kinsangani. Free universities have been founded by Catholic and Protestant churches as in Bakavu and Butembo.

Entrance to degree courses is with the **Diplôme d'Etat d'Etudes Secondaires du Cycle Long**. Students who do not hold sufficiently good school qualifications to be admitted to university or whose course is not homologated, may take an examination leading to the **Certificat du Jury Universitaire**.

Until 1971, courses generally followed the Belgian pattern of *Première Candidature* (year 1), *Deuxième Candidature* (year 2), *Première Année de Licence* (year 3), and *Deuxième Année de Licence* (year 4). Since 1973 the **Candidat** has been extended to three years. This has extended the normal **Licence** to five years. The first two years at university consist of broadly based studies leading to the qualification of **Gradue** – in medicine and law this stage lasts three years. The examinations at the end of the first, second and third years are the first, second or third **Candidature**. The extra year for the **Candidat** often covers a period of practical study (or, in the case of teaching, a year of teaching practice). A further two years leads to the **Licence**, or three to four years to a professional qualification. The examinations at the end of each year are called first, second or third **Licence**.

A further qualification was introduced in 1989: the **Diplôme d'Etudes Supérieures**, which is a two-year course taken after the **Licence**.

Medicine – the title of **Docteur en Médecine** is obtained after six years, including one-year internship.

In arts, philosophy and science, individual research lasting a minimum of three years leads to a **Doctorat**. There are no **Master's degrees**.

Theology – the **Baccalauréat** in theology is obtained after one year of university study. The **Doctorat** is obtained one year after the **Licence** on successful submission of a thesis.

Law – the **Baccalauréat** is awarded after one year of university study. The **Doctorat** is obtained after at least one year of study after the **Licence**; students must obtain the **Diplome d'Etudes Speciales** and then present a thesis.

TEACHER EDUCATION

Primary

There are two levels of course taken in:

Cycle Court – a three-year course consisting of two years' general education followed by one year's in-service teacher-training (*Stage Pedagogique*), leading to the qualification of **Brevet d'Instituteurs**.

Cycle Long – a four-year course followed by one year of in-service teacher/training, leading to the qualification of **Diplôme d'Instituteurs**.

Secondary

Lower – a three-year course for holders of the **Diplôme d'Etat** at the Ecole Normale Moyenne, leading to the qualification of **Gradue en Enseignement**.

Upper – holders of the **Gradue en Enseignement** may undertake a further two-year course at the Institut Pedagogique National or Institut Supérieur Pedagogique (both affiliated to the Ecole Normale Supérieur), leading to a **Licence d'Enseignement**. Holders of the **Diplôme d'Etat** may take a three-year course leading to the **Licence d'Enseignement**. Students who take degree courses in subjects other than education may obtain the **Agregation de l'Enseignement Secondaire Supérieur** if they pass a paper in education and undertake some teaching practice.

Zambia

The education system is centrally controlled but certain aspects of education administration are now being decentralized. The Ministry of Education conducts examinations through its examinations sections, although the awarding body is the Examinations Council of Zambia which has been an independent body since 1987. It conducts the grade VII, IX and XII examinations. The Curriculum Development Centre (CDC) prepares curricula development. Provision of materials has recently been liberalized.

Primary education is compulsory.

The official language and medium of instruction has been English since 1965 (confirmed by the Education Act of 1966). However, a new policy change will implement the local language as the medium of instruction in grades I–IV over the next few years.

The academic year runs as follows:

Schools	–	January–December
Teacher training colleges	–	January–December
University	–	October–July, although this has slipped significantly over recent years.

EVALUATION IN BRITAIN

School

Zambia School Certificate – grades 1–6 are generally considered comparable to GCSE standard (grades A, B and C) on a subject-for-subject basis.

Further

DTEVT Advanced Certificate – generally considered comparable to BTEC National Diploma / N/SVQ level 3 / Advanced GNVQ/GSVQ standard. May be considered to satisfy the general entrance requirements of British higher education institutions.

Higher

Bachelor degree – generally considered comparable to a standard between GCE Advanced standard and British Bachelor degree. May be given advanced standing by British higher education institutions.

MARKING SYSTEMS

School

Zambia School Certificate is graded 1–9, where 9 is a fail.

1–2   distinction

3–4   merit

5–6   credit

7–8   satisfactory (pass)

9   unsatisfactory

Higher

Course work

86 per cent and above	A+	distinction
76–85	A	distinction
66–75	B+	meritorious
56–65	B	very satisfactory
46–55	C+	definite pass
36–45	C	bare pass
35 and below	D	fail

Overall mark

The overall mark is obtained by averaging the course-work percentages. Thus, an overall mark of 66–75 per cent would be B+ meritorious. The final certificate will use the classifications: with distinction, with merit, with credit and pass. The above markings are used at university and secondary teacher training colleges. Certificates issued by primary teacher training colleges show passes but with no individual grades.

SCHOOL EDUCATION

Pre-primary

Most pre-primary education is private and the facilities are limited. In some areas District Councils now run pre-primary education, mostly in urban areas.

Primary

This has covered seven years from age seven since 1974; before then it was from age five. The period is divided into two cycles: lower (grades I–IV) and upper (grades V–VII).

The curriculum includes English, mathematics, science, social studies, practical subjects, Zambian languages, religious instruction, home economics, music and physical education. On completion of grade VII, pupils take the **Primary School Leaving Certificate Examination.** This examination consists of five papers – English, mathematics, science, social studies and Zambian languages, plus one special paper consisting of non-verbal intelligence tests. There are plans to extend the basic cycle to grade IX for all pupils.

Secondary

This covers five years, divided into: junior (grades VIII and IX) and senior (grades X–XII).

Junior

All pupils take English, mathematics, science, religious education, civics, history, geography and agricultural science. Options include French, art, music, woodwork, metalwork, technical drawing, typewriting, office practice, bookkeeping and homecraft. The cycle culminates in the **Junior Secondary School Leaving Examination**; to obtain the certificate, pupils must pass English and five other subjects.

Senior

On completion of this cycle pupils take the examinations for the **Zambia School Certificate** which is awarded by the Examinations Council of Zambia. Until 1980, students sat the **Cambridge Overseas School Certificate**.

It is possible to study for London **GCE Advanced** examinations through private correspondence colleges and some state-run evening classes, but there is no counterpart to this examination within the Zambian school system.

TECHNICAL AND FURTHER EDUCATION

The Department of Technical Education and Vocational Training (DTEVT), originally established in 1969 as a Commission responsible for the restructuring of technical education in Zambia, now operates eleven institutions offering over ninety full-time programmes. Present enrolment is over 5,000 students. DTEVT is part of the Ministry of Science, Technology and Vocational training. Its awards are issued under the approval of the Examinations Council of Zambia and are divided into four categories:

The **Craft Certificate,** and **Certificate,** awarded after two years, with entry level set at grade XII; the **Advanced Certificate (technician level)** consisting of two years and nine months (nine terms at college and two terms in industry) post-**Zambia School Certificate;** and the **Diploma** which lasts three years and three months (ten terms at college and three terms in industry) with the **Advanced Certificate** as the entry level.

A fifth award, 'The Record of Achievement', is issued to those who successfully complete short courses of at least twelve months' duration, not normally considered as full programmes. Broadly speaking, DTEVT administers two types of institution: trades training institutes and higher institutions.

There are eleven trades training institutes. The minimum entry requirement is grade XII. The institutes' trade/craft programmes last two years at the end of which an interim **Craft Certificate** is awarded. Students then need to obtain one year's working experience before the final **Craft Certificate** is given.

The following courses have a minimum entry requirement of grade XII.

Northern Technical College (NORTEC). The three training departments of the College are mechanical, automotive and electrical engineering.

The courses offered by these departments are full-time and lead to DTEVT's own qualifications. There are evening and part-time commercial and office practice courses leading to a variety of external qualifications. **GCE Advanced** courses in mathematics and physics are also offered.

Awards of the City and Guilds of London Institute are also offered.

Zambia Air Services Training Institute (ZASTI) offers diploma and certificate programmes in commercial aviation, aviation electronics, aircraft maintenance, air traffic control, meteorology, telecommunications, and fire services.

Evelyn Hone College of Applied Arts and Commerce offers diploma and certificate courses in a variety of commercial and vocational subjects, for example, business studies, personnel management, secretarial studies, journalism, printing, hotel and catering and paramedical subjects. Awards of the City and Guilds of London Institute may also be obtained.

Nursing

Zambian state-registered nurses take a three-year course. The entry requirement is a **Zambia School Certificate** with passes in five subjects. Zambian state-enrolled nurses follow a two-year course for which minimum entry is grade XI. The University of Zambia offers a three-year **BSc** programme in nursing. There is also a one-year post-registration course in midwifery conducted at schools of midwifery.

Agriculture

At the lowest level are the farmer training centres in each district for training subsistence farmers. Above these are the farm institutes – one in each province – which run a variety of short courses mainly for extension workers.

There are four farm colleges which are run by the Ministry of Agriculture. The minimum entry requirement is usually grade VII and courses last up to three years.

The two colleges of agriculture (one at Monze and the other at Mpika) run identical two-year **Certificate in General Agriculture** courses. Minimum entry is grade IX and the following subjects are studied: agricultural science (first year only but students must pass it), animal husbandry, crop husbandry, farm management, farm engineering (girls study home economics instead) and extension methods (which also covers human nutrition). These colleges are also the responsibility of the Ministry of Agriculture.

The Natural Resources Development College in Lusaka offers three-year diploma courses in agriculture, agricultural engineering, agricultural education and nutrition. Agriculture students can major in their third year in animal science, crop science or business management. The College belongs to the Ministry of Agriculture.

Zambia Forest College offers a two-year diploma course and is planning to run a three-year **Bachelor degree** in forestry with Copperbelt University.

HIGHER EDUCATION

There are two universities, the University of Zambia (UNZA) and The Copperbelt University. The entrance requirement to **Bachelor degree** courses is five passes in the **Zambia School Certificate**.

At the University of Zambia all students enter either the school of natural sciences, the school of humanities and social science or the school of education for the first year.

They may then move from the school of natural sciences to the faculties of engineering, medicine, agricultural science, veterinary education or mines, and from the school of humanities and social science to the faculty of law.

Students at The Copperbelt University enter their chosen schools in the first year. The schools at The Copperbelt University are: business, administration and accountancy; environmental studies; technology (formerly a separate institution known as the Zambia Institute of Technology); forestry and wood science.

Bachelor degree courses in arts, science and law take four years; those in engineering and agriculture five years. There is no division into Ordinary and Honours degrees.

Master's degrees take two further years of study.

Facilities for doctoral study were introduced in the late 1970s.

Medicine: the degree course lasts seven years, but after the first four years students are awarded the **Bachelor of Science in Human Biology.**

Veterinary science: A six-year course in veterinary science is offered to thirty students per year.

Dentistry: a two-year course at technician level is run by the Ministry of Health.

Pharmacy and medical laboratory: three-year diploma courses are available at Evelyn Hone College.

Forestry: a three-year diploma course is available at Mwekera Forestry College.

Correspondence degrees include one to two years' full-time study. They can be taken in social sciences, education and law.

The universities also offers various certificate and diploma courses.

TEACHER EDUCATION

There are ten primary teachers' colleges one of which is for in-service training and one for teachers of people with disabilities. There are also three secondary colleges of which one is for technical and vocational teachers.

Primary

There is a two-year certificate course for which the minimum entry qualification is grade XII with five passes.

Secondary

Junior

A two-year diploma course for which the minimum entry requirement is the **Zambia School Certificate**. There is also a one-year **Advanced Diploma** in maths and science. The Technical and Vocational Teachers' College comes under the DTEVT. The examinations and curriculum of the other two colleges are moderated by the University of Zambia.

Senior

Teachers for grades X to XII come not from the teachers' colleges but from the School of Education at the <u>University of Zambia</u>. The School of Education awards the degrees of **BA** (with education) and **BSc** (with education).

The <u>University of Zambia</u> (UNZA) moderates the junior and secondary teaching examinations (the **Junior Diploma** and the four year **Senior degree**).

Zimbabwe

Formerly Southern Rhodesia, the Republic of Zimbabwe gained independence in April 1980.

Primary education, followed by nearly three million pupils, is free in rural areas. In urban areas parents pay for the education of their children, but the lowly paid are exempted. Were it not for the current economic adjustment programme free education would have been scrapped. In principle primary education is compulsory from the age of five, with school levies for buildings agreed between head-teachers and parents as part of self-help projects. Secondary education, followed by half a million pupils, is available to all who can afford the tuition fees and other charges, but is not compulsory.

The medium of instruction is English, although Shona, Ndebele or other African languages may be used up to primary grade 3.

The school year runs from mid-January to early December and is divided into three terms. The university year, for most faculties, runs from March to November.

EVALUATION IN BRITAIN

School

Cambridge School Certificate – generally considered comparable to GCSE standard (grades A, B and C) when grades of 1 (maximum) to 6 are awarded.

Cambridge Higher School Certificate – grades A–E are generally considered comparable to GCE Advanced standard.

The <u>University of London</u> conducts **GCE O** and **A level** examinations in Zimbabwe.

Higher

Bachelor degree (from the <u>University of Zimbabwe</u>) – generally considered comparable to British Bachelor degree standard.

MARKING SYSTEMS

School

The **Cambridge School Certificate** is marked on a scale of 1 (maximum) to 9.

A/B/C	= 1–6
D/E	= 7–8
U	= 9

The **Cambridge Higher School Certificate** is marked on a scale of A to E with O representing an **O level** pass and F a fail.

Higher

University examination papers are set by lecturers and approved by the heads of department. Papers are marked by the lecturer and also by an external examiner. The papers are marked on the scale: first, upper second, lower second, third, fail.

80 per cent+	= first division
70–79	= upper second division
60–69	= lower second division
50–59	= third division
below 50	= fail

SCHOOL EDUCATION

Background

Before 1979, two separate systems of education operated in Rhodesia: one for Africans, and one for Europeans, mixed races and Asians. For the Africans, schooling was not compulsory; for the rest, it was compulsory between the ages of seven and fifteen but places were not always available.

The 1979 Education Act

The 1979 Education Act, passed by the transitional government, abolished compulsory education and classified schools into three groups: private schools; community schools; and state government schools.

Independence, 1980

After Independence, the new Ministry of Education and Culture introduced free primary education for all children from grades 1 to 7, and secondary education was extended. Areas of expansion have included: improved facilities in the rural areas, greater government participation, mass literacy and numeracy campaigns, increased vocational and technical education, and a non-formal education sector for adults.

The two principal African national languages, Shona and Ndebele, are now taught in all schools, with English still the main medium of instruction.

Primary

In primary schools, grades 1 to 7 lead to a national **Grade 7 Examination**.

Secondary

From grade 7 there is automatic right of entry to form 1 at secondary level. About eighty per cent of primary school students proceed to secondary level. Within the secondary system there is only one stream. All pupils take the **Zimbabwe Junior Certificate** at the end of form 2 but the purpose of this examination is not to weed out pupils, but to stream those with more technical or academic aptitudes. All continue through to form 4 at the end of which the **Cambridge School Certificate** (CSC) or **GCE O levels** are taken. Most pupils then leave school. Equality of opportunity for all pupils to pass automatically from primary to secondary school, and all secondary school pupils to take CSC/**O levels**, has been established. The **Cambridge School**

Certificate or **GCE O levels** are being localized in phases after which the setting and marking of these examinations will be the sole responsibility of the Ministry of Education and Culture.

Pupils with CSC/GCE passes in at least five subjects may go on to the lower sixth form to follow a two-year **Higher School Certificate** (HSC)/**A level** course. The **M level** examination of the Associated Examining Board has been phased out.

FURTHER EDUCATION

Agricultural

Agricultural education is offered at three levels:

Agricultural Institutes

There are four agricultural institutes offering two-year courses leading to a **Certificate in Agriculture**. The minimum entry requirement is the **Zimbabwe Junior Certificate** but CSC/**O level** entry is becoming more widespread.

Colleges of Agriculture

There are two colleges of agriculture. The entrance requirement is five passes at CSC/**GCE O level** which must include English, mathematics and a science. The two-year course leads to a **Diploma in Agriculture**.

Faculty of Agriculture, University of Zimbabwe

The entrance requirement is five CSC/**GCE** passes of which two must be at HSC/**A level**; both must be science subjects. The course lasts three years and includes various practical-work assignments. The faculty also offers **MPhil** and **DPhil degrees** by research.

Technical/vocational

Responsibility for technical and vocational education lies with the Ministry of Higher Education. Various courses are offered leading to skilled worker and technician qualifications. Apprenticeships last three to four years. During this period the apprentice is exposed to both practical and theoretical training – taking 80–85 per cent and 15–20 per cent of the time respectively. Theoretical training is undertaken at technical colleges, usually on either full-time or block release. For all college-based courses, the academic entry requirement is at least **O level** with passes at grade C or better in five approved subjects.

Technical and vocational courses commence in secondary schools, after the **Zimbabwe Junior Certificate**, where students do **National Foundation Certificate (NFC)** subjects. These subjects are equivalent to **O level** subjects.

The course levels available are:

National Certificate
entry level :   CSC/**O levels** or **NFC**.
course length: 900 hours of study requiring six subjects.
                                                      1 year full-time.

National Diploma

entry level: completed **National Certificate** or
two **A level** passes in relevant subjects.

course length: 1800 hours of study requiring six subjects.
2 years full-time.

The ministry runs the following types of institution:

Technical colleges
Polytechnics
Vocational training centres
Management Training Bureau (Harare)

In the private sector there are at least 147 institutions offering a wide variety of vocational courses.

Bachelor of Technology courses were introduced at Harare Polytechnic in October 1985; they are professionally supervised by the University of Zimbabwe.

Courses leading to the awards of City and Guilds of London Institute are also available at some institutions, provided they do not have local equivalents.

HIGHER EDUCATION

In 1988, the Ministry of Higher Education was established.

The University of Zimbabwe was founded in 1957 as the University College of Rhodesia and Nyasaland and later became the University of Rhodesia before assuming its present title at Independence. A third university, Africa University was opened in Mutare in 1992 with United Methodist Church sponsorship.

Entrance is generally comparable to university entrance in Britain, i.e. five passes at CSC/**GCE**, of which at least two must be at HSC/**A level.** All students must have English language at CSC or **O level** standard. The University offers three to four-year **Bachelor degrees**; special diplomas and postgraduate certificates; two to three-year **Master's degrees** and three to four-year **Doctorate** programmes.

TEACHER EDUCATION

There are ten primary and five secondary teachers' colleges. Of the ten primary teachers' colleges five are government conventional colleges, three private and two ZINTEC colleges. Two of the secondary colleges are technical and offer four-year programmes. The remaining three teach mainly non-technical subjects. The colleges are affiliated to the Department of Teacher Education (formerly Associate College Centre) in the faculty of education at the University of Zimbabwe.

The entry requirement for all the colleges is at least five passes at CSC/**O level**, including a language. The course lasts three years and is administered on a 'year-in year-out year-in' basis. To date two secondary colleges have introduced two-year programmes for holders of **A levels**. The courses lead to the **Certificate/Diploma in Education of the University of Zimbabwe.**

The faculty of education at the University of Zimbabwe offers a four-term full-time/three-year part-time **BEd** course. The course is for in-service teachers who already hold a **Certificate of Education**. **BEd** graduates normally teach at senior secondary levels but are trained to teach at any level within the secondary system.

The Zimbabwe Integrated Teacher Education Course (ZINTEC) is a government programme aimed at reducing the number of untrained primary teachers with minimum loss of teaching capacity while students are in training. The course starts with a two-term residential course of lectures and tutorials followed by eight terms of supervised teaching practice and in-service training by correspondence work and vacation courses, and ends with a two-term residential course at a teachers' college. At the end of the four-year cycle, students who are successful in the final examinations and receive adequate assessments are awarded **Standard-Trained** status.

Appendix 1

General Certificate of Secondary Education (GCSE)

SUBJECTS OFFERED AT GCSE

The following list provides details of the main group of subjects examined at GCSE level. There are also other minor subjects, deriving from the main subject groups offered. These are not listed here.

The letters above the columns refer to the examining boards – from left to right:

University of London Examinations and Assessment Council

Midland Examining Group

Northern Examinations and Assessment Board

Northern Ireland Council for the Curriculum, Examinations and Assessment

Southern Examining Group

Welsh Joint Education Committee

SUBJECT	L	M	N	NI	S	W
Accounting	*		*	*	*	*
American studies					*	
Arabic	*					
Archaeology			*			
Art and design	*	*	*	*	*	*
Bengali	*					
Biblical Hebrew	*					
British government and politics	*		*			
British industrial society			*		*	
Building studies		*	*			
Business education						*
Business and information studies	*					
Business studies	*	*	*	*	*	*
Catering						*
Chinese	*	*				
Classical civilization	*	*	*	*		
Commerce			*		*	*
Community issues	*					
Computer studies	*			*		
Craft and design			*			
Critical studies: art	*		*			
Dance			*			
Design					*	

SUBJECT	L	M	N	NI	S	W
Design and communication	*	*	*	*	*	
Design and realization	*	*	*	*	*	
Design and technology	*	*	*		*	*
Design and technology and art	*		*		*	*
Design and technology and auto engineering	*					
Design and technology and automation	*					
Design and technology and business studies	*		*		*	*
Design and technology and catering	*		*		*	
Design and technology and drama						
Design and technology and electronics	*		*			
Design and technology and fashion	*		*			
Design and technology and health						*
Design and technology and music			*			*
Design and technology and product design					*	
Drama	*	*	*		*	*
Economics	*	*	*	*	*	*
Engineering workshop theory					*	
English	*	*	*	*	*	*
English literature	*	*	*	*	*	
Environmental studies			*			
European studies					*	
Expressive arts	*	*	*			
Food studies			*			
French	*	*	*	*	*	*
General studies		*	*		*	
Geography	*	*	*	*	*	*
German	*	*	*	*	*	*
Graphic and product design	*					
Graphic communication	*		*			
Greek	*	*	*	*		
Greek civilization			*			
Gujarati		*				
Health studies		*				
History and appreciation of music			*			
Home economics: child development	*	*	*	*	*	*
Home economics: food	*	*	*	*	*	*
Home economics: home and food			*		*	
Home economics: textiles		*	*	*	*	*
Humanities		*	*		*	*
Information systems	*	*	*		*	
Information technology	*	*	*		*	
Information technology and art			*			*
Information technology and business studies	*		*			*
Information technology and catering			*			*
Information technology and drama						*
Information technology and electronics						*
Information technology and fashion			*			*
Information technology and health						*
Information technology and music			*			*
Integrated humanities		*	*		*	
Irish				*		
Italian	*		*	*		
Japanese	*					
Keyboarding applications	*		*		*	
Land surveying					*	

SUBJECT	L	M	N	NI	S	W
Latin	*	*	*	*		
Latin and Roman civilization		*				
Law		*				
Logic	*					
Marine navigation						
Mathematics	*	*	*	*	*	*
Media studies			*	*		
Modern Greek	*		*			
Modern Hebrew			*			
Motor vehicle engineering			*			
Motor vehicle and road user studies			*			
Music	*	*	*	*	*	*
Nautical studies			*			
Office studies			*			*
Panjabi		*	*			
Personal and social education					*	
Photography						
Physical education	*	*	*	*	*	*
Portuguese	*					
Psychology		*	*			
Religious studies	*	*	*	*	*	
Roman civilization			*			
Russian	*		*			
Sanskrit	*					
Science	*	*	*		*	
Science: agricultural			*			
Science: biology	*	*	*	*	*	*
Science: chemistry	*	*	*	*	*	
Science: electronics	*	*	*			
Science: geology					*	*
Science: horticultural			*			
Science: human physiology and health			*		*	
Science: physics	*	*	*	*	*	*
Science: rural			*			
Science, technology and society			*			
Social science		*	*			
Sociology	*	*	*		*	
Spanish	*	*	*		*	
Speech and drama	*					
Statistics			*		*	
Technical design and graphic communication			*			
Technology	*	*	*			*
Technology and art						
Technology and business studies	*	*				*
Technology and catering						
Technology and electronics	*					
Technology and fashion			*			
Technology and music						
Technology: product and systems design						
Textiles			*			
Theatre arts					*	
Turkish	*					
Ukrainian			*			
Urdu	*		*			
Welfare and society			*			

Appendix 1

SUBJECT	L	M	N	NI	S	W
Welsh language						*
Welsh literature						*
Welsh second language						*
Welsh second language and business studies						*
Welsh second language and drama						*
Welsh second language and information technology						*
Welsh second language and religious studies						*
World development						*

Appendix 2

Overseas GCE Certificates

General Certificate of Education (**GCE**) examinations can be taken overseas in many countries. The University of Cambridge Local Examinations Syndicate (UCLES) offers **School Certificate (SC), Higher School Certificate (HSC), GCE O level, GCE A level** and the more recent **International General Certificate of Secondary Education (IGCSE)**, an international counterpart of the **General Certificate of Secondary Education (GCSE)** which has superseded **GCE O level** and CSE in the UK (see below). UCLES also offers the **Higher International General Certificate of Secondary Education (HIGCSE)** for centres in Southern Africa, and the **Advanced International Certificate of Education (AICE)** which is an international version of the UK **Advanced Supplementary (AS)** examination. The University of London School Examinations Board (ULSEB), now renamed the University of London Examinations and Assessment Council (ULEAC), offers **GCE O level** and **A level** overseas. The University of Oxford Delegacy of Local Examinations offers a special **GCE O level** and standard **GCE A level** overseas. The Associated Examining Board (AEB) offers standard **GCSEs** and **GCE A levels**.

University of Cambridge Local Examinations Syndicate (UCLES)

In many countries, former Cambridge certificates have been taken over by national examination authorities and developed as national awards. In some of these cases UCLES is still involved in setting the syllabus, marking, validation, moderation or monitoring. On those certificates where UCLES is represented as 'in collaboration/conjunction' with the national authority, then UCLES recognizes the certificate as **GCE** equivalent.

Cambridge certificates are still taken in at least fifty countries world-wide, but entry for the **IGCSE, AICE** and other examinations is made by individual schools and there are many more countries where Cambridge examinations are available to individual schools.

In Singapore and Brunei, UCLES is responsible for standards only in those subjects indicated 'Cambridge' on the certificate.

In Malaysia, entry for **GCE O level** is restricted to a special English language syllabus for candidates seeking a UK matriculation qualification.

The **School Certificate** was originally a group certificate, for the award of which pupils had to pass in a specified number of subject groups and pass in a requisite minimum number of these, including English language. In the late 1950s, the Cambridge Syndicate introduced the joint examinations for the **School** and **Higher School Certificates** and **General Certificate of Education** (the **School Certificate** with the **GCE** at **Ordinary level**, and the **Higher School Certificate** with the **GCE** at **Advanced level**). Any student who passed the required number of subjects was awarded a **School Certificate**. A student who did not qualify for the **School Certificate** but passed in at least one subject at grade 6 or better, was awarded a certificate showing the subjects in which he or she was deemed to have reached **GCE O level**.

The **Cambridge Overseas School Certificate** has also been known as the **Cambridge**

School Certificate and **Cambridge Senior School Certificate**. (The **Cambridge Junior School Certificate** used to be available at a stage two years before the **Senior Certificate**.)

The **International General Certificate of Secondary Education (IGCSE)** courses are designed as two-year courses for examination at age sixteen-plus. The aims of the **IGCSE** are to support modern curriculum development, promote international understanding, encourage good teaching practice, set widely recognized standards and to facilitate the mobility of students.

The **IGCSE** is offered in schools and colleges in over sixty countries throughout the world. The Ministry of Education and Culture in Namibia has adopted the **IGCSE** as its senior secondary school leaving examination. The **IGCSE** is only available through and administered by, the University of Cambridge Local Examinations Syndicate (UCLES).

Higher International General Certificate of Secondary Education (HIGCSE) courses are used by schools in Southern Africa, and in particular in Namibia. The **HIGCSE** and **IGCSE** are closely related. The **HIGCSE** grows out of the **IGCSE**; it shares common aims, approaches and content but at a higher level. The **HIGCSE** represents an additional year of study beyond the **IGCSE**.

The **Advanced International Certificate of Education (AICE)** programme is a pre-university course of study, progressive from the **IGCSE**. The **AICE** is an international version of the British **Advanced Supplementary (AS)** examination.

EVALUATION IN BRITAIN

Cambridge Overseas School Certificate – grades 1–5 (until 1960), grades 1–6 (since 1961), A, B and C are equated to **GCSE** grades A, B, C.

Cambridge Overseas Higher School Certificate – grades A–E are equated to **GCE Advanced standard**.

The **International General Certificate of Secondary Education (IGCSE)** has been accepted by British higher education institutions on the same basis as the **GCSE** and **GCE O level** at corresponding grades for the purposes of satisfying general and course entrance requirements.

The **Higher International General Certificate of Secondary Education (HIGCSE)** is taken in Namibia only at present – passes in five subjects, with an average of at least 3 in each subject, may be considered to satisfy the general entrance requirements of British higher education institutions.

The **Advanced International Certificate of Education (AICE)** a minimum score of 30 points may be accepted by British universities as satisfying their general entrance requirements for undergraduate courses.

Appendix 2

MARKING SYSTEMS

The School Certificate/GCE Ordinary level examinations are graded:

1	A, very good	)	A until 1960 only grades 3–5
2		)	were considered as credit passes
3	B, credit	)	B
		)	
5	C, pass	)	C
6		)	
7	pass (in the **School Certificate**)	)	D
8		)	E
9	fail	)	U

The Higher School Certificate/GCE A level examinations are graded A, B, C, D, E. Such principal passes are equated to passes at **GCE A level**. Subsidiary pass (Grade O) is below **HSC/GCE A level**, but is considered above **GCSE** grade C. Grade F is a fail.

The International General Certificate of Secondary Education (IGCSE) can be taken in individual syllabuses. The **IGCSE** is an examination suitable for virtually the whole ability range. It has a seven-point scale of grades: A, B, C, D, E, F and G. Grade A is awarded for the highest level of achievement; grade G indicates minimum satisfactory performance.

The International Certificate of Education (ICE) is awarded to students who have attained passes in at least seven subjects at **IGCSE** level.

The Higher International General Certificate of Secondary Education (HIGCSE) is graded on a four-point scale, 1 to 4, of which Grade 1 represents the highest level of achievement. The Committee of University Principals (CUP) of the South African universities, accepts **HIGCSE** passes at Grades 1 to 3 for entrance to undergraduate courses.

The Advanced International Certificate of Education (AICE) examinations are graded on the scale A (high) to E (low). The full **AICE** certificate is awarded on a points system.

The grade aggregate on which a candidate's general performance for the **School Certificate** is judged is obtained by adding together the best six subject grades. With the exception of Mauritius and Zambia, **School Certificates** are classified as follows:

first division – for an aggregate not exceeding 23, with at least a credit in five subjects (including English language) and at least a pass in a sixth;

second division – for an aggregate not exceeding 33, with at least credit in four subjects and at least pass in two others (subjects passed to include English language);

third division – for an aggregate not exceeding 45, with either at least a credit in one subject and at least a pass in five others, or at least a credit in two subjects and at least a pass in three others (in both these cases, subjects passed to include English language).

The International General Certificate of Secondary Education curriculum consists of five subject groups.

Group I – Languages:

First language

Arabic	Dutch	Japanese
Afrikaans	English	Portuguese
Bahasa Malaysia	French	Sesotho
Chinese	German	Spanish

Second language

English

Foreign languages

Dutch	Indonesian	Spanish
French	Italian	German
Portuguese		

Group II – Humanities and social sciences:

Literature in English, French, German and Spanish	History
	Latin
Development studies	Natural economy
Economics	Sociology
Geography	

Group III – Sciences:

Agriculture	Co-ordinated sciences
Biology	Natural economy
Chemistry	Physical science
Combined science	Physics

Group IV – Mathematics:

Mathematics	Additional mathematics

Group V – Creative, technical and vocational:

Accounting	Computer studies
Art and design	Design and technology
Business studies	Food science
Child development	Music

The **International Certificate of Education (ICE)** is also available. To be eligible for the award of the **ICE** a candidate must pass at least seven subjects at **IGCSE** level, including two from Group I and one from each of Groups II to V. The seventh subject may be chosen from any one of the groups.

The **ICE** is awarded at three levels:

Distinction	Grade A in five subjects and grade C or better in two subjects;
Merit	Grade C or better in five subjects and grade F or better in two subjects;
Pass	Grade G or better in seven subjects.

In the **Advanced International Certificate of Education (AICE)** students follow a balanced course of at least five subjects. One subject must be taken from each of the three subject groups – A, B and C:

Group A – Mathematics and sciences

Biology	Chemistry	Environmental science
Mathematics	Technology	Further mathematics
Physics		

Group B – Languages

Arabic	English	French
German	Spanish	

Group C – Arts and humanities

Economics	History	Business studies
Geography	Music	Art and design

Students may substitute two half-credit courses for one of the full-credit courses listed above.

The **AICE** is awarded on a points system, as follows:

Full-credit		**Half-credit**	
Grade	points	Grade	points
A	10	A	5
B	8	B	4
C	6	C	3
D	4	D	2
E	2	E	1

The **AICE** is awarded at three levels:

Distinction	46 points or more
Merit	30–45 points
Pass	10–29 points

Students who pass **AICE** examinations in individual subjects, but who do not qualify for the full **AICE** certificate, will be awarded a certificate listing their results in subjects passed.

Further information about UCLES' international examinations may be obtained from:

The IGCSE/AICE Co-ordinator
University of Cambridge Local Examinations Syndicate
1 Hills Road
Cambridge CB1 2EU
United Kingdom

Other GCE boards offering overseas examinations

The University of London School Examinations Board (ULSEB) – now renamed the
University of London Examinations and Assessment Council (ULEAC), the Associated
Examining Board (AEB) and the University of Oxford Delegacy of Local
Examinations offer **GCE** and **GCSE** examinations between them in schools in at least
fifty countries world-wide.

Further information may be obtained from:

University of London Examinations and Assessment Council
Stewart House
32 Russell Square
London WC1B 5DN
United Kingdom

The Associated Examining Board
Stag Hill House
Guildford
Surrey GU2 5XJ
United Kingdom

University of Oxford Delegacy of Local Examinations
Ewert House
Ewert Place
Banbury Road Summertown
Oxford OX2 7BZ
United Kingdom

Appendix 3

West African Examinations Council

The West African Examinations Council (WAEC) was established in 1952 to determine the examinations required in the public interest in West Africa, to conduct such examinations in Ghana (the Gold Coast as it then was), Nigeria, Sierra Leone and the Gambia, and to award certificates comparable to those awarded by equivalent examining bodies in the United Kingdom. Liberia became the fifth member country in 1974. The Council is made up of representatives from all member countries.

In its early years, the Council acted as an agent in administering examinations such as the **School Certificate** examination of the University of Cambridge Local Examinations Syndicate (UCLES) and the **General Certificate of Education** examinations of the University of London and maintained a close relationship with these examining bodies. However, with the acquisition of the necessary expertise, the Council started taking on greater responsibilities, and in 1955, the **Cambridge School Certificate**, renamed the **West African School Certificate** (**WASC**), was awarded by UCLES in collaboration with WAEC.

Starting in 1960 with the **School Certificate** examination of the West African Examinations Council (SC/WAEC), renamed the **School Certificate/General Certificate of Education** (**SC/GCE**) in 1963, the Council now independently develops and administers all its own examinations and administers others on behalf of (or in collaboration with) certain examining bodies. Currently, WAEC develops and administers the **Joint Examination** for the **School Certificate** and **GCE O level** and for the **GCE A level**.

As with the **School Certificate**, the Council administered the **Higher School Certificate** examination and also later the **GCE Advanced level** examination on behalf of UCLES and the University of London from its inception until 1972, when WAEC began to develop and administer its own examinations at **GCE A level**. After 1974, the Council discontinued the **Higher School Certificate** examination and adopted the single-subject **GCE A level** examination.

NEW WAEC EXAMINATIONS

The Senior School Certificate Examination (Nigeria)

Following the adoption of a new system of education in Nigeria – the 6–3–3–4 – the Council conducted the first **Senior School Certificate** examination for some candidates in May/June 1988. All school candidates in Nigeria were entered for the new examinations in 1991. Private candidates followed suit in 1992. The **GCE** examinations were phased out in Nigeria in 1990. The level of the **Senior School Certificate** examination is pitched midway between the **GCE O level** and **A level** examinations.

The Senior Secondary School Certificate Examination (Ghana)

Following the recent educational reforms in Ghana, the first **Senior Secondary School Certificate** examinations have been provided for school candidates as from May/June 1993. The last **GCE O level** examinations for school candidates were taken in

May/June 1994. For school candidates, the last **GCE A level** examinations will be taken in May/June 1996. Private candidates will continue to take **GCE O levels** and **A levels** until 1999 when they will be phased out in Ghana.

To check the validity of a WAEC certificate contact:

The West African Examinations Council
Argyle House
29–31 Euston Road
London
NW1 2SD

EVALUATION IN BRITAIN

West African School Certificate/GCE O level – grades 1–6 are generally considered comparable to GCSE standard (grades A, B and C) on a subject-for-subject basis.

Senior School Certificate (SSCE) – grades 1–6 are generally considered comparable to GCSE standard (grades A, B and C) on a subject-for-subject basis. The full **Senior School Certificate** may be considered for admission to access/bridging courses.

Senior Secondary School Certificate (in Ghana is graded using letters A–F) – grades A–C are generally considered comparable to GCSE standard (grades A, B and C) on a subject-for-subject basis.

Senior Secondary School Certificate in Nigeria – grades 1–6 are generally considered comparable to GCSE standard (grades A, B and C) on a subject-for-subject basis.

West African GCE A level – generally equated to GCE Advanced standard.

MARKING SYSTEMS

The pass grades at **School Certificate** and at **GCE O level** are the same. The interpretation of the subject grades in terms of the **School Certificate** is as follows:

Grade	School Certificate	West African GCE O level
1	excellent	excellent
2	very good	very good
3	good	good
4	credit	credit
5	credit	credit
6	credit	credit
7	pass	pass
8	pass	pass
9	fail	fail

To qualify for the award of **GCE O level** the candidate must either have entered the **School Certificate** and, while failing to gain the **Certificate**, have passed in at least one subject or have entered on a single-subject basis and have secured a pass in at least one subject.

Appendix 3

In the case of the **Higher School Certificate** there are seven grades in order of merit. The first five, designated A, B, C, D and E, are pass grades. The sixth grade is designated a subsidiary pass, defined as a standard below **GCE A level** and above **GCE O level**. The last grade represents a failure.

The interpretation of results in terms of the **Senior Secondary School Certificate** in Nigeria is as follows:

Grade	Interpretation
1	excellent
2	very good
3	good
4	credit
5	credit
6	credit
7	pass
8	pass
9	fail

In Ghana the **Senior Secondary School Certificate** is graded using letters. The interpretation of these is as follows:

Grade	Interpretation
A	excellent
B	very good
C	good
D	credit
E	pass
F	fail

For the award of the **School Certificate** candidates must take a minimum of six and a maximum of nine subjects from any four of the following subject groupings, English language being compulsory:

Group	1 –	languages, including English language
	2 –	general, including literature in English
	3 –	mathematics
	4 –	science
	5 –	arts and crafts
	6 –	technical
	7 –	commercial and secretarial.

To qualify for a certificate candidates must:

– pass all subjects at the same sitting;

– reach a satisfactory standard in the aggregate of grades of their best six subjects;

– either   pass in six subjects
    or   in five subjects with credits in at least two
    or   pass with credits in four subjects.

Appendix 3

The **School Certificate** is classified as follows:

Division I with distinction

awarded to candidates who pass in six subjects chosen from any four or more of the subject groups (including English language and either a group 3 or a group 4 subject) with five credits, yielding an aggregate score not exceeding 12 in their best six subjects.

Division I

awarded to candidates who pass in six subjects chosen from any four or more of the subject groups (including English language and either a group 3 or a group 4 subject) with five credits, yielding an aggregate score not exceeding 24 in their best six subjects.

Division II

awarded to candidates who pass in six subjects chosen from any four or more of the subject groups (including English language) with credits in at least four of the subjects, producing an aggregate score not exceeding 36 in their best six subjects.

Division III

awarded to candidates who obtain six passes or three passes plus two credits or four credits, the aggregate score from the subject grades not exceeding 48 in their best six subjects.

For the award of the **Senior School Certificate** in Nigeria, candidates must enter for and sit a minimum of eight and a maximum of nine subjects including the following six core subjects and two or three of several electives:

1   English language
2   one Nigerian language
3   mathematics
4   one of the following alternative subjects: physics, chemistry and biology
5   one of literature in English, history and geography
6   agricultural science or a vocational subject

For the award of the **Senior Secondary School Certificate** in Ghana, candidates must enter for and sit all the core subjects and three elective subjects chosen from one of the seven course programmes available. The core subjects are as follows:

1   English language
2   science
3   mathematics
4   agricultural science and environmental studies
5   life skills
6   one Ghanaian language

Candidates for **GCE A level** may offer up to five subjects, normally three or four **A level** subjects plus a general paper which is a subsidiary paper.

The International Senior Secondary School Examination

Reforms of the educational systems in the other member countries have begun and they are all likely to lead to the phasing out of the **GCE** examinations by the end of the decade. Meanwhile, the Council plans to provide its first **International Senior School Certificate** examination in 1997 in all member countries. If adopted by all or at least some member countries, the WAEC **International SSCE** will replace the national **SSCE**.

899

Appendix 4

Caribbean Examinations Council

The Caribbean Examinations Council (CXC) was established in 1972, and presently covers Anguilla; Antigua and Barbuda; Barbados*; Belize*; British Virgin Islands; Dominica; Grenada; Guyana*; Jamaica*; Montserrat; St Kitts/Nevis; St Lucia; St Vincent and the Grenadines; Trinidad and Tobago*; Turks and Caicos Islands.

(*See separate chapters for further information.)

The examinations offered by the CXC are criterion referenced with a large element of teacher assessment, and are designed for pupils who have completed five years of secondary school education. They are intended to offer greater flexibility and thus assist pupils with limited academic ability or interest in technical studies. Eventually, these examinations will replace those offered by non-Caribbean examining authorities; in the meantime, pupils may still take **GCE O level/GCSE** examinations in subjects not offered by the CXC.

The first examinations (in five subjects) for the **Caribbean Examinations Council Secondary Education Certificate** (CSEC) were offered in 1979. The Council now examines candidates in thirty-two subjects. Additional subjects are currently under consideration.

Candidates may offer subjects for examination under a General Proficiency Scheme and under a Basic Proficiency Scheme. The General Proficiency Scheme is designed for students who intend to pursue further educational programmes and who therefore require an in-depth knowledge of the subject. This scheme is taken by pupils who would normally have taken **GCE O level/GCSE** examinations. The emphasis in the Basic Proficiency Scheme is on the acquisition of skills, since it is intended that students who pursue this option will be preparing to enter the job market. Both examinations are offered to students who have completed five years of education at secondary level. There is also a Technical Proficiency Scheme in certain fields. Students are encouraged to take a combination of basic and general or technical proficiencies, since this allows them to broaden their knowledge of a number of subject areas.

The CXC has had assistance from examining bodies in the United States of America (e.g. Educational Testing Service of Princeton, New Jersey) and Britain (e.g. University of Cambridge Local Examinations Syndicate, University of London Examinations Council, Joint Matriculation Board, Metropolitan Regional Examinations Board, and Scottish Examination Board) in developing its examination capability.

EVALUATION IN BRITAIN

Caribbean Examinations Council Secondary Education Certificate – grades 1 and 2 at general proficiency generally considered comparable to GCSE standard (grades A, B, C) on a subject-for-subject basis; grades 3 and 4 at general proficiency generally considered comparable to GCSE standard (grades D and E).

MARKING SYSTEM

There is no pass/fail-mark.

Grade

1   comprehensive working knowledge of the syllabus

2   working knowledge of most aspects of the syllabus

3   working knowledge of some aspects of the syllabus

4   limited knowledge of a few aspects of the syllabus

5   insufficient evidence on which to base a judgement

In addition to this overall grade, the profile reports (for each subject which has been examined) provide information on the student's specific strengths and weaknesses. The profile report uses the following grades:

A   above average

B   average

C   below average

N/A no assessment possible

The Council is moving towards offering examinations beyond the CSEC level.

Appendix 5

European Baccalaureate

The **European Baccalaureate** may only be obtained by pupils from the small number of European Schools, the first of which was established in 1957, under an agreement signed by the then members of the European Community (EC). The **Baccalaureate** is the final examination certificate of these schools; it generally enjoys the same status as the national final school-leaving certificates of the member countries of the EC.

The character and curriculum of the schools

The schools are comparable with the French *Lycée* or German *Gymnasium* in that lesson time is largely taken up with academic subjects. The curriculum is centrally controlled by the Board of Governors. Subjects compulsory thoughout years 1 to 7 of secondary education are first language (mother tongue), second language (first foreign language), mathematics, history, geography, science (separate sciences from year 4), physical education and ethics. Art and music are compulsory in years 1 to 3, the study of a second foreign language in years 2 to 5 and philosophy in years 6 to 7. Time allocation is predetermined; there is a small range of options in years 4 to 5 and a considerably greater one in years 6 to 7.

Teaching is carried out through the medium of nine languages – Danish, Dutch, English, French, German, Greek, Italian, Portuguese and Spanish. Pupils are members of a language section, normally that of their mother tongue, in which they receive a large proportion of their education; mathematics, natural science and ethics are taught in that language (the first language), as are philosophy and the later options of Latin and Ancient Greek. From the first primary year, a second language (first foreign language) chosen from English, French and German is taught by native speakers using a direct method. It becomes a pupil's language of instruction:

–   from the first secondary year, in creative arts and physical education;

–   from the third secondary year, in history and geography;

–   from the fourth year, in economics, where this is a chosen option, unless it is taught in the language of the country where the school is situated; and

–   in the sixth and seventh years, in some complementary options, though others may be conducted in the second or third foreign language.

In common with the practice of most European countries, there is no intermediate examination at 16+. There is, however, a 16+ leavers' certificate which is awarded to those pupils who will not continue their studies for the **European Baccalaureate**.

Article 5(2) of the Statute of the European School provides that at the end of the seventh year of secondary education pupils may take the examination of the **European Baccalaureate**. Details of this examination are set out in the Annex to the Statute and in the Regulations for the **European Baccalaureate**. As a result of changes in the curriculum and the examination, from the school year 1984–5 pupils have taken the **European Baccalaureate** in the new form agreed by the Member States. Representatives of the Member States signed new Regulations on 11 May 1984 to implement these changes.

Appendix 5

In accordance with Article 8 of the Annex to the Statute, the **Baccalaureate** is administered and directly supervised by an external examining board appointed annually by the Board of Governors. The examining board consists of up to three representatives of each of the Member States, who must satisfy the conditions governing the appointment of examining boards in their countries of origin. It is presided over by a person teaching in higher education, usually a university professor, assisted by a member of the Board of Inspectors of the schools.

Article 5(2) of the Statute provides that holders of the **European Baccalaureate** shall:

–   enjoy in their respective countries all the benefits attaching to the possession of the diploma or certificate awarded at the end of secondary school in those countries; and

–   have the same right as nationals with equivalent qualifications to seek admission to any university in the territory of the Contracting Parties.

For the purpose of the Statute the expression 'university' applies to 'institutions regarded as of university standing by the Contracting Party in whose territory they are situated'. In the UK, therefore, the Article applies to admission to degree and other higher education courses in polytechnics and colleges of higher education as well as to universities.

The first awards of the **European Baccalaureate** were made in 1959. Applications for admission to higher education in the UK have been, and will continue to be made, not only by British pupils but also by nationals of other Member States who have completed their school education in another language section.

The structure of the European Baccalaureate

A pupil is assessed for the purposes of the **Baccalaureate** in each of the subjects he or she studies in his or her sixth and seventh years of secondary schooling. Obligatory subjects account for between 19 and 23 periods of a pupil's weekly timetable. At least two full options are taken, and the programme is made up to a minimum of 31 and a maximum of 35 periods by complementary options. The subjects available are listed below together with the number of 45-minute periods which are allocated weekly to each.

Obligatory subjects

Language I (mother tongue, e.g. English)	4
Language II (first foreign, e.g. French)	3
Mathematics (a)	3 or 5
Geography	2
History	2
Physical education	2
Ethics	1
Philosophy*	2
Biological science (b)	2

(a)   Two mathematics courses are offered, one covering a more extended syllabus.

(b)   Not obligatory if a science full option is taken.

Optional subjects

Full options:

Latin	5
Ancient Greek	5
Economics	5
Language III	3
Language IV	3
Physics	4
Chemistry	3½
Biology	3½
Advanced mathematics*	3
Advanced philosophy*	3
Advanced language I*	3
Advanced language II*	3

Complementary options:

Art		2
Music		2
Irish		3
Advanced geography*		2
Advanced history*		2
Sociology*		2
Computer science*		2
Electronics*		2
Physics*	(Laboratory courses	2
Chemistry*	to complement the	2
Biology*	full options.)	2

School-based options, approved by the Board of Governors, are also available for two periods a week.

'Advanced' is used in the sense of 'additional' indicating further study of a subject at a higher level.

* Studied only in years 6 and 7.

EVALUATION IN BRITAIN

By virtue of its accession to the Statute of the European School, the UK government has accepted that all holders of the **Baccalaureate**, irrespective of nationality, have the same rights as holders of national certificates of education to seek admission to higher education in this country and should satisfy the general entrance requirements of British higher education institutions.

MARKING SYSTEM

Candidates are awarded a final overall mark for the **Baccalaureate**, expressed as a percentage, based on:

i)   Internal assessment of all subjects (other than ethics) studied during the year preceding the **Baccalaureate** examination (between nine and twelve subjects). This is by means of:

    a)   internal school examinations;   25 per cent
    b)   continuous assessment   15 per cent

ii)   A final examination which is in two parts

    a)   written examination set by   36 per cent
the examining board in five
subjects. These comprise
language I, language II, two
full option subjects and either
mathematics, philosophy or a
third full option;

    b)   oral examinations in four   24 per cent
subjects. They are examined in
the language in which they were
taught and comprise languages
I and II, history or geography
and a full or complementary
option subject.

If no mathematical or scientific subject is offered under (a), it must be offered as the fourth oral examination.

During the twenty-minute oral examination candidates are expected to speak and answer questions on a specialized topic, which they have drawn by lot twenty minutes beforehand. The language of the oral examination is the language of instruction, which in at least two of the orals is one of the candidate's foreign languages.

Candidates who achieve an overall mark of 60 per cent or more are awarded the **European Baccalaureate**.

Appendix 6

International Baccalaureate

The **International Baccalaureate** (IB) diploma programme is a two-year pre-university course designed to facilitate the mobility of students, promote international understanding, and provide a widely accepted university matriculation qualification (the **IB Diploma** examination). In addition, the International Baccalaureate Organisation offers a programme for students aged between 11 and 16 years – the **IB Middle Years Programme** (**IBMYP**).

IB programmes are offered in over six hundred schools and colleges in 85 countries throughout the world. The schools have been individually assessed and approved by the International Baccalaureate Office (IBO) which is based in Geneva. The curriculum and assessment activities of the IB Organisation are based in Cardiff, Wales.

There is no formal entry requirement to IB courses but the **Diploma** is intended as a two-year upper secondary programme. For example, in Britain, it is taken as a post-**GCSE** course and provides a broader and more varied general education than the **GCE Advanced** course.

EVALUATION IN BRITAIN

The full **International Baccalaureate Diploma** may be considered to satisfy the general entrance requirements of British higher education institutions.

The **Middle Years Programme** (**MYP**) is assessed and evaluated by the International Baccalaureate Organisation. Assessment is internal but will be moderated externally by subject. A school may opt for programme evaluation instead of or in addition to assessment of student achievement.

Further information about the **IB Diploma** and the **IB Middle Years Programme** may be obtained from:

International Baccalaureate Examinations Office
Pascal Close
St Mellons
CARDIFF
South Glamorgan
CF3 0YP

Tel: 01222 770770
Fax: 01222 770333

Dr Ian Hill
Regional Director
International Baccalaureate Europe/Africa/Middle East
15 route des Morillons
1218 Grand-Saconnex
Geneva, Switzerland

Tel: 4122 7910274
Fax: 4122 7910277

MARKING SYSTEM

At both Higher and Subsidiary level, each examined subject is graded on a scale of 1 (minimum) to 7 (maximum). The award of the **Diploma** requires a minimum total of 24 points in addition to satisfactory completion of the Theory of Knowledge course, the Extended Essay and CAS.

Candidates may also offer single subjects, for which they receive a certificate.

The **IB Diploma** curriculum consists of six subject groups.

Group 1

Language A1: literature course for native or near-native speakers, including the study of selections from world literature.

Group 2

Language A2: language/literature course for highly competent speakers of the target language;

Language B: foreign language course for students with some previous experience of the language;

the ab initio: foreign language course for students who have no previous experience of learning the target language. This course is offered at Subsidiary Level (SL) only.

Group 3

Individuals and Societies: history, geography, economics, philosophy, psychology, social anthropology, business and organization.

Group 4

Experimental Sciences: biology, chemistry HL, general chemistry SL, applied chemistry SL, physics, environmental systems SL, design technology.

Group 5

Mathematics: mathematics HL, mathematical methods SL, mathematical studies SL, advanced mathematics SL.

Group 6

One of the following options:

Art/design, music, Latin, classical Greek, computer science, information technology in a global society, theatre arts.

A school-based syllabus approved by IBO.

Instead of a group 6 subject a candidate may offer:

A third modern language; a second subject from group 3, Individuals and Societies; a second subject from group 4, Experimental Sciences; or advanced mathematics SL.

Appendix 6

Examples of **IB Diplomas:**

Higher Level (HL)	**Subsidiary Level (SL)**	
a) Mathematics (HL)	English A	Extended Essay: chemistry
Physics	German B	Theory of Knowledge
Chemistry	History	
b) French A	Mathematical Studies	Extended Essay: economics
Arabic B	Biology	Theory of Knowledge
Economics	Art/Design	

To be eligible for the award of the **Diploma** all candidates must:

1. Offer one subject from each of the above groups 1–6;

2. Offer at least three and not more than four of the six subjects at Higher Level (HL) and the others at Subsidiary level (SL);

3. Submit an Extended Essay. This is a piece of individual personal research presented in a maximum of 4,000 words. The list of Extended Essay subjects is not the same as the list of IB subjects and the Extended Essay subject chosen by a student does not have to be one of the subjects being studied for the **Diploma;**

4. Follow a course in the Theory of Knowledge;

5. Engage in extra-curricular activities – Creativity, Action and Service (CAS).

Appendix 7

Roman Catholic Ecclesiastical
Education System

The **Holy See** is the organ of government of the Roman Catholic Church and the juridic personification of the Church in its contacts with other members of the international community. The juridic personality of the **Holy See** is by nature international, and thus its academic institutions are found throughout the world.

The medium of instruction for ecclesiastical studies used to be Latin, but this is disappearing; and, except for subjects with a strong Latin component, all the others are taught in the language requested by the majority of students.

In Europe, the academic year runs from October to June; in the rest of the world the time varies according to geographical factors.

EVALUATION IN BRITAIN

School

School-leaving certificates are the same as those granted by state schools in the country concerned.

Higher

Baccalaureate – generally considered to be between British GCE Advanced level and Bachelor degree standard.

Licentiate – generally considered comparable to British Bachelor degree standard.

Doctorate – represents at least one year of postgraduate research; may be accepted for further postgraduate study in Britain.

MARKING SYSTEMS

School

The marking system adopted in state schools in the country concerned is used.

Higher

Marking systems vary from country to country and university to university.

For example, ecclesiastical universities in Rome adopt the following grading system:

magna cum laude probatus	honour
cum laude probatus	credit
probatus	pass
non probatus	fail

Numerical marks assigned to each of these vary from institution to institution.

SCHOOL EDUCATION

Primary and Secondary level education is carried out in Catholic schools throughout the world. These follow the educational provisions of the countries in which they are found and grant the same school-leaving certificates as state schools. Bishops of the areas in which Catholic schools are found have the right of vigilance over them.

Primary

This conforms to the educational provisions offered under the state system of the country concerned and is not designed for future priests.

Secondary

In some cases the secondary and pre-university studies take place in the **Minor Seminary** (*Seminarium Minus*), in others they are followed in secular or Catholic schools.

The educational cycle known as **Minor Seminary** (*Seminarium Minus*) is designed for future priests. The course of study consists of a three-year lower secondary cycle, followed by a five-year upper secondary cycle, organized and denominated differently in each country. At the end of the five-year upper secondary cycle, pupils sit an examination.

For example, in Rome pupils sit an examination for the award of the **Maturitas**. The certificate is known as **Testimonium Maturitatis e Lyceo**.

FURTHER AND HIGHER EDUCATION

Ecclesiastical education continues with two different courses of study.

While in some cases the academic preparation for the Priesthood takes place in a Faculty, in others the intellectual as well as the spiritual and pastoral formation is given in a Seminary.

The **Major Seminary** (*Seminarium Maius*) programme lasts six years.
This follows, with slight variation from one region to another, the completion of the **Minor Seminary** (*Seminarium Minus*) programme, or secondary school and pre-university studies.

The awarding of degrees is not intrinsically related to the Seminary programme; in some places, however, civil degrees are awarded for the studies undertaken.

In some cases, the course of study is known as **Sexennium Philosophico-theologicum** (consisting of a two-year period of philosophical studies followed by a four-year period of theological studies). A diploma is awarded on completion.

Academic

The academic centres at this level for which the **Holy See** bears responsibility are classified according to finality and content of the studies offered, and the authority on the basis of which degrees are awarded. There are two types:

Ecclesiastical universities and faculties

These institutions are engaged in teaching and research in the sciences proper to the Church. Throughout the world they are governed by a common academic legislation – the **Apostolic Constitution 'Sapientia Christiana'** of 15 April 1979 and the annexed **Norms of the Congregation for Catholic Education** of 29 April 1979. They award degrees on the authority of the **Holy See**. There are about 140 of these institutions in the world.

The three major faculties of an ecclesiastical university are theology, philosophy and Canon (Church) law.

The curriculum is organized on a three-cycle basis:

The first cycle, lasting two to three years, depending on the subject of study, is a foundation course at the end of which the **Baccalaureate** is awarded.

The second cycle, normally two years, is a period of specialization, at the end of which the **Licentiate** (until 1929 corresponding to a degree) is awarded.

The third cycle, lasting a minimum of one year, is a period of original research leading to a doctoral thesis and the award of the **Doctorate**.

Thus academic studies take six to nine years, depending on the subject of study.

Detailed information about these cycles and their length according to the subject studied can be found in the above mentioned constitution '*Sapientia Christiana*'.

Entrance requirements:

'To enrol in a Faculty in order to obtain an academic degree, one must present that kind of study which would be necessary to permit enrolment in a civil university of one's own country or of the country where the faculty is located'

('*Sapientia Christiana*' art. 32/1)

'The Faculty, in its own statutes, should determine what, besides what is contained in statute 1 above, is needed for entrance into its course of study, including ancient and modern language requirements'

('*Sapientia Christiana*' art. 32/2)

The entrance to the second and third cycle requires the attainment of the degree of the previous one.

Catholic universities (and other tertiary institutions)

These institutions are also found in many countries of the world. They follow the academic legislation and structure of the countries in which they are found, including their criteria for admission. They teach and research, in the light of the Christian faith, in the disciplines common to all universities. Degrees are awarded on the basis of civil authority. There are about 900 of these institutions in the world.

TEACHER EDUCATION

Holders of qualifications from the ecclesiastical institutions above (**Baccalaureate, Licentiate** and **Doctorate**) are allowed to teach religious instruction in some state schools and in religious secondary schools throughout the world; the **Doctorate** also entitles the holder to teach at ecclesiastical universities.

Appendix 8

South Pacific Board for
Educational Assessment

The South Pacific Board for Educational Assessment (SPBEA) is based in Suva, Fiji. It was established in 1980 to provide an advisory service in educational evaluation to its member countries (the Cook Islands, Fiji, Kiribati, the Solomon Islands, Tonga, Tuvalu, Western Samoa) and to the <u>University of the South Pacific</u>. The Board's membership has grown since that time to include Tokelau, Vanuatu and the Marshall Islands.

The basic function of the Board is to assist the countries in the region in the development and use of national education assessment procedures and in the preparation and moderation of assessment instruments. Such assistance is country based and related to existing or planned national examinations.

The Board's functions were broadened in 1989, in response to a regional request, to enable the SPBEA to become the examining and certifying body for the **Pacific Senior Secondary Certificate** (PSSC). This is a norm-referenced assessment system that is currently used by five countries – Kiribati, the Solomon Islands, Tonga, Vanuatu and Western Samoa.

The PSSC is offered in the five countries at the end of the twelfth year of schooling. Presently, there are ten subjects in the PSSC programme – accounting, agriculture, biology, chemistry, economics, English, geography, history, mathematics, and physics. The number is expected to grow in the future. All subjects have an external end-of-year examination, and most include a school-based assessment component in the overall assessment. School-based assessments are verified at source and then statistically moderated against examination scores. In some subjects practical and field-work skills are assessed in this way.

The Board also acts as a liaison agent in transferring school certificate examinations (the year prior to PSSC) from New Zealand (NZSC) to three member countries viz: Kiribati, Tuvalu and Western Samoa. This involves consultancy services aimed at helping the countries to set up fully independent assessment systems at this school level.

EVALUATION IN BRITAIN

Pacific Senior Secondary Certificate – grades 1–5 generally considered comparable to GCSE standard (grades A, B and C) on a subject-for-subject basis.

MARKING SYSTEM

Students receive a single-digit grade that can range from 1 to 9 (based on their ranking) for each subject that they have taken. The highest achievement grade is 1, the lowest is 9. The idea of 'pass' or 'fail' is discouraged. Descriptors that are used at present in association with these grades are:

Appendix 8

Grade	Descriptor
1	Excellent standard of achievement
2	Very high standard of achievement
3	High standard of achievement
4	Good standard of achievement
5	Satisfactory standard of achievement
6	Adequate standard of achievement
7	Some achievement
8	Lower level of achievement
9	Little level of achievement

Appendix 9

University of the South Pacific

The University of the South Pacific (USP) was established as a regional institution in 1968. It was set up to serve eleven English-speaking countries associated with the United Kingdom, Australia and New Zealand. The countries are Cook Islands, Fiji, Kiribati, Nauru, Niue, Solomon Islands, Tokelau, Tonga, Tuvalu, Vanuatu and Western Samoa. Marshall Islands, formerly a United States territory, became the twelfth member country in 1991. The first campus was established just outside Suva, capital of Fiji.

The University opened with three schools: Social and Economic Development, Pure and Applied Sciences, and Humanities. The South Pacific Regional College of Tropical Agriculture in Western Samoa was later integrated in to USP as the School of Agriculture, giving the University a second campus.

Programmes offered by the University include:

One-year preliminary programme in which English, mathematics and either science or social science subjects are studied. The programme is normally restricted to students from countries which do not offer a form 6 programme of secondary education and is planned as a bridge between school certificate qualifications and the foundation programme. This programme is now offered through University Extension (distance education) only.

One-year foundation programmes are taught on-campus for science students and by Extension for social science students. Students entering at this stage will normally have satisfactorily completed six years of secondary education and obtained passes in an approved sixth form examination.

The general entry requirement to a first degree course is a satisfactory pass in the University's foundation programme or an equivalent qualification e.g. **Fiji Form 7 Examination**. The normal length of a **Bachelor degree** course is three years except for medicine which is an external degree awarded for courses taught at the Fiji School of Medicine and which takes four years. **Master's degrees** normally take one to two years after a first degree and a **Doctorate** a minimum of a further two years.

A number of professional and in-service certificate and diploma courses are available.

The University Extension service, established in 1970, offers distance education throughout the area served by the University. There are university centres in many countries in the area. Printed, audio and video materials are produced and satellite communication is also used. Programmes available include preliminary and foundation courses, courses towards a degree (it is not yet possible to complete a full degree) and continuing education in the form of public lectures, evening classes and seminars.

The academic year runs from February to November divided into two semesters with a break in June/July.

EVALUATION IN BRITAIN

Bachelor degree – generally considered comparable to British Bachelor degree standard. Students with good results may be considered for admission to taught Master's degree courses.

MARKING SYSTEM

Degrees are unclassified.

Appendix 10

University of the West Indies

The University of the West Indies is a regional institution supported by and serving fourteen English-speaking countries in the West Indies. The countries are Antigua and Barbuda, Bahamas, Barbados, Belize, British Virgin Islands, Cayman Islands, Dominica, Grenada, Jamaica, Montserrat, St Christopher and Nevis, St Lucia, St Vincent and the Grenadines, Trinidad and Tobago. In addition, Guyana is a full participant in the Faculty of Law and by agreement, has a limited number of students in the professional faculties.

The institution was founded as the University College of the West Indies in 1949 and was granted university status in 1962.

The University has three campuses: the original site at Mona in Jamaica, St Augustine in Trinidad which opened in 1960, and Cave Hill in Barbados which opened in 1963. There is a Centre for Hotel and Tourism Management in Nassau, Bahamas, which started in 1976. There are university centres in most non-campus countries.

There are two levels of admission to the University: Normal matriculation, or direct entry to full-time degree programmes, requires candidates to have at least two **GCE A level** subjects or equivalent; to qualify for lower level matriculation, or admission to the preliminary science and evening or part-time courses, candidates will hold the **Caribbean Examinations Council (CXC), Secondary Education Certificate (CSEC)** or **GCSE** level equivalents. Certificates and diplomas from a number of post-secondary institutions are regarded as equivalent qualifications. First degree courses leading to a **Bachelor degree** normally take three years, except for certain subjects such as medicine which take longer. **Master's degrees** normally take two years after a first degree and **PhDs** a further two years.

A number of professional certificate and diploma courses are available.

The School of Continuing Studies has a network of centres in both campus and non-campus countries providing education for those who cannot be served by established institutions, classes to achieve university matriculation, and for others who need academic certification. Another area of development has been the Challenge Examination Scheme, which allows students in the non-campus countries (NCCs) to write first-year examinations in social sciences, arts and general studies, and law, at home with limited on-the-spot tuition through the School of Continuing Studies.

The University of the West Indies Distance Teaching Experiment (UWIDTE) links the three campuses and the university centres in non-campus countries providing facilities for distance teaching and teleconferences.

In 1990–1 a two-term semester academic year was introduced. Previously, the academic year consisted of three terms.

EVALUATION IN BRITAIN

Bachelor degree – generally considered comparable to British Bachelor degree standard. Students with good results may be considered for admission to taught Master's degree courses.

MARKING SYSTEM

Bachelor (Honours) degrees:

Class I

Class II upper division

Class II lower division

If performance has been insufficient for Honours, the degree is awarded as a Pass.

UK NARIC invite **all** users of this edition of *International Guide to Qualifications in Education* (IGQE) to complete the following form. We would like to receive your feedback with a view to quality improvement. Please include your contact details if you would like us to keep you informed about amendments to IGQE.

Where did you first hear about:

- IGQE
- UK NARIC

Please rate the country chapters of IGQE in terms of their interest and benefit to you/your organisation – on a scale of 1 to 3: 1 high; 2 medium; 3 low.

	Interest	Benefit
Introduction/background		
Evaluation in Britain		
Primary education		
Secondary education		
Higher education		
Teacher training		

Any other comments that you may have on the quality, design and content of this edition – and ideas for improvement – are welcome.

Please indicate if you would like to receive information about the services offered by UK NARIC in the future: YES/NO

Name

Position

Organization

Address

Telephone	E-mail
Fax	Telex

Please return this form and any other feedback to:

UK NARIC
The British Council
Medlock Street
Manchester
M15 4AA